FOUNDATIONS OF LANGUAGE

to our students

FOUNDATIONS OF LANGUAGE

Brain, Meaning, Grammar, Evolution

Ray Jackendoff

OXFORD
UNIVERSITY PRESS

OXFORD

UNIVERSITY PRESS

Great Clarendon Street, Oxford OX2 6DP

Oxford University Press is a department of the University of Oxford.
It furthers the University's objective of excellence in research, scholarship,
and education by publishing worldwide in

Oxford New York

Auckland   Cape Town   Dar es Salaam   Hong Kong   Karachi
Kuala Lumpur   Madrid   Melbourne   Mexico City   Nairobi
New Delhi   Shanghai   Taipei   Toronto
With offices in
Argentina   Austria   Brazil   Chile   Czech Republic   France   Greece
Guatemala   Hungary   Italy   Japan   South Korea   Poland   Portugal
Singapore   Switzerland   Thailand   Turkey   Ukraine   Vietnam

Oxford is a registered trade mark of Oxford University Press
in the UK and in certain other countries

Published in the United States
by Oxford University Press Inc., New York

ISBN 978-0-19-926437-7

Printed in the United Kingdom by
Lightning Source UK Ltd., Milton Keynes

Contents

PART II ARCHITECTURAL FOUNDATIONS

PART III SEMANTIC AND CONCEPTUAL FOUNDATIONS

Preface

I began my graduate work at MIT in 1965, at a time when generative linguistics was very much the toast of the intellectual world. Everyone from biologists to philosophers to literary critics wanted to know about deep structure in syntax and what it showed us about the mind and human nature. Over the succeeding decades, generative linguistics has certainly flourished. But the price of success seems to have been increasing specialization and fragmentation within the field, coupled with a gradual loss of prestige and influence in the outside world. In the course of those years, I found my own interests slowly drifting away from the mainstream. Yet, unlike most people who have undergone such a shift, I still consider myself a generative linguist.

The reason for this self-assessment, even if it seems paradoxical to some of my colleagues, is that the overarching goals of generative linguistics still resonate strongly for me and guide my inquiry. A vast amount of research since 1965 has enabled us to refine, nuance, and enrich those goals, but nothing has come along that to me justifies rejecting them in favor of something else.

After many years toiling in the terra incognita of lexical semantics, with detours into musical cognition and the theory of consciousness, I returned during the 1990s to syntax, where I had begun my life as a linguist. From the perspective gained in the interim, it struck me that some traditional basic assumptions about the overall roles of syntax and the lexicon in the grammar were mistaken. In 1965 these assumptions looked altogether reasonable. Without them it is unlikely that the field could have progressed with the exuberance it did. However, as such things often do, these assumptions first hardened into dogma and then disappeared into the background, there to be maintained through the many subsequent incarnations of transformational generative syntax: the Extended Standard Theory, Principles and Parameters Theory (more or less alias Government-Binding Theory), and the Minimalist Program.

The first difficulty in confronting these assumptions was bringing them back to the foreground so they could be examined and questioned. The second difficulty was deciding what to put in their place. Fortunately, many of the necessary pieces were already to be found among the numerous non-transformational approaches to generative grammar that developed during the 1980s and 1990s, such as Lexical-Functional Grammar, Head-Driven Phrase Structure Grammar,

Autosegmental Phonology, Autolexical Syntax, Role and Reference Grammar, Construction Grammar, and Optimality Theory. Important pieces of the model also came from the generative music theory that I had developed with Fred Lerdahl in the late 1970s.

To my surprise, the effect of these revisions is a rather radical reformulation of linguistic theory that in some strange sense "turns the grammar inside out." The new framework above all preserves what I consider the genuine insights of generative grammar. But at the same time, it permits us to see more clearly the proper interaction among the various subdomains of grammar, as well the virtues of the various approaches to grammatical theory on the market. To me, it therefore offers the hope of restoring some degree of much-needed unity to the field of linguistics.

In exploring where I thought traditional assumptions of generative grammar had led linguistics astray, I also discovered real scientific reasons (beyond the all too numerous personal and political ones) for the gradual distancing of linguistics from much of the rest of cognitive (neuro)science. And, although my reformulation of grammar was motivated largely on grounds internal to linguistics, it turned out also to permit much more fruitful interactions with research in language processing, language acquisition, language use, spatial cognition, social cognition, evolutionary psychology, and neuroscience. If anything, these interactions have proven to be the most exciting aspect of the enterprise, for to me they revive the promise of the generative linguistics of my intellectual childhood: that the study of linguistic structure can provide an entrée into the complexities of mind and brain. Not the only one by any means, but one with unique insights to offer.

The goal of the present book, therefore, is to present an overview of the new landscape and an exploration of some of the roads through it. I have written it with three concentric audiences in mind. The most central, of course, is linguists of all specialties and all persuasions. The next ring includes those disciplines that look to linguistics for theoretical models: psycholinguistics, neurolinguistics, language acquisition, and computational linguistics. The outer ring includes everyone else who has some professional concern with language, including psychologists, cognitive scientists, neuroscientists, philosophers of language and philosophers of mind, perhaps evolutionary biologists. Naturally I also welcome anyone else who wishes to join in the conversation.

Unfortunately, the reaction of some linguists to foundational discussion of the sort I engage in here is: "Do I (and my students) really have to think about this? I just want to be able to do good syntax (or phonology or whatever)." I acknowledge that, as the field has grown and matured, some degree of specialization is inevitable and necessary. Still: when you're driving you don't just look ten feet in front of the car. You continually shift your gaze back and forth from near to middle to far distance. Once in a while you may even look around and enjoy the scenery. So it should be in scientific research as well. One has both the goal of understanding the problem at hand and the goal of integrating it into the larger context. And if integration seems to call for alteration of the larger context, one should not shrink from the challenge.

In order for such integration to succeed, probably everyone will have to endure some discomfort and give a little. We cannot afford the strategy that regrettably seems endemic in the cognitive sciences: one discovers a new tool, decides it is the only tool needed, and, in an act of academic (and funding) territoriality, loudly proclaims the superiority of this tool over all others. My own attitude is that we are in this together. It is going to take us lots of tools to understand language. We should try to appreciate exactly what each of the tools we have is good for, and to recognize when new and as yet undiscovered tools are necessary.

This is not to advocate a warm fuzzy embrace of every new approach that appears on the scene. Rather, what is called for is an open-mindedness to insights from whatever quarter, a willingness to recognize tensions among apparently competing insights, and a joint commitment to fight fair in the interests of deeper understanding. To my mind, that's what the game of science is about.

A book with a scope this large is well beyond the scholarly capabilities of any single individual. My empirical research for the last thirty-five years has concentrated on semantics and its relation to syntax, and this is what I have the most to say about here. If I have slighted other areas, from phonetics to typology to acquisition to pragmatics, it is not because I don't think these areas are interesting enough. It is just that I can only venture into them with trepidation, relying on (or against the advice of) friends whom I trust. For years the relevant literature has been expanding far faster than anyone can read it. Life is short. Readers who find my treatment woefully incomplete in their areas of interest are hereby invited to write more chapters.

Because I aspire to speak to so many different audiences here, I sometimes have found it necessary to make technical remarks that are more pertinent and more accessible to one audience rather than another. Rather than flag such passages as, say, "only for linguists" or "mostly for philosophers," I have chosen to trust readers to decide for themselves how to read the book.

*   *   *   *   *

As we have a long and tortuous path to travel, I owe the reader some hints of where we are going.

Part I lays out the fundamental issues that motivate generative linguistics.

First, in the interests of recognizing what a theory of language is responsible for, Chapter 1 is devoted to briefly presenting the structure associated with a very simple sentence of English—a wealth of structure that is well established independent of any doctrinal considerations. We then discuss three basic tenets of generative linguistics that I think have stood the test of time: mentalism, combinatoriality, and nativism.

Mentalism (Chapter 2): Language is instantiated in the minds and therefore the brains of language users, so that linguistics is to be regarded as a branch of psychology. We will ask what it means to say linguists are modeling the mind, and we will reinterpret in a more tractable light the important distinction between competence and performance, i.e. between speakers' knowledge of a language and their ability to put that knowledge to use.

Combinatoriality (Chapter 3): One of the most striking features of language is the fact that speakers can understand and construct an indefinitely large number of sentences that they have never experienced before. This leads to the conclusion that a speaker's knowledge is instantiated as a set of generative principles (or rules) for constructing and recognizing sentences; these principles constitute the speaker's mental grammar. After enumerating some of the general types of rule proposed in various frameworks of generative grammar, we will discuss some problems that combinatoriality poses for popular theories of semantic memory and neural nets.

Nativism (Chapter 4): Children obviously learn language through exposure to the environment. However, Chomsky's most famous and controversial hypothesis is that the child brings resources to language learning beyond those used for other sorts of learning: he claims that the ability to learn language is in part a cognitive specialization of our species, a "Universal Grammar" that is "wired into" children's brains.

How should this hypothesis be construed, and how can it be verified? How could the genetic code produce such "wiring," and what role could evolution have played in it? While acknowledging certain criticisms, on balance I will conclude that a suitably nuanced version of the Universal Grammar hypothesis is supportable, and that it should continue to play the central role in linguistic investigation that it has enjoyed since *Aspects*.

Part II is the point where we diverge from standard generative theory. Chapters 5 and 6 are the theoretical core of the book; they expose the traditional assumptions that I find mistaken and develop alternatives.

The role of syntax (Chapter 5): Traditional generative grammar assumes without argument that only syntax is "generative," that is, that the combinatorial complexity of language arises entirely by virtue of its syntactic organization. I will motivate a framework in which phonology, syntax, and semantics are equally generative. Syntax is thus only one of several parallel sources of grammatical organization. The generative components communicate with each other through "interface" components; we will spend considerable time showing that these interfaces are of nontrivial complexity. We will also see that many of the alternative frameworks for generative grammar share this sort of parallel organization.

The lexicon (Chapter 6): Traditional generative grammar makes a pair of related assumptions: first, that lexical items—the stored elements that are combined into larger expressions—enter the combinatorial system by virtue of being inserted into syntactic structures; and second, that lexical items are always words. In the parallel model of Chapter 5, lexical items emerge instead as parts of the interfaces among generative components. Moreover, by taking very seriously the question of what is stored in memory, we will arrive at the view that lexical (i.e. stored) items are of heterogeneous sizes, from affixes to idioms and more abstract structures.

This reconceptualization of the lexicon leads to striking consequences for linguistic theory, in particular breaking down some of the traditional distinction between lexical items and rules of grammar. It also leads to a reconsideration of the formal character of language learning.

Language processing (Chapter 7): The parallel model lends itself rather naturally to addressing issues of language perception and production. In particular, the interface components, including the lexicon, can be interpreted as playing a direct role in language processing. It develops that the notion of modularity is no longer to be couched in terms of an isolated "grammar box," but rather in terms of time constraints on the interaction of the multiple components of the language processor. This view, motivated here in terms of linguistic theory, has in fact emerged independently on experimental grounds within the psycholinguistic community. Thus it seems within reach to integrate the theories of competence and performance much more fully than has been previously possible.

Evolution (Chapter 8): One of the issues raised by the nativist claim is that the capacity to learn language must have emerged at some point in the evolution of the human species. However, it is difficult to see how a capacity of the complexity usually assumed by linguists could have evolved through natural selection. It turns out that the parallel model offers more attractive possibilities for an incremental evolution of the language capacity. We will discuss some possible stages in this evolution, showing how they are reflected in the organization of present-day language.

A glaring lacuna in most approaches to generative grammar has been the absence of a theory of semantics of any sophistication. Part III is devoted to working out the foundations of semantics in a manner compatible with the goals of generative linguistics, incorporating insofar as possible the insights of several (largely incompatible) approaches, including traditional philosophy of language, logic and formal semantics, lexical semantics of various stripes, cognitive grammar, psycholinguistic and neurolinguistic approaches, and my own conceptual semantics and related work.

Mentalism again (Chapter 9): We begin by couching the questions of semantic theory in mentalistic terms, so that semantics will be compatible with generative grammar. We contrast this position with a number of other views of what semantics is about. This chapter also addresses the putative distinction between linguistic meaning and "world knowledge," arguing that various ways of making this distinction do not serve the purpose they are intended for. Rather, if there is a special "linguistic semantics," it is the theory of the interface components between meaning and linguistic expression.

Reference and truth (Chapter 10): The most difficult challenge to a mentalist semantics is the overwhelming intuition that language refers to objects and events "in the world." A direct connection between a language in the mind and objects in the world is severely problematic. I conclude that the proper formulation of reference is as a relation between linguistic expressions and the world *as conceptualized by the language user*. Such a formulation aligns with standard views in perceptual psychology, and permits a far richer ontology of entities for language to refer to than most formal semanticists and philosophers of mind are accustomed to grant. Some of the standard philosophical objections to this view are answered; at the same time, some of the standard puzzles of reference are shown to dissolve.

After these two chapters that lay the groundwork, the final two chapters are devoted to lexical and phrasal semantics respectively. Chapter 11 addresses the issue of lexical decomposition, showing that, although traditional decomposition into necessary and sufficient conditions is not viable, the evidence warrants a far richer notion of lexical decomposition. Chapter 12 develops a theory of phrasal composition, again considerably richer than usually assumed. In particular, the meaning of a sentence consists of more than the meanings of its words combined according to syntactic structure. I motivate separating phrasal and sentential semantics into a number of *tiers*, along the lines of phonological tiers, each of which contributes a different sort of information to the meaning.

Finally, a brief epilogue attempts to pull everything together.

Acknowledgments

The opportunity to write this book arose from an invitation to spend the academic year 1999–2000 at the Wissenschaftskolleg zu Berlin, a research institute whose only purpose is to invite people from many different fields to come, do their work, and talk with one another. And a glorious year it proved to be. Ensconced with my computer in a villa in Grunewald, I went at it day after day, month after month, till a draft was done in June, just in time to pack up and come home. What sustained me was the amenities: the lovely lunches and dinners with colleagues and staff, the weekly colloquia, many many nights at the opera, and the multidimensional fascinations of the city. The staff of the Kolleg was overwhelmingly warm and helpful, and I was privileged to have as friends especially Christine von Arnim, Andrea Friedrich, Reinhart Meyer-Kalkus, Katharina Biegger, Barbara Sanders, and Maria Wirth, and to have as Boss the incredible Wolf Lepenies.

Among my cohort at the Kolleg, David Olson, Angela Friederici, and very particularly Merrill Garrett were valuable sources of discussion and advice on matters pertaining to the book. David Wasserstein, Valentina Sandu-Dediu and Dan Dediu, Fania and Eli Salzberger, Elizabeth Dunn, Barbara Brown, Franco Moretti, Niki Lacey, and Marcello deCecco were constant good companions. My life outside the Kolleg was fortified by frequent excursions to the dives of Kreuzberg, guided by Kai Reimers and the jolly Wiese sisters, Heike and Karen. Cantor Oljean Ingster, Rabbi Chaim Rozwaski, Irene Runge, and the regulars of the Rykestrasse Synagoge took me in as one of their own and introduced me to the richness of Jewish life in Berlin.

During the preceding summer I had the chance to offer a course at the LSA Linguistic Institute at the University of Illinois, based on my plans for the book. To my astonishment, the class kept growing as the course went on; I guess they liked it. I am grateful to the director of the Institute, Adele Goldberg, for making all the arrangements for the course so smooth, and to Gert Webelhuth, Dan Jurafsky, Jila Ghomeshi, Beth Jacobs, and numerous members of my class—as well as Adele again—for many lively discussions of relevant issues.

The final form of the book owes a great deal to colleagues who offered comments, sometimes frighteningly extensive, on earlier versions. These include Henk Verkuyl, Pim Levelt, Edgar Zurif, Merrill Garrett (again), Fritz Newmeyer, Heike Wiese, Ida Toivonen, Katharina Hartmann, Adele Goldberg (again!),

Gert Webelhuth, Dan Dennett, Marc Hauser, Tecumseh Fitch, Marcel Kins-
bourne, James Pustejovsky, Jong Sup Jun, and my editor, John Davey. Effusive
thanks also on general principles to Joan Maling, my Brandeis colleague of
nearly thirty years, and to Lila Gleitman. I must particularly express my debt to
my old graduate school friend Peter Culicover, with whom I've been collaborating extensively over the last ten years. The synergy between Peter's developing
theory of "concrete minimalism" and my own work has helped me step out and
commit to the radically restructured conception of syntax that emerges here.

While I was grinding out the early chapters of the book in Berlin, I received
the news of the passing of my dear friend Vicki Fromkin. Vicki "adopted" me
(as she adopted everyone else) when I arrived in Los Angeles in 1969 as a fresh-
ly minted Ph.D., and she and Jack never stopped being sources of delight. Her
enthusiasm for bringing linguistics to the rest of the world was inspirational; I
can only hope that some of her spirit has rubbed off here. In the same week, we
also lost Alvin Liberman, whom I admired a great deal both professionally and
personally, and who, like Vicki, was concerned with bringing his message to
audiences outside the field. It's important to me to remember both of them here
and to acknowledge their influence on my thought over many years.

Old-timers will remember the journal *Foundations of Language*, which
flourished from the mid-1960s into the mid-1970s. I still retain some fondness
for it, having published my first paper in it in 1968. I hope it does not resent my
having borrowed its name.

Writing a book also takes money. For that, I'm grateful to the Schering Foundation, which funded my fellowship to the Wissenschaftskolleg, and to the
National Institutes of Health, whose Grant 03660 to Brandeis University
helped support this research.

It has been a real pleasure to work with the people at Oxford University Press,
who have taken this project very seriously and made every effort to get the word
out. I especially want to thank John Davey and Sarah Dobson for their help in
making the book both textually clear and physically beautiful, and Jennifer
Morettini, whose creative publicity has brought me some interesting adven-
tures.

Various parts of the text have been adapted from other works of mine, and
appear here by permission. These works include:

"The Representational Structures of the Language Faculty and Their Interac-
    tions," in Colin M. Brown and Peter Hagoort (eds.), *The Neurocognition of
    Language* (Oxford University Press, 1999) (much of Chapter 1).
"What's in the Lexicon?," in S. Nooteboom, F. Weerman, and F. Wijnen (eds.),
    Storage and Computation in the Language Faculty (Kluwer, 2001) (much of
    Chapter 6).

"Fodorian Modularity and Representational Modularity," in Yosef Grodzinsky, Lewis Shapiro, and David Swinney (eds.), *Language and the Brain* (Academic Press, 2000) (parts of Chapter 7).

"Possible Stages in the Evolution of the Language Capacity," *Trends in Cognitive Sciences* 3 (1999) (much of Chapter 8).

"Conceptual Semantics and Cognitive Semantics," *Cognitive Linguistics* 7 (1996) (parts of Chapter 11)

"The Architecture of the Linguistic–Spatial Interface," in P. Bloom, M. Peterson, L. Nadel, and M. Garrett (eds.), *Language and Space* (MIT Press) (parts of Chapter 11)

"Semantics and Cognition," in Shalom Lappin (ed.), *The Handbook of Contemporary Semantic Theory* (Blackwell, 1996) (parts of Chapter 11).

Finally, my deepest personal gratitude and love go to Amy, Beth, and Hildy.

PART I

Psychological and Biological Foundations

CHAPTER I

The Complexity of Linguistic Structure

1.1 A sociological problem

Those of us who make it our business to study language often find ourselves in the curious position of trying to persuade the world at large that we are engaged in a technically demanding enterprise. Mathematicians are not expected to be able to relate their work to others: "Oh, I never could do math!" And although biologists and neuroscientists may be expected to explain the goals of their research in a very general way, the formidable chemical and physiological details that constitute the real substance of their work are freely granted to be beyond the understanding of non-specialists.

But language seems to be a different story. When we begin describing the sorts of issue we deal with, a typical response is "Oh, yes, I know how hard language is: I tried to learn Russian once!" When we try to explain that, no, that's not the half of it, we rapidly lose our audience's attention. The reaction is understandable: who but a linguist wants to hear at a cocktail party or barbecue about current thinking on long-distance extraction or the role of extrametricality in stress assignment?

Language and biology provide an interesting contrast in this respect. People *expect* to be baffled or bored by the biochemical details of, say, cell metabolism, so they don't ask about them. What interests people about biology is natural history—strange facts about animal behavior and so forth. But they recognize and respect the fact that most biologists don't study that. Similarly, what interests people about language is its "natural history": the etymology of words, where language came from, and why kids talk so badly these days. The difference is that they don't recognize that there is more to language than this, so they are unpleasantly disappointed when the linguist doesn't share their fascination.

It may well be that individuals who are attracted into linguistics have a certain talent for metalinguistic reflection—a delight in constructing ungrammatical sentences, finding curious ambiguities and implicatures, hearing and imitating accents, and the like—and that professional training as a linguist only amplifies this proclivity. It would then be no surprise that linguists' sense of what is interesting in language is different from that of our friends in biology, economics, and dentistry. It is just that we linguists have made the mistake of assuming everyone else is like us. We are sort of in the position of an avid opera-goer who hasn't quite caught on that he is in the company of a bunch of rock-and-rollers.

In itself this mutual misperception would be merely a harmless source of social annoyance. But it can have a more pernicious side. A good example is the debate in the middle 1990s over the proposal by the School Board of Oakland, California that the dialect of the African-American community ("Ebonics") be employed as an integral part of class instruction (see Perry and Delpit 1998). The proposal was based on the well-documented structural integrity of this dialect as a language from the point of view of linguistics, and on linguistic research suggesting that instruction in a vernacular can be a valuable scaffolding to support acquisition of literacy in the standard language (Labov 1972; Rickford 1999). However, scientific documentation was of no concern to the general public. During the height of the debate, it was not uncommon to find letters to the editor in newspapers and even scientific journals to the effect that whatever the linguists in their ivory towers might think, Ebonics is a barbaric perversion of English, and it is nonsense to encourage its use.[1]

This example is revealing in two ways. First, it underlines the importance of language to social identity, and the way linguistic issues come to be conflated with broader social attitudes. Unlike cell metabolism, language is something that people have a personal stake in. Second, it demonstrates the way that people feel entitled to enter the conversation in the absence of expertise, and even to demean the experts in the interest of making a point. The behavior is reminiscent of creationists reacting to evolutionary theory, or oil corporations reacting to evidence of global warming.

Of course the experts aren't always right, and often there are dueling experts

---

[1] It is surely significant that few people, even in high places, understood what the Oakland *School Board* had proposed. It was widely thought that they had proposed to "teach children Ebonics." In fact, the actual proposal was to recognize the children's own dialect in the classroom as a legitimate means of expression, and to use it as a scaffolding for teaching literacy in Standard English. An important part of learning to read is appreciating how orthography reflects pronunciation. If one is teaching reading of Standard English to a child who does not speak it, it is difficult to establish this crucial link.

arrayed on opposite sides of a politically charged issue. But one ought to feel obliged at least to consider some of the facts and arguments that the experts have to offer before rejecting them.

Even when broader social issues are not at stake, one finds a curious readiness on the part of the lay public to speculate about the nature of language, and to be satisfied with the answers they arrive at. Unfortunately, such attitudes sometimes extend to influential practitioners of disciplines impinging on linguistics such as philosophy, neuroscience, and computer science. The effect is to divide disciplines from each other when they should be providing mutual support.

The goal of this chapter, therefore, is to establish a baseline of what a theory of linguistic structure must be responsible for. For linguists, the chapter should serve as a reminder of the scope of the enterprise and as an orientation into the outlook of the present study. As for those in neighboring disciplines, I certainly don't expect them to follow every detail of the structure to be described. But I hope the chapter will help them see beyond "natural history" aspects of language and to recognize the subtler issues at stake in linguistic theory, so that in succeeding chapters I can bring these issues to bear on psychological and biological concerns.

To be sure, there are many other aspects to language besides raw structure, such as its role in social identity and its power in poetry. But it is in the study of structure that I think linguistic theory finds its deepest and most characteristic concerns, and it is structure that will be the principal focus here.

1.2 The structure of a simple sentence

A good way to get into the complexity of linguistic structure is through a rather full analysis of a very simple sentence of English:

(1)   The little star's beside a big star.

The structure of this sentence is given in Fig. 1.1 (next page). Fig. 1.1 is organized into four domains or levels, each of which has a characteristic formal structure. I have given a pretty fair articulation of phonological (sound) structure and syntactic structure, though many particulars are still omitted. The gross articulation of semantic/conceptual structure (alias meaning) is given here, but much of the detail is unknown. I have also included a very sketchy articulation of a level I have called spatial structure, the level at which this sentence can be compared with the perception of the world.

Fig. 1.1 serves as a useful baseline because nearly every bit of structure encoded in it represents a broad consensus among linguists—even if there is disagreement

Phonological structure

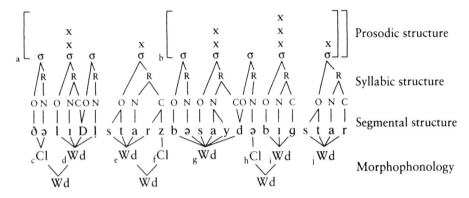

Syntactic structure

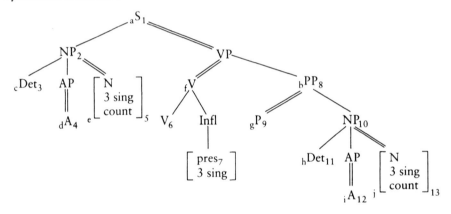

Semantic/conceptual structure

Spatial structure

Fig. 1.1. Structure of *The little star's beside a big star*

about exactly how various aspects are to be systematically formalized. In particular, some variant of the phonological and syntactic structure will be found in every introductory textbook of linguistics.

The format of Fig. 1.1 is, however, a bit idiosyncratic in the way it divides the structure into levels. I have chosen this format in anticipation of the theory of linguistic structure to be developed in Part II: each level of structure is to be thought of as the product of an independent combinatorial ("generative") system.

But this is getting ahead of the story. For the moment let us take a tour of Fig. 1.1.[2]

1.3 Phonological structure

The phonological structure consists of four subcomponents or *tiers*. Down the middle is the *segmental structure*, the string of discrete speech sounds or phonemes, notated here in the phonetic alphabet (representing more or less standard American pronunciation). However, the speech sounds are actually composite, made up of a matrix of *distinctive features*. Fig. 1.2 zooms in on the segmental structure of the word *star*, now broken into distinctive features. These features define a similarity space among speech sounds. Here is a classic example that illustrates their usefulness. The English regular plural suffix has three pronunciations: 's' as in *cats*, 'z' as in *dogs*, and 'əz' ('uhz') as in *horses*. The choice of which to use is determined by the final sound of the word that the suffix is attached to—in particular the sound's distinctive features. The [–voiced] sound 's' is used with words that end with a [–voiced] sound ('t', 'p', 'k', 'f', etc.); the [+voiced] sound 'z' is used with words that end with a [+voiced] sound ('d', 'b', 'g', 'm', etc. plus vowels); and 'əz' is used with words that end with the sounds 's', 'z', 'š' ('sh'), 'ž' ('zh'), 'č' ('ch'), or 'j', all of which have feature compositions

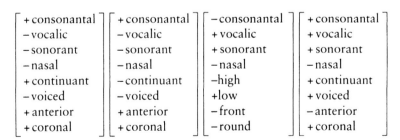

Fig. 1.2. Detail of segmental structure of the word *star*

---

[2] As we will be making reference to Fig. 1.1 extensively in this chapter and then sporadically throughout the rest of the book, readers may find it useful to photocopy the page.

close to those of 's' and 'z'. That is, the generalizations concerning the exact phonetic form of the plural suffix fall out very naturally from the similarity space
defined by the distinctive features. Hundreds of phenomena of this sort have been
studied by phonologists. These features play a role in child language acquisition,
in historical change, and in speech errors, as well as in the description of many
dozens of languages. It is a scientific question what the right set of features is—
one that is gradually being settled through phonological and phonetic research.

However, phonological structure is more than just a sequence of phonemes:
it is organized into a number of semi-independent "tiers," labeled along the
right-hand side of the phonology in Fig. 1.1. One is the grouping of speech
sounds into syllables, indicated by σ. Now it could have been that syllables were
just unstructured strings of phonemes, like this:

(2)

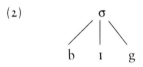

But in fact there are hierarchical distinctions inside the syllable. A syllable has to
have one segment that functions as a Nucleus—the sonorous core around
which the syllable is built. This is designated by N in Fig. 1.1. The nucleus is
usually a vowel, but consonants with the distinctive feature [+sonorant] can
also serve as syllabic nuclei. One of these is 'l', which serves as nucleus in the
second syllable of *little*, as seen in Fig. 1.1.

The rest of the syllable's structure is optional. The nucleus and any following material (called the Coda) are grouped as the Rime (the part of the
syllable that remains the same in rhymes). The material before the nucleus is
grouped as the Onset (the part that remains the same in alliteration). These
are indicated in Fig. 1.1 by R and O respectively. Notice also in Fig. 1.1 that
the segment D in *little* (a "flapped" *d* or *t*) is *ambisyllabic*: it serves both as
coda of one syllable and as onset of the next.

Above the syllabic structure is the tier of *prosodic structure*, which has
two subcomponents. The brackets indicate the organization of the syllables
into *intonational phrases*; pauses in pronouncing the sentence can occur only
between bracketed units. Within the brackets are the *x*s of the *metrical grid*,
which indicates the relative stress of syllables. Syllables with no *x*s above
them are unstressed; more *x*s indicate more stress, so that the word *big*
receives the main stress of the sentence.

Looking now below the phonological string, we find the tier of morphophonological structure—the grouping of the speech stream into words

(indicated by Wd). Notice that the words *the* and *a* do not have the symbol Wd below them. Rather, they are treated phonologically as *clitics*—phonological fragments that attach to adjacent words to form a larger Wd constituent. Finally, notice that the sound '*z*' by itself also is a clitic, notated orthographically in sentence (1) by '*s*.

1.4 Syntactic structure

Consider next the syntactic structure. This is a tree diagram of the familiar sort. The largest constituent, the sentence (S), divides into a noun phrase (NP) (which serves as the subject) and a verb phrase (VP) (which serves as the predicate); the NP divides into a Determiner, a modifying adjective phrase (AP), and a head noun (N), which carries the features 3rd person count singular. (If this were a French or German sentence, the Det and A would also have number, and all constituents of NP would have grammatical gender as well.) The VP divides into a head verb (V) and a prepositional phrase (PP), the PP divides into a preposition and its NP object, and the NP divides like the subject NP. Attached to the V is an Inflection which includes present tense plus the features 3rd person singular, which agree with the subject.

The way I have notated this tree differs from standard convention in two respects. First, it is customary to put the words of the sentence at the bottom of the tree, as in (3).

(3)

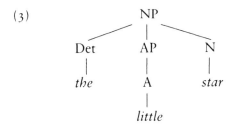

I have omitted the words for reasons to be discussed more fully in Chapter 5. The basic reason is that things like *the* and *star* are actually pieces of phonology, not syntax. The only aspects of words that play a role in syntax are the part of speech (Det, N, etc.) and syntactic features such as 3rd person singular and present tense.

The other way this notation differs from tradition is that some of the connections in the tree are notated with double lines. These are connections between phrases and their heads. The idea is that phrases like NP, VP, AP, and

PP are "projections" of their heads—N, V, A, and P respectively. For example, there couldn't be a prepositional phrase with a noun as head or a verb phrase with a preposition as head. So each phrase is to be thought of as a structural skeleton, indicated by the double lines, supplemented by elaborations, indicated by single lines. This is not a standard notation, but it makes more graphic an insight about syntactic structure that goes back at least to Zellig Harris in the 1940s and that was introduced into modern theory by Chomsky (1970) under the rubric of "X-bar" theory (see also Jackendoff 1977).[3]

In Fig. 1.1, I have continued the double line from V up beyond VP to S, in effect treating the sentence as a syntactic projection of the verb. An important variant, originating in Chomsky (1986), is shown in (4). Here the sentence is the projection of Inflection (Tense).

(4)

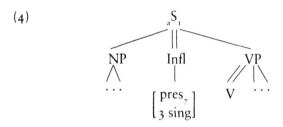

Again, as in phonology, there is ongoing debate about this seemingly simple choice; in section 1.6 we will return to some repercussions. Nevertheless, everyone agrees that overall there is constituent structure of this sort, and that constituents have heads.

A further aspect of X-bar theory has not been notated here: syntactic categories such as Noun and Verb, like phonological segments, are often treated as feature complexes rather than primitives. The most broadly accepted set (dating from Chomsky 1970) analyzes Noun as [+N, −V] and Verb as [−N, +V]; Adjective is [+N, +V] and Preposition is [−N, −V].

---

[3] In most approaches to syntax, this distinction between single and double lines can be regarded as merely a visual aid, of no theoretical significance. However, some versions of syntactic theory take the distinction between the head of a phrase and its other constituents to be marked in the structure. For instance, in Head-Driven Phrase Structure Grammar (HPSG, Pollard and Sag 1994), the head falls under the HEAD–DTR ("head–daughter") attribute, and other constituents fall under the COMP–DTRS ("complement–daughters") attribute. Under this approach the double line has a theoretical interpretation, as it stands for a different kind of connection between the head and the phrase. For the moment I leave open the decision of how to regard the double line notation. It is, however, illustrative of the sort of subtle but significant questions that can arise in syntactic theory.

1.5 Semantic/conceptual and spatial structure

If phonology and syntax are fairly well settled at least at this relatively gross level, there is considerably less agreement about the proper formulation of semantic/conceptual structure, even with respect to whether there is such a thing. Fig. 1.1 unabashedly presents one aspect of this structure in my own version of the notation. Chapter 12 will call this aspect the *descriptive tier*; it corresponds roughly to the information that might be encoded in a predicate logic. Chapter 12 will also motivate other tiers of semantic/conceptual structure, related to this tier in roughly the way the tiers of phonology are related. One is the *referential tier*, which corresponds roughly to the aspects of meaning added when moving from a predicate logic to a quantificational logic. Another is the tier of *information structure*, the division of the content of the sentence into foreground and background (topic/focus and presupposition).

The structure given in Fig. 1.1 is a labeled bracketing, in which each pair of brackets surrounds a *conceptual constituent*. The label on a constituent designates it as belonging to a major conceptual type such as Situation, Event, State, Object, Place, or Property.

Two kinds of relation among conceptual constituents appear in this structure. The first is function–argument structure, notated as in (5).

(5) $[_X F ([_Y \ldots], [_Z \ldots])]$

Here F is a function that maps a constituent of type Y and a constituent of type Z into a constituent of type X. (5) shows a two-place function. BE is such a function in Fig. 1.1. There are also one-place functions (such as BESIDE in Fig. 1.1) and possibly three-place functions. The second kind of relation is modification, notated as in (6).

(6) $\begin{bmatrix} \ldots \\ _X [_Y \ldots] \end{bmatrix}$

(6) is a constituent of type X, in which the inner constituent, of type Y, specifies a further characteristic of the outer constituent. An example of this in Fig. 1.1 is the modification of the first Object constituent by the Property LITTLE.

Using this notation, the conceptual structure in Fig. 1.1 says that there is a Situation in the present, consisting of a State. This State is one of an Object being located in a Place; the function BE maps the Object and the Place into this State.

Now look at the Object that is the first argument of BE. It has three pieces of structure. The first designates the Object as of the category STAR (which presumably has more internal articulation, not notated here: see Chapter 11). The second piece is a marker DEF ('definite'), which indicates roughly that the identity of the object in question can be fixed by either the previous discourse or the context (if there were two little stars around, one couldn't say THE *little star*). The third piece is a modifying constituent of the type Property, which designates the object as having the characteristic LITTLE.

LITTLE has further internal structure, which again I have not formalized: basically it says that the overall size of the object in question is smaller than a pragmatically determined norm. This norm in turn may be chosen from (a) the average size of members of the category in question (here, stars), (b) the average size of stars in the contextual environment (here, only two), (c) the average size of all comparable objects in the contextual environment (as in *The star is little, the circle is big*), and perhaps others (Bierwisch and Lang 1989).

Turning to the rest of the semantic/conceptual structure in Fig. 1.1: the other Object, *a big star*, works the same way as *the little star*. *A big star*, however, serves as the argument of a function BESIDE, which maps the Object into a region or Place—the region in which the first Object is located by the function BE. Again, I can give some detail of BESIDE: the region beside an object X is exterior to X, proximal to X, and in a horizontal direction from X. Hence in (7a) the Y is near but not beside the X. In addition, no other object can come between X and an object next to it; hence in (7b) the Y is also near but not beside the X.

(7)   a. Y
          X

       b. X Z Y

I emphasize again that the notation for semantic/conceptual structure in Fig. 1.1 is by no means universally accepted. However, all the distinctions that have been mentioned here arise sooner or later in every theory of meaning (and what is sooner and what later, and by how much, is one of the major divides among theories).

If the details of semantic/conceptual structure are sketchy and open to dispute, those of spatial structure are hardly even touched upon. One can think of spatial structure variously as an image of the scene that the sentence describes, a schema that must be compared against the world in order to verify the sentence (a "mental model" in Johnson-Laird's (1983) sense), the physical (or nonpropositional) structure of the model in which the truth conditions of semantic/conceptual structure are applied, or perhaps other construals. (I will be more precise in Chapters 9 and 11.)

What is clear is that any such image requires two star-shaped objects (or object-schemas) in it. More interesting is that the features of BESIDE must appear in some way also in this configuration, so that "beside-ness" can be verified in a visually presented array. I have notated the region "beside a big star" very crudely in Fig. 1.1 by means of a dotted line that represents the approximate boundary of the relevant region.

1.6 Connecting the levels

The structure of our sentence cannot just be the collection of these structures. It is necessary also to encode the relationships among them—how the parts of each structure are connected to parts of the others.

I have notated correspondences between units of phonological structure and syntactic structure with pre-subscripts. For example, the phonological clitic *the* carries the pre-subscript *c*, which places it in correspondence with the initial Determiner in syntax. Similarly, correspondences between units of syntax and units of semantic/conceptual structure are notated with post-subscripts. For instance, the initial *Det* in syntax is coindexed with the feature DEF in semantic/conceptual structure. As with the structures themselves, many aspects of the correspondences notated in Fig. 1.1 are somewhat sketchy and imprecise; we will return to some of the details later. Still, their general outline should be clear.[4]

An important feature of these correspondences—whatever their details—is that for the most part they do not obtain between primitive elements of any of the levels: they are rather relations between composite units. The primitive units of phonological structure such as distinctive features and syllables are completely invisible to syntax and meaning. What this means is that the speech sounds are themselves meaningless. Only the assembly of a number of speech sounds into a word or clitic has a connection to syntax and/or meaning. Similarly, the word's syntactic category such as Noun or Verb (itself a composite of syntactic features) is invisible to phonology. In other words, a word's part of speech gives no hint as to how to pronounce it.

Various other primitive units of syntax have no direct connection to phonological structure. They are therefore by themselves unpronounceable. Consider for instance *3rd person*. It must combine with the features *singular* and the element *present tense* before there is a unit that (sometimes) has a pronunciation as the verbal affix -*s*, as in the verb *spins*. In this particular sentence, however, even *3rd person singular present tense* has no independent pronunciation. Rather, it is bundled up with the verb to form a unit that is often pronounced *is*, but that in this case is contracted into *z* (spelled *'s*), a clitic attached to the previous word.

Not every aspect of syntax corresponds to something in meaning either. For

---

[4] In particular, alert readers may wonder how the pre-subscripts *a* and *b* connect the phonology to the syntax, and why the VP in syntax does not connect to anything in phonology. Please wait until Chapter 5.

example, the features *3rd person* and *singular* on the verb are purely syntactic agreement features that have no particular effect in semantic/conceptual structure (in English at least).

Another thing to notice about these correspondences is that the units that are connected between phonology and syntax are not always the same units that are connected between syntax and conceptual structure. For example, the inflected verb (the upper V in Fig. 1.1) is connected to the phonology (subscript f), where it appears as the clitic *z*; but the bare verb and the inflection are connected separately to semantics (subscripts 6 and 7), where they are separate elements.

Generally speaking, the mapping between phonology and syntax preserves linear order, while the mapping between syntax and meaning tends to preserve the relative embedding of arguments and modifiers. In particular, the head of a syntactic phrase tends to map into the outermost function of the corresponding conceptual constituent. For instance, the preposition *beside*, the head of the PP, maps into the function BESIDE that governs the Place-constituent in Fig. 1.1.

In turn, some but not all parts of semantic/conceptual structure correspond to spatial structure—in Fig. 1.1, the two Object-constituents and the Place. Other parts of conceptual structure are harder to represent directly in any spatial format. For instance, LITTLE and BIG raise the problem of how to notate relative size in spatial structure; definiteness (DEF) raises the problem of how to notate uniqueness. My impression is that these explicit pieces of conceptual structure encode distinctions that are only implicit in spatial structure—so it is hard to see how to notate the relationship with a simple co-subscripting.

One aspect of this correspondence merits special attention. As noted a moment ago, the little clitic '*z*' in phonology is of course the contracted verb *is*, which expresses the verb *be* in the 3rd person singular present tense, a smallish part of the syntactic tree. In turn, the verb *be* corresponds to the next-to-largest function in semantic/conceptual structure. The largest function in semantic/conceptual structure is present tense. But this appears as a feature of the verb *be* in syntax, and is not even an independent element in the phonology. So, by virtue of this two-step correspondence, elements of relative insignificance in phonology can correspond to major organizing features of meaning. (A similar situation arises in vision, where tiny features of a boundary can dramatically affect the three-dimensional interpretation of an array.)

This behavior on the part of Tense is a good illustration of the kinds of tensions that arise in syntactic theory. Tense has been notated in Fig. 1.1 as a feature on the verb, making it easy to match to phonology. But as a result it is more difficult to match to meaning, because it is necessary to say, exceptionally, that this feature attached to a verb (rather than the verb itself) maps to the function of largest scope in semantic/conceptual structure. We can improve the mapping to semantic/conceptual structure by adopting the alternative syntactic structure shown in (4), with Inflection as the head of the sentence: now the superordinate syntactic head maps to the largest-scope semantic function. But this creates a problem in mapping to the phonology, since the clitic 'z' now must match two separate pieces of syntax at once, the Verb and the Tense. So changing the syntactic analysis to simplify one mapping makes the other mapping more complex.

A third possibility is to keep both correspondences simple by localizing the complexity in the syntactic component itself. This has been the standard approach in generative grammar. The idea is that the syntactic structure of our sentence contains two different trees. The form given in Fig. 1.1 is the "surface structure," which interfaces easily with the phonology; and the form in (4) is the "underlying (or deep) structure," which interfaces easily with meaning. Then, internal to syntax, these two forms are related by a transformation that combines the underlying Inflection and Verb into the single unit found in surface structure. This approach was the major innovation in Chomsky's *Syntactic Structures* (1957) and has been a staple of syntactic analysis ever since.

Whichever of these three ways to deal with Tense proves correct, the point is that there is a mismatch between phonology and meaning, which has to be encoded somewhere in the mapping among the levels of structure. If this mismatch is eliminated at one point in the system, it pops up elsewhere. Much dispute in modern syntax has been over these sorts of mismatch and how to deal with them. (I don't think most linguists have viewed it this way, though.) We will encounter such mismatches pervasively in the course of Parts II and III.

1.7 Anaphora and unbounded dependencies

For the sake of completeness, let me step away from our little sentence for a moment, to mention briefly two syntactic phenomena that have been the focus of a great deal of research in linguistic theory and that will turn up now and again in the present study: anaphora and unbounded dependencies.

The set of constraints on the use of anaphoric elements such as pronouns and reflexives has come to be called *Binding Theory* (not to be confused with the neuroscientist's notion of binding, to be taken up in Chapter 3). Some standard examples of reflexives appear in (8). (The notation * before a sentence indicates that it is judged ungrammatical.)

(8)   a.   Joe adores himself.   [himself = Joe]
      b.   Joe thinks that Fred adores himself.   [himself = Fred]
      c.   *Joe thinks that you adore himself.

Example (8a) shows that a reflexive pronoun in object position can co-refer with (or be *bound by*) an NP in subject position. (8b) shows that it must co-refer with the subject of the same clause, not just with any subject. (8c) shows that if the reflexive cannot be bound by the subject of its own clause—here because *you* and *himself* cannot co-refer—its use is ungrammatical (in English; certain other languages such as Japanese work differently).

Turning to ordinary pronouns, consider the examples in (9).

(9)   a.   Joe adores him.   [*him* ≠ Joe]
      b.   Joe thinks that Fred adores him.   [*him* = Joe or third party]
      c.   Joe thinks that you adore him.   [*him* = Joe or third party]
      d.   He thinks that Joe adores Fred.   [*he* ≠ Joe or Fred]
      e.   If you tickle Joe, he laughs.   [*he* can = Joe]
      f.   If you tickle him, Joe laughs.   [*him* can = Joe]

Example (9a) shows that a simple pronoun in object position, unlike the reflexive in (8a), must not co-refer with the subject of its clause. (9b, c) show that it can, however, co-refer with an NP in another clause—again unlike a reflexive. (9d) shows that a pronoun cannot co-refer with an NP in a subordinate clause on its right. However, (9e) shows that a pronoun can co-refer with an NP in a subordinate clause on its left. In (9f) the pronoun is, atypically, to the left of its antecedent; but this case is saved by the fact that the pronoun is in a subordinate clause.

Another sort of anaphoric element is the expression *do so*, which stands for a VP rather than an NP. Its relation to its antecedent resembles that of pronouns. Compare (10a–d) to (9c–f).

(10)   a.   Fred impressed the boss without trying to do so.
                                          [*do so* = impress the boss]
       b.   Fred did so without trying to impress the boss.
                                          [*did so* ≠ impress the boss]
       c.   Without TRYING to impress the boss, Fred did so.
                                          [*did so* = impress the boss]
       d.   Without trying to do so, Fred impressed the boss.
                                          [*do so* = impress the boss]

These examples make it clear that it is a complex matter to state the exact conditions under which an anaphoric element can co-refer with an antecedent.

In particular, the conditions crucially involve linguistic structure, and not just linear order. Thus it is no surprise that these conditions have been a constant preoccupation of linguistic research. The main lines of dispute are whether the linguistic structure involved in conditions on anaphora is syntactic structure alone (Chomsky 1981; Lasnik 1989), or whether semantic/conceptual structure plays a role as well or even instead (six independent approaches among many appear in Jackendoff 1972; Fauconnier 1985; Kuno 1987; Levinson 1987; Van Hoek 1995; and Culicover and Jackendoff 1995).

For a different sort of phenomenon, consider the examples in (11). The italicized elements are understood as having a role appropriate to the position marked by *t*. For instance, in (11a), *which movie* is understood as the object of the verb *saw*.

(11)   a. *Which movie* does Susan imagine that Sarah saw *t* last night?
                                                          [*wh*-direct question]
       b. John was wondering *who* Sarah decided she would go to the movies with *t* on Sunday.   [Indirect question]
       c. I didn't like the movie *which* you said that everyone was talking about *t* the other day.   [Relative clause]
       d. You may take *whichever sandwich* you find *t* on the table over there.
                                                                    [Free relative]
       e. *That movie*, I wouldn't recommend that anyone consider taking their kids to *t*.   [Topicalization]

It is significant that the understood position can be within a subordinate clause, in fact deeply embedded within multiple subordinate clauses, as in (11e). For this reason, the relation between the italicized constituent and the understood position is called a *long-distance dependency*.

The analysis of such constructions within mainstream generative grammar is that the italicized constituent is actually *in* its understood position in underlying (deep) structure, and that it moves to the fronted position in the course of a syntactic derivation. The movement leaves behind an "unpronounced pronoun" called a *trace*, which is indicated by *t* in (11). However, other generative frameworks, especially Head-Driven Phrase Structure Grammar (Pollard and Sag 1994), have proposed analyses in which there is no movement, but instead the grammar directly establishes an anaphora-like relation between the italicized constituent and the trace (or a formal equivalent of the trace).

These constructions pose an interesting problem in that there are strong constraints on the structural position that an "extracted" constituent can occupy in relation to its trace. For example, an "extracted" constituent cannot be outside of a conjoined construction (12a), a relative clause (12b), an indirect question

(12c), or a noun complement (12d) that the trace is inside of. The examples in (12) all involve direct wh-questions, but the same thing happens with all the constructions in (10).

(12) a. *What did Beth eat peanut butter and t for dinner?
      b. *Who does Sam know a girl who is in love with t?
      c. *Who does Betty know which professor flunked t?
      d. *What food were you never aware of the hypothesis that you
          shouldn't eat t?

As with anaphora, it has been a preoccupation of linguistic research for three decades (starting with Ross 1967) to characterize precisely the environments from which "extraction" is possible. Again, one of the issues is whether the criteria are completely syntactic or partially semantic as well (Erteschik-Shir and Lappin 1979; Deane 1991; Kluender 1992; Van Valin 1994; Culicover and Jackendoff 1997). But the overall outlines of the phenomenon are clear.

*   *   *   *   *

Any adequate theory of language must begin with the fact that even the simplest sentences contain at least this rich a structure. Although I don't feel comfortable making moral statements, I will make one nevertheless. In my opinion, if one wishes to join the conversation about the nature of language, one must recognize and acknowledge this complexity. One need not have an account of all of it, but one may not willfully ignore it and still expect to be allowed in the game. This is the minimum that scientific responsibility demands.

Having recognized all this complexity, the obvious question is: What can we make of it? That is what the rest of this book is about.

CHAPTER 2

Language as a Mental Phenomenon

2.1 What do we mean by "mental"?

The remarkable first chapter of Noam Chomsky's *Aspects of the Theory of Syntax* (1965) sets in place an agenda for generative linguistic theory, much of which has survived intact for over thirty-five years. The present chapter and the next two will be devoted to evaluating and rearticulating this agenda, and to replying to some of the more common and longstanding criticisms of the approach.

We follow *Aspects* by starting with the issue of the status of linguistic description. The standard techniques of linguistic research lead us to some posited structure, say Fig.1.1, for the sentence *The little star's beside a big star*. How is such a structure to be understood? The fundamental claim of *Aspects* is that this structure is more than just a useful description for the purposes of linguists. It is meant to be "psychologically real": it is to be treated as a model of something in the mind of a speaker of English who says or hears this sentence. What does this claim mean?

Often the answer is put in these terms: Fig. 1.1 is a model of a mental representation of the sentence. Unfortunately, I have to plunge right in and attempt to wean readers away from this terminology, which I think has led to unnecessary and prolonged misunderstanding. The problem is that the term "representation" suggests that it represents *something*—and for something to represent something else, it must represent it *to someone*. But we don't want to say that Fig. 1.1 "represents the sentence to the language user": that would suggest somehow that the language user has conscious access to all the structure in the figure, or could have it with sufficient introspective effort. Nor do we want to say that the figure represents the sentence to some entity within the language user's unconscious mind: that would conjure up the notorious homunculus, the "little person in the brain" who (to use the term of Dennett 1991) sits in the "Cartesian theater" watching the show.

"Representation" belongs to a family of related terms that pervade cognitive science and that raise parallel problems. For instance, it is customary to speak of Fig. 1.1 as part of a *symbolic* theory of mental representation or of brain function; written symbols such as the phoneme *b* or the category NP are taken to model "symbols" in the mind. Now, the written symbols do symbolize something, namely the entities in the mind. But do the entities in the mind symbolize anything? The entity *b* in the mind doesn't *symbolize* the phoneme *b*, it *is* the mental entity that makes the phoneme what it is. Furthermore, a symbol is a symbol by virtue of having a perceiver or community of perceivers, so using this terminology implicitly draws us into the homunculus problem again.

Even the apparently innocuous term "information" is not immune: something does not constitute information unless there is something or someone it can inform. The writing on the page and the linguistic sounds transmitted through the air do indeed inform people—but the phoneme *b* and the category NP in the head are among the things that the writing and sounds inform people *of*.

As some readers will recognize, I am making all this fuss to head off the thorny philosophical problem of *intentionality*: the apparent "aboutness" of thoughts and other mental entities in relation to the outside world. John Searle (1980), for example, argues against the possibility of ever making sense of analyses like Fig. 1.1 in mentalistic terms, on the grounds that having such a structure in one's mind would not ever explain how it can be *about* the world, how it can symbolize anything. Jerry Fodor (1987, 1998), while deeply committed to the existence of mental representations, agrees with Searle that an account of intentionality is crucial; but then (if I may summarize his serious and complex argument in a sentence) he more or less tears himself in half trying to come up with a resolution of the ensuing paradoxes. The philosophical concerns with intentionality have traditionally been addressed to meaning (semantic/conceptual structure in Fig. 1.1); we will treat them in some detail in Chapters 9 and 10. But the same difficulties pertain, if more subtly, to the "symbols" of phonological and syntactic structure.

Accordingly, I propose to avoid all such problems from the outset by replacing the intentionality-laden terms "representation," "symbol," and "information" with appropriately neutral terms. I'll call Fig. 1.1 a model of a "cognitive structure," and I'll call components such as the phoneme *b* and the category NP "cognitive entities" or "structural elements." Instead of speaking of "encoding information," I'll use the old structuralist term "making distinctions". Note of course that a structural element may itself be a structure: for instance *b* is composed of its distinctive features.

Our revised construal of Fig. 1.1 is therefore that it models a cognitive structure in the mind of a speaker. But there is still a problem: the term "mind." The mind is traditionally understood as the seat of consciousness and volition; the "mind–body problem" concerns the relations of consciousness and volition to the physical world. Since at least Freud, we have also become accustomed to speak of the "unconscious mind". Common parlance, following Freud, takes the unconscious mind to be just like the conscious mind except that we aren't aware of it. Hence it is taken to be full of thoughts, images, and so forth that are at least in principle available to conscious introspection.

This notion of the unconscious is then often taken to be as far as one can go in describing phenomena as "mental." From there on down, it's all "body"— brain, to be more specific. This leaves no room in the mind for elaborate structures like Fig. 1.1, which go far beyond anything ever available to introspection. It leaves room only for neurons firing and thereby activating or inhibiting other neurons through synaptic connections. This is precisely the move Searle wants to make and Fodor wants to resist. In order for us to resist it successfully, we have to open up a new domain of description, as it were in between the Freudian unconscious and the physical meat.

In modern cognitive science, essentially following Chomsky's usage, the term "mind" (and more recently "mind/brain") has come to denote this in-between domain of description. It might be characterized as the functional organization and functional activity of the brain, some small part of which emerges in consciousness and most of which does not. Unfortunately, this usage tempts confusion with the everyday sense of the term: "It makes no sense to say you have an NP *in mind* when you utter *The little star is . . .*" Of course it doesn't. To stave off such misunderstanding, I will introduce the term of art "f-mind" ("functional mind") for this sense, to make clear its distinctness from common usage.[1]

The standard way to understand "functional" organization and activity (some people call it "subsymbolic") is in terms of the hardware–software distinction in computers: the brain is taken to parallel the hardware, the mind the software. When we speak of a particular computer running, say, Word 97, and speak of it storing certain data structures that enable it to run that program, we

---

[1] In revising terminology one is faced with a number of choices, none ideal. One can persist in using "mind," in which case readers (especially those picking up the book in the middle) are prone to understand the term in the everyday sense. Or one can create an entirely new and opaque term such as "cognizer" that leaves everyone cold. As a middle ground, I have chosen to adopt the traditional term but with a diacritic that flags it as a special technical usage. I apologize in advance for its awkwardness.

I should also make clear that this sense of "functional" is unrelated to the approach to linguistic theory called "functionalism," which seeks to derive grammatical properties from the exigencies of communication (see section 2.5).

are speaking in functional terms—in terms of the logical organization of the task the computer is performing. In physical (hardware) terms, this functional organization is embodied in a collection of electronic components on chips, disks, and so forth, interacting through electrical impulses. Similarly, if we speak of the mind/brain determining visual contours or parsing a linguistic expression, we are speaking in functional terms; this functional organization is embodied in a collection of neurons engaging in electrical and chemical interaction. There is plenty of dispute about how seriously to take the computational analogy (e.g. Searle 1980 again), but within certain bounds it has proven a robust heuristic for understanding brain processes.

There are limits on this analogy. First, no one writes the "programs" that run in our minds. They have to develop indigenously, and we call this *learning* and *development*—an issue we return to in Chapter 4.

Second, it has become clear that, unlike a standard computer, the brain (and therefore the f-mind) has no "executive central processor" that controls all its activities. Rather, it comprises a large number of specialized systems that interact in parallel to build up our understanding of the world and to control our goals and actions in the world. Even what seems to be a unified subsystem such as vision has been found to be subdivided into many smaller interacting systems for detecting motion, detecting depth, coordinating reaching movements, recognizing faces, and so forth.

Third, the character of the "software" and "data structures" that constitute the f-mind are far more tightly bound up with the nature of the "hardware" than in a standard computer. An early attitude toward studying the f-mind was carried over from experience with computers, where the same program could be run on physically very different machines: the functional organization of the mind was treated as a mathematical function, relatively independent of its physical instantiation in the brain (see e.g. Arbib 1964; Pylyshyn 1984). It now has become clearer that the "software" is exquisitely tuned to what the "hardware" can do (in a way that, say, Word 97 is not especially tuned to the Pentium chip).

As a consequence, discoveries about brain properties are now believed to have a more direct bearing on functional properties than was previously thought, a welcome development. As Marr (1982) eloquently stresses, though, the connection is a two-way street: if it can be demonstrated that humans must in effect compute such-and-such a function in order to perform as they do on some task, then it is necessary to figure out how the brain's neural circuitry could compute that function.[2]

---

[2] I should stress that deciding exactly what function people (or animals) compute is a matter for intense experimental investigation. Such investigation often shows that the f-mind resorts to "cheap tricks" rather than the mathematically most robust solution.

Even with these understandings of the relation between functional organization and neural instantiation, there has been a concerted attack on the usefulness of a theory of functional organization, coming this time not from philosophers but from certain communities in neuroscience and computational modeling (e.g. Rumelhart and McClelland 1986a; Churchland and Sejnowski 1992; Edelman 1992). According to this school of thought, the scientific reality is lodged in the neurons and the neurons alone; hence again there is no sense in developing models like Fig. 1.1.

I can understand the impulse behind this reductionist stance. The last two decades have seen an explosion of exciting new techniques for understanding the nervous system: recordings of the activity of individual neurons and the whole brain, computational modeling of perceptual and cognitive processes, and explanation of nervous system processes in terms of biochemical activity. Such research significantly deepens our understanding of the "hardware"—a quest with which I am altogether in sympathy. Furthermore, some aspects of "mental computation" in the functional sense are quite curious from the standpoint of standard algorithmic computation, but fall out rather naturally in neural network models (see Chapter 6). So there is good reason to relinquish the "Good Old-Fashioned Artificial Intelligence" treatment of the f-mind as a variety of serial and digital Turing machine, functionally quite unlike the brain.

On the other hand, researchers working within the reductionist stance often invoke it to delegitimate all the exquisitely detailed work done from the functional stance, including the work that leads to Fig. 1.1. Yet little has been offered to replace it. All we have at the moment is relatively coarse localization and timing of brain activity through imaging and studies of brain damage, plus recordings of individual neurons and small ensembles of them. With few exceptions (primarily in low-level vision, e.g. Hubel and Wiesel 1968), it is far from understood exactly what any brain area does, how it does it, and what "data structures" it processes and stores. In particular, none of the new techniques has yet come near revealing how a cognitive structure as simple as a single speech sound is explained in terms of a physical embodiment in neurons.

Consequently, the bread-and-butter work that linguists do on, say, case-marking in Icelandic, stress in Moroccan Arabic, and reduplication in Tagalog has no home within this tradition, at least in the foreseeable future. Should linguists just put these sorts of study on ice till neuroscience catches up? I submit that it is worth considering an alternative stance that allows for insights from both approaches.

2.2 How to interpret linguistic notation mentally

Toward such an alternative: No one denies that cognitive structures subsist on a neural substrate. And no one (I think) denies the importance of understanding how the neurons manage to accomplish language comprehension and production. So what might a result like Fig. 1.1 tell us about neural instantiation?

First, it is important to understand exactly what claims are made by the notation. It is obvious that speakers don't have a direct counterpart of the symbol NP in their heads. Rather, what is significant about the symbol is only that it differs from the other syntactic categories, not how it is labeled. Similarly, in saying syntactic structure is modeled by a tree structure, we are not claiming that speakers literally have trees in their heads. In fact, we often replace tree structures such as (1a) with the "labeled bracket notation" illustrated in (1b). Some people even use a "box" notation like (1c), and there are still other notations.

(1)   a.

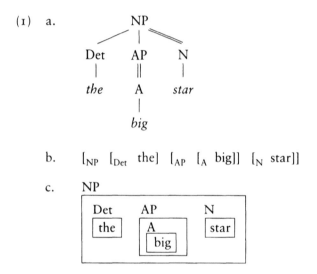

b.   [$_{NP}$ [$_{Det}$ the] [$_{AP}$ [$_A$ big]] [$_N$ star]]

c.   NP

All of these are ways of notating the theoretical claims (a) that words belong to syntactic categories; (b) that words are in linear order; and (c) that words group hierarchically into larger constituents that also belong to syntactic categories. These aspects of the notation, then, must be reflected somehow in neural instantiation. Beyond these aspects, the choice of notation is solely a matter of convenience.

With this understanding in mind, we can think of the combination of the states of all the neurons in the relevant parts of the brain as defining a "state-space" with a huge number of dimensions. When someone hears or produces the sentence *The little star's beside a big star*, their brain can be thought of as being at some point in that state-space; it will be at another point for each different linguistic expression. The notation in which Fig. 1.1 is couched encodes hypotheses about the significant dimensions of the state-space, and each element in the notation encodes a position in one (or more) of those dimensions.

For instance, the notation *b* encodes a position in the subspace of "phoneme choice"; in turn, the phonological distinctive feature notation (Fig. 1.2) encodes subdimensions such as consonanthood, voicing, and position of articulation within that subspace. The notation NP encodes a position in the subspace of "syntactic category." Its feature decomposition (alluded to in section 1.4) positions it in the dimensions of that subspace: it is a "phrasal" category (as opposed to "lexical" categories such as Noun) and "nominal" (as opposed to "verbal," "adjectival," and so forth). The fact that *b* is positioned in phonological structure and NP in syntactic structure encodes a hypothesis that certain dimensions of the overall state-space are more tightly linked than others, in particular that there are significant groupings of dimensions that can in functional terms be referred to as phonology and syntax. In other words, the functional approach is to be taken as making hypotheses about the significant dimensions of variation of brain states, and about the shape of the space of distinctions the brain can make.[3]

At least two interesting problems arise in making this conception work. The first is that the functional state-space in language is usually taken to be discrete or categorial. A phoneme is a *b* or a *p* but not something in between; a syntactic category is an NP or an AP but not something in between. By contrast, neural computation appears to be somewhat graded, a matter of degree of activation and synaptic strength. However, the seeds of accommodation are already present, I think. On the neural side, it is recognized that some neurons have highly tuned responses, making very sharp distinctions between what they do and do not fire to. Still, even the sharpest tuning is not absolute.

Looking at the linguistic side: In acoustic phonetics it has been known for a long time that categorial perception of phonemes is not absolutely sharp. Rather, there is a narrow range of acoustic inputs between, say, *p* and *b* that produce variation and context-dependency in hearers' judgments (e.g. Liberman and Studdert-Kennedy 1977). It has also become clear that in semantics, graded categories are altogether the norm (see section 11.6). And in syntax, indeterminacy has occasionally been recognized around the edges of categories (e.g. Ross's (1972) "squishy categories" and Culicover's (1999) proposal of a continuum of possible categories).

These observations in the functional domain are surely reflections of non-categorial behavior in the hardware. They force us to recognize that the dimensions of linguistic state-space are to some degree continuous rather than digital.

---

[3] Notice how the locution "space of distinctions the brain can make" strikes the ear differently than the more traditional "kinds of information the brain can encode." More austere, less intentional.

They appear to have sharp categorial distinctions because there are loci of relative stability within a dimension of variation. The degree of "discreteness vs. gradedness" in a dimension then reflects the relative steepness of stability gradients in the neighborhood of such loci. The discrete categories of a functional description are therefore to be regarded as a useful approximation to the behavior of the relevant part of the neural substrate, with the recognition that there will be situations where the approximation breaks down and we must resort to more elaborate modes of functional description.[4]

The second problem in bringing neural and functional descriptions into potential alignment is, I think, more severe. It arises from the fact that the functional description of language is inherently combinatorial. For example, we cannot simply say that the position in state-space encoded by Fig. 1.1 is the sum of the positions of all its speech sounds. Each speech sound is a position in phonological space that excludes all other positions. To simply sum them would be to say that the phonological part of state-space invoked by the sentence is simultaneously ð, ə, l, ɪ, and so on—a total mush. Rather it is necessary to specify the overall state (in part) as ð followed by ə followed by l and so on. But it is not clear how to set up a binary relation such as "followed by" in terms of a state-space. Similar difficulties emerge in instantiating hierarchical tree structures in terms of a state-space. Moreover, because the size of utterances is unlimited, the state-space also must be unlimited. We will come back to this problem in Chapter 3, concluding that neural modelers for the most part have not come to grips with the depth of this problem. It thus remains a significant challenge to the possibility of melding the neural and functional approaches.

These first two sections have engaged in a very abstract discussion, not an ideal way to start an exposition of linguistic theory. But it is necessary in order to situate the inquiry properly. In 1965 life was perhaps simpler: Chomsky could just say (1965: 4): "in the technical sense, linguistic theory is mentalistic, since it is concerned with discovering a mental reality underlying actual behavior." He clarifies this statement in a footnote (p. 193) that states the standard functionalist line of the period.

The mentalist, in this traditional sense, need make no assumptions about the possible physiological basis for the mental reality that he studies. In particular, he need not deny that there is such a basis. One would guess, rather, that it is the mentalistic studies that

---

[4] Smolensky (1999: 594) proposes the hypothesis of "Symbolic Approximation": "In the domain of language, the patterns of activation constituting mental representations admit abstract, higher-level descriptions that are closely approximated by the kinds of discrete, abstract structures posited by symbolic linguistic theory." Making appropriate substitutions for Smolensky's intentional terms "mental," "representations," and "symbolic," this is essentially what is envisioned here.

will ultimately be of greatest value for the investigation of neurophysiological mechanisms, since they alone are concerned with determining abstractly the properties that such mechanisms must exhibit and the functions they must perform.

Now, with our greater understanding of brain function at the neural level, the dependency has to be regarded as going both ways. And, although it is clear from this passage that Chomsky intends by the term "mind" a functional description, the intervening years have done little to clear up the confusion the term engenders.

In trying to purge linguistic theory of intentional terms such as "representation," "symbol," and "information," and by introducing the artificial terms "f-mind" and "f-mental," my goal is to clarify an explicit niche of description between the traditional (and Freudian) mind and the neural stance. Within this niche, linguists can do their usual research, arriving at theories of f-mental structure along the lines of Fig. 1.1. It can be recognized that these analyses ride on the back of a neural substrate whose physical structure ultimately determines the character of f-mental structure. At the same time, to the extent that cognitive structures are justified by linguistic and psycholinguistic investigation, they set boundary conditions on the character of the neural substrate that embodies them: the brain must be a structure that can compute *this*.

2.3 Knowledge of language

At the outset of *Aspects* (1965: 3–4), Chomsky says:

Linguistic theory is concerned primarily with an ideal speaker-listener, in a completely homogeneous speech-community, who knows its language perfectly and is unaffected by such grammatically irrelevant conditions as memory limitations, distractions, shifts of attention and interest, and errors (random or characteristic) in applying his knowledge of the language in actual performance. This seems to me to have been the position of the founders of modern general linguistics. . . .

We thus make a fundamental distinction between *competence* (the speaker-hearer's knowledge of his language) and *performance* (the actual use of the language in concrete situations). Only under the idealization set forth in the preceding paragraph is performance a direct reflection of competence.

This passage contains some of the most crucial points of contention between linguists and their critics, so it calls for some exegesis.

Let us start with "know" and "knowledge"; these are terms in which Chomsky sets great store. Here, for example, is a passage from the somewhat later *Reflections on Language*:

Thus it does not seem to me quite accurate to take "knowledge of English" to be a capacity or ability, though it enters into the capacity or ability exercised in language use. In principle, one might have the cognitive structure that we call "knowledge of English," fully developed, with no capacity to use this structure . . . (Chomsky 1975: 23)

The reason for this insistence becomes clearer in the next paragraph, where he mentions "the proper way to exorcise the ghost in the machine," alluding to a term coined by Gilbert Ryle (1949). Ryle famously stressed the distinction between "knowing that," a cognitive relation to a proposition, and "knowing how," a capacity, ability, habit, or disposition to perform an action. "Knowing how" was taken by Ryle to be explicable in behaviorist terms: it could be acquired on the basis of reinforcement and could be verified simply by the organism's behavior. It hence could avoid any mention of mind, which to Ryle smacked of "the ghost in the machine" (our homunculus of Section 2.1). Chomsky, for his part, rightly insists that linguistic theory cannot be reduced to behaviorist explanation. One way for him to do so is to distance himself from any terminology such as "ability" or "habit" that exudes the slightest whiff of behaviorism, as in this passage from early in *Aspects* (1965: 4):

Observed use of language or hypothesized dispositions to respond, habits, and so on, may provide evidence as to the nature of this mental reality, but surely cannot constitute the actual subject matter of linguistics, if this is to be a serious discipline.

In retrospect, I would say the distinction has been somewhat overdrawn. For one thing, disavowing "knowing how" seems to draw one toward the other member of the opposition, "knowing that." But knowing English is not really "knowing *that*" anything.[5] To have a command of, say, the English tense system is not to be acquainted with and committed to any set of propositions (at least in the standard sense). To claim that knowledge of language is a variety of "knowing that" would seem to put it in the conscious sector, or at least in the Freudian unconscious—certainly not in the functionalist domain where we want it.

Moreover, we now believe that any sort of practiced and overlearned ability or expertise, from swimming to playing the clarinet to playing chess, requires complex cognitive structures to support the overt behavior. Motor paralysis

---

[5] Except under a heavily referentially opaque interpretation of *know*. One can for instance say that Beth knows that *every* is a Determiner in English, even if she has never heard the term "Determiner"; one bases this assertion on Beth's linguistic behavior, including perhaps her grammaticality judgments. But this is parallel to saying that Beth knows that the fifth note of *Happy Birthday* is a perfect fourth above the first note, based on the fact that she sings the song in tune—even though she knows no music theory and wouldn't have the slightest idea what a "perfect fourth" is. This is hardly "knowing that" in the sense that Ryle intended.

may mean that one cannot exercise that ability, but, whatever Ryle may have thought, the underlying cognitive capacity need not dissolve. So the distinction between language and other abilities is hardly as sharp as Chomsky wants to make it.

Again, "knowledge" is one of those intentional terms, and this accounts for a lot of the trouble it has raised and that Chomsky has had to fend off. Sometimes (e.g. 1986: 265–69) he suggests substituting a term of art such as "cognize"; then he shows that this term would be used essentially the same way as "know" and, concluding we are free to use any term we feel comfortable with, chooses to stay with "know." Much of his discussion in this vein is in connection with critics who fail to recognize the distinctness of the f-mental domain in which linguistic structure resides. To keep matters straight, I will append the obnoxious "f-" to the term when necessary, speaking of "f-knowledge."

2.4 Competence versus performance

We now turn our attention to the heavily loaded distinction between *competence* and *performance*.[6] In the quote at the beginning of the previous section, Chomsky alludes to the concern with competence—"the speaker-hearer's [f-]knowledge of his language"—as "the position of the founders of modern general linguistics." What is behind this assertion, I suspect, is that he is trying to justify doing what linguists have always done, namely analyze things like case systems, relative clauses, and stress placement—but in an explicitly mentalistic framework. Speaking strictly pragmatically, this sort of inquiry has yielded massive results, some of which are encapsulated in Fig. 1.1; there seems no reason to abandon it.

---

[6] It is important not to conflate the competence–performance distinction with two other distinctions in the literature. One is Chomsky's own distinction between *I-language* ("internal(ized) language") and *E-language* ("external(ized) language"), emphasized in his 1986 book *Knowledge of Language*. I-language is the structure of language regarded mentalistically; it coincides more or less with competence. E-language, however, is (as I understand it) not the mechanisms that speakers use to exhibit linguistic behavior (i.e. performance), but either (a) external linguistic behavior of individuals or (b) language regarded as an object external to human minds, as an abstract object that subsists "in the community." While Chomsky thinks studies of performance are potentially of interest (at least in *Aspects*), he maintains that the study of E-language will yield nothing of theoretical significance.

Another distinction sometimes conflated with competence/performance is Saussure's (1915) often-cited distinction between *langue* and *parole*. *Parole* is supposed to be individuals' speech-acts; *langue* is supposed to be the language abstracted away from the individuals that speak it. Thus nothing here corresponds to either competence or performance in Chomsky's sense; rather both terms correspond to aspects of E-language.

Chomsky makes the competence–performance distinction in part to ward off alternative proposals for how linguistics must be studied. In particular, he is justifiably resisting the behaviorists, who insisted that proper science requires counting every cough in the middle of a sentence as part of linguistic behavior. His resistance was particularly urgent at the time, because of the overwhelming influence of the behaviorist stance on American structuralist linguistics of the period (see Chomsky's remarks on Twaddell (1935) on p. 193 of *Aspects*, for example). Judging from remarks in *Syntactic Structures* (especially pp. 19–20), Chomsky is also trying to defend traditional linguistic practice against finite-state Markov theories that generate or analyze sentences in serial order, moving from state to state; he cites Shannon and Weaver (1949) and Hockett (1955) as instances of this approach. (Such approaches have not gone away: Elman (1990) is a recent reincarnation.)

The factors that Chomsky consigns to performance—the things he thinks a theory of linguistic competence should *not* be concerned with—are quite heterogeneous, and it is worth reviewing some of them to see how they fare in a more contemporary light.

A first factor is memory limitations. Presumably memory limitations account for the impossibility of producing a 6000-word sentence, every part of which is locally grammatical. One could not possibly keep all that in f-mind at once. For a more extreme case, one would die before completing a 60-million-word sentence. The point is that the theory of linguistic competence does not have to bother to rule such things out—there are other and more obvious extraneous factors.

A second factor in Chomsky's notion of performance is "distractions, shifts of attention and interest, and errors (random or characteristic)." There is now a strong tradition of studying speech errors and repairs (e.g. Fromkin 1971; Garrett 1975; Levelt 1989; Dell 1986), which has been used to help justify the division of linguistic structure into domains along the lines shown in Fig. 1.1. If the domains picked out by such inquiry do not coincide with those proposed by linguistic theory, there should be a certain amount of concern. The theories of competence and performance should line up. We take up these issues in Chapter 7.

A third factor in performance is the distinction between knowledge and processing. Chomsky says (1965: 9), "When we say that a sentence has a certain derivation with respect to a particular generative grammar, we say nothing about how the speaker or hearer might proceed, in some practical or efficient way, to construct such a derivation. These questions belong to the theory of language use—the theory of performance." This basic distinction between the grammatical structure of sentences and the logic of sentence processing has remained essential to grammatical theory up to the present. For example, Fig.

1.1 models a cognitive structure in the f-mind of someone who either hears or speaks the sentence *The little star's beside a big star*. A hearer presumably constructs this structure first by deriving a phonological structure from the auditory signal and then using that to arrive at the syntactic and conceptual structures. But a speaker presumably starts out with a meaning to express and develops a syntactic and phonological structure from it. So although the structure is the same, the hearer and speaker produce its parts in different orders.

This is, I think, the essential difference between competence theories and processing theories. Competence theories are concerned with what the total structure is for either speaker or hearer. Processing theories are concerned with how the structure is built in real time, so they naturally bifurcate into different theories for the speaker and the hearer.

Chomsky's intuition that "the study of performance models incorporating generative grammars may be a fruitful study" has of course been borne out: there is now a thriving inquiry into the course of sentence processing and sentence production (sources too numerous to mention, but see Chapter 7), based on the structures uncovered by competence theory.

A final factor in Chomsky's conception of performance has to a degree fallen by the wayside: "intonational and stylistic factors" (Chomsky 1965: 10). For instance, Chomsky cites the natural intonation of (2) as a performance error: "the intonation breaks are ordinarily inserted in the wrong places (that is, after 'cat' and 'rat,' instead of where the main brackets [i.e. the syntactic boundaries] appear" (p. 13).

(2)   This is the cat that caught the rat that stole the cheese.

(2) is now normally recognized as an example of mismatch between prosodic structure (one of the tiers of phonological structure) and syntactic structure, i.e. as not an error at all. We will return to this case in Chapter 5.

Chomsky also cites the following examples of grammatical sentences that are "unacceptable" for performance reasons (1965: 11):

(3)   a. *I called the man who wrote the book that you told me about up.
       b. *The man who the boy who the students recognized pointed out is a
           friend of mine.

(3a) would now most likely be treated as a competence error. The violation comes from the fact that the particle *up* at the end grammatically requires its own intonation contour; however, a short intonation contour at the end of a sentence, especially following a long contour, is highly dispreferred. This is part of the competence grammar of English, but in the prosodic rather than the syntactic domain.

(3b) is the well-known case of a doubly center-embedded sentence. A language that allows nouns to be freely modified by relative clauses cannot help but come up with cases like this, among the many other possible configurations. It would be artificial for the description of relative clauses to single out this particular configuration as ungrammatical. However, Miller and Chomsky (1963) showed that under certain reasonable assumptions about language processing, this configuration, unlike other relative clause constructions, would fortuitously create a major strain on working memory. They therefore concluded that it is a performance violation, not a competence violation—that is, it is one of those extrinsic factors that the competence theory need not mention.

It appears to me that the problem in (3b), like that in (3a), is at least in part prosodic. To see this, notice that the examples in (4) are parallel to (3b) in having doubly center-embedded relative clauses, but sound much better; (4c) in particular is nearly identical to (3b). Hence the problem with (3b) cannot be solely a matter of its syntactic parse. (I suggest reading these out loud; the bracketed commas indicate intonation breaks.)

(4) a. The movie that everyone I know raved about[,] turned out to be lousy.
     b. That professor that the girl you brought home fell in love with[,] won the Nobel Prize last week.
     c. The man who the boy we recognized pointed out[,] is a friend of mine.

These sentences evidently sound better than (3a) because their innermost relative clauses are relatively shorter and therefore can form intonational units with the nouns they modify. For instance, *everyone I know* in (4a) can be an intonational unit in a way that *the boy who the students recognized* in (3b) cannot. Such phenomena involving length are reminiscent of prosodic violations like (3a). This is not to say that the problem with (3b) is *all* prosodic, but more aspects of competence appear to be involved than Chomsky realized in 1965.[7]

To sum up, what Chomsky lumps into performance actually constitutes a wide variety of phenomena. Some fall into basic facts about memory limitations; some into different aspects of the theory of sentence processing; and some now are subsumed under competence theory.

---

[7] A detailed contemporary analysis of center-embedding as a processing violation, with massive reference to the psycholinguistic literature, appears in Gibson (1998). Christiansen and Chater (1999) offer a treatment of center-embedding difficulties in a connectionist framework. However, the task set to their networks is simply to get subject–verb agreement correct. Hence as far as their networks are concerned, a right-embedded structure such as *Bill sees the boys [who like the girl [who eats ice cream]]* is identical to a non-embedded structure such as *Bill sees; the boys like [something]; the girl eats ice cream*; that is, for them, right-embedding is not embedding at all. In the light of this basic error in the linguistic analysis, it is hard to evaluate Christiansen and Chater's claims about center-embedding.

It is interesting how the competence–performance distinction has been misunderstood in the literature. For instance, a 1984 edited volume (Bever et al. 1984) contains three papers with nearly identical pronouncements on competence vs. performance, by Walter Kintsch, Charles Osgood, and Roger Schank and Lawrence Birnbaum. Each of them rejects competence models on the grounds that they are about *syntax*, whereas a really adequate theory should deal with semantics and pragmatics as well (or instead!). Each then proposes his own theory of language processing that in fact incorporates implicitly a theory of language structure, a theory that, while not a Chomskyan generative grammar, is recognizably a competence theory.

These authors are correct in observing that generative grammar's emphasis on syntax is not sufficient to account for language understanding; but so far as I know, Chomsky has never proposed leaving semantic interpretation out of the eventual competence theory. (Pragmatics may be a different story, though.) In fact, their objections to generative grammar are more properly attributed to its "syntactocentrism," the assumption that the combinatorial power of language stems from syntax alone (see Chapter 5).

In the quote at the beginning of the previous section, Chomsky views competence as an idealization abstracted away from the full range of linguistic behavior. As such, it deserves as much consideration as any idealization in science: if it yields interesting generalizations it is worthwhile. Still, one can make a distinction between "soft" and "hard" idealizations. A "soft" idealization is acknowledged to be a matter of convenience, and one hopes eventually to find a natural way to re-integrate the excluded factors. A standard example is the fiction of a frictionless plane in physics, which yields important generalizations about forces and energy. But one aspires eventually to go beyond the idealization and integrate friction into the picture. By contrast, a "hard" idealization denies the need to go beyond itself; in the end it cuts itself off from the possibility of integration into a larger context.

It is my unfortunate impression that, over the years, Chomsky's articulation of the competence–performance distinction has moved from relatively soft, as in the quote above that introduces it, to considerably harder, as suggested by the flavor of passages like this one:

It has sometimes been argued that linguistic theory must meet the empirical condition that it account for the ease and rapidity of parsing. But parsing does not, in fact, have these properties. . . . In general, it is not the case that language is readily usable or "designed for use." (Chomsky and Lasnik 1993: 18)

There turn out to be good reasons that Chomsky has made this shift, emanating from the character of his version of competence theory. The approach to be developed in Part II maintains the competence–performance distinction but lends itself better to integration with performance theory. I take such a relatively soft idealization to be a desideratum. (Bresnan and Kaplan (1982) and Pollard and Sag (1994) argue for a similar position; the theories of syntax they advocate lend themselves to direct interpretation in parsing terms.)

To sum up, I think the competence–performance distinction acknowledges the value of the sort of work linguists do in their day-to-day research, while recognizing that this work eventually must be placed in a broader psychological context. But I regard it as a pragmatic division of labor, a methodological convenience, not as a firewall to protect a certain form of inquiry.

Combining this discussion with that in section 2.1, we might best view the enterprise of understanding the human language capacity as naturally dividing into three lines of inquiry:

• Theory of competence: the functional characterization of the "data structures" stored and assembled in the f-mind in the course of language use.

• Theory of performance: the functional characterization of the use of these data structures in the course of language perception and production.

• Theory of neural instantiation: how the data structures and the processes that store and assemble them are realized in the brain.

Again, the distinctions between these theories are "soft" or methodological divisions, not ideological ones. One should welcome cross-talk among them, and in practice today we indeed find a steadily increasing amount of it.

2.5 Language in a social context (all too briefly)

Of course, as has often been observed, language does not subsist in the f-minds of individuals alone; it also exists in a social context. Some would say it exists *only* in a social context. In a sense this is true—if there were no other individuals with whom one wished to communicate, there would be little point to language as we know it. But on the other hand, the use of a language in a community presumes that the individuals have the cognitive capacity to produce and comprehend the signals they are sending each other. This cognitive capacity is what is being studied in the mentalistic framework.

Herbert Clark (1996) emphasizes that linguistic communication is not a one-way street, a speaker making utterances and a hearer passively taking them in. Rather, virtually all communication (but especially face to face) involves a delicate negotiation between speaker and hearer in a joint effort for both to be assured that the intended message gets across. Drawing on much previous research, Clark shows that many aspects of live speech that are often taken to be matters of "performance", for example hesitations, repairs, and interjected *um* and *like* are often metalinguistic signals designed to help guide the hearer through the process of interpretation, and to elicit feedback from the hearer as to whether the message is getting across. He also shows how gestures, facial expressions, and direction of gaze are often used to amplify the message beyond what the spoken signal conveys.

My interpretation of Clark's work is that it adds to the domains in which it is necessary and possible to describe linguistic competence. In addition to sentence structure itself, language users need cognitive structures that permit them to understand the goals of communication and to attach significance to the associated metalinguistic signals. As Clark emphasizes, many aspects of this communicative competence are subsumed under a larger theory of how people manage to carry out any sort of cooperative activity. Thus this kind of research is a bridge between strictly linguistic competence and more general social competence. And within this domain, we need as well a theory of performance that explains how people create and receive such metalinguistic signals in real time.

But on the other hand, a theory of communicative competence and/or performance doesn't eliminate the need for a theory of grammatical structure. No matter how well speakers can coordinate their activity, they still have to put the verbs in the right place in their sentences. (I don't think Clark would deny this, but one does sometimes see claims to the effect that one doesn't need a theory of grammar because language is all about communicative effectiveness.)

Let us next turn back to Chomsky's idealization of a homogeneous speech community. This has always been a soft idealization: generative linguists have never hesitated to discuss situations where speakers do not all have the same cognitive structures associated with the utterances they present as linguistic output. Such situations occur all the time in language and dialect contact, and above all when adults talk with young children. In these situations, Clark's point becomes even clearer. Communicating requires not just putting a signal out there for the listener and hoping for the best, but mutually verifying that the message has gotten across to both participants' satisfaction.

However, once we acknowledge that people do not necessarily have identical internalized cognitive structures for language, the question arises of what constitutes, say, "English"—or even "Standard American English." I suggest that the use of language names is a harmless reification of the commonality in the linguistic f-knowledge of a perceived community of speakers. When we get down to dialect or individual differences, we can drop the idealization insofar as necessary without any problem. Again, this is common practice in linguistics.

I imagine, then, that to speak of a language in linguistics is a bit like speaking of a species in biology: one acknowledges that members of a species are not genetically identical; and cases sometimes arise where what is apparently one species shades off imperceptibly over some geographical range into another. Does that mean there are no species? Some biologists think so. But as long as we regard the term as a convenient first approximation, there seems no harm in it.

It is worth mentioning, though, that this first-approximation reification of language very easily passes over unnoticed into a harder idealization, especially in everyday parlance. It is this idealization that, for instance, leads people to say that "the language" is degenerating because teenagers don't know how to talk anymore (they were saying that in the eighteenth century too!). It is also behind seeing the dictionary as an authority on the "correct meanings" of words rather than as an attempt to record how words are understood in the speech community. Even linguists adopt this stance all the time in everyday life (especially as teachers of students who can't write a decent paragraph). But once we go inside the heads of speakers to study their own individual cognitive structure, the stance must be dropped.

Now suppose, counterfactually, that speakers did have identical cognitive structures associated with their linguistic communication. There would still be reasons why communication cannot be perfect. For one thing, people are in different states of knowledge: they have different histories and different goals. In addition, one can never be absolutely certain, from the other's behavior, that one's message has been understood the way one intends. Rather, one settles for more or less certainty, depending on the situation. Telling someone how to perform surgery is more exacting than relating a personal anecdote in a bar, and one adjusts one's communicative expectations accordingly.

Moreover, the act of communication presents two conflicting desiderata. One goal is to get the meaning across with a minimum of physical effort on the part of both speaker and hearer. This creates a pressure towards brevity and abbreviation. But another goal is to convey the meaning as clearly as possible, which creates a pressure towards length and redundancy. Individual speech acts as well as the grammatical structure of languages reflect the tension between these two goals.

Of course, the more that both partipants know they can rely on context to fix the intended content, the briefer the actual utterance has to be. Under such conditions, local conventions can arise, some extremely parochial and context-bound. For instance, in the Cafe Espresso Royale in Urbana, Illinois in the summer of 1999, regular customers could be heard to utter, "I'll have a day"— meaning, to those behind the counter, "a coffee of the day." This is incomprehensible out of context, but in its narrow context it served its purpose.

These conflicting pressures of brevity and clarity are present all the time, and are generally considered to be one of the important forces motivating historical change in language. As I understand the functionalist school of grammar (e.g. Bates and MacWhinney 1982, Givón 1995), much of linguistic structure is claimed to be a consequence of the constant problem of balancing these two pressures against one another. Still, this does not eliminate the need for analyses like Fig. 1.1, as is sometimes asserted. In a particular utterance, speaker and hearer both have plenty of structure that has to be accounted for, whatever its historical source.

The inhomogeneity of linguistic populations and the possibility of innovation lead to a fascinating question: how does a particular linguistic usage (word, construction, or grammatical feature) come to be relatively stabilized in a large dispersed population? We have some evidence for how innovations spread through a population over time (e.g. Labov (1994) for phonetic changes, Maling and Sigurjónsdóttir (1997) for a syntactic change), but this doesn't really answer *why* innovations spread. There are doubtless more basic principles of social dynamics that apply not only to language but to cultural innovations as well. Kirby (1998) and Steels (1998) can be understood as exploring the dynamics whereby communicative devices achieve a stable form within a community.

Finally, I should not leave this extremely brief survey of social factors without acknowledging all the issues of social identity (e.g. gender, class, and ethnicity) tied up with language use. These concerns about language certainly arouse greater passions than does the proper formulation of subject–auxiliary inversion. However, they are relatively remote from my concerns here—though not because of lack of intrinsic importance. And to be sure, research on the cognitive structure associated with language has been brought to bear on these issues, for example in the social legitimation of African-American varieties of English (e.g. Labov 1972; Rickford 1999) and the signed languages (Stokoe 1960; Klima and Bellugi 1979). The connections are there for those who wish to pursue them.

CHAPTER 3

Combinatoriality

3.1 The need for an f-mental grammar

From the standpoint of communication systems in the natural world, one of the most striking facts about human language is that its users can create and understand an unlimited number of utterances on an unlimited number of topics. This productivity is possible thanks to an important design feature of language: utterances are built by combining elements of a large but finite vocabulary into larger meaningful expressions. Furthermore, the principles of combination are such as to enable users to construct arbitrarily long expressions, subject only to extrinsic limitations of memory and attention of the sort alluded to in Chapter 2.

As is observed in every introductory linguistics course, language provides many different ways of constructing elaborate utterances. Among them are successive conjunction of phrases (1a) or clauses (1b), multiple adjectival modifiers (1c), successively embedded prepositional modifiers (1d), successively embedded relative clauses (1e), successively embedded complement clauses (1f), plus free mixtures of the above (1g).

(1)   a. We ate apples and oranges and pears and pretzels and stew and . . . and I can't remember what else.
      b. Ducks quack and dogs bark and cats meow and fish swim and worms wriggle and . . . and I don't know what armadillos do.
      c. This is a big, new, imposing, poorly designed, cold, uncomfortable, very expensive building.
      d. There's a sty on the eye on the fly on the lump on the wart on the frog on the bump on the log in the hole in the bottom of the sea.
      e. This is the butcher that killed the ox that drank the water that quenched the fire that burned the stick that beat the dog that bit the cat that ate the goat that my father bought for two zuzim.

    f. I wonder if Susan knows that Fred assured Lois that Clark would
       remind Pat to buy food for dinner.

    g. We have a young child and our chef has twins so we know how difficult
       it is to find a first rate restaurant that doesn't shudder when you show
       up at the door with kids in tow.

The length and complexity of utterances involves not only the number of
words and their syntactic organization. The messages that utterances convey—
and their topics—are equally unlimited. In this respect human utterances contrast sharply with the long and complex songs of certain species of whales and
birds, which, as far as can be told at present (Hauser 1996; Payne 2000; Slater
2000), basically convey only the message "Here I am, everyone!"

In principle, a communication system might construct arbitrarily long messages just by adding more and more new elements to the end of utterances, along
the lines of a shopping list. But human language doesn't work like that: it builds
up large utterances according to structural principles or *rules*. What made generative grammar in the modern sense possible was the development of formal
techniques for describing rules and systems of rules, deriving from work in the
foundations of mathematics during the first half of the twentieth century. (The
very same techniques, of course, led to the development of the digital computer.) And, although there were precursors in post-Bloomfieldian structuralism, in particular Chomsky's teacher Zellig Harris (Harris 1951), it was
Chomsky who developed and made clear the connections between this mathematical work and linguistic description.

Putting the issue of combinatoriality into a mentalist framework adds an
important twist. Since the number of possible utterances of a human language is
unlimited, language users cannot store them all in their heads. Rather, f-knowledge of language requires two components. One is a finite list of structural elements that are available to be combined. This list is traditionally called the
"lexicon," and its elements are called "lexical items"; for the moment let us suppose lexical items are words or morphemes (we will alter this substantially in
Chapter 6). The other component is a finite set of combinatorial principles, or a
grammar.[1] To the extent that speakers of a language (or a dialect) are consistent
with one another (see section 2.5), we can speak of the "grammar of the language" as a useful approximation to what all its speakers have in their heads.

The task of a theory of linguistic competence, then, is to model the lexicon

---

[1] A terminological point: Sometimes "grammar" is taken to encompass rules *plus* lexicon, particularly when, as will be seen in section 3.3, the lexicon is thought to contain rules as well. From
force of habit, I will no doubt fall into this inconsistency, but I will attempt to make clear what is
intended when it makes a difference.

and the grammar in a language user's f-mind, using every sort of empirical evidence available, from speakers' grammaticality judgments to patterns of historical development to brain imaging. Diagrams like Fig. 1.1 are taken to reflect the principles by which sentences are built up from (or can be analyzed into) their constituent parts. The structure one draws comes out differently depending on the principles one claims are involved in its construction.[2]

Chomsky coined the term "generative grammar" to refer to a precise formulation of the combinatorial principles that characterize a speaker's competence. He deliberately used the term ambiguously, to characterize both the principles in the speaker's head and those formulated by the linguist, relying on context to make clear which was intended. For example, if one speaks of "writing a grammar," it is obviously the linguist's grammar; but if one speaks of "a child learning or acquiring a grammar," the principles in the head are intended.

The next two sections will undertake a brief survey of the sorts of grammatical rule that various versions of generative grammar have found it useful to posit. With these examples before us, we will be in a better position to ask how to construe the notion of a rule of mental grammar, a crucial issue in trying to integrate linguistic theory into a larger theory of mind (section 3.4). The chapter will conclude by considering some important implications of combinatoriality for theories of brain processing.

3.2 Some types of rule

Across a broad range of formulations of linguistic theory, three major types of rules emerge, which I will call *formation rules, derivational rules*, and *constraints*.[3] We take up these types in the present section. In addition, many approaches claim that the lexicon is not just a list of unstructured items. Rather, lexical items have their own internal structure which can be characterized by *lexical rules*. These come in at least two types, *lexical formation rules* and *lexical relations*; a special case of the latter is *inheritance hierarchies*. Lexical rules will be the topic of section 3.3.

---

[2] Could there be more than one grammar that predicts the same linguistic behavior, so that it would be a mistake to speak of *the* grammar of English? In principle, yes. In practice, it is usually hard enough to find even *one* grammar that does the trick in sufficient detail. On the other hand, the possibility of multiple grammars at certain points in a language's history is often posited as a source of grammatical change over the course of a generation or two (Kiparsky 1969).

[3] A terminological point: sometimes *rules* are taken to include only formation rules and derivational rules, contrasting with *constraints*. It is convenient here to lump all three types together as rules.

3.2.1 *Formation rules and typed variables*

Formation rules specify how lexical items are to be combined into larger units, and how these larger units in turn are combined into still larger units. Phrase structure rules are the prototypical formation rules. An example is the rule for English noun phrases that permits the construction of units like *the little star*. In the traditional notation it is written like this:[4]

(2)   NP → Det – AP – N

This is traditionally read "Noun Phrase goes to (is expanded as) a Determiner followed by an Adjective Phrase followed by a Noun." The application of this rule is reflected in two places within Fig. 1.1, shown by the circled parts of the syntactic tree structure shown in (3).

(3)

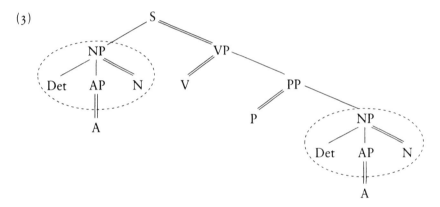

The traditional way of reading (2) suggests that the construction of utterances is to be conceived as proceeding from the top down: one starts with S, expands it to NP followed by VP, and so on. Students are always reminded that this is just an abstract way of characterizing a class of structures, and therefore rules like (2) are to be understood non-directionally. Nevertheless, the aura of directionality remains in the notation, if only because of the arrow.

A more neutral notation for the same formation rule might be the tree fragment (4) (Janet Fodor has suggested the term "treelet").

---

4 This rule is meant only as a sample and is heavily oversimplified. As in Ch. 1, I am assuming NP has a flat structure in which its constituents are simply concatenated. If the structure is more complex, as is standardly assumed, the phrase structure rules must be adjusted accordingly. I am also ignoring the distinction between optional constituents (the Det and the AP) and obligatory constituents (the N) as well as further possible constituents of NP such as postnominal PPs and relative clauses.

(4)

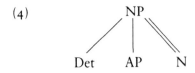

This can be read as "An NP has as parts a Det, an AP, and an N, in that order."
Alternatively, it can be read "bottom-up": "A Det followed by an AP followed
by an N may be taken to constitute an NP." Within this notation, we can think
of constructing a tree as "clipping" treelets together. For instance, (4) would
"clip onto" an NP node at the bottom of another treelet; in turn, a treelet with
AP at the top would "clip onto" the AP node of (4). "Clipping together" can
proceed from top to bottom, bottom to top, or any combination thereof.[5]

Some formulations of generative grammar have found it of interest to separate out the rules for constituency (the parts of an expression) from the principles for linear order. Such a procedure is useful, for instance, in characterizing
languages with freer word order than English. In this case the formation rules
specify only constituency (what is a part of what); principles of linear order are
formulated as constraints (see below). There is no standard notation for rules of
unordered constituency, and I will not bother to invent one here.

Whatever notation one adopts, an absolutely essential feature of formation
rules already emerges: they must be formulated in terms of abstract categories.
A formation rule that mentioned only particular lexical items would not be
especially useful. There may exist such rules in English, for instance the one that
says *hello* and *there* may be combined in that order to form the utterance *hello
there*. But this way of combining items is not going to lead to any sort of productivity. At the very least one must be able to refer to the class of words as a
whole. For instance, suppose we wish to specify something as simple as "An
utterance is a string of concatenated words." This requires a formation rule
which counts anything that falls into the class of words as part of an utterance—
but which excludes non-word entities such as grunts, gestures, and sneezes.
That is, the formation rule must contain a *typed variable*—a specification "anything of *this* particular sort."[6]

Most actual formation rules in language use typed variables narrower than

---

[5] This approach is most explicit in Tree-Adjoining Grammar (Joshi 1987; Frank and Kroch
1995), but it is also essentially the tack taken in all unification-based approaches such as HPSG and
LFG.

[6] One might wonder why we need to introduce something as technical as a typed variable in
order to specify something as loose as "any word." The answer becomes clearer when we notice
that language contains contexts that permit a category *broader* than words. An example is *And
then he went* "* * *," where "* * *" can be any sort of noise at all—or even a soundless gesture such
as shrugging the shoulders.

"any word." For example, (4) has four variables: NP, Det, AP, and N: it says "Any Det followed by any AP followed by any N can constitute an NP." Of these variables, Det and N are categories (or types) of word; let us concentrate on them for a moment. In order for rule (4) to be able to put words together, two things are necessary. First, lexical items must be marked for what category they belong to. For instance, *star* and *cat* belong to the category Noun; *the*, *a*, and *this* belong to the category Determiner. Second, we need a "meta-principle" of *variable instantiation*, which can be seen from two perspectives. From the "top-down" perspective, it allows instances of a category to be substituted for a variable of that category, thus "satisfying" or "saturating" the variable. From a "bottom-up" perspective, it allows an individual word to be analyzed as having a role in a larger structure; this structure can be identified by substituting a variable for the individual word.

Next, consider the categories NP and AP. These are not categories of words, but categories of *phrases*. Such categories allow us not only to string words together, but also to build them into larger units that can then combine further. A phrasal category is more abstract than a lexical category such as Noun and Determiner, in that it is not instantiated just by pulling a single word out of the lexicon. Rather, it is instantiated by a string of one or more words and/or phrases that satisfy the variables in its formation rule (i.e. that are "clipped onto it"). Thus, for instance, NP can be instantiated by *stars*, *the little star*, *this fat cat*, and so forth; AP by *fat*, *very skinny*, *moderately attractive*, and so forth.

The reason for using phrasal variables rather than just strings of lexical types becomes clear when the same phrasal variable appears in several different formation rules. For example, NP appears as a variable in, among other things, the following formation rules of English (assuming a generic introductory-course set of phrase structure rules).

(5) a.   S   b.   VP   c.   PP

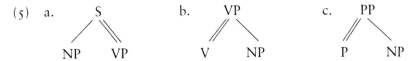

     NP   VP   V   NP   P   NP

In (5a), NP is the subject of a sentence; in (5b) it is the object of a verb phrase; in (5c) it is the object of a prepositional phrase. The fact that the same variable, with the same set of instantiations, shows up in multiple places is part of what convinces us we are dealing with a genuine linguistic unit and not just an analytic artifact.

In introducing formation rules as part of a grammar, we already have to face three important and interlocked empirical questions. First, what are the actual formation rules for the language under analysis? Second, and more generally, what is the available repertoire of types for variables in formation rules? For instance, how many lexical categories are there and what are they, and how many phrasal categories are there and what are they? Third, what is the repertoire of relations induced by formation rules? Do they specify linear order of the parts, like (3), or do they specify unordered constituency? Is the relation of the head to the phrase (shown by a double line in (4) and (5)) distinct from the relation of other constituents (single lines)?

We have alluded to the possibility that some of the work of formation rules (say, linear order) is taken over by constraints. In the Minimalist Program (Chomsky 1995) this possibility has been carried to the extreme position that there is a single formation rule, called Merge: "Any word or phrase can be combined with any word or phrase, subject to all applicable constraints." Similarly, in Optimality Theory in both phonology (Prince and Smolensky 1993) and syntax (Grimshaw 1997), there is a component called Gen ("generate") which essentially says "Combine any units of the appropriate sort (i.e. phonological or syntactic respectively)." In Chapter 6 we will arrive at a more or less parallel position.

A second sort of formation rule specifies a category as composed from a number of more limited variables. For instance, Chapter 1 mentioned the analysis of the category NP as the composition of the three features [+N, −V, +phrasal]). In order for this composition to make sense, the grammar must contain a formation rule that stipulates the range of possibilities, for instance (6).

(6)   Syntactic category = [±N, ±V, ±phrasal]

The variables here are the ± signs, which can be instantiated as + or −. This rule has the effect of creating a set of eight syntactic categories, corresponding to all the combinations of the three variables. Thus instead of a repertoire of eight unrelated categories, we have the broader type "syntactic category" plus a repertoire of three features and their variables.[7]

Here is why we might want such an analysis. Suppose we find that certain categories, say NP and AP, behave in parallel fashion in various respects. We can then formulate the principles governing this parallel behavior in terms of a typed variable that ignores the difference between them—perhaps [+N, +phrasal], which leaves the value of the ±V feature open. That is, feature composition rules like (6) permit us a wider range of typed variables. The empirical issue is always to find the right set of features that permits us to express the generalizations that we in fact find.[8]

---

[7] Again, this is an oversimplification, in that there are other syntactic categories such as Tense and Det that do not fall under (6) as stated.

[8] It is worth mentioning that the idea of formal feature composition was an innovation of the Prague School structuralists such as Jakobson (1940) and Trubetzkoy (1958) in the domain of phonology. It was this innovation that was taken over to broader domains by people like Lévi-Strauss.

To sum up, we find two basic kinds of formation rule: rules of *constituency* and rules of *feature composition*. Both contain typed variables. The "meta-rule" of *variable instantiation* connects these variables to their instantiations.

3.2.2 *Derivational (transformational) rules*

The most exciting innovation of early generative grammar, however, was not formation rules but derivational rules (or *transformations*): rules that take a fully formed structure and change some aspect of it. Sentence pairs like (7) provide a simple illustration.

(7)   a. Dave really disliked that movie.
      b. That movie, Dave really disliked.

These two sentences mean essentially the same, with only perhaps a difference in emphasis. (7a) displays a more "basic" order: the thing that is disliked is in the "normal" direct object position. By contrast, in (7b), *disliked* is not followed by an object, as it should be, and *that movie* is in a curious position before the subject. So, the proposal goes, the grammar can capture the similarity between (7a) and (7b) by saying that (7b) in fact is not generated by the formation rules. Rather, it has an "underlying form" that is more or less identical to (7a) and that *is* generated by the formation rules. However, "after" the formation rules create the underlying form, a derivational rule moves *that movie* to the front of the sentence to create the "surface form."

   This approach carries with it a number of advantages. First, the semantic relation between the two sentences is explicit in underlying form: at that level they are in fact the same sentence (or at least very close). Second, the formation rules are simpler, in that they do not have to include the position at the front of the sentence. Third, the constraint that *dislike* requires a direct object is apparently violated in (7b)—but now this violation is only apparent, since it is explicitly observed in underlying form. These advantages are gained at a price: the introduction of a new and complex type of rule.

   A derivational rule can be thought of more generally as a relation between two structures, one "more underlying" and one "more superficial." Most parts of the structures are the same, but one or more parts are different. In the case of (6), the direct object in the more underlying form moves to initial position in the more superficial form, and everything else remains the same. Of course, in order to state this rule generally, it is necessary to use typed variables again: any NP in the underlying position can correspond to the same NP in the superficial position. Thus a very limited form of the rule responsible for (7) could be stated as

(8). (The subscripts on the NPs in (8) are notational conveniences so we can tell them apart.)[9]

(8)   More underlying: More superficial:

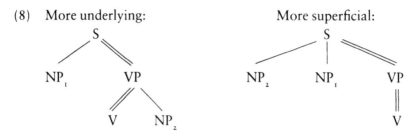

The application of a derivational rule can thus be notated as an ordered pair of trees. Alternatively it can be abbreviated in a single tree, say like (9).

(9)

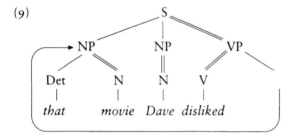

As section 1.7 mentioned, since the middle 1970s (e.g. Chomsky 1975) it has been assumed that movement rules always leave behind a "trace," a sort of unpronounced pronoun, whose antecedent is the moved constituent. In this notation, the application of the rule can be notated as (10), where t is the trace, and the subscripts show the relationship between the trace and its antecedent. (10) can be thought of roughly as *that movie, Dave disliked (it)*, where the parenthesized pronoun is not pronounced.

(10)

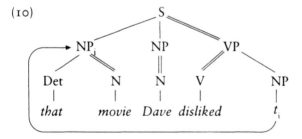

The reason I call the two structures related by (8) "more underlying" and

---

"more superficial," rather than simply "underlying" and "superficial," is that derivational rules can chain up, one applying to the output of another. Let me illustrate. In approaches that make use of derivational rules (i.e. all of Chomsky's successive frameworks), it is standard to treat the subject of a passive sentence as derived from a more underlying object, as sketched in (11). (I give only the string of words; the structure is to be understood.)

(11)   This book$_i$ has been studied t_i by generations of linguists.

Similarly, it is standard to derive the subject of certain predicates such as *seem* from a more underlying subject of a subordinate clause; that is, the underlying form of (12b) is close to the nearly synonymous (12a). The derivational rule involved is called "raising."

(12)   a. It seems [that John likes ice cream].
       b. John$_i$ seems [t_i to like ice cream].

(13) can then be derived as the product of passive followed by raising.

(13)   This book$_i$ seems [t_i to have been studied t_i by generations of linguists.

In other words, we can understand *this book* as the underlying object of *study*, despite its considerable distance from this position. It has achieved this distance by a sequence of independently motivated movements.

   Thus a full derivation for a sentence consists of the creation of an underlying form by means of the formation rules, followed by a sequence of derivational rules to create the ultimate surface form.[10] In the *Aspects* framework the underlying form was called the sentence's "Deep Structure," the most superficial form its "Surface Structure"; in later frameworks these terms were abbreviated to "D-structure" and "S-structure."

   Such a derivation has an inherent directionality, from underlying to surface. Students are always reminded that the notion of movement is intended "metaphorically," and that this directionality is just a way of defining a set of well-formed structures. No claim is implied that speakers actually move phrases around in their heads—this is taken to be a matter of performance. However,

---

[10] In some approaches, such as that of *Syntactic Structures*, the Minimalist Program, and Tree-Adjoining Grammar (Joshi 1987; Kroch 1987; Frank and Kroch 1995), structures created by derivational rules can be inserted for variables in formation rules, so that this strict ordering need not be observed.

the movement metaphor is pervasive, in that it is customary to speak of one rule applying "after" another, as can be seen in the discussion above. We return to this issue in Chapter 7, in connection with processing.

Two of the important empirical questions concerning derivational rules are (a) how explicit they have to be and (b) how their order of application is determined. The tendency in syntactic theory has been to extract more and more of the special properties of particular movements and re-encode them as constraints. This trend reaches its culmination in Government-Binding Theory (Chomsky 1981), which proposes only the maximally general derivational rule Move α (i.e. move anything to anywhere), subject to heavy independent constraints.

3.2.3 Constraints

A constraint is a kind of rule that places extra conditions on structures created by formation rules and derivational rules. It may consist of conditions that structures must necessarily satisfy, or alternatively of conditions that help make a structure more "favorable" or "stable." I will briefly mention some of the different kinds that have achieved some acceptance. Note that all of them require typed variables.

• Lexical items themselves can impose constraints on the structure they inhabit. For instance, the verb *dislike* imposes the constraint that it must be followed by an NP (in underlying structure); this is precisely what it means to say the verb is transitive.

• Constraints can impose extrinsic requirements on a structure created by a derivational rule. Here is an illustration. As mentioned in section 1.7, a major preoccupation of syntactic theory since the middle 1960s has been how movement rules are restricted; it has turned out that all of them are subject to very similar limitations. For instance, no matter what movement rule one tries to apply, it is impossible to remove anything from the inside of the subject of a sentence. Hence putative structures like (14) are grossly ungrammatical.

(14)   a. *Bill$_i$, a rumor about t_i is going around town.
            (from [a rumor about Bill] is going around town)
        b. *Which book$_i$ did a review of t_i appear in the Times?
            (related to [a review of some book] appeared in the Times)

This restriction can be purged from each individual movement rule if we extract it into a more general constraint. This constraint, generally called the Sentential Subject Constraint, applies to the relation between traces and their antecedents. A version of it appears in (15). (Note that X is a typed variable that stands for any constituent; the ellipses are typed variables that stand for any random string of constituents, including a null string.)

(15)   The structure   X$_i$ ...   S   ...   is ungrammatical.

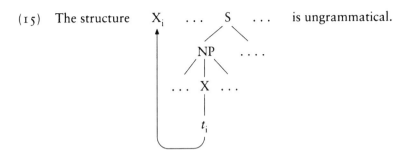

• Constraints can impose conditions on the relation between different stages in the derivation. As mentioned above, the early formulations of movement lacked traces, so constraints on movement had to be stated on stages related by a derivational step. For instance, the equivalent of (15) in this earlier framework (e.g. Ross 1967) would be stated as (16).

(16)   A derivation from   ...S...to   X...S...is illegal.

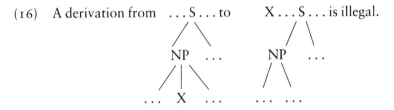

Among more contemporary theories, Optimality Theory (OT) proposes that derivations involve exactly two layers: the Input (which plays approximately the role of underlying form) and a large collection of candidate Output (or surface) structures. The basic principle of OT is to impose constraints on the relation between these two layers, choosing the candidate Output that best meets the constraints. For instance, the "Parse" constraint stipulates that every element in the Input structure should appear in the Output structure. However, constraints in OT are regarded as violable. Therefore, under certain conditions when other constraints override Parse, some element of the Input will fail to appear in the Output; this is how OT treats what would be treated as a deletion in a theory with derivational rules. A major difference between OT and a derivational theory is that OT applies all constraints simultaneously to the Input–Output pair, whereas a derivational theory sees the relation between underlying and surface forms as a potentially unlimited sequence of simple steps.

• All of the rules we have discussed so far involve syntactic structure alone. Another kind of constraint imposes conditions between two structures of disparate types. This type of constraint, which I will call a *correspondence rule* or an *interface rule*, plays an especially important role in what is to come here. Two simple cases are the principles stated informally as (17a, b). They can best be understood in the context of section 1.6, which discussed how corresponding constituents in the phonological, syntactic, and semantic structures in Fig. 1.1 are linked by subscripts.

(17)   a. If the semantic structure of a sentence contains an Agent (the entity bringing an action about), it (normally) corresponds to the subject in syntactic structure.

b. The linear order of elements in phonological structure (normally) corresponds to the linear order of corresponding elements in syntactic structure.

Such principles appear in a wide range of theories of grammar; we will discuss them in Chapter 5. Importantly, in many of these theories, relations such as the active–passive alternation are not captured in terms of derivational rules. Rather, the grammar contains alternative interface rules relating syntactic structure and meaning, such that active and passive syntactic structures map into essentially the same meaning. We see here one of the major divides among theories of grammar: should such semantic relations among sentences be captured by more elaborate derivational rules, or by more elaborate interface rules? (Note how this relates to the alternative treatments of Tense in section 1.6.)

• A more complex type of constraint, which might be called a "meta-constraint," applies not between two levels of structure in the same derivation, but between two or more alternative derivations. A situation where this seems unavoidable is *morphological blocking*. For example, the standard procedure for producing the past tense of an English verb is to add -*d*;[11] this applies to anything that counts as a verb, even new made-up verbs like *fax*. However, this procedure does not work in the 180 or so cases where it is supplanted by an irregular form; thus we say *went* and *shook* instead of *goed* and *shaked*. In other words, the derivation of *go* + -*d*, although in principle legitimate, is blocked because there is another way to express the same combination of meanings. This sort of phenomenon is ubiquitous in principles of morphology (word structure).

Meta-constraints with a much more global spirit appear in both the Minimalist Program and Optimality Theory. In the former, there are in principle many ways to get from an underlying form to an acceptable surface form, but one of these is chosen in preference to the others in part by a meta-constraint called Economy. This constraint gives priority to the shortest derivation that satisfies all the other constraints.

---

[11] In turn, -*d* is pronounced -*t* or -*əd* depending on the final consonant of the verb, along lines similar to those discussed in connection with the English noun plural in section 1.3.

In OT, a large number of different candidate Outputs can be associated with the same Input; typically each of them violates one or more of the constraints. This presents the problem of deciding which violation is least serious. In the solution proposed by OT, the grammar of the language stipulates a ranking among the constraints from most to least important. Each candidate Output, then, has a most important violation. Among the candidates, the one whose most important violation is least important is chosen as the actual Output. This principle of choice among candidates, then, is another sort of meta-constraint.[12]

3.3 Lexical rules

So far we have been thinking of the lexicon as simply a list of items that can be arranged in hierarchical structures by formation rules. This approach is encouraged by Chomsky's (1965: 84) characterization of the lexicon as "simply an unordered list of all lexical formatives"; he cites similar characterizations by Bloomfield (1933) and Sweet (1913).

But lexical items are not just atomic undecomposable units like constants in algebra. It is necessary to say how *they* are built too. Hence a theory of competence must specify the repertoire of possible "sub-lexical" elements and how they combine into actual lexical items. This specification constitutes a set of *lexical rules*. These too fall into a number of different types, including *lexical formation rules*, *lexical redundancy rules* (or *lexical relations*), and *inheritance hierarchies*. We take these up in turn.

3.3.1 *Lexical formation rules*

Perhaps the most frequently cited aspect of Saussurean doctrine is that a word is an arbitrary association of a sign with a meaning. The sign has two aspects: phonological structure (how it is pronounced) and syntactic structure (how it combines with other words in sentences). Thus a basic formation rule for lexical items specifies that they are triples of phonological structure, syntactic structure, and meaning. Every framework of grammar adopts such an assumption, at least implicitly.

Within each of these structures something has to be said as well. In order for an item to be able to instantiate typed variables in syntactic rules, its lexical syntactic structure has to specify what categories it belongs to; these categories will include

---

[12] The idea of violable constraints that interact to produce an optimal choice of output also plays a major role in the theory of musical cognition proposed by Lerdahl and Jackendoff (1983). As pointed out by Smolensky (1999), Dell et al. (1999), and Seidenberg and MacDonald (1999), such constraint systems are attractive for implementation in terms of connectionist networks. However, see section 3.5 for independent problems with network implementations.

at least part of speech, grammatical number and gender, and so forth. In addition, section 3.2.3 observed that a lexical item can place a constraint on its syntactic environment; for instance a verb may be specified as transitive. Such a constraint is called a subcategorization feature; we will see in section 6.6 how these are specified.

Among lexical formation rules we might also include principles of morphosyntax, which make it possible for words to have internal syntactic structure. For instance, the word *perturbation* is built from the verb *perturb*, which is converted to a noun by attaching the ending *-ation*. It is common to analyze words like this in terms of a tree structure altogether parallel to syntactic tree structures, except that the trees are inside of a word, as in (18a). Moreover, the trees can be hierarchical, as in (18b).

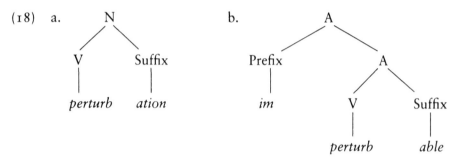

The lexical formation rules must thus include tree fragments from which such structures can be built.

Turning to phonology, an item's phonological structure determines how it is pronounced. The formation rules for lexical phonological structure have to specify the range of possible pronunciations for words in the language: the inventory of phonological segments and how they combine into syllables and larger units. To cite a well-known example, *blik* is a possible word of English but *bnik* is not, because the syllabic formation rules for English permit the onset cluster *bl-* but not *bn-* (even though *bn-* is pronounceable and *is* a possible onset cluster in some other languages). As illustrated in Fig. 1.2, phonological segments themselves have a systematic decomposition into features; the possibilities for such decomposition are stated in terms of formation rules parallel to those for syntactic categories such as (6).

An item's lexical semantic/conceptual structure is also conceived of (in most approaches) as combinatorial. And again, the lexical formation rules must specify the available repertoire of more basic units and how they are combined. We return to this issue in Chapters 9–11.

The reader may have already detected hints that lexical formation rules are really very similar in format to phrasal formation rules. And indeed this is the case, as we will bring out more clearly in Chapter 6.

3.3.2 Lexical redundancy rules

How should the grammar account for the systematic relations among pairs of words such as *construct/construction*, *impress/impression*, and *suggest/suggestion*? In early generative grammar, including *Aspects* and notably Lees (1960), such relations were treated in terms of derivational rules applying to phrases. For instance, the NP *the construction of a wall* was taken to be derived from an underlying clause along the lines of *someone constructs a wall*. It was not too long before this approach was seen to be problematic, for a variety of technical reasons detailed in Chomsky (1970).[13]

The alternative was to admit *construct* and *construction* as separate but related forms in the lexicon.[14] Their relation is partly idiosyncratic, but partly systematic; the systematic part is expressed by a *lexical redundancy rule* (or, in later parlance, simply a *lexical rule*) (Jackendoff 1975). The relevant rule here can be stated informally as (19).

(19)   A verb pronounced /X/ that denotes an action can be related to a noun pronounced /X+šən/ that denotes the performance of such an action (or, alternatively, the product of such an action).

This rule involves correlations in phonology, syntax, and semantics between the paired items. Its effect is to mark the parts of the paired items that are shared, in effect noting the redundancies between them. Such a rule is of interest to the extent that it relates many different pairs of items in the same way.

---

13 Among the reasons:

• There are many apparently "derived" cases for which there is no apparent source. For example, if *the writer of the book* is derived from *someone who writes/wrote the book*, what is the source for the altogether parallel *the author of the book*? There is no verb *auth*.

• When verbs are converted to morphologically more complex nouns, their modifying adverbs are converted to morphologically simpler adjectives: *John suddenly refused* vs. *John's sudden refusal*. Hence there is an apparent conflict in the direction of derivation.

• "Derived" nouns can appear with modifiers that lack close parallels in the sentences from which they are putatively derived, e.g. *John's three criticisms of the book* vs. *John (*three(ly)) criticized the book (three times/three ways?)*.

• Many "derived" nouns mean something other than a simple transformation from the verb would predict. For instance, both *recitation* and *recital* have something to do morphologically with the verb *recite*, but only the former has a meaning pertaining to reciting.

The Generative Semantics movement that flourished in the late 1960s (e.g. Lakoff 1970; McCawley 1968; Postal 1970a) was founded on the idea that one could account for all meaning relations of this sort through derivational rules. Observations like those just cited were the opening salvo in the attacks on Generative Semantics (Chomsky 1972a; Jackendoff 1972; Akmajian 1973; Bowers 1975).

14 Chomsky (1970) actually proposed that there is a single more general lexical item which is pronounced *construct* when used as a verb and *construction* when used as a noun. So far as I know, nobody has ever really worked out this approach.

3.3.3 Inheritance hierarchies

How should the grammar account for the fact that many verbs expressing transfer (or intended transfer) appear in two possible syntactic frames?

(20)   a. Beth gave/handed/sent/offered a teapot to Nancy.
       b. Beth gave/handed/sent/offered Nancy a teapot.
(21)   a. Beth told a story to Nancy.
       b. Beth told Nancy a story.

In early generative grammar, this alternation was accomplished by means of a
derivational rule (often called Dative Shift) that optionally turned the underlying order (20a, 21a) into the surface order (20b, 21b); a variant of this approach
has been revived more recently (Larson 1988). The advantage of this treatment
is that the verbs in question need to be supplied only with a single subcategorization feature instead of two; the price is this single derivational rule.

Howcver, again for a variety of technical reasons (see references in Levin 1993;
Jackendoff 1990b), most linguists have rejected the derivational approach for
this alternation. But this leaves the problem of why all these verbs have two distinct subcategorization frames. One approach that has won some degree of
acceptance (Pollard and Sag 1987; 1994; Michaelis and Lambrecht 1996) is that
the lexicon contains not just the actual lexical items of the language but also more
abstract schemata from which actual items can "inherit" properties. In the present case, the schema might be stated roughly as (22); the subscripts correlate the
syntactic variables with the semantic ones, in the way they did in Fig. 1.1.

(22)   Syntax:
           Part of speech: V
           Subcategorization: __ NP$_1$ to NP$_2$
                           or
           __ NP$_2$ NP$_1$
       Semantics:
           TRANSFER (X$_1$, TO Y$_2$)

This says that a verb that means "transfer" accepts both syntactic frames, with the
same meaning. Because the words in (20) and (21) inherit their properties from
this schema, they "cost less": the extra subcategorization comes in a sense "for
free." New items in the language with the appropriate meaning inherit these properties as well, with no further ado; for instance the new verb *fax* has both forms.

As in the discussion of derivational rules versus constraints, we see here an
important locus of contention among alternative frameworks. Given any particular phenomenon, should it be treated as a derivational rule, a lexical redundancy rule, or an inheritance hierarchy? These are not just matters of notational

preference, as they might appear at a first approximation. Rather, at the second and third approximations, different rule types lend themselves to different sorts of generalization, and so often it is only when one explores the phenomena in depth that the consequences of choosing one theory rather than another begin to emerge. Some such points were sketched in note 13 above, and others will appear throughout the course of our exposition.

3.4 What *are* rules of grammar?

As linguists, we may find it necessary to write rules of all these sorts in order to make sense of the patterns of linguistic use. Our focus is quite naturally on the proper formulation of rules. But with some sample rules in hand, it is worth posing a more general question that is often left to be asked by outsiders:[15] What in the world is a rule of mental grammar supposed to be?

Like the term "knowledge" and other terms discussed in Chapter 2, "rule" has many uses in ordinary language. Is a linguistic rule like any of these? Let us for instance compare the rules discussed in the previous two sections to rules of a game. Players of a game consciously learn its rules, and can consciously invoke them. For example, there are rules of tennis that say what counts as a legal serve, what counts as winning a point, and so forth; and players can cite them. These rules have been agreed upon by some collection of people who have made up the game. By contrast, speakers of English can hardly cite the rules of English (unless perhaps they have studied linguistics): linguistic rules are essentially unconscious. Moreover, the rules of language, though shared by all speakers (to a very good approximation), are not overtly agreed upon by the speakers, and no established body makes them up.

Are linguistic rules like rules of law (e.g. traffic laws)? No, for many of the same reasons. In addition, if one breaks a rule of law, further laws spell out the consequences. By contrast, if a speaker break a rule of grammar (as I just did), the violation may provoke notice, but beyond that, the speaker just communicates less effectively. Are linguistic rules like moral rules, such that one *should* obey them at the risk of social opprobrium? The prescriptive rules of school grammar ("Don't use *ain't*," "Don't end a sentence with a preposition") might have this quality, but the rules of the last two sections certainly do not.

Going to the other extreme from consciously invoked rules, we might try to see rules of grammar as like laws of physics: formal descriptions of the behavior

---

[15] Though it is addressed in detail by Chomsky, for instance in Chomsky (e.g. 1975; 1980). Much of this section recapitulates his discussion, if much more briefly.

of speakers, with no implications for how this behavior is actually implemented. For instance, just as the planets do not solve internalized differential equations in order to know where to go next, we might want to say that speakers do not invoke internalized formation rules and constraints in order to construct and understand sentences.

Some linguists do affect this stance: "The rules I'm working out are just a formal description of languages; I don't care what they have to do with the mind." But this abandons the mentalist thesis that we set out to adopt in Chapter 2. It leads us away from the attempt to understand how people manage to be language users, and hence away from potential connections with psychology and neuroscience. Physicists who have developed insightful formal descriptions of physical behavior always go on to ask what mechanism is responsible for it: if the planets don't compute their trajectories, then what makes the trajectories come out the way they do? The same question should be asked of rules of grammar. If they are not in the mind, then what *is* in the mind, such that speakers observe these regularities?

Another difference between rules of grammar and laws of physics is that rules of grammar differ from language to language, and one does not come into the world automatically following the rules of English or any other language. By contrast, laws of physics are universal and timeless. They are not acquired; they just *are*. One can break rules of grammar; one cannot break laws of physics.

It is sometimes suggested, especially by those of a behavioristic bent, that rules of grammar are like ingrained habits. This is closer to acceptable, as long as we accept the idea of a habit not just as a propensity to behave, but as a complex ingrained cognitive organization of perception and behavior. In particular, the "habit" of using linguistic rules plays a role in producing sentences, perceiving sentences, making grammaticality judgments, making judgments of rhyme, and solving anagrams. It is far more abstract and distant from actual behavior than, say, the habit of going to bed at 10 p.m. or the habit of taking such-and-such a route to work. And unlike these latter two habits, it cannot be acquired deliberately. As we will see in the next chapter, the acquisition of language involves a complex and subtle interaction between the child and the environment.

The proper way to understand rules of grammar, I suggest, is to situate them in the metaphysical domain between the conscious mind and the physical neurons: in the functional mind introduced in the previous chapter. Recalling that discussion, we treated linguistic structures like Fig. 1.1 as functionally characterized "data structures" in the f-mind. In those terms, the rules of grammar for a language are a general characterization of the state-space available to its users.

The lexical rules characterize possible lexical items of the language, and the phrasal rules characterize their combinatorial possibilities. What makes elements of the language *rules* rather than basic elements is that they contain typed variables (i.e. open places)—that is, they describe *patterns* of linguistic elements.

It is an open question how rules of grammar are to be incorporated into a model of performance, and hence into a theory of neural instantiation. Here are three plausible options.

• Rules are (in some sense) explicit in long-term memory within the f-mind, and the language processor explicitly refers to them in constructing and comprehending utterances. Following the computer metaphor, rules are like data structures in a computer.

• Rules are partial descriptions of the operations of the processor itself. In the computer metaphor, the rules as we write them are high-level descriptions of parts of the processor's program.

• Rules are implicit in the f-mind; they describe emergent regularities (perhaps statistical regularities) among more basic elements, but are not themselves implemented in any direct way.

As suggested in section 3.2, the traditional formulation of phrase structure rules like (2) and of derivational rules like (8) is conducive to viewing the rules as like a program for constructing sentences. The connotations of the term "generate" in "generative grammar" reinforce such a view. However, as already mentioned, students are always cautioned to resist this interpretation. In particular they are exhorted to view derivational movement as metaphorical: "We are, after all, describing competence, not performance." The upshot is that the status of such rules vis-à-vis performance models is left unspecified. We return to this issue in Chapter 7.

Feature composition rules and constraints lend themselves better to a "data structure" interpretation, in the sense that they delimit a space of possibilities within which linguistic entities can be located. In the approach to be worked out here, particularly in Chapter 6, a considerable proportion of standard rules of grammar will be interpreted in this light.

On the other hand, we will also conclude in Chapter 6 that certain classes of lexical rules fall into the "implicit" category. Such rules are nowhere present in the f-mind in the form we write them. Rather, these rules *are* indeed just descriptions of regularities in the organization of linguistic memory. I will maintain, however, that such rules still shed light on the nature of linguistic structure, so they are worth studying with traditional linguistic techniques.

3.5 Four challenges for cognitive neuroscience[16]

Just as linguistic structures like Fig. 1.1 are functional characterizations that require neural instantiation, so the functional regularities that we state as rules of grammar must be neurally instantiated. To repeat a point from Chapter 2: although a great deal is known about functional localization of various aspects of language in the brain, I think it is fair to say that nothing at all is known about how neurons instantiate the details of rules of grammar. In fact, we don't even have any idea of how a single speech sound such as /p/—much less a category like NP—is instantiated in neural firings or synaptic connections. The rest of this chapter will lay out four challenges that linguistic combinatoriality and rules of language present to theories of brain function—challenges that to my knowledge have not been widely recognized in the cognitive neuroscience community.

3.5.1 *The massiveness of the binding problem*

Consider what happens in the perception or production of our familiar sentence (23).

(23)   The little star's beside a big star.

Much of the neuroscience of language has been concerned with how words stored in long-term memory are activated ("light up") in the course of sentence perception and production (e.g. Caramazza and Miozzo 1997; Pulvermüller 1999). But activation of words alone is not sufficient to account for the understanding of sentences. If understanding (23) consisted only of activating the words, the sentence in (24a), not to mention the complete nonsense in (24b), would "light up" the same words and hence be understood the same.

(24)   a. The big star's beside a little star.
        b. Beside a the big little star star's.

Clearly a sentence is more than a collection of words: the word meanings are structured into the meaning of the sentence by means of semantic relations among them. These semantic relations are to some degree signaled by the syntactic structure of the sentence, which in turn is correlated with the linear order of the phonological words.

Thus all of the structure modeled in Fig. 1.1 must be functionally present—at once—in order for this sentence to be grasped. Introspectively, the whole seems to be maintained at least for some brief period after the completion of the sentence.

---

[16] This section is based on unpublished work done in collaboration with Maja Matarić. It also draws a great deal on the work of Gary Marcus (1998; 2001).

During this time, all the connections within and among the structures are available: phonologically, one retains the order of words; semantically, one retains the relations among the words; and one knows which sounds (e.g. /əbɪgstar/) correlate with which part of meaning, in particular with the spatial structure. It will not do to say that one hears or utters the words in sequence but that one does not retain the whole in memory.[17]

In order to grasp a sentence, one need not have previously memorized it: one may spontaneously utter it when asked to describe a visual configuration, or one may hear someone else utter it. Our ability to spontaneously produce and perceive it is a consequence of the productive combinatoriality of language. What one *must* have memorized, though, is the words *the, star, big, little, beside*, and *a*, and the clitic *'s*, plus the principles for putting them together.

The need for combining independent bits into a single coherent percept has been recognized in the theory of vision under the name of the *binding problem* (not to be confused with linguists' Binding Theory, mentioned in section 1.7). In the discussions I have encountered, the binding problem is usually stated this way: we have found that the shape and the color of an object are encoded in different regions of the brain, and they can be differentially impaired by brain damage. How is it, then, that we sense a particular shape and color as attributes of the same object? The problem becomes more pointed in a two-object situation: if the shape region detects a square and a circle, and the color region detects red and blue, how does the brain encode that one is seeing, say, a red square and a blue circle rather than the other way around? In fact, under time pressure, subjects can mismatch the features of multiple perceived objects (Treisman 1988). A proposal that has gained a certain popularity (Gray et al. 1989; Crick and Koch 1990; Singer et al. 1997) is that the different representations are phase-linked: the neurons encoding "red" and "square" fire in synchrony, and those encoding "blue" and "circle" do as well, but out of phase with the first pair.

However, the binding problem presented by linguistic structure is far more massive than this simple description. The trivially simple sentence (23) has the four independent structures shown in Fig.1.1. Each structure has multiple parts that must be correlated; in addition, the four structures must be correlated with each other, as notated by the subscripts in Fig. 1.1. Consider just the

---

[17] Nor is it useful to conceive of understanding the sentence in terms of predicting what word will come next—which is what Elman's (1990) connectionist parser does. One might well predict that what comes after *little* in (23) is likely to be a noun (though it might be *blue* or even *very old*), but that still leaves open some tens of thousands of choices. The same is true for every position in the sentence. On the other hand, Pollack (1990) proposes a connectionist parser that does encode an entire hierarchical tree structure. See n. 21 below for further comments on Elman's parser.

prepositional phrase in the syntactic structure. To characterize it properly, the following relationships must be encoded:

(25)   a. It is of the type PP.
      b. It is a part of VP.
      c. It follows V.
      d. It has P and NP as parts.
      e. It corresponds to the Place-constituent in conceptual structure.
      f. It corresponds to the phonological constituent *beside a big star*.

For the object of the preposition:

(26)   a. It is of the type NP.
      b. It is a part of PP.
      c. It follows P.
      d. It has Det, AP, and N as parts.
      e. It corresponds to a particular Object-constituent in conceptual structure.
      f. It corresponds to the phonological constituent *a big star*.

How effectively can firing synchrony be scaled up to deal with such an inter-locking web of relationships? In particular, if the PP is synchronized with its parts, and its parts are synchronized with *their* parts, the whole tree structure is temporally unresolvable. More generally, is there sufficient bandwidth in the temporal resolution of neural firing to distinguish all the parts of the sentence from one another? To me, these questions cast considerable doubt on the feasi-bility of solving the binding problem in terms of temporal synchrony alone—even if temporal synchrony is indeed an important part of the solution.[18]

It should be observed that this complexity is not peculiar to language percep-tion and production. The sorts of visual experiment cited above typically involve two objects with two relevant properties apiece. But consider the com-plexity of an everyday visual field, say one's desk, covered with books, papers, pictures, and office paraphernalia. All these objects—their (partially occluded) shapes, parts, colors, and locations—must be bound together in visual cogni-tion. To be sure, one can perhaps only attend to (and therefore see in detail) some small part of this at once (as observed by Dennett 1991, for example). Nevertheless, much of the unattended spatial layout must still be present in working memory, for if someone says "Now look at the picture" one's eyes go

---

[18] Singer et al. (1997) merely speculate on the possibility that their analysis in terms of syn-chrony will scale up to hierarchically structured relations; though see Shastri and Ajjanagade (1993) for a proposal.

right to it without search; similarly, one can reach for the coffee cup off in the corner without really looking at it. Thus, as in the case of sentences, a full visual field provides a complex web of transient and novel relationships that must be put together out of familiar parts.

3.5.2 The Problem of 2

In much work on language processing (e.g. Barsalou 1992; 1999; Smith and Medin 1981; Caramazza and Miozzo 1997; Elman et al. 1996), the only mechanism available for constructing linguistic expressions is spreading activation among nodes connected in a semantic network or neural net. Thus it is assumed that "lexical retrieval" in processing—i.e. identifying what word one is hearing or speaking—amounts to activating the nodes encoding (or instantiating) that word in long-term memory. We have already seen that such an approach is silent about capturing the relations among the words of a sentence. But there is an even simpler difficulty, which I will call the Problem of 2.

Consider yet again sentence (23), in which there are two occurrences of the word *star*. If the first occurrence simply activates the lexical entry in long-term memory, what can the second occurrence do? It cannot just activate the word a second time, since—as just argued—the word has to remain activated the first time in order for the sentence to receive a full interpretation. Nor can the second occurrence just activate the word more strongly, because that leaves the two occurrences indistinguishable. In particular, the first occurrence is bound to *little* and the second to *big*, so simultaneous binding to both would lead to the contradictory concept of a little big star.

This problem recurs at every level of linguistic structure. For example, in phonological structure, if the detection of the phoneme s consists simply of activating an s-node (or a distributed complex of nodes that together instantiate s), what happens in a word with more than one such sound, say *Sisyphus* or *sassafras*?[19] The same problem occurs in conceptual structure when conceptualizing a relation involving two tokens of the same type (e.g. the meaning of (23)) and in spatial structure when viewing or imagining two identical objects. It also occurs in understanding melodies: if the unit of musical memory is the individual note, then every repetition of the same note raises the problem; if the unit is

---

[19] Rumelhart and McClelland (1986b) attempt to avoid this problem by coding words as "wickelphones," overlapping sequences of three phonemes. But this too is subject to the Problem of 2: how is the word detector to distinguish *sassafras* from the nonword *sassassafras*, which has two occurrences of the medial sequence . . . *assa* . . .—or *great-grandmother* from *great-great-grandmother*, which has two occurrences of the medial sequence . . . *reatgr* . . . ? Pinker and Prince (1988) cite an Australian aboriginal language, Oykangand, whose words *algal* 'straight' and *algalgal* 'ramrod straight' pose the same problem.

the interval between adjacent notes (say a major third), every repetition of the same interval raises the problem; if the unit is a motive, then every repetition of the motive (e.g. the first two occurrences of the text *Happy Birthday* in the birthday song) raises the problem; and so forth. Finally, the problem occurs in action patterns, for example dance patterns that involve things like "repeat such-and-such a step four times, then repeat this other step six times, then repeat the whole pattern."

The Problem of 2 has been recognized (e.g. Pollack 1990; Marcus 2001, ch. 5 says it was well known by 1985), but it does not find a ready solution in classical network models of processing. A solution that is sometimes adopted, especially for phoneme detection, is that multiple copies of each unit exist in memory, one for each possible position it can occupy. Then the first occurrence of *s* in *sassafras* would activate [*position 1: s*] and the second would activate [*position 3: s*]; the first occurrence of *star* in (23) would activate [*position 3: star*] and the second would activate [*position 7: star*]. There are two difficulties with this solution, especially when trying to scale it up to multiple copies of words in sentences. First, it requires duplication of the entire repertoire of units over a large number of possible positions. This is most evident when the units in question are words: ten- to twenty-word sentences, with the words chosen out of a vocabulary of 20,000, are not uncommon. Second, and worse, there can be no generalization among these positions. There is no reason for [*position 1: s*] to be the same phoneme as [*position 3: s*], or for [*position 3: star*] to have anything to do with [*position 7: star*]. The two could be totally different in structural significance.[20] (See Marcus 1998; 2001 for amplification of this argument.)

Such a "brute force" solution might be adequate for domains of brain function where there is a fixed size for the perceptual field and a limited number of distinctions to be made at each position. Primary visual cortex (V1) is a good example of such a domain: it codes a limited selection of visual features (brightness, presence of contour, orientation of contour, etc.), each detectable at each location in the visual field. But when we get to domains of more cognitive brain function—the perceived visual field full of objects, the sentence full of words—the solution does not scale up.[21]

---

[20] A version of this proposal, for instance, appears in Dell et al. (1999). Their model (p. 521) has a bank of consonant nodes that function as syllable onsets, and another unrelated bank of consonant nodes that function as syllable codas. This is saved from obvious intractability only because they confine themselves to monosyllabic words.

[21] Elman (1990), observing this difficulty of providing a large enough frame, proposes instead a solution with a recurrent network, which encodes sentential structure in terms of the sequential dependencies among words. As pointed out by Chomsky (1957) and Miller and Chomsky (1963),

A more old-fashioned computational approach to lexical access (Miller 1956; Neisser 1967; Baddeley 1986) supposes that the accessed word is copied from long-term memory (LTM) into a buffer in short-term or working memory (WM)—in this case in two different positions in WM. This approach meets the objections to the network solution, as it keeps the two occurrences of *star* distinct. On the other hand, how is it implemented neurally? The pure connectionist approaches with which I am familiar do not allow for the possibility of "copying" information from one "register" to another. A spreading activation equivalent of "copying" words into WM would require a set of nodes constituting WM, each of which is connected to (and can be activated by) every single word in the lexicon. This is somewhat better than the "brute force" solution, but still neurally implausible (so far as I know).

Yet another possibility would be that WM is a set of "dummy" nodes which have no content of their own but are bound to lexical items by temporal synchrony of firing, along lines discussed in section 3.5.1. Thus WM serves as a set of "pointers" to LTM, and in addition encodes relationships among the items being pointed to (for example, linear order). (Solutions of this sort are proposed by Potter (1993), citing Kahneman and Treisman (1984), and by Ballard et al. (1997).) Of course the questions raised in section 3.5.1 concerning the adequacy of temporal synchrony arise again. There is also a broader tradition of hybrid models, in which active nodes in a spreading activation network are keyed into an independent frame-and-slot component where larger structures are built (Collins and Quillian 1969; Levelt 1989; Roelofs 1997, among many examples). However, at this point the options are beyond the scope of this study; I hope that the nature of the problem has been made clear enough for those in the relevant fields. The main point is that although spreading activation may be a necessary component of memory, it is not enough for language.

---

though, the sequential dependencies among words in a sentence are not sufficient to determine understanding or even grammaticality. For instance, consider (i).

(i) Does the little boy in the yellow hat who Mary described as a genius *like* ice cream?

The fact that the italicized verb in (i) is *like* rather than *likes* is determined by the presence of *does*, 14 words away; and we would have no trouble making the distance even longer. However, it is not the distance in words that is significant: it is the distance in noun phrases, i.e. *does* is one NP away from *like*, whatever the length of the NP. This generalization, a typical example of what Chomsky calls the "structure-dependence" of linguistic rules, cannot be captured in Elman's recurrent network, which only deals with word sequence. As far as I can determine, a similar objection applies to the dynamical model proposed by Tabor and Tanenhaus (1999). Steedman (1999: 619) points out, in reference to Elman's work and several extensions of it, that "we know from work on symbolic finite-state models such as Hidden Markov Models and part-of-speech taggers [references omitted] that such approximations can achieve very high accuracy—better than 95% precision—without having any claim whatsoever to embody the grammar itself."

3.5.3 *The problem of variables*

The situation is still more problematic. Consider the problem of encoding a two-place relation such as "X rhymes with Y." The brain cannot list all the rhymes in the language. For one thing, we can acquire a new word, say *ling*, and know immediately that it rhymes with *sting* and *bring* but not with *monk* or *mustard*; we do not have to learn all its rhymes individually. Nor can we figure out its rhymes by analogy, reasoning for example, "Well, *ling* sounds sort of like the word *link*, and *link* rhymes with *think*, so maybe *ling* rhymes with *think*." The only words for which such an analogical argument works are the words with which *ling* already rhymes—which is of course of no help.

Another reason rhymes cannot be listed is that one can judge rhymes involving sounds that are not even part of one's language. English speakers can, without knowing German, judge that *Fach* rhymes with *Bach*, despite the fact that the *ch* sound is not a sound of English, and despite the fact that they learned about rhymes entirely through experience with English.

A third reason is that there is a phonological process in Yiddish-influenced dialects of English that creates expressions of sarcasm by rhyming with a non-sense word whose onset is *shm-*: "Oedipus-Shmedipus! Just so you love your mother!" That is, new rhymes can be created on the spot.

Finally, people can judge rhymes that are created through combinatoriality, for example those in (27).

(27) a. try and hide/cyanide   (Tom Lehrer)
      b. tonsillectomy/come direct to me/send a check to me
            (Groucho Marx's Dr. Hackenbush)
      c. a lot o' news/hypotenuse
         din afore/Pinafore
         I'm more wary at/commissariat
            (Gilbert and Sullivan's Major-General Stanley)

One certainly has no significant experience with rhyming "things that sound like *tonsillectomy*", so these can't be done by any sort of analogy either.

Rather, the rhyming relation has to be encoded in the form of a pattern with two typed variables: *any* phonological string rhymes with any *other* phonological string if everything from the stressed vowel to the end is identical in the two strings, and the onset preceding the stressed vowel is different (since normally *ring* does not rhyme with *ring*).

Marcus (1998, 2001) takes up about the simplest possible two-place relation: total identity (*A rose is a rose; a daisy is a daisy; a dahlia is a . . .* : Fill in the blank.) He demonstrates that even this case cannot be formulated without the use of typed variables. His agenda is to defuse the extravagant claims that have been made on behalf of a particular class of spreading activation models, the multi-layer perceptrons of the sort common in connectionist modeling (e.g. Rumelhart and McClelland 1986a, b; Elman et al. 1996). He shows that for principled reasons these models cannot encode variables of the sort necessary for two-place relations such as "X is identical with Y," "X rhymes with Y," and "X is the regular past tense of Y." Space precludes my repeating his arguments here, not to mention his replies to the many reactions his work has produced. Suffice it to say that Marcus has tested all the relevant networks in the literature on the data sets for which he predicts they will fail, and indeed they fail.[22]

This principled failure is fatal to unadorned spreading activation models of language, for, as we saw in section 3.2, all combinatorial rules of language—formation rules, derivational rules, and constraints—require typed variables. Again, this does not mean that spreading activation plays no role in the brain's storage and processing of linguistic f-knowledge; in fact it likely does (see Chapter 7). But some further technical innovation is called for in neural network models, which will permit them to encode typed variables and the operation of instantiating them. I think that upon the development of such an innovation, the dialogue between linguistic theory and neural network modeling will begin to be more productive.

3.5.4 Binding in working memory vs. long-term memory

As alluded to earlier, contemporary neuroscience tends to see transient (short-term) connections among items in memory as instantiated either by spreading activation through synapses or by the "binding" relation, often thought of in terms of firing synchrony. By contrast, lasting (long-term) connections are usually thought of as encoded in terms of strength of synaptic connections. However, the combinatoriality of language presents the problem that the very same relation may be encoded either in a transient structure or in one stored in memory.

Consider, for instance, the idiom *kick the bucket*. This has to be stored in long-term memory, since one cannot predict its meaning from the meaning of its parts. At the same time, it has the syntactic structure of an ordinary verb phrase such as *lift the shovel*, which is built up combinatorially. Hence, when *kick the*

---

[22] Marcus's arguments concerning variables do not appear to be adequately appreciated in the connectionist literature; e.g. I find no reference to them in a recent issue of *Cognitive Science* dedicated to "Connectionist Models of Human Language Processing: Progress and Prospects" (Christiansen et al. 1999).

bucket is retrieved in the course of sentence perception or production, it ought to have the very same sort of instantiation as *lift the shovel* in the parts of the brain responsible for syntactic structure. It does not seem correct to posit that the connections of *kick the bucket* are encoded as synaptic weights and those of *lift the shovel* as firing synchrony.

A different sort of example: By now you have undoubtedly committed our original sample sentence, *The little star . . .* , to memory, so it is stored in your brain as a unit. In the old view of working memory as a buffer, one could claim that its contents are simply shipped off to long-term memory. But this option is not available in a view where the words of a sentence being perceived are related only by temporal synchrony. One cannot store a memorized sentence in long-term memory by constantly rerunning the transient bindings among the words—as it were, constantly rehearsing it. The transient bindings are by hypothesis being used for the sentences one is currently processing, not for the ones one has laid up against future need. But how are transient connections converted to synaptic weights in the course of memorizing the sentence?

It is usually argued that transient connections have the effect of gradually adjusting synaptic weights (so-called Hebbian learning). But what about cases in which one trial is sufficient for learning? For example, you say to me, *I'll meet you for lunch at noon.* I reply, *OK*, and indeed I do show up as agreed. My long-term memory has been laid in on the basis of one trial; there hasn't been any opportunity to adjust synaptic weights gradually.

Again, this is not just a problem for the theory of language. It occurs any time there is one-time learning of a novel configuration of known elements. For instance, to choose a task that a non-linguistic primate might find useful: One is walking along a trail in the woods and suddenly spots some ripe figs up in a tree. The next morning, as soon as one gets up, one may head right back to that spot to look for more. There is no previous association of figs with this location, so the knowledge is acquired on a single trial.

For another case: An experimenter says to a subject: "You will see some words appear on the screen. If a word has an *f* in it, stick out your tongue." Subjects can perform faultlessly nearly immediately; and when they leave the experiment, they do not continue sticking out their tongue every time they see a word with an *f* in it. This is the typical paradigm of a psychological experiment: a subject is confronted with a novel task made of familiar parts—and the task has typed variables! Given all the experiments psychologists do, I find it intriguing that no one ever seems to ask how people assimilate the instructions, turning themselves temporarily into specialized stimulus–response machines. For present purposes, though, the important point is that on the basis of a transient input, a lasting combinatorial connection has been forged (understanding the task) which then is used to formulate transient connections (i.e. the actual responses to stimuli in the experiment).

More generally, any sort of episodic memory (in the sense of Tulving 1972) raises this problem: an episodic memory is by hypothesis something that is remembered on the basis of one occurrence, and it usually involves objects, places, and people with which one is familiar. One cannot just encode an episodic memory by gradually strengthening the associations among the involved characters: the precise relations among the characters are crucial, and they are established at once.

I will offer no speculations on how this transfer from working memory to structured long-term memory is accomplished, given that one can no longer speak simply of "shipping information off to some other area of memory." As with the other three cases of this section, I leave it as a challenge for neuroscience. And as with the other cases, it is not something that can simply be disregarded by ignoring language.

To sum up, a theory of how language is instantiated in the brain must grapple with four problems that arise from the combinatoriality of language: the massiveness of binding in linguistic structure, the problem of multiple instances of a known unit in a novel structure, the necessity for encoding and instantiating typed variables, and the relation between long-term and short-term memory encodings of structure. These problems are not exclusive to language, but they certainly come to the fore in dealing with the linguistic phenomena that linguists deal with every day.

A further issue arises from combinatoriality: that of learning the principles that govern it. This requires a whole chapter of its own.

CHAPTER 4

Universal Grammar

4.1 The logic of the argument

Over the years, the most controversial aspect of generative grammar has been Chomsky's hypothesis that humans have a cognitive specialization for learning language. This hypothesis is what connects linguistic theory most closely to biology, cognitive development, ethology, and evolutionary psychology. It also has been a main driving force in research on language typology, language acquisition, and linguistic change, not to mention day-to-day research on the structure of language. Hence, whatever controversy surrounds this hypothesis, its importance cannot be overestimated. This chapter will therefore be devoted to a fairly careful exegesis of the Universal Grammar hypothesis, the evidence for it, the arguments against it, and the tensions and challenges it presents to linguistic theory and the other disciplines on which it impinges.

The language learner first enters the scene in *Aspects* in a passage worth quoting and discussing at some length.

> [I]t is useful to consider the abstract problem of constructing an "acquisition model" for language, that is, a theory of language learning or grammar construction. Clearly, a child who has learned a language has developed an internal representation of a system of rules that determine how sentences are to be formed, used, and understood. (Chomsky 1965: 25)

Our discussion in sections 2.1 and 3.4 recommended purging intentional vocabulary from the theory. This suggests that Chomsky's phrase "has developed an internal representation of a system of rules" is better expressed as "has internally developed a system of rules." The rules are not *represented* in the learner's mind, they are just there.

Similarly, "learn" has to be handled with care, because of its closeness in meaning to "come to know," an intentional term. In this passage and those to be quoted below, Chomsky speaks of "inventing," "constructing," "developing," "devising," and "acquiring" a grammar, all circumlocutions designed to get away from the idea that the child's activity is anything like learning facts. Unfortunately, many of these terms still carry overtones of conscious activity, which we certainly do not want to ascribe to the child, given that the grammar itself is unconscious.[1] In other words, we must understand "learn" in the functional sense of "come to have f-knowledge" in the sense of Chapter 2.

Whatever locutions are adopted, though, Chomsky's point is clear: if speakers have a grammar in their f-minds, then it is important to ask how the grammar got there—how children come to acquire it.

[W]e can say that the child has developed and internally represented a generative grammar [better: "has internally developed a generative grammar"—RJ]. . . . He has done this on the basis of observation of what we may call *primary linguistic data*. (Chomsky 1965: 25)

A footnote explains the notion of primary linguistic data better than the main text:

It seems clear that many children acquire first or second languages quite successfully even though no special care is taken to teach them and no special attention is given to their progress. It also seems apparent that much of the actual speech observed consists of fragments and deviant expressions of a variety of sorts. Thus it seems that a child must have the ability to "invent" a generative grammar that defines well-formedness and assigns interpretations to sentences even though the primary linguistic data that he uses as a basis for this act of theory construction [substitute "f-rule construction"—RJ] may, from the point of view of the theory ["grammar"] he constructs, be deficient in various respects. (Chomsky 1965: 200–1)

That is, environmental evidence alone is an insufficient basis for the child to f-construct a grammar. This is the essence of the "poverty of the stimulus" argument, to which we will return in section 4.6.

Returning to the main text (with my proposed emendations in brackets):

To learn a language, then, the child must have a method for [f-]devising an appropriate grammar, given primary linguistic data. As a precondition for language learning, he must possess, first, a linguistic theory ["a functional prespecification"] that specifies the form of the grammar of a possible human language, and second, a[n unconscious] strategy for [f-]selecting a grammar of the appropriate form that is compatible with the primary linguistic data. (Chomsky 1965: 25)

The term "Universal Grammar" first appears in *Aspects* in a 1788 quotation from James Beattie, where it is defined as those features that all languages have

---

[1] This does not preclude the child's consciously *practicing* language, as documented as early as Weir 1962. But practicing constructing sentences is distinct from having conscious access to the rules by which the sentences being practiced are constructed.

in common and that therefore do not need to be mentioned in grammars of particular languages (Chomsky 1965: 5–6). This usage apparently derives from the term *grammaire générale* of the 1660 Cartesian "Port-Royal Grammar." Soon afterward in Chomsky's writings (1972b; 1975), "Universal Grammar" comes to be used to denote the "initial state" of the language learner; it thus is conceived of as the aspect of the human mind that *causes* languages to have the features in common that they do. More precisely, Chomsky often uses this term to refer to the child's initial prespecification of the form of possible human grammars. He uses the term "Language Acquisition Device" to refer to the child's strategy for constructing or "inventing" a grammar based on primary linguistic data, using Universal Grammar as the starting point. (Alternatively, "Universal Grammar" is sometimes used more loosely to encompass both of these.)[2]

Another passage further conveys the flavor of what Chomsky has in mind:

[I]t seems reasonable to suppose that a child cannot help constructing a particular sort of transformational grammar to account for the data presented to him, any more than he can control his perception of solid objects or his attention to line and angle. (Chomsky 1965: 59)

This observation is what lies behind Pinker's (1994b) calling the ability to learn language the "language instinct." It is part of being human that a child, in response to language in the environment, learns to speak. In a long passage of *Aspects* (pp. 47–52), further developed in Chomsky (1966; 1972a), the idea of an "instinctive" cognitive structure underpinning the acquisition of knowledge is referred back to rationalist forebears including Descartes, Lord Herbert, Cudworth, Arnauld, Leibniz, and particularly Wilhelm von Humboldt.[3]

Finally, Chomsky brings the issue back to the problems faced by linguists:

As a long-range task for general linguistics, we might set the problem of developing an account of this innate linguistic theory ["innate structure" or "prespecification"] that provides the basis for language learning. (Chomsky 1965: 25)

---

[2] Chomsky proposes the simplifying idealization that the child stores up a lot of data and then selects a grammar instantaneously. As far as I know, this idealization has not played any significant role in research. Essentially everyone sees the problem as describing what stage the child is at such-and-such a point, and how the next stage is achieved.

[3] A more recent tradition which Chomsky rarely cites is the gestalt psychology of the 1920s and 1930s (e.g. Wertheimer 1923; Köhler 1927; Koffka 1935), which pursued arguments about the innate basis for perception and learning along lines remarkably similar to Chomsky's (see Macnamara 2000 for discussion). Based on my recollections of discussion with Chomsky, I suspect that he disregarded the gestalt psychologists because their later speculations about brain mechanisms (e.g. Köhler 1940) had brought them into considerable disrepute in American psychology by the 1950s (Lashley 1956). However (as Pim Levelt has pointed out to me), nativist thinking did remain influential in Europe much longer, e.g. in the work of Michotte (1954).

What are the initial assumptions ["functional prespecifications"] concerning the nature of language that the child brings to language learning, and how detailed and specific is the innate schema (the general definition of "grammar") that gradually becomes more explicit and differentiated as the child learns the language? For the present we cannot come at all close to making a hypothesis about innate schemata that is rich, detailed, and specific enough to account for the fact of language acquisition. Consequently, the main task of linguistic theory must be[4] to develop an account of linguistic universals that, on the one hand, will not be falsified by the actual diversity of languages and, on the other, will be sufficiently rich and explicit to account for the rapidity and uniformity of language learning, and the remarkable complexity and range of the generative grammars that are the product of language learning. (pp. 27–8)

I think it fair to say that the task set in these passages—describing the character of Universal Grammar—lies behind the exuberant flowering of linguistic theory and language acquisition research over the past thirty-five years, including much of the work done by resolute opponents of Universal Grammar, who believe there is no such specialized prespecification. Generative linguists will recognize here the mantra that precedes every exposition of linguistic theory; what they may not be aware of is how widely it is rejected and even reviled, not only in other schools of linguistics (such as Cognitive Grammar) but in the vast reaches of psychology and neuroscience.[5]

I happen to think that the idea of Universal Grammar makes a great deal of sense and deserves the influence it has had. On the other hand, it requires a certain amount of polishing, repair, and retrofitting in order to get it into appropriate shape for the Age of Cognitive Neuroscience. That is the task of this chapter; Pinker (1994b) and Jackendoff (1994) have more extended discussion of many of the points raised here.

4.2 Getting the hypothesis right

In order to get to the substance of the hypothesis, we need first to clear away some common misunderstandings of what it says. The quotes below are generalized from many different sources in the literature, as well as from personal conversations over the years.

• "Chomsky claims that grammar is innate." No. Children have to acquire the grammar of whatever language is present in their environment. Universal

---

[4] Notice how within two pages, an account of Universal Grammar has been upgraded from "we might set as a long-range task" to "the main task must be"; the latter is clearly what is intended all along. Rhetorical strategy aside, there is no denying the task's interest and importance.

[5] See Jackendoff (1988) for some illustrations; the situation has if anything become worse in the meantime.

Grammar is not the grammar of any single language: it is the prespecification in the brain that permits the learning of language to take place. So the grammar-*acquiring* capacity is what Chomsky claims is innate. If the child is not exposed to language, language will not develop (though see section 4.9.4). Perhaps the term "Universal Grammar" is misleading and Chomsky should have called it "metagrammar" or "the seeds of grammar." But in order to preserve historical continuity, we are more or less forced to stick with this term, whatever incorrect connotations it invites.

The term "innate" also requires comment. For a first approximation, it means "present at birth." However, it is customarily used more broadly to denote a characteristic that appears automatically in the course of an organism's development, whether before or after birth. For instance the number and organization of human teeth, which develop after birth, can be said to be innate. The term is normally contrasted with "acquired" characteristics, which are due to the influence of the environment. It is now widely understood that most characteristics of organisms result from an interaction of innate and environmental influences. The strength of one's muscles depends on exercise and nutrition. But the fact that humans develop muscles in the places they have them is innate. So it is meant to be with speaking a language: the capacity for acquiring a language may well develop in the brain over the first two or three years of life. And the child's actual achievements at speaking and understanding result from the interaction of this capacity with the input in the environment.

- "Chomsky claims that there is a universal, innate Deep Structure." Not quite. As seen in the previous chapter, Deep Structure denotes the level of a syntactic derivation prior to the application of derivational (transformational) rules. The content of this level might or might not be universal.[6] However, even if Deep Structure is universal, this cannot exhaust the scope of Universal Grammar, which must also prespecify the possibilities for derivational rules (if any) and for constraints in syntax, not to mention many important facets of phonological structure.

On the other hand, in the *Aspects* view, Universal Grammar does specify *that there is Deep Structure*, even it does not specify the exact content of Deep Structure in any particular language. This is part of the overall form of grammar, one that conditions the sorts of (f-)expectations children will have in trying to make sense of the incomprehensible noises the people around them are making. We return to this in section 4.4.

---

[6] However, the incorrect interpretation is encouraged by such statements as "In general, it should be expected that only descriptions concerned with deep structure will have serious import for proposals concerning linguistic universals" (Chomsky 1965: 209–10). There was a brief interest in the late 1960s in the "Universal Base Hypothesis," in which the Deep Structure of all languages was taken to be the same; this idea has been revived in more recent work such as Kayne (1994).

- "Chomsky claims that there is a universal, innate Deep Structure that encodes the meaning of language." This reading of Chomsky was responsible for the powerful appeal of generative grammar to philosophers and psychologists (as well as the general public) in the 1960s: it promised that generative grammar would at last provide a key to meaning, the holy grail of the study of mind. Unfortunately, Chomsky intended no such thing. As just observed, Deep Structure itself is not necessarily universal. In addition, it is not meaning: it is just a level of syntactic structure. The misinterpretation was encouraged by the fact that in the *Aspects* theory, following a proposal by Katz and Postal (1964), Deep Structure was hypothesized to be the level of linguistic structure that, though not meaning itself, *determines* meaning.[7]

Thereby hangs a tale, if I may be permitted a digression. The *Aspects* theory inspired considerable research into whether Deep Structure could be brought still closer to meaning. One of the outcomes was the very popular theory of Case Grammar (Fillmore 1968), in which semantic relations such as Agent, Patient, and Goal were coded directly as "case-markers" in Deep Structure; this formed the basis for much subsequent research in computational linguistics and cognitive psychology. More radical was the theory of Generative Semantics (McCawley 1968; Lakoff 1971; Postal 1970a), in which Deep Structure was posited to be *identical* with meaning. This led to a startling expansion of the overall size of posited underlying syntactic structures, plus a much more elaborate set of derivational rules and constraints. Outside of Chomsky's immediate circle, Generative Semantics became phenomenally attractive, and with good reason: if it were correct, the holy grail would have been achieved. However, Chomsky (1972a) and his students (e.g. Akmajian 1973; Culicover 1972; Jackendoff 1972) attacked it vigorously; the ensuing intellectual melée has with

---

[7] This misconstrual is further encouraged by occasional passages like these:

"In place of the terms 'deep structure' and 'surface structure,' one might use the corresponding Humboldtian notions 'inner form' of a sentence and 'outer form' of a sentence. . . . The terms 'depth grammar' and 'surface grammar' are familiar in modern philosophy in something roughly like the sense here intended (cf. Wittgenstein's distinction of '*Tiefengrammatik*' and '*Oberflächengrammatik*,' 1953, p. 168) . . . The distinction between deep and surface structure, in the sense in which these terms are used here, is drawn quite clearly in the Port-Royal *Grammar*." (Chomsky 1965: 198–9)

"The deep structure that expresses the meaning is common to all languages, so it is claimed [by the Port-Royal grammarians], being a simple reflection of the forms of thought." (Chomsky 1966: 35)

One can be fairly certain that the authors cited really did not have a level of syntax in mind when they spoke of "inner" or "deep" form; they meant "meaning." The problem for these earlier grammarians was that, lacking the tools of formal logic and the like, the only way they had to talk about the meaning of a *complex sentence* was in terms of simpler related sentences. Chomsky chooses to interpret this practice, for better or for worse, as an implicit version of his own theory of syntax.

some justification come to be known as the Linguistic Wars. In the end, for reasons detailed by Newmeyer (1980), Harris (1993), and Huck and Goldsmith (1995), Chomsky emerged victorious—but with a theory, the so-called Extended Standard Theory, in which Deep Structure no longer had the privilege of determining meaning: rather, this role was shared by Deep and Surface Structure. And then he turned his interest away from meaning, to constraints on syntactic derivations (e.g. Chomsky 1973; 1977).

The reaction in the wider community was one of disillusionment, above all at the bad behavior displayed by both sides in the dispute (including the present author). But the disillusionment was intellectual as well: Chomsky's theory turned out not to reveal meaning after all, at least in the sense that had been anticipated. The consequence was that many researchers felt as though they had been seriously misled by linguistics, and they lost all trust in the field.[8] Many psychologists who had been intrigued with generative grammar and its nativist underpinnings came to reject both. Many philosophers interested in formal theories of meaning turned from Generative Semantics to formal logic (e.g. Montague Grammar, Partee 1975; 1976), with its explicitly apsychological underpinnings. Nor was anyone outside linguistics impressed (if they were even paying attention) when some years later, Chomsky (1981) proposed a new level of syntax, Logical Form, that again was supposed to determine meaning. They had all been there before. In short, this painful episode was an important factor in the alienation of linguistics from the rest of cognitive science.

4.3 Linguistic universals

Returning to our main theme, the claims of the hypothesis of Universal Grammar, let me deal with some common questions about linguistic universals. As mentioned above, the term "Universal Grammar" is sometimes used interchangeably with "linguistic universals." This suggests that Universal Grammar is to be found uniformly in the structure of all languages, leading to the following sorts of questions:

---

[8] This turn away from linguistics is documented in the following quote from Walter Kintsch: "... the work on syntax was the showpiece of psycholinguistics. Linguists were going to tell psychologists what to look for, and psychologists were going to find it sooner or later.

"But this linguistics-gone-psychological disappeared from the scene almost as fast as it came. This was partly because the psychologists wanted to share the fun of theorizing and partly because many linguists between MIT and Berkeley kept changing their minds and contradicting each other. But the chief reason was that the linguists talked syntax and, from a psychological point of view, there seemed to be so many more significant, more pressing problems [i.e. meaning—RJ] about which our linguistic mentors had much less to say." (Kintsch 1984: 112)

In conversation, other prominent researchers have reported similar experiences.

- "How can Universal Grammar claim to be universal, when (at least at the beginning) it was applied only to English?" Answer: In fact, Chomsky's very earliest work (1951) was on Modern Hebrew; other early work in syntax concerned German (Lees 1960; Bierwisch 1963), Turkish (Lees 1960), Latin (Lakoff 1968), Japanese (Kuroda 1965), and the Native American languages Hidatsa (Matthews 1964) and Mohawk (Postal 1962). The number of languages now studied is vastly larger. Generative phonology from the start embraced a wide range of languages: the "language index" in Chomsky and Halle's (1968) *Sound Pattern of English* lists references to over 100 languages.

Still, the syntactic machinery most heavily investigated in Chomskyan versions of generative grammar does indeed betray a pedigree grounded in the study of English-like languages. In reaction, other generative theories, notably Lexical-Functional Grammar (Bresnan 1982a; 2001), Autolexical Syntax (Sadock 1991), and Role and Reference Grammar (Van Valin and LaPolla 1997), have developed syntactic machinery more explicitly designed to speak to the varieties of syntactic phenomena in the languages of the world. This leads to the next question:

- "If languages differ so much from each other, how can there be any universals? And if there aren't, how can Universal Grammar have any content?" Remember, Universal Grammar is not supposed to be what is universal among languages: it is supposed to be the "toolkit" that a human child brings to learning any of the languages of the world. If we find that a certain aspect of linguistic structure is indeed universal, then it is a good candidate for part of Universal Grammar, though other options must also be considered (see section 4.5).

However, non-universal aspects of linguistic structure may be candidates for Universal Grammar as well. When you have a toolkit, you are not obliged to use every tool for every job. Thus we might expect that not every grammatical mechanism provided by Universal Grammar appears in every language. For instance, some languages make heavy use of case marking, and others don't; some languages make heavy use of fixed word order, and others don't. We would like to say that Universal Grammar makes both these possibilities available to the child; but only the possibilities actually present in the environment come to realization in the child's developing grammar.

One prominent version of the "toolkit" approach is Principles and Parameters theory (Chomsky 1981), in which all grammatical variation among languages is localized in a set of universal parameters, whose settings are triggered by environmental input. Learning a language can then be thought of roughly as like customizing the settings in a software package. But there are other, less rigid theories of Universal Grammar as well. In any event, it is commonly understood that Universal Grammar provides possibilities, not just certainties, for the structure of the grammar the child is to develop.

Such an approach is subject to a certain justified skepticism. It is tempting to fall into the trap, upon encountering a new grammatical phenomenon, of positing it as a new component of Universal Grammar—just one that happens to be restricted to this single language. This potentially leads to an inflated estimate of what the child brings to language learning. Although of course researchers do sometimes fall into this trap, in general I think it has been avoided.

Rather, the dialectic goes roughly like this: When one looks at language after language and finds that the tools one has proposed for Universal Grammar are sufficient, one begins to get the feeling that one has the right toolkit. On the other hand, when the same difficulty starts cropping up time after time, one begins to consider proposing a new tool, or revising the tools one has previously proposed. A good example might be the widespread phenomenon of Noun Incorporation, which came to the attention of generative theorists in the middle 1980s. There are many languages in which it is possible to express a direct object by attaching a noun closely to the verb ("incorporating it into the verb"), leaving the modifiers of the noun still expressed in direct object position. (1) is an example from Southern Tiwa, quoted in Sadock 1991; note that 'cat' is part of the verb form, sandwiched between the agreement marker and the verb itself.

(1) Wisi ibi- musa-tuwi-ban
     two   AGR-cat - buy -PAST   'They bought two cats.'

It was clear to everyone that this phenomenon did not lend itself easily to the tools of the then-current theories of syntax, and that some addition had therefore to be made to the toolkit posited by Universal Grammar. The character of the proper mechanism has been subject to lively discussion (Mithun 1984; Baker 1988; Rosen 1989; Sadock 1991; and many others). Is it a new kind of derivational rule, a new kind of lexical formation rule, or a lexical redundancy rule? Does the same tool account for English nouns like *man-eater* and *language learner*, which are built out of a verb and its object? This is not the right place to go into details; the point here is only to give the flavor of the conversation.

At the same time, there is a constant re-evaluation of the inventory of elements posited in Universal Grammar. The goal is to posit the smallest toolkit that can still account for the data. For instance, under the conception of derivational rules in early generative grammar, an account of Noun Incorporation was altogether straightforward; Postal (1964) in fact used Noun Incorporation in Mohawk to construct an important argument for transformational grammar. However, in the interests of constraining the possibilities offered within Universal Grammar, the theory was changed in order to rule out many movement phenomena that had not yet been observed. As it happened, these changes also ruled out the possibility of Noun Incorporation. The problem then faced in the 1980s was to formulate an account that allowed for the observed phenomena without reintroducing the excessive promiscuity of the earlier hypothesis. More generally, the frequent readjustments in Chomsky's theories over the years have been an attempt to propose as lean a version of Universal Grammar as possible; the Minimalist Program (Chomsky 1995) is by far the leanest.

Some of this constant re-evaluation has been driven by explorations into what forms of grammar are mathematically learnable. In particular, many of the early constraints on transformational rules were in part inspired by learnability considerations (Gold 1967; Wexler and Culicover 1980), which applied specifically to the *Aspects* model. And later research has often averted to learnability considerations as well (Baker and McCarthy 1981; Pinker 1989; Gleitman and Landau 1994; Van Valin 1994; and many others).

What I hope the reader can appreciate from this brief discussion is that hypotheses about the content of Universal Grammar constantly raise complex empirical issues about how a multitude of linguistic phenomena are to be described. Continued examination of more and more linguistic phenomena, with attention not only to what happens but also to what does *not* happen, has led to the many reformulations of linguistic theory over the years, with concomitant rearticulation of the content of Universal Grammar.

4.4 Substantive universals, repertoire of rule types, and architectural universals

Another aspect of the problem of universals is addressed in a section of *Aspects* called "Formal and Substantive Universals" (Chomsky 1965: 27–30), which distinguishes two different facets of Universal Grammar. By "substantive universals," Chomsky means the basic building blocks of linguistic structure: phonological distinctive features and the notion of syllable in phonology, and parts of speech and the notion of syntactic tree in syntax. These parts are used differently in different languages, but one cannot construct a human language without them. Chomsky therefore wishes to attribute them to the brain's prespecification.

By "formal universals," Chomsky means the overall organization of the grammar. These might be divided into two subcategories. First, the child has to have a repertoire of rule types—what kinds of rules a language might have for combining the basic units into complex structures. Chapter 3 distinguished phrasal formation rules, derivational rules, several varieties of constraints, lexical formation rules, lexical redundancy rules, and inheritance hierarchies. All of these rule types have to be in the child's repertoire, ready to be filled with content so they can develop into the rules of the child's very own grammar.

Also in the repertoire of rule types belong particular constraints on derivations that have been proposed over the years. For instance, section 3.2.3 mentioned the Sentential Subject Constraint, which prohibits certain kinds of relation between underlying and surface forms. Insofar as every movement rule (or its equivalent in alternative non-movement theories) in every language obeys this constraint—and children don't violate it in the course of learning language—we would like to be able to say that this constraint and others like it come prespecified in the child's toolkit.

As we observed in Chapter 3, a great deal of theoretical dispute concerns which kinds of phenomenon fit under which kind of rule—and whether certain sorts of rules (in particular derivational rules and inheritance hierarchies) exist at all. These disputes concern specifically what repertoire of rule types should be ascribed to the child's prespecification.

Still more basically, the child needs to f-know in what overall linguistic structures the basic building blocks can be arranged. The basic architectural outline of linguistic structure sketched in Fig. 1.1—interconnected phonological, syntactic, and conceptual/semantic structures, each containing substructures and tiers of particular sorts—*is* common to all languages; this sort of formal universal might be called an "architectural universal." Languages can differ considerably in how this architecture is realized, but at the largest scale there is little or no deviation.

Some of the major changes in linguistic theory have concerned architectural universals. For instance, the level of Deep Structure proposed in *Aspects* is meant as an architectural universal: it is a syntactic level that is input to both the transformational component and semantic interpretation. The proposed architecture changed when the role of Deep Structure in semantics was altered in subsequent versions of the theory. Chapter 5 will develop a more extensive revision of the overall architecture.

4.5 The balance of linguistic and more general capacities

Michael Tomasello (1995) voices a common complaint with linguists' hypotheses about formal universals, in the context of a critique of Steven Pinker's (1994b) exposition of Universal Grammar.

[T]he list [of innate aspects of language] contains things that no nonlinguist would ever recognize—such things as the projection principle, the empty category principle, the subjacency constraint, and the coordinate structure constraint. . . . [A]ll of these universals are described in linguistically specific terms such that it is very difficult to relate them to cognition in other psychological domains. (Tomasello 1995: 135–6)

However, Tomasello begs the question: he presupposes that everything innate in language should be explicable in terms of more general psychological phenomena.

One would be laughed at for such a complaint in the case of an undeniably specialized system, say visual stereopsis (perceiving depth from the disparity of images in the two eyes). What makes a system specialized is in part that it performs processes not found elsewhere in the f-mind. If language is indeed a specialized system, one should expect some of its functional principles to be sui generis.

Similarly, Andy Clark (1996) wonders how much brain specialization is necessary for language. The formal structure of language provides part of the answer. Using language requires the ability to process syntactic and phonological structures—two structures qualitatively different from anything else in the brain—in the course of mapping between thoughts and external signals. This seems to me to require a brain specialization of some sort, certainly more than "some additional feedback loops" or the "freeing up of some resources" thanks to a larger cortex, as Clark speculates. In particular, Clark asks whether language could be due just to "some small tweak" in brain architecture. I would counter, "Small compared to what?" It's a small tweak compared to the differences between insects and fish, or to the differentiation of the basic body plan. But then, so is the machinery in the bat's brain that permits echolocation, or the machinery in the elephant's brain that permits it to use its trunk. I doubt that Clark would attribute echolocation just to "some additional feedback loops" or the "freeing up of some resources." As Chomsky (1975) and Pinker (1994b) emphasize, there is no reason to view language any differently.

Part of the trouble is that Universal Grammar has often been construed—by both sides in the dispute—in terms of a cartoonish "grammar box," cut off from the rest of the mind. This is clearly an oversimplification. Tomasello and Clark are correct to the extent that, insofar as possible, we should be conservative in how much linguistic structure we ascribe to an innate UG. We should welcome explanations of linguistic universals on more general cognitive grounds. For example, if there prove to be hierarchical structures and/or instantiation of variables elsewhere in perception, cognition, and action (as argued in Chapter 3), we then need not ascribe these characteristics to a specifically linguistic "toolkit." This point is clearly prefigured in *Aspects* (if only in a footnote):

Notice that we do not, of course, imply that the functions of language acquisition are carried out by entirely separate components of the abstract mind or the physical brain. . . . In fact, it is an important problem for psychology to determine to what extent other aspects of cognition share properties of language acquisition and language use, and to attempt, in this way, to develop a richer and more comprehensive theory of mind. (Chomsky 1965: 207)

On the other hand, even granted the broader applicability of hierarchical structure and variable instantiation, general principles alone cannot explain the character of the specifically linguistic hierarchies and linguistic categories: the units out of which they are built (the substantive universals), the repertoire of rule types that govern them, and the overall architecture. Therefore, in order to see what aspects of language *can* be reduced to more general principles of the f-mind, we cannot just observe, for instance, that hierarchical structures are found in motor control (e.g. tool construction), and thereby claim that these are directly related to the hierarchical structures of language (such an argument seems to be offered by Corballis 1991; see the discussion by Bloom 1994a). Rather, it is necessary to develop a functional description of the cognitive structures in question, parallel to that for language exemplified in Fig. 1.1, so we can look for finer-scale commonalities.

I take David Marr (1982) to have been developing such a functional description for the visual system; unfortunately this goal seems to have receded since Marr's death, shortly before publication of his book. Lerdahl and Jackendoff (1983) develop a functional description for musical cognition. Within this system one can see detailed similarities to both vision and language. In particular, the similarities between musical rhythm and linguistic prosody are striking— although neither is reducible to the other. The two are related more or less like fingers and toes.

At a different scale, connectionist neural network modeling (Rumelhart and McClelland 1986a) has suggested some very general principles of f-mental computation and learning that demonstrably extend over many capacities. These are interestingly echoed in Lakoff's (1987) and Jackendoff's (1983) arguments at the level of functional description for the existence of flexible, violable (and therefore nonalgorithmic) constraints involved in many domains of cognition and perception, including language, and they re-emerge in contemporary linguistics to some degree in Optimality Theory. These general principles may be conceived of as formal universals of the f-mind. They undoubtedly constrain and shape formal universals specific to language. But they do not determine the particular content of the linguistic universals, precisely to the extent that language is a distinct specialization.

On still another scale, the one area where a great deal is known about neural instantiation is the low-level visual system (e.g. Hubel and Wiesel 1968). This system and how it maps to higher visual areas or to visuo-motor coordination are sometimes invoked (e.g. Churchland 1986) as a model for how the rest of cognition works. The trouble is that low-level vision shares very little in the way of functional properties with any aspect of language. For example, as pointed out in Chapter 3, low-level vision does not require freely combinatorial structure mediated by typed variables. Hence we cannot expect arguments about low-level vision to carry over very decisively to language.

On the whole, linguists have taken more interest in establishing universals than in reducing them to more general cognitive capacities, and to this degree Tomasello's complaint is justified.[9] This is an area where sympathetic cooperation with researchers in other areas of perception and cognition would be extremely helpful: an attempt to find detailed functional parallels to linguistic phenomena is usually beyond the professional competence of either an unaided linguist or an unaided non-linguist.

One other possible source for linguistic universals ought to be mentioned here. It is quite possible that there are some constraints that apply to *any* communicative system operating in a community of organisms, and therefore apply to language. Such "systems" effects might not be explicitly present in any single organism but might arise as "emergent properties" of the community as a whole. An example is the architecture of termite mounds, which arises presumably not because any single termite has a grand plan in f-mind, but because each termite is programmed to perform certain far simpler actions which collectively add up to the communal construction of an elaborate structure. I am unaware of any research that demonstrates such effects in aspects of linguistic structure, but it is important to leave the possibility open, especially in the light of interesting work now being done on mathematical and computational modeling of communities of communicating organisms (e.g. Kirby 1998; Steels 1998; Batali 1998; Nowak et al. 2000).

A related line of argument for linguistic universals, which I find less persuasive, appeals to the historical development of languages. For instance, Terrence Deacon says:

Human children appear preadapted to guess the rules of syntax properly, precisely because languages evolve[10] so as to embody in their syntax the most frequently guessed patterns. The brain has co-evolved with respect to language, but languages have done most of the adapting. (Deacon 1997: 122)

But this puts the cart before the horse. Deacon is correct that human languages do not push the envelope of Universal Grammar very much. But our question is: What is this envelope anyway, such that languages, however they evolve over time, must conform to it? Given all the differences among the languages of the world, what is it about them that enables children to "guess the rules of

---

[9] A notable exception is Cognitive Grammar (Lakoff 1987; Langacker 1987). However, the psychological principles invoked by Cognitive Grammar rarely extend beyond the figure–ground distinction and Rosch's (1978) theory of categorization, so the depth of the reduction is somewhat limited.

[10] Note that "evolve" here refers to historical change in languages, e.g. the changes from Middle English to Modern English. This is quite a different sense from the evolution of the brain, and it takes place over a different timescale.

syntax" so well? This something, whatever it is, is what is meant by Universal Grammar.

4.6 The poverty of the stimulus; the Paradox of Language Acquisition

Aspects continually returns to the assertion that the primary linguistic data available to the language learner underdetermine the choice of grammar, and therefore are insufficient for inducing the grammar without the aid of a specialized Universal Grammar. Chomsky frequently adds assertions along the following lines (a similar passage was quoted earlier):

It is, for the present, impossible to formulate an assumption about initial, innate structure *rich enough* [my italics—RJ] to account for the fact that grammatical [f-]knowledge is attained on the basis of the evidence available to the learner. (Chomsky 1965: 58)

That is, he says, the problem facing us is not to reduce the tools we ascribe to the child: it is to give the child enough tools to do the job. This argument has been used to justify major phases of elaboration in the theory of Universal Grammar.

On the other hand, opponents of Universal Grammar have argued that the child has much more evidence than Chomsky thinks: among other things, special modes of speech by parents ("Motherese") that make linguistic distinctions clearer to the child (Newport et al. 1977; Fernald 1984), understanding of context, including social context (Bruner 1974/5; Bates and MacWhinney 1982), and statistical distribution of phonemic transitions (Saffran et al. 1996) and of word occurrence (Plunkett and Marchman 1991). All these kinds of evidence are indeed available to the child, and they do help. Chomsky makes a telling slip here, when he says (1965: 35), "Real progress in linguistics consists in the discovery that certain features of given languages can be reduced to universal properties of language, and explained in terms of these deeper aspects of linguistic form." He neglects to observe that it is also real progress to show that there is evidence enough in the input for certain features of languages to be *learned*.

What the critics do not demonstrate, however, is that these kinds of evidence alone are enough to vault the child into the exalted realm of structures like Fig. 1.1. Bates and Elman (1996), for instance, argue that learning is much more powerful than previously believed, weakening the case for a highly prespecified Universal Grammar. I agree that learning which makes more effective use of the input certainly helps the child, and it certainly takes some of the load off Universal Grammar. But I do not think it takes *all* the load off. It may allow Universal Grammar to be less rich, but it does not allow UG to be dispensed with altogether. (More detailed discussion of this point appears in Gleitman and Wanner 1982 and Shatz 1982.)

To be sure, Bates and Elman end by saying "Even if we assume that a brain ... contains no innate knowledge at all, we have to make crucial assumptions about the structure of the learning device, its rate and style of learning, and the kinds of input that it 'prefers' to receive." Still, it is my impression that many advocates of such arguments either are not aware of or explicitly wish to deny the complexity of linguistic structure; and a less complex structure naturally requires a less elaborate learning theory. As in Chapter 1, I insist that we cannot adequately assess theories of language learning without understanding the character of what is learned: Fig. 1.1 represents a bare minimum that all linguists (not just unreconstructed Chomskyans) agree upon. Vision seems intuitively simple too, yet no one in cognitive science believes any more that the visual system has a simple structure or that the brain just "learns to see" without any specialized genetic support.

It is useful to put the problem of learning more starkly in terms of what I like to call the Paradox of Language Acquisition: The community of linguists, collaborating over many decades, has so far failed to come up with an adequate description of a speaker's f-knowledge of his or her native language. Yet every normal child manages to acquire this f-knowledge by the age of ten or so, without reading any linguistics textbooks or going to any conferences. How is it that in some sense every single normal child is smarter than the whole community of linguists?

The answer proposed by the Universal Grammar hypothesis is that the child comes to the task with some f-preconceptions of what language is going to be like, and structures linguistic input according to the dictates (or opportunities!) provided by those expectations. By contrast, linguists, using explicit reasoning—and far more data from the world than the child—have a much larger design space in which they must localize the character of grammar. Hence their task is harder than the child's: they constantly come face to face with the *real* poverty of the stimulus. No child has to decide the sorts of issues we have been sketching here: whether there is a separate prosodic tier in phonology; whether or not there are derivational rules; whether such-and-such a phenomenon belongs to derivational rules, lexical formation rules, or interface constraints; and what kind of a rule is responsible for Noun Incorporation. And surely no child has to choose among major architectural alternatives such as GB, LFG, HPSG, Cognitive Grammar, OT, and many other yet-to-be-devised alternatives. The Universal Grammar hypothesis supposes that at some level (we might say intuitively or instinctively), the child f-knows the right choices. It may take children a while to sort the phenomena out, but, as stressed in Chapter 2, they all come up with essentially the same solution.

It is worth pointing out that the Paradox of Language Acquisition finds parallels in every cognitive domain. All normal children learn to see, navigate, manipulate objects, and engage in rich social interaction; but we are far from being able to describe the f-mental processes that constitute these abilities, and even farther from being able to specify a simple learning process that leads to these abilities without support from a rather richly specified initial state. There seems no reason why language should be singled out for different treatment.

Nevertheless, sometimes it is objected[11] that positing an innate basis for language acquisition is a counsel of despair or resignation, just pushing the problem downstairs into the genes (which we discuss in section 4.8). But one might justifiably have said the same of the theory of gravitation in Newton's time: it postulated an occult, invisible, inexplicable force that physicists are still trying to explain. There is nothing wrong with such a theoretical move if it is done with care and it leads to interesting conclusions. While there is scientific virtue in desiring a minimum of theoretical machinery in psychology as well as physics, this must not be confused with dogmatically insisting on a minimum regardless of what the evidence might be.

Sometimes it is objected that linguists are trying to figure out the grammar consciously, but children do it unconsciously, so they are more intuitive, less hampered by preconceptions. To me this misses the point: we need a way for children to be *less* imaginative than linguists and *more* hampered by preconceptions—in fact hampered by the very same preconceptions as every other child. It is just that children's preconceptions happen to give them the right solutions.

A way for children to be more hampered than adults has been proposed by Newport (1990) and Elman (1993). They suggest, for different reasons, that children may be able to learn language only because their minds are less developed than those of adults. Linguists and adult language learners have developed many more conscious and unconscious strategies for learning, which only serve to lead them astray when they are faced with a foreign language. By contrast, according to this story, children are constrained to a more limited number of possible choices, so they get language right with less trouble. This suggestion may well have some truth to it. However, as pointed out a moment ago, the limited number of possible choices to which children are constrained had better be the *right* ones, otherwise they won't learn. That is, these constraints on their choices amount precisely to Universal Grammar (or, possibly, more general cognitive constraints that children grow out of).

---

[11] The following two objections are voiced explicitly in Hilferty et al. (1998). But they have been raised in many other places in the literature as well and they come up frequently in conversation.

In claiming that children learn grammar so easily by doing it intuitively rather than consciously, critics also miss another important point: in an information-theoretic sense, children and linguists are facing the *very same* problem. I suspect that this is the part of the argument that people find most difficult. So let me try to make it more concrete, to show how it works out in practice.

Suppose we find that in the (hypothetical) language Urtish, certain direct objects are marked dative case and others are marked accusative. The problem for the child as well as for the linguist is to find out which are which. Of course children don't know anything explicit about case marking: "dative," "accusative," and even "case" are just *our* labels. Children only have to put the right affix in the right place, without knowing why, and perhaps even without knowing *that* they have done so. But they do have to get it right.

So we linguists can ask how children manage to do this. One way might be that they simply memorize the right case for each verb, and this may indeed be the right solution; in a theoretical grammar we would call this "lexically marked quirky case." But suppose when we introduce children to new verbs, they automatically use the right case:

(2) *Experimenter*: Look! This is blizzing. Tell me what I just did.
     Child: You blizzed the cake-os. [where -*os* is the case-marking in question]

Now we have to discover what clues the child used. Are they semantic, phonological, or pragmatic? If semantic, are they based on the nature of the action, the object acted on, the agent's intention, etc., etc.? The theoretical grammar will have to be formulated to capture this distinction. Or suppose children invariably use accusative case on the first try, even when the correct case is dative. Then the linguist might say accusative is the "default" case, and look for the systematicity or lack thereof behind deviation from the default. Having figured this out, then we can ask: Why did the child look for *that* clue rather than something else? Such questions are familiar to every practicing linguist. When we find these questions arising in every corner of every language (as we do), the Paradox of Language Acquisition becomes almost second nature, a fact of daily research life.

One of my favorite illustrations of the Paradox is the following set of sentences, first pointed out by Jeffrey Gruber (1965).

(3) a. Every acorn grew into an oak.
     b. Every oak grew out of an acorn.
     c. An oak grew out of every acorn.
     d. *An acorn grew into every oak.

What is striking about this paradigm is its asymmetry. In (3a–c), we understand each acorn to correspond to an oak, that is, *every* quantifies over *an*. But (3d) has only the absurd interpretation that a single acorn grew into multiple trees. There would be no problem if (3c, d) were both good: we could say that *every* can quantify over *an* under any circumstance. Again, if (3c, d) were both bad, the story would be simple: we could say that *every* can quantify over *an* only if it precedes it (or is structurally dominant over it). Or, if (3b, d) were both bad, we could say that *every* can quantify over *an* only if *every* is connected to a temporally prior stage (*acorn*), not a temporally subsequent stage (*oak*). But the actual data show some weird interaction of linear order in the sentence and temporal order in the semantics, a totally unexpected result. So far as I know there is no "natural" solution to this in the literature, one that does not in essence simply stipulate this asymmetry.

I also know of no data on the acquisition of this paradigm. But all English speakers (so far as I know) have a grammar that produces these judgments. How did they acquire it? One might propose that sentences like (3a, b, c) are present in the child's primary linguistic input, but sentences like (3d) are not; therefore (3d) is never around to be imitated and hence never comes to be uttered. However, such an approach will not do. We routinely assume that children generalize from the input, so if they hear, say, (4a, b, c), they will be willing to produce (4d).

(4) a. The cow bit the horse.
     b. The horse bit the cow.
     c. The horse was bitten by the cow.
     d. The cow was bitten by the horse.

So something is preventing children from making the parallel generalization from (3a, b, c) to (3d)—otherwise (3d) would become grammatical within one generation. This something is what linguists so far have failed to discover but children intuitively f-know.

Linguists are looking for a "natural" or "elegant" solution to (3) rather than a purely stipulative one precisely so they can ascribe a "natural" or "elegant" structure to the child's intuitions—intuitions that result in our all having the judgments shown in (3). If the eventual "natural" or "elegant" solution turned out to rely in part on non-grammatical aspects of cognition, we would be happier; but we cannot rule out the possibility that it is a peculiarity of the language faculty, hence part of Universal Grammar. We cannot prejudge where to look, and grammatical and non-linguistic solutions call for equally rigorous argumentation.

It is important, however, to handle the poverty of the stimulus argument with care. For instance, a crucial issue in syntax is what permits noun phrases (NPs) to appear in the syntactic positions they do. One popular approach (Chomsky 1981) takes its cue from languages like Latin, German, and Russian, where all NPs are marked for case (nominative, accusative, dative, etc.). The proposal is that, universally, NPs are permitted in positions where they can be case marked. In order for this proposal to be carried through consistently, it is necessary to claim that English too is relentlessly case marked, even though it makes no overt case distinctions except on pronouns (*I/me, she/her*, etc.). And even pronouns fail to show an accusative–dative case distinction, needed to distinguish direct from indirect objects. Thus, goes the argument, children learning English acquire the case system even though there is virtually nothing in the linguistic input that tells them about it. Therefore, it is concluded, case marking must be part of UG.

One might find it objectionable that this solution attributes a great deal of invisible structure to English, yet gets this structure in there via innate f-knowledge. In order to answer the argument, though, it is not enough to pronounce it absurd. Two tasks are incumbent on the critic. First, an alternative account of the syntactic positioning of NPs must be offered, one that is either learnable or else based on other plausible principles of UG. Preferably, this account should also be shown to be more empirically adequate in dealing with the distribution of NPs cross-linguistically. Second, an account must be offered of case marking that shows how *it* is learnable in the languages that have it. My impression is that case systems (Blake 1994) cross-linguistically show patterns reminiscent of the cross-linguistic distribution of color names (Berlin and Kay 1969). This suggests that there are at least some innate biases regarding case systems that make them come out as they do. Thus at best the critic might be able to conclude (a) that English speakers do not have an invisible case system, but that the distribution of NPs is determined by some partly innate linguistic principles more "natural" than case; and (b) that the acquisition of case in those languages that have it is guided in part by innate case principles that help the learner structure the primary linguistic input. In other words, perhaps one could arrive at a more input-driven model of the language learner with respect to these phenomena, but it is unlikely that the contribution of UG will go away altogether.

4.7 Poverty of the stimulus in word learning

The discussion so far has been couched largely in terms of the acquisition of grammar, following Chomsky's emphasis. But learning the lexicon poses if anything a far vaster problem. Suppose a grammar has as many as a few hundred rules in it, and compare this to the estimate that an average speaker knows on the order of several tens of thousands of words (this includes passive as well as active vocabulary, since after all one must understand as well as speak the language). By a simple arithmetic calculation, Carey (1978) observes that a child must learn on the order of five words a day in order to achieve the estimated 8,ooo-word vocabulary of a six-year-old. Of course this learning is not for the most part deliberate; it is not like learning foreign vocabulary from flash cards. Rather, at any given time the child is probably "working on" various stages of dozens or hundreds of words. The learning of grammar pales by comparison.

It is often taken for granted that word learning is straightforward. Parents point to an object and say the word (*Doggie! See the doggie?*), and the child automatically makes the association. But behind that apparent effortlessness lies a great deal of complexity, once we think to look for it. Quine's (1960) doctrine of the "indeterminacy of radical translation" was early applied to the problem of word learning: does *doggie* refer to that particular dog (like *Rover* or *Snoopy*), to dogs in general, to (say) poodles in general, to pets, animals, furry things, animate things? Worse, does it refer to the dog's tail, its overall shape, its color, the substance of which it is made, what the dog is doing right now (sitting, panting, slobbering), or (less plausible but still logically possible) the collection of the dog's legs or the combination of the dog and the carpet it is sitting on?

And *dog* is just a concrete count noun. Consider the problems faced when the word is something the parents can't point to, such as *see, think, hungry, ask, from, any, when, but*, and *were*, to pick only a few of the many hundreds of non-concrete words a six-year-old knows. How does the child figure out what these words mean? Jerry Fodor (1975; 1998) proposes to solve the learning problem by making all word meanings innate, an extravagance with which few have concurred (see Chapter 11). But even supposing that he were correct, the child would still face the problem of figuring out which of the tens (or hundreds) of thousands of innate meanings is the right one for each of these words. That is, Fodor's move does not evade the poverty of the stimulus argument.

The semantic/conceptual sophistication of the very early word learner is examined at length in John Macnamara's 1982 *Names for Things*, and a vigorous experimental tradition has ensued, attempting to test exactly what assumptions a child makes about the meanings of newly encountered words (Katz et al. 1974; Keil 1989; Bloom 1994b; 1999; 2000; Carey 1994; Markman 1989; Hall 1999; Landau 1994, to list only a few parochially selected choices). This has led to (or has been connected with) fascinating research on how infants conceptualize the physical world and how this changes over the first couple of years of life (Baillargeon 1986; Spelke et al. 1994; Carey and Xu 1999), which in turn has led to parallel experimentation on non-human primates (some examples are cited in Hauser 2000). What is clearly emerging is that the world of the baby is far from William James's "blooming, buzzing confusion" or Quine's undifferentiated quality space. Children apparently come to the task of learning the world—and the words used to describe it—with a host of built-in biases that constrain their f-hypotheses about what a word can pertain to.

Most of the experimental work cited above pertains to words for objects, with subsidiary emphases on words for substances (*milk*), properties (*heavy*), and locations (*on, under*). A whole other area of research, impinging more closely on the learning of grammar, concerns the learning of verbs, which express actions and states. Different kinds of action involve different numbers and types of character. For instance, sleeping and sneezing involve only one character; eating requires an eater and something eaten; giving requires a giver, a recipient, and something given. This has implications for the corresponding verb's syntactic behavior. For instance, *sleep* and *sneeze* are intransitive, their single character being expressed as the verb's subject. *Eat* is transitive, the thing eaten being expressed as direct object—or omitted. *Give* is ditransitive: the recipient and thing given are expressed as indirect object and direct object respectively—or as object of *to* and direct object respectively. (The principles behind these correspondences will be discussed in sections 5.8 and 5.9.) So the question arises: To what extent do children figure out a verb's meaning and then its syntactic possibilities, and to what extent do they have to hear its syntactic possibilities—including various alternatives as in the cases above—in order to decide what it means? A fascinating and intricate discussion in the literature (e.g. Landau and Gleitman 1985; Pinker 1989; 1994a; Fisher et al. 1994; Grimshaw 1994; Brent 1994; Steedman 1994; Tomasello and Merriman 1995; Gillette et al. 1999) detects influences in both directions. However the answer works out, one has to assume that the child has certain biases as to what to look for.

This is only the semantic side of word learning. As Macnamara (1982) points out, the child must also f-identify the spoken word as a significant perceptual object, in order to have something to link a meaning to. Here too there is a significant body of research (e.g. Cutler 1994; Jusczyk 1997). Statistical regularities in syllabic structure (Saffran et al. 1996; Kuhl 2000) undoubtedly play a role in the child's determining which strings of sounds are words at all. More generally, the connectionist tradition (Rumelhart and McClelland 1986a, b; Elman et al. 1996) has shown that rather elementary statistical procedures can lead to much more sophisticated behavior and learning than could have been imagined in 1965. As pointed out in Chapter 3, such procedures do not come to terms with the all-important combinatoriality of language. However, we will return in Chapter 6 to points where this sort of learning proves useful.

The discussion in this section can hardly do justice to what has by now become a vast tradition of research. I allude to this tradition only to make clear how rich, varied, and difficult the questions of word learning are. Again we meet the Paradox of Language Acquisition at every turn. We should be delighted if some aspects of this problem can be reduced to the child doing some relatively simple statistical analysis of the input; but on the other hand, we should not assume that this approach scales up to a solution of the entire problem.

4.8 How Universal Grammar can be related to genetics

In order for Universal Grammar to be an innate cognitive specialization, it must be transmitted genetically, just like anything else innate. But what does it mean for it to be transmitted genetically?

It is certain that the genes cannot directly code a set of functional principles. All they can do is code the synthesis of proteins under particular environmental circumstances, which in turn guide certain unknown parameters of brain growth. Edelman (1992), Elman et al. (1996), and Deacon (1997) provide fascinating discussions of how brain architecture develops and differentiates. But I think it fair to say that the manner in which this process is guided by genetics or anything else is pretty much a mystery at the moment—and this is only at the level of turning genetic instructions into neural architecture. On top of this lies the mystery pointed out in Chapter 2—how neural instantiation supports functional organization, especially at a level as complex as language. So at the moment I think there is really no hope of understanding in any detail the wonderfully indirect mechanisms for genetic transmission of Universal Grammar. In fifty years, perhaps. . . .

Jeffrey Elman et al. (1996) and, following them, Terrence Deacon (1997) mount a series of important arguments against a detailed innate language-learning capacity, based on this problem of genetic transmission. It is worth addressing these arguments in some detail, as they provide a concise distillation of many arguments in opposition to Universal Grammar over the years.

First, they argue that the only way to control behavior of an organism is through adjustment of synaptic weights. But genes cannot adjust synaptic weights—they can code only general guidelines to brain growth. At the same time, however, these authors explicitly say they are nativists, and they are ready to grant complex inborn instincts to animals. It is only UG that they object to. But then, we might ask, how are animal instincts coded on the genes? There is just as much mystery here. As Chomsky says (1965: 206), "Every known species has highly specialized cognitive capacities"; and all the evidence of the past thirty-five years has amplified this statement substantially.

I suggest that the proper questions to ask on this score are the following:

• How can *any* sort of animal behavior—spatial orientation and navigation, bird songs and nest-building, primate call systems, sexual selection, child-rearing, understanding and producing facial expressions, conducting exchanges of reciprocal altruism (e.g. Darwin 1872; Tinbergen 1951/89; Dawkins 1989; Gallistel 1990)—be composed of innate and learned components? There are many differences among species in exactly what is learned and what is innate, as has been established particularly for bird song (Marler 1984).

• How can the genome code any such innate component of animal behavior so as to guide brain development appropriately? Consider something as simple as sneezing, which I assume we can agree is innate—or the ability of newborn horses to get up and walk immediately. How does the brain code these action patterns, and how do the genes make the brain develop so as to code them?

• To what extent is the human ability to learn language guided by such an innate component? Of these three questions, this is the only one at issue at the moment. Putting the question in terms of "to what extent" permits a wide spectrum of possible answers, rather than a binary decision for or against Universal Grammar.

Sometimes it is argued that innate capacities in animals turn out to be "cheap tricks." For instance, Konrad Lorenz (1952; 1966) discovered that male cichlid fish attack not just other males, but anything that happens to have the right kind of red spot; and that newborn geese imprint not just on their mother, but anything that happens to move the right way. These tricks happen to work well enough in the normal environment of these animals. It is only in the context of perverse experimenters that nature's short cuts are uncovered. The critics of Universal Grammar sometimes suggest that it too will turn out to be a collection of "cheap tricks," rather than a detailed specification of tree structures, constraints on rules, and the like. Still, even a cheap trick is a cognitive specialization —and the genome has to code it, whether in cichlids, geese, or humans.

Another argument offered by Elman et al. and Deacon concerns individual differences. How can Universal Grammar be uniform among humans, if everyone's brain is a little different—for instance, if localization of the language areas is not entirely identical? There are two lines of answer. First, as acknowledged in Chapter 2, not everyone's language is entirely identical—just good enough for both parties in a conversation to be convinced that communication is taking place. These differences might be a consequence of brain differences in the initial state, or of contingencies of learning, or both—no one really knows. Second, this same question can obviously be addressed to animals' cognitive specializations, but we are not going to argue that these are not innate. So why should language be singled out? I would imagine that differences among individuals' brains are more or less like differences among their faces: a bit more here, a bit less there, slightly different placement here, slightly different proportions there, but everything works essentially the same. We don't know how the genes code individual differences in human faces, much less the basic similarities that distinguish human faces from gorilla faces. Yet we have no problem agreeing that faces are partly determined by the genes.

Elman et al. and Deacon also mount an argument against Universal Grammar based on brain plasticity: young children often can recover fairly good language function (low end of normal range) in the face of early damage to the language areas of the left hemisphere (Milner 1974; Vargha-Khadem et al. 1991). This rules out a direct genetic coding of a "language box" fated to be situated in Broca's and Wernicke's areas—or for that matter a "language learning box" situated there.

Again, there are several lines of reply. First, it is not necessary to conceive of Universal Grammar as a "language learning box," isolated physically and computationally from everything else. Section 4.5 discussed the question of balance between Universal Grammar and more general capacities (or even other specializations). Second, as we will gradually see in the course of succeeding chapters, Universal Grammar need not be a single monolithic faculty. Rather, we will come to see it as a collection of smaller components, some of which may be more vulnerable to impairment than others. Third, considering again nonhuman analogies, it might just be important to look at the plasticity of cognitive specializations of other animals, especially primates. Elman et al. do compare the relative plasticity of language to the relative nonplasticity of spatial cognition. But perhaps more data points are called for. We might find similar patterns of recovery in other capacities and we might not, and it might depend heavily on the capacity in question and the species. Given the number of variables involved and the basic mysteries of the gene-to-cognitive capacity connection, I am not prepared to make any prognostications, much less speculate on their significance.

A final argument in this suite concerns the "modularity" of language. Jerry Fodor (1983) argues that many functions of the mind/brain can be treated as "mental organs" or "processing modules." According to Fodor, several factors serve together as criteria for modularity of a mental function: specialized content, automaticity, susceptibility to focal brain damage, and evidence for innateness. We will examine Fodor's notion of modularity more closely in Chapter 7. For the moment, the argument is that language is a module because it exhibits all the other symptoms: it has the specialized content of syntax and phonology; it is automatic in that one cannot help hearing language as language; it is susceptible to aphasias that affect language but not other aspects of mental functioning. Therefore, goes the argument, it is likely to be innate.

Elman et al. and Deacon quite reasonably ask about other exclusively human activities. Reading and driving cars are automatized and have rather specialized subject matter; at least the former is subject to focal brain damage and child-hood impairment. Experts at chess and (in my own case) playing a musical instrument exhibit a great deal of structured and automatized behavior. But we do not believe there are innate specializations for reading, driving, chess, and clarinet-playing. So why single out language as innate?

I think this argument has to be answered first of all by rejecting Fodor's clas-sification of all these characteristics as together symptomatic of a processing module. *Any* well-practiced and overlearned ability seems to be automatic and to have specialized structure to some degree. So we may grant that reading, driving, chess, and clarinet-playing can all behave online like Fodorian mod-ules. However, the issue of innateness of language does not concern how lan-guage is processed online: it concerns how language is acquired. Hence the comparable question to ask about these other abilities is: What must we give learners in advance in order for them to be able to overlearn these abilities, and how much of this learning follows automatically from cognitive capacities they would have anyway? In order to answer this question, we must determine exact-ly what they have overlearned. We have some idea of how language is struc-tured, how hard it would be to learn from scratch, and how children do actually learn it. We have no comparable analysis for these other activities. And, as stressed in section 4.5, we have no comparable analysis for any of the perceptu-al, motor, or cognitive capacities in which these could be embedded.

In short, Elman et al. are right to ask why language should be different from other overlearned abilities, many of which are unlikely to have a direct narrow innate basis. However, I think the question is not just rhetorical: before a prop-er comparison can be made, there is much empirical work to be done on other abilities as well as on language.

A final step is required in the genetic grounding of Universal Grammar. If there is a genetic basis for language learning, not present in apes, where did it come from? The only reasonable possibility is through evolution. Chapter 8 will take up the question of possible evolutionary routes to modern language. For the moment, let me just note that Chomsky points out the balance between learning and evolution (1965: 59): "There is surely no reason today for taking seriously a position that attributes a complex human achievement entirely to months (or at most years) of experience, rather than to millions of years of evolution. . . ." That is, the more properties of language we can attribute to evo-lution, the easier language acquisition is for the child.

But Chomsky immediately hedges his bets on evolutionary justification of Universal Grammar, and continues: "or to principles of neural organization that may be even more deeply grounded in physical law." Though logically pos-sible, this alternative declines to follow the argument through to its inexorable conclusion, and thus it begins to dissociate linguistics from biology. There are two reasons why Chomsky might be wary of an evolutionary argument (he never states them explicitly, so I am speculating here—see Newmeyer 1998a). First, in Chomsky (1972b) he examines and rightly rejects many proposals for antecedents of human language in animal communication: the gap between human languages and other natural systems of communication is vast. Second, Universal Grammar on his conception is so tightly organized that its incremental development through natural selection looks on the face of it unlikely. As will be seen in Chapter 8, the conception to be worked out here is somewhat more amenable to an evolutionary approach. Thus it should be possible to keep evolution in the argument, and to treat Universal Grammar biologically just like any other cognitive specialization in the natural world.[12]

4.9 Evidence outside linguistic structure for Universal Grammar/Language Acquisition Device

Over the years, a large number of phenomena have accumulated that are taken to provide evidence for a human cognitive specialization for language acquisition. It is worth briefly enumerating them, with a few comments. Fuller discussions of most of them appear in Pinker (1994b) and Jackendoff (1994).

4.9.1 Species-specificity

It is an ancient observation that only humans speak. This distinction is undeniable, even if we reject the traditional conflation of this trait (e.g. by Descartes) with the possession of a soul, free will, and a moral capacity. We can also accept the existence of numerous systems of communication in the animal world (Hauser 1996) without denying the uniqueness of language.

The question is, to what is this species-specificity due? After all, there are

---

[12] One sometimes encounters proposals that what evolved was not humans but *language*. For instance, Andy Clark (1996) proposes that "language is . . . an artifact, one which has itself evolved so as to be easily acquired by young humans (perhaps exploiting processing biases inherent in the young)." But what can it mean for language to evolve by "itself"? The *noises* are not subject to natural selection; only the organism is. That is, for language to evolve we must suppose that organisms evolved that were equipped to carry out these particular sorts of sound-to-meaning mappings. The "processing biases inherent in the young" likewise had to evolve so that children could learn to make sense of these noises in the environment. Unlike artifacts such as bows and arrows, language was not designed by people; people evolved so as to be able to have it, just as bats evolved so as to be able to echolocate and elephants evolved so as to be able to pick things up with their noses. See Ch. 8 for further discussion.

many other differences between us and the apes, and in principle any of them might be the factor that makes language possible. The most prominent candidate is sheer brain size. Eric Lenneberg (1967) discounts this possibility with the evidence of "nanocephalic dwarves," individuals whose brains develop only to about the size of those of chimpanzees, with a proportional reduction in number of neurons. Lenneberg claims that, though deeply retarded, these individuals still learn to speak.[13]

Another benchmark for brain size concerns children who have undergone early hemispherectomy, so their brains are half normal size. They too are deeply impaired in certain ways, but in some cases language does develop—not entirely perfectly, but pretty well, even when the missing hemisphere is the left, the one that usually specializes for grammatical function (Dennis 1980; Vargha-Khadem et al. 1991; Curtiss and de Bode 2000).

The other side of the equation comes from the experiments teaching language to chimpanzees, gorillas, and bonobos (Linden 1974; Premack 1976; Savage-Rumbaugh et al. 1998; Seidenberg and Petitto 1978; Terrace 1979). These experiments have been subject to ongoing and heated controversy: have the apes achieved language or not? My own interpretation is in the middle. I am willing to accept that they have achieved the use of symbols for communicative purposes. But, although they do concatenate symbols into strings, they seem not to have achieved any reliable combinatoriality in the sense of Chapter 3. As will become clearer in Chapter 8, we are not required to proclaim whether they "have language" or not. The apparent binarity of the decision is a consequence of seeing Universal Grammar as a unified "grammar box," a position to be rejected here. Rather, we can say that the apes are capable of learning some aspects of language and not others, and that this is partly a reflection of differences in cognitive capacity.

4.9.2 *Characteristic timing of acquisition*

Again this characteristic of language is based on a commonsense observation: adults are not as good at learning languages as children. Any child, taken to any linguistic community at an early age, will come to speak the community's language like a native, while the parents may struggle for years and never achieve fluency.

This observation can be nuanced a bit more closely. All normal children acquire the native language(s) of their community; acquiring a language as a

---

[13] I have encountered no more recent published research on linguistic ability in this syndrome, now called Seckel Syndrome (Shanske et al. 1997). Anecdotal evidence suggests it is not as good as Lenneberg thought.

child is something that everyone does, like walking. By contrast, adults differ widely in their ability to learn a new language, some finding it relatively easy and some finding it nearly impossible. That is, adult language learning is more like playing chess or the stock market or a musical instrument, domains in which individuals differ widely in talent. This wide variation is documented in Klein and Perdue's (1997) long-term study of second language acquisition by immigrant workers. (There is some anecdotal evidence that early multilingualism enhances talent at adult language learning.)

It should not be said, of course, that adults cannot learn second languages *at all*. Even the least talented learn some words and expressions. The norm, given adequate exposure and motivation, is at least some degree of fluency, but with many errors in pronunciation and in grammatical fine points.

The difficulty of language learning for adults is sometimes attributed to their greater self-consciousness and/or lack of the child's innocent motivation. While these may be contributing factors, I imagine we are all familiar with non-native speakers of our own language who have the most outgoing, bubbly, unselfconscious personalities, but have not in many years managed to achieve anything near native fluency. Contrariwise, many of us were terribly self-conscious and inhibited as children, but still we managed to learn to speak our native languages quite fluently, thank you. (We have already discussed in section 4.6 a related putative explanation: the idea that children learn language better because they are simply not as smart as adults.)

Lenneberg (1967) ascribes the disparity between children and adults to a biological "critical period" of brain development. He characterizes this as a time window in which the Language Acquisition Device is available to a child, and he cites as biological analogies the critical periods for maturation of binocular vision, for learning species-specific songs in certain bird species, and for imprinting infants of various species on their parents. More general examples of biological timing include puberty and development of teeth.

Elissa Newport (1990) refines the thesis of a critical period, showing that fluency does not drop off sharply at a particular age. Rather, fluency in certain aspects of second language acquisition correlates inversely with the age at which one starts to learn. On average, people who start at age six get better than people who start at twelve, and still better than people who start at eighteen; after eighteen the curve flattens out to adult levels of incompetence.

Two independent kinds of data confirm the decay of language learning proficiency with age. The first comes from deaf individuals whose first exposure to sign language (and therefore first exposure to *any* language) comes relatively late in life. The results (Newport 1990) parallel those for late second language acquisition. All speakers achieve some competence with sign, but the greatest fluency is reserved for those exposed from birth. Adult competence declines with first exposure at six, more with first exposure at twelve, and still more with first exposure at eighteen or later.

The second kind of data concerns the case of "Genie" (Curtiss 1977), the girl discovered in 1970 at the age of thirteen who had been isolated from human contact since the age of 2. Through intensive training, she did acquire vocabulary rapidly, but even the most basic principles of grammatical structure never emerged. Similar results are reported in the case of a woman who had normal social contact, but was thought to be retarded until her deafness was discovered at age thirty-one (Curtiss 1994). When provided with hearing aids, she rapidly acquired vocabulary, but grammatical structure did not develop. Surprisingly, these cases are a good deal more extreme than the late sign language learners. It would be interesting to know why.

A side point: There seems to be considerable discussion in the literature on second language acquisition (Flynn and O'Neill 1988) over whether adult learners are making use of Universal Grammar or not. I would like to suggest that this discussion has been inconclusive because the wrong question has been asked: again Universal Grammar has been treated as an undecomposable "grammar box" that you either have or do not. If, as has been suggested earlier, we view Universal Grammar as a collection of capacities, it should be possible to ask precisely which parts of it are vulnerable to critical period effects and which are not. We will return to this question in Chapter 8.

4.9.3 Dissociations

In normal brains, language function is localized fairly reliably, though with considerable individual variation (including gender variation). Localization is evident especially in the various forms of aphasia, in which different aspects of language itself are impaired (Zurif 1990). One of the most surprising aspects of localization is that the impairments that turn up in sign language aphasias parallel spoken language aphasias; moreover, they are largely due to lesions in parallel parts of the brain (Bellugi et al. 1989). This fact, along with the thoroughgoing grammatical parallels between signed and spoken languages, has been used to argue that language is the same faculty of mind, whatever its modality.

These are facts concerning adult language and how it plays out in the brain. It might well be that any skilled capacity, say chess playing, has similar properties of localization. So, one might argue, this is not an argument for Universal Grammar, which is supposed to be a cognitive specialization for *acquiring* language. However, I find the parallels between signed and spoken language telling.

On the surface, the two systems are so distinct that one would think, left to their own devices, they would seek out quite different realizations in the brain. Yet they do not. Sign does make use of certain special opportunities of the visual modality, for instance it often expresses verbal modification by modulating the form of the verb's sign rather than by adding an affix. However, aside from these differences we prove to be dealing with the very same system. This suggests that children mobilize the same resources in acquiring sign—that as soon as something in the world can be categorized as symbolic communication, the language machine is engaged.

This case is a dissociation between grammatical capacity and modality of expression. The other cases are dissociations between aspects of language and general intelligence. There are three.

- Smith and Tsimpli (1995) discuss a "linguistic savant," an individual who is deeply retarded on most measures but exhibits a remarkable talent at learning languages. His competence, however, extends only so far as the grammatical system: his translations among languages are grammatically impeccable, but tend to be word-for-word in a way that neglects overall sense.

- Williams Syndrome (Bellugi et al. 1994) was originally described as a genetically based syndrome that results in retardation, particularly in spatial cognition, but preserves language-learning ability. Children with Williams Syndrome are indeed highly verbal, often at first giving an impression of impressive intelligence. However, further study has revealed selective deficits in Williams Syndrome language: for instance, syntactic tasks and regular inflection are unimpaired, but irregular inflection is disrupted (Clahsen and Almazan 1998).

- Specific Language Impairment (SLI) was first brought to the attention of the linguistics community by Gopnik and Crago (1990), who studied a family some of whose members suffered from this impairment and others did not, in a pattern familiar from studies of genetic inheritance of other characteristics. The impairment was said to affect only language, specifically morphology, without affecting general intelligence. Vargha-Khadem and Passingham's (1990) study of this family, however, found a parallel pattern of more general auditory and articulatory problems, a finding that has been widely taken to discredit Gopnik and Crago's argument for a genetically based language specialization. On the other hand, more extensive studies of SLI by Gopnik (1999) and others (e.g. van der Lely 1999; van der Lely and Christian 2000; Clahsen and Almazan 1998), with data from a variety of languages, overall confirm the character of the impairment. What is interesting is that this impairment seems roughly the converse of (one aspect of) the impairment in Williams Syndrome: irregular inflection seems to be acquired, but regular inflection is impaired.

These results and their interpretation are still controversial. However, again, the dispute need not be couched in the oversimplified terms of a "grammar gene" that determines a "grammar box." First, only some aspects of SLI language are impaired, suggesting multiple loci of genetic control. This comports with the view I have been urging throughout this chapter, that Universal Grammar should not be viewed as a monolithic unit. Second, I take it as given that a particular stretch of genetic material normally controls the development of many different and apparently unrelated aspects of the body. So we should not demand a "smoking gun," a genetic defect that affects all and only language. Like all the evidence presented here, the evidence from SLI on its own is only suggestive, not conclusive. But taken as a whole, I think the body of evidence does begin to show an overwhelming pattern.

4.9.4 *Language creation*

What I find the most striking evidence for a prespecified skeleton for language are the situations in which children create a language where there was none before. There are three cases.

• Deaf children whose parents do not know a signed language have been observed to improvise a gestural communication system, sometimes called "home sign" (Goldin-Meadow and Mylander 1990). Though their parents make use of the sign system as well, it is clearly being initiated by the children: at any stage of the system's development, the children use a greater variety of signs with a greater complexity of combination than the adults. To the extent the systems have been studied, they display certain rudiments of grammatical structure: consistent word order and incipient morphological marking. Where can the consistent structuring of these systems come from, if not from the child's f-expectations of what linguistic communication is supposed to be like?

• "Pidgin" languages have developed many times in the course of history, when speakers of several mutually incomprehensible languages have been thrown together. Pidgins typically borrow vocabulary from the parent languages, often in phonologically degraded form. They lack stable word order, and their grammatical organization has a rudimentary "Me Tarzan, you Jane" flavor, lacking inflection and subordination.

The interesting thing is what happens next. Derek Bickerton (1981) documents in detail that children of a pidgin-speaking community do not grow up speaking the pidgin, but rather use the pidgin as raw material for a grammatically much richer system called a "creole." In particular, he traces the transition from the Hawaiian pidgin of imported workers to the Hawaiian creole of their children; speakers of both of these were still alive at the time of his fieldwork in the 1960s. Creoles from all over the world are often found to have grammatical devices not traceable to any of the parent languages of the pidgin.[14] Thus, Bickerton's argument goes, creole grammar must have come from the children's expectations of "what a language has to look like"—i.e. Universal Grammar— and they build these expectations into their linguistic output. The children's parents, on the other hand, do not learn the creole; they continue to speak the pidgin, because they are past the critical period. (See also the papers in DeGraff 1999.)

The case of creolization differs from home sign in some important ways. First, creoles are full languages, with full grammar. By contrast, home sign systems are quite rudimentary, comparable with the language competence of two-and-a-half- to three-year-olds. One possible reason for this is that creoles have some raw material to work with: the antecedent pidgin. Another possible reason is that there is a sizeable community of children "working on the creole together"; by contrast, home sign children are working in isolation, in the sense that they are teaching their parents rather than the other way around. This is a point where one might be inclined to look for an "emergent system dynamics" effect in language learning, of the sort alluded to in section 4.5: the system cannot be developed by an individual alone, without a surrounding community that is co-developing it.

• The final case, documented by Kegl et al. (1999), combines elements of the previous two. In the 1980s a school for the deaf was instituted in Nicaragua, bringing together a community of individuals whose only communication system up that point was through home signs. Within a few years, this community was found to be speaking a brand new sign language of altogether expectable sort, without any formal instruction in sign. Over the ensuing ten years, the language has developed further elaborations in its grammatical structure; these are used by recent learners but not by earlier learners (evidently because the latter have passed beyond the critical period). Besides offering the wonder of a whole language coming out of nowhere, Nicaraguan Sign Language sheds some light on questions about creole. Evidently a community is necessary for language creation, but a common stock of pre-existing raw material is not.

Elman et al. (1996), in reference to the home sign, creolization, and Nicaraguan Sign Language material, respond as follows:

---

[14] This point has been controversial. However, Roberts (1998), through a painstaking examination of written documents from the period of emergence of Hawaiian creole (c. 1900–20), argues in detail that none of the sources from which the creole putatively borrowed grammatical features in fact can have served the purpose.

We would agree that these phenomena are extremely interesting, and that they attest to a robust drive among human beings to communicate their thoughts as rapidly and efficiently as possible. However, these phenomena do not require a preformationist scenario. . . . If children develop a robust drive to solve this problem, and are born with processing tools to solve it, then the rest may simply follow because it is the natural solution. . . . (Elman et al. 1996: 390)

The question, of course, is how one cashes out "a robust drive." Adults too have this robust drive, and they invent pidgins. Pidgins work. Why do children respond to a "drive" to go beyond the adequacy of the pidgin, rather than taking the easy way out and just imitating the grown-ups? And why did Nicaraguan Sign develop beyond a "pidgin" stage? Something extra seems necessary.

My interpretation of the material sketched in this section is that, *en masse*, it offers an overwhelming case for some degree of biological specialization for language learning in humans. My hope is that if, on one hand, skeptics of Universal Grammar work very hard to deal with the real complexity of linguistic material and to flesh out what this "drive" and these "processing tools" are, and if, on the other hand, linguists work very hard to find a version of Universal Grammar that can be shown sufficient for language learning and that strives for biological realism, we stand a chance of eventual convergence. I'm trying in this book to fulfill my part of the bargain.

4.10 Summary of factors involved in the theory of Universal Grammar

A bewildering variety of facts and arguments have been brought to bear in this chapter. Let me conclude this chapter by trying to summarize the situation.

The linguist has to figure out the correct grammar for the language under study from linguistic facts—judgments and behavior in ordinary speech and experimental situations. It is of course a scientific desideratum that this grammar be as simple as possible, consistent with the facts. The need for simplicity is driven not only by an a priori desire for analytic elegance, but also by the need for the learner to acquire the grammar. However, theoretical linguists tend to attempt to be responsible for a greater range of facts than psychologists, philosophers, and neuroscientists, so they typically end up positing more complex grammars.

If some aspects of linguistic behavior can be predicted from more general considerations of the dynamics of communication in a community, rather than from the linguistic capacities of individual speakers, then they should be. This leaves a residue of grammar that has to be present in the language user's f-mind by virtue of the acquisition process.

The acquisition of the grammar in turn has to be divided into factors learned from the primary linguistic input and factors due to the initial state of the organism. Determining the primary linguistic input depends on what actual factors in the language learner's environment count as input for learning. Is there a dependence on special speech modes when talking to babies, on prosody, on statistical regularity, on prior understanding of context, and so forth? All of these count as aspects of the input, and may reduce the share of complexity attributed to the child's initial state. As observed in section 4.6, opponents of Universal Grammar typically attribute more influence to the input than proponents—and perhaps rightly so. But, I have insisted, the input alone is nevertheless likely to be insufficient: the complexity of grammar still leaves a substantial gap for the initial state to fill in.

Turning to the initial state, we might artificially divide it into two factors: learning strategies and prespecification of structure. Again there is a balance to be struck: if the structure of grammar can be more completely prespecified, there is less work for the learning strategy, and vice versa.

Positions in the literature tend to cluster at the two extremes. On one hand, connectionist theories, like most empiricist approaches, want little or no prespecified structure, leaving all the work to the learning strategies. For that matter, they typically want to minimize the complexity of the learning strategies as well. The question I have constantly raised here is whether such an approach is adequate to the complexity of linguistic fact—that is, whether it can yield correct grammars.

On the other hand, Principles and Parameters Theory (Chomsky 1981) and Optimality Theory both take the prespecification of grammar to the extreme. They both conceive of Universal Grammar as containing all the principles necessary for all languages. In Principles and Parameters, the differences among languages are encoded as a set of "parameters" or switches; all the learning strategy has to do is find the appropriate "triggers" for these switches in the input. In Optimality Theory, the differences among languages are encoded as different rankings of the universal constraints; all the learning theory has to do is find readily available cues in the input for constraint ranking.

The truth undoubtedly lies between these two extremes, Pollyannaish though this may sound. There are many possible intermediate positions, one of which we will explore in Chapter 6.

A cross-cutting division of the initial state is between those aspects that belong to a cognitive specialization for language learning and those that belong to more general faculties of the f-mind, such as sociability, ability to conceptualize the world, rhythmic analysis of temporal signals, and the ability to form hierarchical structures. Again, theoretical linguists acknowledge the use of other capacities but stress the specifically linguistic parts, whereas the reverse is true of non-linguists. The discussion here has, I hope, clarified the sorts of evidence one might adduce.

All aspects of the initial state, specialized and general, are in turn governed by a combination of genetic prespecification and principles of brain development. The latter may well depend on certain sorts of inputs being available as triggers. The balance between these factors is far beyond the everyday concerns of linguists, though in the end it must play a role. All aspects of the initial state are also outcomes of an evolutionary process that relates humans to the other species of the world.

We have thus traced a chain of relationships among a diverse set of research programs, from observations about particular languages and how parents talk to their children all the way to genetics and evolutionary theory. As observed at the outset of this chapter, what brings these diverse enterprises into contact is precisely the hypothesis of Universal Grammar.

PART II

Architectural Foundations

CHAPTER 5

The Parallel Architecture

5.1 Introduction to Part II

The last three chapters have surveyed the overall program of generative grammar: situating language in the f-mind, treating it as a formal combinatorial system, and confronting the problem of language acquisition. After more than thirty years, as I have tried to show, this program is still compelling.

However, not all aspects of generative grammar that have survived all this time are so worthy. In particular, I wish to take issue with a fundamental assumption embedded deep in the core of generative theory: that the free combinatoriality of language is due to a single source, localized in syntactic structure. I have come to believe that this "syntactocentric" architecture was an important mistake—perhaps historically unavoidable, but a mistake nevertheless. Part II, comprising Chapters 5–8, develops the alternative assumption that language has multiple parallel sources of combinatoriality, each of which creates its own characteristic type of structure. Fig. 1.1 has already displayed the sort of structure produced by such a parallel architecture: multiple structures partly linked by indices.

In practice, as we will see, theorists in phonology and semantics have ignored the assumption of syntactocentrism for over twenty years; and some of the offshoots of mainline generative syntax also have come to incorporate multiple generative components. However, the consequences of this break with tradition have never been seriously investigated in the context of generative theory as a whole. That is what I propose to do here. The outcome is a theory of grammar which is true to the fundamental goals of generative linguistics, and which at the same time affords a clearer integration among the subfields of linguistics and between linguistics and related disciplines.

5.2 A short history of syntactocentrism

Let me make clearer what I mean by "syntactocentrism." The *Aspects* model begins the derivation of a sentence by generating a structure in the "base" component of syntax. The base consists of two parts: (a) the phrase structure rules, which create initial syntactic trees, and (b) the principle of *lexical insertion*, which selects words out of the lexicon and puts them at the bottom of the trees. The resulting structures, Deep Structures, are the input to principles of semantic interpretation and also to the transformational rules that give rise to Surface Structures. Thus all combinatoriality in language is ultimately the product of the phrase structure rules. The following passages make this explicit:

The syntactic component specifies an infinite set of abstract formal objects, each of which incorporates all information relevant to a single interpretation of a particular sentence. (Chomsky 1965: 16)

I assume throughout that the syntactic component contains a lexicon, and that each lexical item is specified in the lexicon in terms of its intrinsic semantic features. . . . (p. 198, note to above passage)

I shall assume that no ambiguity is introduced by the rules of the base.   (p. 17)

I am assuming throughout that the semantic component of a generative grammar, like the phonological component, is purely interpretive [i.e. all its structure is derived solely from syntactic structure—R.J.].   (p. 75)

These passages also make clear that this organization is purely an assumption. Although *Aspects* does argue that Deep Structure is the syntactic level that determines semantic interpretation, it never offers an argument that syntax is the only generative component, that is, the only component that explicitly gives rise to combinatoriality. And to my knowledge, no argument has ever been offered since.

In context, this assumption is understandable. The assertion that syntax is generative was one of the major innovations of generative grammar, and the battle at the time was simply to establish that *something* is generative. Whether it is the sole source of generativity was the last thing anybody needed to worry about. It seemed altogether plausible to view phonology as a sort of final adjustment to Surface Structure (as in Chomsky and Halle 1968), so phonology presented no opportunities for generativity. Furthermore, at the time virtually nothing was known within the generative tradition about semantics, so it made sense to derive what little semantic structure there might be from the rich structural possibilities emerging from the new syntactic technology.[1]

The assumption of syntactocentrism is preserved in every subsequent version of Chomskyan theory. Fig. 5.1 illustrates the major stages of architectural development from *Aspects* to the Minimalist Program.

---

[1]   Still, from the start there is a curious tension between stressing that language is the means for the free expression of thought, following the Cartesians, and formalizing language in a way that seems to deny thought any independent status.

Standard Theory (*Aspects; SPE*, 1968)

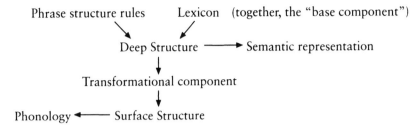

Extended Standard Theory (*Studies on Semantics in Generative Grammar*, 1972)

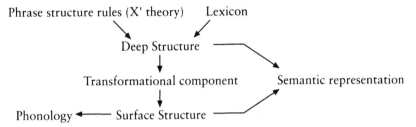

Revised Extended Standard Theory (*Reflections on Language*, 1975)

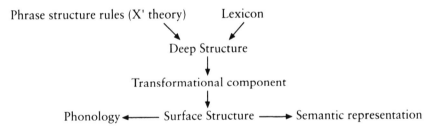

Government-Binding Theory (*Lectures on Government and Binding*, 1981)

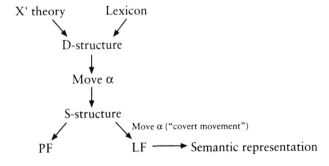

Fig. 5.1. Architecture of Chomsky's theories over the years

Minimalist Program (1993)

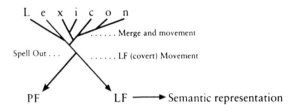

Fig. 5.1 *continued*

As observed in section 4.2, the Extended Standard Theory of 1972 preserved the structure of the *Aspects* model, except that certain aspects of semantic interpretation (notably quantifier scope, focus, and possibly anaphora) were read off of Surface Structure. By 1975, the notion of a "trace of movement" (the *t* in sections 1.7 and 3.2) had been introduced. This permitted all semantic interpretation to take place in terms of Surface Structure, since the Deep Structure positions of constituents could be identified by their traces in Surface Structure.

Government-Binding Theory represents a major shift, in that two new levels of representation are introduced, both derived from Surface Structure (now called S-structure) through further sequences of derivational rules (now simplified to the general form "Move α"), guided by multiple constraints. One of these sequences, resulting in Phonetic Form (PF), more or less duplicates the old phonological component (to the extent that anyone has ever attempted to be explicit about it). The other sequence, which received far greater attention, results in a level called Logical Form (LF). LF begins rather modestly (Chomsky 1975) as a way of explicitly encoding quantifier scope and anaphoric relations in syntax, but by Chomsky (1986: 68) it is called a "direct representation of . . . meaning," an " 'interface' between language and other cognitive systems." Thus it takes over the semantic function assigned to the more extreme interpretations of Deep Structure in the *Aspects* theory. The remnant of Deep Structure, now called D-structure, is still the locus of syntactic formation rules and the insertion of lexical items. Crucially, the derivational rules that connect S-structure to LF are without visible consequences: they perform "covert" movements that account for the mismatches between interpretation and surface form.

The most recent variant, the Minimalist Program, responds to the attenuated roles of D-structure and S-structure in Government-Binding Theory by eliminating them altogether. Syntactic structures are built up by combining lexical items according to their intrinsic lexical constraints; the operation of combining lexical items into phrases and of combining phrases with each other is called Merge. Merge operations can be freely interspersed with derivational operations. However, at some point the derivation splits into two directions, one direction ("Spell-Out") yielding PF and the other LF. Despite all these changes, what is preserved is (a) that syntactic structure is the sole source of generativity in the grammar, and (b) that lexical items enter a derivation at the point where syntactic combination is taking place.[2]

5.3 Tiers and interfaces in phonology

The alternative to be pursued here is that *language comprises a number of independent combinatorial systems, which are aligned with each other by means of a collection of interface systems.* Syntax is among the combinatorial systems, but far from the only one.

The genesis of this alternative comes from developments in "autosegmental phonology" in the middle 1970s, which came to divide phonological structure into a number of quasi-independent subcomponents or *tiers* (Goldsmith 1979; 1990; Liberman and Prince 1977). By way of illustration, let us look again at a representative piece of Fig. 1.1, the phonological structure associated with the phrase *the little star.*

(1)

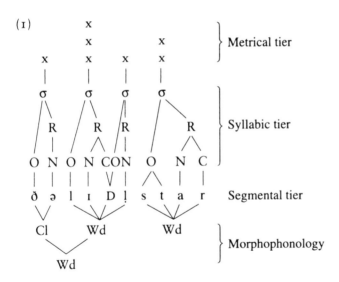

The units of the syllabic structure are individual segments and their combinations into syllables, i.e. structures like (2).

---

[2] A sociological point: Unfortunately, along with the formal syntactocentrism of the framework has come a syntactocentrism of outlook in many practitioners, a reluctance to explore solutions in other than syntactic terms. "We have the tools to deal with this problem syntactically, so why spend effort on some ill-understood and vague semantic/pragmatic framework?" Such a view can be justified to some degree on practical grounds: the approach has led to tremendously productive, detailed, and subtle research on a huge variety of languages. However, as remarked in Ch. 4, the emphasis on syntax to the detriment of semantics has led to criticism from every quarter, deepening the rift between generative grammar and neighboring disciplines.

(2)

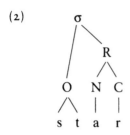

The units that encode stress, however, are abstract organizations of "beats" notated as a "metrical grid" of *x*s. Each *x* in the bottom line stands for a metrical position; the *x*s above them indicate relative degrees of stress. In (3), for instance, the first position has higher stress than the unstressed second position, and the third position has higher stress than either of the first two.

(3)
```
                x
    x           x           x
    x   x   x   x   x   x   x
```

The basic point of autosegmental phonology is that the metrical grid is not *derived* from syllabic structure. Rather, it is governed by an independent set of principles that determine what metrical configurations are possible. These "formation rules" describe (or "license" or "generate"—choose your favorite term) a sequence of abstract positions given by the lowest row of *x*s, to each of which is assigned a certain degree of stress. An important aspect of this little "subgrammar" is that it sets a priority—though not an absolute requirement—on grids: they should have alternating stressed and unstressed beats at all levels. This priority can be stated roughly as (4).

(4)   At any layer of the grid,
```
    prefer  x     x    (alternating stress)
            x x x
    to      x x        (stress clash)
            x x
```

Thus grid (3) is preferred to (5a), which has stress clash in the middle layer, and to (5b), which has stress clash in the top layer (circled elements).

(5) a.

The syllabic and metrical structures, then, are made of different sorts of units with different combinatorial properties—i.e. different formation rules. Since language has both kinds of structure, the structures must be matched up. The rules determining stress in a language concern the interface between these two structures: how a segmental structure is fit to an acceptable metrical grid.

Let us explore the character of this interface a little. The first principle of the interface is that every syllable is matched to an x in the lowest layer of the grid. This matching is notated in (1) by the "association lines"; it could alternatively be notated by co-subscripting, as in the matching of phonology to syntax.[3] A second principle is a strong tendency (universally) for "heavy" syllables (syllables with either a coda or a long vowel) to be associated with relative stress. This principle is most easily seen in words with a lot of syllables, for example (6).

(6)   x
             x   x
          x   x   x   x   x
          Mo-nong-a-he-la

This has alternating stress, in conformance with principle (4); the second and fourth syllables, which are heavy, receive heavier stress. In addition, in order to avoid stress clash in the middle layer of stress, either the second or fourth syllable must have an extra stress. The decision between these two is made by another formation rule for metrical grids, one specific to English, which stipulates a preference for the right-hand member of the pair to get the heavier stress. (Other languages, for instance Hungarian, invariably put the heaviest stress on the left.)

A well-known case involving a more complex interaction is shown in (7).

(7)   a.   b.   ┌─────── x   c.   x
                x   ┌ x   x ┐   x   x
             x   x   x ┆ x   x ┘   x   x   x
             fourteen   fourteen men   fourteen men

Both syllables of the word *fourteen* are heavy, so the principles matching syllable weight to grids do not decide where heavier stress should be placed. Hence the preference in English for right-hand stress makes the decision shown in (7a). However, when *fourteen* is placed adjacent to *men*, the resulting grid has a stress clash, circled in (7b). The strongly preferred stress pattern (7c) overrides the right-hand principle for *fourteen* in order to preserve the rhythm of alternating stress.

The negotation can also go the other way: syllabification can adjust to stress. Compare the syllabification of *Mississippi* and *Missouri*.

---

[3] In Fig. 1.1, the association is notated simply letting the σs stand for the lowest layer of *x*s.

(8)   a.   x   b.

                x   x   x

                x   x   x   x   x   x   x

         Mis-(s)i-ssip-(p)i   Mi-ssou(r)-ri

Mississippi has a regular alternating stress pattern. Consequently, the principles matching the grid to the syllabic tier prefer the first syllable to be heavy and the second light. And so the syllabification adjusts to meet this preference: the first *s* sound is felt to belong to the end of the first syllable (and possibly also to the beginning of the second), giving the first syllable a coda and therefore making it heavy. By contrast, the second *s* sound does not belong to the end of the second syllable, but only to the beginning of the third. This enables the second syllable to be light, comporting with its light stress. This situation is interesting to compare with *Missouri*, whose first syllable is unstressed. Here the *z* sound (spelled *ss*) is felt to belong to the beginning of the second syllable, so as to keep the first syllable light.

Thus the combination of syllabic/segmental and metrical structures results in a complex interaction, of which we have seen here only the tiniest fragment. The principles of stress across the languages of the world have been studied in intense detail and consist in large part of elaborations of principles of the sort presented here: languages vary, for instance, in what grids are allowable and preferable (e.g. are there ternary as well as binary grids?), in exactly what makes a syllable count as heavy, in how stress clashes are mitigated, and in what special provisions can be made at the beginnings and ends of words (Kager 1995; Halle and Idsardi 1995).[4]

The overall architecture of this fragment of the grammar can be schematically diagrammed as Fig. 5.2. Let us next see how this fragment fits into the larger system. The metrical grid has a number of interfaces with other linguistic and non-linguistic subsystems. For a simple case, the main stress in a word or phrase determines the point in time when language will be coordinated with a hand gesture; syllabic content plays no role. Thus beat gestures with the hand can be performed at the positions in sentence (9) marked in line (a), but not at the positions in line (b). The beats need not be perceived visually—they can be performed by pounding on the table (auditory) or poking the hearer (haptic).

---

[4] Given the essentially finite scope of stress systems, and the clarity with which they are understood crosslinguistically, stress would seem to be a prime candidate for attempts at computer modeling of language learning—far better than the syntactic and semantic phenomena usually attempted. Stress is of course a lot less sexy, and requires of modelers an engagement with linguistic materials in exotic languages. But I think the attempt would be well worth the effort, in terms of the insight it would yield about the possibilities and/or limitations of various models of learning. In particular, the sorts of interactions observed in the examples above, which are typical, are reminiscent of the "Harmony Theory" of Smolensky (1999).

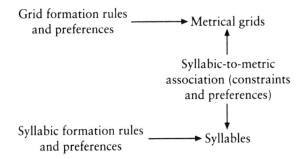

Fig. 5.2. The relation of the subgrammars for metrical grids and syllabic structure

(9)   This is the most riDICulous thing I've EVer heard.
    a.   x   x
    b.   x   x   x

For another case, meter in music also involves a metrical grid, which shares many basic principles with the linguistic grid but differs in other respects. In particular, in music the grid is usually much more rigid than in language (Lerdahl and Jackendoff 1983). The proper setting of linguistic texts to music is, for a first approximation, a matter of aligning the two grids. When a text is sung, the linguistic grid adopts the timing required by the musical grid, often grossly distorting the natural speech rhythm (*Oh beauuuuutiful for spaaaaacious skies*). This adjustment resembles the adjustments in syllabification and stress observed above.

Within language itself, main stress in the metrical grid is used to align intonation contours. For instance, the intonation contour for the end of a declarative sentence in English typically has a high pitch followed by a low pitch. The high pitch aligns with main stress, and the low pitch is stretched or shrunk to fit the space between the main stress and the end (Bolinger 1965b; Liberman 1975; Beckman and Pierrehumbert 1986; Ladd 1996). (10) illustrates; the intonation is notated as a line above the metrical grid.

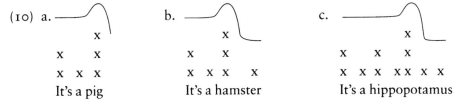

Segmental/syllabic content plays no direct role here, except insofar as it influences the grid.

Finally, the metrical grid also is implicated in the expression of emphasis, contrast, and focus—semantic notions. For instance, the normal stress on *a big star* is as shown in (11a). However, in the context of expressed or implied contrast with another star, stress shifts to *big*, as in (11b). Notice also how intonation shifts with the stress.

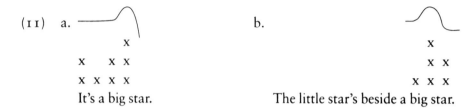

(11)   a.

          x
      x   x x
      x x x x
      It's a big star.

       b.

                                          x
                                       x x
                                     x x x
              The little star's beside a big star.

Notice that the contrastive stress affects primarily the main stress of the contrasting word and not the other stresses; for example the Determiner *a* has the same stress in (11a) and (11b). It is also worth noting that these contrastive effects occur even when there is no appreciable syntactic structure. Consider the utterances in (12), possibly made by a radio announcer during a baseball game.

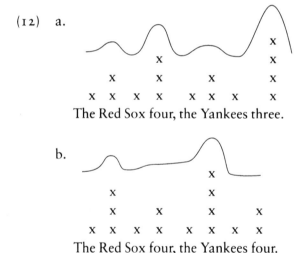

(12)   a.

                                           x
                      x   x
                  x   x   x   x
              x x x x   x x x   x
          The Red Sox four, the Yankees three.

       b.

                  x   x
                  x   x   x   x
              x x x x   x x x x
          The Red Sox four, the Yankees four.

When the scores are the same, as in (12b), the highest stress shifts to the the team names, which still contrast.

Next let us return to syllabic structure. The string of speech sounds grouped *into* syllables has to match up with the string of speech sounds that identifies the words and affixes of the utterance—the *morphophonology* of (1). However, the syllabic groupings do not have to coincide with the morphophonological groupings, as seen in cases like (13).

(13) a.

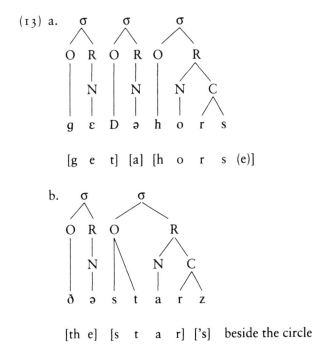

[g e t] [a] [h o r s (e)]

b.

[th e] [s t a r] ['s] beside the circle

The upshot is in addition to being connected to each other, as in Fig. 5.2, syllabic structure and metrical structure each have interfaces with other kinds of structures. Fig. 5.3 sketches the interactions observed here; each double-ended arrow designates a set of interface principles. In turn, each of the other structures on the right-hand side of Fig. 5.3 has its own formation rules and participates in other interfaces.[5]

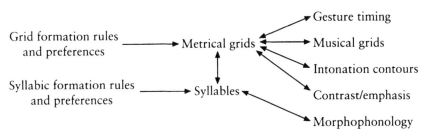

Fig. 5.3. Interfaces of metrical and syllabic structures with other subcomponents

---

[5] I have not mentioned a further important tier of phonology, namely tone. This plays an important role in West African languages such as the hundreds of Bantu languages, and in East Asian languages such as Vietnamese, Thai, and the varieties of Chinese. Tone phenomena were in fact the initial motivation for Goldsmith (1976) proposing Autosegmental Phonology. See Odden (1995) and Yip (1995) for brief discussions of tone.

5.4 Syntax and phonology

The next thing to notice about the structure in (1) and the rule system in Fig. 5.3 is how little they have to do with syntax. The units of syllabic and metrical structure—things like codas and beats—bear no relation at all to syntactic categories. Only the morphophonology has constituents that map cleanly into constituents of the syntactic tree. And even the types of units here—Words and Clitics—are not the same as the syntactic categories Noun, Verb, and so forth. For instance, *the* and *every* are both Determiners, but *the* is a Clitic and *every* is a Word. Moreover, a Clitic can attach in morphophonology to a Word to which it bears no syntactic relation. This can be seen in (14), where the mismatches are boldfaced.

(14)   Morphophonology:

$[_{Wd}[_{Cl}$ a]   very] $[_{Wd}$ old] $[_{Wd}$ **man**$[_{Cl}$'s]] $[_{Wd}$ here]

Syntax:

$[_{NP}[_{Det}$ a] $[_{AP}[_{Adv}$ very] $[_A$ old]] $[_N$ man]] $[_{VP}[_V$'s] $[_{PP}$ here]]

However, even if constituent structure is not preserved, what *is* preserved is the linear order of morphophonological and syntactic units. That is, we can state the general correspondence as rule (15).[6]

(15)   Morphophonology: ...$\xi_1 \xi_2$...

         corresponds to

         Syntax: ...$x_1 x_2$...

         where ξ_i corresponds to x_i

Turning to the scale of the whole sentence, the prosodic unit closest in size to syntactic phrases is the Intonational Phrase (IntP), the part of the sentence that falls under an intonation contour. However, intonational contours do not follow syntactic phrases at all precisely. Consider the sentence in (16). Its syntactic bracketing is (16a). It can be pronounced in at least the two possible ways shown in (16b, c), with no appreciable difference in meaning. Note how different all three bracketings are.

(16)   a. Syntax:

            $[_{NP}$ Sesame St.] $[_{VP}$ is $[_{NP}$ a production $[_{PP}$ of $[_{NP}$ the Children's

                                                                    Television Workshop]]]]

---

[6] This may be actually just a very strong default. There are circumstances, for instance, where a clitic is in the "wrong" order for syntactic generality. A possible solution is that what we see is the phonological ordering, but the syntactic ordering does not match. For one such case involving Serbo-Croatian, see Halpern (1995).

   b. Phonology (one possibility):

     [$_{IntP}$ Sesame St. is a production of] [$_{IntP}$ the Children's Television

                                          Workshop]

   c. Phonology (another possibility):

     [$_{IntP}$ Sesame St.] [$_{IntP}$ is a production] [$_{IntP}$ of the Children's Television

                                          Workshop]

For another case, (17) repeats the well-known example cited in section 2.3, whose intonation Chomsky attributed to "performance."[7]

(17) a. Syntax:

       [$_{NP}$ this] [$_{VP}$ is [$_{NP}$ the cat [$_{CP}$ that [$_{VP}$ caught [$_{NP}$ the rat [$_{CP}$ that

                              [$_{VP}$ stole [$_{NP}$ the cheese]]]]]]]]]

    b. Phonology:

       [$_{IntP}$ this is the cat] [$_{IntP}$ that caught the rat] [$_{IntP}$ that stole the cheese]

But (17b) is not a performance error, it is exactly the ideal intonation for this sentence.

    The right approach to these correspondences sees Intonational Phrases as phonological units that on one hand constrain the domains of syllabification, stress, and intonation, and that on the other bear a loose relation to syntax (Gee and Grosjean 1983, Selkirk 1984, Jackendoff 1987, Hirst 1993, Truckenbrodt 1999). The formation rules for IntPs can be stipulated approximately as (18).[8]

(18) a. An utterance consists of a series of one or more concatenated IntPs forming a flat structure. Each IntP is a sequence of Words.

    b. *Preferably*, the IntPs are of equal length.

    c. *Preferably*, the longest IntP is at the end.

    d. (Possibly, some strong preferences on maximum duration of IntPs, e.g. try not to go over three seconds)

A basic interface constraint relates IntPs to syntactic structure. It can be stated informally as (19a) and slightly more formally as (19b).

(19) a. An IntP corresponds to all of a syntactic constituent C, except that a subconstituent at the right-hand end of C can be omitted.

---

   [7] For non-linguists: CP in (17a) stands for "complementizer phrase," a now-standard term in linguistic theory for subordinate clauses; the term "complementizer" is roughly what traditional grammar calls a subordinating conjunction.

   [8] Connoisseurs will again recognize that I have oversimplified, omitting e.g. details of intermediate-sized groupings of morphophonological words such as Phonological Phrase (Selkirk 1984; Nespor and Vogel 1986).

b. Morphophonology:　　　$[_{IntP} \xi_1, \ldots, \xi_n]_a$

　　　corresponds to

　Syntax:　　　$[x_1, \ldots, x_n ([y_1, \ldots, y_m])]_a$

　　where ξ_i corresponds to x_i

To see how this works, look again at (16) and (17).

• The first IntP in (16b) corresponds to the whole sentence in (16a), except that *the Children's Television Workshop* is "carved out" of the right-hand end (i.e. it corresponds to the optional sequence of *y*s in rule (19b) which are omitted from the IntP). However, rule (18a) says that everything in the utterance must belong to some IntP or other. Therefore *the Children's Television Workshop* is assigned to its own IntP; it can be so assigned, because it is a constituent on its own.

• In (16c), the first IntP corresponds directly to the subject NP. The second IntP corresponds to the VP, but the final PP *of the Children's Television Workshop* is carved out to form its own IntP.

• In (17), the first IntP corresponds to the whole sentence, but the large relative clause *that caught the rat that ate the cheese* is omitted. In turn, this relative clause is further carved: the final relative clause is taken out to form the third IntP. The result is perfectly balanced prosodically.

• Note also the role of rule (18d), which places some sort of bound on absolute duration. It is this rule that prevents (16a) and (17a) from being assigned to a single extremely long IntP.[9]

　　We see from (16) that, although syntactic structure constrains the choice of intonational phrasing, it does not uniquely determine it. Now we can ask: is the relation mutual? Does intonation ever constrain syntax? Consider an example like (20). (The brackets indicate intonational phrasing in (20c, d).)

(20)　a.　　John bought a computer yesterday.
　　　b.　　*John bought yesterday a computer.
　　　c.　　?*[John bought several expensive pieces of hardware that he's been
　　　　　　dreaming about for months] [yesterday]
　　　d.　　[John bought yesterday] [several expensive pieces of hardware
　　　　　　that he's been dreaming about for months]

---

[9] I promised in section 1.6 to explain the strange coindexing marked by the subscripts *a* and *b* in Fig. 1.1. It follows from rule (19). The subscript *a* is marked as in (19b); it corresponds to the first Intonational Phrase in the phonology and the whole sentence in the syntax. Subscript *b* corresponds to the "carved out" constituent: the second Intonational Phrase in phonology and the PP in syntax.

Normally the syntax of English is very insistent that the direct object precede any time adverbials, as seen in the contrast (20a, b). But if the object is very long and the time adverbial short, the reverse order (20d) is far more acceptable. The reason is that this permits the prosody to satisfy conditions (18b, c) much better: the IntPs are much closer in length, with the longer at the end. So evidently the needs of prosody are forcing a non-optimal syntactic structure.[10] In short, the interaction between intonational phrasing and syntax resembles the interaction between stress and syllabification seen in the previous section.

To sum up this section: the relation of syntax to phonology, especially to intonation, is qualitatively just like the relation among the tiers of phonology. Syntax and phonology are independent combinatorial systems, built from distinct sets of primitive elements combined by distinct sets of formation rules. Neither can be reduced to or derived from the other. Certain aspects of each component are related to certain aspects of the other through interface constraints. For instance, small-scale syntactic units such as Nouns and Verbs correspond in linear order to morphophonological Words and Clitics, and larger-scale syntactic phrases constrain Intonational Phrases. But the actual segmental content of phonological words and their syllabification and stress play no role in constraining syntax, and most details of syntactic embedding are invisible to phonology.[11] This sort of relation has in fact been strongly favored among phonologists for some years (Zwicky and Pullum 1983; Inkelas and Zec 1990).

If we take this conclusion seriously, we ought to go on to the further conclusion that syntactic trees do not contain phonological information. As far as syntax is concerned, *star*, *galaxy*, *nebula*, and *comet* are identical: they are just singular count nouns. It is this conclusion that justifies the form of syntactic trees in Fig. 1.1—trees like (21a) rather than the traditional (21b).

---

[10] The traditional approach to this situation is to say that the direct object in (20d) is generated in normal direct object position, like (20c), but it is moved to the end by a derivational rule called Heavy NP Shift. I am aware of no account in the literature that does it exactly the way proposed here, namely through an override of syntactic ordering constraints in the interests of prosody. For a discussion of "heaviness" constraints on syntactic order, see Arnold et al. (2000).

Hawkins (1994) proposes an account of these heaviness constraints in terms of parsing: basically, both speech production and speech perception favor holding off long constituents as long as possible, preferring to integrate shorter constituents first. I don't think his account is necessarily incompatible with the one offered here: it is important that the reordering involved, even if for processing purposes, be stated in terms of intonational constraints. However, a closer comparison of the two views is warranted.

[11] The problems here are the occasional cases where syntactic category has a bearing on word stress. A well-known example is English *permít* (verb) versus *pérmit* (noun).

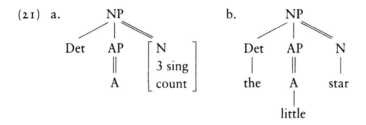

(21) a.   b.

The use of traditional trees need not be proscribed altogether. However, we must understand that the relation between Det and *the* is not the same as that between NP and Det. NP *dominates* Det—a syntactic relation; but Det *corresponds* to morphophonological *the*—an interface relation. Accordingly, when it is convenient to use traditional trees, I'll employ a dotted line for the interface relations, as in (22a). This will abbreviate the more proper notation in (22b).

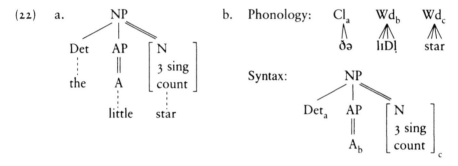

(22)   a.   b.   Phonology:

        Syntax:

Where do traditional phonological derivations *(à la* Chomsky and Halle 1968) fit into this picture? Their input ("phonological underlying form") is given by the interface with syntactic structure, here the sequence of morphophonological elements. The output of phonological derivations is phonetic form, the linguistic structure that interfaces with speech perception and speech production. This consists of the syllabic, metrical, and intonational tiers. As seen in (13), these two do not entirely match in bracketing or segmental content (and the disparity is much greater when we get away from simple English examples). It is this gap (or interface) that traditional phonological derivations fill, converting the morphophonological structure step by step into the phonetic form.

Optimality Theory provides an alternative approach to this interface, with the morphophonological sequence again serving as input and the other tiers as output. The difference between the two approaches (and it is radical in practice!) is that traditional phonology bridges the interface with a sequence of derivational rules, whereas Optimality Theory does it with a set of simultaneously applied violable constraints. (See Jackendoff 1997a, section 6.2 for somewhat more extended remarks on the role of traditional phonological derivations.)

To sum up the last two sections: The overall architecture of grammar consists of a collection of generative components $G_1, \ldots, G_n$ that create/license structures $S_1, \ldots S_n$, plus a set of interfaces I_{jk} that constrain the relation between structures of type S_j and structures of type S_k. (In principle, there may also be interfaces that address three or more structures.) Typically, an interface I_{jk} does not "see" all of either S_j or S_k; it attends only to certain aspects of them. For instance, the syntax–morphophonology interface does not "see" most of syntactic embedding, nor does it "see" syntactic category distinctions such as NP vs. VP. It sees only (primarily) the linear order of words in syntax, plus those syntactic features such as case that map into affixes. So we can think of the distinctions in S_j and S_k to which I_{jk} is sensitive as its "windows" onto S_j and S_k. This overall architecture will be replicated as we move to further components of the grammar.

5.5 Semantics as a generative system

Let us turn our attention next to semantics. Assuming that the function of language is the expression and communication of thoughts, I will identify semantics as the organization of those thoughts that language can express. This is not the only construal of the term "semantics," but Chapters 9 and 10 will argue that this is the appropriate construal for an f-mentalistic theory of language. Anticipating that discussion, let us say that the thoughts expressed by language are structured in terms of a cognitive organization called *conceptual structure* (CS). Conceptual structure is not part of language per se—it is part of thought. It is the locus for the understanding of linguistic utterances in context, incorporating pragmatic considerations and "world knowledge"; it is the cognitive structure in terms of which reasoning and planning take place. That is, the hypothesized level of conceptual structure is intended as a theoretical counterpart of what common sense calls "meaning."

The hypothesis of conceptual structure goes beyond the goals of many linguistic semanticists, who wish to find a kind of specifically linguistic semantic structure that is more limited in scope, excluding all pragmatic or contextual considerations. Sections 9.6 and 9.7 are devoted to showing why this limited goal ought to be abandoned. (However, just in case I am wrong about this, I will also show how such a level too can be worked into the architecture.)

It has become clear from the many approaches to semantics in the literature that semantics is a combinatorial system independent of, and far richer than, syntactic structure. Formal semantics (Chierchia and McConnell-Ginet 1990; Lappin 1996) and Cognitive Grammar (Langacker 1987; Lakoff 1987) differ on just about every issue but this one: they are both theories of meaning as a rich combinatorial system. In neither of these approaches are the units of this system nouns and verbs; they are entities like individuals, events, predicates, variables, and quantifiers. Instead of the relations of domination and linear order found in syntax, semantic structure has such relations as logical connectives, functions that take arguments, quantifiers that bind variables, and the relation of assertion to presupposition. Thus meaning has an inventory of basic units and of means to combine them that is as distinct from syntax as syntax is from phonology.

Moreover, not all semantic distinctions play a role in syntax. Just as the phonological distinctions among *star, galaxy, nebula,* and *comet* have no impact on syntax, neither do the semantic differences among them. This suggests that we ought to attempt to evacuate all semantic content from syntactic structure, just as we removed phonological content: structures like (21a) should be perfectly adequate for syntactic purposes.

In short, we come to see semantics not as *derived* from syntax, but as an independent generative system correlated with syntax through an interface. It instantiates the thoughts that language expresses; syntax and phonology are the means by which thoughts are converted into overt expressions.

We will be dealing at some length with the characteristics of semantics and the syntax–semantics interface in the rest of the book, but a major overall point should be introduced here. There is a recurring tendency to think either that syntax can be derived from semantics or that the syntax–semantics interface must be relatively simple—in other words, that the form of language is a good key to the form of thought. However, generations of philosophers and grammarians have assured us that this is not the case; and we would do well to pay heed.

For instance, to choose about the simplest possible correlation, it is frequently asserted that nouns name "things," such as houses, horses, doctors, and tables; hence the category Noun can be derived directly from (or directly correlated with) semantics. But what about earthquakes and concerts and wars, values and weights and costs, famines and droughts, redness and fairness, days and millennia, functions and purposes, craftsmanship, perfection, enjoyment, and finesse? The kinds of entities that these nouns denote bear no resemblance to concrete objects. To assert that they *must* have something in common semantically with concrete nouns merely begs the question.[12] What they actually have

---

[12] Langacker (1987; 1998) argues that the syntactic category Noun corresponds to the semantic category Thing, where "a 'thing' is . . . defined as any product of grouping and reification" (1998: 19). However, the examples cited above go far beyond Langacker's, and even with his more limited set, he admits, "I have no definite proof for this conceptual characterization of nouns. . . . It is merely offered as a coherent proposal. . . . I personally find it hard to imagine that fundamental and universal categories like noun and verb would not have a conceptual basis" (1998: 19). I think it safe to consider this simply a statement of ideology.

in common is not their semantics but their ability to occur in noun positions in relation to verbs and prepositions, their ability to govern number/gender agreement and take case endings (in languages that have such functions), their ability to occur with certain kinds of quantificational expressions such as *many*, *much*, and *all*, and so forth—all syntactic properties.

To be sure, although not all nouns denote concrete objects, all words for concrete objects are nouns: there is a one-way but not a two-way implication. And the nouns of early child language *do* indeed all denote concrete objects. (What would a two-year-old have to say about perfection and finesse?) The consensus (e.g. Pinker 1989) is that children f-use this one-way implication in their language acquisition. The words for concrete objects are learnable in part because they are visible and people can point them out. Having learned the words for concrete objects, children f-know that these words are going to be nouns. In turn, this enables them to f-look for the grammatical properties of nouns, from which they can start f-figuring out *storm*, *cost*, and the like. Notice that this learning strategy requires a non-zero Universal Grammar: UG must stipulate that Concrete Objects in semantics are encoded syntactically as Nouns.

This is only by way of motivating a distinction between syntactic and semantic categories at the very simplest level. The disparity will accumulate as we proceed.

5.6 The tripartite theory and some variants

Before further exploring the lexicon and the syntax–semantics interface, we can sum up the main point of this chapter: the grammar overall has the tripartite organization sketched in Fig. 5.4.

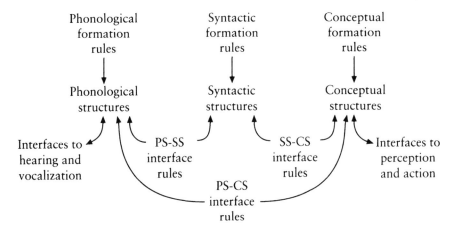

Fig 5.4. The tripartite parallel architecture

In terms of this organization, the linguistic structure elaborated in Fig. 1.1 can be seen as the consequence of constructing structures in all the domains of Fig. 5.4, with phonological structure further differentiated as in Figure 5.3; the subscripts of Fig. 1.1 designate the links among these structures established by the interfaces.

Fig. 5.4 is relatively coarse, and we can "zoom in" on details of these major components, revealing a finer-scale organization of tiers and interfaces such as is found in phonology. In particular, the syntax–phonology interface is a connection to the morphophonological tier, not to phonology as a whole. Similarly, a major component of the phonology–semantics interface is a connection from the metrical grid of phonology to the "information structure" tier of semantics (see section 12.5).

Fig. 5.4 reveals clearly the role of syntax in the parallel architecture. Following traditional views, language as a whole can be thought of as a mapping between sounds and meanings; phonological structure is the specifically linguistic encoding of sounds, and conceptual structure is the encoding of meanings. Syntactic structure serves as a "way-station" between these two structures, making the mapping between them more articulate and precise. Thus, although syntax is in the center in Fig. 5.4, the grammar is no longer syntactocentric in the sense of section 5.2. Rather, syntax is simply one of the three major generative components in the grammar. Syntax is, however, special in the sense that it is the most "isolated" component: unlike phonology and semantics, it does not have multiple interfaces with other cognitive capacities. The reasons for this will emerge in Chapter 8.

Many other theories and sub-theories of grammar in the literature can be viewed as variants and elaborations of Fig. 5.4 or parts thereof. Chomsky's syntactocentric grammars (Fig. 5.1) can all be seen (roughly) as Fig. 5.4 minus the phonological and conceptual formation rules and the phonology–semantics interface: phonology and semantics get their properties entirely through their (rather rigid) interfaces with syntactic structure. Alternatively, a theory that denied the existence of an autonomous syntax would omit the syntactic formation rules, leaving all properties of syntactic structure to be determined by its interfaces with phonology and meaning. Or one could go farther and deny the existence of syntactic structure altogether, leaving only phonology, semantics, and their interfaces.

More interesting are theories that propose more ramified architecture. Modern autosegmental phonology, as we have seen, is an elaboration of phonological structure and its formation rules into independent subcomponents that interact in the same general fashion, as shown in Fig. 5.3. Lexical-Functional Grammar (Fig. 5.5a) elaborates the syntactic component into two parallel components: c-structure

a. **Lexical-Functional Grammar** (Bresnan 1982a; 2001)

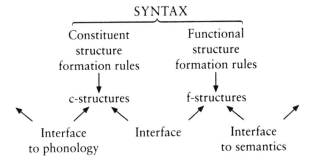

b. **Autolexical Syntax** (Sadock 1991)

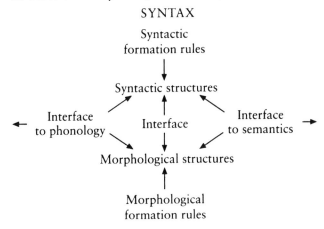

c. **Role and Reference Grammar** (Van Valin and LaPolla 1997)

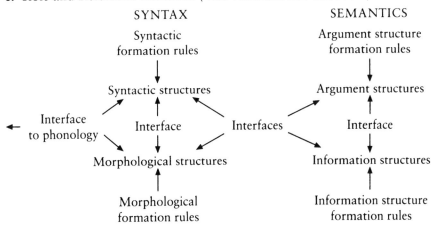

Fig. 5.5. Elaborations on the tripartite architecture

encodes standard constituent structure and f-structure encodes grammatical relations. Autolexical Syntax (Fig. 5.5b) elaborates syntax differently, with independent phrasal and morphological components. Role and Reference Grammar (Fig.
5.5c) pairs the two subcomponents of Autolexical Syntax with two subcomponents of semantics, argument structure (who did what to whom) and information structure (topic/focus organization); interfaces go in every direction among
them. I should also mention an early antecedent: Sydney Lamb's (1966)
Stratificational Grammar, whatever its drawbacks, offered a parallel architecture
carried through the entire organization of the grammar.

   In Chapter 12 we will work out our own elaborations of the semantic component and its interfaces; a somewhat more elaborate version of the syntactic
component will be suggested in section 5.10. Here I confine myself to a remark
on one important elaboration of syntactic structure.

   Figs. 5.5b and 5.5c suggest a division between phrasal syntax and morphosyntax. As observed in section 3.3.1, words, like phrases, can be built up
hierarchically as tree structures. (23) illustrates.

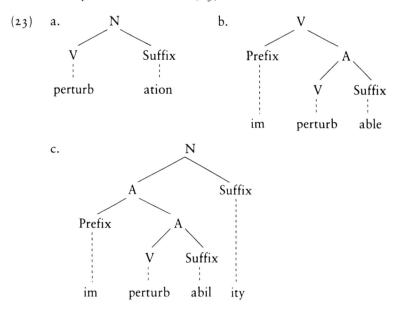

(23)   a.

As has been often remarked (e.g. Aronoff 1976, Selkirk 1982, Di Sciullo and
Williams 1987, Beard 1987, Lieber 1992, as well as Sadock 1991 and Van Valin
and LaPolla 1997), the principles of hierarchical structure inside words are
somewhat different from those for phrases.

• Morphological structures are mostly created by adding closed-class items
(affixes and clitics) to open-class stems (nouns, verbs, adjectives); phrases are
built primarily of open-class items.

- The head of a phrase is an open-class category which determines the category of the phrase; for instance, NPs are headed by nouns, APs by adjectives. By contrast, the category of a morphological structure is determined by its affixes; for instance, -ation forms nouns from verbs, im- forms adjectives from adjectives, and -ity forms nouns from adjectives and verbs.

- When a word bears multiple inflections, these come in a fixed "templatic" order, often with no hint of hierarchical stacking; by contrast, syntax is full of alternative word orders and hierarchical structure.

- Inflection normally marks only relations internal to a single clause; by contrast, phrasal syntax is replete with long-distance dependencies, where a phrase appears in a clause outside its "normal" position.

- Inflection lends itself to a great deal of idiosyncratic irregularity; syntax much less so.

- Most of the structure interior to words is "invisible" to rules of phrasal syntax (the Lexicalist Hypothesis of Chomsky (1972a) and the Lexical Integrity Principle of Bresnan and Mchombo (1995)). The only part of word structure that interacts with phrasal syntax is inflectional morphology (e.g. tense, case, number, gender) (Anderson 1992).

- As stressed by Talmy (1978), among others, the semantic range of the closed-class items (including not just affixes but also grammatically specialized items such as auxiliary verbs and pronouns) is quite limited: prominent among them are expressions of tense and aspect, causativity, valence (e.g. active/passive), mood (e.g. indicative/subjunctive), negation, person, number (singular/plural), reflexivity, gender, social relation of interlocutors (intimate/formal), relative magnitude (comparative, superlative) and speaker's evidence for making a claim (e.g. direct experience vs. hearsay). There are no expressions of absolute category, size, color, rate, manner, location, number (above two), and so forth, which are characteristic of the open-class items.

These differences suggest that phrasal syntax and morphosyntax might be regarded as semi-autonomous tiers with related but not identical organizing principles. Alternatively, they might be treated as different scales of phrasal syntax with different behavior, much as different scales of phonology such as phonological words and intonational phrases have somewhat different principles. Working out even a sketch of these alternatives is, however, beyond the scope of the present work.

Returning to the main point of this section, the architectures illustrated in Fig. 5.5, as well as the architectures of autosegmental and metrical phonology, are of interest here because they explicitly abandon Chomsky's assumption that there is a single source of generativity in grammar. What is new in the present

approach is that the idea of multiple generative components connected by interface components has been extended in thoroughgoing fashion to every part of
the grammar, so that it becomes a fundamental architectural design principle.

A similar overall plan emerges in the musical grammar proposed by Lerdahl
and Jackendoff (1983). There the generative components are *grouping structure, metrical structure, time-span reduction,* and *prolongational reduction.*
The first two of these, together dealing with rhythm, find close parallels in the
prosodic system of language. The last two, dealing with melodic and harmonic
organization, bear no resemblance to anything in language.

More generally, it is abundantly clear that the brain is organized in terms of
numerous interacting areas that together determine our experience of the world
and our intentions to act. A description of the f-mind in terms of independent
components that interact through interfaces thus offers the hope of an interesting account of its instantiation in brain terms. As observed in Chapter 2, such a
possibility is of course a desideratum, even if the connection between functional and neural theories is far in the future.

5.7 The lexicon and lexical licensing

We next turn to the lexicon. For a first approximation, the lexicon is the store of
words in long-term memory from which the grammar constructs phrases and
sentences.

It is widely agreed that a word is to be regarded as a long-term memory association of phonological, syntactic, and semantic features. Many have suggested
that words that denote physical objects also carry with them some sort of image
of a stereotypical instance; in Fig. 1.1 this is notated as the spatial structure associated with the sentence. If a word is concerned with another sensory modality,
for instance the word *acrid*, it will presumably be linked to a structure appropriate to that modality instead. We return to spatial structure and other sensory
structures in Chapters 9 and 11; for the moment we will consider only the
phonological, syntactic, and conceptual features associated with words.

Recall that mainstream generative grammar, following Chomsky (1965), inserts
lexical items as a whole into syntactic structure; their phonological and semantic
features are interpreted later in the derivation by the appropriate components.
While this approach is not formally impossible, it raises the question of why syntax
should drag around all these features that it cannot itself access. As Ivan Sag has
suggested (p.c.), it is as though the syntax has to carry around two locked suitcases
that it turns over at a checkpoint to the components that have the right keys.

A number of people over the years have noticed this anomaly and suggested
a process of "late lexical insertion" (e.g. Otero 1983; den Besten 1977; Fiengo

1980; Koster 1987; Di Sciullo and Williams 1987; Anderson 1992; Büring 1993). The idea is that phrasal syntactic combination takes place as usual in D-structure, but lexical items are not inserted. Syntax goes about its business using only syntactic features until the point when lexical information is needed in order to interface with phonology and semantics—usually S-structure. Another variant is Distributed Morphology (Halle and Marantz 1993): semantic and syntactic lexical features are inserted early, but phonological features wait for insertion until S-structure (or Spell-Out in the Minimalist architecture). These approaches are an improvement, in that syntax doesn't have to carry the locked suitcases as far. But it still has to carry them.

Lexical insertion—in any of these versions—assumes there is a "place" in the grammar where lexical items are put into sentences. Quite a different scenario emerges in the parallel architecture. A word, by virtue of having features in each of the components of grammar, serves as part of the linkage between the multiple structures. For example, (24) shows the material in the lexical entry for *star*.

(24)   Word$_i$ $\begin{bmatrix} N \\ \text{sing} \\ \text{count} \end{bmatrix}_i$ [$_{\text{Object}}$ TYPE: STAR]$_i$
         ⋀⋀
         s t a r

The proper way to regard (24) is as a small-scale three-way interface rule. It lists a small chunk of phonology, a small chunk of syntax, and a small chunk of semantics, and it shows how to line these chunks up when they appear in parallel phonological, syntactic, and conceptual structures. The co-subscripting of the three pieces licenses co-subscripting among them in larger structures such as (22b) and the two occurrences of *star* in Fig. 1.1. A well-formed sentence requires the proper matching of the structures, in part mediated by the lexical entries of its words.

In short, *the function of lexical items is to serve as interface rules, and the lexicon as a whole is to be regarded as part of the interface components*. On this view, the formal role of lexical items is not that they are "inserted" into syntactic derivations, but rather that they establish the correspondence of certain syntactic constituents with phonological and conceptual structures.

In addition to the usual lexical items that match phonology, syntax, and semantics, there exist "defective" lexical items that have phonology and semantics but no syntax. Some examples appear in (25), sorted approximately by semantic class.

(25) a. yes, no
      b. hello, goodbye, thanks
      c. ouch, oops, wow, phooey, hooray, gadzooks, oboy, oy vey, dammit, shit, yuck, upsey-daisy
      d. hey, fiddlesticks, pshaw, humph, oo-la-la

   e. shh, psst, tsk-tsk
   f. abracadabra, hocus-pocus
   g. bow-wow, cockadoodledoo

Unlike ordinary words, these can be used on their own as meaningful utterances. Moreover, they cannot be combined with other words into sentences.[13]

There are also words that have phonology and syntax but no semantics, for instance the *it* in *It's hot in here* and the *do* of *do*-support (*I didn't like him*), which is present just to carry the Tense. In some theories of syntax there are lexical items that have syntax and semantics but no phonology, for instance mainstream generative theory's "empty pronoun" PRO that serves as the subject of infinitives; in this approach, *Bill tried to talk* is taken to have the syntactic structure *Bill tried [PRO to talk]*. Finally, there are some words(?) that are just stored pieces of phonology lacking both syntax and meaning, for example nonsense refrains like those in (26), used to fill up metrical structure in songs and nursery rhymes.

(26)   fiddle-de-dee, hey-diddle-diddle, hickory-dickory-dock, eenie-meenie-minie-moe, she-bop-she-bop, rikiti-tikiti-tin, ink-a-dink-a-doo

This notion of "defective" lexical items will play a crucial role in Chapters 6 and 8.

With this view of the architecture of grammar in place, we take up one aspect of the syntax–semantics interface in some detail.

5.8 Introduction to argument structure

This section and the next sketch the theory of argument structure, one of the most central topics in every version of grammatical theory. My goal here is to illustrate the complexity of this aspect of the syntax–semantics interface. My account draws on many analyses in the literature, but it comes out somewhat differently from any of them, partly as a consequence of being able to take a larger perspective on the problem. For the most part I will refrain from theoretical commitments: like Chapter 1, these sections are meant primarily as an illustration of the complexity of the phenomenon, enumerating facts that everyone essentially agrees on.

The domain of the lexicon where argument structure is most important is verbs. Consider the verb *devour*. For something to be an act of devouring, some character has to be cramming some other character (or some stuff) into its mouth. We will call these characters the "semantic arguments" of the verb; we

---

[13] They can, however, appear within direct quotes, where there are no syntactic constraints: here even phrases of a different language are possible. As quotes they can also be used as nouns, as in *his loud hello*. But this is possible with any word, e.g. *his frequent howevers*. Some animal sounds such as *meow*, *moo*, and *oink* can double as verbs, but the ones in (25g) cannot.

will say that *devour* "licenses" (or "requires" or, more simply, "takes") two semantic arguments. The conceptual structure of the verb can be thought of as a function that maps these two arguments into a conceptualized action. We can schematize the semantic/conceptual structure of *devour* as (27). The arguments X and Y are typed variables that specify what kinds of thing can devour and can be devoured respectively. These type specifications are called the "selectional restrictions" on the arguments, and are part of the essential meaning of *devour*. For now we will consider the function DEVOUR as an indivisible unit: Chapter 11 provides more fine-grained analysis.

(27)   DEVOUR (X, Y)

The roles that the characters play in the event of devouring are often called the characters' *thematic roles* or *theta-roles*. We might call these roles the "devourer" and "devouree." Such terms are not very useful, though, as they apply only to this verb. But they intuitively fall into far more general roles that are shared with many verbs: the "devourer" is a kind of Agent (character performing an action) and the "devouree" is a kind of Patient (character on which an action is performed).

In a simple active use of the verb,[14] both these characters must be expressed, the Agent as subject and the Patient as object:

(28)   The lamb devoured the lion
       [Agent]   [Patient]

We will call the subject and object the "syntactic arguments" of *devour*. That is, *devour* has two semantic arguments and two syntactic arguments.

The very similar verb *eat* has the same two characters in the semantics: there cannot be an act of eating without something doing the eating and something being eaten. But it has two possible syntactic realizations (29a, b); the latter is impossible for *devour*.

(29)   a.   The lamb ate the lion.
       b.   The lamb ate.
       c.   *The lamb devoured.

---

[14] Simple actives are the best criterion for determining syntactic arguments because constructions like passive (*The lamb was eaten*) and imperative (*Eat the lion!*) can eliminate expression of one of the arguments. Many languages permit the character that would ordinarily be expressed in subject position to be omitted and understood as if it were (in English) an appropriate pronoun. For instance, *he/she/it ate the lion* is normally expressed in Spanish as *comía el león*. Such languages are called "pro-drop languages."

Hence one of the semantic arguments of *eat* always corresponds to a syntactic argument, but the other may remain implicit.

It is often said that *eat* "licenses an optional argument." However, this conflates semantic and syntactic argument structure. The character being eaten is part of one's understanding, whether it is expressed or not. This becomes clearer by comparison with the verb *swallow*. Its syntactic behavior is identical to that of *eat: Bill swallowed (the food)*. But although one cannot eat without eating *something*, one *can* swallow without swallowing anything. That is, *swallow* differs from *eat* in that its second *semantic* argument is optional.

The term "argument structure" refers to the specification of and relation between a word's semantic and syntactic arguments. Differentiating the three verbs *devour, eat,* and *swallow* is in part a matter of assigning them different argument structures. More generally, we need at least to be able to say how many semantic arguments a verb licenses, and which of them are obligatorily expressed.[15]

Traditionally excluded from argument structure are expressions of modification such as manner, time, and place expressions. Certainly, if some event occurs, there is a time and place where it occurs. But verbs do not differ in whether they allow expression of manner, time, and place: these are always optional.[16]

---

[15] Many languages, such as Korean and Japanese, are much freer than English in omitting arguments. In such languages there may be no justification for distinguishing between obligatorily and optionally expressed semantic arguments.

There is often an impulse to conjecture that the obligatoriness of arguments is predictable from the semantics. For instance, *devour* is more specific in its semantics than *eat*, so perhaps more specific verbs tend to make their arguments obligatory. This conjecture is immediately counterexemplified by contrasts like *serve/give the food to Sally* vs. *serve/*give the food*, where serving is a more specific form of giving, and *insert/put the letter in the slot* vs. *insert/*put the letter*, where inserting is a more specific form of putting. I also note the verbs *juggle* and *flirt*, which have got to be among the more highly specific verbs in the language, yet take an optional syntactic argument: *juggle (six balls), flirt (with Kim)*. These arguments are not optional in semantics: one certainly can't juggle without juggling something, nor flirt without flirting with someone. I conclude that the obligatoriness of syntactic arguments must be encoded as an idiosyncratic lexical property.

An important and little-mentioned distinction among implicit syntactic arguments is whether they are construed as "indefinite" or "definite." For instance, the implicit argument in *John is eating* is indefinite: it can be paraphrased by *John is eating something*. By contrast, the implicit argument in *I'll show you* is definite: there has to be an understood discourse argument, and the explicit paraphrase is *I'll show it to you*. The choice between indefinite and definite implicit arguments seems specific to the verb (or possibly the semantic verb class). See e.g. Grimshaw (1979), among others, for discussion of this distinction.

[16] A caution here: Certain verbs take place expressions as obligatory syntactic arguments, e.g. *Bill put the book on the table*; certain verbs take time expressions, e.g. *The movie lasted six hours*; and certain verbs take manner expressions, e.g. *Bill worded the letter carefully*. The point is that place, manner, and time are *always* available as optional additions to semantically appropriate sentences.

(30)   Mr. Mustard committed the murder (carefully) (in the attic) (at noon).

I will use the term "modifiers" for the contributions these expressions make to
semantics; in syntax they are traditionally called "adjuncts."

   The range of variation in argument structure is vast; Levin (1993) devotes an
entire book to a fairly exhaustive enumeration of the possibilities. The minimum number of semantic arguments is zero, in "weather" verbs such as *rain*,
snow, and *drizzle*, whose subjects are normally a "dummy" *it*.[17] The largest
number of semantic arguments seems to be four, exhibited by verbs describing
transactions (31a) and wagers (31b). An action cannot be a transaction without
two actors, each of whom is giving the other something; an action cannot be a
wager without two characters, some wagered object or amount of money, and
an event on whose outcome the wager depends.

(31)   a. Pat sold/rented a lawnmower to Chris for $20.
            Chris paid Pat $20 for the lawnmower.
        b. Fran bet Phil a cigar that Mark wouldn't come.

In between, there is a bewildering variety of one-, two-, and three-argument
verbs. The one-argument verbs range from bodily functions (*swallow*, *sneeze*,
sleep, *cry*) to change of size (*grow*, *shrink*) to passage of time (*elapse*) to somewhat uncharacterizable verbs like those in (32), which have a dummy *it* subject
and a clausal syntactic argument.

(32)   a. It (just so) happens that the earth isn't flat.
        b. It figures that John is late (just when we need him most).

Among the two-argument verbs, a major subclass is the transitives, whose
semantic arguments are both expressed as NPs. The stereotypical transitive verb
has an Agent acting on a Patient (33a); but many other possibilities are available, for example (33b–k). This shows that the transitive pattern is not invariably associated with particular thematic roles.

(33)   a. John drank the water. John threw the ball.
        b. John imagined/mentioned his pet elephant.
        c. The audience applauded the clown.
        d. Emily likes/fears/despises cats.
        e. Capitalism frightens/bothers/disgusts Sam.
        f. Liana left/entered the room.

---

[17] One might think that the semantic structure of the verb *snow* is FALL(SNOW), 'snow falls',
where SNOW is an implicit argument. I agree that this is roughly the correct semantic structure, but
would contend that SNOW is not an argument for purposes of argument structure, since it is never
overtly expressed as an argument.

    g. A wall surrounds/divides the city.

    h. This book has/contains/comprises 13 chapters.

    i. The meeting lasted seven hours. The book weighs three pounds.

    j. Harry owns a BMW. Larry lacks money.

    k. My patience equals/exceeds my enthusiasm.

    l. The doctor underwent an operation.

    m. This outcome means trouble.

Other syntactic realizations of two-argument verbs are illustrated in (34).

(34)   a. Bill went into the room.   [NP-PP]

       b. Jill became tired.   [NP-AP]

       c. Phil thinks/supposes/knows that the earth is flat.   [NP-clause]

       d. That the earth is flat bothers/frightens/disgusts Gil.   [clause-NP]

       e. That the dog is sick never occurred to Lil.   [clause-PP]

       f. That Til isn't here proves that he's guilty.   [clause-clause]

       g. It bothers/frightens/disgusts Shmill that the earth is flat.

                                 [dummy *it*-NP-clause]

       h. It seems/appears to Otto that the dog is sick.   [dummy *it*-PP-clause]

    The possibilities for three-argument verbs defy brief enumeration. However, it is important to note again that the same syntactic configuration can support wildly different semantic relations (35), and that verbs with very similar semantics map to different sets of syntactic configurations (36).

(35)   a. Bob gave Janice some breakfast.

                        [stereotypical meaning for this configuration:

                              transfer of something to a recipient]

       b. The administration denied Henry a raise.

       c. The book cost me $78.

       d. The job took Sam 4 hours.

       e. Norbert envies you your high reputation.

       f. They named/called the baby Yael.

       g. Pat considers/deems Fran a genius.[18]

(36)   a. Bob gave/served/*provided/*supplied Janice some breakfast.

       b. Bob gave/served/provided/supplied some breakfast to Janice.

       c. Bob *gave/*served/provided/supplied Janice with some breakfast.

---

[18] The final NP argument of *consider* is a predicate nominal, often thought to be a different syntactic configuration from ordinary NPs. However, I believe that many special syntactic properties of predicate NPs can be made to follow from their expressing a non-referential semantic argument; see sections 12.3 and 12.4.

Nouns too have argument structures. Semantic arguments appear, for instance, with kinship expressions like *the father of the bride* and *the bride of Frankenstein*, with part–whole expressions like *a part of the sentence* and *a component of the grammar*, and with expressions denoting *properties of objects* like *the style of her hat* and *the size of the house*. Argument structure flourishes in nouns that are morphologically related to verbs, reaching a peak in nominal counterparts of the four-argument verbs in (31):

(37)   a. Pat's sale of a lawnmower to Chris for $20
       b. Fran's $5 bet with Phil that Mark wouldn't come

Three points on the argument structure of nouns in English. First, with a few tricky exceptions (Grimshaw 1990), syntactic arguments of nouns are all optional. Second, all syntactic arguments of nouns are either genitive NPs (before the noun) or PPs and clauses (after it).[19] Third, *of* in the examples above is a meaningless preposition used to fulfill the requirement for a noun's syntactic argument to be a PP.[20] In particular, *of* is the most common preposition for nominal counterparts of direct objects (38a), though not the only possibility (38b).

(38)   a. destroy the plans   destruction of the plans
          own a car   ownership of a car
          he fears flying   his fear of flying
          he claims immunity   his claim of immunity
       b. he desires truth   his desire for truth
          X equals Y   X's equality with Y

Thus *of* is another of those "defective" words that have syntax and phonology but no semantics; it is used as a default to satisfy the syntax.

Adjectives too can have semantic arguments that are expressed syntactically as PPs or clauses. Again the default *of* is prominent. I know of no case where an adjective has more than a single syntactic argument.[21]

---

[19] An exception is $5 in (37b). This position is used also for adjuncts of size, cost, and duration, as in *a ten-gallon jug*, *a $20,000 car*, and *a two-year drought*. I don't know of any research on this configuration. Traditional grammar would probably call it adjectival because of its position and semantic function—but it certainly looks like an NP. Another possibly controversial case is *the American invasion of Vietnam*, in which the adjective *American* supplies the Agent role of *invasion*.

[20] Langacker (1992) argues that *of* denotes that there exists some semantic relation or other between the head noun and the NP that functions as its syntactic argument. I find this argument rather empty: there is no constituent of the larger NP that does *not* have some semantic relation or another to the head.

[21] In many approaches, the individual of which the adjective is predicated is considered also to be a semantic argument of the adjective, one that cannot be expressed within the adjective phrase

(39)   a. proud of Bill, afraid of the dark, nervous about the Y2K problem
       b. eager to please, nervous that the computer will crash

The adverbial counterparts of the adjectives in (39) do not admit syntactic arguments: *proudly (*of Bill)*, *nervously (*about the Y2K problem)*, *eagerly (*to please)*. This is a systematic fact about English syntax: whatever the semantics of adverbs, they have no syntactic arguments at all.

Prepositions also have argument structures. This becomes clearest when we consider prepositions that occur with or without objects.

(40)   outside (the house), underneath (the floor), up (the stairs)

Something cannot be outside or underneath without being outside or underneath *something*; that is, *outside* and *underneath* have a semantic argument that is only optionally expressed. On the other hand, one can just go up (i.e. rise) without going up anything like a tree or a pole, so *up* apparently has an optional semantic argument. Thus *outside* and *up* differ in just the way *eat* and *swallow* do. (See Jackendoff 1983: ch. 9 for more details of argument structure of prepositions.)

5.9 How much of syntactic argument structure can be predicted from semantics?

This is the big question. What is at stake is the issue of language acquisition. If a word's syntactic behavior (including its syntactic argument structure) were always tightly linked to its meaning (including semantic argument structure), there would be far less lexical idiosyncrasy for the child to learn, always a desideratum (section 4.7). In the previous section, I have deliberately drowned the reader in data, in order to convey a sense of how daunting it is to answer this question properly. My answer will be: A lot of syntactic behavior is predictable from meaning, but far from all; the syntax–semantics interface is highly constrained but not entirely rigid. I break the question into four parts:

Given a word's semantic argument structure,

- How many syntactic arguments will a words have?
- What syntactic categories will they be?

---

itself. For example, in *Phil is proud of Bill*, *Phil* would express this semantic "external argument." Under such approaches, the adjectives in (39) would all have two semantic arguments, the "external" argument and the "internal" argument. I personally do not subscribe to such an approach (Jackendoff 1983); this is not the place to go through the arguments.

- Where will they be located in a simple active clause?
- Where will they be located in general?

We take these questions up successively in the next four subsections.

5.9.1 *Number of syntactic arguments*

Recall that syntactic arguments are expressions of semantic arguments, and that a verb can either permit or require a semantic argument to be expressed. Therefore the following generalization should obtain:

(41) The number of syntactic arguments that a verb takes on any given occasion is equal to or fewer than the number of its semantic arguments.

(41) is *almost* correct. The flavor of the exceptions is illustrated in (42).

(42) a. Betsy behaved/perjured ***herself.***
          A better solution presented ***itself.***
          Bill prides ***himself*** on his stamp collection.
      b. The chair has a stain on ***it.***
      c. Slim slept ***a deep sleep.***
          Kathy coughed ***a violent cough.***

In (42a), no direct object is possible other than a reflexive: *Betsy behaved/perjured Sam*. Moreover, *behave* can omit the reflexive without a perceptible difference in meaning. This suggests that the reflexive is a supernumerary syntactic argument. Verbs with such argument structure are rare in English but more common in Romance languages, where they are used for instance as decausative versions of transitive verbs (43a), among other possibilities.

(43) (French)
      a. Le vase s' est brisée.
          the vase *self* is broken 'The vase broke.'
      b. Marie   s' en   va.
          Marie   *self* from there goes 'Marie is going away.'

In (42b), the pronoun can be replaced only by expressions that denote a part of the chair, e.g. *The chair has a hole in its/the leg*, but *The chair has a hole in the carpet*; and the sentence can be paraphrased using two syntactic arguments rather than three: *On the chair is a stain*; *In the chair's leg is a hole*. Hence this use of *have* seems to have an extra syntactic argument—perhaps the subject, since this is the argument absent from the paraphrase.

(42c) is the so-called "cognate object" construction. No direct object is possible other than one headed by the cognate object, e.g. *Slim slept a long nap* is plausible but ungrammatical.[22] The object can be omitted without noticeably changing meaning, provided the object's modifiers can be converted into adverbials, as in *Slim slept deeply, Kathy coughed violently*. Again this suggests that the object is a supernumerary syntactic argument, this time duplicating not the subject but the verb.

With these exceptions as a caution, generalization (41) holds most of the time: the number of syntactic arguments is almost always equal to or smaller than the number of semantic arguments.

5.9.2 *Category of syntactic arguments*

Next comes the question whether a semantic argument is expressed as an NP, AP, PP, or clause. To some extent this is predictable from the semantic argument. For the clearest example, suppose the semantic argument denotes a concrete object (including a person). As observed in section 5.5, only NPs can express concrete objects, so the corresponding syntactic argument has to be an NP. On the other hand, properties can be expressed by APs and predicate NPs (though not by clauses) (44a), and propositions can be expressed directly by clauses and mentioned by using NPs (though not APs) (44b).

(44) a. John became $\begin{cases} \text{angry.} \\ \text{a raving maniac.} \end{cases}$

 b. John mentioned $\begin{cases} \text{that Jean had left Fred.} \\ \text{a nasty rumor.} \end{cases}$

The alternating arguments in (44) have been matched as closely as possible for semantics, so that we can with some justification say that the same semantic argument is expressed by different syntactic categories. Thus we can say that the verb specifies only the semantic properties of its argument and specifies nothing about the syntax of the corresponding syntactic argument.

On the other hand, some verbs allow only one or the other of these syntactic argument types.

(45) a. John got/seemed $\begin{cases} \text{angry.} \\ \text{*a raving maniac. [* in intended sense]} \end{cases}$

 b. John expressed $\begin{cases} \text{his innocence.} \\ \text{*that he was innocent.} \end{cases}$

---

[22] This case must not be confused with *sing a song*, where *song* is a real direct object and can be replaced by *aria, tune,* "Stardust," and so forth.

c. John objected $\begin{cases} \text{*his innocence.}^{23} \\ \text{that he was innocent.} \end{cases}$

This suggests that the character of a semantic argument is not always sufficient to constrain the category of the corresponding syntactic argument. To be sure, semantically related verbs usually are rather close in their syntactic behavior (Pinker 1989; Jackendoff 1990a; Levin 1993), but the detailed semantic differences do not seem to correlate reliably with detailed syntactic differences. Thus we tentatively conclude that verbs can stipulate the category of their syntactic arguments, though not every verb does. (The standard term for such stipulation, going back to *Aspects*, is "strict subcategorization.")[24]

Another aspect of syntactic argument structure that cannot be entirely predicted from semantics concerns the "governed prepositions" that are sometimes required to glue heads to their syntactic arguments. (46) offers examples, some repeated from the previous section.

(46) a. Susan provided Amy *with* a cupcake. *vs.*
         Susan served Amy (**with*) a cupcake.
      b. We count *on* you. *vs.* We trust (*in*) you.
      c. The road approaches the castle. *vs.* the approach *to*/**of* the castle.
      d. We talked *with*/*to* Jane. *vs.* our talk *with*/**to* Jane
      e. pride *in*/**of* Bill *vs.* proud *of*/**in* Bill
      f. angry *at*/*with* Harold *vs.* mad *at*/**with* Harold

The members of these pairs differ minimally in their semantics but do differ in their governed prepositions. Sometimes the choice of preposition is semantically motivated (for instance *the approach to*/**with the castle*). But when words are as closely related as the adjectives *angry* and *mad*, there seems little choice for the governed preposition other than pure stipulation. The tentative conclusion is that verbs do at least sometimes specify some of the syntax (and phonology!) of their syntactic arguments. (We return to strict subcategorization and governed prepositions in section 6.6.)

---

[23] *John objected to his innocence* means something else—the PP expresses a different semantic argument of the verb.

[24] Grimshaw (1979; 1990) suggests that a verb can stipulate the syntactic category only of arguments within VP. Thus if an argument appears elsewhere, its category is sometimes constrained only by semantics. The interesting cases are pseudo-clefts: compare (45b) with (i).

(i)   What John didn't express was that he was disappointed.

In (i) a clausal argument is possible, even though the "normal" position in the VP is restricted to NP, as seen in (45b). Thus these syntactically unrestricted positions let the semantic realizations of the argument shine through more clearly.

5.9.3 *Position of syntactic arguments*

We now turn to the question of the order in which syntactic arguments are expressed in a clause. For the moment we continue to confine ourselves to simple active clauses; we discuss the more general case in section 5.9.4.

In English (at least), the problem breaks into two cases: when arguments are of different syntactic categories, and when they are of the same syntactic category. The former case is governed simply by the syntactic formation rules and has nothing to do with semantics. The principle in question can be stated as (47).

(47)   Syntactic Argument Ordering Constraint
       NP > AP > PP > clause (where '>' = 'precedes')

The reader can verify that this generalization holds in all the relevant examples of section 5.8 ((31), (34), (36), and in NPs (37)), and that the order of arguments of different categories cannot be reversed (except under heavy pressure from prosody, as discussed in section 5.4). Further, verbs that have variant syntactic realizations of the same semantic argument yield alternations of order like (48), which conform to the ordering in (47).

(48)   a. John mentioned his sickness to Jean.
       b. John mentioned to Jean that he was sick.

The only exception is the clausal subjects in cases like (34e, f), which precede NPs or PPs.

This leaves multiple arguments of the *same* category. Multiple PP arguments are usually freely ordered, in either VP (49a, b) or NP (49c).[25]

(49)   a. We talked with Max about Martha.
           We talked about Martha with Max.
       b. Barb seems like a genius to Elizabeth.
           Barb seems to Elizabeth like a genius.
       c. the sale of a lawnmower to Bob
           the sale to Bob of a lawnmower

The only remaining case is multiple NP arguments, of which there can be up to three, as in (35). The order of NP arguments is *not* free, as can be seen by

---

[25]   However, PP adjuncts such as manner, place, and time expressions invariably follow PP arguments such as *on the shelf* in (i) and (ii), except under pressure from prosody.

(i)   John put a book on the shelf {with great care/on Tuesday}.
(ii)   *John put a book {with great care/on Tuesday} on the shelf.

attempting to reverse their order in (33) or (35). The consensus in the field is that the order is determined by the thematic roles of the corresponding semantic arguments (Anderson 1977; Bresnan and Kanerva 1989; Grimshaw 1990; Dowty 1991; Van Valin and LaPolla 1997; Jackendoff 1990a). All accounts agree that if one argument is an Agent (an individual that brings about an action), it comes first. More generally, the order tends to work out something like (50) (with some disagreement among different accounts). This does not account for all the cases in (33)–(35)—partly because the semantic roles with verbs like *last*, *cost*, and *mean* are not well understood—but it covers most of them.

(50)   Linking Hierarchy for NP arguments
       Agent > Recipient (e.g. indirect object of *give*, *send*, etc.) > Theme (entity undergoing change or being located) > Location (e.g. object of *enter*, *leave*, *surround*) > Predicate NP

Principle (50) is neither purely syntactic nor purely semantic: it is an interface constraint that matches semantic roles with syntactic position.[26]

With these constraints in place, it becomes possible to specify the argument structure of verbs rather simply: in most cases it is necessary only to list the semantic arguments and whether they are obligatorily or optionally expressed as syntactic arguments. For instance, *devour* and *eat* can be differentiated as in (51); the subscript *obl* designates obligatory expression, and its absence designates optional expression. (See Jackendoff 1990a: ch.11 for a fuller development of this notation and Jackendoff 1993 for an emendation.)

(51)   a.   Wd$_i$ V$_i$ $[\text{DEVOUR } (X_{obl}, Y_{obl})]_i$

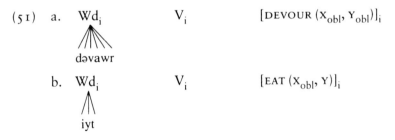

            dəvawr

       b.   Wd$_i$ V$_i$ $[\text{EAT } (X_{obl}, Y)]_i$

            iyt

---

[26] This approach also accounts for the order of arguments in the Dative alternation. When the Recipient is expressed as a PP, i.e. a *to*-phrase, it necessarily follows the direct object because of (47). When it is expressed by an NP, it necessarily precedes the direct object, which has the thematic role Theme, because of (50).

Although something like (50) is the predominant linking hierarchy in English, there are other linking hierarchies, based on animacy and focus information, that are more prominent in other languages. See Aissen (1999).

The syntactic categories and positions of the syntactic arguments mostly follow from (a) the constraints on syntactic expression of semantic categories, (b) constraint (47) on order of syntactic categories, and (c) constraint (50) on the thematic roles of NPs. For instance, because the devourer and devouree are both objects (or substances), they will automatically be expressed as NPs. Because the devourer is an Agent, it will be expressed in subject position.

However, some verbs require further specifications of syntactic argument structure for strict subcategorization, for governed prepositions, and for supernumerary arguments. We will treat the first two of these cases in section 6.6.

5.9.4 Locality of syntactic arguments, and exceptions

We have so far been discussing the placement of syntactic arguments in single clauses. We now generalize to the larger case of clauses embedded in other clauses. Consider a sentence like (52).

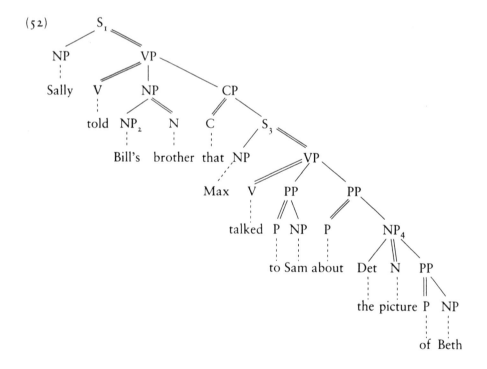

We can see in this tree that the arguments of a verb are "local," in the sense that they are all located in the verb's own clause. For instance, there are no arguments of *tell* inside of NP_2 or S_3, and there are no arguments of *talk* either inside of NP_4 or outside of S_3. This observation might be expressed as the "Head Constraint."

(53) Head Constraint
The syntactic arguments and adjuncts in a phrase express the semantic arguments and modifiers of the phrase's head.

The Head Constraint is subject to various sorts of exception. First, an NP argument can be embedded in a PP whose head is a governed preposition (a so-called oblique complement). *Sam* and *the picture of Beth* in (53) are probably such arguments. Second, there are some situations in which the syntactic arguments in a clause are not arguments of any verb at all; we defer discussion of this case, seldom recognized in the literature, to section 6.6.

However, the most important exceptions to the Head Constraint are cases where syntactic arguments of a verb are found in positions *higher* than the verb's subject position. These situations have been a major focus in generative grammar throughout its history, phenomena that every theory has to contend with. They are by now quite well understood and well differentiated from each other, both in English and in crosslinguistic context.

Consider (54), which we encountered in section 3.2.2: *John* is a semantic argument of *like* but is not its subject.

(54) John seems [to like ice cream].

Classical generative grammar maintained the Head Constraint as a universal by saying that it applies in Deep Structure. Recall the discussion in section 3.2.2: *John* is regarded as being the subject of *like* in underlying form, in conformity with the Head Constraint; and in the course of the derivation it is raised to become the subject of *seem*. In other words, the apparent violation of the Head Constraint is produced by a derivational rule ("Raising") that moves a phrase out of the environment in which it initially serves as an argument. This keeps the semantics-to-underlying syntax interface simple with respect to argument structure, preserving the notion that underlying syntactic structure is relatively close to meaning.

Other generative approaches, notably LFG and HPSG, take a different tack on the sort of syntax–semantics mismatch illustrated in (54). These approaches are committed to the elimination of movement rules from the grammar; the syntactic formation rules create a surface form directly. The greater simplicity in the syntactic component is counterbalanced by a more complex syntax–semantics interface, one that treats the Head Constraint as only a default. In particular, in configurations like (54) where the classical theory uses a derivational rule to move a constituent upward, the non-derivational theories have an interface principle that violates the Head Constraint: through a specification in the argument structure of *seem*, its syntactic subject is "referred down" to the subordinate clause to find its correspondence with a semantic argument. (This is formalized in different ways in different theories, but the basic idea is the same.)

As in many situations we have encountered, then, the issue is a trade-off between different rule types. On either approach, the complexity of language does not go away; it just reveals itself in different ways. In particular, in either approach, the possibility of this "raising" construction depends on a particular lexical property of *seem*.

(55) represents a different type of violation of the Head Constraint, due to a long-distance dependency (discussed in sections 1.7 and 3.2). *Who* is a semantic argument of *see* but is not within the same clause. The "normal" position of the object is a gap notated by ∧.

(55)   Who do you think [that John saw ∧]?

The reason this construction is called a long-distance dependency is that the gap can be deeply embedded within subordinate clauses, as in (56).

(56)   Which book do you think that [Harold told Miriam [to get Richard [to read ∧ next]]]?

This construction, along with many others such as indirect questions, relative clauses, topicalization, exclamations (*How elegant Bill seems to have become!*), and comparatives (*Fred is richer than Bill is thought to be*), is licensed not by particular verbs, but by conditions on the position of the gap and the way each successive clause is embedded in the one above it. The Sentential Subject Constraint, which we met in section 3.2.3, is one such condition; others were illustrated though not named in section 1.7.

In all of Chomsky's successive approaches, (55) satisfies the Head Constraint in underlying syntactic structure: the *wh*-phrase is taken to be generated in D(eep) Structure in the position of the gap, then moved to the front. By contrast, non-derivational theories generate the *wh*-phrase directly in its surface position, but place a "silent pronoun" or other formal marker in the position of the gap. Thus for these theories, long-distance dependencies are genuine violations of the Head Constraint. Whichever account is adopted, these violations of the Head Constraint have quite a different character from the raising cases.[27]

---

[27] Partly as a matter of historical accident, long-distance dependencies have traditionally been characterized as a basically free relation between a position at the front and a gap anywhere in a sentence; the task taken on by Ross (1967) and most subsequent literature has been to find constraints that restrict that freedom appropriately. Postal (1997), though, suggests that it may actually be simpler to characterize *positively* just those positions where gaps are permitted. The

(57) shows three other types of Head Constraint violations.

(57)   a. John is easy [to please]
      b. [A picture] is hanging on the wall [of a famous movie actor].
      c. John put [the blame for the accident] on Bill.

In (57a), *John* is a semantic argument of *please* but not its syntactic object. This construction resembles the "raising" construction (54), in that it is licensed by particular words such as *easy, tough,* and *fun*. It also has some of the character of a long-distance dependency, in that the position from which *John* receives its semantic role can be more deeply embedded:

(58)   John is easy [to get people [to dislike ∧]].

(57b) is a case where an argument or modifier of an NP has been displaced to the end of the clause of which the NP is an argument. Unlike any of the previous displacements, this one is evidently motivated on the sort of prosodic grounds with which we became familiar in section 5.4: notice that (57b) sounds much better than *A picture was hanging on the wall [of me]*, where the displaced phrase is too short to be prosodically appropriate at the end.

(57c) is a case of the so-called "light verb" construction. *John* is doing the blaming, and *Bill* is being blamed, but, in violation of the Head Constraint, neither is in the NP headed by *blame*. In this construction, a verb like *put, take, give, get, make,* or *have* is combined with a nominal that denotes an event or action, and the two together create a shared argument structure. In (57c), for instance, the argument structure is determined by neither *put* nor *blame*, but by the complex *put the blame* (e.g. Jackendoff 1974; Grimshaw and Mester 1988). In some languages such as Japanese and Korean, light verb constructions run rampant: a large proportion of English verbs translate into a light verb plus a nominal (see further remarks in section 8.10).

In classical generative grammar, ways have been sought to treat each of the constructions in (57) as satisfying the Head Constraint in D(eep) Structure, and to produce the surface form by some sort of movement or deletion. In non-derivational theories they are regarded as direct violations of the Head Constraint, in which the offending phrase is linked in a non-canonical way to its semantic role. Whichever way they are accounted for, each of these types of violation of the Head Constraint is amply attested in the languages of the world.

---

minimal case would prohibit gaps anywhere, and a language would deviate from this unmarked case to some degree or another depending how free its long-distance dependencies are. This proposal, if it can be worked out, has the distinct advantage of permitting learning by positive evidence and thereby simplifying UG to a degree.

Thus Universal Grammar must make provision for them in either the syntax or the syntax–semantics interface (depending on one's theory of grammar).

It is time to extract ourselves from the embedded depths of this discussion and see what overall conclusion can be drawn. The past two sections have shown that the syntactic argument structure of a sentence results from a complex interaction of factors:

- The number and type of semantic arguments in a sentence is a consequence of the conceptual formation rules, and is not entirely predictable from the syntax.

- The number, type, and order of syntactic arguments in a sentence is predictable only in part from the semantic arguments.

- Some aspects of the category and order of syntactic arguments are consequences of general syntactic formation rules. For instance,
    a. Adverbs have no syntactic arguments.
    b. NPs and APs have only PP and clausal arguments.
    c. NP arguments precede AP and PP arguments, which precede clausal arguments.
    d. PP arguments are freely ordered.

- Some aspects of the number and category of syntactic arguments are consequences of lexical constraints imposed by particular lexical items.

- Some aspects of the order of syntactic arguments are consequences of a general interface principle that interacts with the semantic argument structure of verbs.

- Some aspects of syntactic argument structure are governed by language-particular violations of the Head Constraint.

The particular formulations given here are by no means universally accepted, but the overall flavor recurs in every serious account of the problem. The solutions, despite differences in theoretical apparatus, reflect similar insights.[28]

In turn, these conclusions about argument structure reflect on the main theme of this chapter: the decomposition of the grammar into independent generative

---

[28] The discussion in this section has concerned verbs primarily. The situation is parallel in NPs, APs, and PPs, but much simpler because there are far fewer combinations of arguments:

- The number of syntactic arguments is always equal to or fewer than the number of semantic arguments. There are no supernumerary arguments of the sort in (42).
- There are some cases of nouns and adjectives that stipulate either the category of their syntactic argument or a governed preposition; some examples are seen in (38) and (39).
- The order of syntactic arguments is governed syntactically by (47), except that nouns and adjectives have only PP and clausal arguments. The only kind of arguments that can occur multiply are PPs, which are freely ordered, as seen in (49c).
- Argument structure in NPs, APs, and PPs observes the Head Constraint as a default. We have seen violations of the Head Constraint in NPs in (57b, c).

components that interact through interface rules. Argument structure provides a rich illustration of this decomposition: it can be accounted for only in a system that discriminates syntactic formation rules, conceptual formation rules, and rich syntax–semantics interface principles. Thus, on one hand, it constitutes an argument against Chomsky's syntactocentric architectures. On the other hand, it also constitutes an argument against purely semantically based theories that deny an independent role to syntax, of the sort often advocated by opponents of the generative approach. We conclude that the detailed facts of argument structure provide important evidence for the parallel architecture.

5.10   A tier for grammatical functions?

An important question lurks around the corners of *Aspects* concerning the status of the traditional grammatical functions: subject, object, and indirect object. *Aspects* suggests that these functions can be defined implicitly, as structural positions in the sentence. The subject in English, for instance, is the daughter of S and the sister of VP; the direct object is the daughter of VP and the sister of V. Hence, Chomsky says, the grammar does not need to make any explicit mention of these roles.

However, Relational Grammar (Perlmutter 1983; Perlmutter and Rosen 1984), Lexical-Functional Grammar (Bresnan 1982a; 2001), and Role and Reference Grammar (Van Valin and LaPolla 1997) stress the fact that grammatical functions cannot always be identified with particular positions in a sentence. Many languages have far freer word order than English, but the grammatical functions are still detectable through patterns of agreement and case marking. Grammatical functions so marked still undergo passive and the like in the usual way—but only if one can define grammatical function in a fashion that abstracts away from its particular realization in the language as position, agreement, and/or case.

Nor, as demonstrated in the previous sections, can grammatical functions be defined in terms of semantic roles; rather, there is a many-to-many relation between the two systems (see especially (33)). Many grammatical principles make reference to grammatical functions rather than thematic roles. For instance, verb agreement pertains to subjects (and, in some languages, objects) irrespective of their thematic roles. With a few semantically motivated exceptions, passive promotes the argument normally in object position to subject position, irrespective of its thematic role.[29] The so-called "structural cases," nominative and accusative, are default

---

[29] The exceptions include the objects of verbs like *weigh* and *cost* (Jackendoff 1972). (It begs the question to say that because of their semantics they are not objects!) Another exceptional case is the way English passive applies to certain prepositional objects, as in *Bill is being talked about*. These

cases for subjects and objects respectively, again irrespective of thematic role (although there are often certain semantic intrusions such as dative-marked subjects for Experiencers) (Maling et al. 1987).

One might also include in this system of grammatical functions the designated position at the front of a clause ("A-bar position" or "Specifier of CP" in GB terminology) that is occupied by question words, relative pronouns, topics, and the like. The semantic roles appearing in this position do not show an overwhelming commonality; they are certainly random in terms of thematic roles; they show a mixture of topic-focus roles and quantificational (variable-binding) status. For convenience I'll call this position "syntactic topic," while recognizing that this term does not do it justice.

That there is something special about subject, object, indirect object, and syntactic topic also emerges implicitly from the fact that so many different theories of syntax are preoccupied with them. Within GB/MP, the "abstract case module" deals with subjects, objects, and indirect objects; and a vast body of research beginning with Ross (1967) has dealt with constraints on the relation between an occupant of syntactic topic position and its trace (the Sentential Subject Constraint in section 3.2.3 is an example). GB/MP singles out these two classes of phenomena (plus anaphora and quantification) as principal components of "core" grammar, while most other phenomena are relegated to the "periphery." Relational Grammar is almost entirely concerned with subject, object, and indirect object; other arguments and adjuncts are called *chômeurs* ('unemployed') and are inert within the system. Lexical-Functional Grammar is founded on the argument that as well as the syntactic level of phrase structure, there is an additional level that codifies grammatical functions—again stressing subjects, objects, and indirect objects and classifying everything else in a relatively undifferentiated "oblique" category. And the Argument-Linking Hierarchy of the previous section pertains specifically to NP arguments—again, subjects, objects, and indirect objects. The fact that all these frameworks arrive at similar notions, though in entirely different terminology, cannot be a coincidence: something must really be going on in language.

The most direct way to incorporate grammatical functions into the architecture is to adopt the proposal of Lexical-Functional Grammar that, in present terms, there is an additional tier of syntactic structure that intervenes between phrasal syntax and semantics. We might present the relevant part of the architecture as in Fig. 5.6.

---

cases present stronger semantic constraints: the surface subject must be construed as somehow being affected by the event (i.e. as a Patient). The classic contrast is *This house has been slept in by George Washington/*my brother*, where having been slept in by George Washington somehow confers status on the house.

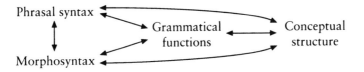

Fig. 5.6. Incorporating a grammatical function tier

This picture differs from the usual LFG architecture in one important respect: it retains some direct connections between syntax and conceptual structure. The idea is that the grammatical function tier provides a sort of "supercharger" on the syntactic expression of semantic relations—a way to regulate more precisely the expression of argument structure. But like tiers in phonology, it deals only with *parts* of the structures it relates, ignoring the rest. In this case the rest is all the periphery/*chômeurs*/obliques, plus matters such as the determiner and auxiliary systems. These aspects of syntax and semantics are "invisible" to the interfaces that engage grammatical functions. Hence the tier that deals with grammatical functions is not a "full" level (as in LFG and RG): rather it is a very limited little "accounting system" that only has to push around a few pieces of structure. Presumably it is this limited character that gives the system its relative efficiency and precision. It is an interesting challenge for future research to see whether a grammatical-function tier of this limited sort can be crafted from the existing theories of grammatical functions, and whether it yields any insight over current approaches. Whether or not this speculation works out, it is most natural to explore it in the context of a parallel architecture.

CHAPTER 6

Lexical Storage versus Online Construction

6.1 Lexical items versus words

This chapter focuses on an issue which to my knowledge has played no significant role in generative theories, but which I have begun to think is absolutely central in working out the instantiation of language in the mind. At first this issue may seem irrelevant to the issues of the previous chapter, but as we go on it will become clearer how intimately they are related.

What aspects of an utterance *must* be stored in long-term memory, and what aspects *can* be constructed online in working memory?

The modalities in the two parts of this question ("must" versus "can") are important. Consider two simple examples. The word *dog* must be stored in long-term memory: there is no way to construct it online from smaller parts. By contrast, the reader probably understands the utterance *My dog just vomited on your carpet* by constructing it online from its constituent words, invoking the combinatorial rules of English grammar. However: since I have memorized this sentence, having used it as an example in many talks, it *is* present in *my* long-term memory. In fact any utterance can be memorized, all the way from little clichés to the words of *Take Me Out to the Ballgame* to the entire text of *Hamlet*. Thus we cannot predict in advance that any particular part of an utterance *must* be constructed online by a given speaker. We can predict only that speakers *can* construct some part online on demand if it hasn't already been memorized.

One might wonder why the possibility of memorizing *Hamlet* should bear on linguistic issues at all. It might be that words are one thing for the brain and f-mind, and long passages of text are something else (e.g. they use a different kind of memory). But notice that memorized texts *are* made up of linguistic units—they are linked phonological, syntactic, and semantic structures that (at least mostly) conform to rules of grammar. Therefore they invoke the language faculty in their production and comprehension. Like individual words, there is no other faculty that they necessarily invoke. Moreover, there is no principled dividing line between little clichés such as *happy birthday* and *signed, sealed, and delivered*, larger units such as *the bigger they are, the harder they fall*, still larger units such as song lyrics, and monsters such as *Hamlet.* The main difference is that the units we call clichés will tend to be in everyone's long-term memory, but linguistic examples, poems, song lyrics, and plays are likely to be known only by some small proportion of speakers. In any event, the longer passages *can* be constructed online (say when hearing them for the first time) but need not be. (For documentation of the number and variety of clichés and other fixed expressions, see Jackendoff 1997a: ch. 7.)

The fact that memorized texts must be stored as linguistic structure is largely overlooked, thanks to a widespread stereotype in linguistic theory (and philosophy and the popular conception of language) to the effect that the memorized units of language are *words.* In fact, the terms "word" and "lexical item" are often used interchangeably. For instance, Chomsky introduces the term "lexicon" in *Aspects* roughly to mean the repository of all the words the speaker knows. Following Bloomfield (1933), he points out that the lexicon must contain all the exceptional, non-predictable features of words. But there is scant attention to larger stored units.

Chomsky further stipulates, without argument, that the lexicon contains *only* non-predictable features, that is, that it contains no redundancy. (It is not clear to me that this was Bloomfield's intention, though.) Here Chomsky likely deviates from psychological reality: there is no reason to think that the brain stores information non-redundantly. We return to this issue in sections 6.5 and 6.8.

To make the distinction clearer, I will use the term "lexical item" exclusively to denote an item stored in the lexicon, i.e. in long-term memory. I will use the term "word" for quite a different notion, based in grammatical theory. In phonology, a phonological word is a constituent such as those dominated by "Wd" in Fig. 1.1; it is a domain over which certain segmental and prosodic constraints are defined. In syntax, a roughly corresponding notion is that of an X° (or so-called lexical) category such as N, V, A, or P. Di Sciullo and Williams (1987) point out the distinction between grammatical words and what are here called lexical items—they call them "listemes"—and they declare from the outset (p. 1) that the theory of listemes is "of no interest to the grammarian." By contrast, I wish to take the theory of listemes quite seriously here: it corresponds precisely to our question of storage vs. online construction. We will see that it is indeed of considerable interest to the grammarian, despite being on the face of it an issue of "performance."

The argument to be pursued here is that, under the definition of lexical item as a unit stored in long-term memory,

- Lexical items may be larger or smaller than grammatical words.
- Not all grammatical words are lexical items.
- There are complex lexical items that contain no phonological material.

In pursuing these points more deeply, we will arrive at two further points that in effect turn the standard theory of grammar "inside out":

- Most of what have previously been called "rules of grammar" also turn out to be lexical items.
- UG can be formulated as a collection of abstract lexical items that "seed" language acquisition.

To begin the argument, let me just briefly mention two basic problems with the stereotype of lexical items as words. First, consider languages with massively productive morphology, say Turkish or Navajo. In such languages, a grammatical word consists of a stem plus potentially a sizable number of affixes. Thus on one hand the number of grammatical words is vast, possibly too large to store in long-term memory; on the other hand it is possible to construct most grammatical words online from units that *are* stored in long-term memory: the independent stems and affixes. These elements are smaller than grammatical words, and cannot be produced in isolation.

Second, consider the treatment of an idiom such as *kick the bucket*. This is a unit larger than a grammatical word—in this case, apparently a VP. Because it means something different from its constituent parts, it must be stored in long-term memory as a unit, in this case a lexical VP. There have been proposals to treat *kick the bucket* and the like as grammatical verbs, and for this particular idiom such a treatment might be plausible. But it is far less plausible for idioms such as *the cat's got his tongue* and *(now) I've got you where I want you*. These are full sentences and so it is hardly plausible to treat them as verbs. We thus must consider the possibility of lexically listed phrases of various sizes. In fact, in the strict sense of lexicon proposed here, we should be able to treat longer memorized linguistic passages as lexical items as well.

We take these two cases in order, then turn to more abstract cases.

6.2 Lexical items smaller than words

As stressed in Chapter 3, the fundamental principle behind generative syntax is the combination of grammatical words into phrases by productive rules of phrasal combination, i.e. "syntax." However, in many "lexicalist" approaches to generative grammar (e.g. HPSG (Pollard and Sag 1994), earlier LFG (Bresnan 1982a), and Hale and Keyser 1993)), the combination of stems and affixes into grammatical words is taken to be accomplished "in the lexicon" by so-called lexical rules (section 3.3), "before" the words are "inserted" into syntactic structures. For example, the word *fortunately* is composed in the lexicon by a lexical rule that converts adjectives into adverbs by adding *-ly* to them; the word *enjoyment* is composed in the lexicon by a lexical rule that converts verbs into nouns by adding *-ment* to them.

However, this treatment neglects an important distinction among word-building rules, between what I will call *productive* and *semiproductive* lexical rules. Let us look at these types in turn.

6.2.1 Productive morphology

Productive morphology is totally regular, except where irregular forms block or supplant regular forms through the "meta-constraint" of morphological blocking discussed in section 3.2.3. A prototypical case is the English present participle (*-ing*) form, which applies without exception to all the verbs of the language. The English past tense affix *-d* is similarly productive (given the predictable phonetic alternations between /-d/, /-t/, and /-əd/), except that it is supplanted (blocked) by irregular forms in about 180 verbs.

Productive morphology is not confined to inflectional morphology (i.e. affixes like agreement, tense, and case); it appears also in derivational morphology. For example, just about any English adjective can be converted into an adverb by adding *-ly*, aside from marked exceptions such as *good–well*, *fast–fast* and adjectives that already end in *-ly* such as *friendly*. Similarly, the prefix *pre-* can be added freely to nouns that denote time periods or events, forming adjectives such as *pre-season*, *pre-summer*, *pre-game*, *pre-puberty*, and *pre-rehearsal*.

In patterns of productive morphology, speakers confronted with a new base form know exactly how to form the derived form and exactly what it means, as seen in the much-cited experiment of Berko (1958):

(1)   *Experimenter*: This funny little thing is a wug. Now there are two of them. There are two . . .
       Child: Wugs.

Berko shows that by the age of five or so children have mastered the regular plural ending of English and can apply it to nonsense words like *wug* that they have never heard before. Moreover, speakers often create and encounter new regular forms, without noticing they are doing anything special. For instance, Dutch speakers affix the productive diminutive suffix *-je* to every noun in sight.

And phrases like *pre-lecture preparation* and *pre-preparation lecture* occasion no surprise; nor do I have any notion whether I've ever heard them before. This property of productive morphology is of particular interest in a heavily affixing language such as Turkish, in which word forms like (2) are not unusual (the first morpheme is the stem, the rest are suffixes):

(2)   gel- emi- yebel- ir- im
       come-unable-possible-aorist-1sg   'I may be unable to come.'
          (Van Valin and LaPolla 1997, 44)
       çalış- tır- ıl- ma- malıy-mış
       work-cause-passive-neg-oblig- infer   'Supposedly he ought not to be
          made to work'   (Spencer 1991, 189)

It is of no consequence whether or not a speaker of Turkish has heard these particular forms before: they can be created and interpreted on the spot.

Now consider what it might mean for such forms to be created "in the lexicon." If "in the lexicon" means "stored in long-term memory," the implication is that speakers store all regular forms. On this hypothesis, when one hears a new noun stem like *wug*, one immediately adds not just *wug* but also *wugs* to one's long-term store. Similarly, Dutch speakers who learn a new noun also add to their long-term memory the diminutive form. For a more striking case, there is a register of American English that permits one to insert an expletive into the interior of a word for emphasis, creating such forms as *manu-fuckin-facture*, *ele-fuckin-mentary*, and so on (McCarthy 1982). (British speakers, I'm told, insert *bloody* instead.) The insertion is possible only if the word has an appropriate stress pattern: roughly, its main stress must be preceded by a secondary stress and preferably an unstressed syllable—hence **ele-fuckin-phant* is not possible. But within this constraint, the morphological process is perfectly productive. Thus the hypothesis that these forms are created "in the lexicon" implies that whenever one learns a new word of appropriate stress pattern, one also tucks away in memory the *-fuckin-* form as well!

These cases are at least technically possible. The case of massively affixing languages like Turkish is more problematic. Hankamer (1989) observes that in such languages every verb has tens of thousands of possible forms, all constructed through productive morphology. If all these forms are created "in the lexicon," then the demands on long-term memory are multiplied by four or five orders of magnitude over a meagerly inflected language like English. When it comes to the capacity of long-term memory one is hard-pressed to say how much is implausible, but cases like Turkish do stretch the imagination.

In fact, the productivity of such large inflectional systems is probably more extensive than that of, say, the Determiner system of English. (3) illustrates, going from simple cases to rather complex ones. (Toward the end, I've added contexts in square brackets to help make sense of the examples.)

(3)   a/the/this/that/what/which/whichever/every/each/some house
these/those/such/some/which/what houses
both/all/enough houses
such a/many a house
{so/too/how} {tall/old/. . .} a house
{much/far} too {tall/old/. . .} a house
{nearly/almost/practically/not quite} every house
{nearly/almost/practically/not quite} {all/enough} houses
how much more expensive a house [*did Bill buy?*]
[*Bill bought*] five times as expensive a car [*as I did*]
[*you can get*] {more than/almost} five times as fast a computer
   [*for cheaper*]
. . .

Nobody would claim that when one learns a new noun, one adds to one's lexicon versions of that noun with all the dozens of possible determiner combinations. Rather, every theory assumes these are built "in the syntax," i.e. by principles of free combination that assemble complex determiner structures and prefix them to nouns, in accordance with syntactic and semantic restrictions on the individual parts.

The same approach seems altogether appropriate for productive morphology. Words can be composed by combining stems and affixes according to principles of free combination, in accordance with the phonological, syntactic, and semantic restrictions on the individual parts. For instance, English progressive -*ing* can be specified phonologically as a suffix, syntactically as something added to a verb to form a participle, and semantically as something that (roughly) operates on an event to form a process. A verb form like *cutting*, then, is the product of free combination of this suffix with the verb stem *cut*.

For our purposes, the important question is: What does it mean to say this free combination is the result of a "lexical rule" that takes place "in the lexicon"? Taking to heart the cases of expletive infixation and Turkish verb inflection, and bearing in mind the parallel to the determiner system, it seems implausible that "in the lexicon" here means "stored in long-term memory." Rather, like the examples in (3), the outputs of productive lexical rules are more likely to be constructed online in working memory. (And like remembered phrases or song lyrics, they *can* be memorized and stored redundantly, but they need not be.) From what material stored in long-term memory are they constructed, then? Obviously, the individual stems and affixes. In other words,

"lexical rule" here means "principle of free combination whose output is something of word size or smaller," and "in the lexicon" means not "stored in long-
term memory" but rather "involving principles that build things of word size or
smaller." That is, "lexical" in these terms really refers to the *grammatical* notion
of "word," not to the notion of the lexicon as stored information. Accordingly,
I will stop using the term "lexical rules" in reference to productive morphology.[1]

6.2.2 *Semiproductive morphology*

The situation is quite different with semiproductive morphology, where there
are only partial regularities. A typical case is the irregular forms of the English
past tense. One can find various generalizations, for example that many irregular verbs form their past tenses by changing the vowel, and that irregularity is confined to monosyllabic verbs (plus bi- and trisyllabic verbs that
begin with the quasi-prefixes *a-*, *be-*, *for-*, *over-*, and *under-*). But even among
verbs that are phonologically very similar, one cannot predict exactly what the
vowel changes to: compare *ring–rang*, *wring–wrung*, *spring–sprang*,
sting–stung, *drink–drank*, *swing–swung*, plus cases that are variable such as
shrink–shrank/shrunk, *stink–stank/stunk*. In addition, this class is interspersed with homophonous regular cases, such as *hang–hanged* and
ring–ringed ('put a ring around') as well as the even more irregular *bring–
brought*. Thus a "lexical rule" of this sort does not apply across the board.
Rather, given a stem form that the rule potentially applies to, one must know
whether the rule *actually* applies to it.

   When a word lacks a specified irregular inflectional form, the inflectional
paradigm must still be completed. For instance, a verb must have a past tense
form. So if there is no irregular form, the regular combinatorial process jumps
in as a default. Derivational morphology, on the other hand, does not demand
a regular pattern that serves as default, so a semiproductive process can just
leave gaps. Consider for example a class of English denominal verbs formed
by zero-affixation, such as *butter (the bread)*, *water (the flowers)*, *paint (the
wall)*, *roof (the house)*. These exhibit a clear regularity, in that they all mean

---

[1] If there is an architectural distinction between phrasal syntax and morphosyntax, as suggested in section 5.6, productive affixes are treated by the latter. But this does not mean that morphosyntax "takes place before" phrasal syntax, as in the "lexicalist" theories mentioned above.
Rather, in accordance with the parallel architecture, morphosyntax generates structures in parallel with phrasal syntax, and the two subcomponents interface with each other via the shared unit
"grammatical word" and shared features of inflectional morphology such as case and agreement
features.

roughly 'put N on something,' where N is the homophonous noun. But for each individual noun in the language, the lexicon must specify whether it gives rise to such a denominal verb. For example, one only asks someone to *mustard the sandwich* or *door the cabinet* ('put a door on the cabinet') as a metalinguistic joke; speakers know that these forms do not exist.

Derivational morphology raises two further complications that can be illustrated with deverbal nouns. First, deverbal nouns can have a variety of meanings, for instance those in (4).

(4) 'put N on': butter, water, paint, roof
     'take N off': dust (the shelves), scale (a fish), skin (a cat)
     'put on N': shelve (books), plate (food)
     'put in N': pocket (the money), bottle (the wine)
     'fasten with N': glue, staple, nail, tape

And just as there are homophonous verbs with different past tenses, such as *hang–hung* vs. *hang–hanged* and *ring–rang* vs. *wring–wrung*, there are homophonous denominal verbs with different meanings. For example, in addition to *dust (the shelves)* 'take dust off', there is *dust (the cake with sugar)* 'put dust-like substance on'; in addition to *roof (the house)* 'put a roof on', my daughters' dialect has *roof (a frisbee)*, 'put/throw onto a roof'. Thus one must know not just *whether* a particular noun has a corresponding denominal verb, but also which variety or varieties of denominal verb meanings it has.

The second complication is that, even if one knows this much, one cannot predict the complete meaning of the denominal verb. To put a clock on a shelf is not to *shelve* it; to just pour wine into a bottle is not to *bottle* it; to spill water on a table is not to *water* it. One cannot *saddle* a table by putting a saddle on it; one cannot *butter* one's toast by laying a stick of butter on it. The verbs *to mother* and *to father* mean very roughly 'act as a mother/father toward someone', but are entirely different in the exact actions that count as relevant. In short, many denominal verbs have semantic peculiarities that are not predicted by the general lexical rule. (See section 11.8 for treatment of the regular part of denominal verb meanings.)

The upshot is that the outputs of semiproductive rules must be listed (at least in part) in long-term memory; they cannot be a product of free combination. Hence in this case the notion of a "lexical rule," a rule applying "in the lexicon," makes sense. Such a rule expresses a generalization in the relationship among pairs of lexical entries. But it does not apply to all entries that satisfy its conditions, nor does it fully predict the information in one member of a pair, given the other. Thus, unlike fully productive morphology, this sort of rule captures the original intention behind "lexical redundancy rules" (section 3.3.2).

6.2.3 The necessity of a heterogeneous theory

The conclusion is that the term "lexical rule" has been applied to two distinct phenomena. The principles that express semiproductive generalizations are indeed lexical rules: they relate lexical items to one another, but speakers must learn one by one the lexical items that the rule relates. That is, the rule expresses the possibility of related forms but not their existence or their details. By contrast, productive generalizations result from the free combination of individual morphemes that are stored as separate lexical items. (This does not preclude high-frequency regular combinations being stored as well, and there is some evidence that they are, e.g. Baayen et al. 1992; Baayen et al. 1993; Booij 1999; Baayen et al. 2000).

On this proposal, then, *devour* is both a word and a lexical item; *-d* is a lexical item but not a word; the regular form *devoured* is a word but not a lexical item, being made out of the lexical items *devour* and *-d*; and the irregular *ate* is both a word and a lexical item.

We can formalize this treatment of affixation along the lines used for words in section 5.9.3. (5) shows the regular past tense.

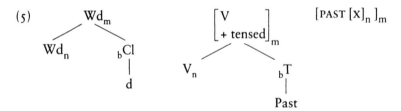

Like an ordinary word, this is an interface rule with feet in all three components: it is a piece of phonology linked to a piece of syntax and a piece of semantics. (On the other hand, some affixes, such as nominative and accusative case in German, have no semantic effects, so they are "defective" in the same way as expletive *it* and default *of*.) Just as a verb has variable positions for its arguments, the past tense affix has a variable position in phonology, syntax, and semantics for the verb to which it attaches.

(5) combines with a regular verb such as *devour* (Ch. 5, (51a)) to form the composite structure (6). (If phrasal syntax and morphosyntax are separate subcomponents, as suggested in section 5.6, this combination is accomplished by the latter.)

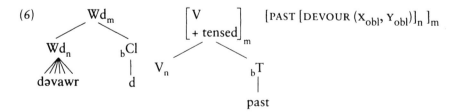

The stored irregular *ate* has the same syntactic and semantic structures as (6), and the same connections between them, but a different connection to the phonology: only the unit as a whole is coindexed with a phonological constituent. This is exactly what it should mean to say the form is irregular.

(7)

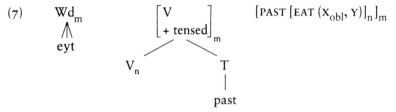

What may seem unintuitive here is the inhomogeneity of the solution. Two forms with the exact same syntactic properties, for instance *devoured* and *ate*, may have different sources: one is a product of free combination and the other comes from the lexicon.[2] In fact, most morphological theories have tacitly assumed that there *must* be a uniform solution for both cases. The result has been a tension between "morpheme-based" or "item-and-arrangement" theories such as Chomsky and Halle (1968) and Di Sciullo and Williams (1987) and "lexeme-based" or "word-and-paradigm" theories such as Halle (1973), Jackendoff (1975), Aronoff (1976), Beard (1987), and Anderson (1992). Morpheme-based theories are perspicuous for productive morphology and spend most of their effort trying to explain semiproductive phenomena. Lexeme-based theories are good at semiproductive phenomena, where whole words have to be listed, but they force one to believe, for instance, that the entire Turkish verb paradigm is stored for every verb.[3]

---

[2] They do however have different combinatorial properties in at least one respect. Pinker (1999 and references therein) points out that irregular plural forms, which are lexical words, enter more readily into compounds than do composed plurals, which are not lexical words. For instance, children spontaneously produce both *mouse-eater* and *mice-eater*, but produce only *rat-eater*, not ??*rats-eater*. Evidently morphosyntax is sensitive to the distinction, but phrasal syntax is not.

[3] The discussion here has implied that all morphology can be analyzed as affixation. To keep myself honest, I have to mention two kinds of exotica here.

Anderson (1992) argues against the view that regular affixes can be treated as independent lexical listemes. His reason is that many morphological changes cannot be treated as adding parts. The clearest sort of case he presents is truncation, when a morphological process *removes* material from the stem, as in pairs like English *virus/viral* (*virusal*), *charity/charitable* (*charityable*). These examples are drawn from semi-regular patterns; however there are also cases of productive truncation morphology (some citations in Blevins 1999). Within the present approach, I suggest that we take a chapter out of the analysis of visually presented shapes, in particular entities like holes and cracks. These seem to be conceptualized (Landau and Jackendoff 1993) as "negative parts" of objects—instead of adding material to the object (like a lump or a handle) we have scooped material out. Whatever innovation must be added to the theory of visual form for such cases might be adapted to phonological structure too: we could treat a truncation process as, say, a suffix with the morphophonological form "negative consonant." In the course of correspondence to phonetic form, the combination of this with the preceding word would result in the "scooping out" of the final consonant of the word to which it is affixed. This is only a preliminary

Looking at the tension between these theories from our present very concrete standpoint of storage in the brain, we arrive at the conclusion that both approaches are correct, but for different classes of words. This not an optimally elegant solution—but of course it is not clear that the brain is always optimally elegant.

The same tension appears among syntactic theories. It was mentioned earlier that many theories such as HPSG achieve a homogeneous treatment of morphology by doing it all "in the lexicon." Such theories level out the distinction between words, a grammatical notion, and lexical items, a notion having to do with storage; they treat all words as lexical items. Thus in this respect they parallel lexeme-based morphological theories. The price is having to claim (usually tacitly) that the entire paradigm of inflection for every word is present in the lexicon. Late Government-Binding Theory (Baker 1988; Pollock 1989) and the Minimalist Program (Chomsky 1995) level out the distinction in the opposite direction: they treat inflectional affixes as X° syntactic categories, and hence like words in their potential to project complement and specifier structure. Because they stress the free combination of affixes, they parallel the morpheme-based morphological theories. The price here is complex derivations that reduce elaborate syntactic structure to the observed morphological forms, and an inadequate treatment of semiproductivity. In both approaches, part of the problem comes from expecting a homogeneous theory.[4]

---

suggestion, and serious consideration is required for these cases, as well as for the more complex cases such as morphological metathesis that Anderson (1992) offers as counterexamples to the additive treatment of morphology.

Another "exotic" and heavily studied case is reduplication, in which affixation results in a copy or partial copy of part of the word to which it is affixed (Marantz 1982; Moravcsik 1978; Spencer 1991). An example is Mandarin *jang* ('sheet')/*jang-jang* ('every sheet'), *ren* ('man')/*ren-ren* ('every man'), etc. Reduplicative morphology is widespread in the languages of the world, associated in different cases with different meanings. For example, reduplication on nouns may be used to mean plurality, universal quantification, diminutives ('little X'), augmentatives ('big X'), and 'Xs and things like that'; on verbs, to mean past tense and continuative aspect ('keep doing X'); on adjectives, to mean 'extremely.' An interesting case from contemporary colloquial English (Ghomeshi et al. 2001) attaches to any syntactic category and means roughly 'most prominent instance of the category': a hostess says, *Would you like wine, or would you like a DRINK-drink?*

Since reduplication is productive in many of these cases, the present theory says there must be a "reduplicative morpheme" listed in the lexicon that can combine freely with other words. What phonological content can possibly be given to such a morpheme? One possibility, roughly following Marantz (1982) and McCarthy and Prince (1986), is a "metaphonological" instruction "REPEAT" that can be part of an item's stored structure, accompanied by a pointer to what is to be repeated. (In partial reduplication, the morpheme would have some specified content that could not be overlaid by the realization of REPEAT (Alderete et al. 1999).)

[4] See Jackendoff (1997a: chs. 5 and 6) for more discussion of morphology in the present framework, including some discussion of allomorphy and morphological classes. The reader is advised, however, to take the treatment of morphological blocking there with a grain of salt. It can't possibly be that complicated.

6.3 Psycholinguistic considerations

The need for a heterogeneous theory of morphology has also been the subject of intense dispute in the psycholinguistics and neurolinguistics community. The genesis of the dispute was the claim by David Rumelhart and James McClelland (1986b) that a connectionist network that performs pattern association could learn the past tense system of English in roughly the way a child does. Steven Pinker and colleagues, in part drawing on work by many others (Pinker 1999; Pinker and Prince 1988; 1991; Clahsen 1999 and references therein) have amassed considerable evidence against this account, arguing that something more than pattern association must be taking place. First consider what the past tense network does. Ostensibly it learns to perform the task "Given the verb X, form its past tense." In fact it actually learns a different task: "Given a sequence of phonemes, produce the sequence of phonemes stipulated to be associated with it." That is, as Pinker emphasizes, the network model has no notion of *word*. Of course it doesn't have to, because it never has to deal with sequences of words, only with words given in isolation. However, because it identifies phoneme sequences rather than words, it cannot distinguish the verb *ring* (with past *rang*) from *ring* (*ringed*) and *wring* (*wrung*), or *hang* (*hung*) from *hang* (*hanged*).

In addition, the network also has no notion of verb or of past tense. This is because the network is not intended as a "general morphology machine": it doesn't have to tell verbs from nouns, so as to be able to decide whether to apply past tense or plural, for example. Nor does it have to decide whether the appropriate ending on a verb in a particular context is past tense or, say, present participle—because there are no contexts. Part of the overall connectionist philosophy (e.g. Rumelhart and McClelland 1986a; Elman et al. 1996) is that discrete symbols such as Verb and Tense are rendered unnecessary by the architecture of networks. But in this case the only reason they appear unnecessary is that virtually everything of linguistic relevance has been bled out of the task the network has been designed to perform.[5] It is therefore hard to take seriously the manifold claims, still being repeated (e.g. Seidenberg and MacDonald 1999;

---

[5] Plunkett and Juola (1999) develop a network that is intended to add both plural to nouns and past tense to verbs, so it appears to be on its way to being a "general morphology machine." However, the authors note (484) that "the network, by design, only has access to phonological information." Thus it has no way of knowing whether the phonological sequence /sædl/ is meant to be the noun or the verb *saddle*, hence how it should be inflected. And the authors admit (484): "Unfortunately, it is not possible in the present simulations to model this process." They then briefly describe a modification that adds random "pseudo-semantics," which is supposed to simulate the distinction between the noun and verb uses of *saddle*, for instance. This hardly models the noun–verb distinction, though; it could just as well simulate the difference between *ring* and *wring*.

McClelland and Seidenberg 2000), that the neural network approach as presently conceived potentially yields the key to the full productivity of language.

Pinker and colleagues also adduce experimental evidence against a pure network account, drawing on the statistical distribution of regulars and irregulars, on speakers' judgments and reaction times in producing and recognizing past tenses of known and novel verbs (Bybee and Moder 1983; Prasada and Pinker 1993), and on the behavior of agrammatics and individuals with Specific Language Impairment (Gopnik 1999; van der Lely 1999) and with Williams Syndrome (Clahsen and Almazan 1998). They show that the pattern association account is satisfactory for irregular verbs (here, semiproductive patterns), and even provides considerable insight. But they also show that the formation of regular past tenses is a phenomenon of quite a different character, not captured by the Rumelhart and McClelland model nor by subsequent connectionist models in a similar spirit such as those of Plunkett and Marchman (1991) and Hare et al. (1995). The experimental results have been replicated with other morphological systems in which a regular default pattern is overlaid by a system of semiproductive patterns: German noun plurals (Marcus et al. 1995; Clahsen 1999), Hebrew noun plurals (Berent et al. 1999), and Japanese noun-forming suffixes (Hagiwara et al. 1999).

I acknowledge that there is a great deal of controversy surrounding these results (see for instance many of the commentaries accompanying Clahsen 1999). But a much more important point has become lost in the debate. Being able to learn to produce past tenses on demand is not enough for learning *language*. In particular, Marcus (1998, 2001) argues that a multilayer network trained by back-propagation—the standard network used in these models—is in principle incapable of extracting the sort of regularity necessary to account for productive morphology. The reason is that such a regularity must be formulated in terms of a *variable*: "this generalization applies to anything I encounter that belongs to such-and-such a category, regardless of its other features." As observed in section 3.5, Marcus shows that pattern associators simply cannot encode variables.

Pinker characterizes the productive process of past tense formation as a rule with a variable: "To form the past tense of *any verb*, add -*d*." Pinker's claim is that a network instantiating pattern association cannot learn *rules*. The present account is slightly different: regular past tenses are formed by the free combination of the lexical entry (5) with a verb stem, in accordance with the affix's structural requirements. Instead of Pinker's special rule or a somewhat more general rule "Add affixes to stems," there is the maximally simple and general rule *COMBINE* or *UNIFY*. Under this interpretation, though, Marcus's argument against the network approach still goes through. The rule has two variables: "Combine *anything* with *anything appropriate*"; and the lexical item *-d* defines what is appropriate using a variable: "I combine with *any verb*." So the present account poses the same principled difficulties for a network of the usual sort.

The present approach in fact makes clearer what is at stake in this argument. As stressed in Chapter 3, the principle of free combination is what makes language what it is. Connectionist approaches do give us considerable insight into semiproductivity. But if a multi-layer network trained by back-propagation in principle cannot account for something as combinatorially trivial as the regular past tense, there is no hope of scaling up current connectionist solutions to the past tense to the rest of language, where free combination reigns supreme. Rather, as suggested in section 3.5, the challenge to network approaches is to develop a robust device for encoding variables—not to continue to try to live without them. Accepting this challenge could, I believe, lead to far more meaningful dialogue between network modelers and theoretical linguists.

To my knowledge it has not been observed that a heterogeneous morphological theory presents an interesting challenge to acquisition. The child, after all, does not have a "Maxwell's demon" that miraculously sorts the words in the environment into regular and semi-regular cases. The same morphological relationship (say causative formation) may be productive in one language (e.g. Turkish) but only semiproductive in another (e.g. English). Nor does relatively high frequency signal a regular pattern. For instance, German regular plural nouns are considerably less frequent than semiproductive plural forms in speech, counting either tokens or types (Marcus et al. 1995). My inclination is to think that the child's brain takes a catholic approach, trying to analyze new morphological patterns both ways at once, and that eventually one mechanism extinguishes the other. We return to this issue in section 6.9.

6.4 The status of lexical redundancy rules

If the irregular *ate* is a separate lexical item from *eat*, then how are they related? As just mentioned, most of the experimental work in Pinker's tradition views the task of relating them as "Given the verb *eat*, form its past tense"; the connectionist tradition treats it similarly but in less structured terms. However, performance on this experimental task is only a reflection of deeper linguistic f-knowledge that is normally employed in tasks more relevant to actual language use. For instance, upon hearing *ate* in a sentence, one does not look in the lexicon for some verb that this is the past tense of, "undoing" the phonological "change" from /iy/ to /ey/. Rather one looks up the phonological form /eyt/ in the lexicon and discovers that it is linked to *[V+past]* in syntax and [PAST [EAT]] in semantics. (See Chapter 7 for extended discussion of lexical look-up.) The relation between *eat* and *ate*, then, is a relation between two stored lexical items, not a derivational process.

Consider now the relationships among semiregular past tense forms. These are analogies among pairs of items, for instance *sing* is to *sang* as *drink* is to *drank*. (8) makes this more explicit.

(8)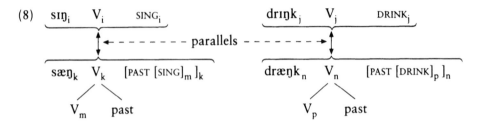

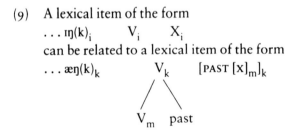

That is, the regularity is in the relation between the items, not among the items themselves. As described in section 3.3.2, this sort of regularity has been called a *lexical redundancy rule*.

A rule that expresses this regularity might be stated very approximately as (9).

(9)   A lexical item of the form
    $\ldots \text{ŋ(k)}_i$ V_i X_i
    can be related to a lexical item of the form
    $\ldots \text{æŋ(k)}_k$ V_k $[\text{PAST } [X]_m]_k$

$$V_m \quad past$$

This can be regarded as a relation between two lexical entries; notice that it has variables in phonology (indicated by "...") and in semantics ("x").[6] And indeed people have written lexical rules in such a format (including Jackendoff 1975; 1997a).

However, if Pinker and the connectionists are correct about semiproductive regularities, no rule like (9) is stored explicitly in the speaker's head. Rather, the relations in (8) are merely implicit for the speaker. They are a consequence of the way the brain stores information associatively, capitalizing on similarity. In any

---

[6] If (9) said "can be converted to" rather than "can be related to," the rule could be regarded as a derivational rule instead. Aside from this, all the conditions would be the same.

event, the pattern suggested by (9) is not a strict regularity; it is shot through with holes. Some of the *-ing/-ink* verbs have *-ung/-unk* pasts, some have regular pasts, and then there is *brought*; moreover the /ɪ/-/æ/ alternation occurs also with *swim*, which isn't covered by (9).

Where does this leave a rule like (9)? Recall from section 3.4 one of the possible views of the rules of linguists' grammars: that they are just epiphenomenal descriptions of implicit regularities in the language user's head, without explicit psychological reality. Generative grammar, of course, has always rejected such an interpretation, claiming that the rules we write are explicitly represented in the brain either as a knowledge base or in the form of the language processor. But such an interpretation can no longer be sustained for semiproductive rules such as (9): they now fall back into the despised epiphenomenal status. They are not "real" rules of grammar, but only descriptions of semi-regularities.

Always ready to turn an apparent dilemma to advantage, I would urge the view that this highlights the psychological reality of the productive rules. In the present approach, productive morphological affixes have emerged as lexical items. Thus "productive rules" are explicit, even if not exactly in the way envisioned by traditional generative grammar. By contrast, there is nothing corresponding to lexical redundancy rules in the language user's head—there are only lexical redundancies. However, this does not absolve linguists from looking for lexical redundancies; it does not make lexical redundancies "less interesting." After all, attempts to be as precise as possible about the character of semiproductive regularities have yielded valuable evidence about the design space of human linguistic competence.

6.5 Idioms

So far we have been investigating lexical items smaller than words, i.e. stems and affixes. As suggested at the outset of the chapter, the lexicon also embraces items *larger* than words, with idioms as a prime case, but also including longer stretches of memorized text. We now take a somewhat closer look at idioms (more detail appears in Jackendoff 1997a: ch. 7).

It is clear that something about idioms must be stored in long-term memory. There is no way to construct the meaning 'die' by combining the morphemes *kick*, *the*, and *bucket*. Moreover, despite a tendency among grammarians to treat idioms as a relatively marginal phenomenon, there are in fact thousands of them—probably as many as there are adjectives. So theories of grammatical structure and of processing ignore idioms at their own risk.

Idioms have been problematic to all the successive architectures adopted by Chomsky since *Aspects*. The difficulty lies in the character of lexical insertion:

words are inserted into syntactic trees under lexical categories such as N, V, and Det. Hence the grammar has to generate a VP dominating a V and a definite NP before inserting *kick*, *the*, and *bucket* individually under V, Det, and N respectively; then the semantic component has to interpret the concatenation of these three words idiomatically. This idiomatic interpretation has to come directly from the lexicon, not from the usual combinatorial interpretive process; but in the insertion of the words one by one, their unity as an idiom has been lost. So how can the lexicon record the idiom as a unit, and how can this unit be inserted into larger combinatorial structures?

One solution (Chomsky 1981: 146, n. 94) treats *kick the bucket* as a lexical verb rather than a verb phrase, giving it the internal structure shown in (10).

(10)

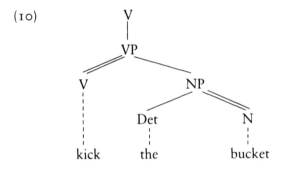

Because (10) is dominated by a V node, it can be inserted as a whole into a V position in syntax. It thus can carry its idiomatic information through to the level of semantic interpretation.

Such a solution has a number of fatal difficulties. First, as pointed out as early as Emonds (1970), there are many discontinuous idioms such as those in (11), in which a direct object intervenes between two constituents of the idiom. (*Pro_e* designates a pronoun that must be coreferential with the subject; *pro_i* designates a pronoun that must be coreferential with the NP subscripted *i*.)

(11)   take NP to task
        take NP for granted
        show NP the door
        give NP the boot
        give NP a piece of *pro_e*'s mind
        put NP_i in *pro_i*'s place

A structure like (10), in which the entire idiom is dominated by V, predicts that these idioms should instead have the form *[_V *take to task*] NP, with the direct object to the right of the entire idiom. One can save the analysis by stipulating that *to task* moves around the direct object in the course of the syntactic derivation.

And then one may try to propose a reason within Universal Grammar that would justify forcing such a movement to take place. But, it is evident that the analysis rapidly becomes forced.[7]

Section 6.1 also mentioned a second difficulty for an analysis like (10): idioms like those in (12) cannot be shoehorned into a lexical category.

(12) a. The jig is up.
      b. That's the way the cookie crumbles.
      c. The cat's got NP's tongue.

These are complete sentences; if they were inserted under V, the underlying structure of the sentence would lack a subject and hence be ill-formed.

The overwhelming generalization about idioms, in fact, is that they have the syntax of garden-variety phrases. A theory with structures like (10) has to predict that this garden-variety syntax arises by obligatorily moving everything out from under the V node into—coincidentally—its normal position.

But even this is not enough. There are a few idioms whose syntax is deviant:

(13) a. all of a sudden
      b. by and large
      c. Far be it from NP to VP.   (usually NP is *me*)
      d. How dare NP VP!

(13a, b) appear in adverbial contexts, but their syntactic structure is not that of an adverbial, nor entirely that of any other category. (13c, d) are complete sentences that cannot be stuffed into a V. Their syntax is at best a relic of some earlier stage of English, but of course they are perfectly acceptable in modern speech.

The upshot is that, although idioms must be stored, the way they must be stored cannot be reconciled with a theory in which only individual words are inserted into sentences. The obvious solution is to admit that, for instance, *kick the bucket* is a lexically stored VP. In the approach to the lexicon sketched in Chapter 5, such a solution is quite natural. (14) illustrates with the idiom *take to task*.

---

[7] Regrettably, such strategies have become so commonplace in certain circles of generative syntax that many linguists no longer recognize their unnaturalness; indeed they may even think highly of the analysis on the grounds that it shows us more about the abstractness of Universal Grammar. Such a stance tends to distance syntactic theory from psycholinguistic and developmental considerations; my overall program (see Part I) is to try to reduce that distance.

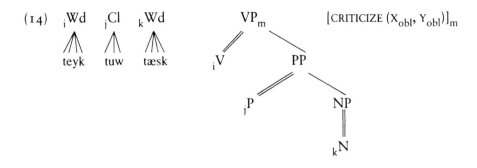

This is somewhat more elaborate than *star* and *devour* (Ch. 5, (24) and (51a)), but the similarities are clear. In particular, the argument structure is just like that of a normal verb: the two arguments in conceptual structure must be expressed, just as with *devour*; one is expressed as the subject and the other as the direct object. However, (14) has two innovations. The first is that the phonological and syntactic components of the item are larger than phonological and syntactic words respectively. Second, the subscripts are now bifurcated into pre-subscripts, which denote phonology–syntax connections, and post-subscripts, which denote syntax–semantics connections. This is necessary because an idiom does not have a standard word-by-word mapping. Here, the first word in phonology maps into the verb, the clitic maps into the preposition, and the second word maps into the noun. But these individual words do not have meanings of their own: only the whole verb phrase does—it means "criticize," as notated by the subscript *m*. That is just what makes (14) an idiom.

The lexical structure in (14) permits a simple account of the idiom's discontinuity. The idiom's second semantic argument maps into an NP in syntax, perhaps automatically, perhaps by strict subcategorization (I leave the question open). Because of the Syntactic Argument Ordering Constraint (Ch. 5, (47)) this NP must precede the PP that is inherently part of the idiom. In turn, the corresponding phonological material falls between *take* and *to task* because of the NP's syntactic position.

The non-homogeneous subscripting across components in (14) bears an interesting parallel to irregular verb forms such as *ate* (7). There we found a regular compositional syntax–semantics connnection but an irregular phonology–syntax connection: the syntactic and semantic units cannot be discriminated in the phonological structure. Idioms like (14) have a regular phonology–syntax connection but an irregular syntax–semantics connection: the words do not contribute individually to the meaning. Thus the two cases are in a way mirror images.

Three important questions are always posed of theories of idioms, and they must be addressed here. The first is why virtually all idioms have perfectly normal syntactic structure, with only rare exceptions such as (13). I would propose an interesting parallel with morphology: apart from their semantics, idioms are like stored regular morphological combinations. A particularly good analogy might be obligatorily plural nouns. For example, *scissors* is morphophonologically regular but does not denote multiple objects (rather an object with multiple parts); and *troops* (in the sense 'soldiers') has no singular form that means 'soldier.' These are morphological idioms with regular morphological form.

Still, the question arises of why there shouldn't be more syntactically *irregular* idioms like (13). One reason is probably that idioms are historical developments from syntactically compositional phrases. Another possibility, suggested by Jackendoff (1975), is that the general principles of free composition, which govern online construction, also place pressure on stored items to conform as well. We will return to this issue in section 6.8.

The second question is why *kick the bucket* cannot form a passive or other standard deformations: *the bucket was kicked by John* has only the literal interpretation. Chomsky has suggested (e.g. 1981) that idioms are somehow "frozen" in their deep structure form. For instance, the NP in (10) is inaccessible to passive because it is inside the V. However, such a solution would preclude moving the PP *to task* out of V and around the direct object. Much worse, as pointed out by Nunberg et al. (1994), many idioms appear only in heavily "transformed" versions. (15) gives some examples.

(15)   NP has it made.   [passive]
        NP is fit to be tied.   [passive]
        play hard to get   ["tough-movement"]
        hard to take   ["tough-movement"]
        a tough nut to crack   ["tough-movement", infinitival relative]
        How do you do?   [Wh-movement]
        (Now) NP$_e$'s got NP$_j$ where *pro$_e$* wants *pro$_j$*.
                                              [Wh-movement, free relative]
        NP$_e$'s not what *pro$_e$*'s cracked up to be.   [Wh-movement, free relative]

This shows that idioms must be specified in the lexicon for their *surface structure*. The best way to accomplish this is for the grammar to check lexical items against surface structures. In a theory with derivational rules (e.g. all of Chomsky's theories throughout the years), this amounts to what has been called "late lexical insertion" (section 5.7): lexical items are inserted not at the initial point in syntactic generation, but after all movement has taken place. Of course, in a theory lacking derivational rules, where surface structure is the *only* syntactic level, lexical insertion/checking/licensing at surface structure is the only option.

There are, however, idioms that do permit a degree of syntactic freedom, for instance *He let the cat out of the bag* vs. *The cat was let out of the bag*; *We must draw the line somewhere* vs. *The line must be drawn somewhere*. It has frequently been observed (Bresnan 1978; Ruwet 1991; Nunberg et al. 1994) that the mobile portion of such idioms has a sort of metaphorical semantic interpretation: *the cat* is a secret, *the line* is a distinction. By contrast, *the bucket* in *kick the bucket* has no such interpretation. The key to mobility appears to lie in the partially compositional semantics of the idiom. A proper solution is beyond the scope of this chapter (but see Jackendoff 1997a: 166–70 for a proposal).

The third question about idioms is whether a structure like (14) might be too specific. Perhaps, for example, one should remove all indication of syntactic order, since it is predictable from the phrase structure rules in any event. And perhaps one should replace the phonological content with pointers to the lexical items *take*, *to*, and *task*, which would provide the idiom with its phonology "on the cheap."

I would see such moves as reflections of the impulse to make the lexicon consist only of non-redundant, unpredictable information. We have already implicitly rejected this position. Consider stored words with regular morphology: they can be generated by free combination, so they are totally redundant. What would it mean to remove all the redundant information from stored regulars? It would amount to deriving them by rules alone—which is exactly what is denied in claiming they are stored! The case of idioms is similar. Parallel to the predictable order of stem and affixes in stored regulars is the predictable word order of idioms. Parallel to the predictable phonological content of stored regulars, which comes directly from the stored stem and affix, is the predictable phonological content of idioms, which comes from the constituent words. I conclude that if such redundancy is tolerable in stored regulars, it should be no problem in idioms. We return to this issue in section 6.8.

6.6 A class of constructional idioms

I now want to move from idioms like those in (11) to a broader class of lexically specified VPs that include free variable positions. All the members of this broader class have the syntactic structure shown in (16).

(16)

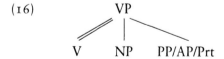

They vary in which parts of the VP are open positions. The idioms in (11) are a subclass that has a specified V and a specified PP but leaves the NP open. We can schematize this subclass as (17), notating the specified idiomatic elements in upper case and the freely chosen elements in lower case (a fuller formalization is as in (14)).

(17)   [$_{VP}$ V np PP]: take NP to task, put NP$_i$ in *pro$_i$*'s place, ...

The familiar verb-particle idioms such as *look NP up*, *screw NP up*, and *put NP off* are a variant of (17) in which the PP is replaced by a particle (Prt). There are also many idioms in which the NP and P are specified and the object of the PP is left open:

(18)   [$_{VP}$ V NP [$_{PP}$ P np]]: take unfair advantage of NP, make much of NP, take umbrage at NP, ...

A much less remarked case (Jackendoff 1997b) is a class of expressions exemplified by *sing one's head off* and *argue one's heart out*. In these, *NP's head off* and *NP's heart out* are fixed, and NP must be a pronoun coreferential with the subject. But the verb is totally free, within pragmatic constraints. One can *talk one's head off*; *drink one's head off*; *cook, knit, swim*, or even *program one's head off*. The most striking constraint is that the verb must have no syntactic argument of its own aside from the subject: although one can *read one's head off*, one cannot be said to **read mysteries one's head off*. Rather, *head* appears to occupy the direct object position, though it is hardly the object of the verb. And *off* is evidently in the particle position, just as in *look NP up*. Another member of this class is *V up a storm*, with the particle in its other possible position.

The meaning of all three of these expressions is roughly 'do to excess.'[8] One would not want to say that all their possible combinations with verbs are listed in the lexicon: that would in effect say that every time one learns a new verb *V*, one also must add to one's lexicon *V pro$_e$'s head off*, *V pro$_e$'s heart out*, and *V up a storm*. This situation should sound familiar from the discussion of regular morphology in section 6.2.1; we are again dealing with the free combination of stored elements. One element is the verb. Because of the idiomatic meaning, the other element has to be *pro$_e$'s head off*. In order to account for the fact that this element occupies positions that would normally be complements of the verb, we have to schematize it as (19).

(19)   [$_{VP}$ v NP PRT]: V pro$_e$'s head/butt off, V pro$_e$'s heart out
       [$_{VP}$ v PRT NP]: V up a storm
            'V excessively'

---

8 One might be tempted to think this construction is a "metaphorical" version of the resultative construction, parallel to, say, *pull the bottle's top off*. But even if it were, the fact that it is a fixed idiomatic unit means that it has to be listed in the lexicon as such; it cannot be derived online like many other resultatives. So the issue is precisely *how* it is listed in the lexicon.

That is, these expressions are VPs in which the NP and PRT are lexically fixed and the V is a free variable. We should also note the idiom *eat one's heart out*, which has the form of (19) but a fixed verb and an idiomatic meaning 'experience envy.'

The next case has a fixed NP and a free V and PP: the *way*-construction (Jackendoff 1990a; Marantz 1992; Goldberg 1995), exemplified by (20). Here the verb can be just about anything that denotes a continuous process, and the PP can be any expression of path in space, time, or even metaphor.

(20) Bill belched his way out of the restaurant.
      Frank drank his way across the country.
      Sue sang her way through dinner.
      Sosa and McGwire have homered their way into the hearts of America.
      Chew your way to a cleaner, fresher mouth.   [ad for gum]

Again it is crucial that the verb have no syntactic argument of its own aside from the subject: one cannot *drink beer one's way across the country* or *hit home runs one's way into the hearts of America*. Evidently, parallel to the class in (19), pro_e's *way* occupies direct object position.

The meaning of the construction is roughly 'traverse the path PP while/by doing V.' (Goldberg 1995 has a detailed discussion of the semantics.) Again, it would not make sense to say each verb combines with *way* "in the lexicon" to form an idiom; this would mean that when one learns a new intransitive verb, one also adds to memory its *way* form (in addition to its *heart out* and *up a storm* forms!). Rather, we are again dealing with free combination, this time combining a verb and a PP with a lexical item of the structure (21).

(21) [$_{VP}$ v NP pp]: V pro_e's way PP, 'go PP while/by V-ing'

This construction too has more specialized versions, including *wend one's way PP* (where the verb *wend* occurs only in this construction), *worm one's way PP* (where *worm* occurs as a verb only in this construction), and the metaphorical *sleep one's way to the top*.

This case blatantly violates the Head Constraint of section 5.9. The PP is a syntactic argument of the VP. But it does not express a semantic argument of the verb. Rather, it expresses a semantic argument of the *construction*—as does the verb. Moreover, the phrase headed by *way* is a syntactic argument, specifically a direct object, but it is not a semantic argument of anything. In order to admit such cases we must treat the Head Constraint as a default rather than a rigid condition.

The next case is exemplified in (22) (more details in Jackendoff 1997b).

(22)   We're twisting the night away.
       Hank drank the whole afternoon away.
       Kathy happily knitted two hours away.

Here the verb is followed by a noun phrase that expresses a time period, plus the particle *away*. Clearly a time period is not a normal semantic argument for the verbs in (22)—one cannot *twist the night*, *drink the afternoon* (except perhaps metaphorically), or *knit two hours* (except in the different sense *knit for two hours*). As in the previous cases, the verb cannot take an object of its own: *drink beer the whole afternoon away*, *knit a sweater two hours away*. The reason is that direct object position is occupied by the time period.

The meaning of the construction is roughly 'spend time period doing V'. By now the scenario is familiar: the best account is not to say that the verb takes the object and the particle as free variables. Rather, the construction is a VP that takes the verb and the NP as arguments, with the NP expressing a semantic argument of the type 'time period.' Thus this is another violation of the Head Constraint. The only phonologically specified part of the construction is the particle *away*, which corresponds to a syntactic argument but not a semantic argument.

(23)   [$_{VP}$ v np PRT]: V NP[time period] away, 'spend NP V-ing'

Again there are specialized cases that use this frame: *while NP[time] away* and *fritter NP away* both have verbs that occur only in this construction (though *fritter* permits a wider range of NPs than just time periods).

At this point we have seen nearly every possible combination of specified constituents and free variables in structure (16). One might wonder whether there is also a situation in which the structure is composed entirely of free variables. This appears to be an appropriate solution for the well-known resultative construction, illustrated in (24).

(24)   Wilma watered the tulips flat.
       Clyde cooked the pot black.
       Drive your engine clean.   [ad for gasoline]

The verb *water* has a semantic argument expressed as a direct object: the thing on which water is sprinkled. But the further result, the tulips acquiring some property (besides becoming wet), is not part of the verb's ordinary meaning. And although one can *cook food* and *drive a car*, one cannot *cook a pot* or *drive a car engine*: these verbs do not license semantic arguments of these types. Thus something special is happening in both syntax and semantics when these verbs are followed by a direct object plus a predicate adjective.

Various discussions in the literature (e.g. Levin and Rappaport Hovav 1991) treat the formation of resultatives as a "lexical rule" that changes and/or adds to the argument structure of the verb. Thus in addition to the regular verb *cook NP* 'cause NP to become cooked', there is also "in the lexicon" a further verb *cook NP AP* 'cause NP to become AP by cooking (with it)'. As usual, to say this is "in the lexicon" in the sense "stored in long-term memory" makes the otiose claim that every appropriate verb carries around yet another extra argument structure frame. The present approach (advocated also by Goldberg 1995 and Jackendoff 1990a) is to say that the lexicon contains an idiomatic resultative construction, and the meaning of (24) is the product of freely composing this construction with four semantic arguments, expressed by the subject, the verb, the object, and the AP. The construction itself comprises nothing but a syntactic frame associated with a meaning—yet another violation of the Head Constraint.

(25)   [$_{VP}$ v np ap], 'cause NP to become AP by V-ing ((with) it)'

This lexical item has no phonology. It is just a pairing of a syntactic and semantic structure. However, this should not be too disturbing. We already know of the existence of other such "defective" lexical items from the discussion in section 5.7: *hello* and *ouch* lack syntax, and *do*-support *do* and expletive *it* lack semantics. So in principle there should be nothing objectionable about a lexical item that lacks phonology. (A more detailed formalization of the resultative appears in section 12.2.)

To sum up, in each of these cases—the *one's head off* construction, the *way* construction, the *time away* construction, and the resultative—we have come to regard the construction not as a lexical rule that creates new verb argument structures "in the lexicon," but rather as a lexical item in its own right that undergoes free combination with verbs. What makes these cases unusual is that the verb does not determine the VP's syntactic argument structure. Rather, the construction itself determines the VP's syntactic argument structure, in violation of the Head Constraint, and the verb satisfies a free position in the construction.

We have still omitted one combination of specified and free constituents: a specified verb with free positions to its right. But this is precisely the case of a verb that strictly subcategorizes its syntactic arguments. For example, as we saw in section 5.9.2, *express* requires an NP argument, even though semantically a clause would be equally appropriate (26b):

(26)   a. John expressed $\begin{cases} \text{his disappointment.} \\ \text{*that he was disappointed.} \end{cases}$

       b. What John expressed was that he was disappointed.

In the *Aspects* framework, strict subcategorization is regarded as a feature on a verb, say [+__ NP] for *express*; various other treatments have appeared over the years. The present approach suggests that we can analyze *express* as having the lexical structure shown in (27).

(27)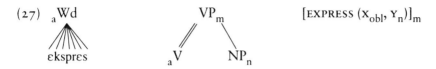

This lexical VP has a phonological reflex only in the V position (the only syntactic position that has a pre-subscript to phonological structure). So on the surface it looks like it is just a verb. But it is not: it is actually a lexical VP with an open object position.[9]

A similar approach recommends itself for governed prepositions. For instance, *depend (on)* is like the idioms in (18) except that it lacks the NP argument.

(28)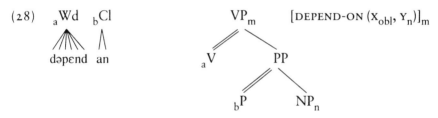

To sum up, we have discovered a cline of lexical VPs, going from verbs that obligatorily subcategorize complements, through verbs with governed prepositions, through idioms, through constructional idioms that specify part of the VP's complement, to the resultative. Each step from one to the next is perfectly natural, but at the ends of the cline we have entities that appear entirely different—and have regularly been so analyzed in the literature. The present approach permits us to see subcategorization by a verb, by an idiom, and by a construction as falling under a common formalization: leaving positions open in a lexical VP. (Williams 1994 and Langacker 1998 point out the existence of such clines in other areas of the lexicon.)

---

[9] I had better say why (26b) is grammatical despite the absence of a syntactic object. Under standard assumptions, the object position is in fact occupied by an NP: a trace or its equivalent, bound to the word *what*. The semantics of the trace, however, comes via its being equated with the clause *that he was disappointed*.

Incidentally, the second semantic argument in (27) is simply co-subscripted with the syntactic argument, instead of being marked optional or obligatory as in previous examples. There are probably better realizations of this detail.

6.7 Generalizing the notion of construction

The last section described a family of constructional idioms in English in which the main verb of the sentence serves as an argument. Most of these idioms are not attested in other languages. The resultative, the most intensively investigated of them, seems to appear only in a relatively limited range of languages (Levin and Rappaport Hovav 1991). The others have hardly been looked for (though Toivonen 1999 finds a close parallel to the *way* construction in Swedish, using a reflexive instead of *way*). But perhaps other languages have construction types not attested in English. Noun Incorporation (section 4.3) might be such a case. Nikanne (2000b) offers some possibilities for Finnish, and Maling and Sigurjónsdóttir (1997) for Icelandic.

Derivational (i.e. Chomskyan) generative grammar has discouraged recognizing constructions as of any theoretical interest—for a principled reason. In this approach, a construction such as passive, question, or free relative is the product of a sequence of movement rules applying to an underlying structure. By definition, the application of a movement rule is free: it is determined only by the rule's own input constraints, not by what sequence of prior movements gave rise to that input. Therefore the emergence of a complex construction can be regarded only as the application of a fortuitous sequence of independent movement rules. In later versions of Chomsky's framework (e.g. Chomsky 1981), a number of interacting sets of constraints together constrain the outputs of derivations. In either case, constructions must be regarded as epiphenomena: the theoretical interest can lie only in the constraints on application of individual movement rules.

By contrast, in the present approach, constructions turn out to be slightly unusual but perfectly respectable lexical items that combine with ordinary words according to ordinary procedures. As further evidence for this alternative, we observe (with Fillmore et al. 1988) that English has some constructions that, like the idioms in (13), are syntactically deviant.

(29) a. One more beer and I'm leaving.
          (General form: NP conj S)   (Culicover 1972; Culicover and
          Jackendoff 1997)
      b. The more you eat, the fatter you get.
          (General form: [the [comparative phrase]$_i$ [$_s$ . . . t_i . . .]],
          [the [comparative phrase]$_j$ [$_s$ . . .t_j . . .]]])
          (Fillmore et al. 1988; McCawley 1988; Culicover and Jackendoff
          1999)
      c. Off with his head! Up to your room with you!
          (General form: PP with NP!)   (Jackendoff 1973)

    d. week by week; book after book; bumper to bumper
      (General form: N P N)[10]   (Williams 1994; Oehrle 1998)

These are far from "core" constructions of English in Chomsky's (1981) sense, but they are used all the time and must be learned by the child. Universal Grammar must therefore make provision for them. Once one bluntly admits the possibility in the grammar of such "syntactic junk"—constructions that cannot be derived in a well-regimented way from any standard structure—it is easier to condone better-behaved constructional idioms such as those in the previous section. (Syntactic "blends" of the sort discussed by Bolinger (1961) might fall in this category as well.)

    This approach leads to a number of theoretical issues for future research. The first is: How structurally complex can constructions be? This issue has been addressed to some extent in the literature on idioms (e.g. Bresnan 1982b; Marantz 1984); I do not know if it has been addressed in terms of the broader class of syntactic constructions. Going to extreme possibilities, it might be intriguing to regard poetic meters and verse forms as phonological constructions that must unify with a text. And since we spoke earlier of song lyrics being stored as large lexical items, we might consider treating as constructions those song lyrics that contain a variable to be filled creatively in successive verses, such as the children's game song (30).

(30)   Let everyone VP like me!
       Let everyone VP like me!
       Come on and join into the game,
       You'll find that it's always the same.
          (where VP is a one- or two-syllable VP naming an action, e.g. *clap hands, laugh, fall down*)

    Another issue is how far the constructional approach extends into "core" grammar. Construction Grammar claims that *all* syntax is built from constructions clipped together. Goldberg's (1995) and Langacker's (1987; 1992) versions of Construction Grammar claim that all syntactic structures are form–meaning pairings, and therefore inherently meaningful; Fillmore and Kay (1993) are more agnostic on the meaningfulness of constructions. My own preference

---

[10] This construction actually falls into "families," some of which are productive and some of which are not. A few cases with non-identical nouns must be listed as individual idioms: *cheek by jowl, hand over fist, head over heels*, etc. Otherwise the nouns must be identical. N *after* N is productive and can appear both in NP and adverbial positions; its pronominal form is *one after another*. N *by* N, N *to* N, and N *for* N are also productive and can be used adverbially or as prenominal adjectives; their pronominal forms are *one by/to/for one*.

(Jackendoff 1996a) is to think that not all syntactic configurations are inherently meaningful—that the relation between form and meaning is often more flexible than in constructions like those we have seen here. For instance, sections 5.8 and 5.9 argued that the range of meanings associated with transitive and ditransitive verb constructions and with N-of-NP constructions is too great for the meaning to be attributed to the construction itself. Rather, all the semantic relations come from the head verb or noun, and the construction is merely a form to be filled.

The view of constructions as lexical items, however, suggests an alternative possibility. If there are "defective" constructions like the resultative that lack phonology, why couldn't there be "doubly defective" constructions that lack both phonology and semantics? Such constructions would be phrase structure rules! For example, (16), the expansion of VP into V plus NP plus PP/AP/Prt, could be such a construction. It could be clipped together with other lexical "treelets" (for example the expansion of S into NP plus VP and the expansion of NP into Det plus N) to form standard phrase-structure trees.

This manner of viewing tree construction begins to blur the distinction between lexical items and what have traditionally been regarded as rules of grammar. It reflects the same spirit as our treatment of regular morphology not in terms of rules that add affixes, but rather as free combination of lexically stored parts. In this approach, the only "rule of grammar" is UNIFY PIECES, and all the pieces are stored in a common format that permits unification.[11] Ordinary words, which encode word-sized linked units of phonology, syntax, and semantics, are on the other end of a scale (or better, at an opposite corner of a multidimensional space) from phrase-structure rules, which encode phrase-sized pieces of syntax without any associated phonology or semantics. But we can attest every step on the scale in between them—and most of these steps are in fact types of unit that have raised difficulties for standard syntactocentric architectures. It is too soon to tell how this program of consolidation will work out, but it sets an interesting agenda for future research.[12]

---

[11] In a sense this proposal thus begins to converge with the Minimalist Program, which creates structure by means of the single operation Merge, and with Chomsky's view (1995) that all differences among languages are encoded in the lexicon. A major difference, of course, is that the present approach has no counterpart to the Minimalist Program's operation Move—not to mention the crucial architectural differences discussed in Ch. 5. A much closer parallel, though, is with unification-based grammars, especially HPSG and Construction Grammar. See section 6.11 for some comparison.

[12] An important problem for the constructional approach that has not to my knowledge been solved satisfactorily is how constructional idioms compose with each other. Examples like (i), a middle construction based on a resultative, and (ii), a relative clause based on a comparative correlative, are sufficiently remote from everyday experience that one would guess that their constructional properties must be composed online.

Having admitted phrasal structures as possible constituents of lexical items, we also open up the possibility of formulating interface constraints as "defective" lexical items. For instance, rules (15) and (19) in Chapter 5, which relate linear order and intonational constituency in phonology to linear order and constituent structure in syntax, are readily reformulated in the terms used in this chapter. Again it is a major challenge to future research to see if such a program can be carried through, but the potential rewards of theoretical consolidation ought to make the effort worthwhile.

Among the interface constraints might be certain default principles that add independent biases of "constructional meaning" to subject and object position when the verb leaves the option open. (31) states two (not mutually exclusive) possibilities.

(31) a. *Preferably*:
        Subject corresponds to Agent; Object corresponds to Patient (entity affected by an action)
      b. *Preferably*:
        Subject corresponds to Figure; Object corresponds to Ground

The effects of (31a) are seen for instance in so-called "spray-load" alternations, illustrated in (32) (Pinker 1989; Levin and Rappaport Hovav 1991).

(32) a. We sprayed paint on the wall.
        We loaded furniture on the truck.
      b. We sprayed the wall with paint.
        We loaded the truck with furniture.

These differ subtly in what is taken to be affected by the action, with somewhat greater emphasis on the paint and the furniture in (32a) and on the wall and the truck in (32b). This can be attributed to the effect of the Patient condition in (31a) on an otherwise ambiguous situation.[13]

The effects of (31b) are seen with so-called "symmetric predicates" such as *resemble* and *be similar*. Compare (33a) to (33b, c).

(i)   That pot doesn't cook black so easily.
(ii) This is a book that the more you study, the more confused you get.

In the traditional derivational formalism, of course, constructions like these arise from the successive application of movement rules. But successive application is not available in a constraint-based formalism.

[13] Much more has been made of this alternation, e.g. by Tenny (1994), who claims that the direct object strongly influences the aspectuality of the event. Jackendoff (1996c) refutes most aspects of this claim.

(33) a. China and Vietnam $\begin{cases} \text{resemble each other.} \\ \text{are similar to each other.} \end{cases}$

　　　b. China resembles/is similar to Vietnam.

　　　c. Vietnam resembles/is similar to China.

(33b, c) are not synonymous; (33a) seems neutral between them (Talmy 1978; Gleitman et al. 1996). The difference in (33b, c) concerns which of the two entities is taken as the standard (or "ground") against which the other (the "figure") is measured. Gleitman et al. (1996) argue that this element of the interpretation is due to a bias introduced by principle (31b), not to an inherent asymmetry in the seemingly symmetrical predicates themselves. By contrast, (33a) introduces no syntactic differentiation between *China* and *Vietnam*, so there is no figure–ground differentiation either.[14]

　　Let me sum up this series of rapid developments. We have come to envision a major consolidation of productive combinatorial phenomena. We have found that the formalism of interface rules among parallel phonological, syntactic, and semantic structures can be adapted to words, productive and semiproductive morphology, idioms, constructions, phrase structure rules, and phrasal interface constraints. With luck, then, the only *procedural* rule will be UNIFY ("clip" structures together). The counterpart of a traditional "rule of grammar" in this system is a lexicalized grammatical pattern with one or more variables in it. In order to retain the term "rule" in the traditional sense, I will henceforth refer to such lexicalized patterns as "l-rules" ("lexicalized rules") when necessary.

---

[14] A less clear but possible case concerns two related classes of verbs that have been the topic of much discussion over the years (e.g. Postal 1971; Belletti and Rizzi 1988; Grimshaw 1990; Pesetsky 1994). Note that the pairs in (i) are close to synonymous.

(i)　a. Jane likes/fears cats.

　　　b. Cats please/frighten Jane.

The assumption is usually that a semantic difference between these verbs predicts their syntactic difference. Yet the difference is relatively subtle. One possibility is that the conceptual relation expressed by these verbs yields an inconclusive or unstable result in the Linking Hierarchy (Ch. 5, (50)), and that particular verbs stipulate one order or the other rather arbitrarily. The order chosen then biases the interpretation so as to be maximally in tune with the Linking Hierarchy and principle (31a). In particular, order (ia) shades towards a sense of Jane as Recipient of impressions coming to her (i.e. *cats* as Theme, lower on the hierarchy); whereas order (ib) brings out the sense of *cats* as Agent, having a psychological effect on Jane as Patient. It is not clear to me whether this approach can account for the multitude of curious syntactic effects associated with this construction (see references above). But it bears examination as a possible instance when syntactic argument position is stipulated by a verb instead of being predicted by the verb's semantics—and then the syntactic position position biases the semantics as it does in (32) and (33).

6.8 The status of inheritance hierarchies

We are now in a position to return to two questions concerning idioms: How does the grammar/lexicon capture the redundancy of idioms? And how do phrase structure rules place pressure on idioms to be regular?

Return to our example *take to task*, repeated as (34). It shares most of its parts with one or another of the lexical entries in (35).

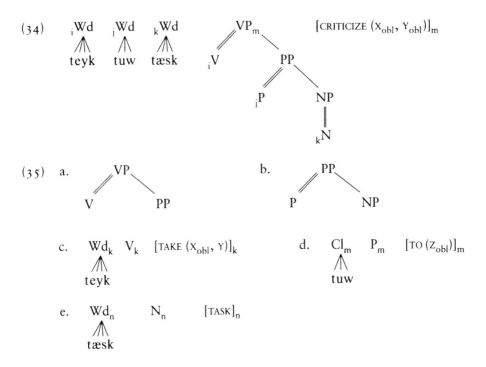

The only part of the idiom that is *not* redundant with some other lexical item is the connection to the idiomatic semantics CRITICIZE. In fact, the redundancy goes deeper than sharing phonological and syntactic form: the idiom's past tense is *took to task* rather than *taked to task*. This shows that in an important sense the idiom is borrowing not just the phonological form *take*, but the *word take*.

A parallel problem arises with irregular verbs, but in mirror image. Take even a completely suppletive pair like *go–went*. Despite its novel phonology, we know that *went* borrows its syntax–semantics connection from the verb *go* and doesn't just repeat similar semantic material, because every idiomatic use of *go* (*go berserk*, *go well with NP* ('suit NP'), etc.) still has the past tense *went*. And we know that *went* borrows from the syntactic past tense as well—not the semantic past—because the use of syntactic past tense for conditional (*If I went berserk, what would you do?*) still yields *went*, not *goed*.

How does the lexicon capture this redundancy, this "borrowing"? One approach, which might be associated with Chomsky's view of the lexicon as a repository of all and only the exceptions of the language, would attempt to bleed all the redundancy out of (34) and encode it as a minimal skeleton from which everything else could be predicted. The difficulty with this approach is in determining what could possibly be left to connect to CRITICIZE, such that one could predict it would be pronounced "take to task." Jackendoff (1997a: section 5.6) shows, for a different case in the same spirit, that it is impossible to take all the redundancy out and still retain a sufficiently coherent structure. There is no place one can draw the line and say "These redundant parts we will take out, but these we will leave in in the interests of coherence." I conclude that this approach cannot be carried out technically, whatever its intuitive appeal.

An alternative in the literature (Pollard and Sag 1994; Goldberg 1995; Michaelis and Lambrecht 1996) appeals to "inheritance," whereby a more highly specified or highly structured item "inherits" structure from less specified or less structured items. Under this approach, we would say that (34) inherits most of its structure from (35a–e); but not all its structure is inherited, since the syntax–semantics links in (35c–e) are overridden. Similarly, *went* inherits its structure from *go* and *past* but overrides the expected phonology–syntax connection. (This would also be true of *sang*, *drank*, etc.) A non-idiomatic stored phrase such as *happy birthday* and a stored regular verb such as *dreamed* (which must be stored in order to compete with *dreamt*) of course inherit everything. The intuitive idea, then, is that the more an item inherits from other stored items, the simpler it is to store.

Inheritance is actually a special case of taxonomic categorization, often expressed in terms of a semantic network along familiar lines like (36).

(36)

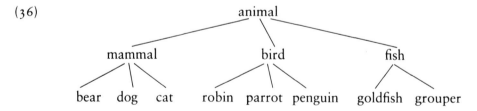

Each element in the hierarchy inherits by default all properties of the elements that dominate it. The inheritance is only a default because, for instance, although birds typically fly, penguins don't. Semantic networks in the literature usually express a strict taxonomy like (36). But it is also possible to set up networks with multiple inheritance, for instance (37), where *pet* is an alternative classification of *animal*, orthogonal to the *mammal–bird–fish* dimension.

(37)

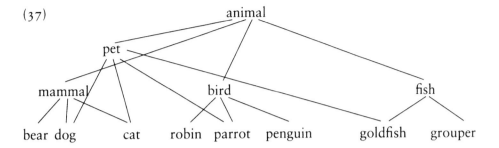

The inheritance properties of *take to task* and *went* can be set up in this format too:

(38)   a.

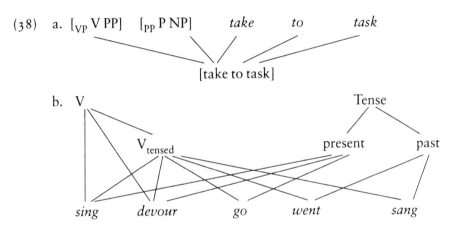

b.

Hence, as many have noted (e.g. Lakoff 1987; Pinker 1999), the hierarchical relations among stored lexical items fall under more general brain mechanisms involved in any sort of memory. This accounts for the fact that lexical memory displays prototypicality effects (some members of a category being more central and others being more peripheral) and family resemblance effects (there being no single set of features shared by all members of a category and no nonmembers). Such a connection permits a welcome reduction of the aspects of language that the theory needs to claim are special.[15]

Now we can ask, just as we did with lexical redundancy rules, whether the inheritance links in semantic networks are explicit in memory, or whether they are epiphenomenal consequences of the nature of neural instantiation of memories. I leave this important issue open. My inclination is to think that inheritance hierarchies, like lexical redundancies, are implicit—that there are no overt

---

[15] Some people (including Lakoff) go on to assert that this shows that there is nothing special about language. I hasten to disagree. Recalling the discussion of special versus general capacities in section 4.5, we can conclude only that there is *less* that is special about language.

inheritance hierarchies in the brain, only inheritance. My sense is that inherit-ance is not very well understood formally yet, particularly in this more general psychological context.

Next we return to the question of why the vast majority of idioms should have perfectly ordinary syntactic structure. Section 6.5 suggested somewhat cryptically that phrase-structure rules not only act as vehicles for free combina-tion but also exert pressure for structuring stored lexical items. This suggestion does not make a lot of sense within the traditional view of phrase structure rules, in which they have nothing whatsoever to do with the lexicon. But in the present context it suddenly looks more natural. A phrase-structure rule is a lexical item with variables in it; free combination is achieved by attaching further structure to the variables. At the same time, as we have just seen, phrase-structure l-rules such as (35a, b) are sitting in the lexicon, available for other lexical items to inherit properties from them. A syntactically regular idiom thus inherits a great deal of its structure and is hence simpler than a syntactically irregular one.

A parallel situation arises in phonology. Principles of syllable structure enable speakers both to syllabify incoming signals online and to constrain stored words. In addition, speakers can use these principles to make distinctions among putative words, for example in Halle's well-known contrast between the possible English word *blick* and the impossible English word *bnick*. And they exert a pressure on the phonological form of borrowings; for instance *Dvorak* is pronounced in English with three syllables in order to avoid the onset /dv/, which is perfectly fine in the original Czech but ungrammatical in English. Moreover, just as there are rare idioms with syntactic violations, there are rare words with ungrammatical syllable structure, for example *kvetch* (pronounced /kfeč / in my dialect).

The claim, then, is that principles of free composition act also as constraints on stored items, both in syntax and phonology. This double role falls out rather naturally in the present approach; it is less natural in traditional approaches (including even Pinker's), where regular rules are entirely distinct from the lexicon.

I am must admit to being uneasy with claiming that the pressure on lexical items from regular l-rules plus historical contingency are together enough to account for the overwhelming syntactic regularity of idioms. Historical contin-gencies surely are responsible for some *ir*regular idioms, such as *far be it from me to VP*, in the same way as they are responsible for the irregular and semi-regular verbs of English (Pinker 1999). But in order to answer whether inher-itance is enough to account for the regularities, we may have to go beyond lin-guistics to explore the general properties of semantic memory. Conversely, evidence from lexical memory can now be brought to bear on the properties of general categorization. I take such potential unification to be a reason for optimism, as it draws a principled connection between two pre-existing robust lines of research.

6.9 Issues of acquisition

Finally we can come back to an important issue raised toward the end of section 6.3:

How do language learners tell the difference between productive and semi-productive processes?

To review the position so far: the difference between semi-regular and regular patterns of morphology is that items in a semi-regular pattern are simply stored, and all the relations among them are implicit. By contrast, regular patterns are distinguished by having an extra item in the lexicon, an l-rule such as the suffix -*d*, with a variable in it. The variable enables the affix to unify with other pieces of structure. The previous section has added a new piece to this story: stored regulars inherit structure from such items.

How does this bear on acquisition? In order to make the question a bit more vivid, let me offer yet another case of contrast between productive and semi-productive morphology, this time in the system of English verb–particle combinations. A curious subclass of idiomatic verb–particle combinations appears to have become semi-productive in the past thirty years. They all mean roughly 'go into an unusual mental state'; the particle is always *out*. Curiously, the "verb" need not be a verb or even an independently attested word. The class is semi-productive because each example (and its meaning) must be learned individually, hence lexically listed. (The judgments of relative recency are only my best guesses; and speakers may differ on their judgments of transitivity.)

(39) a. Intransitives
            [older examples] pass out, black out, conk out, fink out, crap out, chicken out; [more recent] flake out, zonk out, zone out, bliss out, flip out, space out, phase out, crump out, veg out, chill out
        b. Transitives
            [older] knock NP out, bum NP out, fake NP out; [more recent] gross NP out, weird NP out, creep NP out
        c. Intransitive or transitive
            [older] burn (NP) out, poop (NP) out, tucker (NP) out; [more recent] freak (NP) out, wig (NP) out, stress (NP) out, mellow (NP) out

Another apparently recent class involving the particle *out* is totally productive. For example, if I have been knitting or programming for the last six hours straight, I may say (40).

(40)   I'm (all) knitted/programmed out.

But this odd combination is not confined to verbs. If I've drunk fourteen cups of coffee in the course of a morning I might utter (41a), and if I've watched fourteen Edward G. Robinson movies in a row I might even utter (41b).

(41)   a. I'm (all) coffeed out.
       b. I'm Edward G. Robinsoned out.

The model for this construction is rather clear: it is an extension of *tired out*, *worn out*, *burned out*, and so forth. But as in other productive constructions, one does not need to learn which verbs and nouns can be substituted into it. What would seem to be stored in the lexicon for this case is an idiomatic construction, an l-rule containing variables; its syntactic form is roughly (42a) and its meaning (42b).

(42)   a. $[_{AP}$ V/N + -d $[_{Prt}$ out]]
       b. 'worn out from too much V-ing/too much N'

So the question is: how does the language learner distinguish between the productivity of this case and the altogether similar class in (39), which remains only semi-productive? Notice that *neither* of these patterns is especially frequent; my guess is that if anything the semi-regular one is the more frequent of the two. How does it come about that only the pattern in (40)–(41) acquires a schema with a variable?

At the outset, of course, the child has no idea what any of the l-rules are, so we must suppose that the child stores everything. Taking the connectionist approach to heart, we may further suppose that, due to the characteristics of memory, implicit relations of similarity develop spontaneously in the course of storing everything. That is, nothing further need be said about semi-regular patterns.[16]

Something extra has to happen for the regular patterns. They require a further sort of learning process, one that attempts to generalize stored items and extract explicit patterns containing typed variables. Without such a pattern, the language user is restricted to using stored forms and word-by-word analogy. By

---

[16] A reminder, though: an unadorned network model is not sufficient. As Pinker and colleagues have observed, we need at the very least the notion of a discrete lexical entry—not just a string of sounds—to which syntactic category and meaning can be associated.

contrast, when a pattern with a variable develops, the relation among the stored items "goes productive": the pattern can participate in free combination with other lexical items that satisfy its typed variables, and new combinations need no longer be stored.

As we can see from the range of phenomena treated in this chapter, such an approach can apply to all scales of the grammar, from syllable structure to phrase structure, with morphology in between. It applies as well to the learning of idioms and constructions.[17] That is, as Culicover (1999) puts it, rule learning is accomplished by the same process as word learning—because both are types of lexical item. The main difference is the extent to which specific material is replaced by variables.

The process of extracting a pattern that can "go productive" is information-theoretically equivalent to the traditional conception of learning a rule. The same questions about the distribution of the input arise, the same constraints on the child apply. The major difference is in the formal apparatus. Here, stored items and rules are of the same formal character; there is no epistemological divide between the form of stored items and the form of rules. The only innovation necessary in the learning theory is a way to learn variables from instances—which is needed in any event.

There is, however, an interesting substantive difference between this approach and the traditional approach to rule learning. Up to now I have described the difference between a regular and a semi-regular pattern as a binary choice: either a pattern with a variable in it is present in the lexicon (regular) or it is not (semi-regular). Actually, the existence of an l-rule in the brain is more likely a matter of degree. The ease or speed with which an l-rule is activated relative to stored forms undoubtedly plays a role in how freely productive it is in performance. Individual words are only gradually established in the child's vocabulary, first in passive command, then active. We should expect the same of productive patterns. And this is indeed what we observe: although the stereotype in the literature is of a

---

[17] The learning of constructional idioms may call for some comment. Section 4.7 spoke of the overwhelming problems posed by the acquisition of word meanings. Everyone would acknowledge that idioms have meanings just about as idiosyncratic and complex as those of words, so the same problems arise in learning them. In the present story, it is only a short step from the problem of learning idioms to the problem of learning constructional idioms. And the meanings of constructional idioms are also about as complex as the meanings of words. Consider for instance the *time-away* construction, which means roughly 'spend time wastefully or frivolously doing something.' This meaning is comparable in complexity and subtlety to, say, *procrastinate*, 'spend time wastefully in order to avoid doing something', and so it should not be more difficult to learn (however children manage to do it!). On the other hand, the grammatical structure of a construction might be more difficult to learn than that of a word because it has more variables in it and less overt phonology to mark its presence.

regular rule suddenly "popping into place," more careful micro-observation often shows a gradual emergence of constructions, appearing in use with one verb at a time (Tomasello 2000a, with whom I agree that children do not have full adult grammars merely constrained by performance; see also Dąbrowska 2000). In addition, memorization of higher-frequency regulars is to be expected, as nothing in principle prohibits it.

I hardly claim to have provided a thorough account of language acquisition here. Rather, I have tried to show that the parallel architecture leads to an attractive formal view of the lexicon and of rules of language. In turn, this view reframes the acquisition problem, bringing traditional questions of linguistically oriented acquisition research closer to the neuroscientific approach to learning. The gap is still not yet bridged, but perhaps it is now at least possible to see to the other side.

6.10 Universal Grammar as a set of attractors

We are now in a position to make an interesting conjecture about the nature of Universal Grammar and the way it determines particular grammars.

I have alluded a few times to a position taken by both Principles and Parameters Theory (P&P, Chomsky 1981) and Optimality Theory (OT, Prince and Smolensky 1993): Universal Grammar explicitly provides all the grammatical possibilities for the languages of the world. In P&P, acquisition of a grammar involves setting a finite number of innate parameters; in OT, it involves ranking a finite set of innate constraints. Thus learning a grammar is conceived of rather like customizing a software package: everything is there, and the learner has only to set the options to suit the environment.

Such an approach seems improbable on grounds both external and internal to linguistic theory. The external grounds are that Universal Grammar is required to be extremely elaborate and very finely tuned. This lies behind the critiques of Universal Grammar offered by Elman et al. (1996), Tomasello (1995), and Deacon (1997) discussed in Chapter 4. It is hard to imagine all this structure emerging in the brain prior to experience, much less being coded genetically. As mentioned, Chomsky's response (e.g. 1995) has basically been that language simply is unlike any other biological capacity.

But the internal grounds against such an approach are even more compelling. As Newmeyer (1998b), Culicover (1999), and Ackerman and Webelhuth (1999) point out, few of the actual parameters determining differences among languages have been successfully worked out, despite nearly twenty years of intensive research in the P&P tradition. At the same time, this research has uncovered many phenomena across languages whose differentiation from each other would require parameters of such niggling specificity that they are hardly plausible as universal possibilities. Culicover and Ackerman and Webelhuth conclude that the variety of grammars in human languages cannot possibly be regimented by a finite parameterization.

Culicover goes further and argues against the conception of parameter triggering in language acquisition. Chomsky's (1981) strategy is to derive superficial differences among languages from some "deep" or "abstract" parameter. Culicover observes that the learner has to structure the input properly in order to trigger the parameter, which then establishes the proper grammar. Then he asks: Once the child structures the input properly, what further work is there for an "abstract" parameter to do? (Tomasello 2000a makes a similar argument.) Culicover therefore advocates specifying choices among grammars in relatively superficial structural terms, not in terms of elaborate invisible structures that the child needs to f-know in advance.

The view of grammar and of grammar acquisition urged here offers an attractive realization of the alternative suggested by Culicover and by Ackerman and Webelhuth. We have construed rules of grammar as lexical constructions of more or less specificity or generality, involving partial phonological, syntactic, and/or semantic structures and containing one or more typed variables. They are learned by extracting general variables from previously stored items.

Now, we can ask, what guides the extraction of these patterns? The poverty of the stimulus still applies: for any collection of input data, there are numerous ways it could be structured into patterns. Yet children pretty much all pick the same way. What favors this way over others? The answer in Chapter 4 was "Universal Grammar." But we did not specify *how* Universal Grammar might affect choice of l-rules.

Suppose that Universal Grammar consists of a collection of skeletal fragments of l-rules built into lexical memory; Ackerman and Webelhuth call them "grammatical archetypes." And suppose that, in the course of acquisition, alternative l-rules are emerging simultaneously in competition (i.e. in traditional terms, the learner is faced with a choice between two competing generalizations). If one of these emerging l-rules inherits structure from existing fragments of UG—in exactly the same way that an idiom inherits structure from a phrase-structure rule—then that one will emerge more strongly (come to be activated more easily or more quickly) and extinguish the other.

Moreover, inheritance is not absolute; it tolerates partial violations, for instance in irregular verbs and idioms. Thus under this conception, patterns that deviate to some extent from UG could be tolerated, if the primary linguistic data demanded it. Thus we arrive at a nice approach to "markedness" phenomena: the "unmarked" case is the one prespecified by UG, and "marked" rules deviate from the unmarked case qualitatively in just the way irregular verbs deviate from regular forms. In this way UG can be seen to "shape" the emerging grammar without entirely determining it. We can think of the grammatical fragments in UG as "attractors" (in the dynamic systems sense) that establish points of stability rather than absolute standards for grammatical patterns. That is, UG renders certain parts of the design space for words and l-rules more stable and/or accessible, with gradients of relative "markedness" as one moves away from the "core" cases. This leaves plenty of room for linguistic idiosyncrasy at all levels of generality, essentially in line with Culicover's proposal.

Here are a few of the most basic pieces one would want to include in this conception of UG:

(43) $Wd_i = X^\circ_i$

That is, a phonological Word corresponds to a syntactic noun, verb, adjective, or preposition—certainly the prototype, but one we have seen is *only* a prototype.

(44) $NP_i = [\text{PHYSICAL OBJECT}]_i; VP_j = [\text{ACTION}]_j$

That is, the prototypical NP denotes an object and the prototypical VP denotes an action. Lots of counterexamples to this generalization can be cited (section 5.5), but again this seems to be the core from which all deviations proceed.[18]

(45)

$$
\sigma \atop {\diagup \diagdown} \atop {C \quad V}
$$

That is, the prototypical syllable is a consonant followed by a vowel. Languages deviate from this prototypical template in all sorts of ways, but this is clearly the benchmark from which all else springs. Many languages (e.g. Japanese) essentially allow *only* this kind of syllable (plus syllables consisting of just a vowel), and there is no other syllable type that enjoys such exclusivity.

(46)   XP
       ‖
       X°

That is, a phrasal syntactic category dominates a head of the corresponding lexical category ("X-bar theory"). This is an essential and prototypical element of

---

[18] It is significant, though, that the violations are asymmetrical, as observed in section 5.5. Lots of different semantic types can be expressed as nouns, but only events and states of affairs can be expressed as verbs. Conversely, physical object concepts can be expressed only by nouns, but event and state concepts can be expressed by nouns as well as by verbs. A story about violable attractors cannot alone account for this asymmetry. See section 8.10 for more discussion.

phrase structure, but it is violable. For instance, English gerundive noun phrases such as *John's walking the dog last night* (as in *John's walking the dog last night was a mistake*) have no head noun; rather they contain a verb phrase, headed by a verb (Jackendoff 1977: ch. 9).

(47) XP_m $= [F_i (W_j <, V_k>)]_m$

X_i YP_j $<ZP_k>$ [Angle brackets < > express optionality]

This is roughly the Head Constraint on argument structure discussed in section 5.9.4. It says that the head X of a syntactic phrase XP expresses a semantic function F, and its syntactic argument(s) YP (and optional ZP) express the semantic argument(s) W (and optionally V) of F; moreover, the whole syntactic phrase expresses the combination of the semantic function and its arguments.

Many other candidates suggest themselves as structural fragments that might act as UG "attractors" for structural patterns of languages. Among the more elaborate ones are the syntactic "tricks" such as long-distance dependencies (the relation between a wh-phrase or topicalized phrase at the front of a clause and its trace elsewhere in the sentence) and the other major types of violation of the Head Constraint enumerated in section 5.9.4.

More generally, the content of UG boils down in large part to (a) architectural universals—what kinds of structure there are in the grammar and how they interface, and (b) what particular fragments of structure (or "tricks") are prespecified to bias the child's acquisition of generalizations. These pieces *did* have to evolve in the history of the species; it is hoped that their evolution is more plausible than that of a standard syntactocentric "grammar box." (We return to the question of evolution in Chapter 8.) In addition, the present approach permits us to make sense of the "markedness" properties of Universal Grammar, in terms of independent characteristics found in concept formation in other areas of cognition.

I must confess that at this point I hear the linguists screaming: There's not enough machinery! How can this be constrained? He's sold out to the connectionists! And I hear the network modelers screaming: There's too much machinery! How can all this be built in? Will those linguists ever learn? I can only respond that the position here is far from a weak-kneed compromise: it is an attempt to make the most sense I can out of the genuine insights of both sides. Both classes of objections indeed must be met; I take this as another challenge for future research.

Above all, what I would like the reader to take away from this discussion is the importance of psychological considerations in the theory of grammar. By taking very seriously the question of what is stored and what is computed online, we have managed to justify a major reorganization of the theory of grammar. If this is letting the theory of performance intrude on the theory of competence, so be it. For my own taste, such interaction between the two theories is the proper way for linguistic research to proceed in the future.

6.11 Appendix: Remarks on HPSG and Construction Grammar

HPSG and Construction Grammar (CG) lead to a consolidation of grammatical phenomena similar to that developed here, though in a different formalism. Pollard and Sag's (1994) exposition of HPSG is in fact far more rigorous than I have been here, dealing with many of the tricky details of how syntactic combination is accomplished. Much of that machinery appears to be readily adaptable to the present notation.

Beyond the notation, though, there are some interesting conceptual differences between the present approach and HPSG/CG.

• HPSG and CG both insist on the primacy of the *sign* in Saussure's sense: they require lexical items to be complexes of sound (phonology), meaning (semantics), and grammatical properties (syntax). In particular, I have mentioned several times the view of Construction Grammar and Cognitive Grammar that all syntactic structure is inherently meaningful. Thus neither HPSG nor CG admit the possibility of "defective" lexical items that lack one or two of the three components; such items have come up repeatedly as important to the present analysis. (HPSG, however, allows components to be null rather than absent.)

I suspect this insistence on the sign has arisen from a rejection of syntactocentrism. It is a way of giving syntax a cooperative rather than dominant role in the formation of sentences, a stance with which I completely agree. However, insisting on the integrity of the sign is not the only way to achieve this stance. The prototypical word is indeed a Saussurean sign; but no argument is ever given that the entire grammar must be so uniform. That is, the integrity of the sign is basically a stipulation. If we abandon it, lexical structures do become more heterogeneous. But this opens up interesting opportunities for analyses of the sort explored here. As we have seen, abandoning the rigid integrity of the sign hardly forces us to fall back into the clutches of syntactocentrism; in fact it draws us away from them.

• Because unification in HPSG/CG is always complete sign by complete sign, combinatoriality must proceed more or less in lockstep among the three components (though HPSG allows constituents to be rearranged in the course of combination). Such correspondence is fairly natural between syntax and semantics, where it has been worked out intensively. However, the syntax–phonology connection (section 5.4), which has been studied hardly at all within HPSG and CG, is far more problematic. And when we enter the world of the phonological tiers (which to my knowledge has never been addressed in these theories), constituent organization bears no resemblance to syntax and semantics. (Some of the phenomena to be discussed in Chapter 12 raise similar problems of constituent incompatibility on the syntax–semantics side too.) Again, the difficulty comes from mistakenly insisting on the unity of the sign. However, it seems altogether feasible to adapt HPSG's basic formalism to the parallel architecture: phonological, syntactic, and semantic combination could be run side by side, and kept connected not by being united in a single sign but by somewhat looser interface components.

• Section 6.2 mentioned that HPSG assumes a strict distinction between lexical and phrasal combination. The reasons for this are the usual ones: the semiproductive patterns *must* be listed in the lexicon, and therefore, in the interests of a homogeneous morphology, *all* morphology is done there. Again there is no particular reason for maintaining this assumption, given the present analysis. The proper division, I have suggested, is between semiproductive and irregular forms, which are listed, and productive forms, which are the result of free combination but may be listed as well. An HPSG/CG version of this approach has in fact been proposed by Koenig and Jurafsky (1994).[19]

• Finally, HPSG means "Head-Driven Phrase Structure Grammar." "Head-driven" means that the basic combinatorial principles in a phrase are determined by its head. However, the constructions in section 6.6 are precisely cases in which the argument structure of a verb phrase is driven not by the verb, but rather by the lexical verb phrase that constitutes the constructional idiom. That is, these constructions violate the Head Constraint of section 5.9. In order to adapt HPSG to these constructions, it is necessary therefore to slightly weaken the "head-driven" aspect of the theory, but in a way that seems on the whole natural. Such weakening appears in Goldberg's (1995) approach to constructions, and to some extent in Sag's (1997) HPSG treatment of relative clauses.

On the whole, although these proposed modifications to HPSG/CG are important, I think they are more cosmetic than substantial. It should be an interesting challenge for the practitioners of these theories to work out the consequences.

---

[19] A place where the "lexicalism" of HPSG leads to results that I find counterintuitive is in the treatment of the clusters of object clitics in Romance languages, for example the italicized items in (i).

(i)   French:
      Marie *le lui*   donne.
      Marie it to him gives   ('Marie gives it to him.')

Miller and Sag (1997) show how HPSG can treat these clitics as attached to the verb "in the lexicon," so that *le lui donne* is a lexical unit inserted into phrasal syntax. However, some Slavic languages such as Serbian have similar clitic clusters which are not attached to the verb, but rather occupy an independent syntactic position in the sentence; hence they cannot be treated as lexical addenda to the verb (Spencer 1991). More generally, Romance clitics are clear instances of free combination: we don't want to say every verb is listed in the lexicon with a full paradigm of clitic combinations. In the present approach they are therefore treated like all other productive morphology, perhaps in the morphosyntactic tier.

CHAPTER 7

Implications for Processing

Chapter 2 touched on the potential connection and interpenetration between theories of competence—linguistic structure—and performance—language processing. In the last chapter we began exploring this issue, concentrating on the storage of linguistic elements. This chapter goes further toward a rapprochement of theoretical linguistics and psycholinguistics. It concerns itself with the job of the language processor: how stored pieces are used online to build combinatorial linguistic structures in working memory during speech perception and production.

We begin by showing how the architecture proposed in Chapter 5 translates into a processing model, with the interface components playing a crucial role. In particular, the treatment of the lexicon in the parallel architecture turns out to fit nicely into analyses of lexical access in perception and production. We then take up some more general questions about the role of modularity in processing. The overall goal is to show that the parallel architecture offers a theoretical perspective that unifies linguistics with psycholinguistics more satisfactorily than has been previously possible.

7.1 The parallel competence architecture forms a basis for a processing architecture

To review the situation so far: The standard architecture for generative grammar, from *Aspects* to the Minimalist Program, conceives of grammar as syntactocentric and derivational. The generative capacity of language comes entirely from syntax. Linguistic structure, complete with lexical items, is built by an initial stage of syntactic derivation—D(eep)-structure in *Aspects* through GB, and the operation Merge in the Minimalist Program. Then derivational rules of movement and deletion produce levels of syntactic structure that are subjected to phonological and semantic interpretation. Phonological and semantic structures are outputs of a syntactic derivation, with no significant generative capacities of their own.

Of course we were all taught as graduate students that syntactic derivations don't model the course of processing. Speakers don't think of the initial symbol S first, then gradually expand it till they choose the words, then push the pieces around until they finally arrive at what the sentence means and how to pronounce it. So the theoretical notion of derivation, particularly syntactic "movement," has been abstracted away from processing by calling it "metaphorical." The derivation is part of competence but has little to do with performance.

This stance is necessary because the syntactocentric architecture has a logical directionality: it begins with syntactic phrase construction and lexical insertion, and branches outward to phonology and semantics (Fig. 7.1a). This is quite at odds with the logical directionality of processing, where speech perception has to get from sounds to meanings (Fig. 7.1b) and speech production has to get from meanings to sounds (Fig. 7.1c).

Linguistic theory can rhetorically make a virtue of necessity by saying "But of course we're developing a theory of *competence*; we're interested in the character of abstract knowledge." Still, other things being equal, a theory that allows us readily to relate competence to performance ought to be favored over one that creates hard boundaries between the two.

Let me make clearer what I think is at stake. A theory of processing is concerned with how a language user, in real time, creates structures for perceived and produced sentences. And a theory of competence must at the very least account for the range of structures available to the language user. But I now

a. The logical directionality of syntactocentric competence

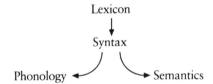

b. The logical directionality of language perception

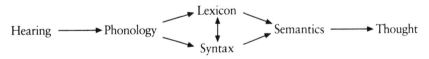

c. The logical directionality of language production

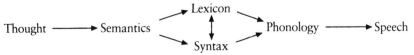

Fig. 7.1. Logical directionality in competence and performance

want to go beyond this to ask: do the principles of the competence theory bear any resemblance to the principles that the language user actually employs in speaking and understanding language? If not, it is not entirely clear exactly what is claimed in attributing psychological reality to the competence grammar.

The parallel constraint-based architecture developed in the past two chapters in fact affords a rather close relation to a theory of processing. To review its overall character: Linguistic structure is viewed as a collection of independent but linked levels of structure: phonology, syntax, and semantics. Each level of structure is characterized by its own set of primitives and combinatorial principles. The linking among levels of structure is established by sets of interface constraints—among which are the words of the language. Thus a well-formed sentence has well-formed structures in each component, connected in a well-formed fashion by linking constraints. Within this organization, syntax is but one among several "cooperating" generative components.

The parallel constraint-based architecture is logically *non*-directional: one can start with any piece of structure in any component and pass along logical pathways provided by the constraints to construct a coherent larger structure around it. For example, one can start with a piece of phonology and, via the interfaces, construct corresponding syntax and semantics; or one can start with a piece of semantics and via the interfaces construct corresponding syntax and phonology. Because the grammar is logically non-directional, it is not inherently biased toward either perception or production—unlike the syntactocentric architecture, which is inherently biased against both![1]

But we can go farther. It is possible to construct a model of processing whose components correspond directly to the components in the parallel model:

• Corresponding to the formation rules and constraints internal to a particular level of structure are processes which, given a collection of fragmentary structures in a particular format, attempt to construct a fully specified structure in that format. The classic example is a syntactic parser, which is given a sequence of lexical categories like (1a) and constructs a fully specified syntactic structure like (1b).

(1)   a. Determiner + Adjective + Noun + Auxiliary + Verb + Noun
       b. [$_S$ [$_{NP}$ Det [$_{AP}$ A] N] Aux [$_{VP}$ V [$_{NP}$ N]]]

Let us call such a process an *integrative* process. For each set of formation rules that defines a level of linguistic structure, the language processor requires an integrative process that uses these principles to construct structures at that level.

• Corresponding to interface constraints are processes that use one form of linguistic structure to create another. The classic example is the conversion of

---

[1] A parallel argument is made for HPSG by Pollard and Sag (1994).

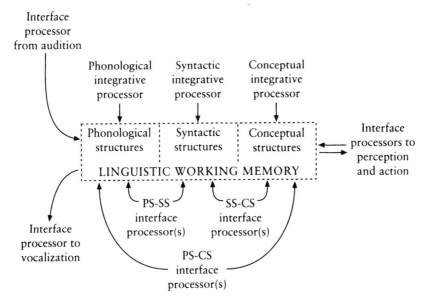

Fig. 7.2. The parallel grammar implemented as a processing architecture

acoustical information—a frequency analysis of a continuously varying speech signal—into a discretely segmented phonetic structure. Another such process uses syntactic parses to construct specifications of semantic roles. Let us call such processes *interface* processes.[2] For each set of interface constraints that links a pair of levels, the processor needs an interface processor that accomplishes such linking—or perhaps it needs one in each direction.

• In addition to these two types, the f-mind needs processes that take as input full or partial structures in a particular format in working memory, and relate them to or construct new structures in the same format. Classic cases are rules of inference, which derive new conceptual structures from existing ones, and principles of mental rotation, which derive new visual/spatial structures from existing ones. Another such case might be checking to see whether two words rhyme, which compares two phonological structures. I'll call these *inferential* processes.

Given these distinctions, it is possible to describe the logic of processing in terms isomorphic to the rule types in the parallel grammar. Fig. 7.2 illustrates.

---

[2] In Jackendoff (1987) these were called "translation" processes. The reason for the change in terminology is that these conversions do not preserve "meaning"—in two respects. First, we are abandoning the view that f-mental structures *have* meaning (Ch. 2), that is, they are not to be viewed as *representing* anything. As far as the brain is concerned they are just pure structure. Second, the relations that an interface implements between structures do not preserve structure in the way the term "translation" would suggest. As seen in Chs. 1 and 5 and section 7.5, it is better to think of interfaces as implementing only partial homologies between two forms of structure.

What is significant is that this is essentially an elaboration of Figs. 7.1b and 7.1c: it provides a route in both directions between sound and meaning, mediated by syntax and by the lexicon, where the lexicon is part of the interface components.

Fig. 7.2 is of course an oversimplification. Among other things, it omits the interior tier structure of phonology, the possible division of syntax into phrasal, morphosyntactic, and possibly grammatical function tiers, and the tiers of conceptual structure to be motivated in Chapter 12. It also leaves open whether the interface processors are bidirectional, or alternatively whether there is one of each for perception (left-to-right) and for production (right-to-left)—an important issue that competence theory alone cannot decide (see Hagoort, Brown, and Osterhout 1999 for discussion).

A crucial role in this processor is played by linguistic working memory. Some aspects of working memory were introduced in section 3.5. In particular, several arguments were offered for why working memory must be a distinct component, something beyond just the currently activated parts of long-term memory. In Fig. 7.2, linguistic working memory is to be understood not just as a static storage space for linguistic material, but as a dynamic "workbench" or "blackboard" on which processors can cooperate in assembling linguistic structures. It has three divisions or "departments" or "buffers," corresponding to the three levels of linguistic structure (alternatively, one can think of it as three functionally separate working memories—it is just a matter of terminology). We return to the character of this component at several points in this chapter.

7.2 How the competence model can constrain theories of processing

Now it is possible to ask: To what extent does the logic of the competence theory dictate the logic of processing? There may of course be constraints on processing that come from the way the processor is implemented in the brain—and the competence theory will have nothing to say about these. Nevertheless, it is interesting to see how far we can go by thinking about processing simply in terms of its logical structure.

In this spirit, here is a preliminary sketch of the course of language perception; we will elaborate on it as the chapter goes on. In brief, one can think of the auditory input as "clamping" linguistic working memory at the phonological end; the constraints then proliferate structure from phonology through syntax to semantics. In slightly more detail: The interface from the auditory system delivers a raw sequence of phonetic segments to the phonological division of working memory. The phonological integrative processor organizes this partial structure in accordance with the phonological principles of the language, in particular creating syllable structures and candidate word boundaries. For instance, given the phonetic string /aybɪltforhawzəz/, it can tell that the only place to put a legal English word boundary in the cluster /. . . ltf . . ./ is before the *f*.

However, in order to determine the actual words being heard, the lexicon must be engaged. So the phonology processor sends out a call to the lexicon: "Does anybody out there sound like *this*?" (i.e. does the phonological structure of any item match this raw input?). And various lexical items pipe up, "Me!" (i.e. become activated). By virtue of becoming activated, though, a lexical item doesn't just activate its phonology: it also activates its syntax and semantics, and thus establishes partial structures in those domains, linked to the phonology. That is, lexical items play a crucial role in the interface processors.

The interface processor from phonology to syntax adds constraints from intonational structure to those provided by lexical linking, creating somewhat fuller syntactic structures in working memory, linked to the phonological structure. However, the syntactic structures are still incomplete, because phonological structure cannot fully determine syntactic embedding (recall section 5.4). So then the syntactic integrative processor—the "parser"—elaborates these partial structures, constructing more complete tree structures. In turn, these provide the cues necessary for the interface to semantics: the syntax–semantics linking rules (sections 5.8 and 5.9) determine the relations among the word meanings that the lexicon has delivered to the conceptual division of working memory. Finally, the conceptual integrative processor combines this structure with contextual constraints ("pragmatics") to construct the interpreted message.

In language production, the processor goes in the other direction, starting with an intended message in conceptual structure. The conceptual processor sends a call to the lexicon: "Does anybody out there mean *this*?" And various candidates raise their hands: "Me!" and thereby become activated. But by virtue of becoming activated, they also activate their syntax and phonology, and thus establish partial structures in those domains and partial linking to the intended message. Then the phrasal constraints proliferate structure through syntax to phonology, until there is a complete phonological structure that can be sent off to the interface to the motor system, there to be pronounced.

In broad outline this story parallels the "blueprints" for the hearer and speaker offered in recent surveys by Cutler and Clifton (1999) and Levelt (1999). What's important here is how naturally it follows from the character of the competence theory.

As just described, the processing model may sound as though it is totally sequential. But that is not necessary. A level of structure need not be completed by its integrative processor in order for the next interface processor to start passing information up or down the line. Rather, any fragment of structure at one level is sufficient to call into action (or activate) any processors that can make use of it. That is, this architecture permits radically "opportunistic" or "incremental" processing (to use Marslen-Wilson and Tyler's (1987) and Levelt's (1989) terms, respectively).

On the other hand, the processor's "opportunism" is not chaotic. It is constrained at any particular moment in time by what structure is already available, and how that structure can affect other structures *through the rules of the grammar*.

The essential role of the grammar becomes more evident when we add intercomponential feedback to the story. Let us work through a typical example. As already noted, the auditory interface delivers a phonetic input bereft of word boundaries (except possibly where there are pauses in the signal). Word boundaries in general must be constructed by the integrative processor for phonology, in part by using lexical look-up. However, consider sentences (2a, b), which are acoustically indistinguishable (at least in my dialect) up to the point marked *. The difference in word boundaries cannot be settled phonologically: the distinction between (2a) and (2b) depends on the semantics as well as the syntax of the phrase following *. (And there is no sense of "garden path" here.)

(2)   a. It's only a PARent, not * a TEACHer.
        b. It's only apPARent, not * REAL.

Hence the phonology processor must potentially entertain alternative structures, both of which get passed on by the interface processors successively to syntax and semantics. When the semantics processor resolves the ambiguity, thus "clamping" the intended meaning, the semantics processor cannot by itself reject the incorrect phonological structure. Rather, the interface processors must pass down the inhibition of the rejected structure in succession to syntax and phonology. In short, what words are *heard* can indeed be affected by semantics—but only through the relation of semantics to phonology through the interface rules.

We see a similar effect in an experiment by Tanenhaus et al. (1995), which shows that visual input interacts with syntactic parsing. Subjects are confronted with an array of objects and an instruction like (3), and their eye movements over the array are tracked.

(3)   Put the apple on * the towel in the cup.

At the moment in time marked by *, the question faced by the language processor is whether *on* is going to designate where the apple *is* or where it is to be *put*. It turns out that at this point, subjects already start scanning the relevant locations in the array in order to disambiguate the sentence (Is there more than one apple? Is there an apple already on the towel?). Hence visual feedback is being used to constrain syntactic structure early on in processing.

The present architecture makes clear how this comes about: the syntax–semantics interface links competing analyses in syntax with competing conceptual structures. In turn, these alternatives are picked up by an interface that connects conceptual structure to the visual system (Macnamara 1978; Jackendoff 1987; Landau and Jackendoff 1993; see also Chapter 11). Visual search is used to "clamp" the contextually appropriate interpretation; inhibition of the inappropriate interpretations is passed back through the interfaces to conceptual structure and then to syntax. This case thus presents a parallel to (2), with the interactions just moved one component over in the system: syntax via conceptual structure to vision instead of phonology to syntax to conceptual structure.

Similar considerations arise in production. For instance, Levelt's (1999) "blueprint of the speaker" (p. 87) includes a component of "self-perception," in which the speaker monitors phonological structure internally ("hears what he/she is about to say") and uses this to revise or repair the conceptual structure being encoded as a sentence. Levelt's diagram treats this component as a direct feedback from phonological structure to conceptual structure. But this is oversimplified, as Levelt notes (p. 88). Phonological structure can affect semantics only through the rules of grammar; thus "what I am about to say" has to be interpreted via the phonology–syntax and syntax–semantics interfaces. In other words, this is the inverse of the situation illustrated by (2) for language perception.

The symmetry of this situation is reminiscent of Garrett's (2000) proposal that the production processors are used in perception and vice versa: the routes used for feedback in one are used for "feedforward" in the other. The present approach explains why this proposal should make sense: the interface constraints don't care in which direction they are applied.

To sum up the argument so far, semantics cannot directly influence phonological analysis—or vice versa[3]—and visual context cannot directly influence

---

[3] Careful readers may note that Fig. 7.2 includes a direct phonology–semantics interface, and may wonder if this might be used for the feedback in these examples. The answer is no: this interface is not sufficient to mediate completely between the two levels. We have seen (Ch. 5) that it includes lexical structure (e.g. /kæt/ means CAT) and the relation of intonation to focus; Ch. 8 will suggest that it also includes some weak constraints between linear order and meaning. But this interface does not include anything about such crucial aspects of meaning as argument structure and modification. These necessarily invoke the interfaces with syntax.

syntactic analysis. The only means for feedback of this sort is through the routes provided by the interfaces. More generally, there is no general-purpose "contextual" mechanism that permits context to affect syntax directly.

The hypothesis that the rules of grammar establish the possible routes of "information flow" in processing can only go so far, of course. It can make predictions about *relative* timing: what structures must be in place before others can be established. For instance, it predicts that semantics cannot constrain phonology until after lexical look-up. For another typical case, in the sentence *Sandy was kissed by Chris*, it is impossible for the perceiver to determine that *Sandy* is Patient of the event (its semantic role) until it is determined that *Sandy* is subject of a passive (its syntactic role). This predicts that there is a necessary time lag between syntactic and conceptual integration, a time lag observed in the numerous experiments designed to test the separation of syntactic from semantic processing. However, the logic of the grammar makes no predictions about *absolute* timing. That is a matter for experimental work to decide.

The competence model may also make predictions about what phenomena go together in what component of the grammar. To the extent that the phenomena of some particular component (say syntactic integration) fall together experimentally in terms of timing, processing load, speech errors, brain wave (ERP) signature, and/or brain localization, and they contrast in these respects with phenomena of other components, we can align the competence model with processing evidence (see Hagoort, Brown, and Osterhout 1999 and also the discussion of aspectual coercion in section 12.2). Ideally, we may even be able to use evidence from processing to help decide in what component of the grammar a particular phenomenon belongs—which, as seen in previous chapters, is often a pressing issue for the competence theory.

Further constraints on the interaction of components may arise from the way the processor is implemented in the brain. Forster (1979) and Frazier (1987), for example, argue that in language perception there is no semantic feedback at all before syntactic processing is complete—a constraint not predicted by the competence theory. Similarly, Levelt (1989) argues that in production, the semantics of lexical items are selected completely before phonological material becomes accessible—again a constraint beyond that predicted by the competence theory. On the other hand, Marslen-Wilson and Tyler (1987), Tanenhaus et al. (1995), and many others argue there *is* semantic feedback on syntax in the course of perception, and Dell (1986; Dell et al. 1997) argues that phonological effects may actually be implicated in semantic selection.

The competence model cannot settle these disputes. The freely incremental possibility looks simpler, but the model is consistent with both possibilities. On the other hand, as seen above, the competence model does tell us that even free interaction of components is constrained by the rules of grammar—that is, it is not *entirely* free.

7.3 Remarks on working memory

One often sees lexical access characterized simply as something like "activating a word node" in memory. This is far too crude, and calls for several refinements.

First of all, the competence theory shows there is no single "word node." A lexical item is a complex association of phonological, syntactic, and semantic structures. I stress here *structures*, not just *features*. One cannot just think of a word node as activating a number of other nodes that together constitute a collection of independent features. Rather, any adequate account has to include provision for hierarchical phonological structure in complex morphological items, for hierarchical syntactic structure in idioms, and for hierarchical conceptual structure in just about any word (see Chapter 11).

Next, let us return to an issue raised in section 3.5. There I argued that working memory cannot just consist of the nodes in long-term memory that are activated in current processing. The most important reason, it will be recalled, is the "Problem of 2": a structure constructed in working memory may contain two or more instances of a type stored in long-term memory. For instance, *The little star's beside a big star* contains two instances of *star*. These two instances cannot be kept distinct if each consists simply of an activation of the lexical entry for *star* in long-term memory.

For this reason, the older view (e.g. Neisser 1967, Baddeley 1986) of working memory as a separate facility in the brain appears more appropriate: material from long-term memory is "retrieved" into working memory where it can undergo transient processing. If we don't like the idea of "copying" material into working memory, an alternative way to think about it might be that working memory is a set of indices or pointers or transient bindings to long-term memory. Although it is still altogether mysterious how such a mechanism can be implemented in neural terms, the nature of the task demands something with these functional properties.

In addition, just having an item in working memory still isn't enough for it to be part of an utterance. It must also be integrated into the larger structures being assembled by the integrative processors—in the phonological, syntactic, and semantic departments of the "blackboard."

It is important to differentiate the present view of working memory from an extensive research tradition associated with such work as Baddeley (1986), Gathercole and Baddeley (1993), and Gathercole (1999). This tradition thinks of working memory as a limited-capacity "phonological loop" in which phonological material is stored, maintained in sequence, and rehearsed. The tasks of processing this information and directing its flow are ascribed to a "central executive." Characteristic experimental tasks used to probe working memory in this tradition are tests of digit span (frontward and backward), recall of lists of words, and repetition of nonsense words.

What strikes me about this tradition is that it apparently neglects what would appear to be by far the most important function of linguistic working memory: understanding and producing spoken language. In order to construct a meaning for a sentence one is hearing, one must do more than retrieve the meanings of the individual words: one must determine the relations among the word meanings, based on the syntactic structure of the sentence—which is in turn based in part on the linear order of the words. Consequently, the string of words must be stored in working memory, not just in order to be able to repeat them back, but in order to understand what is related to what. Similarly, in language production, phonological working memory is the "place" where the pronunciations of words are put in linear order on the basis of the syntactic and semantic relations in the intended utterance, prior to the construction of a motor program that produces the utterance.[4]

---

[4] Logically speaking, the working memory system used for understanding and producing sentences might be different from the one whose capacity is being measured by digit spans and lists of unrelated words. One reason they might seem superficially different is that language processing can deal with much longer strings of words than are observed in digit span tasks. However, the earliest literature on working memory (Miller 1956) observed that its limited capacity depends not on the sheer amount of information, but rather on how that information is "chunked." Phonological processing certainly involves chunking word strings into larger segments—a process that this tradition of research on working memory simply avoids by restricting test stimuli to lists and nonsense words.

Gathercole and Baddeley (1993) do explicitly argue that their "phonological loop" does not play a central role in speech perception and production. Addressing production (ch. 4), they produce evidence that the "phonological loop" is not to be identified with motor programs for speech, and conclude that it is not involved in production. But they fail to sufficiently distinguish levels of structure: phonological structure simply is not a motor program, so phonological working memory should not be expected to contain motor programs. They also cite evidence from Shallice and Butterworth (1977) concerning a patient with "conduction aphasia," whose repetition and digit span skills were impaired but who spoke fairly normally. Problems with repetition, however, surely involve lexical access as well as phonological working memory, so without further analysis of the task it is not clear how to interpret this case.

Turning to perception (1993: ch. 8), Gathercole and Baddeley give evidence that working memory load impairs only complex language processing (embedded relative clauses, reversible passives, and the like). They also cite patients whose digit spans are impaired but whose language comprehension is not impaired except with complex sentences. They therefore make a distinction between "online" comprehension based on "raw input forms" and "offline" comprehension based on storage in the "phonological loop"; they claim only the latter is affected in the cases they cite. Again,

The processing architecture sketched in Fig. 7.2, of course, treats phono-logical working memory as only one department or "blackboard" in linguistic working memory. And to repeat a point from the last section, I want to think of working memory not just as a shelf where the brain stores material, but as a workbench where processing goes on, where structures are constructed. There seems no point in relegating processing to a "central executive," when it has become abundantly clear that the brain is thoroughly decentralized.[5]

7.4 More about lexical access

As a sample of how the parallel competence model can play a role in theorizing about processing, we will spend a little time deconstructing the notion of lexical access in processing. The objective is not to pass judgment on experimental work but to clarify the questions that experimental work addresses.

7.4.1 Lexical access in perception

Elaborating the discussion in section 7.2, consider what is involved in a simple "call to the lexicon" in language perception. At this point in processing, the auditory–phonological interface has presented a certain amount of sequenced phonetic structure to the phonology "blackboard," and the phonology integra-tive processor has made some preliminary guesses about syllable and word boundaries, based on the phonotactics of the language.

Now, when the lexicon is called, should we think of the processor calling the lexicon for a match? Or should we think of the lexicon, as part of the interface processor, as actively attempting to impose itself on the input? This perhaps awaits a better understanding of brain dynamics. (One thing ought to be cer-tain, though: lexical access cannot be a serial search, as was envisaged by some in the early days.)

---

they do not ask what could possibly be meant by "raw input form." It is surely not acoustic: it must already be converted into phonological form before it can invoke lexical access and give rise to semantics. My intuition is that an impaired phonological working memory in the sense proposed here (Fig. 7.2) would have just the desired effect: it would work acceptably for easy sentences that could be rapidly "chunked," but would break down if "chunks" could not be determined without extensive subsequent processing.

To be sure, it is of interest to know which elements of a list are more likely to be remembered after different time intervals and under different simultaneous loads. But it would by now seem time to establish a meaningful line of communication between this enterprise and psycholinguistic research.

[5] For the relation between linguistic working memory, attention, and consciousness, see Jackendoff (1987: esp. chs. 6, 13, and 14).

In any event, lexical entries can be matched with the phonology blackboard only through their phonological structure. It doesn't matter what contextual information is present on the conceptual blackboard, because this material is not linked to the phonology blackboard. The processor, trying to understand the incoming sentence, can get around to integrating with the context only when it comes to conceptual integration. But we're not there yet—we're still trying to find a phonological match.[6]

Suppose a match is found. Then the phonological structure of the lexical item comes to be bound to the material already on the blackboard. This binding is the step of the processor saying "this is the word I'm hearing." The literature on lexical access traditionally calls this part of the process "selection" of a long-term memory lexical item as a candidate in working memory.

In practice, the lexicon will often contain many different items or combinations of items that match the phonological structure in working memory (e.g. *a parent* and *apparent*). The processor, which for the moment must take a purely phonological point of view, cannot distinguish among these—this awaits integration on the other blackboards. Hence it stands to reason that we should obtain the well-known results dating back to Swinney (1979) and Tanenhaus et al. (1979) showing that lexical access is semantically promiscuous—it activates every lexical item that has the right phonology, regardless of meaning. In the present approach, we can interpret this as multiple items binding to the same phonological structure in working memory, in competition with each other. (Cutler and Clifton 1999 offer a survey of models of word recognition that incorporate concurrent competing analyses.)

When a lexical item establishes a phonological connection to working memory, this also activates its syntactic and conceptual structures and connects them to the appropriate departments of working memory as well—in competition with other candidates, of course. In practice, the activation of syntax and semantics is not instantaneous, given that activation has to spread through the lexical structure. The syntactic and conceptual material, unlike the phonological material, is not yet integrated: this is the function of the syntactic and conceptual integrative processors. And, as mentioned earlier, conceptual

---

[6] Actually, in the general case a match with the phonetic input is not what has to be sought. A point rarely addressed in studies of lexical access in perception is the necessity to negotiate between phonetic input and the morphophonological form in which the item is stored. I am thinking, for instance, of cases in which rapid speech degrades the phonetics, of cases where regular sound change creates predictable phonetic alternants, and—for an extreme situation—cases where a morphological affix is realized as reduplication or where the lexical phonological form is broken up by an infix, as in forms such as *Mononga-fuckin-hela* (see section 6.2.1). Here the "call to the lexicon" must be mediated by the phonology integrative processor, which has to construct active hypotheses about what morphophonological forms to attempt to call.

integration often will have to wait for results communicated from syntactic integration through the syntactic–conceptual interface.

Finally, there normally comes a point where all the competing multiple analyses but one are extinguished, because of ill-formedness, contextual bias, or other factors. At this point the remaining analysis is the one the hearer understands as "the sentence." Sometimes this process of *resolution* fails and the hearer construes the sentence as ambiguous or perhaps a pun. On the other hand, sometimes the processor resolves multiple competing possibilities prematurely, as in "garden path" sentences such as (4).

(4)   The horse raced past the barn fell.
      (= 'The horse that was raced past the barn fell').

In example (2) (*It's only a parent, not a teacher*), resolution affects what actual lexical item is heard as part of the sentence. That is, the final choice of words in the sentence is not complete until resolution has taken place—in this case following conceptual integration.

7.4.2 *Priming*

Let us pursue a bit further the logic behind the semantic promiscuity of lexical access. In the experiments that demonstrate this promiscuity, it is found that, for a brief period, the word *bug* heard in any sentential context primes (speeds up reaction time to) the "lexical decision task" of recognizing either *insect* or *spy* as a word; these words are semantically related to different senses of *bug*. After this brief period, only one of these words continues to be primed: the one related to the sense of *bug* in the presented sentence. How can this come about?

Bug has to prime *insect* and *spy* via the semantics of the items—there is no phonological resemblance. The assumption is that priming amounts to a degree of "pre-activation": the primed lexical item *insect* is already somewhat active when the probe stimulus is detected, so it takes less time for it to reach the threshold necessary to trigger a response.

In order to trigger a response, the lexical item *insect* has to be bound to the encoded probe in working memory (or "selected into working memory"). But it can only be bound to the probe via its phonology (or orthography, if visually presented). In other words, the preactivation of the item's semantics leads also to the preactivation of its phonology, which in turn leads to quicker binding to the probe. Finally, this binding is picked up by unknown processes (see remarks in section 3.5) that lead to the experimental response, namely pushing the button that signals "yes, it's a word."

Fig. 7.3 illustrates all the processes involved in leading to the sped-up response

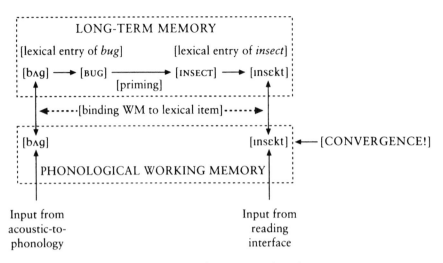

Fig. 7.3. How hearing *bug* primes identifying *insect*

to lexical decision for *insect*. Crucially, priming is through the semantics of *bug* to the semantics of *insect*, but the judgment on the lexical decision task is through the phonology of *insect*. (We discuss the "reading interface" in section 7.5.)

However, suppose one hears *bug* but doesn't immediately encounter *insect*— as surely happens in the vast majority of situations. From the point of view of language perception, the enhanced activation of *insect* seems to serve no purpose. The primed item is not connected with working memory, so it does not show up on the "blackboard." In other words, it makes sense to think of priming as essentially a long-term memory phenomenon, not engaging working memory at all. (On the other hand, we can *detect* priming only through its potential to affect working memory processing!)

To sum up the past two subsections, we see the importance of distinguishing four components of lexical access.

• *Activation* of a lexical item in long-term memory. This can be accomplished by a call from phonological working memory to the item's phonological structure. But a lexical item can also be activated by priming: spreading activation from associated items within the lexicon.

• *Binding* (or copying) of a long-term memory item to working memory—placing the item in play on the "blackboard" (or in traditional terminology, *selecting* the item for the "blackboard"). Binding entails activation; but, as we have just seen in the case of priming, activation does not necessarily entail binding.

• *Integration* is the process of combining an item on the "blackboard" with a larger structure being built, for example determining its position in a syntactic parse. In case there is more than one possible structure into which the item might fit, it is initially integrated "promiscuously." Likewise, if a position in a structure can be identified with more than one possible item, they are initially all integrated with the position, in competition with one another.

• *Resolution* is the collection of processes by which multiple possibilities for integration are pared down. These come in at least two subvarieties. First, the integrative processors must check for full integration of the input. For instance, the phonology integrative processor rules out the choice of *a* plus *apparent* in example (2) above, because the same segment is assigned to two words at once. Second, if a structure at one level is incoherent or disfavored by its integrative processor (i.e. loses out to competitors in the integration process), the interface processors can send inhibition up- or downstream to the associated structures at other levels. The overall goal of resolution is to produce a maximally favorable single structure at all levels.

It should also be remembered that each of these subprocesses is realized neurally. Thus they are not instantaneous, but rather have a time course—a rise time before maximum intensity is achieved; furthermore, the maximum intensity may differ from item to item. It is here, for instance, that it makes sense to localize the fact that reaction time in lexical decision tasks depends on word frequency (Oldfield and Wingfield 1965).

7.4.3 *Lexical access in production*

Because most work on language perception is concerned with syntactic parsing, theories of perception cannot help dealing with combinatoriality. However, a great deal of the production literature (e.g. Caramazza and Miozzo 1997; Engelkamp and Rummer 1998) seems to have focused on relatively non-combinatorial tasks like picture naming. They have therefore been able to conceptualize production simply in terms of spreading activation in a static network: a visual stimulus drives one end of the network, and the phonology of a word comes out the other end. Such a conception, however, is simply not up to the task of producing real language, since its machinery leaves no room for actually building sentences.

A more sophisticated tradition (e.g. Levelt 1989; 1999; Roelofs 1997; Levelt et al. 1999; Dell, Burger, and Svec 1997) recognizes the critical importance of combinatoriality. Lexical access is still treated in terms of spreading activation, but when it comes to building a sentence, the theory appeals to a more algorithmic view in which linguistic items are integrated into a skeleton of slots. Using a stricter distinction between long-term and working memory, and the distinction among the four subprocesses above, we can perhaps refine this view a little.

Suppose the conceptual department of working memory contains some thought that the speaker wishes to express. (Along with Levelt, I will not concern myself with (a) how the thought got there, nor with (b) what events in the f-mind trigger the language faculty into expressing it.) The initial event has to be a call to the lexicon: what words potentially express parts of this thought? As in perception, it is an open question whether the call to the lexicon should be thought of as an actual "call" from working memory or as the lexicon actively intruding itself on working memory.

Following Levelt and many others, it appears that the call to the lexicon results in the activation of a variety of lexical items of varying degrees of appropriateness for the part of the thought in question. In present terms, this can be thought of as binding the candidate items to working memory, where their conceptual structures compete for integration into the thought in conceptual working memory. At some point a best candidate wins the competition (the competition is resolved), based among other things on its match to the intended thought. This last step is standardly called "lexical selection" in the production literature.[7]

Two kinds of speech error result from incorrect lexical resolution/selection. If for some reason the wrong competitor is chosen, we get word substitutions based on similarity in meaning, say *He shot him through with a sword* for . . . *arrow*. If resolution/selection gets fouled up and two words remain in competition, we get blends such as *troblem* for *trouble* plus *problem*. (The mechanisms for the latter as we pass through to the phonology are not so clear, though.)

Once a lexical item's conceptual structure is bound to working memory, its syntactic and phonological structures ought to follow suit shortly and bind to their respective "blackboards"—without yet being integrated into structures. It is a point of logic that phonological integration has to await the completion of syntactic integration. The syntax determines what order words come in, which determines the order of phonological integration (remember, this is all being done incrementally: the processor doesn't have to finish the syntax or even the word choice for the whole sentence before starting to integrate the phonology).

In addition to linear order, the phonology must also know what morphological forms of words to choose, depending on the syntactic context. For instance, it has to know whether a verb is, say, in past tense or stem form, as in *He went* versus *Did he go?*—which is determined by syntactic context. It also has to know whether to put in morphemes that lack semantics, for instance *It's raining, He didn't go, a picture of Bill*, and, in languages such as German and

---

[7] It appears therefore that different subprocesses are called "selection" in the perception and production literatures: they correspond to what are called here "binding" and "resolution" respectively.

Italian, gender agreement endings on adjectives; these have no counterpart in the conceptual structure to be expressed.[8]

A similar but more complex story is told in perhaps the most detailed and influential tradition in speech production, that of Levelt and colleagues, referred to above. Levelt et al. argue, on the basis of substantial experimental evidence, that lexical access proceeds in two stages, selection of lemmas and selection of word forms or lexemes. Levelt (1989) characterizes the lemma (following Kempen and Hoenkamp 1987) as the complex of a word's semantic and syntactic features; in some later work it is characterized instead as the syntactic features alone. The initial process of lexical access is argued to involve only lemma selection; no phonological forms have yet been activated. After conceptual and syntactic integration and resolution have been achieved, there is a second call to long-term memory to retrieve a word form (or lexeme) that provides the phonology associated with the lemma's syntactically integrated form. Since the syntactically integrated form includes grammatical inflection and the like, we can say that *go* and *went* are different word forms associated with the same lemma GO, and that grammatical *it* and *do* are word forms without associated lemmas.

This is not the place to go through the extensive experimental evidence adduced in favor of this view—and against it (e.g. Dell 1986; Dell, Schwartz et al. 1997). However, two things make me uneasy about it on theoretical grounds. First, recall the logic of priming in speech perception. Phonological activation of *bug* has to result in semantic activation of *bug* in long-term memory, which in turn activates the semantics of *insect*, which activates the phonology of *insect*. If the lexicon is divided into lemmas and word forms, then the claim must be that lemmas can activate word forms in perception, but not in production. There may indeed be such an asymmetry, but it does not follow from anything.[9]

---

[8] Caramazza and Miozzo (1997) champion a lexical network in which semantic features activate phonology, which in turn activates syntactic features. They fail to consider the need for syntactic integration and for an independent working memory; their theory is based on a picture-naming paradigm, where syntactic integration is unnecessary. The sorts of phonological choice mentioned here, which depend on syntactic integration, are therefore completely unavailable to their model.

[9] People occasionally talk about having two different lexicons, one for perception and one for production. I find this odd, given that they involve the same kinds of structure, and given that perceived words can prime production. I tend to think that the differences between the two tasks are due to different processing problems rather than different lexical data bases. For one thing, perception is recognition memory for lexical items, while production is the much more difficult recall memory. Production also requires the assembly and execution of a motor program, adding to its difficulty. Finally, access to the lexicon through semantics in production may be inherently less stable than access through phonetics in perception—production has no external signal to which processing can be "clamped."

What disturbs me more is that, within the competence theory of the lexicon developed in the past two chapters, I cannot find a way to cleanly divide lexical items up into separable lemma and word form portions. Suppose, for instance, a lemma is a pairing of conceptual features with syntactic features, and a word form is a pairing of phonological features with syntactic features. The problem is that syntactic features alone are far too coarse for matching lemmas with word forms. For instance, as we have noted in previous chapters, the words *dog*, *cat*, *kangaroo*, *airplane*, and *calendar* all have the same syntactic features: [singular count noun]. Thus a match of lemmas to word forms based on their common features will be unable to distinguish these words from each other.[10] That is, the semantics is necessary to individuate the phonology; this is possible only in the standard tripartite organization of lexical entries. Other possible ways of dividing the lexicon into lemmas and word forms either suffer from similar problems or make it altogether impossible to establish linking (I leave the verification of this point to the interested reader).

Let us see how close we can get to the conclusions of the Levelt et al. tradition within the present theory, whose lexicon is not differentiated into lemmas and word forms. At the moment in time when a lexical item is initially activated, only its semantics is of interest. The conceptual integrative processor, which binds the lexical item to part of the thought being expressed, sees nothing but meaning. The next step is to use the semantics–syntax interface to put some material on the syntax blackboard. For this process, it is crucial to activate and bind the item's syntax. Then the syntactic integrative processor can begin to work this item into the syntax of the utterance being built. None of the processors invoked so far can see the item's phonology—so for all intents and pur-poses they are working with the item's lemma. And whether or not the item's phonology is activated in long-term memory at this point is irrelevant to these processors. Similarly, the later step of phonological integration is carried out by the syntax–phonology interface processor and the phonology integrative processor. These can see only the relation of the item's syntax to its phonology, and are oblivious to its meaning. Hence they are in effect working with the item's word form.

What this means is that it may not be necessary to reify the lemma and word form as components of the lexical item in long-term memory. Rather, lemmas and word forms emerge naturally as functional realizations of what the various processors can see. The fact that lemmas are invoked ahead of word forms in

---

[10] Most treatments in the literature evade this point by having a "syntactic node" [cat] that can serve as the link between semantic CAT and phonetic /kæt/. But, as stressed in Ch. 5, there should be no such syntactic node. It is only the custom of drawing syntactic trees with informal phonological information at the bottom that leads us to think there is one.

speaking is a natural consequence of the logic of the processor. This is very close to the Levelt story; it remains to be seen if the differences are more than rhetorical.[11]

7.4.4 *Speech errors and tip-of-the-tongue states*

As early as Lashley (1951) we find a basic account of the logic of speech errors. Consider Reverend Spooner's *our queer old dean* in place of *our dear old queen*. Lashley points out that, in order for the *kw* sound to be inserted in the intended word *dear*, it must already be present in working memory, waiting its turn for phonological integration. Lashley uses this to argue that speech cannot be produced by simple chaining of words one to another; rather some overall planning must be going on in advance.

An observation by Victoria Fromkin (1971) sets up speech errors as a paradigm for studying modularity in language processing. Fromkin points out that when morphemes are exchanged, they are treated phonologically as if they are completely normal in their new environment. Consider an example like *I'd hear that if I knew it*, uttered when what was intended was *I'd know that if I heard it*. The exchanged verbs appear in the appropriate form for their new environment—including *know* taking on its characteristic irregular past tense form. This suggests that the exchange has taken place in the course of syntactic integration, where the tense is still independent from the verbs. It is only at the stage of phonological integration that the tense is combined with the verbs into the

---

[11] I should address one important experimental result. Van Turennout et al. (1998) show that in a picture-naming task, syntactic information about a noun (its grammatical gender) is available a tiny amount of time (40 milliseconds) ahead of phonological information. This is taken as evidence for successive lemma and word-form stages in production. In the present story there are two possible interpretations. The first invokes the logic of processing. A spoken response cannot be produced without integrating the lexical item in question into working memory. And perhaps syntactic integration must precede phonological integration even in a picture-naming task, where the output is a single word.

A second interpretation invokes the neural instantiation of processing. Consider what it takes to activate an item's syntax and phonology in long-term memory. We have been assuming that when an item's semantics is activated, its syntax and phonology follow suit immediately; let us now go beyond this first approximation. A lexical item's syntactic structure is far sparser than its phonological structure: a part of speech plus a few inflectional features and perhaps a syntactic argument structure. The phonological structure, by contrast, has to spell out all the distinctive features of every segment. This might well have a consequence for activation: the syntax, having fewer features, in effect has less "inertia," and therefore might well rise above threshold activation faster than the phonology.

Either of these interpretations makes it possible to imagine the Van Turennout et al. results without invoking a lemma/word form split in the lexicon itself. Sorting the possibilities out experimentally is a challenge for future research.

irregular forms. However, phonological integration has no idea that the wrong verbs are there; it can't see the intended meaning. So it goes its merry way producing *knew*. Another such example, this time at the phonological level, is *an unkey's muncle* [intended: *a monkey's uncle*]. Here, since the *m* has been removed from *monkey*, the word now starts with a vowel. This triggers the automatic phonetic process of replacing *a* with *an*; this process doesn't care whether what it precedes is a real word or not.

Garrett (1975), through an extensive categorization of speech errors, maps out a sequence of stages in speech production that is close to what emerges from the present model. At the beginning of the process is lexical selection, which results in the semantic substitutions and blend errors mentioned in the previous section. The other main classes involve different stages of integration.

• Sound exchanges and shifts such as *our queer old dean* and *a but-gusting meal* [intended: *gut-busting*].

• Word exchanges and shifts: examples are *any guys you time . . .* [intended: *any time you guys. . .*] and *the crazy idea who had a good idea . . .* [intended: *the crazy guy. . .*]. Here words are moved around complete with their affixes. This case contrasts with

• Morpheme exchanges and shifts: examples are *I'd hear it if I knew it*; *naming a wear tag* [*wearing a name tag*]; *I hate raining on a hitchy day* [*hitching on a rainy day*]. In these examples, stems move around, leaving affixes in place.[12]

Garrett shows that each type of error has a characteristic maximal span over which shifts can take place, and characteristic constraints on what can substitute for what. Subsequent research (e.g. Shattuck-Hufnagel 1979; Levelt 1989; Dell 1986; Bock 1995) has refined the constraints and tendencies found in these different classes of errors. For present purposes, the main point is that Lashley was basically right about errors resulting from improper integration of material lying around in working memory.

Moreover, the stages of processing identified by Garrett correspond nicely to stages of integration in the present model. Sound exchanges and shifts are clearly problems in phonological integration. The word exchanges/shifts and morpheme exchanges/shifts are both problems in syntactic integration. Section 5.6 suggested dividing the syntactic component into phrasal and morphosyntactic tiers. Given this division, the word errors fall naturally under phrasal integration and the morpheme errors under morphosyntactic integration. This is hardly news. However, the close correspondence between the competence and

---

[12] Most of these examples are from Shattuck-Hufnagel's (1979) corpus of actually observed speech errors.

performance models now gives us a clearer chance to use speech error evidence in refining the balance of power among components in the competence theory.

Next consider tip-of-the-tongue (TOT) states. In a TOT state, speakers have selected a lexical conceptual structure and can accept or reject proffered words as what they had in mind. They just can't locate the phonology ("No, it's not THAT, but damned if I can remember what it is!"). As readers will surely recognize from personal experience, one may be able to recall *part* of the phonology or prosody ("It sounds like *da-DUM-dum*"); Caramazza and Miozzo (1997) show that in, say, Italian, one may also recall the grammatical gender ("It's *LA* something-or-other"), more or less independently of the phonology.[13]

The problem in TOT states could conceivably fall at three different points in lexical access. First, it could be a problem of activation: the lexical conceptual structure activated by the intended thought could fail to pass sufficient activation on to the corresponding phonology and/or syntax. Second, it could be a problem of binding: the phonology could be appropriately activated in long-term memory but fail to find its way into working memory. Third, it could be a problem of integration: the phonology could get onto the "blackboard" but fail to be integrated into the utterance. I am in no position to decide among these. Perhaps a correct solution or at least further experimentation may emerge from a closer consideration of the data (including from anomia and conduction aphasia) in light of the more fully articulated model of lexical access and modularity developed here.

7.4.5 *Syntactic priming*

Bock and Loebell (1990) give experimental evidence that not only do words prime other words, but syntactic structures prime other syntactic structures. Bock (1995: 199) explains:

For example, a speaker who employs a double-object dative in one utterance (perhaps, "The governess made the princess a pot of tea") is subsequently more likely to use a double-object dative than a prepositional dative, even in a completely unrelated utterance (so, "The woman is showing a man a dress" becomes relatively more likely than "The woman is showing a dress to a man").

This raises a problem for the usual approach to syntactic structure (p. 200):

[S]ince structural repetition does not appear to depend on the repetition of particular words or thematic roles or features of word meaning . . . , its explanation rests on the

---

[13] They use this independence to argue that lexical phonology and syntax are independently activated by lexical semantics, with which I concur. But they go on to argue for a model of lexical organization that is indefensible for reasons discussed in note 8 above.

transient enhancement of general structural procedures rather than the enhanced retrieval or use of specific stored information. If this is so, it becomes difficult to use frequency effects as symptoms of simple retrieval processes.

Bock is assuming the standard distinction between words and rules ("general structural procedures"), espoused even by Pinker (see discussion in section 6.2.3). She therefore finds syntactic priming rather puzzling, since priming is supposed to be characteristic of words.

However, recall how we ended up treating principles of phrase structure in Chapter 6. We found a cline of stored linguistic forms, from ordinary words, through idioms (which have complex syntactic structure), through constructions (which have syntactic structure and a meaning but contain variables), all the way to phrase structure rules—which have syntactic structure containing variables but no meaning. That is, in terms of storage, pieces of phrase structure are not as unlike words as Bock assumes. The only *procedural* rule in the grammar—what Bock calls a "general structural procedure"—is the operation UNIFY.

Our view of lexical storage thus suggests that syntactic integration involves not only integrating words into a structure in working memory, but also building that structure by retrieving stored "treelets" of phrase structure from long-term memory. Thus perhaps within the present view the priming of syntactic structure is less of a surprise: it follows from exactly the same principles as word priming. So here is a case where the appropriate competence theory helps make better sense of a performance phenomenon.

7.5 Structure-constrained modularity

7.5.1 Fodor's view and an alternative

We now leave the details of processing behind and turn to one of the dominating issues in the study of language processing: the question of its *modularity*. The most prominent exposition of modularity, of course, is Jerry Fodor's *The Modularity of Mind* (1983); Fodor has maintained the essentials of the position as recently as Fodor (2000a). As in the treatment of *Aspects*, I will concur with Fodor's overall agenda and many specifics, but I will offer a different realization.[14]

---

[14] I should caution the reader that I will be reading Fodor very literally. My impression is that modularity is understood somewhat differently—and more reasonably—in the lore, without anyone noticing that this is not what Fodor proposed.

The basic outlook of modularity is that we should not conceive of the f-mind as a giant maximally interconnected net, such that, for instance, one's language processing can potentially be affected by what one ate for breakfast or the color of the speaker's hair or millions of other ridiculous things. Fodor intends his book as an argument for the specialization of mental functional architecture, and as an argument against generalized association, general-purpose problem solvers, general connectionism, heavily top-down AI, and top-down "New Look" psychology.

Fodor's realization of this agenda is the hypothesis that input and output systems are organized into faculty-sized *modules*; the putative module devoted to language perception is the main topic of the book. The general idea is that modules are almost reflex-like: they are fast in operation and mandatory, so that, for instance, one cannot help hearing speech-like signals as speech. They are also reflex-like in that they are relatively stupid—in two important respects. First, they are domain-specific; for instance the language perception module deals only with linguistic structures, not with visual or social or historical information. Second, they are informationally encapsulated, which means that no other cognitive processes such as general inference or contextual understanding can "break into them" to affect their operation. In addition, Fodor claims, modules have characteristic brain localization and an innate basis; however, we observed in section 4.8 that many overlearned abilities behave like modular processors but are by no means innate.

Fodor contrasts the modularity of input and output systems with the process of "belief fixation," a central capacity which he claims is not modular in his sense. Fodor's chief example of belief fixation is scientific theorizing and discovery. But in general, belief fixation is less grandiose: it is the process of deciding whether you think that what someone tells you is true or not. Fodor's basic argument is that, unlike the process of determining what sentence you have heard, deciding whether it is true can take a long time and can draw on all sorts of disparate knowledge. More precisely, Fodor characterizes belief fixation as relatively slow, non-domain-specific, "isotropic" (i.e. potentially drawing on any kind of mental information), and "Quinean" (i.e. potentially resulting in the revision of any kind of mental information).

The view of processing advocated here leads to a variant of Fodor's position that I'll call "structure-constrained modularity" (I'll call Fodor's position "Fodorian modularity"). We can see already from Fig. 7.2 that, like Fodor, we are regarding the brain as a collection of specialists rather than an all-purpose cognizer. However, the locus of modularity in Fig. 7.2 is not large-scale faculties such as language perception, but the smaller scale of individual integrative, interface, and inferential processors. There is no extrinsic border around modules.

Rather, modules are *implicitly* differentiated, by what formats of cognitive structure they access and derive. Such a view of modularity has been espoused by Townsend and Bever (1982), Jackendoff (1987),[15] Arbib (1987), Levelt (1989), Prather et al. (1991), Bever (1992), and Coltheart (1999), among others. As we will see, it provides a natural explanation of many of the phenomena with which Fodor is concerned.[16]

Each module is strictly domain-specific in Fodor's sense: integrative and inferential processors deal with only one level of structure each; interface processors deal with two (we might therefore want to call them "bi-domain-specific"). Similarly, each module is informationally encapsulated: the only kind of information that can influence it is its designated input level. Through the chaining of integrative and interface processors—and the possibilities for constrained feedback among them—we achieve the overwhelmingly complex mapping between acoustic information and meaning. Furthermore, if each processor is mandatory and fast, then the chain will be mandatory and (almost as) fast. That is, the effect of Fodor's faculty-sized module is created by the chaining of a series of structure-specific modules.[17]

Much of the dissent concerning modularity (e.g. Crain and Steedman 1985;

---

[15] In Jackendoff (1987; 1997a; 2000) I used the term "representational modularity." The new terminology is adopted here as part of the effort to expunge "representation" from the theoretical vocabulary, for reasons discussed in Ch. 2.

[16] A somewhat different scale of modularity is invoked in the work of Cosmides and Tooby (e.g. Cosmides 1989; Tooby and Cosmides 1992), who sometimes speak of such modules as "cheater detection," "friendship," and "kin-oriented motivation." My inclination is to regard these as too small a domain for modularity: each of them is embedded in a rich system of cognitive structures and inferential processes concerning values and social interaction. It is this larger system that (to me at least) appears to be on a more appropriate scale for modular processes in the present sense (Jackendoff 1992a; ch. 4; 1994: ch. 15). Within such a system, cheater detection and so forth might be regarded as principles of social inference whose acquisition is highly favored by the genome, more or less akin to the "attractors" of Universal Grammar proposed in section 6.10. It appears to me that such a perspective does no damage to the genuine results of the Cosmides–Tooby program, but has the effect of making the rhetoric more compatible with that for language.

[17] We return to the "slow" central processes posited by Fodor, which apply to conceptual structure, in Chs. 9 and 10. To the extent that Fodor is correct about belief fixation being relatively slow, isotropic, and Quinean, these properties are now confined to inferential processors which compare newly constructed conceptual structures to those present in long-term memory, and which construct further inferences and judgments on the basis of this comparison. If, as I believe, there is a further system of central cognitive structure concerned with spatial understanding (Ch. 11), this too may well support slow and isotropic inferential processes: consider spatial problems like optimally packing a carton, designing a better mousetrap, and deciding the best route to drive to the other side of town. Such a division between propositional/conceptual structures and spatial structures is a central aspect of Stephen Kosslyn's (1980; 1996) research program. The upshot is that central processes may well be modular too, though of a different sort than the input and output processes.

Marslen-Wilson and Tyler 1987; Tanenhaus et al. 1995) has been about the relation between syntax and semantics—in particular, whether or not syntactic parsing (inside the language module) is influenced by semantics (outside the language module). The usual argument goes: such-and-such a property of meaning or context has a measurable influence on syntactic parsing, therefore language perception is not informationally encapsulated, therefore modularity is wrong. The usual reply (e.g. Forster 1979; Altmann 1987; Clifton and Ferreira 1987; Frazier 1987; Fodor et al. 1992) goes: If you look at the phenomena more subtly and do the following experiments, you find that up to a certain point in time, in fact syntax is *not* influenced by semantics, therefore modularity is right.

But notice that the argument concerns *Fodorian* modularity, where syntax is claimed to be insulated from semantics. Fodorian modularity might be wrong without requiring a reversion to indiscriminately general-purpose processing. In structure-constrained modularity, as we have seen, semantic effects on syntax are indeed possible, but they are constrained by the need to pass through the semantics–syntax interface. In language perception, such feedback will necessarily follow previous steps of syntactic integration, syntax–semantics interfacing, and semantic integration. Thus the logic of processing predicts, as observed, that there is an initial feedback-free period in syntactic parsing, but thereafter feedback is possible. That is, the observed timing of processing is a function of what information is available when, not some extrinsic constraint.

7.5.2 *Interface modules are how integrative modules talk to each other*

People often seem to think of a modular capacity as entirely independent of the rest of the f-mind. This is part of what underlies the widespread conception of a modular language capacity as an isolated "grammar box" (Chapter 4). Domain specificity and informational encapsulation indeed seem to imply such a position. However, notice that an entirely domain-specific and informationally encapsulated module would be functionally disconnected from the rest of the (f-)mind, and could therefore serve no purpose in the larger goal of helping the organism perceive and behave. So there is a problem with such a caricature of modularity: how do informationally encapsulated modules "talk to each other"? Structure-constrained modularity provides an answer: levels of structure communicate with each other through interface modules.

This solution closes a crucial gap in Fodor's conception of modularity. Fodor proposes that the output of the language perception module is some language-specific "shallow" structure, perhaps a syntactic parse or a "logical form"—he is not entirely specific. He *is* specific in denying that this output is a form of cognitive structure in terms of which rules of inference and/or meaning postulates are stated, and in terms of which judgments of truth are determined—what I call here "conceptual structure" and what Fodor would call "narrow content" or "the syntax of the Language of Thought."

Notice, however, that the process of language perception is supposed to lead to belief fixation, i.e. determining the truth value of the heard utterance. The difficulty is that *in order to be fixed, a belief has to be formulated in terms of conceptual structure.* A *linguistic* structure is simply the wrong vehicle for belief fixation. Fodor's faculty-sized module is therefore stranded without access to the cognitive structures it needs to attain.[18] Structure-constrained modularity does not face this problem: the transition from linguistic structure to conceptual structure is accomplished by an interface module that is altogether parallel in character to the one that mediates between phonology and syntax. (The latter is not a module for Fodor either: it is just some unexamined subcomponent within the larger Fodorian language perception module.)

This gap in Fodor's account of the modularity of language is an instance of a more pervasive problem in theorizing about cognitive processes, which arises from failing to observe the distinction between integrative and interface processors. The problem is revealed in the common practice of drawing diagrams of processing along the lines of (5),

(5)   syntactic processor → semantic processor

and saying things like "the output of the syntactic processor (or module) is sent to the semantics."

Although this makes sense intuitively, it neglects an important step. A syntactic processor is concerned strictly with elements of syntactic trees like Ns, VPs, complementizers, and case marking. Its parse of a sentence is still made out of syntactic units. A semantic processor knows nothing about NPs and case marking; rather it knows about things like conceptualized objects and events, and about claims to truth and falsity. Hence the syntactic information that a certain NP is the object of a verb is useless to the semantic processor. The semantic

---

[18] This point is made in different ways by Marslen-Wilson and Tyler (1987) and Jackendoff (1987). See Jackendoff (2000) for further discussion and examples.

Many people with whom I have discussed this point deny that Fodor really intends the language module to stop at syntax. However, Fodor's text is quite explicit. For instance, he has a long excursus (1983: 79–82) on the lexical priming experiments we discussed in section 7.4.2. He goes to great lengths to deny that *bug* primes *insect* by virtue of its meaning—which for him is inaccessible to the language module. He appeals instead to "stupid" "interlexical associations" that are supposed to be something *other* than meaning-based. While this might be possible for pairs like *salt* and *pepper* that are often heard in juxtaposition, it is less likely for *bug* and *insect*. As far as I know, the literature has rightfully neglected this aspect of Fodor's proposal.

processor needs to know that the individual denoted by this NP plays a certain thematic role (say Patient) in the action denoted by this verb. Similarly, consider a classic example of ambiguous PP attachment such as *Fran painted the sign on the porch*. The syntactic processor can say that the final PP may be attached to either the NP object or the VP. But this is of no use to the semantic processor, which is concerned with whether the speaker is specifying the location of the sign or the location of the action of painting. In both these cases, it is the linking rules, implemented by the syntax–semantics interface processor, that are needed to make the connection.

We see from these examples that syntactic structure can play no role in semantics except by being correlated with its semantic consequences. In other words, "sending" syntactic information to the semantic processor actually entails a process of correlation between one level of structure and another, a non-trivial process. It is not like sending a signal down a wire or a liquid down a pipe. It is, rather, a computation in its own right, just the sort of computation that an interface processor performs.[19]

7.5.3 The "bi-domain specificity" of interface modules

So far I have spoken of an interface module as if it simply accesses its characteristic input structure and produces its characteristic output structure. But we can be more precise.

For a simple case, consider the auditory system. Alvin Liberman and colleagues (e.g. Liberman 1996; Liberman and Studdert-Kennedy 1977) have argued at length that the auditory–phonetic interface processor is a specialized modular device that runs in parallel with ordinary auditory processing (e.g. church bell and thunder perception), starting with the same auditory input but analyzing it differently. In addition, two other specialized devices, voice recognition and auditory affect (tone of voice/emotion) perception, use the auditory signal in still different ways. Each of these two is known to be subject to differential dissociation due to brain damage (Etcoff 1986; 1989). That is, the

---

[19] This of course applies with double force to the eye-tracking experiments discussed in section 7.2. What the human eye tells the human brain is useless to the syntactic processor unless it can be converted into syntactic format, using the standard interface principles from vision into conceptual structure and from conceptual structure into syntax.

Clifton and Ferreira (1987: 290) make the tentative hypothesis that "some representational vocabulary—for instance, thematic roles [an aspect of conceptual structure—RJ]—may even be shared between the modules of the grammatical system and the general-purpose system for representing knowledge and beliefs." What should be emerging from the present discussion is that it is absolutely *essential* for modules to share information, and that they do so through interface modules.

auditory–phonetic interface is only one of several specialized interfaces that take auditory signals as input.

Each of these interfaces "sees" different parts of the auditory signal. The auditory–phonetic module pays attention to timing and distribution of formant transitions and to short-term variations in intensity and pitch—the distinctions it needs to derive phonetic structure. But it is oblivious to overall amplitude, pitch, and timbre, which serve instead as cues to voice and affect recognition. Conversely, the modules for identifying voice and affect are oblivious to the distinctions that identify phonetic segments, but they do detect the cues relevant to their own domains. That is, each of these interface modules makes use of only a subset of the distinctions available in the auditory input. Conversely, an interface module need not provide all the distinctions possible in its output domain: think again of how the auditory–phonetic module does not provide word boundaries.

This characteristic is replicated in other interface modules. The phonology–syntax module correlates linear order in its input and output structures. But, as observed in section 5.4, it knows nothing about aspects of phonological structure such as syllabification, which are relevant to pronunciation but not to syntax, and it knows few details of embedding in syntactic structure, which are more relevant to semantics than to phonology. Similarly, the interface that relates conceptual structure to visuo-spatial understanding knows nothing about such important aspects of conceptual structure as scope of quantification, conditionals, illocutionary force, or value. It recognizes only those aspects of conceptual structure that deal with objects, their parts, their location, their motion, and perhaps the forces among them. It also does not know everything there is to know about spatial structure: in particular, it probably does not have access to detailed analogue shape information about objects (Landau and Jackendoff 1993; Jackendoff 1996c; see also section 11.5).

Thus, in general an interface module can be more domain-specific than the integrative modules that construct its input and output structures. Its "bi-domain specificity" is limited precisely to those aspects of the two formats that can be directly correlated, while other aspects of each format are treated as irrelevant, "invisible" to the interface. Hence, to reinforce a point made in section 1.6, we ought to think of the connection created by an interface not as a "translation" from one format to another, but rather as a sort of partial homology.

In this light, consider some visual phenomena that interact with language perception. In the McGurk effect (McGurk and MacDonald 1976; Massaro 1997), experimental subjects are presented simultaneously with visual *ba* and acoustic *da*; they actually experience a heard *ba*, with no awareness of the presented mismatch. In other words, the visual input actually overrides the acoustics. In more ecologically realistic situations, the visually detected motion of the speaker's mouth contributes to phonetic perception and actually helps us hear in noisy environments. Within structure-constrained modularity, the McGurk effect can be attributed to an additional interface processor that uses visual input to contribute fragments of structure to phonological working memory. But this interface can't tell phonology about all aspects of phonological structure—only about those distinctive features that can be detected by visual inspection (lip closure and rounding, and perhaps vowel height) plus perhaps some weak information about degree of stress. Similarly, its input is not all of visual structure, but only those aspects that pertain to the external appearance of the vocal tract. So it implements an extremely limited partial homology between the visual input and phonological structure.

A different partial homology appears in the use of gesture accompanying language. As observed in section 5.3, beat gestures basically set up a metrical grid; these must be placed in optimal coincidence with the metrical grid in phonological structure. Every other aspect of phonological structure is irrelevant. A similar though more complex problem occurs in setting texts to music: the musical and linguistic stresses must coincide (within certain degrees of latitude). And of course visually detected beat gestures are available to music processing too: that's how the orchestra follows the conductor. In each of these cases, what is required is a highly bi-domain-specific interface processor that attempts to correlate metrical grids, ignoring all other aspects of the structures involved.

Reading requires yet another type of visual–phonological interface. This operation is fast, mandatory (try seeing writing as mere design!), and subject to domain-specific brain damage—again hallmarks of modular processes. Reading (at least in alphabetic orthographies) provides phonology with predominantly segmental information; punctuation gives some information about prosodic bracketing that is also derivable from the auditory signal. Unlike the auditory–phonological interface, reading does not give information about stress, except through use of underlining or italics. But on the other hand, reading gives more reliable information about word boundaries than auditory input. So the output of the reading interface partially overlaps with that of the auditory–phonological mapping, but is far from complete. The visual information "visible" to the reading interface is also partial. The phonological content of what you're reading doesn't change if you change the colors on your computer screen or carve the letters in a tree or put them up in neon lights. That is, reading does not exploit the full capabilities of the visual system, and it overlaps in complex ways with general-purpose vision. In short, like the other interfaces we have seen, reading implements a partial homology between its input and output structures.[20]

Sign language presents a more complex case. It evidently replaces one of the phonological tiers—the segmental structure—with a new one linked to visual input and motor output; its distinctive features are things like hand shape and hand movement. But the rest of phonological organization—syllabic, prosodic, and morphophonological structure—is preserved. Again, it appears that the replacement parts in the system are still highly domain-specific and encapsulated.

Thus we have at least four distinct interfaces between aspects of the visual system and aspects of phonology. Each is exquisitely specialized in the mapping it performs; each is bi-domain-specific in its own particular way. They cannot together be subsumed under a "general vision–phonology" processor.

What begins to bother me here is the proliferation of special-purpose interface processors. The situation is better than an indiscriminate general-purpose processor, because each processor is so limited in what it can do. On the other

---

[20] Suppose Fodor were right that the language module's input is transducers at the ear and its output is syntactic structure. Since phonological structure is a level intermediate between these two, it is by hypothesis informationally encapsulated. That means that the visual system should be unable to affect phonological structure—as it clearly does in reading. In other words, if we take Fodor's claim of informational encapsulation literally, there should be no such thing as reading.

Fodor might reply (and has done so) that we really don't know the exact extent of the language module, and that a full characterization would include this second class of possible inputs. Still, such an answer has to finesse a serious problem of how orthographic information is segregated and processed differently from the rest of visual input in the *visual* module.

Garfield (1987), a volume devoted to discussion of Fodorian modularity, contains a number of papers that mention reading, but curiously, none observes this challenge to Fodor's position. For instance, Clifton and Ferreira (1987) speak of a "lexical-processing module (which processes both visual and auditory information)" (279), which sneaks in reading without further notice. Yet the visual information involved in reading is not raw visual input: identifying letters and their linear order would appear to require a level of visual processing at which size and shape constancy have been established, and at which shapes can be abstracted away from the peculiarities of typeface. Moreover, the linear order of written words can't be detected by a purely "lexical" module. Hence much of the "vision module" must be invoked in reading—one input module coupled into the middle of another.

Moreover, Clifton and Ferreira (1987), Carroll and Slowiaczek (1987), and Frazier (1987) all discuss the effects of parsing difficulty on eye movements in reading, without noticing that such effects constitute a strong violation of the tenets of Fodorian modularity. Within Fodor's conception, how can the inner workings of the domain-specific and informationally encapsulated language module interact with the inner workings of the domain-specific and informationally encapsulated vision module, such that, say, "the eye-movement control system interrupts the word-recognition processor and switches into reanalysis mode, under the control of the language processor" (Carroll and Slowiaczek 1987: 234)? Unlike the other two papers, Carroll and Slowiaczek at least recognize vision and language as "two systems that are biologically and functionally distinct" (235); but they overlook the severe consequences for Fodorian modularity.

hand, where do they come from? Do all these pathways of information flow, complete with all their constraints, have to be innate?

I see a couple of possibilities. My inclination is to think that all the levels of structure—the integrative processors—are innate, and that some of the interface processors are innate but others are not. The process of reading, for instance, acts like a module in an accomplished reader, but it requires intensive training for most people in a way that the phonology–syntax module does not. At this point I don't fully understand the logical and neurological issues involved in making a claim that an interface module is learnable, so I will have to leave it at that.[21]

7.5.4 Multiple inputs and outputs on the same "blackboard"

Let us return briefly to the function of working memory as a "blackboard." Because of the independence of modules, any single level of structure can be fed simultaneously by multiple interface processors, all of whose outputs are taken into account by the integrative processor in constructing a maximally coherent structure. We have seen this abundantly within the language processor already: for instance, in perception, the phonological integrative processor is working on material being provided by the acoustic–phonetic interface, by the lexicon, and (through feedback) by the syntax–phonology interface.

We can now add to this mix the McGurk effect, where an interface processor with visual inputs (specifically mouth configuration) provides information to the phonological "blackboard" about the composition of phonetic segments. The phonology integrative processor doesn't know which interface processor has provided the input; it just puts together the fragments of structure on the "blackboard" as best it can. (And in the case of conflict between auditory and "McGurk" input, it sometimes chooses the latter!) In other words, the phonology integrative processor is still domain-specific and informationally encapsulated.

A parallel case in an altogether different domain is the sense of body orientation (Lackner 1981; 1988; Lackner and DiZio 2000). Here inputs converge from a wide variety of sensory systems: stretch receptors in the muscles, touch and pressure sensors in the skin, the semicircular canals and otolithic organs in

---

[21] A possibly wild suggestion: Suppose there are cortical areas for whose use more than one integrative module competes, and which shift allegiances depending on attention. Such an area would be in a position to detect and record fortuitous correlations between two modules that are capable of using it. It might therefore be possible for it to *develop* into an interface processor without having any special use for that purpose wired into it from the start. This speculation is encouraged by the fact that in the congenitally deaf, visual function can invade areas that are normally auditory cortex, and vice versa in the blind (Neville and Lawson 1987; Kujala et al. 2000).

the ear, and of course the visual system and auditory localization. The result is a unified sensation of body position and orientation, which in the present framework can be seen (for a first approximation) as the consequence of a single integrative processor reconciling the inputs from a large number of independent interface modules. Here, if anywhere, is a modular system in Fodor's sense: it is certainly a fast, mandatory, and cognitively impenetrable input system—but with multiple sources of input.

These are cases where multiple processors converge on a single "blackboard." The converse also exists: multiple interface processors that read from the same "blackboard." One case, discussed in the previous section, is the four interface modules that all read different aspects of auditory input: interfaces that feed general-purpose audition, phonology, voice recognition, and affect recognition. Similarly, conceptual structure is used as input for speaking (via the conceptual structure–syntax interface), drawing inferences (a process creating new conceptual structures from old), and acting (i.e. converting an intention—a kind of conceptual structure—into a structural format that can drive body motion such as navigating or reaching). Through the interface to the visual system, conceptual structure can also be used to check a belief, an inference, or a verbal claim against a visual input. Thus conceptual structure fulfills its central function by virtue of its "blackboard" being accessed by interfaces to many different capacities.

A different sort of situation arises in reading aloud. Here visual input drives phonological structure through an interface, but then the information flow goes in both directions: toward pronunciation via the phonology–motor interface, but also toward understanding via the phonology–syntax interface (except when reading aloud in a language one does not know!).

7.5.5 Informational encapsulation among levels of structure

As observed earlier, a totally informationally encapsulated module would be isolated from the rest of the f-mind, hence useless. The interface modules are what prevent such isolation. But Fodor's idea of informationally encapsulated modules still reflects an intuition that is worth capturing.

It seems to me that we can't talk properly about *the* informational encapsulation of a module. Rather, we have to talk about informational encapsulation in relative terms: to what degree does a distinction in one level of structure have a bearing on distinctions in some other level? For instance, word boundaries in phonology have a rather direct reflection in syntactic structure; so syntax is not at all encapsulated with respect to this aspect of phonology. Similarly, embedding in syntactic structure is closely related to embedding in corresponding conceptual structure, so there is little encapsulation here.

For a far more distant case, someone's hair color *can* affect conceptual structure through the spatial–conceptual interface, and, if expressed in language, have an indirect effect on produced phonological structure through the chain of interfaces (the speaker may say *Hey! You dyed your hair!*). Even the output of the semicircular canals may have an effect on phonological structure (*I'm dizzy!*), but the effect is distant, mediated by a long chain of intermediate levels of structure and interfaces.

On the other hand, the motion of the speaker's *lips* may have a *direct* effect on the hearer's phonological structure, through the "McGurk" interface. So here, in a very small domain, gerrymandered in both input and output components, we have more information flow, and more direct information flow, than in random aspects of vision and phonology.

In other words, the presence of an interface between two levels of structure is what makes them *not* informationally encapsulated from each other. The richness of the information flow depends on the degree to which the interface module is more domain-specific than the structures it connects. The phonology-syntax interface is relatively rich; the "McGurk" interface is not.

In principle, an interface module might be precisely as domain-specific as the structures that serve as its input and output: every distinction in the input structure could make a difference in the output structure, and every distinction in the output structure could be affected by something in the input structure. In such a case, though, it would hardly make sense to speak of two distinct "modules" any more, since their interactions would be more or less unconstrained. We might as well see the union of their domains as a single larger domain, and we might as well see the interface module just as embodying some of the principles involved in integrating this larger domain.

It therefore begins to make sense to speak of "degrees of modularity" rather than absolute modularity. Two domains connected by a narrow "information bottleneck" will be relatively modular: not very many parts of each domain can affect the other. As the interface becomes richer, more parts can interact. If communication between the two domains is wide open, it is impossible to say where one leaves off and the other begins. Given the gradual nature of this transition from relatively modular to nonmodular, it is impossible to draw a precise boundary on modularity.

A cynic might say therefore that the issue of modularity is dissolved. I would disagree. Rather, it develops into a more nuanced set of questions: What families of distinctions form richly interconnected and well-integrated domains, and where are there more restricted "information bottlenecks"? The correlates in processing are as they always have been: Can one identify particular stages of informational integration, enhanced by priming or disrupted by concurrent load in the same domain? Can these stages be identified with discrete levels of structure in the formal theory? To what extent can these stages be temporally distinguished in the course of processing and/or spatially distinguished by brain imaging? To what extent can they be differentially disrupted by brain damage? It seems to me that this more nuanced viewpoint leaves unaffected all the standard issues in processing; perhaps it can spare us continuation of some of the needless debate of the past fifteen years.

*   *   *   *   *

This survey of the relation between the competence and performance models has of course been exceedingly sketchy. I have mainly tried to show how the parallel architecture, supplemented by a robust notion of working memory, lends itself quite naturally to addressing processing issues. With luck this can lead to a refinement in framing questions for both linguistic theory and psycholinguistics—and for more fully cooperative enterprises.

CHAPTER 8

An Evolutionary Perspective on the Architecture

8.1 The dialectic

We now return to an important aspect of the hypothesis that the ability to acquire a language is a human cognitive specialization. As observed in section 4.8, such cognitive specialization must be coded somehow in the genes, which determine, very indirectly, how the brain is built. In order for these genes to come into existence, some evolutionary step is required at some time since humans diverged from our nearest relatives, the chimpanzees, about five million years ago.

If we are to take full responsibility for the hypothesis, then, it is incumbent on us to address the evolution of the language capacity. This chapter suggests some elements of a possible scenario, in part because of its intrinsic interest, in part towards justification of the UG hypothesis, but also in part as a way to further investigate and refine the architecture of the language faculty proposed in Chapters 5 and 6.

A number of factors stand in the way of developing evolutionary arguments concerning language. First of all, it is a running joke that in 1866 the Linguistic Society of Paris expressly prohibited papers on the origins of language. Evidently too many people had made fools of themselves; today's linguists don't want to fall into the same trap. On the other hand, 1866 was only nine years after the publication of *The Origin of Species*, and in recent years our understanding of evolutionary principles in general and of human origins in particular has expanded vastly. Now that evolutionary talk is rampant, plenty of other people are happy to speculate about evolution of language (e.g. Calvin 1990; Corballis 1991; Deacon 1997; Dennett 1991; Donald 1991)—without taking into account much of what is really known about language. So, as Derek Bickerton suggests (Calvin and Bickerton 2000), it is important for linguists to participate in the conversation, if only to maintain a position in this intellectual niche that is of such commanding interest to the larger scientific public. Some linguists have indeed risen to the challenge, as will be seen below. The present chapter too is offered in this spirit: I am not sure how seriously I want to take it, but as long as there is a debate, it is worth taking part.

Beyond the sociological issues, proposals about language evolution face two major difficulties. One is a question of data. There is no direct evidence for early forms of language until the advent of writing about 5,000 years ago, and by then we are dealing with fully modern language. Languages may change and "evolve" in the sense of *cultural* evolution, but as far as can be determined, this is in the context of a fully *biologically* evolved language capacity. For the prior five million years, we can make only very indirect inferences based on the nature of artifacts such as tools and pictures, and on equivocal hints about the structure of the brain and the vocal tract.

Indeed, the latter have over time proven less telling than originally thought. For instance, one of the early pieces of evidence (Lieberman 1984) concerned the fact that the Neanderthal larynx, like that of apes, is situated much higher in the vocal tract than that of modern humans, a position not conducive to producing the modern human variety of speech sounds. (Darwin pointed out this difference between humans and other primates, but Lieberman actually worked out the acoustics.) On the other hand, Fitch (2000) shows that, although the larynx of monkeys and goats is positioned much like that of Neanderthals, it descends substantially during the animal's vocalizations—to something much closer to the modern human position. There is no reason not to assume the same was true of Neanderthals, in which case certain aspects of Neanderthal acoustics would have more closely approached the modern standard than Lieberman claimed.

Fitch also reviews fossil evidence from brain endocasts (which can reveal hemispheric differences), from fossil hyoid bones (the attachment point for many vocal tract muscles), and from the size of the canal in the base of the skull for the hypoglossal nerve that controls the tongue. Though each of these has been offered as evidence for or against speech in hominids, Fitch concludes that recent results have rendered all this evidence rather equivocal. And even though Lieberman's arguments about the more limited acoustic possibilities of the upper Neanderthal vocal tract (tongue position and so forth) have not been challenged, this still tells us little about whether Neanderthals *spoke*, and, more important, about what they had to say. In short, there is virtually nothing in the paleontological record that can yield strong evidence about when and in which stages the language capacity evolved.

Moreover, although there are numerous systems of animal communication, none of them has anything like the expressive capacity of human language (Hauser 1996). They consist either of small collections of discrete messages (such as vervet monkey call systems), messages that vary along a very limited number of dimensions (such as honeybee communication about location of food sources), or messages in which greater elaboration of the signal conveys greater intensity or charisma but not a concomitant elaboration of the message (as in bird songs). As observed already by Darwin (1872), most aspects of primate communication have good human analogues in our systems of facial expression, tone of voice, and "body language." Thus there is no comparative basis in other species for most of the distinctive characteristics of language, and in particular no evidence for significant precursors of language in the apes.

Accordingly, the main evidence I will adduce here comes from the structure of language as we see it today; I will look within modern language for traces of its past. This is to some extent a justifiable methodology in evolutionary theory. For instance, there is virtually no fossil evidence for the evolution of the structure of eyes, as soft tissue is only rarely left behind. Therefore the main evidence for evolution is comparative study of the eyes of modern organisms. Of course we do not have comparative studies of language in other species; but in partial compensation we have comparative linguistic typology as a source of hints.

A second major difficulty in thinking about the evolution of the language capacity is internal to linguistic theory. The common view of Universal Grammar treats it as an undecomposable "grammar box," no part of which would be of any use to hominids without all the rest. The syntactocentric perspective in particular presents serious conceptual difficulties to an evolutionary story. Syntax is useless without phonology and semantics, since it generates structures that alone can play no role in communication or thought; so syntax could not have evolved first. But phonology and semantics could not have evolved first, because (in this architecture) they are simply passive handmaidens of syntax.[1]

There therefore has arisen a characteristic dialectic which if anything has hardened over time, as evolutionary arguments about cognition have gained in ascendancy and at the same time generative grammar has retreated from direct connections with performance and brain instantiation. Opponents of UG argue that there couldn't be such a thing as UG, because there is no evolutionary route to arrive at it. Chomsky, in reply, has tended to deny the value of evolutionary argumentation. For instance, section 4.8 cited an allusion in *Aspects* (59) to a

---

[1] Chomsky (1981) subdivides GB syntax into a number of components or "modules," such as case theory, binding theory, theta-theory, and so on. But these are not candidates for independent evolution either; each is useless in the absence of the others.

possible alternative to natural selection, "principles of neural organization that may be even more deeply grounded in physical law." Perhaps Chomsky's most famous quote about evolutionary argumentation is this one (among several cited in Newmeyer 1998a):

We know very little about what happens when 10^{10} neurons are crammed into something the size of a basketball, with further conditions imposed by the specific manner in which this system developed over time. It would be a serious error to suppose that all properties, or the interesting properties of the structures that evolved, can be 'explained' in terms of natural selection. (Chomsky 1975: 59)

As Toulmin (1972), Newmeyer (1998a), and Dennett (1995) point out, this is virtually a retreat to mysticism, appealing to the simple increase in brain size plus the convergence of unknown physical principles. We must not discount the possibility that Chomsky is right; but surely it is worth attempting to make use of the tools at our disposal before throwing them away.

Piattelli-Palmerini (1989) argues, along more evolutionarily defensible lines, that language is nothing but a "spandrel" in the sense of Gould and Lewontin (1979).[2] In his scenario, a number of unrelated developments motivated by natural selection coincidentally converged on a brain structure that happened to instantiate UG, which itself was not selected for. A similar hypothesis appears in Toulmin (1972: 459): "the physiological prerequisites of language developed, in proto-human populations, in a manner having nothing whatever to do with their subsequent 'linguistic' expression." Toulmin ends up hoping that "language might then turn out to be the behavioural end-product, not of a unitary and specific 'native capacity' precisely isomorphic with our actual linguistic behaviour, but rather of more generalized capacities" (465). That is, he specifically wishes to deny the UG hypothesis. As Newmeyer (1998a) points out, one cannot both have a specialized eccentric UG, as Piattelli-Palmerini would like, and claim that it is merely a consequence of general capacities, as Toulmin would like.

Chomsky, Piattelli-Palmerini, and Toulmin all are in effect taking the position that UG was not something that natural selection directly shaped—that it is in some way just a fortunate accident. The former two are using this position to answer the critics of UG; Toulmin is using a similar position to deny a special UG. Without further evidence, then, this argument is a standoff.

Pinker and Bloom (1990) argue for a different position: that the communica-

---

[2] Dennett (1995) observes that Gould and Lewontin's use of the term "spandrel" is not analogous to the architectural sense of the term on which they claim to draw. However, the term has taken on its own life in evolutionary theory, like "Universal Grammar" in linguistics, so I suppose we have to live with it.

tive advantages of human language are just the kind of cognitive phenomenon that natural selection is sensitive to. Therefore our best hypothesis is that language has evolved incrementally in response to natural selection. This is the position I will take here; I will therefore attempt to provide some parts of a plausible evolutionary scenario. Two basic insights contribute to breaking the logjam posed by Chomsky's version of UG. First, Chapters 5 and 6 have begun to decompose the language capacity into many semi-independent parts. It thus becomes possible to ask to what extent they could have emerged either independently or in sequence. In this respect I will concur with Toulmin's incremental story—with the major difference that the pieces added incrementally are specifically linguistic rather than general-purpose.

The second insight that contributes to breaking the evolutionary impasse posed by a "grammar box" is Derek Bickerton's proposal for two incremental steps in the evolution of language (a similar and somewhat more highly structured proposal is offered by Givón 1995). Although the proposal to be developed here differs from Bickerton's in many respects, he provides an excellent starting point for substantive discussion.

8.2 Bickerton's proposal and auxiliary assumptions

In his book *Language and Species* (1990), Bickerton proposes that the human capacity for language evolved in two stages. His second stage is language as we know it—let's call it "modern language." He calls the first stage "protolanguage"; for a first approximation one can think of it as modern language minus syntax. His hypothesis is that for several million years, hominids spoke only in a protolanguage, and that the development of modern language is perhaps as recent as 50,000 years ago, with the appearance of *Homo sapiens*.

What elevates Bickerton's story above mere speculation is his claim that protolanguage is still present in the modern human brain. It surfaces when modern language is disrupted; examples are pidgin languages (Bickerton 1981), "Genie," the woman isolated from human contact from age three to thirteen (Curtiss 1977), and possibly agrammatic aphasics. It also surfaces in situations when modern language has not developed: on one hand in early child language, and the other hand in the experiments in teaching language to apes (Linden 1974; Savage-Rumbaugh et al. 1998). Thus evolution did not throw a Good Idea away; rather it built on it. (This story is reminiscent of Rod Brooks's (1986) notion of a "subsumption architecture," in which new, more refined systems are added on top of less articulated existing ones.)

Bickerton (1990) still views the development from protolanguage to modern language as a single rather miraculous leap (in Calvin and Bickerton 2000 he takes a more gradualist position). Nevertheless, his insight is the opening wedge in conceiving of a more graceful incremental evolution of the language capacity. Lewontin (1990: 741), in a reply to Pinker and Bloom, presents the challenge:

The explanatory reconstruction of the origin of the camera eye by natural selection requires a particular ordering of light receptor and ennervation first, followed by lens, followed by focusing distortion of the lens and iris diaphragm. The reverse order would not work, if every stage was to be an improvement in vision. Is there an unambiguous ordering for the elements of natural language? Did we have to have them all at once, in which case the selective theory is in deep trouble?

I will argue that one actually can reconstruct from modern human language a sequence of distinct innovations over primate calls, some prior to Bickerton's protolanguage, and some later, each of which is an improvement in communicative expressiveness and precision. Like Bickerton, I will look for traces of these stages in degraded forms of modern language, and relate these stages to what apes have been trained to do. But in addition—and I take this to be an important innovation—in some instances I will be able to show, not just that these earlier stages are still present in the brain, but that *their "fossils" are present in the grammar of modern language itself*, offering a new source of evidence on the issue.

The consequence is that it will no longer be meaningful to ask the divisive question, "Does primate P (e.g. Sarah, Washoe, Koko, Kanzi) and did hominid H have language?" We can only ask "What *elements* of a language capacity might primate P have, and what elements might hominid H have had?" If nothing else, opening this room for a middle ground should be a useful contribution to discourse.

I will make a number of assumptions without justification. All are arguable, but they either make little difference or would take us too far afield here.

• I will not be concerned with the question of "what makes humans unique." There seems often to be an impulse to find the single innovation from which flowed everything distinguishing humans from apes, whether it is walking upright, having opposable thumbs, eating more meat, females having continuous sexual receptivity, or something else. All kinds of things make humans unique, just as all kinds of things make every species unique.

• I assume that language arose primarily in the interests of enhancing communication, and only secondarily in the interests of enhancing thought. (See Chapters 9 and 10 and Jackendoff 1996b; 1997a: ch. 8 for my position on the relation of language and thought.)

• I assume that language arose in the vocal-auditory modality, not in the gestural-visual modality, as has been proposed by Corballis (1991) and Givón (1995), among others. This is just a matter of convenience in exposition; a gestural-visual origin would not materially change my story.

- Along with Pinker and Bloom (1990), I assume that the complexity and specialization of language precludes it being simply a natural development from (or spandrel of) increased memory, planning abilities, motor functions, or other more general functions.

- Most importantly, I assume that any increase in expressive power and precision of the communicative system is adaptive, whether for cooperation in hunting, gathering, defense (Pinker and Bloom 1990), gossip, "social grooming," or deception (Dunbar 1998; Power 1998; Worden 1998). I see no reason to champion any particular one of these as *the* driving force behind language; they would all have benefited from increased expression.

- I will not inquire as to the details of how increased expressive power came to spread through a population (I agree with practically everyone that the "Baldwin effect" had something to do with it),[3] nor how the genome and the morphogenesis of the brain accomplished these changes. Accepted practice in evolutionary psychology (e.g. Dawkins 1989; Barkow et al. 1992) generally finds it convenient to ignore these problems; I see no need at the moment to hold myself to a higher standard than the rest of the field.

- I will not be concerned with establishing the absolute timing of the successive innovations in the language capacity. What concerns me here is the logical progression of stages, hence only their relative timing.

Following the lead of Bickerton and many others, I will draw on evidence from child language, late second language acquisition, aphasia, pidgin languages, and ape language experiments. It is of course never clear how relevant such evidence is for evolutionary concerns—in particular, to what degree ontogeny really does recapitulate phylogeny. Nevertheless, this is all the evidence we've got, so we must make the most of it, while recognizing that it should be taken with a grain of salt.

Finally, I take my cue from an important observation of Wolfgang Köhler (1927) in connection with his studies of animal problem-solving: cognitive steps which appear to us altogether natural may decompose into some parts that are natural for another organism and some parts that are very difficult. The evolutionary counterpart of this observation is that no matter how natural and adaptive some aspect of cognition might appear, it is by no means inevitable that evolution should immediately chance upon it. Thus, for instance, I cannot concur with Corballis's (1991) assumption that an organism with hierarchically

---

[3] The "Baldwin effect": If organisms are capable of learning some task that is important in their environment, natural selection may favor those individuals who, by virtue of genetic variation, happen to have an innate "leg up" on learning the task. The effect is that innate knowledge will gradually develop over generations, making learning easier. (See Dennett 1995, among many others.)

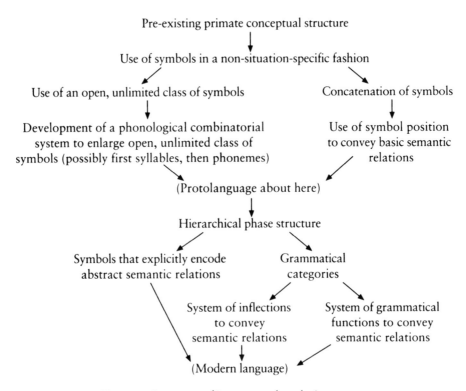

Fig. 8.1. Summary of incremental evolutionary steps

organized behavior is therefore poised to invent syntax (see discussion by Bloom 1994a). Rather, each expansion in the range of the organism's behavior must potentially be regarded as an independent evolutionary step.

The steps I propose are summarized in Fig. 8.1. Logically sequential steps are ordered top to bottom; logically independent steps are presented side by side.

8.3 The use of symbols

The most important preconditions for language are already demonstrably present in primates: there must be a community of individuals who have thoughts worth communicating to each other. I take it as established by decades of primate research (Köhler 1927; Cheney and Seyfarth 1990; de Waal 1996; Tomasello 2000b, among many many others) that chimpanzees have a combinatorial system of conceptual structure in place, adequate to deal with physical problem-solving, with navigation, and above all with rich and subtle social interaction incorporating some sense of the behavior patterns and perhaps intentions of others.

However, primates are strictly limited in the sorts of information they can communicate.[4] The most important step in getting human language off the ground is the voluntary use of discrete symbolic vocalizations (or other signals such as gestures). Achieving this stage is a major evolutionary step: Deacon (1997), Donald (1991), and Aitchison (1998) are correct in seeing symbol use as *the* most fundamental factor in language evolution. I will not join them in speculating how this ability arose in the hominid line, nor on what precursors had to be present for this ability to evolve. Instead I will concentrate on what had to happen next—on what many researchers shortsightedly view as a straightforward and inevitable development of language from such humble beginnings.

Deacon in particular seems to think that symbols require grammatical combination; he therefore attempts to vault immediately into grammar without any intervening step. However, a single vocalization, as in a one-year-old's single-word utterance, can clearly serve symbolically. I therefore concur with most speculation on the subject in thinking that this initial stage consisted of single-symbol utterances, lacking combinatoriality.

Single-symbol utterances in young children go beyond primate calls in important respects that are crucial in the evolution of language. Perhaps the most important difference is the non-situation-specificity of human words. The word *kitty* may be uttered by a baby to draw attention to a cat, to inquire about the whereabouts of the cat, to summon the cat, to remark that something resembles a cat, and so forth. Other primates' calls do not have this property. A food call is used when food is discovered (or imminently anticipated) but not to suggest that food be sought. A leopard alarm call can report the sighting of a leopard, but cannot be used to ask if anyone has seen a leopard lately (Cheney and Seyfarth 1990; Hauser 1996).

In addition, the child's one-word stage shows considerable conceptual subtlety. For instance, as demonstrated by Macnamara (1982), very young children already appreciate the logical distinction between proper nouns (symbols for tokens—mostly token humans, pets, and places) and common nouns (symbols for types or kinds of any sort). Considerable inquiry has been focused on how children may acquire (or innately have) this aspect of semantics (e.g. Bloom 1999; 2000; Carey and Xu 1999; Hall 1999). Notably, all the famous ape language training experiments of the past three decades seem to have achieved this stage (at least on the more enthusiastic assessments such as Savage-Rumbaugh

---

[4] Sometimes when I claim that primate thought is in many respects like ours, people ask, "But if apes can think, why can't they talk?" The answer is that they don't have a capacity to acquire phonological and syntactic structures that map thought into linguistic expression. That's exactly what it means to say language is a cognitive specialization, separate from thought.

et al. 1998): non-situation-specific use of a repertoire of single symbols, including both symbols for individuals (proper names) and symbols for categories (common nouns).[5]

However, we can potentially go back further in evolution than the one-word stage: certain little-remarked aspects of modern language are if anything *more* primitive than the child's one-word utterances. Consider the "defective" lexical items mentioned in Chapter 5. These items have no syntax and therefore cannot be integrated into larger syntactic constructions (other than direct quotes and the like). One group of them is associated with sudden high affect, for instance *ouch!*, *dammit!*, *wow!* and *oboy!* These can remain in the repertoire of the deepest aphasics, apparently coming from the right hemisphere (Jackson 1874). Another group includes situation-specific utterances such as *shh*, *psst*, and some uses of *hey* that have almost the flavor of primate alarm calls. Though the *ouch* type and the *shh* type both lack syntax, they have different properties. *Ouch* is often used non-communicatively, but *shh* calls for a hearer; and the *ouch* type are more likely to be uttered involuntarily than the *shh* type, which are usually under conscious control. Also among single-word utterances are the situation-specific greetings *hello* and *goodbye* and the answers *yes* and *no*. The latter are not completely situation-specific: in addition to answering questions, one can use *yes!* to encourage or congratulate the addressee and *no!* as a proto-command for the addressee to cease what (s)he is doing. It is important to notice that no animal call system includes a signal of generalized negation like *no*, which as all parents know is one of the earliest words in child vocabulary.

I would like to think of such words as these as "fossils" of the one-word stage of language evolution—single-word utterances that for some reason are not integrated into the larger combinatorial system. English probably has a few dozen of these—let us not forget exotica such as *abracadabra* and *gadzooks*—and I imagine every language has parallels. Their semantic and pragmatic diversity suggests that they are island remnants of a larger system, superseded by true grammar.[6]

---

[5] It is an interesting question why apes have this capacity, if in fact they do. Why should they be able to acquire and use symbols, despite the fact that it is not something they ever encounter in the wild? I don't know. What I do know is that they don't spontaneously invent symbols, the way deaf children do in inventing "home sign" (section 4.9.4). My inclination is to think symbol use is a "spandrel" for apes, a consequence of other capacities, but that it has been ramped up into a robust specialization in humans, perhaps by the "Baldwin effect."

[6] Just to be very clear: I am not suggesting that the actual "defective" lexical items of English are historical holdovers from this stage of evolution. Rather, what is a holdover is the possibility for a language to contain such "defective items"; those of English are realizations of this possibility.

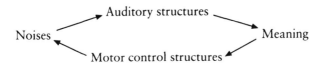

Fig 8.2. Architecture of early single-symbol stage

At this point, then, the system has an architecture like Fig. 8.2. The symbols of the system are long-term memory associations between meanings and auditory/motor codes; we might call them "paleo-lexical items." The arrows in this diagram stand for interfaces of the sort described in Chapter 5.

8.4 Open class of symbols

To go beyond single symbols toward modern language, we need two major innovations. The first is to permit an unlimitedly large class of symbols in the system (a large lexicon); the second is the concatenation of symbols into larger utterances (the beginning of syntax). These two are logically independent: one could have a communicative system involving only one or the other. This is reflected in Fig. 8.1 in the two parallel tracks descending from "use of symbols."[7]

Let's think first about the open vocabulary, the repertoire of meaningful linguistic units stored in long-term memory. By contrast with primate call repertoires (the closest appropriate comparison), which number roughly in the dozens at most, the vocabulary of an average speaker is estimated to run into the tens of thousands. Beginning around the age of two, children learn these in droves, and we keep picking up new words all our lives (Carey 1978). As stressed by Donald (1998), such a large vocabulary places significant demands on long-term memory and rapid retrieval.

The language-trained apes, by contrast, acquire at most several hundred symbols, mostly through extensive training, but in some instances (e.g. Savage-Rumbaugh's bonobo Kanzi) appearing to "just pick them up." At present it is unknown what accounts for the hundredfold difference in vocabulary size. It might be a consequence of the larger human brain, or alternatively of some special human "tuning" that makes vocabulary learning vast and effortless. Some indirect evidence suggests the latter. Reports of children subjected to early hemispherectomy (Vargha-Khadem et al. 1991) do *not* observe massive vocabulary

---

[7] Intuitively, it makes sense that development of an open vocabulary probably went on concurrently with the advent of combinatoriality. I keep them separate so as to make clear the logical independence of the two developments.

deficits despite a half-size brain. Similarly, Lenneberg's (1967) discussion of Seckel Syndrome ("nanocephalic dwarfs") did not report massively impaired vocabulary learning in these individuals with chimpanzee-sized brains. This evidence hints that the effortlessness of vocabulary acquisition is indeed a human cognitive adaptation. Though apes can learn vocabulary, I suspect that this learning is qualitatively different, rather like children's learning of reading: a largely effortful undertaking requiring much motivation and instruction, quite unlike children's spoken (and signed) word learning, which is rapid and spontaneous.

Late second-language learners can be counted on to acquire substantial vocabulary, even when their grammar and especially pronunciation is far from fluent. In the famous case of "Genie" (Curtiss 1977), vocabulary acquisition began immediately upon her discovery, and her rate of vocabulary acquisition approximated that of young children. Yet after years of training, her grammar remained exceedingly rudimentary. Parallel results obtained in a similar case are reported in Curtiss (1994). These well-known facts suggest that the capacity for an open vocabulary is independent of that for grammatical elaboration.

At some point, then, the hominid line had to adapt to learning this vast number of symbols. As Donald (1991) observes, the uniquely human ability to imitate—yet another important cognitive adaptation—obviously plays a role here in the acquisition of the sounds of words. And given the importance of pointing (both by parents and children) in early language acquisition, it is surely significant that apes do not appear to appreciate pointing in the way that human infants do from before one year of age (Povinelli et al. 2000). Imitation and pointing are both important preadaptations for the acquisition of an open vocabulary.

In turn, in order for there to be this vast number of symbols to learn, hominids had to be adapted to be able occasionally to invent *new* symbols, yet another adaptation. It is not clear to me how much metasymbolic capability this would require; the issue requires more investigation, perhaps by looking at the metasymbolic abilities of very young children.

8.5 A generative system for single symbols: proto-phonology

As the class of symbols becomes larger, the perceptual problem arises of making all the utterances discriminable and memorable. If the symbols were holistic vocalizations like primate calls, even a thousand symbols would be impossible to keep distinct in perception and memory (Nowak et al. 1999). Modern language deals with this problem by building words up combinatorially from a repertoire of a few dozen smaller meaningless speech sounds. Using concatenated speech sounds to construct conventionalized vocalizations makes the distinction among vocalizations a categorical/digital matter rather than a graded one.

Recall Lieberman's (1984) observation that, as late as the Neanderthals (however they are related to us), the shape of the vocal tract did not allow the multitude of easily perceptible distinctions among speech sounds found in modern language (this point is disputed by Aiello 1998). Lieberman, however, points out that an open vocabulary is still possible with a less highly differentiated phonological system. For example, with a repertoire of ten distinct phonemes, one could still construct thousands of words of reasonable length; after all the modern language Hawaiian makes do with only thirteen phonemes. The evolution of the vocal tract—and of the brain machinery that operates it—can be seen as driven by the adaptivity of a larger vocabulary, made possible in part by more rapid articulation and enhanced comprehensibility.

An intermediate stage in evolving a phoneme-based vocabulary might have been based on the syllable rather than the phoneme as the generative unit. The syllable is basically a unit of articulatory gesture, and, as we saw in Chapter 5, the rhythmic organization of language (stress and timing) revolves around the syllable rather than the individual phoneme. Its basic organization is a move from some relatively closed position of the mouth, through a relatively sonorous segment (usually a vowel but occasionally a "syllabic consonant," as in the final syllable of *syllable*), to relative closure again (either the close of the syllable or the beginning of the next). MacNeilage (1998) proposes that this basic form is an adaptation from the mouth's basic close–open–close cycle used for chewing.

The syllable demonstrably plays an important role in speech perception and production. Levelt and Wheeldon (1994) offer psycholinguistic evidence that the repertoire of most frequently used syllables (generally numbering around a few hundred) is stored in what they call a "syllabary"; among other things the syllabary includes a repertoire of motor scripts that aid in rapid articulation.

Clara Levelt (1994) suggests that children around one year of age organize their phonetic articulation in terms of syllables that are not entirely decomposed into independent phonemes. The earliest words tend to have a uniform place of articulation: the mouth opens and shuts but tongue and lip position are held constant. Thus child prefers words such as /tɪn/, in which the tongue tip is near the teeth throughout, or /pom/, where the lips form the major vocal tract constriction throughout. Then the child begins to vary the place of articulation within the syllable, producing things like /pɪn/, where the closure starts at the lips and ends with the tongue on the teeth. It is at this point that we can begin to speak of the child having a real differentiation into phonemes.

In terms of conscious control of speech, children can be taught to count syllables (in my experience) quite readily at three. They cannot be taught to individuate speech sounds until five or six, the age when most children are ready to learn to read; reading alphabetic orthography depends on decomposing words into speech sounds. Even very young children, of course, intuitively appreciate rhyme, which depends on everything in the syllable from the vowel onward. And many cultures have developed syllabic scripts (one character per syllable), whereas by contrast alphabetic script seems to have been invented only once. All these bits of circumstantial evidence point to a certain cognitive primacy to the syllable, despite its being phonetically composite.

Thus we might speculate that the earliest open-ended class of protowords in hominids was composed not from individual speech sounds but, as suggested by MacNeilage, (proto)syllables, each of which was a holistic vocal gesture. A repertoire of ten such gestures could be used to build 100 two-protosyllable vocalizations and 1,000 three-protosyllable vocalizations—well on the way to being open-ended. I imagine that a system of this sort would be possible with the Neanderthal vocal tract. The differentiation of protosyllables into modern syllables analytically composed of phonemes could then be seen as a further step in language evolution; this would make possible a larger and more systematically discriminable class of syllables, in the interests of adding an order of magnitude to the size of the vocabulary. At the same time, the syllable retains some primacy as a phonological unit owing to its longer evolutionary pedigree.

As many linguists (e.g. Hockett 1960; Lieberman 1984; Studdert-Kennedy 1998)—but not many non-linguists—have recognized, the innovation of phonological structure is a major cognitive advance. It requires us to think of the system of vocalizations as *combinatorial*, in that the concatenation of inherently meaningless phonological units leads to an intrinsically unlimited class of words. This is not the fancy recursive generativity of syntax, but, as observed in Chapter 5, it is generativity nonetheless: it is a way of systematizing existing vocabulary items and being able to create new ones, based on the principle of concatenating syllables fairly freely. In turn, syllables are built up from concatenated speech sounds, following fairly strict universal principles of sonority plus arbitrary restrictions and elaborations that differ from language to language.[8] A generative phonological system is thus a crucial step in the evolution of language, necessary for the vocabulary to achieve its presently massive size. (I

---

[8] It is interesting that the constraints on English syllable structure are violated by some of the single-word English utterances mentioned in the previous section, for instance *shh, psst, ʔm-hm* ('yes'), *ʔm-ʔm* ('no'), and the apical click of disapproval usually spelled *tsk-tsk*. Perhaps this attests to their primitivity in the linguistic system, "fossils" of the protosyllabic stage.

have not touched at all upon the evolution of other aspects of the phonological system: tone in tone languages, stress, speech rhythm and intonation.)

As mentioned above, child language develops phonological organization very early. By contrast, to my knowledge none of the ape experiments has achieved this step (or even tested it). In the cases where the "language" being taught is visual symbols (lexigrams), each symbol seems to be an unanalyzed visual form. In the cases where sign language was taught, I am not familiar with any evidence that the apes learned the signs in terms of the analytic features of handshape, position, and movement that (as argued by Wilbur 1990 among others) constitute the parallel to syllabic structure in spoken languages.

It should be mentioned, however, that creative concatenation of meaningless elements does appear in the songs of certain bird species, whose repertoire is enlarged by recombination of discriminable song fragments (Hauser 1996; Hultsch et al. 1999; Slater 2000). At the moment the consensus seems to be that no meaning differences accrue from the newly created songs. Rather, larger song repertoires appear to be associated with relative social dominance. Given that the function of this recombination is so different, and given the phylogenetic distance between humans and songbirds, I see no reason to believe there is any inherent link between birdsong and phonology. This is just one of those cases where evolution happened to come up with the same trick on different occasions. Similar concatenative procedures appear to exist in cetacean songs and in possibly some primate "long calls" (Marler 1998; Ujhelyi 1998; Payne 2000); only in the last case is there justification for a possible evolutionary link with human phonology.

8.6 Concatenation of symbols to build larger utterances

A baby's use of single-word utterances is highly context-dependent and must be interpreted in any given situation with a liberal dose of pragmatics. Still, communication *does* take place—a baby's needs are much easier to understand when (s)he has a few dozen words than when there are no words at all. I therefore take it that a communicative system entirely of this sort—where all words behaved grammatically like *hello*—would still be useful to hominids, especially if it had a sizable vocabulary.

One virtue of Bickerton's proposed two-stage evolution of language is in pointing out how one can go beyond single-word utterances without having modern syntax. Much of the rest of this chapter will involve pulling syntax apart, seeking plausible evolutionary steps to the modern state of affairs.

The first essential innovation would be the ability simply to concatenate two or more symbols into a single utterance, with the connection among them dictated purely by context. For example, *Fred apple* (imagine this uttered by an eighteen-month-old or a signing chimp) might express any number of connections between Fred and apples, expressible in modern language in sentences such as *That's Fred's apple, Fred is eating an apple, Fred likes apples, Take the apple from Fred, Give the apple to Fred,* or even *An apple fell on Fred.* Though still vague, then, *Fred apple* is far more precise than just *Fred* or *apple* in isolation. Moreover, it isn't totally vague: it probably wouldn't be used to express *Fred has incorrect beliefs about the color of apples* or *Apples frighten Fred's sister.* That is, although there are many possible connections, the pragmatics are not unlimited.

Concatenating more than two symbols multiplies the number of pragmatic possibilities. Much depends on the symbols in question. *Bread cheese beer* might well express *I want bread, cheese, and beer. Bread cheese Fred* is less obvious, *Bread Fred cheese* even less so.

This is clearly a different kind of combination than that discussed in the previous section. Phonological generativity is a way of analyzing meaningful symbols and producing new ones in terms of a repertoire of smaller meaningless units. The present sort of combination puts together meaningful symbols to form larger utterances whose meanings are a function of the meanings of the constituent symbols. The two kinds of combination could have evolved simultaneously or in either order.

This sort of combination has not been attested in the ethological literature. As mentioned above, the units of bird songs, cetacean songs, and primate "long calls" are not meaningful on their own, and/or different combinations are not distinctively meaningful. (As Hauser 1996 points out, however, this may be for lack of means to assess such combinations.) On the other hand, the language-trained apes do show this capability, at least to some degree, on some assessments.

To see if this is where apes' capability stops, it is most revealing to look at the less controlled cases, in which free utterances were possible: the experiments with sign. Terrace (1979) claims that his chimp Nim reached this stage and this stage only, producing large numbers of concatenated (and repeated) signs in an utterance, but without any further organization. He claims that a careful look at the full data from the other signing experiments reveals similar results (see also Seidenberg and Petitto 1978; Ristau and Robbins 1982; Kako 1999), though more enthusiastic researchers have claimed greater organization.

8.7 Using linear position to signal semantic relations

Concatenating symbols opens up many opportunities for enhancing expressive power and precision. Two important classes of innovations are orthogonal:

using the linear order of concatenated symbols to express relations between them, and introducing new sorts of vocabulary item that convey relations explicitly. We take these up in turn.

With just symbol concatenation, *eat apple Fred* and *eat Fred apple* might be used to convey exactly the same message. In this particular case there would be no problem, because of the pragmatics of the words involved. But in *hit tree Fred*, did Fred hit the tree or did the tree hit Fred? Though the larger context might tell us, the pragmatics of the words alone do not. Pinker and Bloom (1990) point out this problem and argue that using principles of word order would be communicatively adaptive.

However, one needn't advance to a full generative syntax, replete with recursive trees, in order to improve the situation. Modern languages display some robust principles that are in some sense prior to syntax, and that reveal themselves more clearly in less fully developed situations. An important piece of evidence comes from Wolfgang Klein and Clive Perdue's (1997) massive longitudinal study of adult second-language learners with various native languages and target languages. The subjects, immigrant workers who "picked up" the target language without explicit instruction, uniformly achieved a stage of linguistic competence that Klein and Perdue call "The Basic Variety" (BV); some, but not all, went beyond this stage in their competence at the new language.

The relevant features of BV are (a) lexical competence; (b) absence of inflectional morphology, e.g. verbs always appear in a fixed form rather than undergoing tense and agreement inflection; (c) omission of contextually supplied arguments, i.e. no obligatory subjects or objects; (d) absence of sentential subordination (no relative clauses, indirect quotes, etc.); (e) simple, largely semantically based principles of word order. The most prominent of these principles are Agent First and Focus Last.[9] So BV is quite far from full linguistic competence. (And, given that many subjects in the study never went beyond this stage, it belies occasional claims that adult second language learning, aside from pronunciation, is usually pretty close to complete).

Agent First and Focus Last are of interest here. A speaker employing Agent First would use *hit tree Fred* to mean only that the tree hit Fred and not that Fred hit the tree; this principle enables one to disambiguate a large proportion of utterances involving two characters. It remains quite powerful in structuring word order in modern language: it appears as the default principle "Agent is expressed

---

[9] In addition, if there is more than one noun argument in a sentence, the verb regularly falls after the first argument, i.e. there is SVO order. However, this may be an artifact of the target languages in the study, all of which were verb-second in main clauses.

in subject position," which can of course be mitigated by constructions such as the passive (Givón 1995; Van Valin and LaPolla 1997). We saw this principle in section 5.9 as the most robust component of the Argument Linking Hierarchy, and also as one of the principles of constructional meaning in section 6.7.

Agent First seems to be observed as well in pidgin languages (Givón 1995). Piñango (1999; 2000) argues that agrammatic aphasics also fall back on this principle to some degree; this explains some of their errors on reversible passives (*The boy was hit by the girl*), object relatives (*The boy who the girl kissed is tall*), and (in a previously unattested class of errors) certain *because*-clauses (*The girl that drowned because of the boy is tall*). To my knowledge, no one has tried to train an ape in a language that violates this principle, so we don't know whether apes spontaneously observe it or not. (The "home signs" invented by deaf children of non-signing parents (Goldin-Meadow and Mylander 1990) appear to use instead the converse, Agent Last.)

Agent First concerns an element in the system of thematic roles, the specification of who did what to whom (sections 5.8, 5.9, 11.8). By contrast, Focus Last concerns an element in the discourse coding of given and new information—the "information structure" tier (section 12.5). English shows some reflections of Focus Last, for instance in the construction *In the room sat a bear*, where the subject appears at the end for focal effect.

The two principal designated roles in the information structure tier are Focus and Topic. Thus a natural mirror image of Focus Last is Topic First. This is observed in pidgin (Bickerton 1981) and is prominent in the grammatical structure of Japanese. More generally, in many languages of the world, discourse coding plays a far greater role than it does in English; Japanese, Hungarian, and Tagalog are prominent examples (Lambrecht 1994; Van Valin and La Polla 1997). To my knowledge, no one has investigated discourse coding in language-trained apes; I also know of no results from home sign.

Next consider an utterance like *dog brown eat mouse*. Assume this obeys the Agent First principle, so that the dog is doing the eating. There still remains the question of what is brown. It is natural to assume that it's the dog—but notice that this judgment relies on a principle of "Grouping": modifiers tend to be adjacent to what they modify. Although such a principle might follow from general properties of cognition, it is by no means inevitable. Indeed, it can be violated in modern language in constructions like *Bill ate the hot dog naked*. Still, like Agent First, it is a default principle in modern language (Givón 1995; Newmeyer 1998b) and appears in pidgins (Givón 1995) and BV (Wolfgang Klein, p.c.) And like Agent First and Focus Last, Grouping is a purely semantically based principle that maps into linear adjacency without using anything syntactic like a Noun Phrase.

BV is fairly close to what Bickerton (1990) describes as "protolanguage," under which he lumps the organization of pidgins, the grammatical competence attained by Genie, and the achievements of the language-trained apes. His characterization in particular agrees with features (a)–(e) of BV. However, Bickerton attributes to protolanguage a less stable word order than that of BV; this may be partly because his evidence comes from pidgins, which are heavily influenced by the native languages of their speakers.

I suggest, then, that Agent First, Focus Last, and Grouping are "fossil principles" from protolanguage, which modern languages often observe and frequently elaborate. Like the features Bickerton discusses, they often survive in degraded forms of language, which may serve as evidence for their evolutionarily more primitive character. Crucially, these principles correlate linear order with semantic roles. They do not require syntactic structure: the linear order of words can be determined directly in terms of phonological concatenation.

Another possible protolinguistic "fossil" in English is the formation of compound nouns such as *snowman* and *blackboard*. About the only solid principle of meaning in English compounds is that the second word is the "head," the word that denotes the larger category into which the compound noun falls. For instance a snowman is basically a kind of man, not a kind of snow. (And even this is violated in cases like *pickpocket*, which is not a kind of pocket, and *bonehead*, which is not a kind of head but a kind of person.) Within the constraints of this "Head Principle," a wide variety of semantic relations is possible between the nouns, in large part mediated by their meanings. (1) offers a sample (the presence or absence of a space between the nouns is purely an accident of spelling).

(1) a. Locative relations:
       doghouse = house for a dog to live in
       housedog = dog that lives in a house.
    b. Part–whole relations:
       wheelchair = a chair with wheels as parts
       chairleg = leg that serves as part of a chair
       snowman = man made of snow
       cake flour = flour that cakes are made of
    c. Resemblance relations:
       zebra fish = fish that resembles a zebra
    d. Actions performed by or on objects:
       garbage man = man who carries away garbage
       fruit man = man who sells fruit
       sun hat = hat that protects against the sun
       butter knife = knife used for spreading butter

However, the relation between the nouns is not totally free: while *snowman* might have meant a man who shovels away snow or who makes snow at a ski area, it is not likely to have meant a man whose sister once fell in the snow. Thus the situation resembles the possible meaning relations conveyed by raw concatenation. Jackendoff (in preparation), based on earlier work such as Lees (1960), Levi (1978), Gleitman and Gleitman (1970), and Downing (1977), finds a repertoire of perhaps twenty relations that can be conveyed in a compound through pragmatics alone—though the reason for this particular set of relations remains for the moment unclear. These relations are enriched and constrained by the meanings of the particular words in the compound, along lines suggested by Pustejovsky (1995). It is this reliance on pragmatics and the details of word meaning that has made the analysis of compounds resistant to standard analytic techniques of generative grammar.

Thousands of compounds with partially idiosyncratic meanings are stored in long-term memory. But in addition, one constantly encounters novel examples such as *health management cost containment services* and *two-axle diesel electric engine dump truck* (examples from the Boston *Globe*), whose meanings can be computed on the spot. Thus this is a productive concatenative system involving only words. As observed by, for instance, Sadock (1998), this system is an entirely different sort of combination than other forms of morphology. Klein and Perdue report that noun compounding is the only kind of morphology found in the Basic Variety; and children improvise compounds very early (Clark et al. 1985).

The facts of compounding thus seem symptomatic of protolinguistic "fossils": the grammatical principle involved is simply one of concatenating two nouns into a bigger noun, and the semantic relation between them is determined by a combination of pragmatics and memorization. Determining the meaning of a newly encountered compound is hence much like determining the meaning of *hit tree Fred* discussed above—one uses the Head Principle, plus the repertoire of possible semantic relations, plus a dose of pragmatics, to put together a meaning that makes sense in context.

Whatever the particular details of these sorts of principle that map between semantic roles and pure linear order, they sharpen communication. They are therefore a plausible step between unregulated concatenation and full syntax. In fact, unregulated concatenation need not necessarily have preceded the appearance of these principles: the evidence in modern language is scant, and only possibly the case of Nim shows us raw concatenation without semantically based ordering principles. Notably, the free utterances of the bonobo Kanzi seem to show some limited use of semantically based word order (Savage-Rumbaugh et al. 1998; but see Kako 1999 for a less positive assessment).

The architecture at this point thus looks like Fig. 8.3, in which the new generative system of phonology has been interposed into the mapping between meaning and the auditory/motor levels. This is a parallel generative system without a level of syntax.

The interface between phonology and meaning includes on one hand lexical items and on the other hand principles that map phonological linear order to semantic relations. At the same time, the older interfaces straight from meaning to the auditory/motor systems need not have gone away. In fact they are still used in modern language in tone of voice and perhaps (modulated by phonology) in onomatopoeia.[10]

A final note: Bickerton insists that protolanguage is *not* language, while Klein and Perdue claim that BV *is* language. Yet the two phenomena are incredibly similar. How do they arrive at these opposed positions? Bickerton wants to stress the difference between protolanguage and modern language (in particular creoles), and hence wants to distance protogrammar from Universal Grammar, the essential part of modern language. Klein and Perdue, in contrast, want to stress the role of UG in late second-language acquisition, so they want UG to be involved in BV. Therefore, they tentatively assert that BV represents the default settings of all the parameters in a Principles-and-Parameters type of Universal Grammar. But, as Bierwisch (1997) and Meisel (1997) point out, this either attributes too much sophistication to BV or not enough to UG.

I suggest that Bickerton and Klein and Perdue are each forced into their position because they assume a discrete "grammar box" with a syntactocentric architecture. UG for both of them *is* syntax, and you either have it or you don't. Moreover, they forget that phonology is part of UG too. The present approach allows us to make the appropriate compromise: we can say that protolanguage and BV both have *part* of UG—and approximately the same part.

At the same time, protolanguage/BV is still a long way from the expressive possibilities of modern language. We now progress through some further steps.

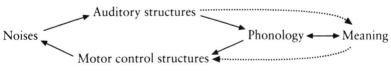

Fig. 8.3. Architecture of protolanguage/Basic Variety

---

[10] The standard line on onomatopoeia is that it is illusory. After all, dogs go *bow-wow* in English but *gnaf-gnaf* in French, and roosters go *cockadoodledoo* in English but *kikiriki* in German. Still, there is some degree of sound symbolism here. I doubt there's a language where dogs go *kikiriki* and roosters go *thud*.

8.8 Phrase structure

All the phenomena discussed so far use word order to signal semantic relations among *words*; but this is not sufficient for modern language. For example, in the sentence *The little star smashed into a big star*, the entire phrase *the little star* enters into a semantic relation with the verb *smash*. This collection of words functions as an elaborated version of the single word *star*, the head of the phrase. More generally, for purposes of both syntax and semantics, a noun phrase counts as sort of a fancy version of Noun, an adjective phrase counts as a fancy version of Adjective, and so forth. As stressed in Chapters 1 and 5, this is a crucial design feature of modern language, called in the generative tradition "X-Bar theory."

The provision of headed phrases in grammar allows principles of *word order* to be elaborated into principles of *phrase order*. For example, Agent First now applies not to the word that denotes the Agent, but to the *phrase* that denotes the Agent, yielding a major increase in the complexity of conveyable messages: not just *dog chase mouse* but *[big dog with floppy ears and long scraggly tail] chase [little frightened mouse]*. In particular, phrase structure makes possible expressions with hierarchical embedding such as *[the dog [that bit the cat [that chased the rat]]]*—which expresses an equally hierarchical conceptual structure. Such hierarchical embedding in syntax, one of the hallmarks of modern language, is not so simple or inevitable. It does not occur so relentlessly in phonological structure, for example.

Most of the discussion of ape syntax has concerned word order. However, it is not so clear that apes have hierarchical phrase structure. Similarly, discussion of pidgin languages has not made a clear distinction between word order and phrase structure. This distinction thus deserves closer examination.

The potential complexity offered by phrase structure raises new problems of communicability. When there are only three words or so in a sentence, the semantic relations among them can be conveyed by simple word order plus pragmatics. But when sentences get longer and are grouped into phrases, it becomes a pressing issue for the speaker to make the phrase boundaries and the semantic relations among the words more explicit to the hearer. Since the only perceptible signals of abstract phrase structure are linear order and to some extent intonation, language needs further devices in order to make semantic relations explicit.[11]

---

[11] Kayne (1994) and (following him) the Minimalist Program have taken linear order to be absent from syntax. In this approach, all phrase structure is strictly binary branching, so that the phonological component can read linear order directly off the branching in an inherently unordered tree. Bickerton's most recent work (Calvin and Bickerton 2000) adopts this position as

8.9 Vocabulary for relational concepts

One possible way of encoding semantic relations among words and phrases is to invent words that express them. At the one-word stage, relational words are pointless. But once multiple-symbol utterances are possible, many classes of "utility" vocabulary items offer themselves as design possibilities. In modern language, some are words, some are morphological affixes, and some are realized as variants of word order ("constructions" in the sense of Chapter 6). Here are a few types.

- *Spatial relation terms.* To give someone directions to some spatial location, we don't do a dance like the honeybees. We say "Go up the stream to a tree next to a big rock. Behind the tree and a little to the side you'll see a bush that has great fruit on it." Such description is impossible without all the words that indicate spatial relations: *up*, *to*, *next to*, *behind*, *to the side*, and *on*.[12]

- *Time terms.* These include explicit time terms such as *now*, *yesterday*, and *Tuesday*; temporal relational terms such as *before*, *after*, and *until*; and (once inflection develops) tense and aspect inflection.

- *Marks of illocutionary force and modality.* These differentiate declaratives from questions, commands, and exclamations. They appear in modern language sometimes as variations in word order, sometimes as verbal inflection, sometimes as differences in intonation, and sometimes as a particular word that marks the

---

well. I take this approach to be profoundly anti-evolutionary. Given that linear order is already present before the advent of phrase structure (and is in any event necessary for discourse!), there is no point in throwing it out of syntactic theory. Rather, syntactic theory should make as much use as possible of linear order, which is after all present in the overt signal. See Culicover (2000) for more extended discussion of this issue.

Carstairs-McCarthy (1999) asks the intriguing question of why so many languages show a major syntactic split between subject and predicate (VP) constituents, where the latter includes (at least) the verb and the direct object. Such a split is not so natural from a logical point of view: after all, first-order logic has no constituent containing the predicate and all but one privileged argument—and neither do computer languages. Carstairs-McCarthy proposes that this asymmetry of subject and predicate—[N [V N]] rather than just [N V N]—is exapted from the asymmetry of the syllable, which (as seen in Chs. 1 and 5) has the structure [C [V C]] rather than [C V C]. Hence, he says, the asymmetry of syntactic structure arose not from the logic of what sentences mean, but rather from the accidental availability of a structure elsewhere in cognition. Although this asymmetry had good acoustic or articulatory reasons in phonology, in syntactic structure it is just one of those accidents of evolution. Whether or not one endorses this argument, I find it does have the right sort of flavor. Another possibility, however, is that subject–predicate structure arose from Topic–Comment organization in information structure. It subsequently became grammaticalized and overlaid with lots of other grammatical phenomena, so that some languages (including English) came to reinvent another pre-subject topic position.

[12] Some of these, for example *up*, are already present in children's vocabulary at the one-word stage. At this point the child probably uses *up* to denote upwardly directed motion, so it is verb-like rather than relational in its semantics.

force of the utterance. A familar case of the last of these is the use in French of *est-ce que* as a fixed formula that converts a declarative sentence into a yes–no question. Perhaps also in this class goes sentential negation, which often seems to get tied up in the tense and question systems, *doesn't it?* We might also include expressions of conditionality such as *if*, *may*, and *can*; these meanings also appear in the tense system, as in the subjunctive and conditional of French.

• *Markers of discourse status.* These include at least the determiners *a* and *the*, which serve to inform the hearer whether the item being mentioned is new to the discourse or identifiable by the hearer from context. At least in English, these are also reliable markers for the beginning of an NP, so they give the hearer help with parsing as well as with keeping characters in a discourse straight.

• *Quantification.* These include the standard logical quantifiers *some*, *all*, and *every*, as well as numerals, expressions like *a lot of* and *oodles of*, and temporal quantifiers like *often* and *always*. A notable case is *more*, which cuts across noun, verb, and adjective modification (*more pudding, run more, more beautiful*), and which is often acquired by children even at the one-word stage, where what it quantifies must be inferred pragmatically.

• *Purposes, reasons, and intermediate causes.* Compare *You live in this house* and *This house is for you to live in.* The latter can be expressed only if one has a vocabulary item with the meaning of "purpose," here the word *for.* Or compare *I threw the spear and it hit the pig* to *I hit the pig with the spear.* The latter makes explicit my ultimate agency in the pig's fate (while making implicit exactly how I did it). Similarly, compare *He ate the apple and he died* with *He died because he ate the apple.* Only the latter is explicit about the nature of the connection between the two events: one is the reason for the other. Without explicit expressions of reason, one cannot ask *Why?* and therefore seek explanation.[13]

• *More general discourse connectors.* These include words such as *but, however, therefore, moreover, what's more*, and *and so forth.*

Each of these classes presents a different challenge to the evolution of the language capacity. Having symbolic utterances or primitive word order or hierarchical structure does not automatically provide any of these classes; nor would organisms that had one class necessarily discover any of the others automatically. The evolution of these possibilities in the language capacity can be speculated about only through the sorts of evidence we have been considering so far: child and adult language acquisition, aphasia, ape experiments, and so on. (Pidgins would be less telling because they draw upon the vocabulary of their source languages.)

---

[13] Does the famous explosion of *why*s in young children represent their discovery of reasons, as suggested by Kelemen (1999)?

Relational vocabulary plays an important role in thought. It has been argued (Dennett 1991; Jackendoff 1996b, among many others) that language enhances thoughts by making them available as perceptual objects (namely sentences), so that they can be attended to, focused on, modified, and remembered. Upon the invention of this "utility vocabulary," it would all of a sudden be possible explicitly to wonder if *p* and suppose that *p*, and to give reasons and purposes for actions, with a tremendous effect on the power of individual and communal reason and planning. ("What *should* I say to so-and-so? *If* he says this, *then maybe* I'll do that; *but if* . . . ." Try to perform this reasoning without the italicized words.)

Suppose we add phrase structure and all this utility vocabulary to a protolanguage. We still don't yet have modern language. In particular, there is no notion of subject and object of a sentence—only semantically defined notions like Agent and Patient. There is no grammatical differentiation of parts of speech, only Object words versus Action words. There is no inflection for case and agreement, and no use of pronouns and other proforms. There is no regimented way of constructing long-distance dependencies such as the relation of a *wh*-phrase at the front of a clause to the "gap" or "trace" elsewhere within the clause, as in *[Which bananas]ᵢ do you think Fred advised us to buy tᵢ for our soup?*

However, we are moving towards something that begins to be recognizable as modern language. In particular, we find "fossils" of this stage in the very productive system of "sentential adverbials" of various syntactic categories that appear freely at the beginning of the sentence, after the subject, or at the end. Consider the examples in (2).

(2)   a.   Obviously,
           In my opinion,
           With a sigh,
           Susan having gone,   } Fred left town.
           Having nothing better to do,
           Sick at heart,
           Though basically a happy guy,

      b.   Fred,   { obviously
                     in my opinion,
                     with a sigh,
                     Susan having gone,   } left town.
                     having nothing better to do,
                     sick at heart,
                     though basically a happy guy,

c.   Fred left town, $\left\{ \begin{array}{l} \text{obviously.} \\ \text{in my opinion.} \\ \text{with a sigh.} \\ \text{Susan having gone.} \\ \text{having nothing better to do.} \\ \text{sick at heart.} \\ \text{though basically a happy guy.} \end{array} \right.$

The use of these expressions is governed only by rudimentary syntactic principles. As long as the semantics is all right, a phrase of any syntactic category can go in any of the major breakpoints of the sentence: the front, the end, or the break between the subject and the predicate.

Another such subsystem comprises the prepositional phrases and "adverbials" denoting time, place, instrument, accompaniment and so forth. These are freely ordered at the end of the verb phrase; syntax apparently just lets one lump them there any old way:

(3)   a.   Sam struck gold last night in Alaska with his trusty pick.
          Sam struck gold in Alaska last night with his trusty pick.
          Sam struck gold with his trusty pick last night in Alaska.
    b.   Beth bought a book yesterday for her sister for $10.
          Beth bought a book for her sister yesterday for $10.
          Beth bought a book for $10 for her sister yesterday.

Again, this freedom bespeaks a somewhat protosyntactic phenomenon. The relation of each phrase to the sentence is determined more or less pragmatically, using the meaning of the noun as a guide: *last night* is a time because *night* is; *for Bill* is a recipient because *Bill* is a person, *for an hour* is a duration because *an hour* is a time, and *for $10* is a quantity of exchange because *$10* is an amount of money. Similarly, **with a knife** denotes an instrument, **with Bill** denotes a collaborator, and **with care** denotes a manner. *For* tends to be used for relations directly or indirectly involving purposes, but it is not entirely consistent; *with* is even less characterizable in general.

The architecture at this point is a true tripartite system, as shown in Fig. 8.4.

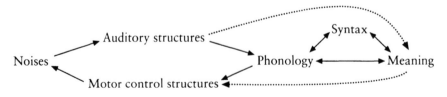

Fig. 8.4. 'Early modern' tripartite architecture

The syntax in this architecture determines a set of syntactic categories which are domains of word and phrase order regularities. For instance, the word order possibilities within a phrase are the same no matter where the phrase occurs in the sentence. In addition, syntactic phrases are domains for interface principles to semantics; for instance, Agent First is now an interface principle between noun *phrases* and thematic roles rather than between *nouns* and thematic roles.

At the same time, because evolution is incremental, the direct relation between phonology and meaning does not go away. In particular, the connection between word meanings and word pronunciations is direct, bypassing syntax. And this important characteristic remains in modern language: as has been observed several times already, syntactic features of words are far coarser than phonological and semantic features. For instance, as far as syntax is concerned, *dog, cat, worm, amoeba*, and *tree* are indistinguishable: they are all just singular count nouns. Similarly, verbs with identical argument structure such as *jog, walk, shuffle* and *strut* are syntactically indistinguishable. Thus the syntactic features serve only to tell the syntax how this word can fit into a phrase structure; they correspond only very coarsely to meaning. (As Levelt 1999 puts it, "Syntax is the poor man's semantics." See also Pinker 1989, where the semantic coarseness of argument structure plays an important role in the theory of children's acquisition of verbs.) The mapping between phonology and fine-scale meaning differences ought therefore to be maintained as part of a straight phonology–semantics interface without syntactic intervention. (And the "defective" words like *ouch* have *only* this connection.)

8.10 Grammatical categories and the "basic body plan" of syntax

So far we have managed to do without the distinction between nouns and verbs. Everything is done semantically. How does this grammatical distinction arise along with the further differentiation of adjectives, prepositions, and so on? I have only a very speculative story here, but I will offer it anyway.

An important asymmetry between nouns and verbs came up in section 5.5. Nouns can express any semantic category whatsoever: not just objects but situations (*situation, concert, earthquake, perusal*), properties (*size, intelligence, redness*), spatial concepts (*distance, region, place*), times (*Tuesday, millennium*), and so on. But verbs can express only situations (events, actions and states). In section 5.5 this was left as an unexplained design feature of the syntax–semantics interface.

Carstairs-McCarthy (1999) observes another significant asymmetry in language, one that is not at all necessary to its expressive power. The sentence (4a) and the noun phrase (4b) convey the same information in their words, and yet only the sentence is acceptable as an independent non-elliptical assertion.

(4) a. Fred perused a book yesterday.
    b. Fred's perusal of a book yesterday

More generally, an utterance cannot stand on its own without a verb.[14] Sometimes this is even at the price of adding dummy items. Why do we have to say the full sentence (5a) rather than the cryptic (5b)?

(5) a. There was a storm last night.
    b. a storm last night

Carstairs-McCarthy observes that we could easily design a language that lacked the noun–verb distinction, in which (4a) and (4b) would translate into the same utterance, and in which something closer to (5b) than to (5a) would be grammatical. But there are no human languages like that.[15]

    A telling case of this asymmetry is provided by Japanese and Korean. These languages make heavy use of the "light verb" construction mentioned in section 5.9.4. An example of this construction in English is *Sally took a walk*, where *take* is a "light verb," contributing little to the meaning, and where the nature of the action is conveyed by the noun *walk*. (6) is an example from Korean (thanks to Jong Sup Jun); note that the word translated as *study* receives an accusative case marker like other nouns.

(6) Inho-ka   hakkyo-eyse yenge-lul   kongpu-lul yelsimhi ha-n-ta
     Inho-NOM school-at   English-ACC study-ACC hard   do-Pres-
                                                                Declarative
     'Inho studies English hard at school.'

It turns out that a sizable proportion of Korean verbs are actually such complexes of nominal plus light verb, and there is no simple verb with the same meaning. (6) is such a case; examples in English might be *take umbrage* and *make a deal*. According to a count by Jee-Sun Nam (Nam 1996), about 9000 out of 13,500 "verbs" listed in Korean dictionaries are actually light verb complexes. That is, despite so many actions being expressible only as nouns, Korean and Japanese still need a verb in the sentence.

---

[14] Some might say that what is necessary is Tense rather than a verb; and since Tense normally requires a verb, the verb comes along automatically. If anything this only exacerbates the puzzle.

[15] There is one notable exception to this generalization. Many languages, e.g. Russian and Hebrew, have no present tense form of the verb *be*, so that *Beth is hungry* comes out *Beth hungry*. There are various resolutions to this case. For the moment I will take the easy way out and say that present tense *be*, the verb with the least possible content, is expressed in these languages by a "defective" lexical item that lacks phonology but still appears in syntax.

Is there a connection between these two asymmetries between nouns and verbs? Suppose at some point in the evolution of UG, words expressing situations took on a special function in governing phrase structure and word order. These are, after all, the relational words par excellence, the ones that have the most articulated semantic argument structure. This special function might consist in (or develop into) their becoming grammatically essential to expressing an assertion. That would leave everything else as the default class. This is not too far off the noun–verb distinction: verbs are situation words and are essential to expressing an assertion. Nouns are everything else. In fact, when situation words are not used with their special grammatical function, they can easily fall into the default class, so nouns can express situations too. In other words, we get both asymmetries from the supposition that syntactic categories first emerged as a result of distinguishing verbs from everything else.

We might think of these special features of verbs versus nouns as a "basic body plan" for language. Japanese and Korean might be thought of, then, as languages whose vocabulary is not optimally suited to this plan: they could be more concise by just dispensing with the light verb most of the time. But they are stuck with it. Just as whales cannot go back to using gills and are therefore hampered by having to go to the surface to breathe, these languages cannot abandon the need for a verb in the sentence.

As we will see in a moment, once the noun–verb distinction is present, many other design features can collect around it.

8.11 Morphology and grammatical functions

To move from this point to modern language, two independent sets of machinery must be added: morphology and further aspects of syntax. Bickerton (along with many modern generative linguists) treats these as a completely integrated whole that forms the core of the "grammar box." On the other hand, as seen in section 6.2, attempts within generative theory to integrate morphology and phrasal syntax seamlessly have (to my taste) resulted in a certain artificiality.

How might the *brain* treat morphology and phrasal syntax? A good analogy elsewhere in the brain is depth perception, where we find a variety of disparate mechanisms, ranging from very sensory (lens accommodation) through perceptual (stereopsis and occlusion) through very cognitive (knowing what sizes things should be). These all converge on a single aspect of perceptual representation—the distance of visible surfaces from the viewer. Sometimes they are redundant; at some distances one or another predominates; and in illusions they may conflict.

A similar approach to phrasal syntax and morphology, advocated by Autolexical Syntax (Sadock 1991), Role and Reference Grammar (Van Valin and LaPolla 1997), and recent Lexical-Functional Grammar (Bresnan 2001), treats them as somewhat independent systems that accomplish partially overlapping functions. Section 5.6 referred to these systems as the tiers of phrasal syntax and morphosyntax, and pointed out some of the differences in the sorts of combinatoriality they offer. These systems, like those involved in depth perception, interweave with each other, sometimes redundantly, sometimes not, but both helping make explicit the semantic relations among components in an utterance. For instance, phrasal syntax may signal thematic roles (who did what to whom) through the order of phrases in relation to the verb. Inflection may do the same thing by means of verb agreement with the subject (and in some languages, with the object as well). Inflection may alternatively express semantic roles through a system of case marking, as in German, Russian, and Latin. In particular, many of the so-called "semantic cases" in these languages have much the same character as the phrasal markers *for* and *with* discussed in the previous section. And parallel to verbs in English that require "governed prepositions" (section 5.8), case-marking languages often have verbs that govern so-called "quirky case" on an argument. Languages tend to mix and match these strategies in different proportion; languages with rich inflectional systems often allow more freedom in word order for different purposes, usually for focus–topic information. On the other hand, inflection can be used (freely or redundantly with word order) to indicate focus or topic as well, for example the Japanese suffix -*wa*, which typically marks topic redundantly with initial position in the clause.

Thus we might think of phrasal syntax and morphosyntax as independently evolved systems, each built on top of the system of protolanguage, each refining communication through its own expressive techniques. In a similar vein, Casey and Kluender (1995) suggest that agreement inflection evolved as an extra system to provide redundant (and hence more reliable) information about semantic relations of arguments. I see no immediate reason to assert the temporal priority of one of these systems over the other in the course of evolution.

Notice that parts of these systems, especially inflection, depend strongly on the noun–verb distinction. Verbs are marked for agreement with nouns; nouns are marked by verbs for case.

An important innovation that remains is the system of grammatical functions: subject, object, and (in some languages) indirect object. Section 5.10 suggested that this system may well form a separate tier of syntax, "GF-structure," interfacing with both phrasal syntax and morphosyntax and relating them to semantic functions. The present evolutionary context invites the intriguing hypothesis that grammatical functions were perhaps the latest-developing part of the architecture—an extra bit of power for efficiently regulating the syntactic expression of semantic relations. Deviating from practice in Lexical-Functional Grammar and Relational Grammar, section 5.10 proposed that this tier applies basically only to NP arguments, and that oblique arguments (i.e. arguments introduced by prepositions), adjuncts, and "adverbials" such as those illustrated in (2) and (3) above are "invisible" to it.

In section 5.10, the idea of such a limited system was justified by analogy with phonological tiers. Now a more powerful analogy suggests itself. Phrasal syntax regulates only a limited aspect of the connection between phonology and semantics, while leaving other, evolutionarily prior aspects (including the all-important word-to-meaning mapping) to the "earlier" system. We can see grammatical functions in a similar light: the syntax–semantics interface is partially regulated by the supervening, more "advanced" system of grammatical functions; but the "earlier" system is left in place, revealing itself around the corners of the "new" system.

The architecture now comes out like Fig. 8.5. It is not elegant. But then again, this is what we have come to expect of the brain. It hardly matches the connectivity of the visual system in its complexity.

8.12 Universal Grammar as a toolkit again

Suppose we take Fig. 8.5 as a sketch of "architectural universals" of language. How much of it is actually universal?

At rock bottom, the open vocabulary, phonology, and word concatenation are surely universal. But then we start running into exceptions. Some Australian languages, for example Warlpiri, Jiwarli, and Wambaya (Hale 1983; Nordlinger 1998; Austin 2001) show no consistent evidence of phrase structure. Their word order is almost entirely free, and adjectival modifiers are routinely separated

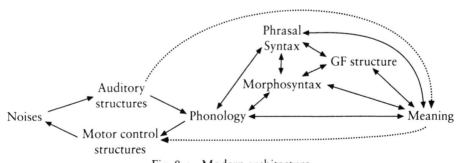

Fig. 8.5. Modern architecture

from the nouns they modify. Semantic relations are regulated by an exuberant case system; modifiers are connected with their heads by a shared case. Subordinate clauses are kept together, but within them order is also totally free. Of course, the rich morphological system requires use of the morphosyntax component. (Stephen Anderson has suggested (p.c.) that Classical Latin too may fit this characterization.)

As mentioned earlier, even in the usual cases when phrase structure is demonstrably present, there is wide variation among languages in how rich a use is made of phrase order and how rich the morphology is.

Turning to grammatical functions, Van Valin and LaPolla (1997) argue that Acehnese (an Austronesian language from Sumatra) does not make use of grammatical functions. Recall that the argument *for* grammatical functions is that there are grammatical principles that refer to subject and/or object independent of their semantic roles. Van Valin and LaPolla show that all analogous grammatical principles in Acehnese actually are dependent on the semantic roles Actor and Undergoer (Patient), so there is no justification for syntactically independent subject and object roles. They mount a similar argument for Mandarin Chinese, where the relevant semantic roles are Topic and Comment. They also argue that in intransitive sentences, Warlpiri acts like it has grammatical subjects, but in transitive sentences, the relevant notion is Actor.

In English, of course, grammatical functions play a role with respect to the arguments of verbs. But for the arguments of nouns the issue is not so clear. For instance, there is something that looks rather like a passive in noun phrases. Parallel to the active and passive sentences (7a) and (7b) are the "active" and "passive" noun phrases (7c) and (7d).

(7) a. The enemy destroyed the city.
     b. The city was destroyed by the enemy.
     c. the enemy's destruction of the city
     d. the city's destruction by the enemy

But such "passive" noun phrases are highly quirky and subject to ill-understood semantic factors (see Grimshaw 1990). For instance, the paradigms in (8) and (9) admit a verbal passive but not a nominal "passive."

(8) a. John observed Bill.
     b. Bill was observed by John.
     c. John's observation of Bill
     d. *Bill's observation by John

(9) a. John knew the answer.
     b. The answer was known by John.

    c.   John's knowledge of the answer
    d. *the answer's knowledge by John

This suggests that the grammatical-function tier applies to verbal structures in English, so that verbal passives are governed by grammatical functions; but that NP structures, including their "passives," are left to the more "primitive" semantically based system. Stiebels (1999) argues that in Classical Nahuatl, by contrast, nouns and verbs are totally symmetrical with respect to argument structure properties, suggesting that perhaps the grammatical-function tier in this language has a more extensive interface with syntax than in English.

My (perhaps self-centered) impression is that English rather than Acehnese or Classical Nahuatl represents the typical situation. Thus again we face an important grammatical asymmetry between verbs and nouns, with verbs typically playing a much more intricate role in determining sentence structure. This accords with the account suggested in the previous section, in which verbs were at the forefront of the evolution of syntactic categories, and therefore are syntactically more specialized.

Faced with this range of variation, what is the appropriate position to take on Universal Grammar? Van Valin and LaPolla's position is that if a characteristic is not universal, it is not part of Universal Grammar. Yet if Universal Grammar is to be the unlearned basis from which language is learned, it had better be available to help children learn case systems, agreement systems, fixed word order, and grammatical functions in case the language in the environment happens to have them. These are after all the most abstract parts of language, the ones least amenable to semantic and pragmatic support. This leads us back to the view of Universal Grammar as a "toolkit," introduced in section 4.3: beyond the absolutely universal bare minimum of concatenated words—the components of protolanguage—languages can pick and choose which tools they use, and how extensively.

This view of the evolved architecture of language has ramifications for other phenomena adduced as evidence for Universal Grammar. Section 8.7 discussed the apparent conflict between calling the Basic Variety an instance of UG but the very similar pidgin languages *not* an instance of UG. The difficulty was that UG was being thought of on both sides as an indivisible "grammar box." Here we were able to resolve the paradox by saying that both make use of part but not all of modern UG.

With this observation in hand, consider the critical period in language acquisition (section 4.9.2). As has been observed in the course of this chapter, some parts of language do not display critical period effects, in particular the acquisition of vocabulary, the concatenation of words, and the simple semantically based principles of word order. Other parts of language, such as details of phonology, phrase structure, and in particular the inflectional system, can be severely impaired in late language learning, yielding Basic Variety and pidgins. Similarly, morphology above all is vulnerable to agrammatic aphasia and to Specific Language Impairment (at least as currently described).

We can localize these problems through viewing Universal Grammar as built out of layered subcomponents. UG is not simply on or off in these abnormal situations. Rather, some of its subcomponents are particularly impaired—significantly, the same ones in case after case. The robust remnant is protolanguage.

The overall conclusion is that grammar is not a single unified system, but a collection of simpler systems. Many of these systems are built up as refinements of pre-existing interfaces between components. Hence the evolution of the language capacity can be seen as deeply incremental, adding more and more little tricks to the cognitive repertoire available to the child faced with acquiring a language.

We should also observe that these subsystems are added specializations *for language*. For instance, a system of grammatical relations and a system of morphological agreement make a lot of sense as refinements of a syntax–semantics mapping. But they are totally useless to any other cognitive capacity; they are exquisitely specialized. This should occasion no surprise: the successive refinements of the structure of the eye—and the visual parts of the brain such as stereopsis—are useless for anything else too. In other words, there is no need to appeal to changes in general-purpose capacities, *à la* Piattelli-Palmerini and Toulmin, to explain the incremental development of the language capacity.

What is also new here is the hypothesis that certain design features of modern language resemble "fossils" of earlier evolutionary stages. To some degree, then, the examination of the structure of language can come to resemble the examination of the physical structure of present-day organisms for the traces of "archaic" features.

Semantic and Conceptual Foundations

CHAPTER 9

Semantics as a Mentalistic Enterprise

9.1 Introduction to Part III

As observed in Chapter 4, meaning is the "holy grail" not only of linguistics, but also of philosophy, psychology, and neuroscience—not to mention more distant domains such as cultural and literary theory. Understanding how we mean and how we think is a vital issue for our intuitive sense of ourselves as human beings. For most people, meaning is intuitively the central issue in the study of language—far more important than understanding details of word order or morphology.

I think linguists have tried over the years to make a big deal out of how the study of language teaches us about human nature. In the days when Deep Structure was claimed to be the key to meaning, such advertising was properly seductive. But more recently, when the parade examples have concerned nitty-gritty phenomena like pronoun use and word stress, the public has been less impressed. To be sure, there are important points to be made here about the nature of learning and innateness—but what people really want to know about is still meaning. And generative grammar on the whole has not made good on the promise so tantalizingly held forth in *Aspects*.

There is more at issue than philosophical discussions of human nature. As pointed out as long ago as Bar-Hillel (1970), potential practical applications of linguistic theory such as machine translation are hobbled without an account of meaning. Computational linguists, I am told, joke that every time they hire a theoretical linguist, their programs become less effective. The problem is that fancy syntax alone isn't that much use for machine understanding.

Most of my own work for the past thirty years has been directed toward developing an account of meaning that is compatible both with the psychological foundations of generative grammar and with the spirit of its formal technology—thus parting company with mainstream concerns in generative grammar. In the process, I have found it necessary also to part company with much of the main-stream in semantics and philosophy of mind, in part on first principles, and in part because the sorts of linguistic generalization I have wished to express are incomprehensible in more standard frameworks. This final part of the book is devoted to a survey of the landscape of meaning from the perspective thus achieved.

The present chapter and the next are concerned with foundational issues; they are followed by two chapters that sketch a broad range of empirically based results in lexical and phrasal semantics. However, the reader should understand that in practice one cannot first establish the foundations and then go on to do the work. Rather, the empirical results are part of what motivates the search for new foundations. I am interested in constructing a stance on meaning from which it is possible to make sense of the sort of detailed empirical investigation that linguists do. The relation between the philosophy and the dirty work has to be a two-way street.

*   *   *   *   *

I propose to begin from the following surely uncontroversial postulate:

People find sentences (and other entities) meaningful because of something going on in their brains.

That is, we are ultimately interested not in the question: What is meaning? but rather: What makes things meaningful *to people*? This anchors the enterprise both in the theory of psychology and in ordinary human experience.

A second postulate is:

There is no magic.

That is, we seek a thoroughly naturalistic explanation that ultimately can be embedded in our understanding of the physical world.

Such an explanation comes at a heavy price. The overall point to bear in mind is that:

Meaning is central to everything human.

If you are not prepared to deal with at least language, intelligence, consciousness, the self, and social and cultural interaction, you are not going to understand meaning.

9.2 Semantics vis-à-vis mainstream generative grammar

As already intimated, generative grammar has on the whole had little to say about meaning. Early contributions by Katz and Fodor (1963; Katz 1972), Bierwisch (1967; 1969), and Weinreich (1966), among others, were developed in the context of the *Aspects* theory, which took Deep Structure to be directly connected to meaning. For many years Jerry Fodor (e.g. 1975; 2000a) has made a significant attempt to establish theoretical foundations for semantics in concurrence with (what he takes to be) the goals of generative grammar. But, as we will see, his conclusions are at such odds with all detailed empirical work on meaning as to discredit the enterprise in the eyes of practical semanticists.

In the wake of the Generative Semantics dispute (section 4.2), most mainstream generative grammarians turned away from the systematic study of meaning, leaving the field largely to practitioners of the newly emerging disciplines of formal semantics, computational linguistics, cognitive psychology/neuroscience, and, somewhat later, Cognitive Grammar. Although all these approaches have made important advances in understanding meaning, none makes full contact with the overall goals of generative linguistics discussed in Part I. In fact, in many instances they espouse wholesale rejection of generative grammar because of its neglect of meaning. Often this manifests itself as rejecting the notion of an "autonomous formal syntactic component" and in some cases even the notion of grammar itself. Usually the notion of innateness is vilified; and some traditions even question the notion that language is in the mind.

I suspect that the underlying reason for this crashing wave of rejections is the syntactocentrism of mainstream generative grammar: the assumption that the syntactic component is the sole source of generative capacity in language (Chapter 5). This assumption, so fundamental that it was already subliminal by 1975, has the implicit effect of (pardon the term) emasculating semantics—of giving the messages conveyed by language a far lesser role than the messenger. The alternative approaches, in revenge, have shot the messenger.

This is really a mistake. Consider our poor little sentence from Chapter 1, repeated here as (1). It is certainly a fact about meaning that (1) must be differentiated from infinitely many other sentences that mean different things, for example those in (2).

(1)   The little star's beside a big star.

(2)   a. A little star's beside the big star.
      b. Every big star is beside some little star.
      c. Is the little star beside a big star?
      d. The little goat is inside a big tent.
      e. John falsely believes that the little star's beside a big star.
      f. Throw Momma from the train.

But it is a fact about English syntax, not about meaning, that (1) must be differentiated from the strings of words in (3)—which could be the way the same meaning is conveyed in some other language.

(3) a. The star little a star big beside is.
     b. Big star beside little star.
     c. The(masc. nom.) little(masc. nom.) star is beside a(masc. dat.)
        big(masc. dat.) star.

That is, one needs formal principles of syntax to account for basic facts concerning language-specific word order, phrase order, and functional categories
such as determiners, the verb *be*, and case endings. Whether a language chooses
verb-second or verb-final word order, whether it puts its adjectives before or
after the noun, and whether it has a robust system of case endings or none at
all—these have nothing to do with semantics.

There are indeed substantive issues about how independent syntax is from
semantics. We went over some of this ground in section 6.7, where we discussed
the possibility that some, though not all, syntactic structure does bear some
inherent load of meaning, for instance that subjects tend to be interpreted as
Agents if possible. Another relevant case prominent in the literature concerns
the scope of quantification in sentences like (4a), which is ambiguous between
the two interpretations suggested by the continuations in (4b, c).

(4) a.   Everyone in this room knows two languages.
     b.   ——namely German and English.
     c.   ——Jeff knows Georgian and German, Herb knows Hebrew and
          Hausa, I know Italian and English.

To be sure, these different interpretations must be distinguished in the cognitive
structures associated with meaning. The question is whether they are distinguished in syntactic structure as well, at some level other than surface structure.
Early generative grammar (e.g. Chomsky 1957) thought not; the *Aspects* theory (Chomsky 1965) was ambivalent; Generative Semantics (Lakoff 1970)
thought so; Government-Binding Theory after the introduction of Logical Form
(Chomsky 1981) thought so; to lay my cards on the table, I think not
(Jackendoff 1972; 1996c). Whatever the answer, the point is that it is a major
research problem, debated for the past forty years, to determine how much of
meaning is directly signaled in syntax. To throw formal syntax out makes it
impossible even to acknowledge the possibility of such problems.

The proper move, I suggest, is not to throw out syntax (not to mention generative grammar as a whole), but to throw out syntactocentrism. These questions can then be stated in terms of the balance of power among various
generative and interface components, along lines explored in Parts I and II. We
can speak of syntax as "*semi*-autonomous," if we like; the issues then concern
the degree (rather than the fact) of autonomy. And we can still acknowledge that

a theory of language is woefully incomplete without a serious account of meaning. So let us begin.

9.3 Meaning and its interfaces

Given the welter of overlapping positions on the issues, it makes most sense for me first to state my own aspirations for semantic theory, then compare them to various alternative traditions. I take the basic problem to be to situate the study of meaning in the study of the f-mind:

(5) **How can we characterize the messages/thoughts/concepts that speakers express/convey by means of using language?**

(6) **How does language express/convey these messages?**

I leave the terms "messages/thoughts/concepts" and "express/ convey" deliberately vague for the moment. Part of our job is to sharpen them. In particular, one has to ask:

(7) **What makes *these* f-mental entities function as meanings?**

Unfortunately, the intellectual politics begin right here: this is not the way everyone construes the term "semantics." Rather than engage in arguments based on terminological imperialism, I will use "conceptualist semantics" as a term of art for this enterprise.[1] Above all, I don't want to get trapped in the question: Is this enterprise really a kind of semantics or not? The relevant questions are: Is this enterprise a worthwhile way of studying meaning? To what extent can it incorporate intuitions and insights from other approaches, and to what extent can it offer insights unavailable in other approaches?

In order for a theory of conceptualist semantics to be embedded in a larger theory of the f-mind, it must be recognized that the messages/thoughts/concepts conveyed by language serve other purposes as well. At the very least, they are used by the following cognitive processes:

• Processes that integrate a linguistically conveyed message with existing f-knowledge, including understanding of context.

• Processes that draw inferences and make judgments, based on the interaction of a linguistically conveyed message with other f-knowledge.

• Processes that use linguistically conveyed messages to direct attention to and make judgments on the world as perceived through the senses.

---

[1] My own particular set of proposals, which I have called Conceptual Semantics (Jackendoff 1990a), is an exemplar of the approach but not the only possible one.

• Processes that connect linguistically conveyed messages with one's physical actions on/in the world.

This collection of interactive processes can be collected into an architectural diagram of the sort familiar from Part II. The main innovation is a dashed line marking the boundary between the f-mind and the "world," a feature to which we will return in a moment.

In Fig. 9.1, phonology and syntax have been compressed into a single interface that connects thoughts in the f-mind to noises in the world, there to be transmitted from one speaker to another. Were we to zoom in on this "language box" we would see all the elaborate architecture of tiers and interfaces in phonology and syntax discussed in Part II.

What is of interest here, however, is the part to the right of phonology and syntax: the cognitive structures I have called "thoughts" and the multiple interfaces that access them. Chapter 3 argued that the combinatoriality of language serves the purpose of transmitting messages constructed from an equally combinatorial system of thoughts: a sentence conveys a meaning built combinatorially out of the meanings of its words. So part of our job is characterizing this combinatorial system, represented by "formation rules for thoughts" in Fig. 9.1. This falls under question (5) above. In Chapter 12, we will see that "zooming in" on this component yields an interesting architecture of tiers, just like phonology and syntax.

Another part of the job is to characterize the interface rules that map these combinatorial structures into the purely linguistic structures of syntax and phonology—question (6). In particular, we would like to be able to account for

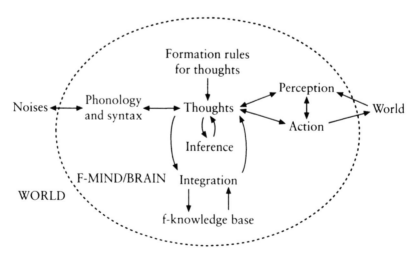

Fig. 9.1. The place of conceptual semantics in the f-mind

the way that (more or less) the same thought can be mapped into expressions of different languages, allowing for the possibility of reasonably good translation.

These two enterprises—characterizing the combinatorial system of meaning and its interfaces to linguistic expression—are closest to what is often called "linguistic semantics." Now consider the other interfaces. The use of thoughts/concepts to produce further thoughts/concepts is what is typically called "inference" or "reasoning." Since we are interested in the study of real people and not just ideals, this interface must include not only logical reasoning but also making plans and forming intentions to act—so-called "practical reasoning" (Bratman 1987; Kahneman et al. 1982; Gigerenzer 2000) and "social reasoning" (Tooby and Cosmides 1992).[2] For present purposes, what is important is that all these processes operate on the very same kinds of cognitive structure that can be expressed/conveyed by language. Thus these theories place boundary conditions on each other.

Similarly for the integration of thoughts conveyed by language with previous f-knowledge or f-beliefs. Part of previous f-knowledge is one's sense of the communicative context, including one's sense of one's interlocutor's intentions. Thus the work of this interface is closest to what is often called "pragmatics."

The interfaces to the perceptual systems are what permit one to form a thought based on observing the world (including an internal sense of one's own body). In turn, by using such thoughts as the input to language production, one can talk about what one sees, hears, tastes, and feels. These interfaces operate in the other direction as well: language perception can direct attention to some particular part of the perceptual field (*Do you see that bird over there? Pay no attention to the little man behind the curtain!*). Turning to the interface with the action system, this is what permits one to execute an intention—including carrying out an intention formed in response to a linguistically conveyed command or request.[3]

Again, it is important to stress that, in order for the kinds of interaction just enumerated to take place, all these interfaces need to converge on a common cognitive structure. Looking at thought through the lens of language alone does not provide enough constraints on possible theories. A richer, more demanding set of boundary conditions emerges from insisting that thought must also make contact with inference, background knowledge, perception, and action.

An important aspect of the present view is that thought is independent of language and can take place in the absence of language. This goes against the common

---

[2] I am inclined to think that the study of deranged (e.g. neurotic and paranoid/schizophrenic) reasoning, as well as the "logic" of dreams, fits in this department as well (Jackendoff 1992a: ch. 5).

[3] It should need no emphasis, of course, that if we "zoom in" on the perception and action interfaces in Fig. 9.1, we find systems at least as richly ramified as the linguistic interfaces. The vision system alone is vastly complex; it no doubt makes language look trivial by comparison. Of course it has had a lot more time to evolve too.

intuition that thought takes place "in a language," as in "Do you think in English, or in French?" My position is that linguistic form provides one means for thought to be made available to awareness (another is visual imagery); we "hear the little voice in the head" and thereby "know what we are thinking." Notice however that the form of the awareness in question is essentially phonological. What we "hear" is *words*, pronounced with *stress patterns*. At the same time, one cannot define rules of inference over phonological structure, so it is not an appropriate medium for reasoning. The correct level for carrying out reasoning is conceptual structure, and reasoning can take place even without any connection to language, in which case it is unconscious. The upshot is that there is a disconnection between the form taken by awareness and the unconscious form responsible for understanding. In Jackendoff (1987, 1997a: ch. 8), I argue that recognizing this disconnection helps solve a great many of the traditional puzzles surrounding consciousness.

This view of thought permits us to make contact immediately with evolutionary considerations as well. Suppose we erase the phonology/syntax interface from Fig. 9.1. We then have an architecture equally suitable—at some level of approxima- tion—to non-linguistic organisms such as apes. They too display complex integra- tion of perception, action, inference, and background knowledge, in both physical and social domains (Köhler 1927; Goodall 1971; Byrne and Whiten 1988; de Waal 1996). It makes evolutionary sense to suppose that some of the fundamental parts of human thought are a heritage of our primate ancestry. As observed in Chapter 8, evolution does not throw Good Ideas away, rather it elaborates and refines them.

To presume that one can invoke evolutionary considerations, of course, is also to presume that some of the overall character of thought is determined by the genome—this time in part shared with closely related species. I won't belabor the point here; we spent enough time in Chapter 4 going over what it means for a cognitive capacity to have a genetic basis. As in the case of syntax and phonolo- gy, there are two conflicting desiderata in working out a theory of the innate aspects of thought. First, other things being equal, it is desirable to keep the genetic contribution at a minimum, and of a sort that could actually be coded on the genes (if we only knew what that was!). But second, the innate basis must be rich enough, architecturally and substantively, to support the acquisition of human concepts and the role of thought in ongoing activity and experience.

Again laying my cards on the table, I see at least three major domains of thought that cry out for substantial support from a genetic basis. The first is the understanding of the physical world: the identification of objects, their spatial configurations with respect to each other, the events in which they take part and interact, and the opportunities (or affordances) they offer for action on and with them. The second is the understanding of the social world: the identification of persons, their social roles with respect to each other (including such issues as kinship, dominance, group membership, obligations, entitlements, and morals[4]), and characterization of their beliefs and motivations (so-called "theory of mind"). The third is a basic algebra of individuation, categorization, grouping, and decomposition that undergirds both the previous systems as well as many others. We will see pieces of these systems in chapters to come.

In short, conceptualist semantics should aspire to offer a common meeting ground for multiple traditions in studying cognition, including not only linguistic semantics but also pragmatics, perceptual understanding, embodied cognition, reasoning and planning, social/cultural understanding, primate cognition, and evolutionary psychology. A high aspiration, but certainly one worth pursuing.

The rest of this chapter, alas, must be devoted to fending off various attempts to limit the scope of semantic theory. I hope nevertheless that something positive will come of it—that the reader will get a feel for the enterprise, and that these preliminary skirmishes will build some courage for the more difficult encounters in the next chapter.

9.4 Chomsky and Fodor on semantics

One reason that semantics has played such a relatively minimal role in mainstream generative grammar is Chomsky's own apparent ambivalence. On the one hand, he has argued vigorously for an internalist (here called "conceptualist") approach to meaning, for instance in the papers collected in Chomsky (2000). On the other hand, aside from presenting a few telling examples, he has never attempted to develop a systematic internalist approach.

Moreover, when pressed, Chomsky expresses strongly conflicted feelings about the term "semantics" itself. I want to quote a few passages from a recent interview with him (Cela-Conde and Marty (1998). 'An Interview with Noam Chomsky.' *Syntax* 1: 19–36, by permission of Blackwell Publishers).

> From the outset, work in generative grammar was motivated primarily by issues that are usually called "semantic". . . .: the fact that a person who has had limited experience with language somehow comes to understand new expressions in highly specific ways. . . .
>
> Personally, I prefer to use the term "syntax" to refer to these topics; others use the term "semantics," which I would prefer to restrict to the study of what are often called "language–world" connections—more properly, in my view, connections between language and other parts of the world, some within the organism (presumably, the articulatory

---

4 As in language, the innate component cannot specify particular social roles, morality, and so forth. It specifies only the design space within which human social systems are located, thereby aiding children in learning the social system in which they find themselves growing up. See Jackendoff (1994: ch. 15).

organs and conceptual systems, among others), some outside, like the computer I am now using. (27)

The property of referential dependence [the relation between a pronoun and its antecedent] is often called "semantic" because it plays a role in what expressions mean and how they are understood. I prefer to call it "syntactic," because the inquiry does not yet reach to language/world relations; it is restricted to what is "in the head." Analogously, we should clearly distinguish the inquiry into how the sensorimotor systems relate expressions to sounds from the study of the information that the language provides to the sensorimotor systems, and how it is constructed by internal operations. I would prefer to reserve the term "phonetics" for the former inquiry, and to regard the latter as part of syntax, in the general sense of the term, including what is called "phonology." It is important to keep the distinctions in mind. (27–8)

Use of the term "semantics" to refer to study of language–world relations and "syntax" to refer to the study of properties of the symbolic systems themselves seems to me fairly conventional. (30)

To the best of my understanding, the study of mental aspects of the world leads us to postulate the existence of a variety of cognitive systems (language among them), which have their own properties and interact in various ways. The internalist study of these systems is what I would prefer to call "syntax." The study of how people use these systems is often called "pragmatics." If semantics is understood to be the study of the relation of "words/concepts and things," where "thing" has some non-mentalistic interpretation, then there may be no such topic as the semantics of natural language. . . . In contrast, if semantics is understood to be the study of relations of language (or concepts) to the outer and inner world, then there is such a topic; it is more or less on a par with phonetics, understood as the relation of (internal) linguistic elements to (external) motions of molecules in the air and the like, but involving no notions similar to *reference*, in its technical sense. (31–2)

Clearly Chomsky has some notion of semantics in mind quite distinct from conceptualist semantics in the sense of the previous section. Carnap (1964) and Davis (1999) attribute this way of dividing up syntax, semantics, and pragmatics to the logical positivist Charles Morris. In fact, the sense of "syntax" in these passages is much broader than its normal use in linguistics: it denotes the organization of any combinatorial system in the mind. In this sense, phonology and even music are syntax too. But in the usual narrower sense of linguistic theory, "syntax" denotes the formal organization of units like NPs and VPs.

The claim of just about every theory of linguistic semantics is that meanings/concepts form a combinatorial system, that is, they have a syntax in the broad sense. But the elements of the system are distinct from those of syntax in the narrow sense.[5] It is the study of this system that seems to me to fall under the "conventional" use of the term "semantics."

---

[5] The couple of exceptions that I know of include Generative Semantics, where meaning was identified with underlying syntactic structure (Lakoff 1971), and the approach of Anna

Chomsky is certainly free to prefer using "syntax" in the broader sense. This is apparently the sense intended when he characterizes the syntactic levels PF (phonetic form) and LF (logical form) as "direct representations of sound on the one hand and meaning on the other" (Chomsky 1986: 68). Phonologists, phoneticians, and semanticists might be justifiably excused if they have been baffled by this characterization, given that the actual formal theory invoked in all Chomsky's writing since 1970 has been that of syntax in the narrow sense. The statements quoted above help clarify Chomsky's intention; they do not, however, clarify his practice.

In particular, consider Chomsky's example of referential dependency. He is of course correct that the relation between a pronoun and its antecedent is "in the head," and therefore syntactic in the broad sense. But since the 1960s the literature has been full of discussion about whether this relation is directly encoded in narrow syntax or whether it is encoded partly or even primarily in semantic/conceptual structure (Lees and Klima 1963; Ross 1967; Jackendoff 1972; Chomsky 1981; Lasnik 1989; Kuno 1987; Van Valin 1994; Van Hoek 1995; Culicover and Jackendoff 1995; Levinson 2000, to mention only a few of hundreds of references). To just say, "Well, I prefer to call it all syntax," without distinguishing broad from narrow syntax, is the rhetorical counterpart of the move by the opponents of generative grammar, "It's all semantics." The effect is to make it impossible to clearly articulate the issues at stake.

Let us look also at what Chomsky wishes to call "semantics." As far as I can understand this characterization, he is groping for the notion of an interface component: "semantics" is a relation between one kind of structure and another, just what interface components are designed to instantiate. But it is unclear what interfaces he has in mind. In one passage above, he speaks of the connection between language and conceptual systems and then, in the next breath, of the connection between language and his computer; in another passage, he speaks of the relation between "language (or concepts)" and the "outer and inner world." Is semantics supposed to be the connection of language to concepts, or that of concepts to something else? And nowhere does he address what I take to be the central question, the formal organization of the conceptual system. He is, however, correct in being deeply skeptical of the ordinary non-mentalistic notion of "thing," an issue to which we return at length in the next chapter.

Jerry Fodor (e.g. 1975; 1983; 1990; 1998) has spent much of his career addressing some of the problems faced by a serious theory of meaning. His approach concurs with conceptualist semantics in insisting on the importance of placing this theory in a mentalistic framework. He argues that meanings must

Wierzbicka (e.g. 1988; 1996; Goddard and Wierzbicka 1994), who contends that word meanings are to be explicated in a sort of "Basic English," using ordinary linguistic forms.

be instantiated in a combinatorial system, and therefore that a simple semantic network account of meaning is not feasible. He is also properly concerned with issues of concept acquisition. We will come back later to his proposals for the combinatorial structure of concepts and for the nature of acquisition. For the moment I wish to concentrate simply on the term Fodor has chosen for this combinatorial system: the Language of Thought (LoT).

Like "syntax," "language" has a number of senses. First is the everyday sense: English, French, Chinese, and so forth. Languages in this sense are systems composed of phonology, syntax, and semantics, plus the relations between them established by interfaces (including the lexicon). Fodor clearly cannot have this sense in mind when he speaks of the Language of Thought: LoT has no phonology, and no (narrow) syntax. Nevertheless, the term is sometimes interpreted in this sense. For example, one sometimes encounters statements to the effect that "Mentalese/The Language of Thought is like a natural language" (e.g. Barnden 1996). This is misguided; it is comparable to saying, "A wheel is like a bicycle." Similarly, sometimes LoT is taken to be composed of "sentences in an inner/private language." But a sentence has phonology and (narrow) syntax; a thought doesn't. The same goes for the term "proposition": if it is supposed to be the thought expressed by a sentence (so that one can express the same proposition in different languages), it cannot be conceived of as sentence-like. The sentences that we use to express propositions have phonology and (narrow) syntax; the propositions themselves don't. Part of our job here (questions (5) and (6) in the previous section) is to figure out the proper form for propositions, and how syntax and phonology express them in different languages.

A second sense of "language" comes from the study of formal languages: a language is a set of expressions and/or the principles that generate them. For instance, we can speak of the strings in (8a) as expressions in a formal language generated by the principles in (8b).

(8) a. ab, aabb, aaabbb, aaaabbbb, . . .
     b. S → aSb
         S → ab

This sense of "language" includes the broad sense of "syntax" in Chomsky's use, but is not restricted to formal organizations in the mind: formal logic in this sense is a language, as are programming languages and possibly even the artistic style of Rembrandt. This sense is appropriate to the notion of "thought" as a combinatorial system in Fig. 9.1. It is not, however, what Fodor has in mind.

Rather, there is a third sense of "language," in which it denotes a set of expressions in a formal language *plus* a set of mapping principles that "interpret" these expressions into some domain. For instance, the sequences of *a*s and *b*s in (8a) might be interpreted as designating rows of different kinds of coins, or sequences of different kinds of sounds, or ordered *n*-tuples of elements chosen from different sets. In this sense of "language," the organization of the formal expressions is often called its "syntax" and the mapping into the other domain its "semantics." This is the sense that Fodor has in mind, concurring with Chomsky's explication of "semantics" above. Fodor intends that LoT has a syntax (in the broad sense) *and* a semantics. The expressions in LoT are *mental representations*, and they *represent* something: entities in the world. Put differently, Fodor insists that LoT is *intentional*: it is *about* something.

Fodor admits that his view is intensely problematic: after all, how do expressions in the head make contact with the things they are supposed to be about? Fodor (1991), for example, aspires to develop a "naturalized" semantics, that is, "to say in *non*semantic and *non*intentional . . . terms what makes something a symbol." In short, he is correctly trying to live by the postulate "There is no magic." His proposal is that *true* uses of a symbol such as *platypus* are somehow *caused* by actual platypuses (how? acting on the speaker's perceptual system? Fodor doesn't say). He then faces the problem of what licenses (a) incorrect uses of *platypus* in response to, say, cows, and (b) "representational" uses of *platypus* when the speaker is just imagining a platypus or thinking about platypuses in general. He concludes tentatively that these cases are "asymmetrically dependent" on the true cases, in a fashion left unexplained.[6]

Notice how drastically different Fodor's view is from what has been advocated here. Here, natural language has phonological, syntactic, and semantic/conceptual structure. Semantic/conceptual structure does not *have* a semantics, it *is* the semantics for language. As a first step in working out this view, I am going to suggest again the radical surgery on terminology advocated in Chapter 2. Fodor's problems arise from treating the combinatorial structures that constitute meanings/thoughts as symbols for something, representations of something, information about something. Instead, I am going to try to take them just as pure non-intentional structure, as we did (less controversially, I hope) with phonology and syntax. The problem will then be to reconstruct the intuitions that the notion of intentionality is supposed to account for. This will be part of the subject of the next chapter.

My approach might in a way be seen as hedging one's bets. I am hoping that we can indeed arrive at a naturalized view of meaning without invoking intentionality. On the other hand, Fodor might be right: conceptual structure might indeed need to be intentional in some sense. Whichever is the case, we still have to work

---

[6] Fodor is clearly worried by these gaps, as evidenced by asides like "No doubt it's wrong of me to be inclined to think this" and, in the final footnote, "Deep down, I think I don't believe any of this. But the question what to put in its place is too hard for me."

out the details of the combinatorial system constituting semantic/conceptual structure/LoT, as well as its interfaces with language, inference, perception, and action—which is what I take as the task of conceptualist semantics. And, as will be seen, there are lots of details worth working out. There is no reason to be paralyzed by the absence of a solution for intentionality, as Fodor seems to be.

9.5 Some "contextualist" approaches to meaning

Various approaches to meaning seek to treat it as something other than a mental phenomenon, as part of the "environment." Perhaps the most extreme is behaviorism, now mostly extinct, which claimed (e.g. Watson 1913) that thinking is nothing but subvocal speaking, and that the idea of a "concept" behind the language is nonsense. However, behaviorism never attempted to explain more than the most trivial of linguistic facts, and those in dubious fashion (Chomsky 1959).

A different sort of argument emerges from some strains of linguistic philosophy, often with appeal to Wittgenstein (1953). This view is that there is no fixed meaning associated with linguistic expressions; rather the best one can do is catalog the contextual uses of expressions. There is a germ of insight here, in that the message conveyed by an expression is indeed heavily influenced by one's understanding of the context (Sperber and Wilson 1986; Pustejovsky 1995). But on the other hand, the expression must convey *something* with which the context can interact. If it did not, a hearer could in principle know from the context what message was intended, without the speaker saying anything at all! It is important to factor out the respective contributions to understanding made by linguistic expressions and by context; this cannot be done by focusing on context alone.

Another view in a similar spirit focuses on the interaction between speaker and hearer: meaning is something not in either one of them alone, but "negotiated" in the interaction between them; it is a "social construction." This view is advocated, for instance, by Dufva and Lähteenmäki (1996), drawing on the "dialogic" tradition of Bakhtin. A less extreme version of this view appears in Herbert Clark's *Using Language* (1996), which offers a detailed analysis of how speaker and hearer collaboratively verify that the speaker's message has been adequately formulated and received. I have no quarrel with the idea that communicating linguistically is a socially engaged cooperative enterprise. I disagree only with the claim that that is *all* it is. Dufva and Lähteenmäki seem to be saying that at the end of a linguistic interaction there is just a disembodied "meaning" out there in interpersonal space. By contrast, I think—and I think Clark would agree with me—that there is something in the hearer's head that was not there before; and perhaps the negotiation results in something different in the speaker's head too. It is these things in the speaker's and hearer's heads that are the focus of my concern. So the question I am asking is:

(9)   What is present in people's f-minds when they grasp a meaning?

Looking at the complexity of the communicative act only adds to the task:

(10)   a. How does social interaction among individuals shape the meanings
            and thoughts that those individuals hold?
            and
        b. How do interacting individuals arrive at the sense that they have
            ideas in common?

We return to the issue of social construction in section 10.11.

Another version of this issue arises in connection with one aspect of Hilary Putnam's (1975) important paper "The Meaning of 'Meaning.'" Putnam observes that there are many words whose meanings we do not fully know; for instance, he knows that *elm* and *beech* both denote kinds of tree, but he himself could not tell, given two trees, which is the elm and which the beech. He proposes that there is a "linguistic division of labor," where we ordinary folk defer to experts who are in possession of the full meaning. This description applies nicely also to the situation of the language learner, who is trying to use clues from "experts," that is, fluent speakers, to figure out what words mean. Putnam takes this to show that meaning is not in the heads of speakers so much as somehow "in the community." But again, for speakers to differ in their competence at applying a word, they must each have some concept, precise or vague, associated with the word. Thus the issue boils down again to question (9), plus question (10a), plus the following questions:

(11)   a. How do interacting individuals recognize that they have *different* ideas?
        b. Under what conditions does an individual choose to defer to the
            ideas of another?

A case where one individual does *not* choose to defer to another is in the case of duelling "experts" arguing about (to pick a random example) how to understand the term "semantics." Here there is no determinate meaning "in the community" and each "expert" is striving to impose his or her own preference.

This way of stating the issues of social/cultural construction of meaning does not alter the intuitions and evidence behind them. What it does do is show how this enterprise fits into conceptualist semantics.

9.6 Is there a specifically linguistic semantics?

The rest of this chapter is devoted to quite a different impulse to constrain the scope of semantics, this time from within linguistic theory. The idea is that it is possible to delimit a specifically *linguistic* part of semantics, distinct from non-linguistic knowledge, thought, and contextualized meaning. The distinction has been proposed along a variety of lines, not mutually exclusive:

(12)   a. It is necessary to distinguish the "dictionary" meaning of lexical items
          from their "encyclopedic" meaning, the latter including at least all
          personal associations with words. Only the former is supposed to be
          in the purview of linguistic semantics.
       b. Certain semantic properties such as analyticity, logical entailment,
          and truth conditions belong to linguistic semantics, while others, such
          as heuristics, default logic, and connection to the real world, belong to
          some other enterprise, perhaps pragmatics.
       c. Certain semantic properties, such as argument structure, aspectual
          structure, illocutionary force, and the mass/count and singular/plural
          distinctions, have grammatical reflexes; these belong in linguistic
          semantics. Others, such as color, metrical size, and species (beyond
          human/non-human), do not; these belong to general knowledge.
       d. Languages differ in their semantics, because of the semantic distinc-
          tions they grammaticalize and because of their patterns of lexicaliza-
          tion. Therefore each language must have its own language-specific
          semantics, which may or may not be separate from a language user's
          general patterns of knowledge and belief.

While these proposed distinctions are based on sound intuitions, I think they
are not in the end viable; we must consider the domain of linguistic semantics to
be continuous with human conceptualization as a whole. In order to see why, let
us first see how a proposal to separate linguistic semantics from contextualized
meaning fits into Fig. 9.1 and discuss some general issues. The next section will
examine proposals (12a–d) in turn.[7]

There are two ways the separation could be effected. One is to propose that
there is a form of cognitive structure distinct from both linguistic form (phonology and syntax) and contextualized meaning, lying between them and connected to each by an interface, as in Fig. 9.2.

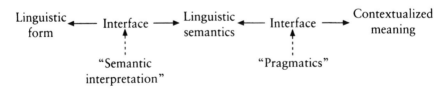

Fig. 9.2. "Linguistic semantics" as a separate level of structure

---

[7] Levinson (2000) presents many parallel arguments against separating linguistic semantics
from contextualized meaning.

This presumes that linguistic semantics is made up from different kinds of units than contextualized meaning—they are different levels of structure in the same sense that phonology and syntax are. In effect, this breaks the interface between linguistic form and meaning of Fig. 9.1 into two stages: "semantics first and pragmatics afterwards." Such is the position, as I understand it, in Katz (1972), Chomsky (1975), and Sperber and Wilson (1986), for instance.[8]

Alternatively, linguistic semantics could be a "stripped down" version of contextualized meaning, comprising only a subset of its units and/or distinctions (perhaps parallel to the relation between the sound structures encoded by lexical phonology and phonetics respectively). We might sketch this organization as Fig. 9.3.

This still keeps semantic interpretation separate from its integration with nonlinguistic elements of meaning ("pragmatics"). The only difference is that we can see the latter process as an enrichment of linguistic meaning rather than a mapping into an separate format of structure.

What might lie behind the desire to separate semantics from conceptualization? One motivation, I suspect, is a lurking fear that general-purpose knowledge and belief are a bottomless pit, and that in order to make the enterprise of semantics manageable it must somehow be restricted. And therefore *some* distinction must be made so we can stop before drowning in endless detail.

My own attitude is that the seams of the mind must be determined empirically, not on the basis of our fears. A priori, it would make more sense for there *not* to be any special level of linguistic semantics: this would just require one more bit of work for evolution to do beyond evolving phonology and syntax. In addition, there is a methodological issue: we can't tell whether there is a seam without establishing what lies on both sides of it. Thus investigating linguistic semantics

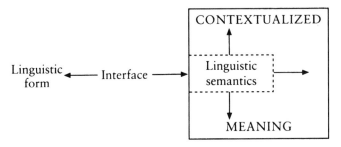

Fig. 9.3. "Linguistic semantics" as a subset of contextualized meaning

---

[8] Chomsky (1975: 105) has a diagram almost identical to Fig. 9.2. He calls linguistic semantics "logical form," and considers the left-hand interface (his *SR-1*) a part of sentence grammar. He characterizes the right-hand interface (his *SR-2*) as "other semantic rules." Of course his arrows go only from left to right, because his grammar is syntactocentric.

without also investigating contextualized meaning cannot in any event tell us whether our hypothesized distinction is correct.[9]

A more worthy motive for trying to separate semantics from conceptualization might be Frege's (1892) quite legitimate desire to eliminate "personal association" from semantics. Frege makes the all-important distinction between the *reference* of an expression—what it denotes—from its *sense*—the manner or route by which it denotes the reference. But he is also careful to distinguish sense from the idea in the language user's mind, which he finds too subjective and variable for his purposes. He therefore takes sense to be an abstract, objective property conventionally associated with a linguistic expression. This approach thus can idealize away from personal associations—such as the endearing way one's dog comes bounding up to visitors, which probably should not be part of the meaning of *dog* as it functions in interpersonal communication.

However, it is difficult if not impossible to draw a principled line between the "public" meaning of a word and its personal associations. Therefore the desire to draw such a line is not a justified motive for separating linguistic meaning from contextualized meaning. Here is why.

Suppose two people have the same personal associations for certain words, perhaps because they have grown up together. This permits them to use these words with each other, and the personal associations have a "public" meaning, albeit for a very restricted public. But as far as the rest of the world is concerned, these are just "personal associations" that cannot be recovered from hearing the words in question.

The same holds at a larger scale when we consider special uses of words by a technical subcommunity. When I use the term *language* in speaking to a linguist, I can invoke associations that come from shared experience in the linguistics community. When I use the word in speaking to my dentist, though, I cannot presume these associations and must put them aside in attempting to get my message across. But it's not as though I have two words *language* in my vocabulary, one for linguists and one for dentists. Moreover, there is a spectrum of intermediate communities, from psycholinguists to philosophers to neuroscientists to biologists, for which some of my "personal associations" are appropriate and others are not; successful communication depends on careful gauging of which to presume. Do I then have a multiplicity of words *language* in my vocabulary? I would rather say that I have intuitions about what aspects of the word's meaning for me are appropriate for my hearers. And when I don't know what

---

[9] And if linguists abdicate from studying general-purpose knowledge and belief, who is supposed to study it? None of the other cognitive sciences has better tools to do the work in its full glorious combinatorial detail.

my audience is (aside from being speakers of English), I will have to presume an appropriately "neutral" or "minimal" sense that might be the one Frege intends as the "public" sense.

I am therefore advocating that the exclusion of "personal associations" from "public" meaning is not a consequence of a strong dissociation in kind between the two kinds of information. Rather it is a consequence of a sort of Gricean principle of conversation: one produces utterances in such a way that one can expect the hearer to reconstruct the intended message. Avoiding ambiguity is just another subcase of the same principle, as is speaking in a language you think the hearer understands. It's my impression that young children are not very good at applying this principle, but gain sophistication at it as they mature. (Though some people never seem to learn it very well.)

Consequently, I don't see any need to make a strong theoretical distinction along Fregean lines to distinguish "public" from "private" meaning. In the next section, as we consider in turn proposals (12a–d) for separating semantics from conceptualization, we will see in any event that none of them captures the desired distinction.

9.7 Four non-ways to separate linguistic semantics from conceptualization

9.7.1 *Semantics = "dictionary"; pragmatics = "encyclopedia"*

The idea behind this distinction, proposal (12a), is that some aspects of a word are not part of its meaning, but are "world knowledge" about the entity the word names. For instance, on this view, the fact that a dog is an animal is part of its "dictionary entry," but the fact that dogs allegedly like to chase cats is "encyclopedic information" that plays no role in the linguistic behavior of this item, only in its pragmatics.

Note right away that this distinction does not correspond to the "public"/ "private" distinction. The fact that my dog likes to chase mailmen may be a personal association with the word *dog*, so somehow connected to *dog* in *my* f-mind. But the alleged fact that dogs like to chase cats is part of common lore and can be alluded to in conversation without difficulty. So a great deal of "public" meaning is "encyclopedic" information and is thereby (on this view) excluded from linguistic semantics.

This approach makes most sense as a version of Fig. 9.3, where dictionary information is a subset of encyclopedic information, but not formally distinct from it. For example, even if the fact that dogs characteristically chase cats is encyclopedic, still the notion of chasing must be part of the dictionary entry for the verb *chase*. More generally, some of the content of encyclopedic information for one item may well be dictionary information for another.

The problem is that it is hard and perhaps impossible to draw the line between what is in the dictionary and what is in the encyclopedia for any particular item (Bolinger 1965a; Jackendoff 1983; Lakoff 1987; Langacker 1987). For example, the difference between *murder* and *assassinate* is that the latter implies a political motive on the part of the agent. Is this dictionary or encyclopedia information? If the former, then something as complex as a political motive can be in the dictionary, and we have hardly simplified the repertoire of "dictionary semantics." If the latter, there is no distinction between the dictionary definitions of these two words. But this latter conclusion is impossible: linguistic semantics, if it is to explicate the matching between form and meaning, *must* be able to distinguish the meanings of these two words.

Jerrold Katz (1980) proposes that the dictionary contain only factors that lead to sharp (or analytic) judgments, and that any sort of graded (or defeasible) factors belong in the encyclopedia. This too is unsatisfying, since it says that color distinctions, which are well known to be graded, fall into the encyclopedia. Consequently, on this analysis, *Green things are not colored* is anomalous on the basis of dictionary information (since green is analytically a color), but *Green things are blue* is anomalous on the basis of encyclopedia information. For my taste, this is quite a curious outcome of the theory. Again, because *green* and *blue* are not synonymous, a theory that relegates their semantic difference to "encyclopedic," hence "non-linguistic," meaning, cannot be a satisfactory theory of linguistic semantics.

Here is a more complex case, arising from work of James Pustejovsky (1995) (see section 11.9). How does the f-mind encode what one typically does with objects, for example that one typically reads books, cooks on a stove, and stores things in sheds? Being *typical* actions, they certainly don't fall under Katz's notion of dictionary. My impression is that most people proposing the dictionary–encyclopedia distinction would consider them the beginning of "drowning in complexity," hence encyclopedia.

Now, think of verbs like *finish* or *enjoy*, which are understood as pertaining to an activity. When these verbs take physical objects as their complements, as in *finish/enjoy the book*, *finish/enjoy the beer*, one readily interprets them in terms of these typical actions one performs on them: one finishes or enjoys *reading* the book but *drinking* the beer. Thus, by hypothesis, a full understanding of these sentences requires encyclopedic information about the objects in question.[10] This

---

[10] *Finish*, but not *enjoy*, requires that this typical activity have a sequential structure. Thus *enjoy the stove* is fine but *finish the stove* is odd without some contextual support, e.g. the understanding that one is cleaning the kitchen.

interpretation can be overridden by circumstance, for instance if the agent cannot carry out the typical activity. Thus *The goat finished the book* can only be
interpreted as the goat eating the book or some such—unless it's a talking goat
in a fairy tale, which *can* carry out the activity. Such delicate discourse dependencies are what make people want to relegate information like "typical activity" to pragmatics.

Consider, however, an example of a semantic anomaly involving these interpretations, for instance *Bill finished the book, and so did the goat.* The joke
comes from the fact that the two clauses are normally interpreted with different
understood activities. This discrepancy, though, has the very same flavor as an
anomaly due to improper use of a polysemous item, as in *The chef cooked all
afternoon, and so did the roast.* Now, if the former case is due to pragmatic conflict in encyclopedic information and the latter to semantic conflict in dictionary
information, a clear generalization is being missed.

The pattern from these examples—*murder, green,* and *finish*—ought to be
clear. For any distinction you may propose between dictionary and encyclopedia, I can find a semantic fact such as a pattern of anomaly that cuts across them.
This was essentially Bolinger's (1965a) argument against Katz and Fodor's
(1963) way of making the distinction, and it holds just as well against any other
proposal of the same sort. So this way of avoiding the full complexity of contextualized meaning fails.[11]

9.7.2 *Logical vs. nonlogical semantic properties*

The idea behind proposal (12b) is that linguistic semantics is concerned only
with properties that lead to logical entailments and that are involved in establishing analyticity; all non-logical semantic properties belong in pragmatics.
Katz's approach is one version of this hypothesis; another version appears in the
psychological literature on semantic memory (e.g. Smith and Medin 1981); yet
another seems to be advocated by Levinson (2000). The idea is that certain parts

---

[11]   A further point may be illustrated by the meaning of the word *remove*. At some coarse level
that we might want to call the "dictionary" meaning, *remove X from Y* means roughly 'cause X to
come not to be on/in Y.' Now consider the problem faced by Bonnie Webber's research group at
the University of Pennsylvania. They were attempting to program a virtual robot (a robot on a
video screen) to respond to natural language commands. It had to know what to do when told to
remove something. But removing wallpaper from a wall requires a different action than removing
a lid from a jar, and than removing a jar from a refrigerator. Where should such knowledge be classified? As part of the "encyclopedic" meaning of *remove*, part of the "encyclopedic" meaning of
wallpaper, etc., as "general world knowledge," or what? I must say that I don't know, and leave it
at that. In any event, this knowledge must appear as part of contextualized meaning for the verb
phrases in question. This problem recurs massively in an account of phrasal meanings, and cannot
be brushed off lightly when thinking about practical reasoning.

of a word's meaning are necessary conditions ("dictionary"), and other parts, less central, may have exceptions. This proposal is compatible either with Fig. 9.2, where logical properties are encoded one way and non-logical properties are encoded some other way, or with Fig. 9.3, where logical properties are a subset of all semantic properties.

Like the previous proposal, this one excludes much of "public" meaning from linguistic semantics. Our utterances communicate a great deal beyond logical implications or necessary conditions—and we count on their doing so. So this proposal should not be construed as satisfying Frege's objection to mentalistic semantics.

This proposal is subject to the counterarguments of the previous subsection, plus three more. The first is Wittgenstein's (1953) reason: many words have no exceptionless distinctions that differentiate them interestingly from other words. Wittgenstein's most famous example is *game*, for which he can find only the necessary condition that it be an (intentional) activity. (Lakoff 1987 in particular elaborates this argument in great detail.) Hence they have no "dictionary definition" in this sense. (More examples in section 11.6.2.)

Second, a condition may result in logical entailment in one word and only in a defeasible (i.e. "pragmatic") assumption in another. For instance, both *rise* and *climb* carry content pertaining to movement in an upward direction. But *climb downwards* is perfectly sensible while *rise downwards* is anomalous. Thus the very same piece of conceptual content may belong either to "pragmatics" or to "semantics," depending on the word. This certainly argues against a layout like Fig. 9.2, where the two types of condition are in different components.

A third reason is developed in Chapters 5 and 6 of Jackendoff (1983). I argue there that if one has formal machinery to make judgments on sentences like (13a) and (13b), this machinery is also sufficient to evaluate the truth of sentences like (13c).

(13) a. That [*pointing*] is a dog.
      b. That [*pointing*] is an animal.
      c. A dog is an animal.

The former sentences certainly involve pragmatics, for they require examination of the visual field to determine the object being pointed to, followed by comparison of that object itself to the features of the predicate (see the next chapter). The latter sentence, of course, is supposed to be analytic, its truth determinable on the basis of linguistic meaning alone. The point of the argument is that there is no special status to be accorded to analytic sentences in terms of the features of meaning they invoke or the formal machinery they require for their evaluation. It misses a generalization to set their treatment off as special. They don't require different resources, just a subset of the ones needed to evaluate sentences in context.

The upshot is that there is little to be gained in theoretical economy or explanatory adequacy by making a strict cut between logical and non-logical properties. Logical properties alone don't make enough distinctions among lexical items; the semantic features involved in logical properties don't form a disjoint set from those involved in non-logical properties; and any system that can deal with non-logical properties can easily deal with logical ones as well. So logical properties are just some heterogeneous subset of semantic properties, and there seems no point in recovering them "first" from linguistic form then adding the other properties on "later."[12]

9.7.3 Grammatically realized vs. grammatically irrelevant content

Proposal (12c) seeks to segregate as "linguistic semantics" just those features of meaning that play a role in syntax and morphology, for instance the distinction between singular and plural but not that between red and green. Various versions of this idea have been proposed by Bierwisch (e.g. Bierwisch and Lang 1989), Pinker (1989), and Grimshaw (1993). Of course, different languages grammaticalize different semantic distinctions. For instance, many European languages base grammatical gender distinctions in part (but in part only) on semantic gender distinctions, but English makes no such grammatical distinction. Similarly, many languages make a mood distinction based in part on evidentiary status (indicative vs. subjunctive), but English does not. We could therefore envision two versions of this proposal, one in which the elements of linguistic semantics are language-specific, and one in which they are universal, but different languages happen to grammaticalize different subsets of linguistic semantics. The former position will fall under the proposal to be discussed in the next subsection, so we will restrict ourselves to the latter here.

According to this proposal, the difference between red and green, between dog and cat, and between twenty-seven and thirty-eight make no grammatical difference, so they are not part of linguistic semantics. Hence this version of linguistic semantics is even narrower than the previous two. It provides no basis

---

[12] Levinson (2000) is correct in pointing out that the necessary conditions must still be distinguished from the defeasible ones, say by notating them in "different colors" or under different logical operators. But he thinks that this difference comes from the kind of rule that leads to the condition in question—semantic or pragmatic. The position here is that the difference simply is a lexical property of the condition in question; e.g. 'upwardness' is simply marked necessary in the lexical entry of rise and defeasible in that of climb. See section 11.6.2 for more discussion.

for any sort of inference, and it ignores the fact that linguistic theory must ultimately account for the mapping between the phonological structure /kæt/ and the meaning of the word *cat*. Still less, of course, can this approach satisfy Frege's desire to separate "public" from "private" meaning.

On this construal, should linguistic semantics be considered a separate level of cognitive structure (Fig. 9.2) or a subset of conceptualization (Fig. 9.3)? I believe that Bierwisch has on different occasions endorsed both possibilities. Chomsky's notion of LF (at least the 1981 version) seems to be an instantiation of Fig. 9.2, in that LF contains semantic features, but only those that are "strictly determined by linguistic rules."

The place where this approach has been most successful, in my opinion, has been Pinker's work (1989), where he shows that the argument structure of verbs—and certain significant cases of argument structure alternation—depend on relatively coarse distinctions in verb meaning. Thus if the language learner can place a verb in a particular coarse class by virtue of its meaning, (s)he can pretty well predict its syntactic behavior.

So let us ask which semantic features are involved in grammatical distinctions across languages. They form quite a heterogeneous set: singular vs. plural, animate vs. inanimate, mass vs. count, male vs. female, quantifierhood, causativity, motion, being a "psychological predicate," rough shape (in classifier systems), and relative social status, among other things. Pinker's "narrow classes," motivated by argument structure distinctions, involve factors such as whether a substance tightly fills a space (verbs like *stuff, pack*, and *cram*) versus whether it is distributed on a surface (*smear, spread*, and *slather*). In Levin and Rappaport Hovav's (1996) discussion of argument structure alternations, we find that sound emission verbs can appear in motion verb frames if the sound emission can be associated directly with the action of moving (e.g. *The car squealed around the corner* but not *The car honked around the corner*). Thus it does not seem that the semantic features that play a role in grammatical structure form a particularly simple or natural class. In fact the association of sound emission with motion surely involves what other proposals would consider "encyclopedic" knowledge.

This suggests to me that little is to be gained from positing a separate level of structure for linguistic semantics (as in Fig. 9.2), since this level exhibits no interesting semantic constraints beyond its coarseness relative to lexical distinctions. This leaves us with the option in Fig. 9.3, in which the semantic features relevant to grammatical structure are a subset of those relevant to meaning in general.

But there is a way to achieve such a subset other than simply to carve it out within the theory of conceptual structure itself. Recall from Part II that part of the theory of linguistic structure involves specifying the interface constraints that relate contextualized meaning to linguistic form. The lexicon forms an important part of this interface; but it also must include phrasal interface rules that specify how syntactic combinations of words are mapped to complex contextualized meaning. With this in mind, an alternative proposal is simply this:

(14)   The subset of semantic features relevant to grammar is just the subset that is (or can be) mentioned in phrasal interface rules—the part of conceptualization that is "visible" to these rules.

Under this approach, the fact that these "grammatically visible" features form a heterogeneous set still remains to be explained, but at least we are no longer required to give them a revealing formal characterization: the phrasal interface rules can see whatever they can see, and if what they can see is a weirdly structured subset of semantics, well, that's how it comes out. At the same time, the fact that this subset is relatively coarse now comes as no surprise. Phrasal interface rules are *supposed* to apply to classes larger than individual lexical items, so it stands to reason that they lump classes of items together, sometimes in broad classes, sometimes in narrow ones. Put in the terms of Chapters 5 and 7, the phrasal part of the syntax–semantics interface is only a partial homology between the two structures, not a full mapping.

As far as I can tell, this perspective is consistent with everything Bierwisch and Pinker say. (In fact, Bierwisch 1996 seems to me only rhetorically different from this, not substantively.) Under this view, the formation rules for conceptual structure do not have to concern themselves with whether a particular distinction has a grammatical counterpart or not; this simplifies the theory of the formation rules. The question of grammatical counterparts for semantic distinctions is asked only in the theory of the syntax–semantics interface constraints.

9.7.4 *Language-specific semantics implying a special linguistic semantics*

It is sometimes suggested (position (12d)) that each language has its own semantics, so there has to be a theory of language-specific semantics separate from the theory of contextualized meaning. Here are three basic arguments adduced for this position:

(15)   a.   Languages can have different sets of lexical items that presuppose different (and incompatible) cultural systems. Therefore semantics cannot be universal, because there is no direct translation between languages.

b. Going beyond individual items, languages have different patterns of lexicalization. For instance, Talmy (1980) observes that Romance languages typically conflate path and motion together in a verb, while English typically conflates manner and motion (though it has its share of path+motion verbs too). These differences in pattern are correlated with differences in grammatical patterns as well.

c. Languages have inflectional categories that reflect different partitioning of semantic space—different gender/classifier systems, different tense/aspect systems, different politeness systems. Linguistic semantics must enable us to characterize these differences.

The answer to these arguments is the same as in the previous subsection. All of these arguments concern the way elements of linguistic form map into complexes of meaning, not with the contents of meaning itself. Thus they can be characterized as language-specific differences in the interface rules—either (a) in the mapping associated with particular cultural vocabulary, (b) in the general pattern of mappings encoded by classes of lexical items (which, recall, are interface rules), or (c) in the phrasal interface rules associated with grammatical and morphological features. This, then, is specifically linguistic semantics, not because it invokes a different sort of cognitive structure, but rather because it involves how the vocabulary and grammar of different languages map onto the *same* level of conceptual structure, thereby creating different natural groupings of meanings for users of different languages.

Position (12d) is not far from a well-known position emerging from linguistics and anthropology, often called the Sapir–Whorf hypothesis (Carroll 1956). This stresses the dependence of thought on language, claiming that differences among languages strongly affect the thought processes of their speakers. Again there is a certain degree of plausibility to this claim, particularly in the realm of vocabulary. In fact, it is unnecessary to look to other languages: we can simply look to technical sub-vocabularies in our own language (say, chemical, medical, cultural, or religious terms) to see how much greater precision is afforded in discourse and thought by virtue of having a more finely divided vocabulary.[13]

Whorf's more radical claim was that grammatical structure fundamentally affects thought. He claimed, for instance, that the Hopi language contains no elements that refer to time, and therefore that monolingual Hopi speakers have no concept of time; both aspects of this claim have been refuted by Malotki

---

[13] Incidentally, the "urban legend" that Eskimo languages have dozens of words for snow can be traced to a far less extreme claim by Whorf; the actual range is not that different from English *sleet, slush, blizzard, powder*, etc. (Pullum 1981).

(1983). More recently, experiments reported by Levinson (1996) have shown some interesting differences in non-verbal spatial understanding in speakers of certain Australian and Mayan languages, compared to speakers of European languages; the differences appear to be related to the way these languages encode spatial relations, thus offering support to a limited version of the Sapir–Whorf hypothesis. (Li and Gleitman 2000 disputes even these modest results, though.)

The upshot is that the character of thought may be to some limited extent affected by the proclivities of its interface with different languages: certain thoughts may be more easily accessible because one's language makes it easier to *express* them. Such a conclusion is still compatible with there being no specific *level* of linguistic semantics. Rather, again, the language-specific character of a speaker's concepts, such as it is, is a consequence of the language-specific *interface* between syntax/phonology and meaning—including the lexicon.

To sum up our discussion of the ecological niche for specifically linguistic semantics in the f-mind: there is such a niche, but not as a separate level of structure. Distinctions like "logical/non-logical" and "dictionary/encyclopedia" seem impossible to draw, and don't appear to make any useful functional distinction in an account of the f-mind. Rather, linguistic semantics per se is the study of the interface between conceptualization and linguistic form (phonology and syntax). It therefore studies the organizations of conceptualization that can be expressed or invoked by language. In particular, *lexical* semantics studies the organizations of conceptualization that can be bundled up in a single word (or to be clearer, in an interface rule whose other end is a morpheme). But all such work can be pursued in the framework of a functional architecture simply like Figure 9.1, where there is no level of "strictly linguistic meaning" intervening between linguistic form and concepts.

CHAPTER 10

Reference and Truth

10.1 Introduction

A crucial part of semantic theory is to explain how reference and truth value are attached to linguistic expressions. Common sense tells us that linguistic expressions say things about the world. When I say *Russell was a great philosopher*, I am referring to Russell, a real person in the real world. When I point at something and say *That is a chicken*, my deictic term *that* is intended to refer to the thing in the world that I'm pointing at. Sentences intuitively have truth values by virtue of how they relate to the world. *Snow is green* is false because snow isn't green. *My name is Russell* is true if uttered by somebody named Russell (e.g. Rosalind Russell, Kevin Russell, Russell Stover), and false if uttered by anyone else. *It's raining outside* is true if at the moment of utterance there is rain coming down outside the enclosure in which the speaker is located and false otherwise.

The predominant traditions in Anglo-American semantics and philosophy of language take for granted this common-sense position. They therefore consider it the task of semantic/pragmatic theory to explain how linguistic expressions say things about the world and have truth values based on their relation to the world.

The next two sections will show that a mentalistic theory of language proves not so easy to reconcile with this common sense position on reference and truth. After exploring a couple of not very promising alternatives, I will conclude that *it is necessary to thoroughly psychologize not just language, but also "the world."* The intent behind this perhaps mysterious statement will become clearer as we go along, and many perils must be avoided in order to make sense of it.

I must make clear from the outset that my goal is not to show that the common-sense view of reference and truth is false and should be rejected out of hand. Consider by analogy the notion of *sunset*. The scientific view of sunsets does not say that the sun doesn't really go down and therefore that there is no such thing as a sunset. Rather, it says that (a) a less intuitive account in terms of the earth's rotation yields a better explanation in terms of physics as a whole; and (b) human psychology is nevertheless such that, no matter how much physics we know, the sun still compellingly *appears* to be going down. Try to watch a sunset and see it (feel it!) as the earth rotating. And "What a beautiful sunset!" is not to be superseded by a scientific reduction.

Similarly, in approaching reference and truth, my goal here is to show that for scientific purposes a position at odds with intuition yields a deeper understanding of the phenomena. But I also wish to show why the common-sense view is nevertheless so intuitively compelling and why it therefore cannot be eliminated from everyday discourse.[1]

10.2 Problems with the common-sense view: "language"

Here are four rather typical statements of the standard position.

... linguistic expressions refer to things out in the world. (Abbott 1997)

In general, to determine whether a sentence is true or false, two things are necessary: (1) you must know what the sentence means and (2) you must face the sentence with some situation in the real world and see whether it corresponds to the meaning of the sentence. (Bach 1989: 8)

What is a semantic theory? Following Tarski I view semantic theories as theories that deal with concepts relating language to the world (in a broad sense): "We shall understand by semantics the totality of considerations concerning those concepts which, roughly speaking, express certain connexions between the expressions of a language and the objects and states of affairs referred to by these expressions." (Tarski 1936: 401)
... Reference is a relation between a term and an object it refers to, and satisfaction is a relation between a formula and an object ... satisfying it ... Truth is definable in terms of reference and satisfaction because it has to do with objects and their relations to language. Truth holds ... of a given sentence *s* iff the objects referred to in *s* possess the properties (stand in the relations) attributed to them by *s*. (Sher 1996: 531)

The first family of theories can be labeled "referential" or "denotational." This kind of theory is outward looking; its main emphasis is on the informational significance of language, its aboutness. Meaningfulness lies, according to this view, in the relations of symbols and configurations thereof to objects of various kinds. The study of meaning is the study of such relations. This tradition is the basis of the semantic techniques that

---

[1] The approach to reference and truth developed in the present chapter has roots in Jackendoff (1983; 1987; 1992a: ch. 8); here I go somewhat beyond those treatments. Lakoff (1987) develops some parallel critiques of the main philosophical positions on truth and reference (what he calls "objectivism"), but he does not to my way of thinking establish sufficiently detailed foundations for his alternative.

have been developed within mathematical and philosophical logic.² (Chierchia and McConnell-Ginet 1990: 46)

These statements accord nicely with common sense; the latter two sharpen the common-sense position. But I would like to dig a bit deeper and question how one is supposed to construe "language" on the one hand and "objects" on the other.

Let us first think about the construal of "language." As will be recalled from Chapter 9, Frege wished to eliminate personal associations or "ideas" from semantics, and therefore he settled on a theory of meaning whose central notions were the reference of an expression and a speaker-independent "sense." Hence Frege and much of the tradition following him take language to be independent of its human users: it relates directly to the world. This is the usual construal of the quotes above, and might be diagrammed as Fig. 10.1.

Later semanticists (e.g. Kripke 1972; Lewis 1972; Stalnaker 1984) replace this simple conception with an approach in which language maps to "possible worlds," as in Fig. 10.2. Among other things, this move enables semantic notions like analyticity and necessity to be captured in terms of "true in all possible worlds."

In formal semantics (Montague 1973; Partee 1975; 1976), "world" comes to be replaced by "model," a set-theoretic construct that enables the theory to be completely formalized. In principle formal semantics is neutral about its metaphysics. But on the whole "language" is taken to retain its common-sense status as something "out there in the world." For instance, the four quotes above are from formal semanticists. David Lewis is equally plain:

I distinguish two topics: first, the description of possible languages or grammars as abstract semantic systems whereby symbols are associated with aspects of the world; and second, the description of the psychological and sociological facts whereby one of these abstract semantic systems is the one used by a person or population. Only confusion comes of mixing these two topics. (Lewis 1972: 170)

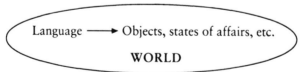

Fig. 10.1. An "objectivist" or "realist" view of language

<hr />

² Chierchia and McConnell-Ginet's "second family" of theories are "psychologistic" or "mentalistic," presumably including the theory to be developed here. The burden of the present chapter is to surmount their criticisms of such theories, to be summarized below. Their "third family" consists of the "social" or "pragmatic" theories discussed in section 9.5.

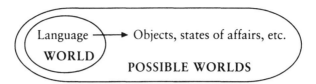

Fig. 10.2. Language in possible worlds semantics

This view of language is of course profoundly at odds with the outlook of generative grammar, which places language in the f-mind of language users. A few formal semanticists have worried about this inconsistency (e.g. Partee 1979; Bach 1986a; Zwarts and Verkuyl 1994), and some formal semantic approaches such as Discourse Representation Theory (Kamp and Reyle 1993) lend themselves better to mentalistic interpretation than others. But by and large the issue has been neglected.[3]

So let us address it. How is the realist view of language to be reconciled with the mentalist approach? One approach would be to jettison the mentalism of generative linguistics, but retain the formal mechanisms: to take the position that there is an objective "language out there in the world," and that this is in fact what generative grammar is studying. But this disconnects generative linguistics from all sources of evidence based on processing, acquisition, genetics, and brain damage. Good riddance, many people would say. For example, Katz (1981) retreats (well, he would say "advances") from his early mentalist position (Katz 1966) to the view that language is an abstract object, independent of the f-mind; he takes the study of language in the mind only to concern issues of performance.

But look what this forces us to give up. As Chapter 4 stressed, the fundamental motivation for positing Universal Grammar and for exploring its character comes directly from the observation that languages come to be instantiated in the f-mind by virtue of being learned by children. Without this mentalistic boundary condition, the subject matter of linguistics becomes limited to the mere description of languages, and the study of Universal Grammar becomes at best an exercise in statistical tendencies and/or formal elegance. Some people don't mind such an outcome, and often when one is enmeshed in the gritty details of an endangered language it makes little practical difference. However, for reasons detailed in Part I, I think that abandoning the mentalist outlook gives up one of the major conceptual advances of our time.

An alternative position might be that of Frege (1892): language is indeed "out in the world" and it refers to "objects in the world"; but people *use* language by

---

[3] Macnamara and Reyes (1994) is an important (though completely non-mainstream) exception, attempting to build a formal semantics based on psychological principles.

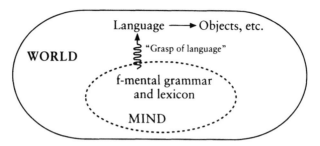

Fig. 10.3. The mind grasping "language in the world"

virtue of their grasp of it, where "grasp" is a transparent metaphor for "the mind holding/understanding/making contact with" something in the world. Fig. 10.3 might schematize such an approach.

Generative linguistics, it might then be said, is the study of what is in the mind when it grasps a language.[4] This would make it possible to incorporate all the mentalistic methodology into linguistics while preserving a realist semantics.

One might interpret Katz's program this way. He is personally interested only in the part of language that is an abstract object "in the world"; but one could conceivably be concerned with the mental side of language as well. However, this approach faces a curious methodological problem. We can determine properties of "language in the world" only through its manifestations in human linguistic intuition and behavior. Thus we have no independent fix on what parts of human language are due to its mental instantiation and what parts are due to characteristics of the abstract object "Language." Katz, for one, is inclined to attribute all the logical properties of human language to the abstract object and to be noncommittal about the rest. Other decisions might be possible as well. The problem is that they are just that: decisions. There is no empirical way to determine how to divide up the pie.[5]

But there is a still more fundamental problem. What sense are we to make of

---

[4] Notice how close this is to the standard phrase in generative grammar, "knowledge of language." This phrase carries with it the implication of an external entity, "language," that is known. Thus Chomsky's disclaimers that there is such an external language are subtly undermined by his choice of terminology.

[5] A similar objection applies to Rey (1996), who wants to "divorce the issue of definitions from the issue of anyone's ability to provide them," and proposes that "the correct definition of a concept is provided by the optimal account of it, which need not be known by the concept's competent users" (293). Here the term "concept" stands for an external abstract object; somehow the "optimal account" of it is supposed to come from science. This may appear apposite for words like *gold*, where science seeks the "true nature" of the substance—but it is surely misguided for such words as *puddle*, *groceries*, and *pie*. Moreover, it directs us away from what language users f-know, which is precisely what a mentalistic account cares about. What is the relation between their f-knowledge and the user-independent definition?

the notion of "grasping" an abstract object? We know in principle how the mind "grasps" concrete objects: by constructing cognitive structures in response to inputs from the senses. This process has a physical instantiation: the sense organs respond to impinging light, vibration, pressure, and so forth by emitting nerve impulses that enter the brain. But an abstract object by definition has no physical manifestations that can impinge on the nervous system. So how does the nervous system "grasp" them? Without a careful exegesis of the term—which no one provides—we are ineluctably led toward a quasi-mystical interpretation of "grasping," a scientific dead end.

Common sense is also a bit strained when it comes to the provenance of abstract objects. If languages are abstract objects, was Nicaraguan Sign Language lying around in the abstract domain until the 1980s, when it was at last grasped by someone? Come to think of it, has modern English been lying around since the Big Bang, and do the abstract objects also include all the languages ever spoken on other planets, which we humans could not possibly grasp? These questions may seem hopelessly naive, but I don't recall ever seeing them addressed. It seems to me that they have only one sensible answer: the conceptualist view that abstract objects are human creations. But creations out of what? (Dennett's (1991) ironic term "figment" comes to mind.) It becomes clear that we have no way to understand "abstract objects" except through metaphor based on concrete objects (Lakoff and Johnson 1980); the metaphor remains apt only if we don't push it too hard.

Proponents of treating language as an abstract object (Katz included) respond that there *must* be a way for the mind to grasp abstract objects. After all, we do manage to grasp numbers and other mathematical objects, not to mention logical truths. These are surely eternal, abstract, and independent of humans. Two plus two would still equal four, five would still be a prime, and [p and q] would still entail p even if we weren't around to appreciate it. So, the proponents say, whatever mechanism allows us to grasp mathematical and logical truths will do for grasping abstract Language as well. If we can't figure out how to instantiate our grasp of arithmetic and logic in materialist terms, well, so much the worse for science.

This response does raise the stakes. Surely a theory of mind has to explain how we come to understand number and logic. But I am not sure a satisfactory theory is going to come from the assumption that we do so by making mystical contact with abstract objects. Rather, within conceptualist semantics, the problem turns inside out: we should be asking what it is about human beings that (a) permits them to deal with mathematical and logical concepts and (b) leads them to believe that these are true independent of human observers. At the moment I have no proposals to offer; Macnamara (1986) and Lakoff (1987) have interesting

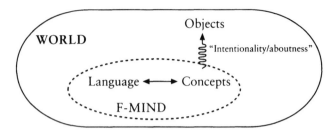

Fig. 10.4. Concepts in the f-mind that are "about" objects in the world

discussions on logic, Gelman and Gallistel (1978), Wynn (1995), Makkai (1999), and Wiese (forthcoming) on number.

One way to eliminate the problem of how the mind grasps language is to push language entirely into the mind—as we have done here. We might then arrive at a semantic theory structured like Fig. 10.4.

This is Fodor's position (see section 9.4): for him, language is a mental faculty that accesses concepts (expressions in the Language of Thought). In turn, concepts have a semantics; they are connected to the world by virtue of being "intentional." The trouble, as already complained of in section 9.4, is that one cannot make naturalistic sense of intentionality. It suffers from precisely the same difficulty as "grasping" language in Figure 10.3: there is no physically realizable causal connection between concepts and objects.

In short, there appears to be no way to combine a realist semantics with a mentalist view of language, without invoking some sort of transcendental connection between the mind and the world. The key to a solution, I suggest, lies in examining the realist's notion of "objects in the world," to which we now turn.

10.3 Problems with the common-sense view: "objects"

Consider again the quotes at the beginning of the last section. To be sure, "objects," "states of affairs," and "things out in the world" have an entirely intuitive construal. "Objects" invites us to think of Bertrand Russell, Noam Chomsky, trees, refrigerators, apartment buildings, screwdrivers, and so on. These are things you can see and touch; you can count them, tell two of them apart, in some cases move them around. "States of affairs" invites us to think of snow being white, dogs being animals, Russell's having been a philosopher, the door to my office being open (at the moment of writing), and so on: observable facts about observable objects.

But we refer routinely to all sorts of "objects" that are not so simple to put our hands on. I am deliberately going to overwhelm you with examples, just to give a flavor of the scope of the problem.

(1)   Fictional and mythical characters
      a. Sherlock Holmes
      b. the unicorn in my dream last night

Sherlock Holmes exists only as a character in stories, yet one can say true and false things about him, for example it is true that he was English, false that he was Romanian, and—false that he existed! There are no unicorns in "the world," but one can experience one in a dream "as if it were real"; and within this context, it is true that it did such-and-such and false that it did something else.

(2)   Geographical objects
      a. Wyoming
      b. the Mississippi River
      c. the distance between New York and Boston

There is nothing tangible about Wyoming, no great geographical features that mark it off, no lines drawn across the landscape (unlike the Land of Oz, where things are all red in one region, yellow in another, and so forth). There may be billboards along the road that say "Welcome to Wyoming", but these are not what make it Wyoming. It is a purely politically constructed entity, its rectilinear boundaries fixed by a stipulative act.

We can touch the Mississippi River, and swim in it. But is the river the water contained in it, the bed of the river, the complex of the two? Exactly where does it end in the Gulf of Mexico, and exactly where does its tributary, the Missouri, end in it? One can draw arbitrary lines on a map, but these are understood as matters of convenience and not some sort of "natural truth about the world."

The distance between New York and Boston is not tangible. Nor is there an absolute truth about it: how should it be measured? From center to center, from nearest border to nearest border, along some particular highway, on a straight line through the earth's crust? Much depends on one's purpose.

(3)   Virtual objects
      a. the square formed by the four dots below

     •   •

     •   •

      b. the horizontal rectangle that goes behind the vertical one below

The square and the horizontal rectangle simply aren't there physically. What does it mean to say they are "objects in the world"?

(4) Social entities
     a. the value of my watch[6]
     b. the first dollar I ever earned
     c. Morris Halle's Ph.D. degree
     d. your reputation
     e. General Motors
     f. the score of tomorrow's Red Sox game

These are all intangible entities (one hesitates to call them objects) that are the result of social practices and conventions. As Searle (1995) points out, they are nevertheless treated referentially, as parts of the "real world." I have chosen a wildly heterogeneous group of examples (with the future reference to "tomorrow's game" thrown in for the pleasure of extra complexity); doubtless the reader can come up with many more.

(5) Auditorily perceived objects
     a. Mahler's Second Symphony
     b. the words *banana* and *despite*

One cannot identify Mahler's Second as a particular performance, or as a score or a recording. It is in some sense the entity that lies behind all of these, of which these are all realizations. Those of a logical frame of mind might try to treat it as a type rather than a token. But this doesn't really solve the problem: a type of what? There is the type expressed by "performances of Mahler's Second," the type expressed by "scores of Mahler's Second," and the type expressed by "recordings of Mahler's Second," each of which has its own particular tokens; but it is mere sleight of hand to assert that Mahler's Second is, say, the union of these types, or, following Goodman (1968), "the set of performances in conformance with the score." Especially since Mahler's Second existed and was the same symphony before there were any recordings of it. In fact it presumably existed in Mahler's imagination before there were any performances and before the score was completed. And of course many musical traditions are not regulated by written scores at all. The problem only becomes more confusing when we consider variant editions and arrangements of Mahler's Second, where the notes and instrumentation are different. Yet we certainly

---

[6] This is a favorite example of Chomsky's, which he uses to illustrate his own skepticism with the notion of "thing in the world," noted in section 9.4. The present section is in a sense an amplification of his point, as well as of a point stressed in Jackendoff (1983).

refer to *Mahler's Second* without any sense of complex circumlocution. It is as much an entity "in the world" as the Sistine Chapel. (Makkai 1999 makes a similar point with respect to poems.)

I leave it as an exercise for the reader to see that words like *banana* and *despite* present the same problems as symphonies. But this is of crucial importance to the theory of reference: exactly what are we *using* to refer to "entities in the world"?

(6) Other
    a. the set of all possible worlds
    b. the best of all possible worlds

I am totally at a loss as to what it could possibly mean to claim these are "in the world," particularly since "the world" is included in *them*. But we do refer to them.

Here is the point: The quotes above assert that we refer to "objects in the world" as if this is completely self-evident. It *is* self-evident, if we think only of reference to middle-sized perceivable physical objects like tables and refrigerators. But as soon as we explore the full range of entities to which we actually refer, "the world" suddenly begins to be populated with all sorts of curious beasts whose ontological status is far less clear. For each of the types of entity cited above, one can construct some elaborate story, and some of them have indeed evoked an extensive philosophical literature. But the effect in each case is to distance the notions of reference and "the world" from direct intuition. The cumulative effect of considering all of them together is a "world" in which direct intuition applies only to a very limited class of instances.

10.4 Pushing "the world" into the mind

To sum up so far: The common-sense position on reference, which standard approaches to semantics take as their starting point, suffers from two complementary problems. First, if language is in the minds of language users, it is necessary to invoke some mystical connection from the mind to the world, either at the level of language (Fig. 10.3) or at the level of the concepts the language expresses (Fig. 10.4). Second, the notion of "objects in the world" is itself suspect.

I propose to cut the Gordian knot by abandoning the unexamined notion of "objects in the world," and, for purposes of the theory of reference, pushing "the world" down into the mind of the language user too, right along with language. The change is in how we are supposed to understand statements about reference. (7) and (8) give the two opposing alternatives.

(7)   Common sense realist theory of reference:
       Phrase P of language L, uttered in context C, refers to entity E in the world
       (or possible worlds).

(8)   Conceptualist theory of reference:
       A speaker S of language L judges phrase P, uttered in context C, to refer to
       entity E in [the world as conceptualized by S].[7]

That is, in a conceptualist theory, reference is taken to be at its foundation
dependent on a language user—just as relativistic physics takes distances and
times to be dependent on an observer's inertial frame. And just as it is often convenient to revert to Newtonian dynamics when relativistic effects can be
ignored, we can often take the (7) as a convenient abbreviation for (8), temporarily ignoring the "reference frame"—the presumption of agreement among
members of a (relatively) homogeneous speech community.

   As initial motivation for exploring the conceptualist position, observe that a
language user cannot refer to an entity without having some conceptualization
of it. Consider an example such as (9).

(9)   I don't know what *that* was, but here it comes again!

In order to utter (9) (and mean it), the speaker must have conceptualized some
relevant entity, though certainly without a full characterization. That is, a referent's being in the world as conceptualized is a necessary condition for a speaker
to refer. However, being in the *real* world is *not* a necessary condition: speakers
can refer to entities like *Sherlock Holmes* and *the unicorn in my dream last
night*. And an entity's being in the world is not sufficient for reference either: one
has to conceptualize it in at least some minimal way. In short, an entity's being
in the real world is neither a necessary nor a sufficient condition for a speaker's
being able to refer to it. Rather, the crucial factor is having conceptualized an
entity of the proper sort.[8]

   Still, I would not blame the reader who is a bit suspicious of this expression
"the world as conceptualized by the language user." It smacks of a certain solipsism or even deconstructionism, as though language users get to make up the

---

[7] Ch. 2 has discussed the tropes needed in order to relativize the idealized term "speaker of language L" to "non-ideal speakers," and to explain the relative uniformity within a speech-community. Likewise, "judges" is a stand-in for a collection of tasks involving language use, including not
only conscious judgment but also appropriate use in normal conversational conditions, evidence
of understanding in normal conversational conditions, behavior in psychological experiments, and
so on.

[8] However, conceptualization is not a sufficient condition for reference, because one can conceptualize an entity without speaking of it at all, or even having a word for it. Moreover, there are
concepts that do not support reference, for example the concept expressed by the word *if*.

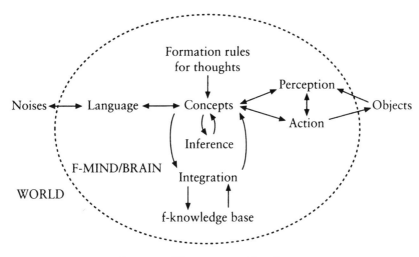

Fig. 10.5. The conceptualist view

world any way they want. Abbott (1997) compares this view to Berkeleyan idealism, which claims that one is referring to one's mental representations rather than to the things represented.

And indeed, there seems little choice. Fig. 10.5, which repeats Fig. 9.1, has no direct connection between the form of concepts and the outside world. On this picture our thoughts seem to be trapped in our own brains.

This outcome, needless to say, has come in for harsh criticism, for example:

Suppose that we adopted an approach . . . that studied meaning by relating symbols to mental representations or mental procedures of some sort, and stopped there. That would amount to limiting the domain of semantics to the relations between a language, which is a form of representation, and another representation . . ., translating our public language into an internal mental code, our "language of thought," say. But how can mapping a representation onto another representation explain what a representation *means* . . .? . . . [E]ven if our interaction with the world is always mediated by representation systems, understanding such systems will eventually involve considering what the systems are about, what they are representations of. (Chierchia and McConnell-Ginet 1990: 47)

. . . words can't have their meanings *just* because their users undertake to pursue some or other linguistic policies; or, indeed, just because of any purely *mental* phenomenon, anything that happens purely 'in your head'. For "John" to be John's name, there must be some sort of *real relation* between the name and its bearer . . . something has to happen *in the world*. (Fodor 1990: 98–9)

Semantic markers [i.e. elements of conceptual structures in the present sense—RJ] are *symbols*: items in the vocabulary of an artificial language we may call *Semantic*

Markerese [here, conceptual structure⁹]. Semantic interpretation by means of them amounts merely to a translation algorithm from the object language to the auxiliary language Markerese. But we can know the Markerese translation of an English sentence without knowing the first thing about the meaning of the English sentence: namely, the conditions under which it would be true.

Semantics with no treatment of truth conditions is not semantics. Translation into Markerese is at best a substitute for real semantics. . . .

The Markerese method is attractive in part just because it deals with nothing but symbols. . . . But it is just this pleasing finitude that prevents Markerese semantics from dealing with the relations between symbols and the world of non-symbols—that is, with genuinely semantic relations. (Lewis 1972: 169–70)

. . . [T]he brain's causal capacity to produce intentionality [i.e. the "aboutness" of concepts—RJ] cannot consist in its instantiating a computer program [i.e. in its being nothing but a system of cognitive structures], since for any program you like it is possible for something to instantiate that program and still not have any [intentional] mental states. Whatever it is that the brain does to produce intentionality, it cannot consist in instantiating a program since no program, by itself, is sufficient for intentionality. (Searle 1980: 424)

How is it possible to escape this barrage? Only by going deeper into psychology, and by dealing even more austerely with the notion of thought. From the standpoint of neuropsychology, we must recognize that the neural assemblies responsible for storing and processing conceptual structures indeed *are* trapped in our brains. They have no direct access to the outside world. Hence, as stressed in Chapter 9, we must explicitly deny that conceptual structures are symbols or representations of anything in the world, that they *mean* anything. Rather, we want to say that they *are* meaning: they do exactly the things meaning is supposed to do, such as support inference and judgment. Language is meaningful, then, because it connects to conceptual structures. Such a statement is of course anathema to the authors quoted above, not to mention to common sense. Still, let's persist and see how far we can go with it.

10.5 A simple act of deictic reference

Consider about the simplest act of using language to refer to a "middle-sized object": a use of referential deixis such as (10).

(10)   Hey, look at that!   [*pointing*]

---

⁹ However, note that Lewis is making the category mistake criticized in section 9.4: he is identifying Markerese as a language "like" a natural language, neglecting the fact that Markerese is intended as a *component* of natural languages alongside syntax and phonology.

The deictic pronoun *that* has no intrinsic descriptive content; its semantics is purely referential.[10] In order to understand (10), the hearer not only must process the sentence but must also determine what referent the speaker intends by *that*. This requires going out of the language faculty and making use of the visual system.

Within the visual system, the hearer must process the visual field and visually establish an individual in it that can serve as referent of *that*.[11] The retinal image alone cannot do the job. The retina is sensitive only to distinctions like "light of such-and-such color and intensity at such-and-such a location on retina" and "dark point in bright surround at such-and-such a location on retina." The retina's "ontology" contains no objects and no external location. Nor is the situation much better in the parts of the brain most directly fed by the retina: here we find things like local line and edge detectors in various orientations (Hubel and Wiesel 1968), all in retinotopic format—but still no objects, no external world. This is all the contact the brain has with the outside world; inboard from here it's all computation.

However this computation works, it eventually has to construct a cognitive structure that might be called a "percept." The principles and neural mechanisms that construct the percept are subjects of intensive research in psychology and neuroscience, and are far from understood. The outcome, however, has to be a cognitive/neural structure that distinguishes individuals in the perceived environment and that permits one to attend to one or another of them. One can stop attending to a perceived individual and then return to it; one can track a perceived individual as it moves through the perceived environment and as it changes properties such as orientation, color, and shape. The cognitive structure that gives rise to perceived individuals is non-linguistic: insofar as human infants and various animals can be shown experimentally to identify and track individuals more or less the way we do, the best hypothesis is that they have percepts more or less like ours.

Of course percepts are trapped inside the brain too. There is no magical direct route between the world and the percept—only the complex and indirect route via the retina and the lower visual areas. So all the arguments directed against

---

10 Well, it has a little descriptive content: it denotes something in a relatively distal position, by contrast with *this*.

11 I am bypassing all the fascinating issues of how the hearer follows the pointing gesture to the intended referent. This is quite possibly a feat of which even chimpanzees are incapable (Povinelli et al. 2000), hence another of those cognitive prerequisites to language acquisition that had to evolve in the last 5 million years. Even if the hearer follows the pointing, there is the question of precisely what the speaker has in mind, whether the rabbit or the collection of the rabbit's legs or whatever (Quine 1960). How children manage to accomplish this in word learning is addressed by Macnamara (1982) and Bloom (2000), among many others.

conceptualist semantics apply equally to percepts. This may bother some philosophers, but most psychologists and neuroscientists take a more practical approach: they see the visual system as creating a cognitive structure which constitutes part of the organism's understanding of reality, and which helps the organism act successfully in its environment. If there is any sense to the notion of "grasping" the world perceptually, this wildly complex computation is it; it is far from a simple unmediated operation.

And of course a visual percept is what will be linked to the deictic *that* in (9) and (10), through the interfaces between conceptual structure and the "upper end" of the visual system. Thus language has indeed made contact with the outside world—but through the complex mediation of the visual system rather than through some mysterious mind–world relation of intentionality. Everything is scientifically kosher.

A skeptic may still be left grumbling that something is missing: "We don't perceive our percepts in our heads, we perceive objects out in the world." Absolutely correct. However, as generations of research in visual perception have shown, the visual system populates "the world" with all sorts of "objects" that have no physical reality, for instance the square subtended by four dots and the "amodally completed" horizontal rectangle in (3). So we should properly think of "the perceptual world" (or "phenomenal world" in the sense of Koffka 1935) not as absolute reality but as the "reality" constructed by our perceptual systems in response to whatever is "really out there."

Naturally, the perceptual world is not totally out of synch with the "real world." The perceptual systems have evolved in order that organisms may act reliably in the real world. They are not concerned with a "true model of the world" in the logical sense, but with a "world model" good enough to support the planning of actions that in the long run lead to better propagation of the genes. Like other products of evolution, the perceptual systems are full of "cheap tricks," which is why we see virtual objects: these tricks *work* in the organism's normal environment. It is only in the context of the laboratory that their artificiality is detected.

Thus *the perceptual world is reality for us*. Apart from the sensory inputs, percepts are entirely "trapped in the brain"; they are nothing but formal structures instantiated in neurons. But the perceptual systems give us the sense, the feeling, the affect, of objects being "out there." We experience objects in the world, not percepts in our heads. That's the way we're built.[12]

---

[12] To put it in the terms of Dennett (1991), the perceptual system is a "syntactic engine that mimics a semantic engine," where "syntactic" and "semantic" are intended in Chomsky's and Fodor's sense: syntax = 'formal manipulation internal to the organism' and semantics = 'relating formal objects to the world'.

In speaking about how we experience the world, we are beginning to venture into the sacred realm of consciousness, a topic not for the faint of heart. So let us pause and take stock. We have been attempting to create a conceptualist account of the intuition that linguistic expressions refer to things in the world. The answer so far is that a deictic linguistic expression like *that* in (10) can be linked with a percept. In turn, a percept is an f-mental structure constructed by the perceptual systems in response to stimulation from the outside world. Although a percept does not necessarily correspond exactly to what is "actually out there" (especially with virtual objects), the experience that accompanies having a percept in one's f-mind is that of an object in the world. Hence we experience the deictic expression as referring to this object.

In short, the problem of reference for the intuitively clear cases is not at bottom a problem for linguistic theory, it is a problem for perceptual theory: how do the mechanisms of perception create for us the experience of a world "out there"?

Some readers will no doubt find this stance disquieting. My dear friend John Macnamara, with whom I agreed on so much, used to accuse me of not believing there is a real world. Similarly, Jerry Fodor, in response to similar conceptualist arguments by Chomsky (2000), says:

> ... in what way is the plausible claim that there are banks (that is, that there "really are" banks) not warranted? There is, for example, the bank that holds my mortgage. That is not just a way of talking; they make me pay up every month, cash on the barrel. How on earth could that be so if there really are not any banks at all? (Fodor 2000b: 4)

One reply would be that mortgages are just as much a mental construct as banks. But there is a deeper reply: we are ultimately concerned with *reality for us*, the world in which we lead our lives. Isn't that enough? (Or at least, isn't that enough for linguistics?) To paraphrase Dan Dennett, who subtitles his book *Elbow Room* (1984) as *The Varieties of Free Will Worth Wanting*, it's useful to ask what varieties of reality are "worth wanting." The reality in which you are reading this book and Jerry Fodor is paying his mortgage is certainly worth wanting; my claim here is that this world is a product of our human modes of perception and conception. If you want to go beyond that and demand a "more ultimate reality," independent of human cognition, well, you are welcome to, but that doesn't exactly render my enterprise here pointless.[13]

I think one could be perfectly justified in stopping at this point, satisfied that reference has been "reduced to a previously unsolved problem." But I am going

---

[13] Smith 1996 is an attempt to build the metaphysics of "reality for us" from the ground up, one that dovetails attractively with the approach taken here.

to push on a bit, in the interests of uncovering further aspects of the theory of reference.

10.6 The functional correlates of consciousness

Let us confine ourselves here to simple perceptually mediated consciousness, for example the experience of seeing a refrigerator, tasting an apple, or feeling an itch. For present purposes we fortunately can ignore more loaded issues such as consciousness of self and the sense of free will, which, while of paramount importance in the overall conception of human nature, play a lesser role in the theory of reference.

Francis Crick and Christof Koch (1990; Crick 1994) make an admirable case for searching for the "neural correlates of consciousness," in particular the correlates of visual awareness. Complementary to their search is an inquiry into what might be called the "functional correlates of consciousness," the structures and processes in the f-mind that give rise to visual awareness (or *accompany* visual awareness, depending on one's overall theory of consciousness). Works such as Dennett (1991) and Jackendoff (1987), among many others, outline theories of the functional correlates of consciousness. The hope, of course, is that research at the neural level and at the functional level will converge. Here, as in our treatment of language, we will be thinking functionally, without by any means excluding neural approaches.

Suppose (10) (*Hey, look at* that!) is uttered in response to a particularly large and disgusting bug scuttling across the floor. In the course of processing the sentence, the hearer's visual system must construct a percept that on one hand results in (or corresponds to) the experience of the bug and on the other hand is bound or linked to the deictic pronoun *that*. What features must be present in this percept?[14]

The kinds of features that visual psychologists concentrate on are obvious candidates. The percept has a shape, a size, a color, and can be decomposed into shaped and joined parts (a body, eyes, lots of legs). It also has a location, motion, and a "character of motion" (the way the legs move and the body twists in the course of the bug's moving). Let us call all these features, however they come to be characterized theoretically, the *descriptive* features of the percept. It is these features that the speaker of (9) (*I don't know what* that *was!*) cannot reconstruct or report.

---

[14] I use the term "features" as a shorthand for "distinctions the system must make," without prejudging whether these distinctions are in binary, digital, or analogue dimensions, and without commitment as to appropriate formal notation.

More basically, the bug-percept is a visual percept. The hearer is not hearing, tasting, smelling, or (we hope) feeling the bug. Thus percepts must be distinguished by modality. Thinking functionally, this could simply be a consequence of the fact that the descriptive features are those appropriate to the visual modules. Similarly, in neural terms, this could be a consequence of where in the brain the percept develops (this is essentially the position being explored by Crick and Koch).

Another basic characteristic of the percept is that it constitutes a figure distinguished from the background on which it is located and it moves. Suppose that I utter (10), and you stare at the patterned rug and see nothing; then suddenly the bug "pops out" in experience (*Oh god, there it is! Eeuww!*). Nothing has changed in "the world" or the retinal image. All that has changed is the organization of percepts "trapped" in the hearer's brain: the bug-percept has emerged as figural. Let us call this figural characteristic the *indexical* feature of the percept. It gives the f-mind a "something" to which descriptive features can be bound. The speaker of (9) has an indexical feature lacking identifiable descriptive features.

The f-mind establishes indexical features in response to perceptual input. But once established, they need not go away in the absence of perceptual input: we intuitively sense that objects continue to exist when we're not seeing them. When an object disappears behind an obstacle and reappears on the other side, is it the same object? To what extent do the descriptive features have to remain constant in order to make this judgment? If an object disappears behind an obstacle and two objects reappear on the other side, which (if any) is the original object? These questions of "tracking" involve the behavior of the indexical feature.[15]

Indexical features can undergo "splitting," for instance when we break a lump of clay in half to form two distinct individuals. They can also undergo "merger," as when we mold two lumps of clay into an undifferentiated mass. Or suppose we spot a red circle on one occasion and a blue circle on a second occasion; then on a third occasion we spot what we take to be the red circle again, and there before our very eyes it turns blue. We are perhaps now inclined to think there was only one circle all along: again an indexical merger.

Suppose our bug starts crawling up your leg. A whole new set of descriptive features in a different modality develops in your f-mind. How are you to experience them as a manifestation of the same entity in the world? I suggest we

---

[15] Baillargeon (1986) and Spelke et al. (1994) pose similar questions to babies. Their results, on the present interpretation, show that babies track indexical features (the identity and number of individuals) but they are far less sensitive than we would expect at tracking descriptive features (exactly what those individuals look like).

think of the descriptive features as being linked to a common indexical feature. Such linking is an act of f-mental construction, not just something to take for granted: think of the (illusory) experience of hearing figures on a movie screen speaking, on the basis of noises emerging from loudspeakers at another location.

Beyond the descriptive features, the modality, and the indexical feature, one other type of feature needs to be considered. My graphic description of hearing (10) in response to a bug may have evoked in you a *visual image* of a bug. And when I spoke of the bug crawling up your leg, maybe you felt one too—you had a *tactile image*. Such experiences arise from cognitive structures in your f-mind; let's call these cognitive structures "functional images" or "f-images." So now I want to ask: How do f-images differ from percepts?

None of the features discussed so far is appropriate to make the difference. Consider indexical features. The experienced bug-image is individuated and stands out as a figure from the (imaged) ground, so the f-image has an indexical feature. What about modality? One can distinguish visual from tactile in images just as well as in perceived objects, so this isn't the difference we want. What about descriptive features? One might be first tempted to appeal to location: the experience corresponding to a percept is "out in the world" and that corresponding to an f-image is "in the head." But I suspect that the tactilely imaged bug crawling up your leg was experienced on your leg, not in your head. So images *may* be in one's head, but need not be.

One might alternatively claim that images are fuzzier and more fleeting than objects, reflecting a difference in their functional structure in the f-mind. But compare for example hearing music way off in the distance, which is indeed fuzzy and fleeting, with hearing in your head some music you know very well, right down to the rasp of John Lennon's voice, for instance. In this case relative clarity goes in the wrong direction: the "real" music is fuzzier than the image. More generally, the range of descriptive distinctions available in any modality of imagery is essentially the same as that in the corresponding modality of perception.

In the old days one might have tried to make the distinction by claiming that there is an "imaging" part of the brain separate from the "perception" part. But we don't believe this anymore (Kosslyn 1980; 1996; Jackendoff 1987): we think that imagery uses most of the same brain areas—as well as the same functional features—as perception. So this way out is not available either.

The distinction I think we need comes from a family of features proposed in Jackendoff (1987: ch. 15, 1997a: ch. 8). These features register not the perceptual qualities of an entity but the associated "feel," so to speak. I called these the "affects" or "valuation" of the percept. One of these features is the distinction *external* versus *internal*. Associating *external* with a cognitive structure results in its being experienced as "out in the world," *internal* results in its being experienced as an image.

Some other features in this family are *familiar* vs. *novel* (which distinguishes not only familar from novel percepts but also memories from acts of imagination), *self-produced* vs. *non-self-produced* (which distinguishes voluntary images from hallucinations), *meaningful* vs. *non-meaningful* (or *coherent* vs. *incoherent*), and *mattering (positively or negatively)* vs. *non-mattering* (which registers emotional effects such as an object's being delightful or disgusting).[16] These features apply equally to all modalities: visual, auditory, and tactile experiences can all be experienced as real or not, familiar or not, self-produced or not, meaningful or not, and important or not.

Valuations, like size, shape, and color, are subject to illusions. For instance, one can think one saw or heard something real but have just imagined it. Déjà vu is a sense of familiarity associated with a situation known to be novel. Schizophrenics find many more things meaningful than they ought to; perhaps autistics find things less meaningful than they ought to. Dreams feel external and non-self-produced but are of course internal and self-produced. People with phobias attach illusory negative value to all manner of inappropriate entities in the environment. Hence valuations too are constructions of the f-mind.[17]

Returning to our bug, it is not simply experienced "out there" automatically: it is "out there" because the percept that gives rise to the experience contains the valuations *external* and *non-self-produced*. Visual processing normally settles on these valuations in response to retinal input: "seeing is believing." However, it also assigns this valuation to the virtual square in (3) despite there being nothing directly corresponding on the retina. By contrast, the imaged bug has the valuations *internal* and *self-produced*.

To sum up, the character of a consciously experienced entity is functionally determined by a cognitive structure that contains the following feature types:

- An indexical feature to which descriptive features can be attached.

- One or more modalities in which descriptive features are present.

- The actual descriptive features in the available modalities.

- A valuation that registers the status of the entity in a number of modality-independent dimensions.

---

[16] Damasio's (1994) notion of "somatic marker" might correspond to this feature.

[17] Section 12.4 will show how valuation features are appropriate for the characterization of "intensional" contexts such as the contents of someone else's beliefs.

Of these feature types, to my knowledge only the modality and descriptive features have been investigated in neural terms.

Within the context of our psychological concerns, it seems to me that this overall organization of feature types is not something that can be ascribed to learning. This is a bare skeleton of the framework in terms of which learning can take place. On the other hand, since this organization plays a role in perception, imagery, and action as well as language, we do not have to ascribe it to narrow Universal Grammar: it is a central part of all cognition.

10.7 Application to theory of reference

Section 10.5 showed how the act of creating or understanding an expression with deictic reference can be reduced functionally to the association or binding of a linguistic entity with a percept. We are now in a position to sharpen and generalize this account.

The indexical feature of a percept is the crucial feature for linguistic reference. If there is no indexical feature to which descriptive features can be bound, there is nothing to which a deictic or other referring linguistic expression can be attached either: there is no *'that'* there.

We have already seen how this account extends to some of the problematic entities mentioned in section 10.3. Consider again virtual objects such as the square subtended by four dots. Although there is nothing "actually out there," the visual system constructs a percept with all the right features for "something out there." Hence there is something "out there" in the *perceived* world, and we can refer to it. Next consider the unicorn in my dream. There is a remembered entity which has an indexical feature and descriptive features in the visual modality (in particular a one-horned shape). In memory, it is assigned the valuation *internal*, so it is not experienced any more as having been "in the world." Still, because it has an indexical feature, it can be connected to a referential expression.

Returning to the standard literature on reference: Frege (1892) made the distinction between the sense and the reference of an expression by citing the well-known example *The morning star is the evening star*. In his analysis, two senses are attached to the same reference. We can understand Frege's example in present terms as reporting the merger of indexicals associated with different descriptive features, exactly as in our example of the circle that is sometimes red and sometimes blue. So Frege's problem is not a uniquely *linguistic* problem; rather, it lies in a more general theory of how the f-mind keeps track of individuated entities.

The reverse of merger can also take place. For a long time I thought the literary/cultural theorist Allan Bloom and the literary/cultural theorist Harold Bloom were the same person. In present terms, the descriptive features of both were linked to a single indexical. Then one day, believing that (Allan) Bloom had died a couple years back, I was astonished to come across a new book by (Harold) Bloom. The embarrassing realization "Ohhh! There are *two* Blooms!" forced me to split the indexical and divide the (admittedly minimal) descriptive features among them; in particular, only one was dead. (In a realist theory of reference, who was I referring to by *Bloom*, before my epiphany?)

More generally, the indexical features proposed here play a role altogether parallel to the discourse referents in various approaches within formal semantics such as Discourse Representation Theory (Kamp and Reyle 1993), File Change Semantics (Heim 1989), and Dynamic Semantics (Groenendijk et al. 1996). Hence many of the insights of these approaches can be taken over here, with the proviso that the "model" over which reference is defined should be a psychologically motivated one. (We return to these approaches in sections 12.3 and 12.4.)

10.8 Entities other than objects

Let us go a bit more into what a psychologically motivated model would include, by extending our analysis of deictic reference in sentences like (10), *Hey, look at that!* The main point to be established is that indexical features do not always identify *individual objects*: these are just one sort of entity that can be identified by an indexical.

For instance, consider (10) uttered in reaction to muddy water pouring out of a pipe. Here the intended reference may well be the *substance* rather than any particular bounded quantity of it. This distinction is reflected in the mass-count distinction in grammar and more generally in aspectual distinctions such as perfective versus imperfective (see Jackendoff 1991 and references there).

The simple deictic *that* can also be used to refer to non-material entities such as sounds and tactile sensations:

(11)   a. Goodness! Did you hear *that*?
       b. [Dentist:] Did *that* hurt?

Hankamer and Sag (1976) notice that English contains a substantial number of other deictic expressions that can be accompanied by gestures. Jackendoff (1983) points out that they are every bit as referential as the deictic in (10).

(12) a. Pro-PP:
          Please put your coat *here* [pointing] and put your hat *there* [pointing].
          He went *thataway* [pointing].
      b. Pro-VP:
          Can you *do that* [pointing]?
          Can you *do this* [demonstrating]?
      c. that . . . happen:
          That [pointing] had better not *happen* around here.
      d. Pro-manner adverbial:
          You shuffle cards *thus/so/like this/this way* [demonstrating].
          I used to walk *that way/like that* [pointing to someone walking in a
          funny fashion].
      e. Pro-measure expression:
          The fish that got away was *this/yay* long [demonstrating].
          There were about *this many* people at Joe's party too. [gesturing
          toward the assembled throng]
      f. Pro-time-PP:
          You may start . . . right . . . *now*! [clapping]

The analysis of (10) suggests parallel analyses for these examples: the deictic
expressions refer to entities in the conceptualized world that can be picked out
with the aid of the accompanying gesture. But the entities referred in (12) are not
objects. In (12a), *here* and *there* refer to locations or places; *thataway* refers to a
direction. *Do this* and *do that* in (12b) and *that . . . happen* in (12c) refer to
actions or events (goings-on). The expressions in (12d) also refer to actions but
draw attention to the manner in which the action is performed. The expressions
in (12e) refers to sizes and amounts, and *now* in (12f) refers to a time.

In order to accommodate these possibilities for reference, it is useful to introduce a kind of "ur-feature" that classifies the entity being referred to into an
ontological type. Each of the ontological types—objects, actions, locations, and
so forth—has its own characteristic conditions of identity and individuation. It
is a task both for natural language semantics and for cognitive psychology/
neuroscience to work out the logic and the characteristic perceptual manifestations of each type. Events, for instance, play a role in many versions of formal
semantics, following Davidson (1967); some of the psychophysics of visually
perceived events is explored by Michotte (1954) and Cutting (1981). Locations
and directions have not played much of a role in formal semantics, but are central in Cognitive Grammar (e.g. Langacker 1987; Talmy 1983; Herskovits
1986; Vandeloise 1986) and have figured in recent experimental research, much
of which is described in Bloom et al. (1996).

The ontological categories of sounds, tactile sensations, manners, and distances have not to my knowledge received significant attention in the literature. Let us look for a moment at the logic of sounds. Notice that the two sentences in (13) can be used to describe the same situation.

(13)   a. There's that noise again!
       b. There's another one of those noises!

(13a) describes the situation as the recurrence of the same individual—hearing the noise again is like seeing the sun again the next day. By contrast, (13b) describes the situation as hearing another sound of the same type (we get to types shortly). A similar ambivalence attaches to other temporally dependent ontological types, for example *There's that pain in my leg again* vs. *There's another of those pains in my leg!*; *It's sunrise/Tuesday again* vs. *It's another sunrise/Tuesday*.

Words appear to be classified as a species of sounds (even when written): *'Star' appears twice in that sentence* vs. (slightly less natural) *There are two 'star's in that sentence*. *Mahler's Second* (example (5a)) leans more strongly in the direction of the (13a) conceptualization: *They played Mahler's Second six times on tour* is much more natural than *They played six Mahler's Seconds on tour* (musicians do, however, say this sort of thing).[18]

Are all the sorts of entities in (11)–(12) "in the world"? They are certainly not like refrigerators—you can't touch them or move them. In fact, it is odd to say they all *exist* in the way that refrigerators exist ("the length of the fish exists"??). Yet (11)–(12) show that we can pick them out of the perceptual field and use them as the referents of deictic expressions. So we must accord them some dignified status in the conceptualized world—the "model" that serves as the basis for linguistic reference.

Now notice what has just happened. Up until this section we have been concerned with reference to objects, and we have used perceptual theory to ground the theory of reference. Now all of a sudden we have turned the argument on its head: if this is the way reference relates to perception, perception must be providing a far richer range of entities than had previously been suspected. It is now a challenge for perceptual theory to describe how the perceptual systems accomplish this. In other words, examples like (11)–(12) open the door for fruitful cooperation between linguistic semantics and research in perception.

Glancing back at an issue raised in Chapters 5, 8, and 9, consider the degree

---

[18] Given that the use of *six Mahler's Seconds* is confined to a small community, I suspect it is shorthand for *six performances of Mahler's Second*, i.e. it is a conventionalized *coercion*, parallel to the more widespread *three coffees* for *three cups/portions of coffee*. See section 12.2.

to which syntactic distinctions mirror semantic distinctions. It turns out that the correspondence, such as it is, pertains above all to ontological category features. For instance, sentences map into situation- and event-concepts; PPs map primarily into place-, direction-, and path-concepts; APs map into property-concepts; and NPs map into just about anything. Going in the other direction, object-concepts map invariably into NPs, place-concepts map into PPs or NPs, and so on. This mapping is evident in the syntactic categories of the deictic forms in (12). In other words, ontological category features, unlike most descriptive features of concepts, *are* "visible" to the syntax–semantics interface. This means that they play an important role in grammar as well as in perception.

The repertoire of ontological types seems to me another good candidate for a very skeletal unlearned element of cognition. Again, because it is central not just to language but to perception and action, we need not call it part of Universal Grammar, the human specialization for learning language. But we do have to call it part of the innate human cognitive endowment.

One last comment before moving on. We have developed here a repertoire of major feature types: indexical features, valuation features, modality, descriptive features, and now ontological category as well. This classification, it seems to me, reveals a major sociological split among approaches to semantics. Formal semantics, growing out of the logical tradition, has concentrated on indexical features and valuations (which, as we will see in section 12.4, include negation, quantification, possibility, and attributions of mental states). By contrast, most traditions of lexical semantics, including cognitive grammar, have been primarily concerned with the descriptive features. A full semantic theory, of course, has to account for both.

10.9 Proper names, kinds, and abstract objects

So far we have been primarily considering referential uses of deictic expressions. Using the machinery developed for these cases, we can begin to construct the basics of other important elements of natural language semantics.

10.9.1 Proper names

It is standard to say that a proper name denotes an individual. In the present approach this translates into saying that a proper name has an indexical in its associated concept.

We can now attribute the distinction between names of real people like *Bertrand Russell* and names of fictional people like *Sherlock Holmes* to the valuation attached to the name: *Russell* has the valuation *external* and *Holmes* has the valuation *imaginary*.

We may also note that there are proper names for entities of other ontological categories. For example, *World War II* names an event, *Wyoming* a place, *Symphonie Fantastique* a sound, *1946* a time period, and *General Motors* an organization (whatever sort of ontological category *that* is).[19]

10.9.2 Kinds

All the concepts we have discussed so far have been individuals. Now consider the possibility of a cognitive structure that has descriptive features (including modality and ontological category), but lacks an indexical and a valuation. I suggest that this is just the structure we need for *kinds* or *types*.

To see the virtues of this approach, consider first the alternative possibility that the difference between an individual (or token) and a kind is that the latter is less specific in its descriptive features. The difficulty here is there are kinds whose descriptive characteristics are very sharp indeed—for instance manufactured objects such as 1998 Lincoln pennies, copies of the Boston *Globe* for April 4, 2000, and size 6-32 half-inch round-head brass bolts. What a kind really lacks is the possibility of pointing to it: one can only point to *instances* of it. Omitting the indexical feature from the concept would have exactly this effect.

This yields a nice formal consequence: one can form an instance from a kind simply by adding an indexical feature. This is paralleled in linguistic expression. Suppose that (as most semanticists think) a common noun such as *penny* denotes a kind, and that, as we have seen above, a demonstrative such as *this* or *that* expresses an indexical feature. Then it is no surprise that the full NP *that penny* denotes an individual that instantiates the type expressed by *penny*—semantically it is the unification of the descriptive features of *penny* and the indexical feature of *that*.[20] Conversely, given an individual, one can form a kind of which it is an instance, simply by deleting the indexical. This does not fall into

---

[19] Something should be said about the "causal theory of reference" for proper names (Kripke 1972). It is obvious that named entities normally get their names by virtue of some agentive event of naming; we assume a named individual has such an event in his/her/its history. I don't see anything especially profound here. I am inclined to think that having a name is conceptualized as a property of an object—a descriptive feature—not unlike having a size or shape. And of course houses get their size and shape by virtue of some agentive act of building; we assume a house has such an event in its history. But perhaps I am being too flip.

I cannot resist a personal anecdote that reveals something about children's implicit causal theory of reference (though I'm not quite sure what): each of my daughters, at about the age of 5, asked me, "If there weren't people when the dinosaurs were around, how do we know what they were called?"

[20] Quantifiers like *every* combine with common nouns in a different way, of course, since they do not express (simple) indexical features. See section 12.4.

linguistic expression quite so readily, but an apt expression is *things like that [pointing]*.

This relation of kinds and their instances also leads to a simple formal description of type-learning from a presented example: the learner deletes the indexical feature from the associated percept (in addition perhaps manipulating or thinning out the descriptive features). Such an approach parallels the approach to linguistic rule-learning advocated in Chapter 6: constructing a rule from an instance involves replacing one or more constants in a structural schema by variables that are now free to be used in a wide range of instantiations.

Language is not always entirely strict in marking the type–token distinction. For instance, *the same* can be used to express either token or type identity, with the choice being only a matter of pragmatics:

(14) a. John wore the same hat he always wears.   [probably token-identity]
      b. John ate the same sandwich he always eats. [probably type-identity!]

We would like this minimal difference to correspond to a minimal difference in conceptual structure. In the present analysis, it is a simple matter of letting *the same* be indifferent to whether an indexical feature is present or not. Similarly, an NP can denote an individual or a kind depending on its context in the sentence. In particular, a *predicate NP* is one that is not associated with an indexical feature.

(15) a. A professor walked in.   [*a professor* = individual]
      b. John has become a professor.   [*a professor* = kind][21]

(15b) does not name two different individuals, John and a professor; rather it says that the descriptive features of professors have come to be associated with the individual John.

Most kinds come without valuations. One can perceive a real bug or experience an imaged bug, and they are both bugs. But some kinds do carry inherent valuations. Unicorns, for instance, are specified as mythical beasts, so the kind *unicorn* must carry the marked valuation *imaginary*.

And kinds come in various ontological categories. In addition to object types such as those expressed by *cocker spaniel* and *6-32 half-inch brass bolt*, there are event types, such as those expressed by *my eating breakfast* (on an unspecified occasion) and *its having rained yesterday* (in an unspecified place). Similarly, in

---

[21] Of course some other languages do mark this difference, as in French *Un professeur est arrivé* ('a professor has arrived') vs. *Jean est devenu (*un) professeur* ('John has become (*a) professor').

addition to specific locations such as those expressed by *in that cup over there*, there are location types such as those expressed by *in people's ears*.

On the other hand, some of the other ontological categories do not so clearly display a type–token distinction. For instance, I find it odd to think of the space between my hands and the length of the fish in (12e) as different instances of the general type expressed by, say, *nineteen inches*. I also find it hard to imagine a type–token ambiguity like that in (14) for sentences about distances, such as *John stayed the same distance from me he always stays*. This suggests that perhaps this ontological category formally lacks the possibility of an indexical feature. For a different case, the last section mentioned the ambivalent behavior of sounds, twinges of pain, sunrises, and Tuesdays with respect to the type–token distinction. I leave the question open as to how these phenomena are to be treated formally.

I want briefly to compare this treatment of kinds with the basic treatment in predicate logic and its derivatives, including many versions of formal semantics. There an individual is formalized as (or named by) a constant and a kind is formalized as a predicate with a variable. An individual that belongs to a particular kind is formalized in terms of an existential quantification over the predicate in question. So, for instance, the kind expressed by *professor* is notated as a one-place predicate Px ('is a professor'), and we get logical expressions like (16).

(16) a. John is a professor = $P(J)$
   b. A professor walked in =
      i. $\exists x(Px \,\&\, Wx)$
         'there exists an x such that x is a professor and x walked in'
      or
      ii. $\exists x_{Px}(Wx)$
         'there exists an x, x being a professor, such that x walked in'

An advantage of this notation is that it is hallowed by tradition and all practitioners know how to read it. I see three drawbacks. First, it tends to muddy the distinction among ontological categories: the object type expressed by the noun *professor* is always rendered logically by 'x is a professor', which in the present system is a type of state-of-affairs. Second, this notation makes it difficult to see the similarity between the two uses of *same* in (14). Third, once we recognize that language makes reference not just to objects but to events and places, it is necessary to clutter logical expressions with existential quantifiers. For instance, (17a) expresses an event containing two objects and a place, so its logical treatment has to be something like (17b).

(17) a. A boy sits on a chair.
   b. $\exists e \exists x_{BOYx} \exists p \exists y_{CHAIRy} \ (e = SIT(x,p) \,\&\, p = ONy)$

The event-variable e is now commonly accepted since being championed by Davidson (1967); the place-variable p is as far as I know a neologism.

These objections to standard notation are not fatal by any means—it can, with appropriate tinkering, code the same set of distinctions. In any event I see no reason not to experiment with alternative notations in an effort to find something more perspicuous and more easily adaptable to a wide range of linguistic phenomena. The next two chapters will work out some alternative possibilities.

In denotational theories of meaning such as Kripke (1972), Montague (1973), and Putnam (1975), kinds are taken not to be f-mental structures consisting of descriptive features, but rather sets, such as the set of individuals (in all possible worlds) who are professors. This cannot be maintained in a mentalistic theory, as one does not carry the members of such sets around in one's head. Rather, at best one can carry a list of some prominent instances, plus a schema that allows one to generate and identify members of the set (i.e. instances of the kind)—if you like, a functional or intensional delineation of the set. But that is exactly what the descriptive features are for. The extension of the set of professors, the collection of its members, plays no role in the f-mind.

A justification for positing the set is the presumption that the reference of a phrase should be built up compositionally from the reference of its words: the set provides a reference for the common noun *professor* that can undergo Boolean combination with other sets. In the present approach, by contrast, *professor* simply has a sense without a reference. The *sense* of a phrase is built up compositionally, and if the composition happens to provide an indexical feature, then we get a referring phrase. I don't see any particular harm in this stance, as long as the indubitably referential phrases are taken care of.[22]

10.9.3 *Abstract objects*

Up to now we have been talking mostly about perceivable entities. What makes them perceivable is that they have features that connect to the perceptual interfaces in Fig. 10.5. Now suppose that conceptual structure contains other features that do not pertain to a perceptual modality, but which connect instead to the inferential system in Fig. 10.5. Such features would provide "bridges" to other concepts but no direct connection to perception. That is, they are used in reasoning rather than in identification. Let's call these "inferential features," by contrast with perceptual features.

What would be candidates for inferential features? Consider an object's

---

[22] Note that although *professor* is on its own non-referential, the phrases *the word 'professor'* and *the kind 'professor'* are referential, referring to a word and an abstract object (the meaning of the word) respectively.

value. This is certainly not perceivable, but it influences the way one reasons about the object, including one's goals and desires concerning the object. Value can be established by all sorts of means, mostly very indirect. Thus value seems like a prime candidate for a type of inferential feature. Another candidate is high-level taxonomic category. For instance, the classification of a particular object as an artifact predicts only that people typically use this object for something. But it does not predict what it looks like, how it works, or what one does with it. Rather, beyond the ontological feature 'physical object', which does have perceptual consequences, *artifact* is not on the whole a collection of perceptual features; rather it bridges to all sorts of inferences that can in turn potentially engage perceptual features.

Now suppose there were a concept that had *only* inferential features. This then would be an abstract concept such as those expressed by *the value of my watch* and *the meaning of this word*. From the point of view of language, abstract objects cannot be distinguished from concrete objects: all that is necessary for reference is an indexical feature. The interfaces to language cannot "see" whether a concept's descriptive features are perceptual or inferential. Thus as far as language is concerned, reference proceeds in the same fashion whether or not there is a conceptualized physical object out there in the world.

If abstract concepts have indexical features and descriptive features, in principle they should have ontological category features and valuations as well. An interesting issue for future research is to explore what ontological category features might pertain to abstract entities. As for valuations, compare *belief* and *opinion* with *value, meaning,* and *obligation*. The former two are understood as "subjective": they are objects in people's minds, hence *internal* relativized to a subject. By contrast, the latter three are normally understood as "objective parts of the world"—even though on reflection nothing has value without someone to value it, nothing has meaning without someone to understand it, and there are no obligations in the absence of individuals who understand the social system. That is, talking about someone's beliefs is like talking about their mental images or dreams (Jackendoff 1983: ch. 11); while talking about someone's obligations is more like talking about their car (Jackendoff 1999). In short, what causes something to be judged "real" is its having the valuation *external*—even when it is a patently abstract object![23]

It is a fascinating question why values, meanings, and obligations should be understood as "objective," and I am not in a position to answer it here.

---

[23] Thus an individual's having a "theory of mind" (in the sense of Premack and Woodruff 1978 and Wimmer and Perner 1983) could functionally depend on their being able to recognize the valuation *internal* as attributed to other individuals. The literature suggests that children do not develop this ability until about 5 years of age, and that most animals lack it almost entirely.

However, if indeed they are, it helps explain the intuitions behind the realist stance on language, in which words are "out there in the world," meanings are "out there in the world," and therefore our job is to explain how they connect to the rest of the world. Here, instead, we have asked why words and meanings "present themselves" to us as "out in the world," why "the world" presents itself to us the way it does, and how the cognitive connection between language and the experienced world is established. This is a more roundabout route, but in the end I hope a more fruitful one.

Returning for a moment to abstract concepts, it is worth asking whether animals could have them at all. Social concepts seem to me to have the right flavor. Consider the sophisticated way that monkeys operate with kinship relations and dominance hierarchies (Cheney and Seyfarth 1990). There is no space to go through the arguments here, but I am persuaded that these notions are in no sense directly visible "in the world," reducible to simple visual (or, say, olfactory) stimuli. Rather, they are abstract relationships that bridge a vast number of different inferences and behaviors. Such concepts are no longer "cheap tricks" that govern behavior; they are "expensive tricks" that coordinate a large number of disparate behaviors. There is no doubt that humans have many more abstract concepts than animals, and that language is instrumental in the exuberant proliferation of such concepts. But abstract concepts do not develop out of nowhere: the evolutionary precedent is there.

10.10 Satisfaction and truth

An important piece has been left out of the story so far. Linguistic expressions used in isolation cannot refer: they can only *purport* to refer. For example, suppose I utter *Hey, will you look at THAT!* to you over the telephone. You understand that I intend to refer to something; but you cannot establish the reference and therefore cannot establish the contextualized meaning of the utterance.

A referential expression *succeeds* in referring for the hearer if it is *satisfied* by something that can serve as its referent. In realist semantics, satisfaction is a relation between a linguistic expression and an entity in the world; in conceptualist semantics, the entity is in [the world as conceptualized by the language user]. It is this latter notion of satisfaction that must be worked out here. Lest this notion be thought too subjective and/or solipsistic, I wish to remind the reader of the commitments of the conceptualist program set out at the beginning of Chapter 9. We are interested in how people (including ourselves) understand the world, not in some notion of absolute truth.

To work out a conceptualist notion of satisfaction, we invoke one component in Fig. 10.5 not yet discussed: the integration of concepts with one's f-knowledge base. Suppose I say to you: *I talked to David Wasserstein today*. In isolation, the proper name *David Wasserstein* purports to refer; you assume that I intended it actually to refer. If you know David Wasserstein (i.e. he is part of your knowledge base), you can establish the intended reference in your own construal of the world. If you do not know him, the proper name is unsatisfied *for you*.

More generally, four different situations can arise.

(18) a. The purported referent is present in your f-knowledge base or the readily available context, and it satisfies the referential expression.
  b. The purported referent is not present in your f-knowledge base or the readily available context, and so you add a new character into your f-knowledge base to satisfy the referential expression. If I anticipate this situation for you, I will use a specific indefinite expression like *a friend of mine* or *this friend of mine, David Wasserstein* rather than a definite description or an unadorned proper name.
  c. The purported referent is in conflict with your f-knowledge base, as in Russell's famous example *the present king of France*. Or it is in conflict with the readily available context, for example in a situation when I speak of *the apple on the table* and you see either no apples or two apples on the table. In this case you have to fall back on some repertoire of repair strategies (H. H. Clark 1996: ch. 9): guessing what I intend,[24] asking me for clarification, deciding to ignore me altogether, and so on.
  d. The purported referent contains descriptive features that inherently conflict with each other, so that nothing can possibly satisfy the expression. In such a case, for instance *the square circle*, you find the expression anomalous, and must again fall back on repair strategies.

This is all clear with the reference of NPs. We next turn to the reference of sentences. The standard custom in the formal semantics tradition, going back to Frege (1892), is that the intended referent of a (declarative) sentence is a truth value. I must confess I have never understood the argument for this position (e.g. Chierchia and McConnell-Ginet 1990: ch. 2); to unravel it is beyond the scope of the present text (see however the discussion in Seuren 1998: 375ff.). I

---

[24] This would include the well-known situation described by Donnellan (1966), here adapted to the conceptualist approach: Joan speaks to Ida of *the man drinking a martini* and gestures toward Edgar. Ida, however, happens to know/believe that Edgar is drinking water, and hence cannot take him to satisfy Joan's description. Nevertheless, Ida will probably be charitable and understand Joan to intend the phrase to refer to Edgar. We do not have to worry about whether the phrase *really* refers, only about how language users treat it.

am going to explore instead the alternative position that the intended reference of a declarative sentence is a situation (an event or a state of affairs) (Jackendoff 1972). Traditionalists should not worry—truth values will get their due shortly.

The view that sentences refer to situations is motivated largely by linguistic parallels to referentiality in NPs—a kind of evidence not frequently cited in the literatures of philosophy of language and formal semantics. First notice the parallel in phrases that accompany deictic reference:

(19)   a. Will you look at *that*! A blimp!
       b. Will you look at *that*! The baby's walking!

(19a) draws the hearer's attention to an object in the environment; (19b) to an event—not to a truth value. Second, notice that discourse pronouns can corefer with sentences as well as with NPs.

(20)   a. A blimp appeared in the sky. It was huge.
       b. Suddenly the baby started walking. It astounded her parents.

The antecedent of *it* in (20b) is the whole preceding sentence, so it presumably has the same referent. But *it* certainly does not refer to a truth value: *it astounded her parents* does not assert that the parents are astounded by the truth of the proposition expressed by *the baby started walking*; they are astounded by the *event* of the baby walking. Hence this event must be the referent of the preceding sentence as well.

Next consider embedded *that*-clauses in a context where they alternate with NPs.

(21)   a. The apple on the table astounded Max.
       b. That the Red Sox won today astounded Max.

What astounded Max in (21b) was not a truth value; it was an event (a truly astounding one!). Parallel to the four possible situations in (18) for satisfaction of an NP's purported referent, there are four possible situations for the referent of *the Red Sox won today*.

(22)   a. Your f-knowledge base includes the event of the Red Sox winning, and this satisfies the intended referent of the clause.
       b. Your f-knowledge base does not include the event of the Red Sox winning, so you add this to the f-knowledge base as the referent of the clause.
       c. Your f-knowledge base includes something in conflict with the purported event of the Red Sox winning (say your take on the world is that the Red Sox didn't play). Then your have to engage in some repair strategy.

d. The descriptive features of the purported event are inherently in conflict, so that there is no possible referent. In such a case, for instance *That the square is a circle astounded Max*, you judge the clause anomalous and again have to resort to repair.

There are of course other cases of *that*-clauses that do not come out this way, notably in so-called intensional contexts such as the complement of *believe*. However, NPs in this position are subject to the same distortions of referentiality:

(23) a. Max believes that there is a tooth fairy/the square is a circle.
b. Max believes in the tooth fairy/in square circles.

In both of these, the speaker makes no commitment to the existence of the tooth fairy or to square circles. In present terms, this context imposes a non-default valuation on the material contained in it, permitting reference to imaginary, nonexistent, and even anomalous entities. This valuation is indifferent as to whether the entities in question are objects or events. We take this up again in section 12.4.

So far, then, we have seen that it makes sense to regard a clause as referentially satisfied by a conceptualized situation. The judgment of a declarative sentence's truth value then follows from how it is referentially satisfied.

- In case (22a), where the intended referent of the sentence is present in the hearer's f-knowledge base (or can be deduced from it), the sentence is judged true.
- In case (22b), where there is no conflict with the hearer's f-knowledge base, the sentence is normally taken to be informative and presumed true.
- In case (22c), the sentence is judged false.
- In case (22d), it is judged analytically false.

Thus truth is defined in terms of reference and satisfaction, just as proposed by Sher (1996), following Tarski, in the quote at the outset of the chapter.

In short, the parallelism in the reference of NPs and sentences lies in the parallelism between conceptualized objects and conceptualized situations. The notion of satisfaction applies identically to both. However, sentences have an additional layer, in which they are characterized as true or false on the basis of how they are referentially satisfied.

Of course, truth and falsity pertain only to sentences that are asserted, that is, that have assertive illocutionary force—declarative main clauses. Many other sorts of illocutionary forces are possible, for example those in (24) (Austin 1962; Searle 1969; Bach and Harnish 1979; H. H. Clark 1996).

(24) a. Where is my hat?   [Question]
      b. What's the capital of New York?   [Pedagogical or quiz-show
                                                                question]

      c. Would you please open the window?   [Request]
      d. Open that window, young man!   [Order]
      e. Shake well before using.   [Instruction]
      f. Suppose there were a bug on your leg. (What would you do?)
                                                          [Supposition]

      g. What a great theory this is!   [Exclamation]
      h. Have a great day!   [Greeting]
      i. Thanks for the lovely party.   [Acknowledgement]
      j. If only it would rain!   [Invocation]
      k. Let's take a vacation.   [Suggestion?]
      l. Let x = 4y.   [Postulate/Axiom/Stipulation]
      m. I promise to finish this book by June.   [Promise]
      n. One more step and I'll shoot.   [Threat]
      o. I name this baby Herman.   [Dubbing]

There are also uses of simple declaratives that are not intended as assertions, that is, that are not intended to be referentially satisfied. Their truth value is not at issue in what the speaker intends to communicate.

(25) a. Once upon a time there was a little girl who lived in a forest.
                                                      [Beginning of story]
      b. There's a priest, a minister, and a rabbi in a boat . . .   [Joke]
      c. Joe can eat 3 candy bars in a minute. (How many can he eat in an
         hour?)   [Pedagogical problem]
      d. Your mother wears army boots!   [Ritual insult (cf. Labov 1972)]
      e. We all live in a yellow submarine.   [Song lyrics]

For present purposes it is not too important to sort out which of these are distinct cases and what the full repertoire is. The only point, going back to Austin, is that making assertions that can be true or false is only one of many things we can do with language. Theorists' concentration on truth value, which seems to go all the way back to Plato, blinds us to the full vivid range of possibility.[25]

    In the present approach, the problem of characterizing the conditions under which a sentence is judged true does not go away. It is just demoted from the

---

[25] People sometimes say that we need to deal with truth as an important part of the problem of meaning, then go on to ignore all the rest. And some (e.g. Katz 1977 for instance), recognizing the other possibilities, attempt to construct the meanings of sentences of all non-assertive illocutionary forces on the basis of truth values of corresponding assertions.

paramount problem of semantic theory to one among many problems. What seems more basic here is the conditions of satisfaction for referential constituents and how they interact with the f-knowledge base. In fact, a great deal of research in "truth-conditional" semantics can easily be reconstrued as addressing this issue. For instance, the question of whether sentence S_1 entails sentence S_2 has nothing to do with their truth values—they may describe thoroughly fictional or hypothetical situations. Rather, S_1 entails S_2 if adding the situation referred to by S_1 to an otherwise blank f-knowledge base enables the situation referred to by S_2 to be satisfied. The factors involved in such satisfaction, and the form of the rules of inference, may remain essentially unchanged from a truth-conditional account.

Above all, the conceptualist approach shifts the focus of semantics from the question "What makes sentences true?" to what I take to be the more ecologically sound question, "How do we humans understand language?"—"ecologically sound" in the sense that it permits us to integrate semantics with the other human sciences. I take this to be a positive step.

10.11 Objectivity, error, and the role of the community

We're not yet quite done escaping the accusation of solipsism. A good entry into the remaining difficulty is through the problem of error. The problem is usually stated something like this:

(26) a. Joe says "Look at that duck!"
      b. But in actuality he points to a platypus.
      c. How does his phrase *that duck* manage to refer?
      d. Does *duck* still refer to ducks in (26a)?

Within common-sense realist theories of meaning, in which words refer to the world, the problem lies in (26c, d): how the phrase could refer to something it is not supposed to, or how the phrase could get its meaning despite being on occasion misused.[26] Within a conceptualist theory this is not a problem: in Joe's conceptualization of the world, that thing "out there" is a duck, so for Joe the phrase succeeds in referring.

The problem for the conceptualist theory lies rather in sentence (26b): *But in*

---

[26] Famous cases in the literature that have the form of the argument in (26) include Putnam's (1975) "cats turn out to be robots radio-controlled from Mars" scenario; Putnam's (1975) "Twin-Earth" scenario; Donnellan's (1966) " 'the man with the martini' is really drinking water" scenario; and Kripke's (1979) scenario of Pierre who thinks London is ugly and "Londres est jolie." My case of the two Blooms (section 10.7) could also be couched in this form.

actuality he points to a platypus. By pushing the world into the mind, we no longer have a standpoint in objective "actuality," independent of the minds of Joe and the other people observing the situation. All we can say is something like "But in the conceptualized worlds of other observers, he points to a platypus." What is to stop them from all having different conceptualizations? How can we speak any more of Joe's being mistaken? And why should we care? Are we therefore doomed to a radical relativism about knowledge?

A way out comes from recognizing the sequence (26a, b) not as a disembodied piece of language "out there in the world," but as originating from a speaker who is communicating his or her conceptualization of the world. This conceptualization includes the judgment that Joe said something with intent to refer to some entity, and that this entity was a platypus. And now we can ask how the speaker came to this judgment.

The judgment has to be based on the match between two concepts: the descriptive characteristics of the entity in question and the descriptive characteristics associated with the word *platypus*. How did the speaker acquire these concepts? The characteristics of the entity Joe names may have come through observation of the reported scene, or they may have come through hearing someone else's report of such an observation. The characteristics of the kind *platypus* have to come through the speaker's learning the word. This in turn relies on a history of observation of others' usage (including instruction and demonstration).

I belabor this point because it poses the same difficulty for conceptualism as (26) itself. How can anyone rely on someone else's report of an observation, and how can anyone count on others' usage of language? Turned a different way: if conceptualization is essentially personal, how can we communicate?

This is now getting quite speculative, but I am inclined to think that human beings have a need to "tune" their conceptualizations to those of others—to have a common understanding of the world. Since we cannot read minds, the only way we can assess our attunement is by judging whether the behavior of others—including what they say—makes sense. To the extent that all members of a community are effective in acting on this drive, there will be a tendency for conceptual convergence, including in the use of language.

A learner faced with a community that has already converged will see the problem of tuning as one of adapting oneself to the community's conceptualization: "This is how things are done." On the other hand, if the community has not converged, the learner will be faced with some difficulty sorting out what to do. This is as true of cultural and technological learning as of language learning.

Of course there are many reasons people's conceptualizations do not converge. People may have access to different information, due to their different experiences. Conflicts may arise because people have different goals and needs, which affect what they find important in any given situation. Conceptualization based on one's own observation or imagination may conflict with the "received" conceptualization with which one desires to tune oneself. The worst is probably when two groups with different communal conceptualizations come into contact, leading to massive breakdown of the sense of attunement.

There are various ways to seek attunement. One way is reliance on an "expert," as in Putnam's (1975) "division of linguistic labor." This includes of course how children learn their culture. When the information is social information, another way is gossip. And apparently the members of a community can dynamically "co-tune" each other, for example when the children of a pidgin-speaking community together converge on a creole that did not exist before.

An individual faced with a perceived lack of attunement has certain choices. One is to accede to the perceived consensus—"accepting the truth." Another is to attempt to tune others to oneself, "convincing them they are wrong," through the exertion of social coercion, whether explicit ("You're wrong. How can you be so stupid?") or implicit ("That approach isn't interesting."). A third way requires a brief digression.

Searle (1995) introduces the idea of a conceptualized *joint intention*. Typically we think of an intention as a cognitive structure that strictly concerns only the performance of one's own action. You can't intend for someone else to perform an action, except indirectly: by intending to do something yourself that brings it about that the other person performs that action (Jackendoff 1995). However, in a joint intention, the intended action is to be carried out by oneself plus others; one's own intended actions fulfill a role in the joint action. For instance, each member of a team has a joint intention to fulfill the team's goals, along with an individual intention to play a role within the team's joint action. Searle makes the case that any sort of deliberately cooperative behavior requires a conceptualized joint intention on the part of the participants, and that the operation of most social institutions relies on an understanding of joint intentions.

Herbert Clark (1996) argues persuasively that (in these terms) a speech act requires not just an intention on the part of the speaker to convey information, but a joint intention on the part of the speaker and hearer towards the conveyance of information. Most of his book is about the delicate negotiations and signals that go on during speech in order for the participants to keep in synchrony and to verify that the joint intention is being fulfilled. It is clear that he means this coordination as a special case of a more general phenomenon of cooperative behavior: he constantly compares conversation to tasks like moving furniture and playing chamber music. In fact it is hard not to see joint intention in the collaborative actions of highly social mammals such as wolves and especially chimpanzees.

Establishing and maintaining a joint intention is yet another way of tuning conceptualizations. It differs from the other ways of tuning conceptualizations—either accepting or fighting the status quo—in that it is not one-sided: the participants are cooperating in establishing a tuning and actively maintaining it.

However, such cooperation is subject to defection. An all-too-common example occurs when one participant takes the common enterprise to be one of cooperation in solving a problem (i.e. presumes tuning), and the other takes it to be one of social coercion ("the truth is what *I* say it is"). The first participant, on discovering the defection, justifiably accuses the second of a swindle or worse.

This brief discussion of "tuning" may evoke in readers a rich range of associations, from education to politics to mental illness to multiculturalism to postmodernism. This is not the place to go on; I encourage others to explore the connections.

For present purposes, the point is that "tuning" seems to me the last piece we need to close the loop in creating a conceptualist account of reference and truth. Not only is our conceptualized world our own reality, we constantly check whether it converges with everyone else's. To the degree that we sense that it converges, we take the common view as flowing from the "objective character of the world." On the other hand, to the degree that we sense conflict, we are forced to acknowledge subjectivity, and the sense of what is "objective" becomes less stable.

This is not to say that objectivity and truth reduce to consensus (a view urged by Rorty 1979, for instance). Rather, objectivity is understood as an ideal that we aspire to achieve. Consensus or "co-tuning" is one important factor that the f-mind weighs (and often *we* weigh consciously) in judging objectivity and truth. But there are others. The rebel trusts his or her own perception and inference and holds out against the consensus ("The emperor has no clothes!"). Achieving the proper balance is often difficult, and the line between courage and madness can be a tough call.

Here is where I think we are, after pursuing a rigorously mentalist approach to meaning. We have not ended up with the rock-solid rigid notion of truth that the realists want. Rather, I think we have begun to envision something that has the promise of explaining our human sense of truth and reference—and of explaining why philosophical and commonsensical disputes about truth and objectivity so often proceed the way they do. I have no illusions that this work is over, but it strikes me as a path well worth exploring.

CHAPTER II

Lexical Semantics

II.I Boundary conditions on theories of lexical meaning

Back to the trenches. An overall framework for studying meaning is not enough: an important part of its value lies in the opportunities it offers for understanding the gritty details of language. Accordingly, this chapter discusses a potpourri of issues concerning the concepts associated with words; the next chapter turns to larger linguistic units.

The mentalist stance of generative grammar, as extended to meaning in the past two chapters, leads us immediately to three important boundary conditions on a theory of lexical concepts—concepts that form the conceptual structure component of lexical items. First, since lexical items must be stored in long-term memory (Chapter 6), so must lexical concepts. As emphasized in the previous chapter, this precludes explicating word meanings in terms of the extension of sets to which the speaker has no access, for example treating the conceptual structure of *dog* as the set of all dogs in all possible worlds. Rather, the meaning of *dog* has to be specified in terms of a set of conditions or features that speakers of English use to distinguish dogs from other entities.

A second boundary condition on the theory of lexical concepts is that they must somehow get into long-term memory. Almost everyone who thinks about it takes it for granted that lexical concepts are learned—though many recognize that this presents formidable problems (section 4.7).

A third boundary condition on a theory of lexical concepts concerns their contribution to the meanings of sentences. The contextualized understanding of a novel sentence (perceived or produced!) has to be composed online in working memory (Chapters 6 and 7). It must be built from the following sources:

- The meanings of its words (the lexical concepts).
- Conceptual structure conveyed by the grammatical structure of the sentence.
- Overall conditions on composed conceptual structure: Is the structure well-formed? Is it plausible?
- Conceptual structure derived from context.

Lexical concepts must be rich and specific enough to play their necessary role in this mix. It may be possible to reduce the richness of lexical concepts by enriching the theories of the other three components, but in the end it is necessary to show that the contributions of the four components add up to the full interpretation.

11.2 The prospects for decomposition into primitives

Let us begin by focusing on the necessity for lexical concepts to be learned. Nearly everyone thinks that learning *anything* consists of constructing it from previously known parts, using previously known means of combination. If we trace the learning process back and ask where the previously known parts came from, and where *their* previously known parts came from, eventually we have to arrive at a point where the most basic parts are *not* learned: they are given to the learner genetically, by virtue of the character of brain development. We went through this trope in Chapter 4; I hope nothing further need be said. Applying this view to lexical learning, we conclude that lexical concepts must have a compositional structure, and that the word learner's f-mind is putting meanings together from smaller parts.[1]

The major exception to this view of lexical learning is Jerry Fodor, who takes the position (e.g. 1975; 1998) that all lexical concepts (or at least all morphologically simple lexical concepts) are innate. This includes, for instance, the meanings of *telephone, carburetor, merlot, soffit,* and *yarmulka*: even if some of these words are absent from someone's vocabulary, their meanings are present in his or her f-mind, just waiting to be triggered. Fodor arrives at this position because he maintains that lexical concepts are monadic: they *have* no parts, hence no parts that could be previously known. Hence he is forced to say that all lexical concepts are innate. He never addresses the question of how they could all be coded genetically, nor how evolution could have come up with them. I take it that this is a position we want to avoid.

Fodor believes that lexical concepts have no parts because he assumes an extremely limited view of what the parts could be and how they could combine. His argument that lexical concepts are monadic stems from a paper entitled "Against Definitions" (Fodor et al. 1980). The title of the paper gives the game away. Observing (correctly) that one usually cannot find airtight definitions that work all of the time, Fodor concludes that word meanings cannot be decomposed.

---

[1] By attributing the composition of word meanings to the learner's f-mind, I am distancing myself from the claim that the word learner is putting pieces together *consciously*, which is surely false. We are as usual talking in functional terms here.

However, his notion of definition is the standard dictionary sort: a phrase that elucidates a word meaning. So what he has actually shown is that word meanings cannot be built by combining other word meanings, using the principles that also combine words into phrases.[2] But there are other options.

A comparison with phonology is useful. The phonology of a word is certainly not monadic and innate; it is built from known parts. At the first layer of decomposition, we find a repertoire of language-specific syllables; at the second, a repertoire of partly language-specific speech sounds; at the third, a universal repertoire of distinctive features. What we take to be innate is the repertoire of features, plus general principles for building them into language-specific repertoires of sounds, syllables, and words.

Notice what happens as we decompose further and further. Among the syllables of a word, many could be words on their own (e.g. within *syllables*, *sill* and *bulls*). At the next layer down, most speech sounds cannot be words on their own (vowels can, but individual consonants can only be clitics, as in *cats*, *he'll*, *I'm*, *named*)—but at least they can be intuitively discriminated. However, at the next layer down, distinctive features not only can't be words on their own, they can't even be *sounds* on their own. We have no conscious access to them, and it requires a theory of phonology to uncover their differentiation and their role in building words. Moreover, although speech sounds combine into syllables by concatenation, and syllables combine into words by concatenation, and words combine into phrases by concatenation, distinctive features do not combine into speech sounds by concatenation.

Whether or not we suffer physics envy, a physical parallel is also suggestive. In explaining the variety of substances in the world, a first layer of decomposition gives us a limited repertoire of substances such as oxygen, boron, sulfur, and gallium, combined by chemical bonds. The next layer down gives us entities that can exist in isolation but are not substances: electrons, protons, and neutrons, combined by electromagnetic and nuclear forces. The next layer down gives us quarks, which not only are not substances but cannot exist in isolation; they are as it were features of elementary particles.

I suggest that the same is true of lexical concepts. As we explore the parts from which they are built, suppose we find layers of structure whose units cannot individually serve as possible word meanings. This would preclude an explication of

---

[2] For more detailed critique of Fodor's position, see (Jackendoff 1983: 122–7; 1990a: 37–41, 150–2). As far as I am aware, Fodor has not replied to these critiques. He does offer an argument against my type of decomposition in Fodor (1998: 49–56) (also discussed in Laurence and Margolis 1999: 58–9). But his argument is made only on methodological grounds and completely ignores all empirical generalizations captured by the decompositional approach. We return to this argument briefly in section 11.8.

lexical meanings in terms of linguistically expressed definitions, i.e. synonymous phrasal expressions. In addition, suppose the principles by which sublexical units combine into word meanings are not the same as the principles by which word meanings combine into phrase meanings. Then, even if the sublexical units composing a word meaning could themselves be expressed as words, no phrase composed of those words could express what the original word expresses. And of course, just as we have no conscious access to phonological primitives, we should not be able to expound on word decomposition on the basis of raw intuition.

So here is the answer to Fodor's argument against definitions: although he has shown that lexical meanings cannot be decomposed definitionally, he neglects the possibility that there are non-definitional forms of decomposition of the sort found in phonology and physics. Since his alternative to non-definitional decomposition is genetic transmission of the whole meanings of *quark* and *fax*, our choice ought to be clear.

An important question often raised about lexical decomposition is the justification of primitives. Where does decomposition end? When do we know to stop? I don't think the parallel question in physics worries its practitioners too much. The history of the last two hundred years is a continual quest to explain deeper and deeper regularities. Semantics is just getting started; let's show some patience. In the meantime, we do the best we can to extract and characterize relevant generalizations.

A quick example here might be helpful to illustrate both the non-definitional character of lexical decomposition and the issue of primitives. A staple of lexical semantic analysis (going back at least to Gruber 1965, McCawley 1968, and Lakoff 1970) has been the extraction of causation as a significant component of many verb meanings. For instance, the sentences in (1) are related to those in (2) by a common approximate paraphrase relation, shown in (3).

(1)   a. The window broke.
      b. The door opened.
      c. The ball rolled down the hill.
      d. Harry received a flower.
      e. Harry died.
      f. Harry decided to talk.

(2)   a. Beth broke the window.
         [≈ Beth caused the window to break]
      b. Beth opened the door.
         [≈ Beth caused the door to open]
      c. Beth rolled the ball down the hill.
         [≈ Beth caused the ball to roll down the hill]

    d. Beth gave Harry a flower.
      [≈ Beth caused Harry to receive/get a flower]
    e. Beth killed Harry.
      [≈ Beth caused Harry to die]
    f. Beth persuaded Harry to talk.
      [≈ Beth caused Harry to decide to talk]

(3)   Beth V_2 NP X ≈ Beth cause NP to V_1 X

In cases (a–c) the verbs in (1) and (2) are morphologically identical, in cases (d–f) they are different; but the paraphrase relation is uniform throughout. As Fodor (1970) points out, this paraphrase relation is not exact (see McCawley 1978 and Jackendoff 1990a: ch. 7 for some reasons why); Fodor uses this as an argument against lexical decomposition. But the fact that the very same not quite paraphrasable relation occurs over and over, in language after language, suggests that something of linguistic importance is going on—but not at the level of decomposition into words.

    So, following custom, let us introduce an abstract term CAUSE for the semantic element the verbs in (2) have in common. In many approaches to lexical semantics this is taken as a primitive. However, Talmy 1985 (reanalyzed in Jackendoff 1990a: ch. 7 and Jackendoff 1996a; an earlier partial analysis is Gruber 1965) shows that CAUSE is not simplex; it is one of a family of concepts related through feature decomposition. They all invoke a basic situation involving two characters; one, the "Antagonist," is trying to get something to happen to the other, the "Agonist." CAUSing is a situation in which the Antagonist succeeds in opposition to the Agonist's resistance or inaction. For instance, in (2a) Beth (Antagonist) acts on the window (Agonist), which would not tend to break (Action) unless Beth acted on it. But there are other combinations, for example:

(4)   a. Beth pressured/urged Harry to talk (but he didn't talk/and he did talk).
      [Beth acts in opposition to Harry, possibly not succeeding.]
    b. Beth helped/aided/assisted Harry in washing the dishes (but they didn't finish/and they finished)
      [Beth acts in concert with Harry, possibly succeeding]
    c. Beth let Harry talk/allowed Harry to talk.
      [Beth ceases to oppose Harry]

There is no word that expresses the basic function these all have in common; Jackendoff calls it CS, and Talmy resorts to an annotated diagram. The two analyses differ in the features posited to distinguish causing, pressuring, helping, and letting; but on either analysis the features involved have no simple lexical paraphrase.

A further generalization of the analysis extends it to verbs expressing propositional relations: at the proper degree of abstraction, *entail* and *imply* are analogous to verbs of causation, *permit* and *be consistent with* are analogous to verbs of letting, and *reinforce* and *support* are analogous to verbs of helping. These patterns of commonality are recognized as significant by many lexical semanticists. But we cannot pull them out without resorting to considerable sublexical formal abstraction, not readily expressible as definitions. And once we do so, are we down to primitives? We don't know. All we know is that we are three stages of generalization away from actual words.

It is all well and good to extract significant parts from word meanings; but what about the part that is left? For example, suppose we accept, even approximately, McCawley's (1968) famous analysis of *kill* as [CAUSE [BECOME [NOT [ALIVE]]]] (where I use words written in small capitals to designate the meanings of those words). The first three elements are widespread among lexical concepts and are candidates for primitives or near-primitives. But what about ALIVE? Can it be decomposed, or do we have to accept it as a primitive? Laurence and Margolis (1999) call this the "problem of *completers*."

This problem also arises in analyzing variation among closely related words. For instance, how does *break* differ from *shatter* and *crumble*? It does not appear likely that the differences among them are elements of any larger generality, such that we would find other groups of verbs that differ in exactly the same dimensions. Such facts, which we confront at every turn, threaten to undermine the prospect of completely decomposing words into primitives that are descriptively useful and that have some plausibility for innateness.

For some linguists this is not taken to be a problem. Pinker (1989: 167): "I will not try to come up with a small set of primitives and relations out of which one can compose definitions [*sic*] capturing the totality of a verb's meaning." Grimshaw (1993): "Linguistically speaking, pairs like [*break* and *shatter*] are synonyms, because they have the same structure. The differences between them are not visible to the language." Pustejovsky (1995:58): "What I would like to do is to propose a new way of viewing decomposition, looking more at the generative or *compositional* aspects of lexical semantics, rather than decomposition into a specified *number* of primitives." For Pinker and Grimshaw, all that is at issue is the syntactic behavior of words; since the syntax–semantics interface cannot "see" all of meaning, a complete decomposition is unnecessary and even irrelevant (section 9.7.3). Pustejovsky is interested in previously unexplored aspects of lexical meaning that go beyond mere feature decomposition (see sections 11.9 and 11.10), so he too can bypass the question of primitives.

However, the requirement of learnability forces us to take the problem of primitives seriously. If children can acquire the fine-scale differences among words, they must have some resources from which the differences can be constructed. Therefore it ought to be a long-range goal for conceptualist semantics to characterize these resources.

A particularly austere approach to primitives would be the thoroughly empiricist claim that meaning is built entirely from primitives provided by sensation or perception, and that all else is built by association or statistical inference. I take it that this is a non-starter. For instance, it was shown as long ago as David Hume's *Treatise on Human Nature* that the notion of causation, here CAUSE, cannot be built up by these means (see discussion in Macnamara 2000). And words like *function, any,* and *nevertheless* seem altogether unapproachable perceptually. In the terms of Chapter 10, perceptual descriptive features alone are not sufficient for characterizing meaning; and there is no way to construct inferential descriptive features from perceptual primitives. Thus there is no question that we are going to have to accept some abstract primitives.[3]

In view of these considerations, we will adopt as a practical policy the necessity for lexical conceptual decomposition. And we will note as we go the prospects, good and bad, for finding primitives.

11.3 Polysemy

Another much-discussed question of lexical semantics is how the theory should deal with polysemy. How should we treat apparently different senses of a lexical item that bear some intuitive relationship, for instance the two uses of *break, open,* and *roll* in (1) and (2)? Let me lay out some cases, mostly not new, that illustrate the complexity of the problem; others will appear in the course of the chapter.

First, a baseline for how rigorous it is possible to be. *Gooseberry* and *strawberry* have nothing to do with geese and straw. Yet given the chance to create folk etymologies, people will invent a story that relates them. Overcoming the strong intuition that there *must* be a relation is not easy, and one must not insist on closer relations than there really are. But how can we tell when to give up and

---

[3] For an interesting case that also bears on non-definitional decomposition, it has often been noticed (Talmy 1978; Jackendoff 1991) that the substance–object (mass-count) distinction in nouns (*water* vs. *bowl*) parallels the process–event distinction in verbs (*run* vs. *arrive*), and that there are often strong interactions between the two distinctions in the meanings of sentences. This parallelism motivates a semantic feature [±*bounded*] that contributes to both domains: objects and events have inherent boundaries, substances and processes do not. As shown in Jackendoff (1991), it is in part this common distinction that allows us to say that both a table (object) and a speech (event) can have an *end*. But there is no perceptual similarity between the end of a table and the end of a speech.

call some putative explanation a "gooseberry etymology"? I don't know in general; I only know that doing so is an honorable last resort.

Next consider some cases where it is easy to make a judgment. On one extreme, I think everyone agrees that the *bank*s in *river bank* and *savings bank* represent separate homonymous concepts listed in the lexicon, not a single polysemous concept. On the other extreme, I doubt anyone thinks that the mental lexicon lists *ham sandwich* as potentially referring to a person, or *Russell* as referring to a book, or *John* as referring to a car, even though they are understood that way in (5).

(5)   a.   [One waitress to another:]
           The ham sandwich in the corner wants some more coffee.
      b.   *Plato* is on the top shelf next to *Russell*.
      c.   *John* got a dent in his left fender.

Rather, these "extended" meanings are built up online from lexically listed meanings by general principles; we take this process up in section 12.2.

The cases between these two extremes are of greater interest. One that I find uncontroversial is the sort of multistep chaining of association found in *cardinal*. According to the *Oxford English Dictionary*, the earliest meaning is 'principal,' as in *cardinal points of the compass* and *cardinal virtues*. From there it extended to the high-ranking church official, then to the traditional color of his robes, then to the bird of that color. All of these senses are still present in English, but they surely do not constitute a single polysemous word—especially the first and last member. The reason is that the basis for connection changes en route, so that one cannot trace the connection without knowing the intermediate steps. What should we say about these cases? They are more closely related than plain homonyms, but not closely related enough to be said to form a unified concept. One might call them "opaquely chained concepts."[4]

We find a quite different situation in the related senses of *open* in (6), which are related by semiproductive lexical relations; the relation between (6b) and (6c) is the causative relation illustrated in (1) and (2).

(6)   a.   The door is open$_1$.
      b.   The door opened$_2$. [≈ the door became open$_1$]
      c.   John opened$_3$ the door.
           [≈ John caused the door to open$_2$ = John caused the door to become open$_1$]

---

[4] I have the same sense about Lakoff's (1987: 104–9) analysis of the Japanese classifier *hon*: among the entities to which it applies, there is a motivated route from candles to Zen contests and to TV programs, but I find it hard to think of them as constituting any sort of unified category, as Lakoff claims.

This chaining, unlike the chaining of *cardinal*, is semantically transparent, in that the original concept is contained in both the derivative concepts. This sort of transparent chaining is a standard case of polysemy.

One might try to claim (with Deane 1996 and Ruhl 1989) that these three uses are not separate senses that must be learned individually, but rather form a single sense that can be extended from the simple core prototype (6a). This treatment runs into problems, though, when we start dealing with long branching chains. An example is the word *smoke*. The core is the noun *smoke*, the wispy substance that comes out of fires. From this we get at least the senses in (7).

(7) a. $smoke_1$ = 'wispy substance'
    b. X $smokes_2$ = 'X gives off $smoke_1$'
    c. Y $smokes_3$ X = 'Y causes X to $smoke_2$, where X is a pipe, cigar, etc., by putting in the mouth and puffing, taking $smoke_1$ into the mouth, etc.'
    d. Y $smokes_4$ = 'Y $smokes_3$ something'
    e. Y $smokes_5$ X = 'Y causes $smoke_1$ to go into X, where X is a ham, herring, etc., by hanging X over a fire in an enclosure'

Although all the steps in (7) are transparent, I would be reluctant to say that these five uses together form a single concept for which $smoke_1$ is the prototype. In particular, there is really no relation between $smoke_4$ and $smoke_5$ other than the presence of $smoke_1$ as a character in each action. One reason for this is that each step of the chain adds idiosyncratic information. For instance, it could only be a joke to speak of $smoking_3$ a herring by setting it on fire and putting it in your mouth and puffing, or of $smoking_5$ a cigar by putting it in a smoky room.

Because of these multiple branches and idiosyncrasies, it makes more sense to say there are five senses arranged in two transparent chains branching outward from $smoke_1$ (1–2–3–4 and 1–5). These senses are not any more closely related to each other than they are to, say, *smoky* and *smoker* (the latter meaning either 'a person who $smokes_4$' or 'a vessel in which one $smokes_5$ things'). And in a morphologically richer language than English they might be morphologically distinct; for instance German has *Rauch* for $smoke_1$, *rauchen* for $smoke_{2-4}$, and *räuchern* for $smoke_5$. In other words, even if all these senses are related, the language user must learn them individually.

A check on the validity of such putative relationships is the extent to which they occur in other lexical items. Here are the linkages for *smoke*, listing other words that show the same relationships among their senses:

(8) $smoke_1$ → $smoke_2$ (V = 'give off N'):
      steam, sweat, smell, flower

smoke$_2$ → smoke$_3$ (V = 'cause to V'):
  open, break, roll, freeze

smoke$_3$ → smoke$_4$ (V = 'V something'):
  eat, drink, read, write

smoke$_1$ → smoke$_5$ (V = 'put N into/onto something'):
  paint, butter, water, powder, steam

Notice that each relationship affects a different group of verbs. Each pairwise relationship is semi-productive, but the entire branching structure of senses for *smoke* is unique. This means that no general process of extension from a prototype can predict all the linkages: they are different for every word.

A linking relationship among senses is more suspicious when it is impossible to find *any* other lexical items that participate in the same relationship. An example is the two senses of *into*:

(9) a. into$_1$ X = 'path terminating in the interior of X'
         (*run into the room*)
     b. into$_2$ X = 'path terminating in violent contact with X'
         (*run into the wall*)

I am happy to treat these senses as related only in that they both express termination (the 'to' portion). The morpheme *in* in *into$_1$* is the usual sense of *in*; but I am inclined to see the morpheme *in* in *into$_2$* as like the *goose* in *gooseberry*, having nothing to do with normal *in*. Deane (1996), by contrast, asks for more: he wishes to analyze *into$_2$* as 'path which would have carried an object to the inside of X if the boundary had not impeded it.' There is something not quite correct about this analysis, since you can crash into a mirror, even though you could never fit inside it. But more troubling is that there are no other prepositions that have this counterfactual sense. For instance, you cannot crash *under* a table by landing violently on top of it—though you would have ended up under the table if its boundary had not impeded your motion. Consequently, there is nothing to gain by extracting out this relation between the two *intos* as a subregularity. Moreover, there is no general process of extension of a prototype that will get to *into$_2$* from *into$_1$*, or that will get both from a more abstract sense they have in common.

Any theory of the lexicon will have to make these distinctions in types of polysemy. In Cognitive Grammar, a theory that takes issues of polysemy seriously, there is sometimes a tendency to assume that much of this machinery will be rendered unnecessary by assuming a general process of extension from a prototype. I have tried to show that in the present cases such a strategy won't work.

This is not to say that there are no general processes of concept extension in language. In fact, there are without question general processes such as metonymy and metaphor, as well as the processes illustrated in (5), which apply productively to any conceptually appropriate expression, so that the derived meanings don't have to be listed in the lexicon. I have taken pains to show that the cases discussed in this section are not like this: we still need lexical polysemy of various sorts.

The distinction between productive processes of meaning extension (such as (5)) and semiproductive instances of polysemy such as *open* and *smoke* is strongly reminiscent of the distinction between productive and semiproductive morphology discussed in Chapter 6. My sense is that the same solution is applicable: the semi-regular cases are listed in the lexicon, related by inheritance hierarchies, whereas the regular relations are extracted as independent rules, which (with luck) can themselves be formulated as lexical items. A couple of the latter cases will be addressed in section 12.2.

11.4 Taxonomic structure

One sort of structure universally acknowledged as part of lexical semantics is taxonomic structure: poodles are kinds of dog, dogs are kinds of animal, animals are kinds of living thing, living things are kinds of physical object. The point of such structure is that it provides more general access to rules of inference: any inference rule that pertains to dogs or to animals in general will automatically apply to poodles.

However, there are some problems about how taxonomies are to be arranged formally. Suppose we list under each category only its immediate antecedent in the hierarchy, so that POODLE only says it is KIND-OF [DOG]. Now suppose we need to draw an inference based on a poodle's being a physical object, say that it continues to exist over time: we have to construct a chain of inferences from POODLE to DOG, from DOG to ANIMAL, and so on till we reach PHYSICAL OBJECT. This seems like an inefficient way to arrange matters.[5] In addition, there is the problem of how many layers the taxonomy should contain. For example, should MAMMAL be inserted between DOG and ANIMAL? If so, this would appear to further lengthen chains of inference. If not, where does MAMMAL fit in?[6]

---

[5] Well, maybe this is just a competence theory, and nothing follows about performance. But, as urged in previous chapters, such a move is dangerous.

[6] The same problems crop up if we conceive of the taxonomic structure as an arrangement of nodes in a semantic network, linked by IS-A relations: from POODLE we have to go all the way up the taxonomy in order to find out what can happen to it by virtue of being a PHYSICAL OBJECT. An approach based on meaning postulates (e.g. POODLE → DOG) faces parallel difficulties. I encourage advocates of these approaches to recast all the arguments of this section in their own terms.

Alternatively, one could conceive of *all* taxonomic structure appearing in *each* lexical entry. Then POODLE would contain KIND-OF [DOG], KIND-OF [ANIMAL], KIND-OF [PHYSICAL OBJECT], and so on. This makes it a one-step process to compute an inference based on any taxonomic relation, and we do not have to decide exactly how many layers of taxonomy go into a concept. Of course, the price is crushing redundancy in lexical concepts.

A parallel problem occurs in dealing with knowledge of individuals. Should we include in the lexical entry for *Dan Dennett* just that he is a male human (or a male philosopher?), and then should we derive the fact that he can move under his own power by going up the taxonomy to ANIMAL? Or should we include in his entry all the superordinate categories he belongs to, and accept all the attendant redundancy?

This dilemma is reminiscent of the one we faced in the encoding of morphological and constructional structure in Chapter 6. There I suggested that the proper solution probably lies in how long-term memory hierarchies are instantiated in the brain, not in some choice of notation in the competence theory. Similarly, Chapter 7 invoked taxonomic relations in discussing lexical priming, without saying how the brain actually encodes these relations. For present purposes, I suggest that we leave our options open.

It has often been noted that inferences based on taxonomy are not altogether strict. For example, one would want to characterize birds as animals that fly— but then there are ostriches and penguins. This too resembles the semiproductive relations found in morphology (section 6.2) and especially inheritance hierarchies; Pinker (1999) draws an explicit parallel betwen the two phenomena, suggesting that morphological and conceptual taxonomies are two manifestations of the same brain process.

More controversial perhaps is the question of whether a lexical concept carries structure relating it to *lower* members in the taxonomy. For instance, does TREE carry a list of its subkinds, including PALM, PINE, and PLUM? To carry things to an extreme, does PHYSICAL OBJECT carry within it a list of all its known subkinds? Implausible. On the other hand, people do use information derived by going down the hierarchy in order to draw inferences: this is "case-based reasoning." Of course, case-based reasoning is notoriously unreliable ("Welfare should be eliminated, because let me tell you about this woman who took advantage of the system"), but people use it all the time nevertheless.

It seems clear that at least some downward links from kinds to their instances are readily accessible. For most people in cognitive science, *linguist* evokes *Chomsky* and *bonobo* invokes *Kanzi*. For dog owners, *dog* likely evokes their own as an exemplar. Moreover, concept learning is often based on the presentation of exemplars ("This is a kangaroo"), and there is no reason that such links, which get concept learning off the ground, should necessarily be abandoned.

When the subordinate is another kind rather than an instance, the strength of a downward link may correlate with the judged "typicality" of the subordinate as a subcategory (Rosch and Mervis 1975; Smith and Medin 1981). For instance, *fruit* evokes *apple* more quickly and reliably than it evokes *pomegranate* or *prickly pear*. A category such as *furniture* has no independent perceptual characterization (what does a piece of furniture look like?), so the collection of its prominent subcategories—chairs, tables, sofas, and so on—comes more prominently to the fore.

There are other categories for which taxonomic information seems to play little role. What larger category includes *puddle*? It doesn't really fit into *bodies of water* along with lakes and rivers. And it doesn't have subcategories or permanently remembered prominent instances. The same goes for *junk*. So simple taxonomic structure is often useful, but not always. As will be seen, this is typical of every kind of lexical information we find.

11.5 Contributions from perceptual modalities

Next let us ask how perceptual features are structured. In order to learn a category from presented instances ("This is a dog"), one must make use of levels of cognitive structure in the visual system that encode what the instances look like. Memories stored in terms of these levels of structure are used to identify new instances of a category on the basis of their appearance ("Is THIS a dog?"), and to recognize known individuals (people, objects, and scenes). Structures in other sensory modalities must be stored as well: the sound of a flute or of a particular individual's voice, the taste of curry, the feel of the key in your front door lock, the sensation of hunger.

If such structures are stored, there is no reason they should not be linked up in long-term memory with lexical items. One might wonder: Are they still part of "meaning," or are they somehow "encyclopedic" information? Such a question grows out of the usual assumption that the domain of meaning is a uniform, homogeneous level of structure, say some form of logic.[7] But this is an oversimplification. After all, phonology and syntax are built out of formally distinct interacting subcomponents. Why shouldn't "meaning" also subdivide into natural subcomponents?

A major division in the structure of meaning appears to lie between what I

---

[7] Fodor (1975; 1983) shares this assumption, in his claim that the Language of Thought is homogeneous and non-modular.

have called *conceptual structure* (CS) and *spatial structure* (SpS) (Jackendoff 1987; 1996d; Landau and Jackendoff 1993).[8] CS, with which most of the rest of this chapter will be concerned, is a hierarchical arrangement built out of discrete features and functions; it encodes such aspects of understanding as category membership (taxonomy) and predicate–argument structure. SpS, by contrast, is concerned with encoding the spatial understanding of the physical world—not just moment-by-moment appearance, but the integration over time of the shape, motion, and layout of objects in space (and possibly the forces among them). Although for a first approximation SpS can be thought of as the "upper end" of the visual system, it also receives and integrates inputs about shape and spatial layout from the haptic system (sense of touch), auditory localization, and the somatosensory system (felt position of one's own body). This integration is what enables you to know by looking at an object where to reach for it, and what it should feel like when you handle it. Thus SpS should be thought of as a system of central cognition, to some degree modality-independent.

The drawing of two adjacent stars in Fig. 1.1, labeled "spatial structure," is only the crudest and most tentative sketch of this level's content. To be more precise: in order to serve as a locus of spatial understanding, SpS must encode the shape of objects in a form that is suitable for recognizing an object at different distances and from different perspectives, i.e. it must solve the classic problem of object constancy.[9] It must be able to encode spatial knowledge of parts of objects that cannot be seen, for instance the hollowness of a balloon. It must be able to encode shape variations among objects of similar visual type, for example making explicit the range of shape variations possible among different cups. That is, it must support visual object *categorization* as well as visual object *identification*. It must be able to encode the degrees of freedom in objects that can change their shape, for instance human and animal bodies. It must be suitable for encoding the full spatial layout of a scene, and for mediating among alternative perspectives ("What would this scene look like from over there?"), so that it can be used to support reaching and navigating.

The best articulated (partial) theory of spatial structure I know of is Marr's (1982) 3D model, with Biederman's (1987) "geonic" constructions as a particular variant. Some of the factors listed here go beyond the Marr and Biederman theories of object shape; but nothing prevents these theories in principle from serving as components of a fuller theory of spatial understanding, rather than

---

[8] I replace my earlier term "spatial representation" with "spatial structure," with the usual goal of eliminating any hint of intentionality.

[9] As a corollary, SpS must support the generation of mentally rotated imaged objects whose perspective with respect to the viewer changes during rotation—a fact noted by Kosslyn (1980).

strictly as theories of high-level visual shape recognition. In particular, the 3D model does not have an intrinsically visual character—it is no longer retinotopic, for example; nor, as Marr stresses, is it confined to the observer's point of view.[10]

It is important to see how abstract the hypothesized level of SpS is. Although SpS is geometric in character, it is not "imagistic" in the sense of the "percepts" of section 10.5: it is not to be thought of as encoding "pictures" or "statues in the head." An image is restricted to a particular point of view, whereas SpS is not. An image is restricted to a particular instance of a category, whereas SpS is not (recall Berkeley's objection to images as the vehicle of thought: how can an image of a particular triangle stand for all possible triangles?). An image cannot include the unseen parts of an object—its back and inside, and the parts of it occluded from the observer's view by other objects—whereas SpS does. An image is restricted to the visual modality, whereas SpS can equally well encode information received haptically or through proprioception. Nevertheless, even though SpSs are not themselves imagistic, it makes sense to think of them as encoding image-schemas: abstract structures from which a variety of images can be generated and to which a variety of percepts can be compared.

The work of understanding the conceptualized world is divided between CS and SpS (and probably other levels). Judgments and inferences having to do with predicate–argument relations, category membership, the type–token distinction, quantification, and so forth can be formulated only in terms of CS. Judgments and inferences having to do with exact shapes, locations, and forces can be formulated only in terms of SpS. On the other hand, there is overlap between the two levels, in that the notions of physical object, part–whole relationships, locations, force, and causation have reflexes in both systems. It is these shared components that enable the two systems to communicate with each other through an interface of the usual sort. This division of labor is thus a more abstract version of Paivio's (1971) old dual-coding hypothesis: CS is sort of

---

[10] Some colleagues have objected to Marr's characterizing the 3D sketch as "object-centered," arguing that objects are always seen from some point of view or other—at the very least the observer's. However, I interpret "object-centered" as implying only that the encoding of the object is independent of point of view. This neutrality permits the appearance of the object to be computed as necessary to fit the object into the visual scene as a whole, viewed from any arbitrary vantage point. Marr, who is not concerned with spatial layout, but only with identifying the object, does not deal with this further step of reinjecting the object into the scene. But I see such a step as altogether within the spirit of his approach.

I recognize that Marr's 3D model is now out of fashion in the vision community. Still, the criteria for SpS must be satisfied by *some* cognitive structure or combination of structures. Readers more conversant than I in the vision literature should feel free to substitute their favorite theory of high-level vision here, as long as it satisfies the criteria we need to provide a "perceptual front end" for language.

"propositional," though not strictly linguistic, and SpS is sort of "imagistic," though not strictly visual.[11]

My working hypothesis at the moment (Jackendoff 1996d) is that the grammatical aspects of language make reference only to CS, not to SpS. Nothing in grammar depends on detailed shapes of objects.[12] On the other hand, SpS is language's indirect connection to visual, haptic, and proprioceptive perception, and to the control of action; it is through the SpS connection that we can talk about what we see. This leads to the diagram of components and interfaces in Fig.11.1, in which the "meaning" component of Fig. 9.1 is opened out into CS and SpS.

Going back to lexical semantics, a stored piece of SpS can take the place of what many approaches (e.g. Rosch and Mervis 1975; Putnam 1975) informally term an "image of a prototypical instance of the category." For example, *cat* will have a CS that identifies it as an animal and a member of the feline family and that specifies its typically being a pet. It will also have an SpS that encodes how cats are shaped and colored and how they move. Not all lexical items, of course, have an SpS component. Those expressing abstract concepts such as *fairness* and *value* and those expressing logical concepts such as *and*, *if*, and *not* come to mind as prominent examples. These will have only CS components. I would imagine that words denoting sounds, tastes, smells, and feelings have components relating to those sense modalities instead of to SpS.

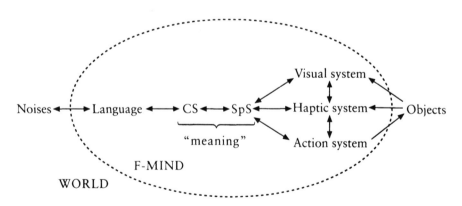

Fig. 11.1. Incorporating the CS–SpS split in meaning

---

[11] One can interpret Kosslyn's (1980) experiments on the distinction between "propositional" and "imagistic" processing as confirming this division of labor.

[12] However, some languages have classifier systems that depend on coarse shapes (e.g. Lakoff's 1987 example of Japanese *hon* that goes with long skinny objects); these might or might not be encoded in CS, an interesting and as yet unaddressed empirical issue.

a. Lexical items supplemented by SpS

| Phonology + Syntax + CS | + SpS |

LANGUAGE ???

b. Non-linguistic concept attached to words

| Phonology + Syntax | + | CS+SpS |

LANGUAGE "CONCEPT"

Fig. 11.2. Two ways of thinking about the CS–SpS connection

Let us return to the issue of the homogeneity of linguistic meaning. One might fear that the linguistic integrity of lexical items is violated by allowing the meaning of a word to contain an SpS component: as sketched in Fig. 11.2a, SpS falls outside the standard tripartite organization of language into phonology, syntax, and semantics. But consider the evolutionary perspective. Suppose one deletes the phonological and syntactic structures. What is left is a non-linguistic association of cognitive structures in memory, much of which could be shared by a non-linguistic organism. Phonological and syntactic structures can then be viewed as further structures tacked onto this concept to make it linguistically expressible. Such a perspective is suggested in Fig. 11.2b.

With or without language, the mind has to have a way to unify multimodal representations and store them as units (that is, to establish long-term memory "binding" in the neuroscience sense). The structures that make this a "lexical item" rather than just a "concept" simply represent an additional modality into which this concept extends: the linguistic modality.

Admitting SpS as a component of lexical meaning provides immediate and welcome aid on the problem of "completers." For instance, Katz (1972) offers, as part of the semantic structure of *chair*, features like [HAS A BACK] and [HAS LEGS]. But what kind of features are these? They are not very general: the kind of back appropriate for chairs will not do for people, camels, houses, or books; and something would not be a chair by virtue of having insect legs. What's really going on is that we *call* some part of a chair the *back* because of (a) its spatial configuration with respect to other parts of the chair and (b) possibly its proximity to the back of the sitter. We call chair legs *legs* because they are skinny vertical supports. With the provision of SpS, much of this difficulty vanishes: SpS can encode what a chair looks like, including its part structure. The fact that certain parts of chairs are called *legs* and *back* is encoded in the lexical entries for *these* words, not necessarily in the entry for *chair*.

More generally, many perceptual properties can be encoded directly in SpS. *Yellow*, for instance, may be encoded in CS as simply KIND-OF COLOR, a reasonable primitive; the distinction between it and all the other colors then is a matter of SpS, where color distinctions need to be encoded anyway for perceptual purposes.

More interesting are the verbs. For instance, *walk, jog, limp, strut,* and *shuffle* are similar in being verbs of self-locomotion. They differ only in manner of motion, one of those things that is extremely awkward to characterize through algebraic features. However, we can distinguish these words by their appearance (and how they feel in the body). Assuming SpS can code dynamic as well as static spatial configurations (Who knows how? Well, *some* level must!), it would make sense to leave the distinctions of manner of motion among these verbs to the geometric/topological encoding of SpS, and abandon the attempt to find primitive algebraic features for this purpose.

As with all interacting components, interesting questions of balance of power arise between CS and SpS. How far can content be bled out of CS into SpS? For example, *slither* and *slide* are somewhat more distant from the verbs above; are they still differentiated from *walk* only in SpS, or is there a CS difference as well? At present I don't know how to decide. (For some other cases, see Jackendoff 1996d; van der Zee 2000; Bloom et al. 1996.)

Notice that pushing some semantic distinctions into SpS does not simplify lexical semantics as a whole. All distinctions must still be encoded somehow (and I hope researchers on vision and action might be persuaded to collaborate in the task). However, this move takes a great deal of the burden off the feature system of CS, where the problems with "completers" arise. It also accounts for the fact that it is so hard to define words part of whose content is spatial: after all, a picture is worth ten thousand words (and an image schema is worth a dozen pictures!).

This position further predicts that lexical items distinguished only by SpS structure will have identical grammatical behavior, which for a first pass seems to be correct. For instance, this explains the intuition behind Grimshaw's claim that *walk, jog,* etc. are "synonymous" for linguistic purposes.

We will make further use of SpS in subsequent sections. But it is time to move on to the next amplification of semantic structure.

11.6 Other than necessary and sufficient conditions

As may have already become apparent, the study of lexical meaning has given rise to considerable investigation into categorization: how humans place individuals into categories, and how systems of categories are constructed mentally. In traditional semantic terms, the problem can be framed in terms of stating the truth-conditions for the sentence *This is an X*, where *X* is the category in question.

However, a mentalist approach to "truth-conditions" differs from the philosophical/logical tradition in two important respects.

First, as stressed in Chapter 10, "truth-conditions" are not taken to constitute absolute truths in the world or in possible worlds. Rather, they are taken to be the conditions by which a language user *judges* that some conceptualized individual is a member of a category; and the form of these conditions is constrained by human psychology, not by logical necessity. Such psychological conditions can be studied experimentally, as a rich research tradition has shown.

Second—and this is the burden of the present section—the main philosophical tradition adopts rather uncritically Tarski's assumption (1956) that the truth-conditions for a sentence constitute a set of conditions that are individually necessary and collectively sufficient to guarantee truth of the sentence: "*Snow is white* is true if and only if the following conditions hold: . . . ." Even the avowed mentalist Fodor, in arguing against definitions, assumes that necessary and sufficient conditions are the appropriate way to accomplish semantic decomposition of lexical items, e.g. "Something is a *bachelor* if and only if it is human, male, adult, and unmarried."

By contrast, much conceptualist semantic research (e.g. Jackendoff 1983; Lakoff 1987) stresses the insufficiency of Tarskian conditions to characterize the richness of human categories. This section presents examples of some of the problems that have arisen.

11.6.1 *Categories with graded boundaries*

Consider the category *red*. This cannot be identified with a particular perceived hue, since a broad range of hues are all called *red*. However, as hues shade imperceptibly from red toward orange, there comes a point where observers are no longer clear about their judgments. Observers may hesitate or disagree with one another. In addition, the judgment of a particular hue may depend on what hues have immediately preceded it in presentation (if presented after focal red, it is judged orange, but if after focal orange, it is judged red). That is, there is a focal range in which judgments are secure and consistent, but it shades into a borderline range in which there is conflict with a neighboring category, and in which judgments become less secure and more context-dependent.

This "fuzziness" in the boundary of a category is not a matter of speakers "not knowing the meaning of *red*"; rather, it is inherent in the structure of the concept itself. One can make *red* more "Tarskian" by stipulating rigid boundaries with orange, pink, purple, and brown, but then one is not dealing with the ordinary meaning of the word. Similarly, one can create a new category *red-orange* at the boundary, but then the same sort of fuzziness occurs at the boundary of red and red-orange. (The existence of such phenomena is noted by Putnam 1975; Berlin and Kay 1969 is the classic work on color judgments.)

Similar boundary problems arise with words like *hot* and *tall* that express significant deviation from a norm. What is the lower bound of temperature for, say, *hot soup*, or the lower bound of height for *tall woman*? (Recall also the classic puzzle about how few hairs are needed to be *bald*.) It is inherent in the structure of these concepts that the boundaries are not classically sharp: there is no way to place every woman definitively either in or out of the set of tall women.

Returning to a theme from Chapter 9, these adjectives also present evidence for the interdependence of "linguistic meaning" and "encyclopedic knowledge" in judgments of truth. For, as has often been observed, a *small elephant* is bigger than a *big mouse*: the norm to which the adjective is applied depends on one's knowledge of the standard size of the animals in question. (Bierwisch and Lang 1989 discuss in detail adjectives that relate an instance to a norm.) Similarly, as Talmy (1978) points out, what counts as a *nearby* star is metrically quite different from a *nearby* piece of furniture; nearness too is defined in terms of the normal distance expected among individuals of the category in question.

These examples all have to do with perceptual properties of objects. But any evaluative adjective presents the same problems. As we all know, the boundary between a *good* term paper and an *excellent* one is far from sharp, as is the boundary between a *smart* student and a *brilliant* one; and a dull student is usually smarter than a brilliant rat. And at what point does one consider oneself *well-paid*? It takes far less to be a well-paid academic than to be a well-paid CEO, and so on. Katz's (1966) treatment of *good* is an early treatment of such a case: a good knife is good *for cutting*; a good book is good *for reading*, and so on: the evaluation of an object is relativized to its normal function (see section 11.9 for more on normal function).

11.6.2 *"Cluster" concepts*

In the cases so far, necessary and sufficient conditions cannot be stated because of a blurred and/or context-dependent boundary. A different situation arises when multiple conditions interact in such a way that none of them is necessary. The classic example of this phenomenon is Wittgenstein's (1953) analysis of *game*, in which he demonstrates that there is no single necessary condition that distinguishes games from other activities. He suggests that the word is understood in terms of "family resemblance": there is a cluster of conditions that define games; but no games satisfy all of them, and none of them is shared by all games. That is, none of the conditions is necessary for an individual to be judged a member of the category, but various suitable combinations of them are sufficient. Such categories are now called "cluster concepts."

This analysis is amplified by Rosch (1978; Rosch and Mervis 1975), who shows experimentally that categorization judgments may contain a cline of "typicality," ranging from typical exemplars of the category (e.g. a robin is a "typical" bird) to atypical exemplars (e.g. a penguin is an "atypical" bird). There are various sources for typicality effects; but among them is a set of conditions that form a cluster concept.[13] Examples that satisfy fewer of the conditions are generally regarded as less typical than examples that maximally satisfy the conditions.

The effects of cluster concepts can be observed in concepts involving as few as two conditions. A case first discussed by Fillmore (1982) is the verb *climb*. Consider the following examples:

(10) a.   Bill climbed (up) the mountain.
     b.   Bill climbed down the mountain.
     c.   The snake climbed (up) the tree.
     d. ?*The snake climbed down the tree.

Climbing involves two independent conceptual conditions: (a) an individual is traveling upward, and (b) the individual is moving with characteristic effortful grasping motions (clambering). On the most likely interpretation of (10a), both conditions are met. (10b) violates the first condition and, since snakes cannot clamber, (10c) violates the second; yet both examples are acceptable instances of climbing. However, if both conditions are violated, as in (10d), the action cannot be characterized as climbing. Thus neither of the two conditions is necessary, but either is sufficient. Moreover, the default interpretation of (10a), in which both conditions are satisfied, is judged to be more prototypical climbing; (10b) and (10c) are judged somewhat more marginal but still perfectly legitimate instances.

One possible account of this would be to say that *climb* is ambiguous or polysemous between the readings 'rise' and 'clamber.' But this does violence to intuition: (10a) is not ambiguous between these two senses. Rather, other things being equal, it satisfies both of them. Another possible account would be to say that the meaning of *climb* is the logical disjunction of the two senses: 'rise *or* clamber.' But this is too crude: a disjunction isn't "more prototypically satisfied"

---

[13] Other sorts of typicality judgments occur, for instance, in color concepts, where a focal red is judged more typical than a red tinged with orange. Armstrong et al. (1983) show that typicality judgments can be obtained even for sharply defined concepts; e.g. 38 is judged a less typical even number than 4, and a nun is judged a less typical woman than a housewife. Thus typicality in and of itself is only a symptom for a number of underlying phenomena in categorization. But the existence of multiple sources for typicality does not undermine the existence of cluster concepts, as Armstrong et al. claim it does. See Jackendoff (1983: ch. 7, n. 6) and Lakoff (1987: ch. 9).

if both disjuncts are true, as *climb* is. If we want to think of constructing meanings by means of conditions connected with logical operators, we could introduce a new non-Boolean operator with this curious property. We might call it "ψ-or," ("ψ" for "psychological"), so that *climb* means 'rise ψ-*or* clamber.'

Parallel analyses have been proposed for the verbs *lie* ('tell a lie') (Coleman and Kay 1981) and *see* (Jackendoff 1983, based in part on Miller and Johnson-Laird 1976). Similar phenomena arise in lexical entries for nouns as well. For instance, a prototypical *chair* has a prototypical form and a standard function. Objects that have the proper function but the wrong form—say beanbag chairs—are more marginal instances of the category; and so are objects that have the right form but cannot fulfill the function—say chairs made of newspaper, or giant chairs. An object that violates both conditions—say a pile of crumpled newspaper—is by no stretch of the imagination a chair. Lakoff (1987: ch. 4) applies such an analysis to the concept *mother*, which includes the woman who contributes genetic material, the woman who bears the child, and the woman who raises the child. In today's arrangements of adoption and genetic engineering, not all three of these always coincide, and so the term is not always used prototypically.

Garrod et al. (1999) suggest that even prepositions may display this sort of component structure. For instance, *in* has a geometric and a functional component. The geometrical component stipulates that if X is in Y, X must be geometrically within the interior of the region subtended by Y. The functional component is "containment": roughly, X is not attached to Y, but if one moves Y, X is physically forced to move along with it. The prototypical instances of *in*, such as a stone in a bottle, satisfy both conditions. However, there are well-known counterexamples to the geometrical condition, such as the pear in the bowl shown in (11a) and the knife in the cheese shown in (11b).

(11)   a. The pear is in the bowl.   b. The knife is in the cheese.

These do satisfy the functional condition. One might suggest therefore that the functional condition is the correct definition of *in*. But when the objects being related are such that the functional condition cannot be satisfied, such partial geometrical inclusion is far less acceptable:

(12)   a. ?The square is in the circle.   b. ?The plane is in the cloud.

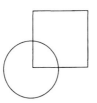   

Thus we see again the characteristic non-Boolean interaction of conditions to form a cluster concept.

In Jackendoff (1983) I called a system of conditions of this sort a "preference rule system"; Lakoff (1987) calls it (one aspect of) an "idealized cognitive model"; the *frames* of Minsky (1975) have similar effects. Concepts organized this way, like Tarskian concepts, are combinations of conditions. They differ from Tarskian concepts in that the conditions are combined differently, namely by "ψ-or." Thus a proper theory of word meanings must go beyond traditional philosophical assumptions. (Default logic comes closer to capturing the effect of such conditions, which function as default values where there is no evidence to the contrary, for instance in (10a).)

Appealing to the psychological goals of conceptualist semantics, such enrichment of the theory proves to be plausible on broader grounds. The manner in which conditions interact in cluster concepts is central in visual perception (Wertheimer 1923; Marr 1982), in phonetic perception (Liberman and Studdert-Kennedy 1977), in musical cognition (Lerdahl and Jackendoff 1983), and in Gricean implicature (Bach and Harnish 1979) (see Lerdahl and Jackendoff 1983: ch. 11 for discussion of all of these). Moreover, such an interaction can be plausibly instantiated in the brain, where the firing of a neuron is normally not a rigid function of other neural firings (like a logical conjunction), but rather a composite of many excitatory and inhibitory synapses of varying strengths. Thus cluster concepts, even though unusual in a logical framework, are quite natural in a psychological framework.

A different interpretation of cluster concepts appears to be more widespread in psychology. Laurence and Margolis (1999: 27), for instance, say "According to the Prototype Theory [e.g. Smith et al. 1988], most concepts—including most lexical concepts—are complex representations whose structure encodes a statistical analysis of the properties their members tend to have. . . . [A]pplication is a matter of satisfying a sufficient number of features, where some may be weighted more significantly than others." The present analysis is not inherently statistical, although learning doubtless involves some statistical correlation of attributes. However, the differences between the two approaches remain to be explored.

The present account must also be distinguished from the view that a concept is a representation of a prototypical instance. On the present account, the prototype is simply an instance that happens to maximally satisfy the cluster conditions. This does not preclude concepts from being linked to standard instances (section 11.4)—it's just that this creates distinct effects from the cluster conditions.

Most of the arguments against cluster concepts are directed against this latter version of the prototype theory. For instance, Fodor (1998) argues that the standard *pet fish* (goldfish, guppy, etc.) cannot be derived from the intersection of prototypical *pets* (dog, cat, etc.) with prototypical *fish* (trout, flounder, etc.). Quite right. This is because we know about pet fish: *pet fish* is lexicalized and anchored as a unit to its own standard examples such as goldfish. In a similar case that is *not* anchored to standard examples, as in *pet marsupial*, we are likely to imagine precisely the prototypical marsupial, a kangaroo. In terms of conditions, though, *pet fish* comes out about as one would expect: it's a fish that people keep in their house for amusement. I don't see any problem in principle here, as long as one distinguishes knowing standard examples from knowing defeasible conditions. Both are potential parts of a concept.

11.7 The same abstract organization in many semantic fields

A foundational result in conceptualist semantics originates with Gruber (1965), who showed that many grammatical patterns used to describe physical objects in space also appear in expressions that describe non-spatial domains.

The groups of sentences in (13) through (16) illustrate this result. Notice especially the parallels indicated by the italicized words.

(13) Spatial location and motion:
    a. The messenger *is in* Istanbul.   [Location]
    b. The messenger *went from* Paris *to* Istanbul.   [Change of location]
    c. The gang *kept* the messenger *in* Istanbul.   [Caused stasis]

(14) Possession:
    a. The money *is* Fred's.   [Possession]
    b. The inheritance finally *went to* Fred.   [Change of possession]
    c. Fred *kept* the money.   [Caused stasis]

(15) Ascription of properties:
    a. The light *is* red.   [Simple property]
    b. The light *went/changed from* green *to* red. [Change of property]
    c. The cop *kept* the light red.   [Caused stasis]

(16)   Scheduling activities:
    a. The meeting *is on* Monday.   [Simple schedule]
    b. The meeting was *changed from* Tuesday *to* Monday.
                                                        [Change of schedule]
    c. The chairman *kept* the meeting *on* Monday.   [Caused stasis]

Each of these groups contains one sentence with the verb *be*, one with *go* or *change*, and one with *keep*. When *be* appears with a preposition (as in (13a) and (16a)), the same preposition can appear with *keep*; if *be* appears without a preposition (as in (14a) and (15a)), so does *keep*. On the other hand, *go* and *change* characteristically appear along with the prepositions *from* and *to*.

These grammatical patterns cannot be motivated by the physical nature of the situations expressed. Changing possession does not necessarily entail changing location: the sale of a house or of stocks does not involve motion at all. An object's color has nothing to do with where it is or who owns it. Setting the appointed time for a meeting or trip bears no apparent relationship at all to the other three.

On a more abstract level, however, the meanings of the four groups of sentences are parallel.

• The *be* sentences all describe some state of affairs in which some characteristic is ascribed to the subject of the sentence: location in a region in (13), belonging to someone in (14), having a property in (15), and having an appointed time in (16).

• The *go*/*change* sentences all describe a change involving the subject of the sentence, in which it comes to have the characteristic ascribed by the corresponding *be* sentence. The subject's characteristic at the beginning of the change is described by the phrase following *from*, and at the end of the change by the phrase following *to*.

• The *keep* sentences all describe the subject of the sentence causing the object of the sentence to have the characteristic ascribed by the corresponding *be* sentence, and this characteristic persists over a period of time.

In other words, the linguistic parallelism among these sets reveals an underlying conceptual parallelism. Thus it is not accidental that many of the same lexical items recur in (13)–(16).

Gruber's insight behind the conceptual parallelism is this: The characteristics that things can be conceived to have fall into broad families or "semantic fields" such as the headings in (13)–(16). Within a field, *be* sentences express simple characteristics such as being in a particular location, belonging to a particular person, being of a particular color, or being scheduled at a particular time. But in addition, the conceptual system contains complex concepts that can be applied to any field, among which are (a) a change from one characteristic to another (the *go/change* sentences) and (b) something making something else have a particular characteristic over a period of time (the *keep* sentences). Because similarly structured complex concepts appear in many (and possibly all) semantic fields, it is convenient for the language to use the same words as it switches from one field to another.[14]

This underlying abstract system is most evident in semantic fields that vary along a one-dimensional range of values: they invariably are expressed in terms of the linear opposites *up* and *down* or *high* and *low*. Numbers (and hence prices, weights, and temperatures) go up and down, military ranks go up and down, pitches on the musical scale go up and down, and so does one's mood. (Time concepts, however, are a partial exception to this generalization. In just about every language, they are expressed by terms that also apply to space; but instead of *up* and *down*, they use a front-to-back continuum, for example *before* and *after* in English.)

Similar grammatical and lexical patterns appear in language after language. Cognitive linguists such as Talmy (1978; 1985) and Langacker (1987) essentially take them for granted and build theories of conceptual structure around them. Lakoff and Johnson (1980; Lakoff 1987; 1990) argue that they are part of a vast system of metaphor, inextricably embedded in the conceptual structure expressed by language. They further argue that the pervasiveness of metaphor makes it impossible to base a semantic theory on a simplistic notion of "literal truth," and impossible to treat metaphor as non-truth-conditional and therefore marginal.

While acknowledging the ubiquity of metaphor in thought, I would argue for a finer-grained account for these particular phenomena (Jackendoff 1983; 1992a: ch. 3; Jackendoff and Aaron 1991). Lakoff and Johnson use the term "metaphor" for *any* extension of terms from one semantic field to another. By contrast, the traditional notion of metaphor is reserved for creative, novel expressions, often with a patent semantic clash, used to make speech more colorful. The parallels illustrated in (13)–(16) exhibit no semantic clash, and they are the only ways available in English of expressing the concepts in question. Thus they are not metaphorical in the traditional sense. I would contend rather that they reflect a set of precise abstract underlying conceptual patterns that can be applied to many different semantic fields. These patterns are the basic machinery that permits complex thought to be formulated and basic entailments to be derived in any domain. Among these domains, the spatial domain exhibits a certain degree of primacy due to its evolutionary priority

---

[14] "Convenient for the language" is an abbreviation for a variety of factors. Among them: speakers who lack a word for something they want to say will press a conceptually related word into service; learners figure out less concrete meanings more easily if more concrete (especially spatial) parallels are made evident by phonological identity.

and its strong linkage to perception. At the same time, Lakoff and Johnson's insight about the pervasiveness of metaphor still stands, if in a more limited fashion.

These cross-field parallels raise an interesting question of polysemy. Does *keep*, for instance, have a single sense that is neutral as to what field it appears in? Or does it have four related senses? I am inclined to take the latter route, because of the syntactic and lexical peculiarities in each field. For instance, in three out of the four fields above, *keep* requires a direct object and a further complement; but in the possessive field, *keep* takes only a single argument, the direct object. *Go* appears in three of the four fields, but we cannot say **The meeting went from Tuesday to Monday* in the scheduling sense—we can only say *was changed/moved*. *Change* appears with the simple *from–to* syntax only in ascription and scheduling; in the spatial field we have to say *change position/location* and in the possessional field we have to say *change hands*. We also have to know that in English, we say **on** *Monday* rather than **in** *Monday*, the latter certainly a logical possibility. All these little details have to be learned; they cannot be part of the general mapping that relates these fields to each other. This means that each word must specify in which fields it appears and what peculiarities it has in each. Thus we are dealing with semiproductive alternation in the sense of Chapter 6 again. If this be polysemy, so be it.

I have described these as senses related by feature variation. This differs from the usual view in cognitive linguistics that (14)–(16) are derived from (13), the spatial field, by metaphor or image-schema transformation (Lakoff 1987). The two views are compared in (17).

(17) a. Conceptual semantics
          to in (13) = $\text{TO}_{\text{Spatial}}$
          to in (14) = TO_{Poss}
          TO is a path-function that is field-neutral, and the subscripts
          specialize it for a field
      b. Cognitive linguistics
          to in (13) = TO
          to in (14) = $\text{F}_{\text{Poss}}(\text{TO})$
          TO is a spatial path-schema, and F is a function that maps the field of
          spatial images into possessional images

That is, cognitive linguistics tends to view cross-field parallelisms as derivational. Hence the polysemy of *keep* is a multiply branching chain, rather like *smoke* (section 11.3). By contrast, I view them as parallel instantiations of a more abstract schema (Jackendoff 1976, 1983: ch. 10, 1992a; Jackendoff and Aaron

1991; Fauconnier and Turner 1994 propose a somewhat similar view in terms of a "generic space"). Here the polysemy is the result of a feature variation, with no fully specified sense as core.

However these disputes are resolved, all major schools of thought in conceptual and cognitive semantics agree that the linguistic parallelisms shown in (13)–(16) reflect substantive parallelisms in the concepts these sentences express, and thereby reveal fundamental organization in human conceptual structure.

11.8 Function–argument structure across semantic fields

11.8.1 Some basic state- and event-functions

Every theory of semantics back to Frege acknowledges that word meanings may contain variables that are satisfied by arguments expressed elsewhere in the sentence. In Chapter 5, for example, we treated the meaning of eat as a two-place function EAT(X,Y), where X is expressed as the subject of *eat* and Y is optionally expressed as its object. (And we recall that such organization constitutes a challenge for neural network theories of language). Many approaches, including most of formal semantics, leave it at that, simply expressing verb meanings as unanalyzed functions written in capital letters.

However, other approaches take the decomposition of verb meanings seriously, asking if there is a set of primitive functions out of which the semantic argument structure of verbs (and other argument-taking words) can be built. Schank (1973) was an early attempt in the AI tradition; Miller and Johnson-Laird (1976) offered extensive analysis with an attempt to ground verb meanings in psychological primitives; Wierzbicka (1985; 1987; 1996) has offered extensive analyses of verbs in terms of a small set of English words (the latter two in fact deal with far more than just verbs).

My own approach to verb decomposition (Jackendoff 1976; 1983; 1990a) grew initially out of the insights of Gruber discussed in the previous section; a similar approach in quite a different notation appears in cognitive grammar (Langacker 1987). The most basic unit is a two-place function BE(X,Y), supplemented by a *field feature*. The field feature determines the character of the arguments of BE and the sorts of inferences that can be drawn. If the field feature is *Spatial*, X is an object and Y is a location where X is located. This configuration in CS interfaces with the SpS conceptualization of space and the associated inferences; it is the configuration expressed, for instance, in our old favorite, *The little star is beside a big star*. If the field feature on BE(X,Y) is *Possession*, X is an object and Y is a person who owns it; this configuration invokes inference rules about rights to use and so forth.[15] If the field feature is Ascription, X is just about anything and Y is a Property or a Kind to which it belongs; this configuration invokes whatever inferences follow from the ascribed Property or Kind. If it is Scheduling, X is an Event and Y is a time period; the inferences concern the time at which there is an opportunity to participate in the event.

BE(X,Y) is of the ontological category *State*: it is the conceptualization of a static configuration that can be localized at a point in time or throughout an interval of time. This is the function underlying all the "be" verbs in (13)–(16). Another basic function is STAY(X,Y), which is just like BE except that it is of the ontological category *Event*: it is the conceptualization of a static configuration being maintained over a period of time. This underlies verbs like *stay, maintain,* and *continue*; for instance notice the difference between *the little star was beside a big star* and *the little star stayed beside a big star*. STAY is a component of the "keep" verbs in (13)–(16).

Underlying the *go* verbs in (13)–(16) is a function GO(X,Y). In each field, X is as before, but Y is now a Path or Trajectory, and GO(X,Y) is the conceptualization of the Event of X traversing Y. One way to build a Path is illustrated in (13)–(16): designate a beginning point (or Source), marked by *from*, and/or an endpoint (or Goal), marked by *to*. Some early approaches such as Gruber (1965), Schank (1973), and Jackendoff (1976) recognized only this possibility. However, particularly in the spatial domain, there are other possibilities. The simplest is to designate a *direction: The airplane went up/north/thataway.* Another is to designate the shape of the trajectory, as in *round and round* and *zigzag*. A third way, for instance *go along the river/past the house*, does not say where motion started or ended, but specifies the configuration of an intermediate point; I have called such Paths "Routes."

Paths can have some of this structure in certain other semantic fields as well. For instance, in Ascription one can specify a direction (*The temperature went up*) or an intermediate point (*The temperature passed through 100 degrees on its way to record heights*). On the other hand, Possession is a discontinuous "space," with no intermediate points between one possessor and another: something can be halfway between two spatial locations A and B, but something cannot be halfway between belonging to A and belonging to B. Thus, by virtue of the inference patterns having to do with Possession, the only Paths in this field are Source–Goal Paths.

---

[15] I glide over the distinction between ownership and merely temporary control, as when one borrows something. Both of these are distinct from "inalienable possession," which often uses the same vocabulary, as in *The house has a roof*. The latter involves things having parts, bringing yet another set of inference rules into play.

When the Path is a Source–Goal pattern (*from W to Z*), the second argument of GO has its own function–argument structure—which is why Path-prepositions take syntactic objects. We can notate the composite as (18), where Z is the Source and W the Goal.

(18)
$$
\text{GO} \left(\text{X}, \left[\begin{array}{l} \text{FROM (W)} \\ _{\text{Path}} \ \text{TO (Z)} \end{array} \right] \right)
$$

The characteristic inference from (18) can be stated informally as (19).[16]

(19)   At the beginning of (18), BE(X,W)
       At the end of (18), BE(X,Z)

(19) is independent of semantic field. However, the consequent clauses of (19) lead to the characteristic field-specific inferences for BE described above, which add further aspects of interpretation.

In much of the literature, Paths are recognized only in the context of motion along a path, and therefore Path has been thought of as a partly temporal notion (e.g. Hinrichs 1985 and Verkuyl 1993). (18) recognizes Path as a distinct ontological type, and motion or change over time is expressed solely by the function GO. Paths themselves are atemporal, and can appear as arguments of other functions, including the two kinds of state-function shown in (20).

(20)   a. EXT(X,Path)
           Non-temporal extension: *The road goes across the river.*
       b. ORIENT(X,Path)
           Orientation: *The sign points across the river.*

The inferences from these functions are quite different than from GO. In a motion event (GO), X is located at different parts of the Path at different times. In a state of extension like (20a), different parts of X occupy different parts of the Path, all at once.[17] In a state of orientation like (20b), the sign is oriented along the Path, but it neither travels along it nor occupies it. Without an independent category of Path, it would be impossible to unify these disparate uses, showing why they can all be expressed by the same preposition.

---

[16] Making it more formal requires characterizing 'beginning' and 'end', for instance as in Jackendoff (1991; 1996b).

[17] It is often contended (e.g. Talmy 1996a) that extension is "metaphorical" or "fictive" motion, giving the sense of an observer scanning the extended object. Although this has some intuitive appeal, I just don't see how it can account for the difference in inference patterns. Jackendoff (1996c) offers a formal decomposition of GO and EXT that brings out their similarities and differences.

The five functions listed so far (BE, STAY, GO, EXT, and ORIENT) are major members of a family of "core functions" around which situations (States and Events) are organized. Another family constitutes "aspectual functions." The most prominent of these is Inchoative, INCH(X), a one-place function whose argument is a State; it denotes an Event of this state coming about. For instance, the relation between the adjective *open*$_1$ and the intransitive verb *open*$_2$ (examples (6a, b)) is that *open*$_2$ conceptualizes the coming about (INCH) of the state of being *open*$_1$. A sort of converse of INCH is the Perfective, PERF(X), a function whose argument is an Event, and which denotes the State of that Event being complete. It is seen most clearly as the perfect tense in sentences like *Sue has eaten lunch*—roughly, 'Sue is presently in the state of having completed eating lunch.' We will see more formally how INCH combines with the core functions in a moment.[18]

A third family of functions is the causative family, which includes CAUSE, LET, and HELP in various Eventive and Stative versions, again relativized to semantic field. CAUSE has two obligatory arguments, the Agent and the Effect, and an optional argument, the Patient. (21) makes these options clearer.

(21) a. The wind made it rain.
        CAUSE (WIND, [$_{Event}$ IT-RAIN])
            Agent   Effect
        'the wind caused the event of its raining'
    b. The wind made me fall down.
        CAUSE (WIND, ME,   [$_{Event}$ I FALL DOWN])
            Agent Patient Effect
        'the wind, acting on me, caused the event of my falling down'

My intuition is that the three-argument version (21b) is preferred when possible; but in the absence of an identifiable Patient on which the Agent can act, the two-argument version (21a) is a fallback. LET works the same way; HELP has only the three-argument version. These three functions are related by features in a fashion sketched in section 11.2.

Readers more familiar with standard formal semantics may recognize in

---

[18] An important result of Jackendoff (1991) is that INCH and TO have identical further decompositions, except that one pertains to situations and one to space: they both denote a one-dimensional directed entity end-bounded by their argument. This leads to a quark-like feature decomposition of the ontological categories, as suggested in section 11.1. Jackendoff (1996c) shows how this common decomposition contributes to the computation of aspectuality of a sentence.

these families of functions a nonstandard version of type logic.[19] Instead of the usual primitive types e and t (individuals and truth values, respectively—the two possible types to which expressions can refer, according to Frege), this approach has a much broader range of primitive types: the major ontological categories Object, Event, and so forth. Using the standard notation $<a,b>$ to denote a function from semantic objects of type a into semantic objects of type b, we can encode the types of these functions as follows:

(22)　a. BE: $<(x,y),$ State>, X and Y an ordered pair, where the types of X and Y depend on semantic field[20]

　　b. STAY: $<(x,y),$ Event> (same stipulations as 22a)

　　c. GO: <(Object, Path), Event>

　　d. EXT, ORIENT: <(Object, Path), State>

　　e. TO, FROM: <x, Path>, where the type of X depends on semantic field

　　f. INCH: <State, Event>

　　g. PERF: <Event, State>

　　h. CAUSE, HELP, LET (three-argument version):
　　　　<(Object/Event, Object, Event), Event>

　　i. CAUSE, LET (two-argument version):
　　　　<(Object/Event, Event), Event>

(22) may seem like a major departure from type logic. However, I have encountered no empirical arguments that e and t are the correct choice of primitive types—only methodological arguments based on the desire to minimize primitives. In the end, the parsimony of a logic containing only two primitive types must be weighed against the potential explanatory power of a richer system; it is an empirical issue, not just a methodological one. Another difference from a more standard type logic is that the category corresponding to a sentence is an Event or State rather than a truth value, as argued in Chapter 10. A truth value can be seen as the evaluation of the Event or State expressed by the sentence with respect to world as conceptualized. Again, this choice is to be weighed on empirical grounds.

11.8.2 Building verb meanings

These functions can be used to build up revealing skeletons of verb and preposition

---

[19] A different interpretation of this notation as a type logic is worked out in Zwarts and Verkuyl (1994).

[20] There is no problem in principle reducing the functions of two and three variables in (22) to the more standard successively embedded functions of a single variable; however, I have found no particularly compelling reason to do so at the present level of detail of the theory.

meanings that explain their argument structure.[21] For instance, (23) shows how a simple sentence of motion expresses a conceptual structure in this format. (I omit the semantic field feature, which is Spatial, as well as the interpretations of the Tense and the definite article.)

(23) a. Syntax and phonology:
          [John]$_i$ went$_j$ [into$_k$ [the room]$_m$]
      b. CS:
          [$_{Event}$ GO ([$_{Object}$ JOHN]$_i$, [$_{Path}$ TO ([$_{Place}$ IN ([$_{Object}$ ROOM]$_m$)])]$_k$)]$_j$

In this example, the verb *went* expresses the function GO(X,Y); the other constituents—the NP *John* and the PP *into the room*—express its arguments. *Into* means roughly 'to in': it expresses a Path-function whose argument is a Place, which itself has a function–argument structure (not discussed in the previous subsection—see Jackendoff 1990a). The syntactic argument of *into* expresses the argument of this Place.

As the labeled bracketing (23b) may be a bit difficult to read, I offer the alternative tree notation in (24), where functions are attached by double lines and their arguments by single lines. (*John* and *room*, as phrasal heads, are treated as a zero-argument functions, i.e. constants.) The contributions of each word are picked out by dashed lines; the overlaps between them are the points of attachment where variables are satisfied.[22]

(24)

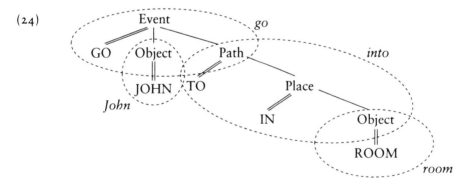

Another way to express the structure (23b) is *John entered the room*. In this case the verb "incorporates" the Path- and Place-functions, as in (25a); the lexical entry of the verb thus decomposes as (25b).

---

[21] This strategy was recognized already by Gruber (1965), and, in a different guise, it played an important role in the Generative Semantics analyses of verb meanings (McCawley 1968; Postal 1970a). A recent version of the Generative Semantics approach has resurfaced in Hale and Keyser (1993); see Jackendoff (1997a: 231–2) for commentary.

[22] Yet a different notation is offered by Nikanne (1990; 2000a).

(25) a.

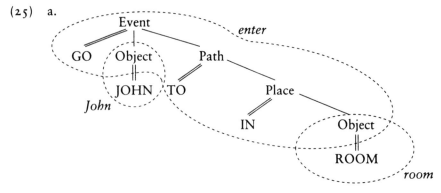

b. /ɛntr/$_i$ V$_i$ [$_{Event}$ GO ([$_{Object}$ X]$_{obl}$, [$_{Path}$ TO ([$_{Place}$ IN ([$_{Object}$ Y])])])]$_i$

The two open arguments X and Y in (25b) are both Objects, which must both be expressed by NP arguments. Hence *enter* is a transitive verb. A similar analysis gives us the transitive verbs *approach* ('go toward'), *leave* ('go from'), and *pass* ('go past').

Now suppose we "incorporate" the Path-function DOWNWARD into a verb along with GO: [$_{Event}$ GO ([$_{Object}$ X], [$_{Path}$ DOWNWARD])]. Since DOWNWARD requires no argument, only one argument is left to be satisfied. This gives us the meaning of the intransitive verb *fall*. Next suppose we incorporate something into the remaining argument of GO, lexically specifying what falls. Then there are no arguments left for the syntax to satisfy, and we get zero-argument verbs such as *rain* and *snow*.

Let me do one more such case. The verb *put* requires three syntactic arguments: *Fran put the food in the fridge.* It decomposes as a causative inchoative: 'Fran caused the food to come to be in the fridge.' In tree form, the decomposition looks like (26).

(Recall that 'INCH' is inchoative, 'come to be'. I use here the three-argument

(26)

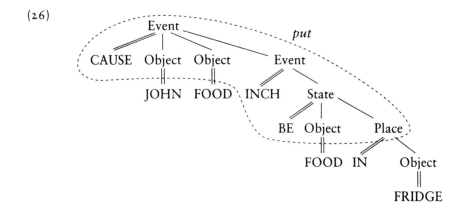

version of CAUSE, as in (21b), with *food* as an explicit Patient.). The very same conceptual configuration can be realized lexically in other ways, by "incorporating" larger parts of the tree in (26). Here are two possibilities, representing two classes of transitive denominal verbs.

(27)   a. Bill buttered the bread

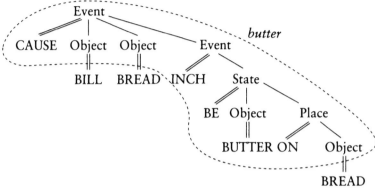

b. Paul pocketed the penny

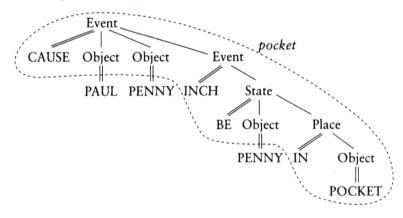

Similar incorporation structures are involved in some of the cases of polysemy discussed in sections 11.2 and 11.3. For instance, if the meaning of the adjective *open₁* is (28a), then the intransitive verb *open₂* is (28b) and the transitive *open₃* is (28c). (28c) is identical to (27a) aside from the arguments of BE.

(28)   a. open₁ = Property
                     ‖
                    OPEN

b. NP$_a$ open$_2$ =

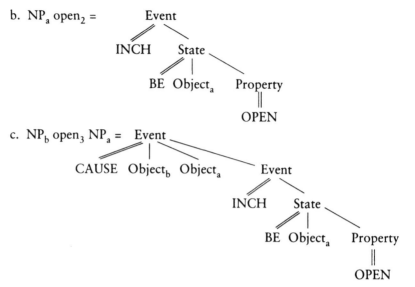

c. NP$_b$ open$_3$ NP$_a$ =

The cores of the verbs *smoke*$_3$, 'smoke (a cigar)', and *smoke*$_5$, 'smoke (a ham)', can be seen as variants on the structure (27a) as well. Ignoring the specialized manner modifiers discussed in section 11.3, these are roughly 'cause smoke$_1$ to go out of a cigar' and 'cause smoke$_1$ to go into a ham' respectively. (I leave the tree structures as an exercise for the compulsive reader.)

This exercise shows how decomposition into functions brings out explicit similarities and differences among verb meanings, how these cut across patterns of syntactic expression, and how relations among readings of polysemous items can be made explicit. In particular, "thematic roles" such as Agent, Patient, Source, and Goal are determined in structural terms in CS, so their partial lack of systematicity in syntax (section 5.8) is a function of the way CS maps into words and syntactic structure.

There is no room here to go into more detail, in particular the fascinating cross-linguistic differences in patterns of incorporation, first brought to light by Talmy (1980); the way semantics affects alternations in the syntactic argument structure of verbs (Pinker 1989; Levin 1993; Jackendoff 1990a); the maximal event structure associated with a clause (Levin and Rappoport Hovav 1996; Rappaport Hovav and Levin 1998; Nikanne 1990), and the decomposition of preposition meanings (Brugman 1981; Herskovits 1986; Vandeloise 1986; Landau and Jackendoff 1993; and many papers in Bloom et al. 1996). The overall picture, however, is that it is of great interest to construct such decompositions. Each primitive function, relativized to semantic field, gives a concept access to characteristic inference patterns; and in the spatial field, to perceptual patterns as well.

Fodor (1998) objects to such decomposition, on the grounds that we have gotten no closer to explicating meaning if the meanings of the primitives have not themselves been explained (this is also Lewis's 1972 objection to "Markerese", quoted in section 10.4). My working hypothesis is that the meaning of the primitives is exhausted by (a) their capacity for combination with other primitives and (b) their use in triggering inference rules and interface rules, individually and in combination. But I acknowledge that this remains to be demonstrated.

Another major challenge is to enumerate the primitives and the inference rules. The spatial field has been well served, but other fields such as mental verbs and verbs of social interaction have hardly been touched (though Wierzbicka 1987 goes into considerable detail within her somewhat less structural approach). Finally, functional decompositions such as (24)–(27) are only skeletal, and there is the usual problem of "completers": can we characterize the rest of the meaning? Even as greater success is achieved in functional decomposition, it is important to keep these larger questions in mind.

11.9 Qualia structure: characteristic activities and purposes

By comparison with verbs, the compositional semantics of nouns has been relatively neglected. James Pustejovsky (1995) proposes two major innovations that take the theory of noun meanings beyond mere lists of features: qualia structure and dot objects. We take these up in order.

Pustejovsky's theory of qualia structure includes three major points. First, following suggestions of Aristotle (via Julius Moravcsik), one can partition the properties of lexical concepts into a number of distinct types called "qualia." Second, these properties need not be single monadic features like [HAS-A-BACK]; they may themselves have rich internal structure. Third, the meaning of a sentence cannot be constructed by the simple technique of gluing together the meanings of its words. Rather, the information within the qualia structure plays an active role in constructing the connections among word meanings in a sentence, a process called "co-composition."

Pustejovsky identifies four qualia: formal, constitutive, agentive, and telic. I do not take this to be an exhaustive list, but it is useful in classifying properties of a great number of concepts.[23] The formal quale includes the taxonomic structure discussed in section 11.4, for instance that a dog is a kind of animal, a kind of living thing, and a physical object. It might also look downward in the tax-

---

[23] In the interests of coherence, I have distributed certain properties among the qualia somewhat differently than Pustejovsky. I do not take these differences to be of any great theoretical significance.

onomy, specifying what subtypes of dogs there are and perhaps some salient instances.

The constitutive quale includes information about an entity's structural attributes. These attributes appear to divide into three subtypes:

• The entity's sensory attributes: dimensionality, shape, size, color, texture, weight, smell, and so forth.

• The material(s) the entity is composed of.

• The entity's part structure; if it is itself inherently a part (such as a wing), what larger structure it is a part of.

When the entity is a physical object, much of this structure will interface with the associated Spatial Structure, as suggested in section 11.5.

The other two qualia are more complex in that they involve actions in which the entity is a character. The agentive quale encodes information about how the entity comes into existence: if an artifact, how it is made; if an organism, its life-cycle stages. Pustejovsky views this as encoding primarily the entity's past. However, this quale might also encode information about what an entity will develop into. For instance, an *embryo* is characterized as something that will grow into an animal; a *fiancée* is someone who is to be married. Of course, an embryo might in fact be aborted and a fiancée might break off the engagement, so a specification of future developmental course must be properly modulated, a point to which we return below.

The telic quale gives information about activities in which the entity takes part. Pustejovsky envisions this quale primarily as encompassing an object's purpose, for instance that a pencil is for writing with. However, it makes sense to include here a range of other sorts of action. For instance, the moon has no purpose per se, but we need to encode our knowledge of its characteristic actions, for instance that it moves across the sky and changes shape in a monthly cycle. The telic quale is the natural place to localize this information.

Another important sort of information is how the entity "works." For instance, pencil sharpeners all have the purpose of sharpening pencils, but different subtypes accomplish this function through different actions on the part of the user. These different subtypes can be differentiated by form in the constitutive quale, and the way each works will be differentiated in the telic quale. (By extension, the fact that pencils need to be periodically sharpened presumably belongs in the telic quale of *pencil* too.)

Another possibility in the telic quale is an activity in which the entity is currently engaged. This is necessary to characterize words such as *pedestrian, passenger*, and *customer* (Busa 1996; Macnamara and Reyes 1994). I may often walk to work, but on those occasions that I drive I am not a pedestrian. As many have observed, such a specification results in an entity's being individuated by occasions in which it takes part in the activity: American Airlines may have carried three million *passengers* but only one million different *people*, thanks to lots of frequent flyers.

Returning to purposes, consider a word like *mail*. What makes something *mail* rather than a piece of paper is (in part) that it is intended to be sent and delivered; for instance being burnable is not an essential part of being mail. But let us be a bit more specific about "intended to be sent and delivered." Sometimes it happens that a piece of mail is not sent, or, more commonly, alas, that it is not delivered. So these activities do not constitute necessary conditions for something to be mail. On the other hand, they are too important to the understanding of the concept of mail to be described as mere "tendencies" or "probabilistic associated activity." I believe the correct characterization is to be found in Ruth Millikan's notion of "proper function." Roughly, "having a proper function is a matter of having been 'designed to' or of being 'supposed to' (impersonal) perform a certain function" (Millikan 1984: 17). An object need not *actually* ever perform its proper function. Millikan's striking example is a sperm, only one of millions of which ever performs its proper function of fertilizing an egg. This can hardly be described as a "tendency" or a "probabilistically associated activity." This modality for proper functions—the possibility that the activity never takes place but is yet essential—is also just what we need for the cases of *embryo* and *fiancée* discussed above.

What kinds of things can have proper functions? There are two major classes. The first is *artifacts*: objects constructed by volitional beings who have some function in mind for the objects, or who benefit from their functioning. As Millikan is quick to point out, we want to include here not just concrete artifacts such as pencils and beaver dams but also abstract artifacts such as myths and contracts. Millikan is particularly concerned with claiming that beliefs have a proper function, namely to guide reasoning and action. She can then say that false beliefs still have a proper function; it is just that, like undelivered mail, they fail to fulfill it.

A second important class of objects with proper functions is *parts*. In the case of parts of artifacts such as the back of a chair, the proper function is clear: it serves as a part of the proper function of the artifact. But in addition the parts of organisms have one or more proper functions: the heart is to pump blood, the kidney is to remove wastes from the blood, the leaves of a plant are to perform photosynthesis, and so forth.

A possible variant on proper function is occupation, which is in complementary distribution with proper function: only humans (and perhaps animals like sheepdogs, bloodhounds, and packhorses) have occupations; only artifacts and object parts have proper functions. One might therefore consider occupation to be a special type of proper function, relativized to humans and domestic animals.

I am inclined to see proper function as a basic element of human conceptualization (and here I fundamentally diverge from Millikan's realist approach). It is not without significance that children are inclined to ascribe proper functions to more things than adults do (Kelemen 1999), for example *A lake is to swim in*, *The sun is to keep us warm*. A lot of science (including evolutionary theory) has been concerned with removing unwarranted teleology from our understanding of the natural world; Skinner just went too far in trying to remove it from our understanding of behavior.

In sum, an entity's telic quale encodes actions in which the entity takes part, modulated by a modality such as characteristic action, current action, characteristic function, and proper function. The telic quale is the locus for forming the meaning of so-called agentive (*-er*) nominals (Aronoff 1980; Busa 1996). For instance, *driver* has a telic quale 'X drives'. If a person, it can denote a person who is currently driving or whose occupation is driving; if an artifact, it denotes something whose proper function is driving (e.g. a golf club or a driving wheel on a locomotive).

A somewhat more complex relation appears in words like *violinist*. A violinist is someone whose activity (telic quale) is playing the violin. But the activity 'playing' is not overtly specified (as in *violin player*). Rather it comes from the meaning of *violin*. A further expansion yields 'person whose activity is using a violin in its proper function (namely playing it).' In addition, the playing of a *violinist* can be either an occupation (29a), a characteristic activity (29b), or even just a current activity (29c).

(29) a. Linda is a violinist in the symphony, but she hasn't played for months, since they've been on strike.
  b. Jerome is an occasional violinist.
  c. Oddly enough, none of the violinists in the orchestra tonight have ever played the violin before—that's why they sound so bad.

Words don't have to be derived morphologically in order to have this sort of complexity in their telic quale. For instance, *fuel* is a substance whose proper function is to burn, this function in turn forming a part of the proper function of something else. The something else can be made explicit in a variety of ways, for instance *fuel for a rocket, rocket fuel*.

Pustejovsky motivates qualia structure by showing that it is necessary for understanding the direct objects of verbs like *begin* and *enjoy*. These verbs require an activity as their semantic argument: one begins *doing* things and enjoys *doing* things. Yet they occur syntactically with direct objects such as *begin/enjoy the book* and *begin/enjoy the beer*. Such sentences are understood (in the default case) as 'begin/enjoy *reading* the book' and 'begin/enjoy *drinking* the beer' (an observation appearing also in Newmeyer 1969/75). Pustejovsky observes that the default activity necessary to understand these direct objects comes from the telic quale of the nouns themselves: books are for reading, beer is for drinking. Thus, he argues, qualia structure is on occasion necessary in order to accomplish the semantic composition of a verb and its object, normally the province of simple variable satisfaction. (Section 12.2 takes up other cases where simple variable satisfaction is insufficient.)

Finally, qualia structure can also be adapted to activities, whether expressed by verbs or nouns.[24] In particular, argument structure falls into the formal quale; for instance, the formal quale of *sprint* will say it is a type of locomotion, and therefore involves a character traversing a path. The constitutive quale will include the rapid (and effortful?) character of the motion. The agentive quale will perhaps specify that the activity arises from the character's will to move, i.e. it is not a passive motion like falling. More generally, the agentive quale would include causes and reasons that give rise to the activity in question. Purposes (proper functions) also occur as part of verb meanings. For example, the meaning of *chase* must specify that the subject's purpose is to catch the object. This information might be encoded in the telic quale (or possibly in the agentive quale, as proper outcome).

11.10 Dot objects

Pustejovsky's other important innovation grows out of the observation that certain classes of objects belong to more than one taxonomy. One such class consists of information-bearing objects such as novels and newspapers. As a physical object, a novel has a size and weight, and it has covers and pages as parts. But a novel also bears information which is about a topic and represents certain events pertaining to that topic. As a physical object, the novel came into existence by being printed and bound; as an information object, it came into existence by being written. And yet the word *novel* is not ambiguous or polysemous, since both aspects can be invoked at once: *That novel about the Crimean War has a red cover.*

Pustejovsky formalizes this dual aspect of an information-bearing object by

---

[24] It is not clear to me that Pustejovsky's way of carrying out this extension is altogether optimal or consistent. In this informal account I will attempt to express the basic insight as I myself see it; Pustejovsky is not to be held responsible.

concatenating its two taxonomic features within the formal quale, as in (30). He calls this concatenation a *dot object*.

(30)   [PHYSICAL OBJECT•INFORMATION]

In turn, each of these aspects gives rise to further qualia structure. The physical object's constitutive quale describes the physical makeup of a book; the telic quale includes how books are sold and stored; the agentive quale includes how books are printed and bound. The information's constitutive quale describes what the information depicts—if a novel, under a modality designating the information as fiction. The telic quale says the information is intended for amusement; the agentive quale says that the information is made up by a novelist. In addition, there are two crucial links between the dual qualia structures. The constitutive qualia are linked by the fact that the physical object bears the information. The telic qualia are linked by the fact that people read books, a physical activity whose outcome is the reader's assimilation of the information borne by the physical object. The upshot of this innovation is that qualia structure goes even further beyond a list of features. Dot objects have a richly interconnected pair of qualia structures.

And there can be dot-object activities. We have already come across one: *reading* consists of two "dotted" actions: the action of visually scanning a writing-bearing (dot-)object, combined with the action of assimilating the information therein. Another prominent case is speech acts, which involve both making a noise and transmitting information of which the noise is the vehicle.

Perhaps the most important dot-object in the conceptual system is the concept of a person. On one hand, a person is conceptualized as a physical object, and all the predicates pertaining to physical objects can be applied to people: spatial extent and location, construction out of parts, the possibility of motion and of contact with other physical objects, susceptibility to gravity, and so on. On the other hand, a person is conceptualized simultaneously as a mind or a self or (dare we say it) a soul. This aspect is *not* physical, and if it has parts, they are things like memory and will rather than arms and legs. The predicates pertaining to the mind are mental and social predicates, having to do with volition, memory, understanding, social roles, rights and obligations.

These two components are universally conceptualized as separable. In particular, every culture is concerned with what happens to the mind/self/soul after death, when the body reverts to a mere physical object. All cultures I've ever read of have a notion of spirits or ghosts—minds/selves/souls lacking a body, but capable of acts of will and memory, and of entering into social relationships with each other and with ordinary people. The notion of reincarnation is widespread—minds/selves/souls coming to occupy a different body. On a more mundane level, we sometimes have dreams in which someone who looks like one person is "really" someone else (*I was talking to Uncle Harold but for some reason he looked like Bill Clinton*). In such cases a mind/self/soul has been "dotted" with a different body.

The "dotted" aspects of speech acts are each connected to the appropriate "dotted" aspects of the speaker: the body makes the noise, thereby conveying the information "contained in" the mind. Interestingly, social roles, which are abstract concepts in the mental/social domain, are often embodied in the physical domain by "dotting" them with aspects of physical appearance such as uniforms, costumes, or haircuts. These physical aspects thus become symbols of the social role: a symbol is one object regarded as simultaneously something else, hence yet another sort of dot-object.

It remains as a challenge for future research to work out the details of dot-objects and their qualia structure, and to sort out which aspects are innate (surely some of them must be) and which are culturally determined. In particular, what kinds of ontological entity can be "dotted" with each other and how can they be connected in qualia structure? Are the possibilities totally open, or is there a delimited set (say several dozen or a hundred) of dot-object types? However the answer turns out, it raises further questions of principle and of detail for learning and evolution.

11.11 Beyond

I want to touch briefly on one further layer of complexity in lexical semantics before closing this chapter.

One of the classic examples of lexical decomposition is *bachelor*, analyzed by Katz and Fodor (1963) as 'unmarried adult human male.' This is often taken as a parade case of analytic decomposition. But consider the putative feature 'unmarried': what sort of feature is this anyway? It is approximately on a par with [HAS-A-BACK] in the analysis of *chair*. It is certainly not primitive, but any attempt to further decompose it requires a whole analysis of the social institution of marriage. That is, the meaning of *bachelor* is inseparable from the understanding of a complicated social framework in which it is embedded. Lakoff (1987) makes much of this fact; he observes, for instance, that it is odd to speak of the Pope as a bachelor, because the Pope falls outside the social institutions in which marriage is an available option. In addition, of course, it is odd to consider an adult unmarried man living in a long-term relationship with a woman as a bachelor. Obviously 'unmarried' is not a sufficient condition. The upshot is that the prospects for a simple analytic feature decomposition for *bachelor* dissolve *in favor of* something with a great deal more implicit structure, in particular overall understanding of larger social frames.

Another such case, raised by Searle (1995), is a *point* in a game. The idea behind points is that they are abstract units that you acquire in the course of a game, and in order to win you need more of them than the other player at the end of the game. How you get points depends on the rules of the game; your reasons for wanting them make sense only in the context of understanding games and what it means to win or lose them. In other words, the conceptual structure of *point* cannot be constructed independently of its embedding in a whole elaborate social frame.

A third example, from Fillmore and Atkins (1992), is the semantics of *risk*. This word has multiple argument structures and is thus polysemous in the sense of section 11.3. (31) gives four of the many frames in which it occurs.

(31) a. We decided to risk going into the jungle.
      b. We risked our lives by going into the jungle.
      c. We risked getting sick by going into the jungle.
      d. There's quite a bit of risk in going into the jungle.

On Fillmore and Atkins's analysis, all these uses advert to a common conceptual frame: the subject is choosing an action which in turn leads to a chance of either benefit or harm; the subject of course hopes to get the benefit. In (31a), *going into the jungle* refers to the chosen action; in (31b), *our lives* is the thing potentially harmed; in (31c) *getting sick* is the harmful action itself. In all of these, *risk* is a verb that appears to refer to the making of the risky choice. In (31d), *risk* is a noun that appears to refer to the chance of harm versus benefit. The point is that all these meanings are different, but they are related by virtue of picking out different parts of the common conceptual frame. Hence again a word meaning cannot be explicated without making use of a larger implicit frame of related circumstances.

I think a larger implicit frame of reference is also necessary to understand proper names of fictional characters. *Santa Claus* is understood properly only in the context of the "Santa Claus legend" of reindeer, going down the chimney with presents, and so forth; *Hamlet* makes sense only in the context of the play.

My inclination is to think that these examples are just the tip of the iceberg and that there is a great deal more complexity to be explored in word meanings. One may be tempted to shrug all this off as "encyclopedic" meaning, hence not part of linguistics. However, as Chapter 9 argued, on the one hand there is no principled dividing line between linguistic and encyclopedic meaning, and on the other hand *someone* has to study these more complex aspects of meaning eventually. So why not linguists?

In closing this chapter, let me briefly return to the issue of lexical decomposition raised in section 11.2. It should be clear by now that the generalizations of word meaning cannot be studied without a theory of lexical decomposition. The kind of decomposition required, however, is not a simple list of necessary and sufficient features of the sort envisioned by Tarski and Fodor. Rather, it is a richly textured system whose subtleties we are only beginning to appreciate: division into CS and SpS components, conditions that shade away from focal values, conditions that operate in a cluster system, features that cut across semantic fields, function–argument structure, qualia structure, and dot-object structure. It does remain to be seen whether all this richness eventually boils down to a system built from primitives, or if not, what alternative there may be. And it does remain to be seen whether lexical meaning can be exhaustively constituted by the techniques discussed here. But even if the ultimate answers are not in sight, there is certainly a sense of progress since the primitive approaches of the 1960s.

It should be recognized that there are fundamental methodological and expository difficulties in doing lexical semantics. What does it take to be properly systematic? It is all too easy to build an industry on the endless details of a single word; good examples are *belief* and *knowledge* in the traditional philosophical literature and *over* in the cognitive linguistics tradition. The unfortunate result is that one loses sight of the goal of a systematic account of the *patterns* of meaning. Alternatively, one can look for the patterns by covering a broad range of words somewhat less deeply; but the result is all too often a tiring list, impossible for any but the most dedicated reader to assimilate. Alas, Pinker's (1989) study of verb frames and much of Anna Wierzbicka's work (e.g. 1987), although amazingly clever and insightful, tend to fall prey to this problem; the present chapter may as well. Perhaps there is no way out: there are just so many goddamned words, and so many parts to them.

On the other hand, these difficulties in themselves point out one of the fundamental messages of generative linguistics: *We language users know so much*. And hence *as children we learned so much*—starting with some innate conceptual basis of unknown richness. Next to lexical semantics, the acquisition problem for grammar pales by comparison.

CHAPTER 12

Phrasal Semantics

This chapter is concerned with how the meaning of a phrase or sentence is composed, using in part the meanings of its words. An account of phrasal semantics is in a sense the most demanding overall task for grammatical theory: the whole point of having a grammar is in order to express phrasal semantics, and practically every resource of the system ends up playing a role. Thus it is also a fitting end for the present study, in that it allows us to bring many different threads of our discussion together.

We begin with the simplest cases, in which the word meanings plus the syntactic structure are sufficient to determine the relevant aspects of phrasal meaning. We continue to more elaborate cases where phrasal and sentence meaning take on a life of their own, incorporating elements not present in the words. We then motivate dividing conceptual structure into tiers, along the lines of phonological structure, each tier conveying a different aspect of sentence meaning. We conclude with a brief foray beyond the sentence, asking what makes larger units such as conversations and narratives cohere.

12.1 Simple composition

The simplest cases of phrasal combination in semantics fall into three types: variable satisfaction, modification, and lambda extraction. In each of these cases, the meaning comes entirely from the words in the phrase plus some minimal structural organization.

12.1.1 *Argument satisfaction*

Chapters 5 and 11 have already presented one of the major ways that word meanings combine into sentence meanings: through satisfaction of argument structure. The standard case involves verbs. As shown in section 5.8, a verb typically expresses a conceptual function of zero to four open variables; these variables are satisfied by the meanings of the subject and complements of the verb's clause. For example, the meaning of the verb *like* includes two variables, the "liker" (an animate Object) and the thing liked (for now an Object, but we will be more general shortly). The general principles of linking (section 5.9) connect these two variables with subject and object position in syntax respectively. Therefore, the lexical entry of *like* plus the linking rules can establish the correspondence shown in (1) between phonological, syntactic, and conceptual structure. (We use LIKE to stand in for the meaning of the verb, for the moment leaving further decomposition aside).[1]

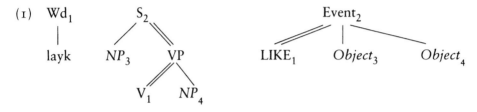

(1)

In (1) the open variables are notated in italics; these must be satisfied in order to make (1) into the structure of an actual sentence. Variables come to be satisfied by being unified with constituents of the appropriate type—in this case NPs in syntactic structure and Objects in conceptual structure. But in addition, (1) stipulates that the NP variables must be linked with the Object variables. Hence they must be satisfied by linked constituents.

The simplest way to achieve such linking is through the lexicon, using proper names as syntactic arguments. The proper names *Beethoven* and *Schubert*, for instance, look like (2a, b).[2]

(2)   a. Wd_5 NP_5 Object_5 b. Wd_6 NP_6 Object_6

      beytowvn   BEETHOVEN   šuwbṛt   SCHUBERT

---

[1] The notation for indices shows its weakness here. The crucial factor is not what actual letters or numbers we use for indices, only which indices are the same and which different. In this chapter I will simply number indices sequentially as I need them.

[2] Persons, the prototypical case of proper names, are actually dot-objects of the type Object•Mind, as argued in section 11.10; we ignore this important detail. In addition, as argued in section 10.9, proper names include an indexical feature, whose role in phrasal semantics we take up in sections 12.3 and 12.4.

To construct the sentence *Beethoven like(s) Schubert* (ignoring tense[3]), we unify the indices numbered 3 in (1) with the indices numbered 5 in (2), and similarly the 4s with the 6s. Note that phonology has no 3 and 4 indices, so nothing in the words alone tells us in what order they are pronounced. Rather, the linear order in phonology comes from the general interface rule that lines up phonological and syntactic linear order (Chapter 5, example (15)).

(3)

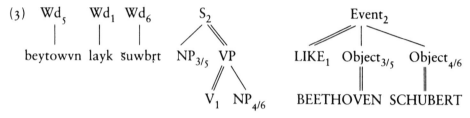

The doubly indexed nodes in (3) are notationally equivalent to the intersecting dashed lines in section 11.8.2: these are nodes that unify the open variable in the material above with the material below, which satisfies the variable.

An overall condition on the well-formedness of a sentence is that all its open variables must be satisfied. For instance, if only one of the variables in (1) is satisfied, we get the ungrammatical **Beethoven like(s)* or **like(s) Schubert*.[4]

Argument satisfaction is not confined to arguments of verbs. For instance, the noun *bride* has a semantic argument, optionally expressed in syntax. If it is expressed, the general linking conditions between syntax and conceptual structure result in the following two possibilities:

(4)

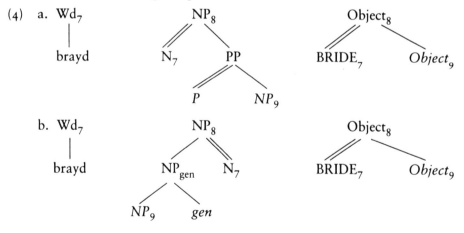

Unifying (2a) with the 9s in (4a) yields the following structure:

(5)

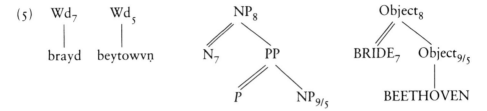

This is still not well-formed, since the syntax of English requires the open syntactic variable *P* to be filled—by an element unlinked to meaning. At this point the defective lexical item *of* steps in to satisfy this remaining variable, without affecting the semantics.

(6)

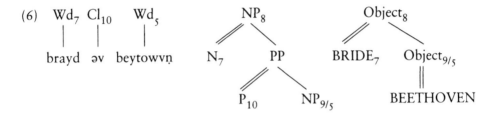

If (2a) is unified with (4b) instead, we get *Beethoven's bride*, in which the -'s affix, like *of*, is a defective lexical item.

The process of variable satisfaction leads to parallel embedding in syntax and semantics. For instance, we can use the composed structure *Beethoven's bride* to satisfy the first argument of *like*, giving us, say, *Beethoven's bride like(s) Schubert*, shown in (7a). *Like* also allows its second conceptual argument to be a situation expressed as a clause. Using this argument structure we can construct a sentence such as *Beethoven likes that Schubert writes music*, (7b). (In the interest of typographical clarity I now notate the phonology in ordinary orthography.[5])

Mechanisms for accomplishing this are available in theories such as HPSG and LFG, and I won't go into them here. Such an analysis may be more generally applicable to "pro-drop" languages such as Italian and Spanish, in which *any* contextually understood subject can be left unexpressed in syntax and phonology, and still more generally to languages like Korean, where all syntactic arguments are optional (section 5.8). The theory does not require us to represent unexpressed semantic arguments as empty NPs, as demanded in syntactocentric architectures.

    [5] I have treated the complementizer *that* in (7b) as a unit needed to fill in the syntax but lacking semantic content, by analogy with the empty preposition *of* and the genitive affix. This may or may not be right, but it's simplest for now.

(7)   a. Beethoven$_5$'s$_{10}$ bride$_7$ like$_1$ Schubert$_6$

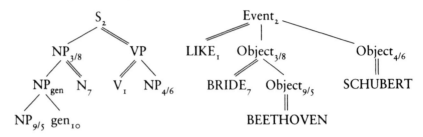

b. Beethoven$_5$ like(s)$_1$ that$_{16}$ Schubert$_6$ write(s)$_{11}$ music$_{15}$

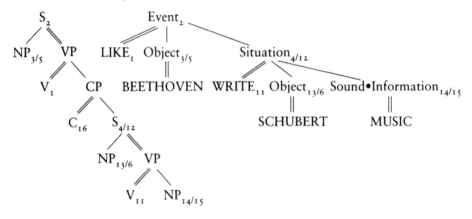

The important thing to see here is that syntactic heads (verbs and nouns) map into conceptual functions (e.g. LIKE, WRITE, BRIDE), and that syntactic subjects and complements map into arguments. Thus the double lines that mark heads correspond in the two structures, as do the single lines that mark arguments.

Glancing back at issues from Chapter 3, recall that it is a mystery how purely associationist neural nets, actual or modeled, can instantiate the satisfaction of open variables of the sort in these structures. Furthermore, each index in these structures needs to be a binding site in working memory—a point where multiple structures are maintained in registration. As remarked in section 3.5, the proliferation of such variables in even the simplest structures such as these also remains a challenge for theories of neural realization.

12.1.2 Modification

Not all cases of phrasal combination involve variable satisfaction. The prototypical example is modification of a noun by an adjective. In *red car*, for instance, *car* does not have a variable position for color. Rather, the property RED simply supplements the other characteristics of the category CAR. Chapter 1, following my earlier practice (Jackendoff 1983; 1990a), notated modification as (8a). The tree notation for conceptual structure might notate it as (8b), where the dotted line stands for a modification relation.

(8) red$_4$ car$_2$

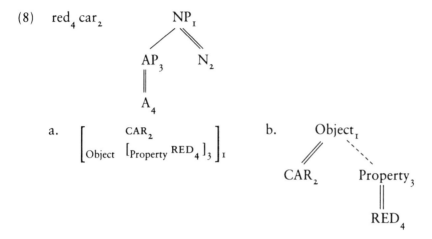

In basic predicate logic, modification is taken to be equivalent to predicate coordination; for example, a red car is something that is a car and is red. However, many cases of modification cannot be so easily paraphrased. For one thing, modification is possible with many combinations of modifier and host, in many different grammatical and conceptual categories, for instance (9).

(9) a. run slowly　　　　　　　[verb/Event, modified by adverb/Property]
　　 b. a house on the hill　　　　[noun/Object, modified by PP/Place]
　　 c. extremely fat　　　　　　[adjective/Property, modified by adverb/Degree]
　　 d. somewhat slowly　　　 [adverb/Property, modified by quantifier/Degree]
　　 e. high on the wall　　　　　[PP/Place, modified by adjective/Property]

Each of these requires a different adjustment in predicate logic notation; I will not dwell on details. By contrast, they all map uniformly into the conceptual structure notation. (10) shows *high on the wall*, where the AP *high* modifies the PP and *the* is taken to be a modifier contributing a conceptual feature of definiteness (as in Chapter 1).

(10)　high$_8$ on$_6$ the$_{11}$ wall$_{10}$

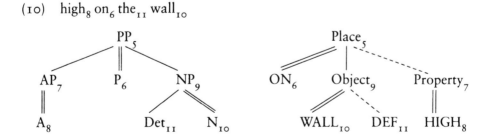

A more potent argument that modification cannot be reduced to predicate conjunction is that many modifiers do not modify their host as a whole, but rather one of its qualia. For instance, a *good knife* is not something that is both a knife and good, as the simple predicate logic translation would have it. Rather it is a knife that *cuts* well, that is, that serves the proper function of knives well. Hence *good* actually modifies the telic quale of *knife*. Similarly, a *fast typist* is not someone who *is* fast, but someone who *types* fast, where the telic quale of *typist* is the function or occupation of typing (section 11.9). And a *train at 10:00* is not something that is a train and that is at 10:00, but a train that leaves or arrives at 10:00, where leaving and arriving are part of the telic quale for *train*. For another sort of case, we remarked in section 11.6 that size modifiers are relativized to the standard size of their hosts: a *big mouse* is smaller than a *small elephant*. This suggests that the modifier is attached within the constitutive quale, which records standard sizes.

This option of attaching modifiers inside qualia structure is widely and systematically available; it is based on the interaction of the noun's and modifier's meanings. These interactions constitute one of Pustejovsky's (1995) important pieces of evidence for qualia structure. Pustejovsky builds a formal description of qualia structure, in a formalism quite different from the one here. A full adaptation is beyond the scope of the present work, though a hint will appear in section 12.1.4.[6]

12.1.3 Lambda extraction and variable binding

A further technique of phrasal combination is necessary to build, for example, the meaning of relative clauses. Consider a phrase like *the man who Beethoven likes*. This contains two departures from what we have done so far. First, the second argument of *like* is not satisfied in the normal fashion by a direct object; rather this argument is satisfied by the relative pronoun *who*. Second, the relative clause functions as a modifier of *man*. But connecting it as a modifier, in the style of (8) and (10), would be incoherent: an Event on its own cannot add further specification to *man*. Rather, a relative clause identifies an individual by virtue of his/her participation in the Situation (State or Event) denoted by the clause. "Beethoven likes someone: *that's* the person we're interested in." The second argument of *like* is understood as this designated individual. And it is being this individual that further characterizes *the man*.

Semantic theory therefore needs a means of picking out such designated indi-

---

[6] See Jackendoff (1997a: ch. 3) for an account of adjectives such as *fake* and *alleged*, which modify their nouns in a still different fashion.

viduals. The logician's paraphrase *the man such that Beethoven likes him* provides a suggestive model: the designated individual, *him*, is in the normal position for satisfying the variable of *like*, but it has a special connection to *the man*, expressed by *such that*. Here are a couple of possible notations. (11a) is based on the formal logic notation for *lambda-extraction*; (11b) is loosely modeled on the cognitive grammar notation for *profiling* (Langacker 1987).[7]

(11)   the man who Beethoven likes

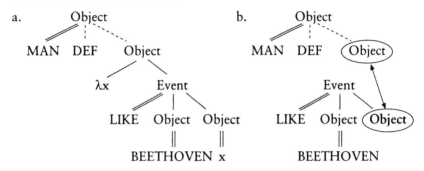

In (11a), *x* is a *bound variable* (in the logician's sense of binding, not the neuroscientist's sense); the bolded Object-constituent in (11b) linked to the upper Object has a similar intent. In either case, it is necessary to add a new way to satisfy an open variable besides filling it with content: in (11a), filling it with a bound variable; in (11b), profiling and externally linking it. I will adopt the (11a) notation, with no prejudice intended.

Bound variable constructions in conceptual structure correspond closely to syntactic constructions such as relative clauses and *wh*-questions which involve long-distance dependencies. In some constructions in some languages, the bound variable is expressed in syntax at a position corresponding to the upper *x* in (11a), i.e. at the front of the clause. Such is the case in English *wh*-relative clauses and questions, where *who/which/what*/etc. appears at the beginning; standard generative grammar calls this "*wh*-movement." In other constructions in other languages, the bound variable is expressed at a position corresponding to the lower *x* in (11a); this is generally called "*wh*- in situ," as in Chinese and also in English echo-questions such as *Beethoven likes WHO?* Finally, the bound variable may be left totally unexpressed, as in English relative clause constructions such as *the man Beethoven likes* and *the man for Beethoven to hire*. The choice among these three possibilities is a syntactic option that has to be

---

7 Again, I am finessing many details, in particular how the relative clause meaning is attached to that of the noun. For instance, some people might want to connect it through the definiteness feature; I would not be averse to trying this out. In particular, it would more closely parallel the equatives to be discussed shortly.

learned by the child; but the fact that a long-distance dependency in syntax expresses a lambda extraction of a bound variable would appear to be a linguistic universal, hence one of the "tricks" in the UG toolkit.

It is worth mentioning that lambda extraction is not confined to Object-constituents. The equative and comparative constructions in adjective phrases closely parallel relative clauses both syntactically and semantically (Bresnan 1973; Postal 1974; Jackendoff 1977; Chomsky 1977). This is best brought out by corresponding paraphrases.

(12)   a. Relative clause: I met the man who Beethoven likes.
           Paraphrase: Beethoven likes some man; I met *that* man.
       b. Equative: John became as rich as Bill became.
           Paraphrase: Bill became rich to some degree; John became *that* rich.
       c. Comparative: John became richer than Bill became.
           Paraphrase: Bill became rich to some degree; John became rich to a
           degree greater than *that*.

A conceptual structure for the equative can be constructed along the lines of (13), using the lambda-extraction notation (the comparative is a bit more complex, and I forgo it).

(13)   as rich as Bill became

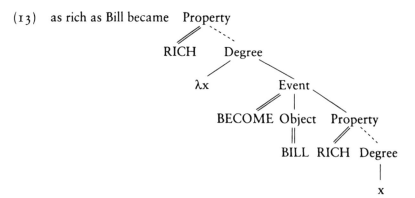

12.1.4 *Parallels in lexical semantics*

The sort of conceptual combination associated with variable satisfaction is already familiar from section 11.8. There we built up complex verb meanings by filling variables of primitive functions like CAUSE, GO, and BE with content, sometimes leaving new variables (as in *enter*) and sometimes eliminating variables altogether (as in *snow*). We see from this that the same principle of conceptual combination can function either in lexical or in phrasal semantics.

The other principles of phrasal combination introduced in this section also occur in lexical semantics. For instance, *brother* and *sister* express the same kinship function but differ in the modifier MALE vs. FEMALE. More generally, any lexical decomposition into a list of independent features can treat these features as separate modifiers.

As for lambda extraction, recall (section 11.9) what the agentive and telic qualia in a noun's meaning encode: how the object comes into being and what it does. For instance, the telic quale of *waitress* says that it is someone who serves food to someone. But just to list the activity of serving as part of the meaning of *waitress* would not say whether the waitress is the person doing the serving, the person being served, or even the food. Lambda extraction provides just the device we need to pick out the correct character in this activity. It is precisely parallel to the lambda extraction in the relative clause of the paraphrase "person who serves food to someone." *Customer*, 'person being served,' has a similar Event in its modifier but lambda extraction over a different variable.

Let us return for a moment to the issue of definitions discussed in section 11.2. These three devices of composition—variable satisfaction, modification, and lambda extraction—are present in both lexical and phrasal semantics. Thus, to the extent that a word's meaning is built up using only these devices, it can be straightforwardly defined; a fairly good example is *approach* = 'go toward.' On the other hand, to the extent that a word's meaning uses a principle of lexical composition that lacks a phrasal parallel, for example a system of cluster conditions, a good definition will be impossible. This incomplete overlap seems to be a basic design feature of language: the interface principles that can "see" syntactic combinations in working memory map into a more limited range of semantic combinations than do the principles that can "see" lexical items.[8]

12.2 Enriched composition

The principles of composition in the preceding section, in conjunction with the general linking principles of section 5.9, yield the default relation between syntactic and conceptual structure: a close correspondence between the configurations of lexical items in syntax and conceptual structure. I have termed these principles "simple composition" (Jackendoff 1997a).

However, we have already noticed that even this default relation is not entirely tight. For instance, modifiers often attach not to their host as a whole but to

---

[8] Note that the broader set of lexical semantic combinations is available not only to word-sized items but also to phrase-sized items such as idioms and constructions.

one of its internal constituents such as the telic quale. In such a case, the same structural configuration in syntax can correspond to a variety of configurations in conceptual structure, depending on the meanings of the words being related.

We now turn to situations in which bits of a phrase's semantic content do not correspond to anything at all in syntactic and phonological structure. Such cases of "enriched composition" show how the understanding of sentences is a rich interaction between grammar, independent well-formedness conditions on conceptual structure, and the construal of context. (These cases overlap closely with what Levinson 2000 terms "generalized conversational implicatures.")

A good first case is Nunberg's (1979) well-known example of *reference transfer*, in which one waitress says to another:

(14)   The ham sandwich over in the corner wants more coffee.

If simple composition alone were used to construct the meaning of (14), the sentence would entail that some ham sandwich has a desire, in violation of conceptual well-formedness. The intended interpretation can be paraphrased as (15); the italicized words are parts not present in (14).

(15)   The *person* over in the corner *contextually associated with a* ham sandwich wants more coffee.

There are three possible lines of approach to this example. The first is to say that *ham sandwich* is lexically polysemous, having an extra meaning 'person contextually associated with a ham sandwich,' perhaps derived by "lexical rule" from the ordinary meaning. But let us go back to the discussion of "lexical rules" in Chapter 6. One certainly does not store this extra meaning in long-term memory. Any word within the bounds of plausibility can be used freely in a reference transfer. Therefore reference transfer is a productive rather than semiproductive process and should not require lexical listing.

A second line of approach is to dismiss this as "mere pragmatics," not part of grammatical competence at all. However, given that we are, after all, aspiring to account for contextualized meaning, we cannot get off the hook so easily. In any event, it turns out that such an approach is insufficient: reference transfer has a striking interaction with the use of reflexive pronouns, an indubitably grammatical phenomenon. Consider the following case (Jackendoff 1992b, based in part on Fauconnier 1985). It is possible to use the name of a character in a play or opera to denote the actor playing the role, as in *Tosca wasn't in very good voice tonight.* This is also a reference transfer, though of a slightly different sort than (14) (see Jackendoff 1992b for some of the different types). Now suppose Richard Nixon goes to see the opera *Nixon in China,* in which the character of Nixon is played by James Maddalena (yes, this is a real opera!). We can then say:

(16)   Sitting in the audience, Nixon was astonished to hear himself sing a
       foolish aria to Chou En-Lai.

Here the reflexive has undergone reference transfer: it refers to Maddalena playing the character Nixon. From this we learn that reflexive pronouns need not
always be coreferential with their antecedents—already an important grammatical effect of reference transfer. But there is more: we cannot use the reflexive in the reverse situation, when its antecedent has undergone reference
transfer and it has not.

(17)   *Up on stage, Nixon was astonished to see himself get up and walk out
       of the opera house in disgust.

(16) and (17) have syntactically identical relations between the reflexive and its
antecedent, but they differ sharply in grammaticality.[9] We conclude that reference transfer cannot be simply dismissed as irrelevant to grammar.

   A third line of approach to reference transfer takes its cue from regular morphology: like regular affixes, reference transfer is a piece of language that can be
used freely online to construct novel utterances. Unlike regular morphology,
though, it has no syntactic or phonological reflexes: it is just a conventionalized
piece of meaning that has no overt expression. (18) shows approximately the
piece necessary for the *ham sandwich* cases, an "operator" that means 'person
associated with.'

(18)

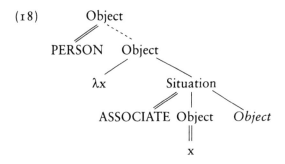

(19) shows how this integrates into the conceptual structure of (14). A dashed
line surrounds the unit (18), which satisfies a variable of *want* and whose own
variable is satisfied by *ham sandwich*. (Jackendoff 1992b shows how such an
approach permits an interesting solution to the reflexive problem posed by (16)
and (17).)

---

[9] One might attempt to escape this conclusion by positing an invisible syntactic difference
between the two cases. Jackendoff (1992b) explores this option in detail and shows it cannot be
sustained.

(19)

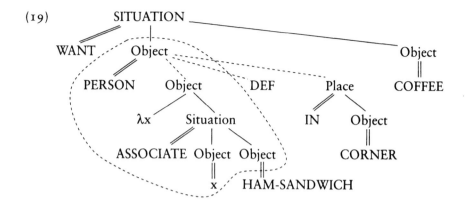

What does it mean to say there is such a conventionalized unit in the lexicon? It means that speakers can "abbreviate" their utterances by leaving this unit unexpressed and can trust hearers to "reconstruct" it in the course of interpretation. In some cases of reference transfer such as the *ham sandwich* example, the hearer is cued by the anomaly of the simple (or literal) reading. In other cases such as *Tosca wasn't in good voice tonight*, the hearer has to rely on contextual cues outside the sentence itself.

This account seems to me to reflect intuition precisely. It says that reference transfer *is* "pragmatics," in the sense that it is part of contextualized interpretation but not part of the utterance. On the other hand, it is also part of language—part of grammar—in the sense that (a) it is conventionalized and (b) it is integrated into conceptual structure just as if it were a word or fixed phrase such as *person who is contextually associated with*. . . . Harking back to the discussion of section 9.7: only if we insist on an ideologically fixed boundary between semantics and pragmatics is such an account problematic; taken on its own terms it seems to me perfectly satisfactory.

This is a typical, if unusually clear, case of enriched composition. I want to briefly mention one other characteristic case (see Jackendoff 1997a: ch. 3 for several more): the widely discussed phenomenon of *aspectual coercion* (Talmy 1978; Verkuyl 1993; Jackendoff 1991; Pustejovsky 1995; and many others). Compare the following sentences.

(20)   a. Sam slept until the bell rang.
       b. Sam jumped until the bell rang.

(20a) implies that Sam's sleeping was a single continuous process, whereas (20b) implies that Sam jumped repeatedly. What makes the difference?

The insight behind all approaches to this problem is that *until* (along with various other expressions like *for an hour*) expresses a temporal bound at the end of an ongoing continuous process. Sleeping is a continuous process, so *until* bounds it by simple composition. However, a verb that denotes a temporally bounded action cannot be further bounded by *until*: consider **Dave died until the bell rang*. A jump also has an inherent ending: when one lands. But unlike dying, jumping can be repeated, and *repeated* jumping is potentially an ongoing process. By construing jumping as repeated, it can compose in a well-formed fashion with *until*.

What is the source of the construed repetition? One might propose that *jump* is lexically polysemous, meaning either 'jump once' or 'jump repeatedly.' However, such a proposal fails on two grounds. First, *every* verb that describes a repeatable temporally bounded action is understood as repeated in the context of *until*. Thus, as in reference transfer, we are dealing with a regular process that should not have to be listed in the lexicon with every verb. Second, and worse, the sense of repetition can depend on the free composition of the verb phrase and on various pragmatic factors. Consider (21).

(21) a. Sue slept all night.   [Continuous sleeping, one night]
      b. Sue slept all night until she started drinking too much coffee.
                               [Multiple acts of sleeping, multiple nights]
      c. Sam sang until the bell rang.   [Continuous singing]
      d. Sam sang the scale until the bell rang.
                               [Multiple performances of the scale]

In (21a), *sleep* has been bounded by *all night*, making it into a closed action. Hence when it combines with *until* in (21b), repetition is generated again. In (21c), *sing* is a continous ongoing action, and *until* tells us when Sam's singing ceased. But in (21d), *singing a scale* is an action that ends when one gets to the top (or gets to the top and returns to the bottom). Hence the only way to construe it with *until* is that Sam sang the scale over and over.

We conclude that there is no way to code every individual verb as polysemous between singular and repeated action; rather construed repetition is a consequence arising from the combination of all the words in the verb phrase. Hence the sense of repetition must be "coerced" into the sentence: it is constructed online in working memory, with no overt phonological or syntactic evidence. Its role in the sentence's meaning is similar to that of adverbials like *repeatedly* or *over and over*, so from the point of view of conceptual structure it is nothing special. All that is unusual about it is its lack of syntactic and phonological form. As with reference transfers, I suggest we can think of it as a conventionalized element of meaning that speakers can use to "abbreviate" their utterances, trusting that hearers can reconstruct this element when it is absent from the signal. Again, in this case, the hearer is cued to the need for coercion by the ill-formedness of the simple reading.[10]

There is actually some psycholinguistic evidence for this conclusion. Piñango et al. (1999) asked subjects to listen to sentences like (20) for comprehension; they tested the subjects for processing load after *until* was heard, at a point in time that comported with semantic rather than syntactic composition (about 250 msec. after *until*). Subjects revealed more load in the *jump* sentences than in the *sleep* sentences, suggesting the construction of a more complex meaning. Piñango (1999) also tested aphasics with an offline task involving this construction. Broca's aphasics, whose semantics is preserved but whose syntax is impaired, were able to answer whether Sam jumped one or many times. By contrast, Wernicke's aphasics, whose syntax is passable but whose semantic integration is disrupted, answered at chance. Though there are other interpretations of both the linguistic facts and the experiments, this is a case where a particular competence theory did make predictions about an experimental outcome; it is not clear that this can be said for any of the other interpretations.[11]

Section 6.6 introduced the idea of constructional idioms—pieces of syntactic structure that bear inherent meaning. These too can be profitably viewed as instances of enriched composition. Consider examples of constructional idioms such as (22).

(22) a. Kim cooked the pot black.   [Resultative]
      b. The train rumbled down the tracks.   [Sound emission+motion]
      c. Nora knitted the afternoon away.   [Time-*away*]

None of the words in these sentences account for our understanding that Kim *caused* the pot to *become* black, that the train *traveled* down the tracks, and that

---

[10] However, there exist cases in which the hearer needs some extrinsic contextual cue. For instance, *Bill kept crossing the street* is ambiguous between 'Bill crossed the street repeatedly' and 'Bill continued toward the other side of the street.' The first of these is the coerced repetition reading we have just been discussing; the second is another type of aspectual coercion. The need for coercion is signaled by the fact that *keep* requires an ongoing process as its complement, and *cross the street* is bounded. However, having established the need for coercion, the hearer must still determine from context *which* coercion is appropriate to the situation. A similar case is *Bill drank two beers last night*, which may mean either of the coerced readings 'two glasses/bottles of beer' or 'two kinds of beer.'

[11] In particular, we show that the experimental results are not what one would expect on an account of *jump* as lexically polysemous between single and multiple jumps.

Another example of enriched composition involves Pustejovsky's (1995) co-composition in sentences like *John finished the book*, which, as pointed out in section 11.9, is understood as 'John finishing *reading* the book.' These cases too have received some psycholinguistic investigation: McElree et al. (2001) found that reading time for such sentences shows a characteristic lengthening by comparison with *John bought the book*, which is understood by simple composition.

Nora *spent* the afternoon knitting. Rather, in the account of section 6.6, these bits of meaning come from constructional VP idioms. The hearer can tell that a constructional idiom is being used because the simple composition of the verb with its complements is ill-formed: there are too many arguments or they are of the wrong type. In (22c) the particle *away* also serves as an overt cue.

In each case, the complements are treated not as semantic arguments of the verb but as semantic arguments of the constructional meaning. Chapter 6 left this unformalized; we can now work it out more precisely. (23) illustrates the resultative construction; the others have similar structures. In particular, the verb (subscripted 2 here) corresponds to a function deep inside a modifying Event, whereas in simple composition it would correspond to the main function.[12]

(23)

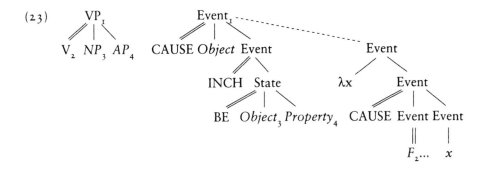

More speculatively, it seems possible to regard various discourse phenomena also as instances of enriched composition. Take, for example, the possibility of answering a *wh*-question with an isolated phrase.

---

[12] Some details of (23):

• I am following the standard paraphrase of resultatives: *Kim cooked the pot black* = 'Kim caused the pot to become (INCH BE) black by cooking (in it).' This should be self-explanatory in (23) except for the final means phrase 'by cooking (in it).'

• The means phrase is a modifier of the main Event. It is a lambda extraction over an Event expressible as 'Kim's cooking caused *this*.' (Alternatively, HELP or FACILITATE might be more appropriate than CAUSE.) That is, on this analysis a means phrase is semantically parallel to the relative clauses discussed in section 12.1.3.

• The upper CAUSE in (23) has an Agent argument that is open but lacks a subscript. It does not need one because the general linking rules of simple composition will map it into subject position, as is standard for Agents. (23) uses the two-argument version of CAUSE; probably the three-argument version is more appropriate.

• (23) leaves blank the argument structure of F_2, which corresponds to the syntactic verb, e.g. *cook* in *Kim cooked the pot black*. A refinement is necessary to show how we know that Kim did the cooking.

(24) a. A: When does the train leave?
          B: (At) 6:30.
       b. A: How do you keep from getting nervous?
          B: By drinking.

Speaker B's utterances in isolation are ill-formed syntactically and semantically. In early generative grammar, one would have claimed that these phrases are derived by deleting the rest of a full answer. Such a solution, however, has been unacceptable since the early 1970s, when such wholesale deletion was rejected. The alternative is to let the grammar generate them as is.[13] Speaker A must interpret them by incorporating conceptual information borrowed from the preceding question. Thus in a strict sense this too is enriched composition: the reply has conceptual structure that comes from neither its words nor its syntactic structure. We discuss some related cases in section 12.5.

I mention this case only to open the door. It remains to be seen to what extent other discourse phenomena might be integrated into the framework of enriched composition, including important phenomena such as conversational implicature.

12.3 The referential tier

A major concern of formal semantics is absent from the semantic theory worked out so far in this chapter and the last: the existential or referential claims a sentence makes about the entities named in it. I am going to take a somewhat novel approach to this aspect of meaning without (I hope) discarding the traditional insights. This approach, based most directly on the work of Piroska Csuri (1996), might be taken to be a version of Discourse Representation Theory (Kamp and Reyle 1993) or of Dynamic Semantics (Groenendijk et al. 1996); it also bears some resemblance to Fauconnier's (1985) theory of "mental spaces," within cognitive grammar.

Csuri's basic idea is that, just as phonology breaks naturally into semi-independent tiers, so does conceptual structure. The semantic structures presented so far in this chapter and the last constitute the *descriptive tier*, the organization of conceptual functions, arguments, and modifiers. But conceptual structure also contains a *referential tier*, which organizes the referential claims about the

---

[13] An intermediate possibility would be that they have the full syntactic structure of a sentence, but almost every node is phonologically empty. This solution, proposed in Jackendoff (1972), is in a way forced by the syntactocentric model, where interpretation must be a consequence of syntactic structure. However, there is no evidence for such syntactic structure other than the interpretation. Therefore the parallel model should do without it.

entities of the sentence.[14] In more standard approaches, the two kinds of organization are conflated into a single formal expression along the lines of (25).

(25)   A fox ate a grape.

$$\exists x_{FOXx} \exists y_{GRAPEy}(EATx,y)$$

The descriptive material consists of the predicates FOX, GRAPE, and EAT, plus their functional organization, which consists of the first two being arguments of the third. The referential material consists of the two existential quantifiers, which make claims that two individuals exist.

Here we will break these two kinds of organization apart. (26) offers the barest start on the referential tier; we will elaborate it gradually.

(26)   Syntax/phonology: $[_S [_{NP} \text{ a fox}]_1 [_{VP} \text{ ate } [_{NP} \text{ a grape}]_2]]_3$

Descriptive tier: $[_{Event} \text{ EAT } ([_{Object} \text{ FOX}]_1, [_{Object} \text{ GRAPE}]_2)]_3$

Referential tier: 1   2 3

The syntax/phonology in (26) is a traditional labeled bracketing; by now I hope the reader can easily understand this as an abbreviation for the two independent syntactic and phonological structures. In the interests of space I have collapsed the descriptive tier back into labeled bracket notation. (See section 11.8 for the equivalence between labeled brackets and the tree notation.)

The new part here is of course the referential tier, which at the moment consists just of three indices, correlated with the two Object-constituents and the Event-constituent of the descriptive tier. The presence of these indices on the referential tier encodes the existential claims that go with the sentence. The indices 1 and 2 correspond to $\exists x$ and $\exists y$ in (25). Index 3 is the claim that the event of the fox eating the grape took place; this corresponds to existential quantification over a Davidsonian event variable. In the terms of the theory of reference in Chapter 10, these indices are the "indexical features" invoked by the sentence: they pick out what constituents of the sentence are intended to correspond to individuals in the world as conceptualized by the speaker.[15]

If the referential tier simply copied the indices out of the descriptive tier, it

---

[14] This idea was primordially present in Jackendoff (1972), which proposed separate semantic components for "functional structure" (here the descriptive tier), "table of coreference" and "modal structure" (here combined into the referential tier), and "focus-presupposition structure" (here information structure—see section 12.5). In 1972 this idea was decidedly kooky. For one thing, the formalization was unusable. More important, at that time we didn't know anything about tiers; it took the phonological precedent to legitimate the idea.

[15] Signed languages typically individuate the characters in a discourse by assigning each one its own position in signing space (Lillo-Martin and Klima 1990). It is interesting to speculate whether this phenomenon might be a direct encoding of the referential tier.

wouldn't be very interesting. So consider: what if an index were *not* copied? This seems precisely the proper account of predicate NPs, which do not pick out an independent individual. For instance, in *Eva became a doctor*, there are not two separate individuals, Eva and the doctor; there is only Eva, of whom doctorhood is predicated. Accordingly, we could set up this sentence as in (27).

(27)   Syntax/phonology: $[_S [_{NP} \text{Eva}]_4 [_{VP} \text{became} [_{NP} \text{a doctor}]_5]]_6$

Descriptive tier: $[_{Event} \text{INCH} ([_{State} \text{BE} ([_{Object} \text{EVA}]_4, [_{Object} \text{DOCTOR}]_5)])]_6$

Referential tier: 4   6

The structural configurations of (26) and (27) are the same in syntax, and nearly the same in the descriptive tier. The main structural difference is in the referential tier: there is no index corresponding to the predicate NP *a doctor*. Thus the sentence asserts that one individual, describable as 'Eva,' has come to be describable also as 'a doctor.' This captures the traditional sense in which predicate NPs are sort of like adjectives: they contribute only description but no new individual.

On the other hand, suppose an independently referential NP such as a proper name is placed in predicative position, for instance *Superman is Clark Kent*. In this case, the referential tier will contain an index for a second individual, and the sentence will assert that the two individuals are identical—that is, it creates a "merger of indexicals" in the sense of section 10.7. (Whether this requires a different sense of *be* is an interesting question; I have argued (Jackendoff 1983: ch. 6) that it does not.)

The distinction between ordinary and predicate NPs leads to an important observation. Some NPs such as proper names are inherently referential. But other NPs, particularly indefinites, are referential only by virtue of their role in the sentence as a whole. In most roles they are referential. But some roles, in particular the predicative role, do not carry referential claims. The formalization of verb semantics in sections 11.7 and 11.8 allows us to localize the predicative role precisely: it is the second argument of the function $BE_{Ascription}$. Other conceptual functions that affect referentiality will appear in the next section.

The separation between the descriptive and referential tiers leads to an interesting account of two different kinds of anaphora. Standard definite pronouns such as *he*, *she*, and *it* are understood as coreferential with their antecedents. This coreference can be notated in the referential tier by equating the pronoun's index with that of its antecedent, as in (28). (I abbreviate syntax/phonology (S/P) and the descriptive tier (DT) still further, eliminating self-explanatory brackets and labels. The pronoun *it* is taken to have the descriptive content '3rd person singular neuter'.)

(28) S/P: [[Joan]$_1$ bought [a car]$_2$]$_3$. [[Fred]$_4$ liked [it]$_5$]$_6$

DT: [BUY (JOAN$_1$, CAR$_2$)]$_3$ [LIKE (FRED$_4$, [3SingNeut]$_5$)]$_6$

RT: 1   2 3   4   5=2 6

The notation 5=2 indicates an indexical merger between the individuals described as *a car* and *it*.

There is, however, a second kind of anaphoric expression, so-called *identity-of-sense* anaphora. The clearest example of this is the pronoun *one*. This denotes an individual with the same description as its antecedent, but not necessarily with the same referential index. (29) illustrates.

(29) S/P: [[Joan]$_1$ bought [a car]$_2$]$_3$. [[Fred]$_4$ bought [one]$_5$ too]$_6$

DT: [BUY (JOAN$_1$, CAR$_2$)]$_3$ [BUY (FRED$_4$, [3Sing]$_{5=2}$)]$_6$

RT: 1   2 3   4   5   6

Here the notation 5=2 indicates that the individual with index 5 falls under the description indexed 2, i.e. it's another car. The referential tier does not specify whether these two individuals are identical—this depends on pragmatic factors. For instance, in *Joan saw a car, and Fred saw one too*, it is possible that the two cars are the same, but the sentence doesn't tell us.

Both kinds of anaphora appear at once in the expression *another one*. This designates an individual that, because of *another*, is referentially distinct from its antecedent but, because of *one*, satisfies the same description.

(30) S/P: [[Joan]$_1$ bought [a car]$_2$]$_3$. [Then [she]$_4$ bought [another one]$_5$]$_6$

DT: [BUY (JOAN$_1$, CAR$_2$)]$_3$ [BUY (SHE$_4$, [3Sing]$_{5=2}$)]$_6$

RT: 1   2 3   4=1   5≠2 6

Conversely, so-called *anaphoric epithets* such as *the poor guy* and *the bum* require identity of reference with an antecedent, but offer a different description:

(31) S/P: [[John]$_1$ bought [a car]$_2$]$_3$. [Then [the bum]$_4$ sold [it]$_5$]$_6$

DT: [BUY (JOHN$_1$, CAR$_2$)]$_3$ [SELL (BUM$_4$, [3SingNeut]$_5$)]$_6$

RT: 1   2 3   4=1   5=2 6

And *anaphoric definite descriptions* express coreference with a previously mentioned character of compatible description:[16]

---

[16] Not all definite NPs are anaphoric definite descriptions, though. Consider an expression like *the richest man in America*. Here the definite article expresses a claim—on the descriptive tier—that a unique individual satisfies this description (more or less as in Russell's 1905 explication of definite descriptions). I am inclined to think that the anaphoric and uniqueness aspects of definiteness often overlap, forming a cluster concept in the sense of section 11.6—which is why neither of them constitutes a full and exclusive explication of definiteness.

(32) S/P: [[a boy]$_1$ met [a girl]$_2$]$_3$ [[The girl]$_4$ was tall$_5$]$_6$
      DT: [MEET (BOY$_1$, GIRL$_2$)]$_3$ [BE (GIRL$_4$, TALL$_5$)]$_6$
      RT: 1   2 3   4=2   6

Next, recall that predicate NPs have no index on the referential tier. This predicts that predicate NPs should be possible antecedents of identity-of-sense
anaphora, since a description is present, but not of referential anaphora, since
there is no referential index. The prediction is correct: *Joan became a doctor, and
Sue became one/*it/*her too.*

Both referential and identity-of-sense anaphora can be applied to Event-vari-
ables as well.

(33) S/P: [[Sam]$_1$ fell out of [a tree]$_2$]$_3$. [[Fred]$_4$ saw [it]$_5$]$_6$
      DT: [FALL (SAM$_1$, OUT-OF [TREE]$_2$)]$_3$ [SEE (FRED$_4$, [3SingNeut]$_5$)]$_6$
      RT: 1   2 3   4   5=3 6

The second sentence of (33) is syntactically parallel to the second sentence of
(28). But the antecedent of the pronoun is different: this time it is the entire event
of Sam's falling out of a tree, as noted in section 10.10. So we have a clear analogy to standard identity-of-reference anaphora. Next consider (34).

(34) S/P: [[Sam]$_1$ fell out of [a tree]$_2$]$_3$. [Then [he]$_4$ did [it]$_5$ again]$_6$
      DT: [FALL (SAM$_1$, OUT-OF [TREE]$_2$)]$_3$ [DO (HE$_4$, [3SingNeut]$_5$)]$_{6=3}$
      RT: 1   2 3   4=1   6

The second sentence in (34) asserts that a distinct event occurred, with the same
description as the first sentence. Hence it parallels identity-of-sense anaphora.[17]

12.4 Referential dependence and referential frames

So far the referential tier consists of a list of indices or indexical features that

---

[17] The notation in (34) is not quite precise enough. In particular, it is possible to use *do it*
anaphora with non-coreferential subjects: . . . *and then Fred did it too.* Working this detail into the
analysis requires a better account of topic-focus structure. Some hints appear in section 12.5.

Again and *too* in these examples seem to have an effect similar to *another*: they mark events of
similar or related description as referentially distinct. The temporal use of *then* likewise marks two
events as temporally distinct, hence referentially distinct.

An important problem with VP anaphors is how their understood constituents acquire referential
status. For instance in (34), the second event of falling out of a tree makes a claim about there being a
tree, not necessarily the same one as in the first event. A robust tradition (e.g. Fiengo and May 1994)
treats this in terms of "syntactic reconstruction" of the anaphor. Here we are committed to there
being no second event expressed at any level of syntax; Culicover and Jackendoff (1995) show this
leads to insuperable technical problems. However, at the moment I have no explicit alternative.

record the active referents in the discourse. A new referent is introduced by adding a new index that is not marked coreferential with any of the previous indices.

We now impose some structure on the list. Consider the event of a woman buying a car. In order for this event to be conceptualized, there must also be a conceptualized woman who does the buying and a conceptualized car that she buys. Of course, this woman and this car might be on the list of available referents even if the event of her buying it never took place. Thus there is a sense in which the event is *referentially dependent* on its characters, while the characters are not referentially dependent on the event.

Let us notate this asymmetric referential dependence in the referential tier like this:

(35)   S/P: [[a woman]$_1$ bought [a car]$_2$]$_3$
       DT: [BUY (WOMAN$_1$, CAR$_2$)]$_3$
       RT: 3

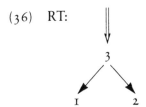

The arrows pointing from 3 to 1 and 2 can be understood in either of two ways: (a) The claimed existence of the event *depends on* the claimed existence of the characters. (b) The claimed existence of the event *entails* the claimed existence of the characters. For the moment we leave open which interpretation is best. (This notion of referential dependence comes from Csuri 1996; a similar notion appears in Erteschik-Shir 1998.)

Now consider what happens if (35) is turned into a question: *Did a woman buy a car?* Suddenly there is no claim that the event took place; rather the speaker wishes the hearer to assert whether or not it did. In the absence of this claim, suddenly *a woman* and *a car* lose their existential force as well: we need not be able to identify either of them. Thus there is a difference in the referential structure of assertions and questions. We will express this in the referential tier by adding a further arrow that denotes assertive force, terminating in the index for the event variable. Thus the referential tier of (35) will become (36), while the corresponding question lacks the assertion arrow.

(36)   RT:

The assertion arrow "grounds" the chain of referential dependence: it allows us to infer that the event took place. If the event is conceptualized as having taken place, then its characters are conceptualized as existing. Without the assertion arrow we still have referential dependence, but the chain of inference can't get started. Accordingly, we can think of the assertion arrow as referentially licensing the event, which in turn referentially licenses its characters.

A proper name, of course, does not lose its existential claim when placed in a question: *Joan* is still identifiable in *Did Joan buy a car?* We can notate this in the referential tier by licensing *Joan* with its own "grounding" arrow, which comes by virtue of *Joan* being a proper name. The arrow is present whether the sentence is declarative or interrogative. (I abbreviate even more severely in (37), conveniently omitting the descriptive tier.)

(37) a. [Joan$_1$ bought a car$_2$]$_3$ b. [Did Joan$_1$ buy a car$_2$]$_3$

RT:

Something similar happens with anaphoric pronouns. In (38), the licensing of an existential claim for *it* comes not through a grounding arrow but through the anaphoric connection to something with its own existential claim:

(38) a. [Joan$_1$ bought a car$_2$]$_3$ [Did you$_4$ see it$_5$]$_6$

RT:

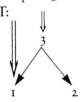

We are now in a position to make an important observation (Jackendoff 1972; Csuri 1996; Roberts 1996). Consider (39a) and the three alternative continuations in (39b, c, d).

(39) a. [Did Joan$_1$ buy a car$_2$]$_3$ b. *. . . [Fred$_4$ sold it$_5$]$_6$

RT:

        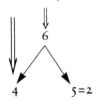

c. ... [and sell it$_7$ again]$_8$ d. ... [Fred$_4$ sold one$_{9=2}$]$_{10}$
RT:

(39a) is a question, so the indefinite *a car* lacks existential force. However, since (39b) is declarative, it has an assertion arrow, which in turn leads to an implication of existential force for the pronoun *it*. This turns out to be unacceptable. The basic principle seems to be that *an anaphoric expression on the referential tier cannot have stronger existential force than its antecedent*. This is of course just a descriptive generalization. One would hope to base it on more fundamental first principles, but I will not do so here.

To see that this is the proper formulation of the principle, consider the other continuations in (39). In (39c) the pronoun *it* is acceptable, unlike (39b). The reason is that here the pronoun also falls under the question, so it also lacks existential force. Hence the pronoun can acceptably corefer. In (39d), the pronoun *one* has its own existential force. But it is acceptable because it is not coreferential with its antecedent; its anaphora is on the descriptive tier.

Negation, the future tense, and the *may* of possibility have an effect on the referential tier similar to that of questioning. In (40), there is no claim that an event of Joan's buying a car takes place, nor that any specific car is referred to.[18]

(40) a. Joan didn't buy a car.
      b. Joan will/may buy a car.

The tests with referential and descriptive anaphora work exactly as they do in questions.

(41) Joan didn't buy a car ...
      a. *She parked it on the street.
      b. and park it on the street.
      c. Fred bought one.

---

[18] The car becomes specific if we replace *a car* by *a certain car*, *that car*, or various other expressions that serve to ground this entity independently of the event described in the sentence. The modals *will* and *may*, like questions, cause indefinite subjects as well as objects to be nonspecific: *A woman will/may buy a car*. With negation, however, an indefinite subject simply sounds odd: ??*A woman didn't buy a car*. We leave this difference aside here.

(42)   Joan will/may buy a car . . .
      a. *She parked it on the street.
      b. and park it on the street.
      c. Fred already has bought one.

Within certain subordinate clauses we find similar behavior. For instance, the adjective *possible* is close in meaning to the modal *may*, and it is no surprise that its complement clause is free of referential commitment: if we say something is possible, we are obviously not committing ourselves to its having happened. Similarly, the verb *want* carries a strong implication that the desired situation does not yet obtain.

(43)   a. It is possible that Joan bought a car.   [No implication that she did]
      b. Joan wants to buy a car.   [No implication that she has or will]

Moreover, the anaphoric tests apply to *a car* in the same way as they do in (41) and (42) (*It is possible that Joan bought a car . . . and parked it on the street/*She parked it on the street*, etc.). So as in the earlier examples, *a car* is referentially licensed by the event of buying.

However, the main clauses in (43) do make existential claims: they claim that something is possible and that Joan does want something. Hence NPs in these main clauses can serve as antecedents for definite pronouns in a succeeding sentence (italics indicate antecedent and pronoun).

(44)   a. It seems possible to *a friend of mine* that Joan bought a car. *He* thinks she's rich.
      b. *A friend of mine* wants to buy a car. *He* doesn't have much money, though.

In order to encode the referential tier for such cases, we cut the graph of referential dependency above the index for the subordinate clause; the cut-off portion lacks assertive force. It is notationally convenient to enclose the cut-off portion in a frame, labeled with an "operator" that notates the alteration of existential claims. (45) shows the resulting structure for (44b); connoisseurs of Discourse Representation Theory should begin to see the resemblance at this point.[19]

---

[19] In this example, the subject of *buy* is notated in the descriptive and referential tiers as if it were a definite pronoun called PRO. Whether this appears also in syntactic structure depends on one's school of thought: Standard generative grammar gives *buy* a syntactic subject, most constraint-based theories do not.

(45) S/P: [[a friend of mine$_2$]$_1$ wants [to buy [a car]$_5$]$_6$]$_3$
      DT: [WANT ([FRIEND (ME$_2$)]$_1$, [BUY (PRO$_4$, CAR$_5$)]$_6$)]$_3$
      RT:

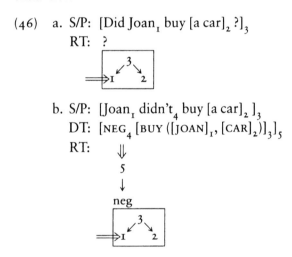

The box notation introduced in (45) is actually useful in earlier examples as well. For example, in order to distinguish the different ways in which indefinite NPs fail to have existential claims, we can encode questioning, negation, and so forth as operators on a box that encloses the non-asserted portions of the referential tier:[20]

(46) a. S/P: [Did Joan$_1$ buy [a car]$_2$?]$_3$
         RT: ?

b. S/P: [Joan$_1$ didn't$_4$ buy [a car]$_2$]$_3$
   DT: [NEG$_4$ [BUY ([JOAN]$_1$, [CAR]$_2$)]$_3$]$_5$
   RT:

At this point the character of these operators in the referential tier begins to become clearer: they are *valuations* of concepts in the sense of section 10.6. A constituent whose index is connected to a grounding arrow has the valuation *external*, i.e. it is understood as referring to a real entity. A constituent whose index is cut off from grounding has a nonspecific or irrealis construal. Different operators encode different valuations that lead to such construals.

---

[20] (46b) contains one further innovation that requires comment. The event of Joan's buying is claimed not to have taken place; therefore its index, 3, falls inside the *neg* box in RT. However, the sentence asserts something about what *didn't* happen. This corresponds to the index 5 on the entire sentence in the DT and RT. The question (46a), by contrast, makes no assertion, so the extra index outside the operator is absent.

The complements of so-called "factive" verbs such as *know* and *realize* are distinguished by being presupposed as true regardless of the status of the main clause itself. Thus, *Fred realized that Joan bought a car*, *Fred didn't realize that Joan bought a car*, and *Did Fred realize that Joan bought a car?* all presume that Joan bought a car. We can incorporate this in the referential tier by saying that these verbs, instead of putting a box around their complements, add a grounding arrow, as in (47).

(47)   S/P: [Fred$_1$ didn't realize that [Joan$_4$ bought a car$_5$]$_2$]$_3$
       RT:

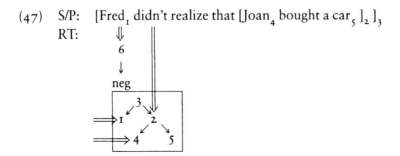

As a side consequence, an indefinite within a factive clause, such as *a car* in (47), has an associated existential claim.

Another important RT configuration occurs in conditional sentences. A sentence of the form *If P, then Q* asserts neither *P* nor *Q*, but rather that *P* is referentially dependent on *Q*. To make this clearer, recall what referential dependence is. In *a woman bought a car*, the buying is referentially dependent on the woman and the car; hence there cannot be an existential claim about the act of buying without a concurrent existential claim about the woman and car. Similarly, in *If P, then Q*, the sentence asserts that there cannot be an existential claim about the situation *P* without a concurrent existential claim about the situation *Q*—precisely the correct meaning. Conditionals can be expressed in a variety of syntactic forms: *if–then* constructions (48a), subordinate clauses (48b), or successive sentences in discourse (48c); but the referential dependency remains constant. Note that definite anaphora within the *then*-clause can have an antecedent in the *if*-clause, indicating that the two are both in the same referential frame.[21]

(48)   a. [If [a verb$_1$ takes an object$_2$]$_3$, (then) [it$_4$ governs accusative case$_5$]$_6$]$_7$
       b. [That [a verb$_1$ takes an object$_2$]$_3$ entails that [it$_4$ governs accusative case$_5$]$_6$]$_7$

---

[21] This parallelism between indefinite NPs and the *then*-clauses of conditionals comes out most clearly if, as advocated in section 10.10, we take the reference of a sentence to be a situation rather than a truth value.

c. [[Suppose [a verb$_1$ takes an object$_2$]$_3$. Then [it$_4$ governs accusative case$_5$]$_6$]$_7$

RT: ⇓

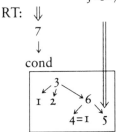

What is unusual about the *if–then* construction is that the referential dependency goes in the opposite direction from usual. Normally, clauses referentially license their constituents, as in (37). But in the *if–then* construction, the subordinate *if*-clause referentially licenses the main clause (optionally preceded by *then*). If one presumes a single structure incorporating both descriptive and referential information, this reversal is difficult to capture. The situation is even worse if one expects *syntactic structure* (say LF) to reflect referential dependency directly. However, if referential dependencies are sorted out into a separate tier, we can keep syntactic, descriptive, and referential dependence separate. The precedent from phonology leads us to expect that a system of tiers will exhibit just such mismatches.

Notice that in (48c) the "scope" of the conditional operator stretches over two sentences. As Fauconnier (1985) and H. Clark (1996) observe, we can extend this idea to deal with the valuation of fictional narratives: the entire "world" of the narrative is enclosed in a frame, in which characters have their own identity. Proper names within a narrative may be grounded either within the narrative itself (like Sherlock Holmes) or in the "real world" (say, as in the opera *Nixon in China*); the difference is only in where the grounding arrow comes from. Similarly, events in the narrative are usually taken to be fictional, but it is also possible for a narrative to refer to "real" events such as the election of Nixon. However, the narrative itself need not be explicit about the source of grounding; this is for the hearer to figure out, hence an instance of enriched composition.

Narratives also provide a simple example of embedded referential frames. If the narrative speaks of Holmes wanting to buy a cigar, it refers neither to a real cigar nor to a fictional cigar, but to a fictionally desired cigar. This is easily expressed in the formalism by embedding the *want* box inside the *fiction* box, as in (49). Note also that *Holmes* is grounded not to the "real world" but to the interior of the *fiction* box.

(49)   S/P: [Holmes₁ wanted [to buy a cigar₂]₃]₄
       RT: fiction

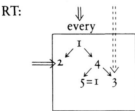

As Clark points out, characters in a narrative have "referential access" only to characters and events within the narrative; they cannot "escape" the narrative and refer to the "real world." This helps account for the ungrammaticality of example (17) (*Up on stage, Nixon saw himself walk out of the opera house); it is yet another case of the interaction of the referential tier with anaphora.

A final case of referential dependency involves quantification. In traditional quantificational notation, the two readings of our old favorite *Every person in this room speaks two languages* would come out something like (50a, b).

(50)   Every person in this room speaks two languages.
       a. For each person, there are two languages (narrow-scope reading of *two languages*)

$$\forall x_{\text{x in this room}} \exists (y,z)_{\text{y,z languages}}(\text{SPEAK } (x, y\&z))$$

       b. Two languages each of which is spoken by everyone (wide-scope reading of *two languages*)

$$\exists (y,z)_{\text{y,z languages}} \forall x_{\text{x in this room}}(\text{SPEAK } (x, y\&z))$$

In the present framework, *speak* imposes normal referential dependencies on its arguments: there cannot be an act (or ability) of speaking without a speaker and a language. In addition, though, the quantifier *every* has the effect of placing *speak* in a special referential frame: the sentence does not assert a single act (or ability) of speaking, but rather one ability per person in the room. Thus each person individually licenses an act of speaking. Now: if *two languages* is referentially licensed in the normal way by *speak*, then there are two languages per person; but if *two languages* is independently grounded, then we get the reading in which the same two languages are known by everyone. (51) gives a tentative structure; the dashed arrow indicates the optional grounding for *two languages*.

(51)   S/P: [[Everyone in [this room]₂]₁ speaks [two languages]₃]₄
       RT:

The index 1 corresponds to the "lifted" quantifier in the standard logical expression; it is placed in accordance with its logical scope in the sentence. The index 5 corresponds to the bound variable. Thus we end up again with referential dependencies that do not strictly mirror embedding in syntax.[22]

The issue for linguistic theory is then whether either syntax or the descriptive tier needs to encode the "lifted" quantifier, the bound variable, and/or relative quantifier scope. The standard approach in generative grammar (the theory of LF) is that they do. But this assumption is based on the syntactocentric architecture, in which all differences in meaning have to stem from differences in syntax. Under the present architecture, with the possibility of mismatches among tiers, we can explore the possibility that relative quantifier scope is (at least often) a matter of enriched composition, unexpressed in syntax. Given that I have elsewhere (Jackendoff 1997a: ch. 3) offered arguments against the very possibility of constructing a theory of LF that incorporates quantifier scope, my own preferences ought to be clear. But here I will officially leave the question open.[23]

A more general set of questions would concern the "operators" that create frames. First, how many different operators are needed? The practice in formal semantics has been to try to cut them to a bare minimum; however our experience with ontological categories (section 10.8) might indicate that a somewhat greater degree of profligacy is worth considering. Second, how do we elaborate the semantic values of these operators so they can drive inferences? Third, we have seen such operators coming from illocutionary force (question), sentence operators (negation, future tense, *may*), adjectives and verbs (*possible* and *want*), conjunctions (*if*), and quantifiers (*every*). Why should referential dependencies be affected by so many different grammatical factors? Fourth, what are the overall principles for mapping between the descriptive and the referential tier?

More generally, the theories of quantification, negation, and modality are among the most richly explored areas of formal semantics. It is a major challenge to see if this tradition of research can be recast in terms of the referential tier.

---

[22] The reversal of the normal referential dependence (1 above 4 in (51)) explains the close paraphrase with a conditional: *If someone is in this room, (s)he speaks two languages.* I leave it to the reader to work out the structure of this latter sentence, using the model of (48), and to observe the similarity.

[23] See Jackendoff (1996c) for one proposal about how distributed quantification shows up in the descriptive tier. It is worth mentioning that Csuri (1996) derives certain constraints on long-distance dependencies from referential tier structure; Erteschik-Shir and Lappin (1979) offer related results. Thus certain evidence for syntactic movement vanishes in favor of independently motivated constraints on referential dependency.

12.5 The information structure (topic/focus) tier

Across a range of theoretical approaches, there is a broad consensus that part of the phrasal semantics/pragmatics of a sentence is an organization in terms of *information structure*, which invokes such distinctions as focus/presupposition, topic/comment, theme/rheme, and old/new information (Bolinger 1965b; Jackendoff 1972; Stalnaker 1978; Sgall et al. 1986; Rochemont and Culicover 1990; Lambrecht 1994; Rooth 1996; Ladd 1996; Büring 1996; Van Valin and LaPolla 1997; Vallduví and Vilkuna 1998; Roberts 1998; McNally 1998; Erteschik-Shir 1998; Prince 1998; Steedman 2000). The present section is an attempt to sort out the main insights of these approaches and to sketch how they might be integrated into the present framework.

Information structure is concerned with the role of the sentence in the speaker–hearer interaction—the means by which the speaker intends the sentence to inform the hearer, in the context of previous discourse. The simplest illustrations of information structure phenomena are question–answer pairs such as (52) and (53). In English, prosody plays a crucial role in the expression of information structure, so I have indicated stressed words in capitals. (In judging the replies in (52) and (53), it is important to stress *only* words that are marked as stressed!)

(52) J: Who went to the party?
     K: a. PAT went to the party.
          b. *Pat went to the PARTY.
          c. PAT.
          d. *The PARTY.
          e. The one who went to the party was PAT.
          f. *The place where Pat went was the PARTY.

(53) J: Where did Pat go?
     K: a. Pat went to the PARTY.
          b. *PAT went to the party.
          c. The PARTY.
          d. *PAT.
          e. The place where Pat went was the PARTY.
          f. *The one who went to the party was PAT.

Part of K's reply corresponds to the *wh*-phrase in J's question: *Pat* in (52) and *the party* in (53). This piece can appear as a stressed element in an ordinary sentence used as an answer, as in (52a) and (53a). Alternatively, it can stand alone as a sentence fragment, as in (52c) and (53c). Or it can appear as the "clefted" element in a "pseudo-cleft" construction, as in (52e) and (53e). The remaining replies show that this correspondence is not random: it reflects a regular relation between the question and the answer.

There is a clear semantic/pragmatic intuition behind these results: the stressed part of the replies in (52) and (53) is information[24] that K intends for J to add to their joint belief (in the sense of section 10.11), or to the "common ground" in the sense of Stalnaker (1978). The *wh*-phrases in J's questions indicate what information J wishes; the inappropriate answers do not supply it. The standard term for this newly supplied information is the *focus* of the sentence (alternatively *rheme*). The remaining part of the sentence can be called the *presupposition*; we will refine this shortly.

Turning for a moment to the *questions* in (52) and (53): we would like to say that the question–answer pairs share a common presupposition, and that the stressed phrase in the answer is a focus. By analogy, then, it makes sense to say that the *wh*-word in a question is also a focus, but with a twist: instead of supplying new information, it supplies a variable to be filled with new information.

What sort of a grammatical entity is the focus? Many writers (including Jackendoff 1972) have identified it in terms of a feature [+F] or the like marked in syntax. But this misses the point. First of all, one still must account for the semantics/pragmatics of focus. A syntactic feature can at best correspond to or express this semantic/pragmatic property of the sentence, which properly belongs in conceptual structure. Second, in (52/53a), the focus is expressed through prosody alone, with ordinary garden-variety syntax. Here a syntactic feature [+F] serves only to "pass information" from semantics to phonology. Third, the syntactic expression of focus is enormously varied, as seen already for English in (52) and (53). Many of the writers cited above (see especially Van Valin and LaPolla 1997) stress that the variety of expression is far greater when one looks across the languages of the world, and many languages are far more grammatically obsessive than English in expressing focus. Hence a simple feature (or node) really does not do much work in syntax—one needs in addition complex ways to work out the actual realization of this feature in each language.

From the present perspective, we can see that a syntactic feature [+F] is simply an artifact of syntactocentrism, the assumption that everything in meaning has to be derived from something generated in syntax. The parallel architecture permits us to separate the semantic/pragmatic property of being focussed from

---

[24] Note, by the way, that we can relinquish the ban on the term "information" here, since we really are talking about a speaker informing a hearer, not just about structural distinctions rattling around inside a brain.

the syntactic and phonological devices used to express it; the interface components encode how particular grammatical devices correspond to semantic focus.
In cases such as (52/53a) that lack syntactic effects, the interface connects focus
only to the prosodic tiers of phonology. On the other hand, if a syntactic structure does have inherent focussing effects, as in the pseudo-clefts (52/53e), we
can treat this structure as a constructional idiom that serves as an interface with
focus. (The "protosyntactic" principle Focus Last of section 8.7 belongs in this
category as well.) As for elliptical answers such as (52/53c), section 12.2 suggested that they have no further syntactic structure and that they are interpreted by enriched composition. We can now be slightly more specific: they are
taken to be the focus of a statement whose presupposition is recovered from the
preceding question.

How should focus be coded in conceptual structure? As seen already in (52)
and (53), the choice of focus is orthogonal to argument structure: any argument
role can be focussed. Therefore focus does not have a natural home in the
descriptive tier. Is it in the referential tier? No, because nonreferential constituents such as adjective phrases and predicate nominals can be focussed.

(54) a. It's a BIG star, not a LITTLE star.
      b. What Susan is is a PROFESSOR.

Following the standard terminology, let us call this tier *information structure*.
So far it is fairly trivial: we could see it just as an element [Focus] coindexed with
a constituent of the descriptive tier in semantics. The interface with phonology
coindexes [Focus] with high stress,[25] and various syntactic constructions in various languages coindex [Focus] with a particular syntactic constituent.
Therefore, when we say, for instance, that *PAT* is Focus in (52a), this is shorthand for saying that this syntactic/phonological constituent is coindexed with
[Focus] on the information structure tier.

There seem to be a number of varieties of Focus, supplying slightly different
kinds of new information. Various authors make the distinctions differently,
and therefore I will only be suggestive here. The type illustrated in (52) and (53)
is probably the most general. It might be thought of as resolving an uncertainty
in the common ground with a more highly specified entity: *Someone went to the
party; who was it? It was Pat. Pat* may be someone already present in the discourse, or someone entirely new. I'll call this *ordinary focus*. In a second type,

---

[25] How does high stress end up on the right word? Ideally, the transitivity of coindexation would
be sufficient to do the job. The descriptive tier is coindexed through syntax to segmental phonology; now it is also coindexed through the information structure tier to high stress. With luck, this
will be enough. But the problem is tricky (see many of the sources cited above on the focus–stress
interface), so I would be wise here to leave the issue open.

the uncertainty is limited to a specified set of individuals. This type of focus is evoked by question types such as (55).

(55)   Which one of them—David, Pat, or Joe—went to the party?

In English, the cleft construction (56) seems specifically to pick out this sort of focus. For instance, (56) seems a more felicitous answer to (55) than to (52).[26]

(56)   It was PAT who went to the party.

Here the focus is an individual presumed to be already known to the hearer; it is only this individual's role in the situation that is new. I'll call this *restrictive focus*. A third type is illustrated in (54a): it is used to contrast two entities along some dimension or to correct the hearer's presumption about something in the common ground. I'll call this *contrastive focus*. A special type of contrastive focus is *metalinguistic focus*, where the speaker is commenting on the choice of words or pronunciation:

(57)   a.   You didn't hear me right: I said BILL, not JILL.
       b.   You say to-MAY-to, and I say to-MAH-to.

These types of focus might be encoded by diacritic features on [Focus] in the information structure tier; various interface rules (including lexical items such as *which* and constructions such as cleft) would be sensitive to these features.

The communicative function of focus is to specify what information in the sentence is new to the hearer. Given that the overall function of communication is to inform the receiver of something new, it stands to reason that every sentence should have a focus.[27] The communicative function of the rest of the sentence, the presupposition, is to link the new information to what the hearer already knows.

There exist sentences in which everything is new, that is, the entire sentence is focus.

---

[26]   As an answer to (52), (56) reads more into the question than the question literally asks—which commonly happens, of course.

[27]   A number of people have suggested to me that this statement is overblown. For example, the use of language in religious ritual is not to inform anyone (even God) of anything. The same is true in ritualized greetings (*Hey, pal, howya doin'?*). So maybe we're only talking about the kinds of examples typically discussed when people study information structure. It bears looking into. Even in such cases, exactly what the speaker intends as new may have to be worked out pragmatically by the hearer (i.e. by enriched composition). A good example is Lambrecht's *You LIED to me!* Presumably the hearer knows this already; what is new is the information that this is now part of the common ground.

(58) a. JOHNSON died!
      b. Once upon a time there was a little girl who lived in a large, dark,
         forest.

(58a) could be used to answer the question *Who died?*, treating *JOHNSON*
as focus and "someone died" as presupposition. But it can also be used to
announce the event of Johnson's death "out of the blue," with no previous
common ground in the conversation that bears upon either Johnson or this
event. (58b) is obviously the beginning of a story. As a scene-setter, it cannot
presume any previous information; the little girl and the forest are both new
characters. Lambrecht (1994) adopts the term *thetic judgments* for presuppo-
sitionless sentences like (58), following the usage of Marty (1918), a pupil of
Brentano.

Another important component of information structure is *topic*. Like the
focus, the topic in English receives a stress peak, usually with a rising intonation.
The clearest expression of topic in English is the *as for* phrase that introduces a
sentence:

(59) As for BILL, I think you'll LIKE him.

The topic is often said to be "what the sentence is about." More precisely, it
serves to draw the hearer's attention to an entity about which some new information is to be provided.

Lambrecht (1994), under the standard definition, wishes to treat unstressed
anaphoric pronouns, especially subject pronouns, as parts of the topic; for
instance, *She's COMING* is "about" *her*. This creates a curious disjunction
between the sorts of topics that are specially marked, as in (59), and those that
are pronominal or even tacit. My inclination is to divide the notion of topic into
"continuing topic" and "new topic." When an anaphoric pronoun is topic in
Lambrecht's sense, it is a "continuing topic," and no special attention needs to
be drawn to it. By contrast, *as for Bill* in (59) introduces a "new topic" to which
the hearer's attention must be drawn. For purposes of the present section, I will
use "topic" to mean "new topic" only.

Not all (new) topics are introduced with special expressions like *as for*. The
stereotypical expression of topic (in English at any rate) is as a subject NP carrying its own intonation contour. The stereotypical information structure in
English divides the sentence into the topic, consisting of the subject, and the
comment, consisting of the verb phrase (or predicate). The topic introduces
what the speaker is talking about and the comment says what there is to say
about it.

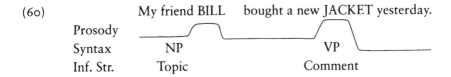

(60)   My friend BILL   bought a new JACKET yesterday.

Prosody		
Syntax	NP	VP
Inf. Str.	Topic	Comment

In (60), the major syntactic break between NP and VP aligns perfectly with the major prosodic break and with the major information structure break. Such an alignment or resonance among structures is highly favored in cognition, and language goes out of its way to make it possible. For instance, as many writers have remarked, a major functional motivation for the passive construction is that it puts into subject position an intended topic that in the normal active form would be postverbal.

The cognitive salience of the topic-comment form, I suspect, is what gave rise to the Aristotelian formulation of logic in terms of predicates applied to subjects. In fact, it also likely accounts for the very use of the term "subject" (= 'topic') for the initial NP in a sentence (see discussion in Seuren 1998: 120–33). Lambrecht, again following Marty, calls a sentence in topic-comment form a *categorical judgment*. In the present approach, of course, it is useful to notice also the *mis*matches between syntax and information structure that the organization into tiers leads us to expect. Not every sentence falls so cleanly into either the thetic or categorical type. For instance, the subject of (52a) (*PAT went to the party*) is Focus rather than Topic, so the sentence is neither thetic nor categorical.

We are now confronted with two overlapping notions of information structure: the focus is picked out in opposition to the presupposition (which includes topic), and the topic is picked out in opposition to the comment (which includes focus). To reconcile the two, I will use the term "common ground" specifically to designate the part of information structure that is neither topic nor focus. In other words, the "presupposition" is an informal term for topic plus common ground; the "comment" is common ground plus focus. Focus is obligatory, topic and common ground are optional. If topic and common ground are both absent, the sentence expresses a thetic judgment.

One other piece of information structure needs to be mentioned. Consider answers to questions that contain two *wh*-phrases.

(61)   A: Who danced with whom at the party last night?
       B: Well, FRAN danced with DAVID, ELI danced with FANIA, and
          ELIZABETH danced with BARBARA.

Following our treatment of answers to questions above, we would like to say that each of the highlighted NPs in B's reply is a focus, hence that there are two foci per clause. But the foci in each clause are not independent of each other; they form ordered pairs. We can paraphrase the reply rather closely by using topic-comment form:

(62)   Well, as for FRAN, SHE danced with DAVID; as for ELI, HE danced with FANIA; as for ELIZABETH, SHE danced with BARBARA.

So these paired foci behave a bit like a list of topic–focus pairs. Should we treat the first stressed element in each clause of (61B) (*Fran, Eli, Elizabeth*) as a Focus or as a Topic? It is somewhere in between.

In the proper setting, it is just barely possible to embed paired foci under a larger topic:[28]

(63)   As for bad reLAtionships [*topic*], JOHN hates his MOTHER, FRAN hates her SISTER, and my BROTHER can't STAND [*contrastive focus*] ME.

This suggests that the first element of a paired focus construction has a different status from an ordinary topic. We might call it a "first focus," preserving the generalization that wh-phrases and the phrases answering them are always foci. Or we might call it a "subtopic," emphasizing its topic-like realization in syntax and phonology. The terminology doesn't really matter.

What matters is this: There are three roles in information structure that can be coindexed with constituents in the descriptive tier, each of which displays characteristic prosodic and syntactic effects: Focus (obligatory), Topic (optional), and First Focus (optional). The remaining material, which does not necessarily form a unified constituent, is Common Ground. So the formation rule for the information structure tier can be simply (64).

(64)   (Topic) (Common Ground) (First Focus) Focus

Compared to all the other structures we have investigated, this is trivially simple. One might wonder whether it permits any sort of embedding, say whether relative clauses or indirect quotations can have their own subordinate information structure. I am not familiar with any proposals to this effect in the literature. Though the question seems worth exploring, I will not do so here.

Let us see how (64) can be coindexed with the descriptive tier. As already mentioned, Topic and Focus map to constituents, but Common Ground does not appear to. For instance, consider (65).

---

[28] I am grateful to Jong Sup Jun for bringing such examples to my attention, in the context of a discussion of topic-marking in Korean.

(65) a. BILL took SALLY to school, and FRANK took PHIL there.
      b. BILL took Sally to SCHOOL, and FRANK took her to the MOVIES.

Each clause in (65) contains paired contrastive foci, each of which is clearly a
constituent. On the other hand, the rest seems to be a nonconstituent: *take . . .
to school* in (65a) and *take Sally . . .* in (65b).[29] So it looks on the surface as
though Common Ground cannot be coindexed with anything.

A solution arises from the observation (Chomsky 1972a; Jackendoff 1972;
Akmajian 1973) that the Common Ground is actually something like *someone
took someone to school* in (65a) and *someone took Sally somewhere* in (65b).
That is, the Common Ground is the result of replacing the Focus and First Focus
constituents with variables. In the present framework, the proper place to do
this is not in syntax, but in the descriptive tier—where it turns out that the variables are already there! They are the open variables that serve as attachment
points for the Focus and First Focus constituents. (66) illustrates. The dashed
lines enclose the pieces of the descriptive tier that correspond to the pieces of
information structure, overlapping at the attachment points.

(66) S/P: $[_S$ BILL$_1$ $[_{VP}$ took$_2$ SALLY$_3$ $[$to$_4$ school$_5$ $]_6$ $]$ $]_7$
      DT:

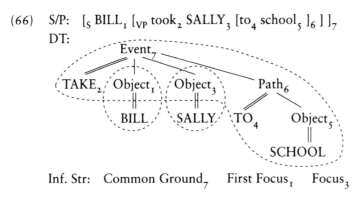

      Inf. Str: Common Ground$_7$ First Focus$_1$ Focus$_3$

In other words, we can think of the foregrounded elements Topic, First Focus,
and Focus as "carving pieces out" of the descriptive tier, leaving behind a
Common Ground with variables in it.

This approach to the Common Ground yields an elegant account of certain
kinds of ellipsis. Consider the examples in (67).

(67) a. JOHN likes PIZZA, and BILL(,) BANANAS.   [Gapping]
      b. JOHN threw his BOOK in the garbage, and FRED did the same
          thing with his TERM paper.   [*Do the same* ellipsis]

---

[29] There have been proposals in the literature that make one or the other of these into a syntactic constituent. Larson (1988), through heavy-duty invocation of syntactic movement, even manages to have it both ways. But I think the proper conclusion is that neither is a constituent and that
the VP has the flat tripartite structure V– NP–PP. See Culicover (2000).

How is the second clause of (67a) interpreted as *Bill likes bananas*, and how is the second clause of (67b) interpreted as *Fred threw his term paper in the garbage*? In particular, there is no way to syntactically reconstruct the antecedent of *do the same thing* in (67b), since *throw . . . in the garbage* is a non-constituent. The answer proposed by Akmajian (1973) is that these kinds of ellipsis involve paired foci, and they take as their antecedent the Common Ground of the first clause. With the formalization of Common Ground suggested in (66), this antecedent is easily accessible, with no further ado.[30]

There are also connections between information structure and the referential tier. In particular, since Topic is something independently known to the hearer, and to which the hearer's attention can be drawn, it cannot be referentially licensed by something in the comment, as observed by Partee (1991). Thus it has to be independently grounded. The effect is that it is outside the scope of quantifiers in the comment. Consider (68).

(68) a. Every girl danced with one of the boys.
      b. One of the boys was danced with by every girl.
      c. One of the boys, every girl danced with.

(68a) preferably has the narrow scope reading of *one* in which each girl danced with a different boy. (68b), with *one of the boys* in subject position, favors but does not require a wide-scope reading, in which the same boy danced with each girl. This is because subject position is preferably interpreted as Topic. (68c) has *one of the boys* in a construction that *requires* it to be understood as Topic, and so the wide scope reading is obligatory.

Furthermore, section 12.4 showed that *every* requires a bound variable that is referentially licensed by the event in the scope of the quantifier. Thus the variable cannot be independently grounded in the referential tier. We therefore predict that *every N* cannot serve as a topic. This seems correct. *Every N* can of course appear as a subject, but subjects need not be Topics. On the other hand, *every N* is ungrammatical in the preposed position that marks topics:

(69) a. *Every girl, one of the boys danced with.
      b. *As for every girl, one of the boys danced with her.

Thus we can perhaps get certain scope effects simply through the meaning of the information structure tier, without appealing to further machinery such as quantifier lifting or lambda extraction.

---

[30] In particular, there is no need for syntactic reconstruction or for semantic lambda extraction, solutions that have been popular in the literature. See however n. 17 for a problem that arises in the referential tier.

This exposition of the information structure tier has been extremely sketchy. The idea has been only to show its general properties and their role in the present system. It is again a matter for future research to integrate the sizable literature in this area into the framework, and to see what advantages or disadvantages may ensue.

12.6 Phrasal semantics and Universal Grammar

We have not talked about the mentalistic basis of semantics much in this chapter. It is time to come back to it, if only briefly. What parts of phrasal semantics have to be learned, and what parts come from Universal Grammar? Of the parts that come from UG, which are aspects of more general-purpose capacities, and which are specific to language?

First, it is clear that all these aspects of phrasal meaning are available in all the languages of the world. As has been mentioned here and there, languages differ in their syntactic strategies for expressing phrasal semantics; but the organization of what is to be expressed seems universal. The elements of the descriptive, referential, and information structure tiers seem the same across languages, and the principles of combination, especially in the descriptive tier, seem universally available. At least on preliminary reflection, the possibility of learning any of this would seem severely limited by the poverty of the stimulus. Thus I find it plausible that the basic architecture of conceptual structure is innate.

On the other hand, conceptual structure is supposed to be the medium of thought—the mental structure that language evolved to express—rather than part of language per se. So it seems reasonable to guess that this architecture is not a part of Universal Grammar, narrowly construed. What *is* part of Universal Grammar, of course, is the architecture of the interface components that allow conceptual structures to be expressed in syntactic and phonological structures.

Is there independent evidence for such a conclusion? Consider the descriptive tier. Monkeys, especially in the realm of social relationships, appear to be working with abstract relations such as kinship and dominance, whose variables are filled with known individuals (Cheney and Seyfarth 1990). On the other hand, in the absence of language, it is hard to establish whether they use function-argument relations recursively in the manner pervasive in linguistically expressed concepts. Turning to the referential tier, any animal that distinguishes individuals from each other on a lasting basis has concepts with indexical features, hence a referential tier of at least a primordial sort. Again, though, in the absence of language it is not clear how to test whether for instance they have indexical features embedded under irrealis frames.

The information structure tier, unlike the other two, is concerned with packaging a complex concept for the purpose of communication. Thus it seems a less likely candidate for an aspect of general-purpose thought. On the other hand, cognitive grammarians (e.g. Talmy 1978; 1996b; Langacker 1987) have consistently used the terms "figure" and "ground" in connection with information structure issues, suggesting that Topic and Focus have something to do with the distribution of attention. If so, perhaps the packaging in expression simply reflects the way we are built to package perception. The issues are at the moment wide open and well worth exploring.

Finally, are these all the tiers there are in meaning? Another candidate, somewhat distanced from "logical meaning," might be register: the use of words, constructions, and phonology to convey degree of formality, presumed relationship to the hearer, and so forth. Some lexical items, constructions, and other stored elements are lexically marked for their register (e.g. *Daddy* is informal, *Father* is formal); other items (e.g. *some* and *banana*) are registrally neutral. The phrasal computation of register would simply ensure that no marked items conflict with one another. I am not in a position to address whether this leads to any significant formal complexity.

12.7 Beyond: discourse, conversation, narrative

I have skipped over many of the usual topics of pragmatics such as conversational implicature, irony, and metaphor, in the hope that connoisseurs will be able to determine for themselves how to integrate them into the present framework. I wish to conclude by very briefly mentioning some issues that arise from pushing the scale of analysis still larger, to multi-sentence assemblages.

First, we have clear intuitions about the semantic connections between adjacent sentences. (70) illustrates a few possibilities.

(70) a. The dog was fat. The cat was thin.   [Simultaneous states]
      b. You pick up that end. I'll pick up this end.   [Simultaneous events]
      c. I can't come. I feel sick.   [S_2 is reason for S_1]
      d. I feel sick. I can't come.   [S_2 is result of S_1]
      e. John walked in. He took off his shoes.   [S_2 follows S_1]
      f. The bottle fell off the table. It crashed into a million pieces.
                          [S_2 follows S_1 and is a consequence of it]
      g. John walked in. He looked angry.   [S_2 is a state revealed by event S_1]

The examples in (70) can all be paraphrased by conjoined forms like *the dog was fat and the cat was thin*. But this is not always possible, particularly if one of the sentences is nondeclarative.

(71)   a. Put your coat in the bathroom. It's wet.

$$[S_2 \text{ is reason for (saying) } S_1]$$

(note *Put your coat in the bathroom, and it's wet)

       b. Why should I have to do that? I'm an old man.

$$[S_2 \text{ is reason for (saying) } S_1]$$

(note * Why should I have to do that and I'm an old man]

Since there is no lexical or structural expression of the connection between the sentences, it is left for the hearer to figure out the connection on general grounds of plausibility. Thus the specification of the connection is a classic case of enriched composition, now at the multi-sentential scale.

Two important questions are posed by Asher (2001) regarding these intuitions. First, is there a limited repertoire of connections from which hearers can select? Second, what semantic factors in S_1 and S_2 lead hearers to select one connection rather than another? We can add to these questions a third: How do language users learn to do this? Interestingly, these questions precisely parallel the questions we asked in section 8.7 about compounds like *doghouse* and *armchair*, in which the range of semantic connections possible between the two nouns is a complex function of the nouns' meanings. This is a point where grammar fades out and we are dealing purely with conceptual structure. But, given that the phenomena arise from language use, it certainly falls to linguists to investigate them.

When we move to discourses longer than two sentences, the problems multiply. For instance, Herbert Clark (1996) suggests that conversations have a sort of embedding structure. Consider the following conversation, which Clark (343) quotes from Merritt (1984: 140). C is a customer and S a salesperson.

(72)   a. C: Hi, do you have uh size C flashlight batteries?
       b. S: Yes sir.
       c. C: I'll have four please.
       d. S: Do you want the long life or the regular?
       e.   See the long life doesn't last ten times longer than the regular battery.
       f.   Usually last three times as long. . . .
       g. C: Guess I better settle for the short life.
       h. S: How many you want?
       i. C: Four please.
       j. S: Okay. That's a dollar forty and nine tax, a dollar forty-nine.

The indenting in (72) reflects Clark's analysis of the embedding. After hearing (72c), the salesperson realizes she needs more information and in (72d) begins a "subtask" of asking what type of battery the customer wants. Before the customer can answer, though, the salesperson realizes there is a sub-subtask of giving the customer a reason to choose one type rather than the other. The customer could have initiated this sub-subtask by asking after (72d), *What's the difference between them?* But the salesperson, having anticipated this question, embarks on the lengthy explanation (72e, f). Once the explanation is over, the customer can complete the subtask of answering (72d) with (72g). At this point the salesperson has forgotten how many batteries the customer wants, already present in (72c). She therefore must initiate yet another subtask (72h) to reestablish this point, which the customer completes with (72i). Finally the conversation can return to the main task of concluding the transaction.

What makes this an embedding structure is that the connections among sentences are not just local. (72d) and (72g) are connected as question and answer, but this connection is interrupted by (72e, f), which have their own local connection to each other. Similarly, (72j) is ultimately a completion of a transaction initiated at (72c), with all the other material treated as an interpolation.

So the same questions arise: What sorts of connection can be used non-locally? What kinds of connection can there be between embedded constituents and the larger units into which they are interpolated? How do hearers negotiate these connections? And how do they *learn* to do it?

Going to a case that is still more complex analytically but totally transparent intuitively, here is the opening of a novel by Raymond Chandler:

(73)   The first time I laid eyes on Terry Lennox he was drunk in a Rolls-Royce Silver Wraith outside the terrace of The Dancers. The parking lot attendant had brought the car out and he was still holding the door open because Terry Lennox's left foot was still dangling outside, as if he had forgotten he had one. He had a young-looking face but his hair was bone white. You could tell by his eyes that he was plastered to the hairline, but otherwise he looked like any other nice young guy in a dinner jacket who had been spending too much money in a joint that exists for that purpose and for no other.

There was a girl beside him. Her hair was a lovely shade of dark red and she had a distant smile on her lips and over her shoulders she had a blue mink that almost made the Rolls-Royce look like just another automobile. It didn't quite. Nothing can. (Chandler 1953: 3)

Some sentences and clauses place the narrator in the scene; others are presented from a distant, omniscient point of view. Some passages describe action; others are just decorative description. The reader's attention is drawn sequentially now to one character, now to another. Some clauses describe events taking place before the scene begins.

The first question we might ask is: What sort of cognitive structure does this narrative build, such that the meaning of each sentence has its proper place in it? It has a multidimensional complexity in time, point of view, tone, and narrative rhythm far beyond anything we have looked at so far. Given this structure, then we have to ask yet again: how do readers derive this structure from the printed page, and how do they learn to do it? What are the cognitive antecedents that allow narrative to take such forms?

A final question: What is wrong with this narrative?

(74)   Once upon a time there was a little duck who lived with an armadillo in a burrow underneath a stop sign, next to a big purple fire station. In the fire station lived a dog named Spot who had been born on a farm in Florida. His parents belonged to a man named Harry Thistlethwaite who grew tobacco for cigars. One day Harry was out walking when he spied a little girl walking down the street. The girl's name was Monica, and she was 10 years old. She owned three umbrellas, one of which was manufactured by a company in Singapore that went bankrupt four years later. Its owner was so distressed he went to Las Vegas and drowned himself in a swimming pool. . . .

Conversations at dinner parties sometimes go like this. Everything is locally connected, but there are no larger connections. This kind of random walk from topic to topic is however unacceptable in narrative. We understand that topics opened and characters introduced must eventually result in narratively significant events, and that threads of narrative opened at one point must eventually be tied up. Again it is of interest to ask what cognitive structures are associated with narrative that demand this sort of large-scale coherence.

Speaking of large-scale coherence, I fear that the range of issues and topics covered in this book may by now feel to readers a bit like a large-scale version of (74). So I will close by trying to summarize what makes it all hang together.

CHAPTER 13

Concluding Remarks

The promise of generative grammar in the 1960s was that it would give us insight into the nature of mind and brain. The path we have traveled in the past several hundred pages has, I think, put us in a better position to realize that promise. A quick review will help see why.

The goal of Part I was to show that the promise should not be relinquished. The most rewarding way to investigate language is still from the mentalist point of view—focusing especially on what it takes for a child to acquire facility in a language. The last thirty years have brought phenomenal progress in understanding linguistic structure, language acquisition, language processing, and language deficits. These years have also brought many important advances in understanding the brain and the learning capacities of animals, humans, and computationally modeled neural systems. Everything about language appears richer and more complex than it did thirty years ago, thanks in part to the better tools we have for looking at it now, but thanks also to decades of patient and impassioned research, exploring more ground more carefully.

The upshot of all this work, on balance, is that we can considerably sharpen the questions posed by mentalism. Instead of simply asserting that language must be lodged in the brain *somehow*, and debating whether children must come to language acquisition with *some* innate capacities specific to language, it is now possible to articulate the issues more clearly. Among the questions that have emerged here as critical are these:

- How are discrete structural units (such as phonological features and syntactic categories) instantiated in the nervous system?

- How are hierarchical structures, composed of such units, instantiated in the nervous system?

- How are variables instantiated as elements of such structures in the nervous system?

- How does the brain instantiate working memory, such that structures can be built online from units and structures stored in long-term memory, and in particular so as to solve the Problem of 2 (multiple instances in working memory of a single long-term memory type)?

• How does the brain instantiate learning, such that pieces assembled in working memory can be installed into long-term memory?

• How does one-trial learning differ from slow, many-trial learning?

• How is innate specialized f-knowledge instantiated in the brain, and how does it guide behavior and learning?

• How is innate specialized f-knowledge coded on the genome, and how does it guide brain development, including the characteristic localizations of different functions?

One of the things I tried to stress about these questions as they came up is that they are not particular to language. The same questions are posed by the visual system and the formulation of action—for any organism that finds its way around its environment and behaves with any degree of complexity. Language just happens to be a domain where some of the questions have been more a matter of open debate than elsewhere.

In reconciling linguistic theory with a mentalistic instantiation, it has been important here to abandon the idea that linguistic entities in the brain are *symbols* or *representations*. We have instead been able to treat them simply as *structures* built of discrete combinatorial units. In the case of phonology and syntax this was not too painful. But in the case of semantics it was necessary to spend much of Chapter 10 working out an alternative to the mystery of intentionality: how it is that language seems to refer to the world despite the fact that all the machinery instantiating language is trapped in our brains. However, again the issues prove not to be particular to language; rather they pertain as well to vision and other perceptual/cognitive modalities—in any organism that perceives the physical world roughly as we do. It is just that this particular way of framing the issues traditionally comes to us from philosophy of language.

A more technical question about memory arises from the discussion of semiregular patterns and inheritance hierarchies in Chapter 6. In the present framework (as well as some related frameworks), a great deal of theoretical weight has come to rest on the idea that the taxonomic relations and redundancies among items somehow allow them to "cost less." For example, in some sense the idiom *take advantage of* ought to be in some sense "cheaper" than *take umbrage at*, because *advantage* is an independent word and *umbrage* occurs only in this idiom. Similarly, the irregular past tense *brought* should be "cheaper" than *went* because (a) *brought* bears some phonological similarity to *bring* whereas *went* bears no relation to *go*, and (b) *fought, taught, bought, sought,* and *caught* share the same distant relation to their present tenses. Yet standard notations within linguistic theory don't allow us to extract just the non-redundant parts of idioms and irregular morphology as distinct lexical entries. Hence we cannot codify their "cost" in terms of number of symbols on the page, the traditional methodological criterion for generality. I have therefore tentatively suggested that, as far as traditional linguistic notation is concerned, these sorts of relation are tacit or implicit; they are a consequence of how memory for related items is organized in the brain. I am given some encouragement in this conclusion from the behavior of some connectionist models, but much remains to be worked out, both within linguistics and within neuroscience. Yet again, though, the same problems accrue to the taxonomic organization of concepts, so this is not a problem peculiar to idioms and irregular verbs.

What we have learned about the brain from studying language, then, is how to frame the hard questions more sharply. I don't think that's so bad. My guess is that these questions are likely not going to be answered in terms of language alone. If they are answered through experiments on, say, a pigeon's homing behavior plus some creative combination of brain recording and computational modeling, that's fine too. But language gives us a benchmark of uneliminable and well-understood problems that make clear what is at stake.

The goal of Part II was to move linguistic theory itself closer to the possibility of explanation in terms of the brain. Not by reducing it or denying any of its complexity—quite the opposite: by embracing its complexity and reorganizing its architecture accordingly. The crucial insight comes initially from phonology. Phonological structure since the late 1970s has been viewed as composed of a number of independent generative subcomponents, each of which is responsible for its own characteristic form of structure or *tier*. The tiers are linked by interface rules that establish not one-to-one correspondences among the structures, but rather partial homologies in which mismatches of structure are to be expected.

Here we have extended this approach to the whole of language. Each of the major components of linguistic structure—phonology, syntax, and semantic/conceptual structure—is the product of an independent generative system, and each is further subdivided into independent tiers. The notion of a generative system is of course nothing new here—even within the individual components. What is new, I think, is the explicit recognition that this is the way the grammar is put together globally.

The key to formulating the parallel generative architecture more clearly is a full-blown theory of the interface components: how an interface component is structured in general, exactly what interface components are necessary, and what role interfaces play in the determination of grammatical structure. In particular, all the usual problems of learnability and balance of power among components pertain to interfaces as well as to the generative components. If I have concentrated more on interface components than generative components here, it is because in my opinion they have not previously received enough attention. People speak of "the phonology–syntax interface" but not "the phonology–syntax interface *component*," failing to recognize interface rules as qualitatively different from generative and derivational rules.

The move that most decisively sets the present framework apart from mainstream generative grammar is its treatment of the lexicon as an essential part of the interface components. A word like *cat* is not a list of phonological, syntactic, and semantic features that is inserted into syntax and carried around in the course of a derivation. Rather, it is a small-scale interface rule that helps correlate the parallel structures. Its phonology appears only in phonological structure, its syntax only in syntactic structure, and its semantics only in conceptual structure; and the word as a whole establishes the linking among the three in the overall structure of a sentence. Here we concur with some of the constraint-based frameworks, especially HPSG.

This sets the stage for a second step in reconceptualizing the lexicon. The notion of lexicon traditionally conflates two very different notions (at least informally): a list of words and a list of things that are memorized. The foundational observation of generative linguistics, of course, is that productive combinatoriality cannot in general be the consequence of memorization, but must be composed online by applying rules. By taking this dictum very seriously, we are led to recognize that lexical items include not just words but also productive morphological affixes and idioms. The treatment of lexical items as interface rules makes this move not only plausible but conceptually and formally natural. From idioms it is a small step to recognize idiomatically meaningful constructions as lexical items of a new and previously unrecognized sort—more or less as advocated by Construction Grammar, but in my opinion better integrated into the system as a whole. And finally, this puts us in a position to recognize such things as phrase structure rules as lexical items consisting entirely of variables. Quite possibly the only combinatorial or "procedural" rule remaining in the grammar, then, is UNIFY.

From the point of view of traditional generative grammar, we have by this point come to live in a very strange and perhaps uncomfortable land. I cannot myself claim to have come to terms with it entirely. However, I have tried to be as clear as I can about where traditional issues in syntax, phonology, and morphology fit into the new system. My hope is that the large-scale map I have offered may motivate exploration of more of the details, especially at the boundaries where major portions of the map have to match up. The treatment of argument structure in Chapter 5, of VP constructions in Chapter 6, and of lexical and phrasal semantics in Chapters 11 and 12 were offered as samples, these being topics on which I personally have spent a lot of effort over the years.

Another aspect of the theory that comes out quite unfamiliar is the theory of learnability. Here I must be still more speculative. But the conviction has grown on me that the dominant view of Universal Grammar as a a highly complex specification of all possible grammars—whether in terms of parameters or ranked constraints—is untenable. It does not allow enough room for the range of idiosyncrasy in language, as evidenced for instance by the variety of constructions in English. The present framework tentatively offers the possibility of seeing Universal Grammar as a much more limited (though hardly trivial) set of "attractor" structures that, through inheritance hierarchies, guide the course of the child's generalizations over the evidence. Whether this proposal can be worked out depends not only on facts from language and language acquisition, but also—heavily—on the resolution of the questions above about the relation of language to the brain. At the moment, anyway, this seems to be a promising direction for bringing linguistic learnability within reach of the brain.

The second half of Part II and all of Part III were spent exploring ways in which this reconfiguring of generative grammar offers a new degree of psychological and biological relevance. A standard criticism of mainstream generative grammar is that the principles of linguistic f-knowledge that the competence theory ascribes to the language user relate to models of language processing only in the most indirect fashion. Linguistic theory has often replied to this criticism by hiding behind the competence/performance distinction. But if the goal is to relate language to the mind, such a reply is less than satisfactory in the long run.

The parallel architecture, which is motivated largely on grounds internal to the competence theory, proves to offer a more positive response to this criticism. It translates quite directly into a model of processing, one in which the constraints on processing follow directly from the rules of grammar. The interface components play a particularly important role in the processing model, for they are what enable a processor to relate sound and meaning "opportunistically" or "incrementally." In particular, the effects of modularity emerge as a consequence of which components of the grammar and of the rest of the mind are related by interfaces, and how rich and direct such relations are. Moreover, treating lexical items as part of the interfaces immediately brings the competence theory to bear directly on heavily studied issues of lexical access in comprehension and production.

A less immediate but still telling criticism of generative grammar concerns evolutionary issues. Even if there is no direct evidence for the evolution of the language faculty, it is reasonable to ask for a plausible scenario by which it could have evolved in all its complexity. Again, mainstream generative grammar does not lend itself to incremental evolutionary development, largely because the parts of language that seem likely to have evolved first—phonology and semantics—are conceived of as the output of syntactic derivation, which has the feel of a relatively late innovation. It is of course hard to bring evolutionary concerns to bear on the gritty details of language. Nevertheless, the central claim of generative grammar is that the language faculty is a cognitive specialization, and we claim that cognitive specializations in every other species are the consequence of natural selection. So it behooves us to take responsibility for an evolutionary scenario, even if at the moment the picture is far from clear.

The parallel architecture turns out to permit a nicely articulated story of incremental evolution. The initial innovation is permitting sounds to be used symbolically in a non-situation-specific fashion. This is admittedly a mysterious advance over primate calls, but vastly less expressive than modern language. From there we are able to see the evolution of the language faculty as the successive addition of more and more "tricks" to the toolkit, in the interest of greater expressiveness and precision in conveying thought. In particular, syllabic and then segmental structure within phonology developed as a way of reliably increasing vocabulary size, and interface principles relating semantic roles to linear word order supplied a first rough cut on expressing relations among word meanings. Phrase structure, inflection, and grammatical functions then developed successively as machinery for expressing more complex hierarchical relations. The more recent innovations are the ones most subject to disruption, critical period effects, and above all variation from one language to the next. And even within the grammar of modern languages it is possible to find remnants of more "primitive" stages that have not been completely overlaid by modern grammar, as well as a "basic body plan" for syntax that has consequences throughout the grammar.

Finally, mainstream generative grammar has lacked a developed theory of semantics. In reaction, the two most prominent (American) schools of semantics have rejected generative grammar, in different ways: psychological issues play virtually no role in formal semantics, and issues of syntactic combinatoriality are downplayed in cognitive grammar. The parallel architecture acknowledges an important insight of both schools: that meaning has its own characteristic combinatorial structure, one that is not simply "read off" syntax. But our global approach to the language faculty has yielded more: a valuable perspective on the relation between syntax and semantics. In particular, the syntax–phonology interface, the interfaces among the phonological tiers, and the interfaces between phonology, acoustics, and gesture give us a fix on what to expect from the syntax–semantics interface. We should not expect an isomorphism: syntax should not (alone) determine semantics, as in mainstream generative grammar and many versions of formal semantics; but neither should semantics entirely determine syntax, as often asserted in cognitive grammar. It is in the character of interfaces everywhere in the f-mind to be "dirty"; there is no reason to expect more here.

A theory of meaning compatible with generative grammar must be psychological through and through: it should aspire to study the nature of thought. The parallel architecture, because it is embedded in a larger theory of the f-mind, gives us a natural way to study the interaction of language with perception and to pose questions for research in perception. It also gives us a way to pose questions about conceptualization in non-linguistic organisms such as babies and apes, and to ask questions about the innateness and the evolutionary basis of human thought.

The two final chapters, surveying issues in word and phrase meaning, give a sense of the complexity of the theory of meaning. Word meanings are compositional, in some respects paralleling the combinatoriality of phrases but in some respects proving more complex and more flexible. Phrasal semantics, like phonology, is organized into a number of tiers, each of which carries an independent aspect of meaning. Aspects of phrasal meaning, in particular referential structure and information structure, lead us on into issues of discourse structure, where further complexity awaits us.

A major benefit of the parallel architecture has emerged in the course of the last chapter: enriched composition and the multiple tiers of semantics liberate syntactic theory from a great deal of the complexity with which it has become encumbered over the years. In retrospect, we can see that this complexity has arisen from the demand that syntax be the sole generative component, responsible for all combinatorial structure in semantics. Now that semantics has its own generative organization, syntax needs to share with it only enough structure to get words into the right order for phonology. We can therefore envision a far leaner syntactic component, taking some of the burden off the learner and off UG as well.

My intuition is that this is as it should be. Phonology and syntax, after all, evolved to *express* meaning, which has a far longer evolutionary pedigree. Moreover, as we have seen, much of conveyed meaning is tacit, not expressed at all in the words uttered or the syntactic structure combining them. Why, therefore, should meaning not be a great deal more complex than the language that expresses it?

This is not to say syntax will go away altogether. There is still plenty of work for syntacticians. We still have to get the verb in the right place and supply agreement, case marking, and epenthetic *it*. We have to say which languages have ditransitive constructions and which don't, which languages require subjects and which don't, how phrasal syntax and morphology interact, how each language forms questions and relative clauses, and what offbeat constructions it has. And, as we have seen, it is a fascinating enterprise to choreograph the balance between pure syntax and its interfaces with the other components.

I have no illusion that such a thoroughgoing reconstruction of linguistic theory will be easy. Perhaps the hardest part will be maintaining the sense of global integration, keeping the subdomains of the field more closely in touch than they have recently been. If we choose to accept the challenge, I think the structure of language can still give us the best possible entrée into the mysteries of thought. The tools we have developed in the past thirty years are cause for encouragement. But linguistics alone cannot sustain the weight of the inquiry. We need all the help we can get from every possible quarter. Above all, my hope for the present work is that it can help encourage the necessary culture of collaboration.

References

Abbott, Barbara (1997). 'Models, Truth, and Semantics'. *Linguistics and Philosophy* 20: 117–38.

Ackerman, Farrell, and Gert Webelhuth (1999). *A Theory of Predicates*. Stanford, Calif.: CSLI.

Aiello, Leslie (1998). 'The Foundations of Human Language'. In Jablonski and Aiello (1998: 21–34).

Aissen, Judith (1999). 'Markedness and Subject Choice in Optimality Theory'. *Natural Language and Linguistic Theory* 17: 673–711.

Aitchison, Jean (1998). 'On Discontinuing the Continuity–Discontinuity Debate'. In Hurford et al. (1998: 17–29).

Akmajian, Adrian (1973). 'The Role of Focus in the Interpretation of Anaphoric Expressions'. In S. R. Anderson and P. Kiparsky (eds.), *A Festschrift for Morris Halle*, 215–26. New York: Holt, Rinehart & Winston.

Alderete, John, Jill Beckman, Laura Benua, Amalia Gnanadesikan, John McCarthy, and Suzanne Urbanczyk (1999). 'Reduplication with Fixed Segmentism'. *Linguistic Inquiry* 30: 327–64.

Altmann, Gerry (1987). 'Modularity and Interaction in Sentence Processing'. In Garfield (1987: 249–58).

Anderson, Stephen R. (1977). Comments on the Paper by Wasow. In P. Culicover, T. Wasow, and A. Akmajian (eds.), *Formal Syntax*, 361–77. New York: Academic Press.

—— (1992). *A-morphous Morphology*. New York: Cambridge University Press.

Arbib, Michael (1964). *Brains, Machines, and Mathematics*. New York: McGraw-Hill.

—— (1987). 'Modularity and Interaction of Brain Regions Underlying Visuomotor Coordination'. In Garfield (1987: 333–64).

Armstrong, Sharon Lee, Lila R. Gleitman, and Henry Gleitman (1983). 'On What Some Concepts Might Not Be'. *Cognition* 13: 263–308.

Arnold, Jennifer E., Thomas Wasow, Anthony Losongco, and Ryan Ginstrom (2000), 'Heaviness vs. Newness: The Effects of Structural Complexity and Discourse Status on Constituent Ordering'. *Language* 76: 28–55.

Aronoff, Mark (1976). *Word Formation in Generative Grammar*. Cambridge, Mass.: MIT Press.

—— (1980). 'Contextuals'. *Language* 56: 744–58.

Asher, Nicholas (2001). 'Computation and Storage in Discourse Interpretation'. In S. Nooteboom, F. Weerman, and F. Wijnen (eds.), *Storage and Computation in the Language Faculty*, 283–311. Dordrecht: Kluwer.

Austin, J. (1962). *How to Do Things with Words*. Oxford: Clarendon Press.

Austin, Peter W. (2001). 'Word Order in a Free Word Order Language. The Case of Jiwarli'. In Jane Simpson, David Nash, Mary Laughren, Peter Austin, and Barry Alpher (eds.), *Forty Years On: Ken Hale and Australian Languages*, 305–23. Canberra: Pacific Linguistics.

Baayen, Harald, Willem Levelt, and Alette Haveman (1993). Research reported in Annual Report of the Max-Planck Institut für Psycholinguistik, 6. Nijmegen: Max-Planck Institut.

—— Maarten Van Casteren, and Ton Dijkstra (1992). Research reported in Annual Report of the Max-Planck Institut für Psycholinguistik, 28. Nijmegen: Max-Planck Institut.

Baayen, R. H., R. Schreuder, N. H. De Jong, and A. Krott (2001). 'Dutch Inflection: The Rules that Prove the Exception'. In S. Nooteboom, F. Weerman, and F. Wijnen (eds.), *Storage and Computation in the Language Faculty*, 41–73. Dordrecht, Kluwer.

Bach, Emmon (1983). 'On the Relation between Word-Grammar and Phrase-Grammar'. *Natural Language and Linguistic Theory* 1: 65–90.

—— (1986a). 'Natural Language Metaphysics'. In R. Barcan-Marcus, G. Dorn, and P. Weingartner (eds.), *Logic Methodology, and Philosophy of Science*, 573–95. Amsterdam: North-Holland.

—— (1986b). 'The Algebra of Events'. *Linguistics and Philosophy* 9: 5–16.

—— (1989). *Informal Lectures on Formal Semantics*. Albany, NY: State University of New York Press.

Bach, Kent, and Robert M. Harnish (1979). *Linguistic Communication and Speech Acts*. Cambridge, Mass.: MIT Press.

Baddeley, Alan (1986). *Working Memory*. Oxford: Clarendon Press.

Baillargeon, Renée (1986). 'Representing the Existence and the Location of Hidden Objects: Object Permanence in 6- and 8-Month-Old Infants'. *Cognition* 23: 21–41.

Baker, C. L., and John J. McCarthy (eds.) (1981). *The Logical Problem of Language Acquisition*. Cambridge, Mass.: MIT Press.

Baker, Mark (1988). *Incorporation: A Theory of Grammatical Function Changing*. Chicago: University of Chicago Press.

Ballard, Dana H., Mary M. Hayhoe, Polly K. Pook, and Rajesh P. N. Rao (1997). 'Deictic Codes for the Embodiment of Cognition'. *Behavioral and Brain Sciences* 20: 723–42.

Bar-Hillel, Yehoshua (1970). 'The Outlook for Computational Semantics'. In Bar-Hillel, *Aspects of Language*, 357–63. Jerusalem: Magnes Press.

Barkow, Jerome H., Leda Cosmides, and John Tooby (eds.) (1992). *The Adapted Mind*. Oxford: Oxford University Press.

Barnden, J. (1996). 'Unconscious Gaps in Jackendoff's "How Language Helps Us Think" '. *Pragmatics and Cognition* 4: 65–79.

Barsalou, Lawrence (1992). 'Frames, Concepts, and Conceptual Fields'. In A. Lehrer and E. Kittay (eds.), *Frames, Fields, and Contrasts*, 21–74. Hillsdale, NJ: Erlbaum.

—— (1999). 'Perceptual Symbol Systems'. *Behavioral and Brain Sciences* 22: 577–609.

Batali, John (1998). 'Computational Simulations of the Emergence of Grammar'. In Hurford et al. (1998: 405–26).

Bates, Elizabeth, and Jeffrey Elman (1996). 'Learning Rediscovered'. *Science* 274 (13 Dec.): 1849–50.

—— and Brian MacWhinney (1982). 'Functionalist Approaches to Grammar'. In E. Wanner and L. Gleitman (eds.), *Language Acquisition: The State of the Art*, 173–218. Cambridge: Cambridge University Press.

Beard, Robert (1987). 'Morpheme Order in a Lexeme/Morpheme-Based Morphology'. *Lingua* 72: 1–44.

Beckman, Mary, and Janet Pierrehumbert (1986). 'Intonational Structure in English and Japanese'. *Phonology* 3: 255–309.

Behrens, Heike, and Michael Tomasello (1999). 'And What about the Chinese?' (commentary on Clahsen 1999). *Behavioral and Brain Sciences* 22: 1014.

Belletti, A., and L. Rizzi (1988). 'Psych-verbs and θ-theory'. *Natural Language and Linguistic Theory* 6: 291–352.

Bellugi, Ursula, Howard Poizner, and Edward S. Klima (1989). 'Language, Modality, and the Brain'. *Trends in Neurosciences* 12: 380–8.

—— Paul P. Wang, and Terry L. Jernigan (1994). 'Williams Syndrome: An Unusual Neuropsychological Profile'. In S. Broman and J. Grafman (eds.), *Atypical Cognitive Deficits in Developmental Disorders: Implications for Brain Function*. Hillsdale, NJ: Erlbaum.

Berent, Iris, Steven Pinker, and Joseph Shimron (1999). 'Default Nominal Inflection in Hebrew: Evidence for Mental Variables'. *Cognition* 72: 1–44.

Berko, Jean (1958). 'The Child's Learning of English Morphology'. *Word* 14: 150–77.

Berlin, Brent, and Paul Kay (1969). *Basic Color Terms: Their Universality and Evolution*. Berkeley, Calif.: University of California Press.

Bever, Thomas G. (1992). 'The Logical and Extrinsic Sources of Modularity'. In M. Gunnar and M. Maratsos (eds.), *Modularity and Constraints in Language and Cognition*, 179–212. Hillsdale, NJ: Erlbaum.

—— John M. Carroll, and Lance A. Miller (eds.) (1984). *Talking Minds: The Study of Language in the Cognitive Sciences*. Cambridge, Mass.: MIT Press.

Bickerton, Derek (1981). *Roots of Language*. Ann Arbor, Mich.: Karoma.

—— (1990) *Language and Species*. Chicago: University of Chicago Press.

Biederman, Irving (1987). 'Recognition-by Components: A Theory of Human Image Understanding'. *Psychological Review* 94: 115–47.

Bierwisch, Manfred (1963). 'Grammatik des deutschen Verbs'. *Studia Grammatica* II.

—— (1967). 'Some Semantic Universals of German Adjectivals'. *Foundations of Language* 3: 1–36.

—— (1969). 'On Certain Problems of Semantic Representation'. *Foundations of Language* 5: 153–84.

—— (1996). 'How Much Space Gets into Language?' In Bloom (1996: 31–76).

—— (1997). 'Universal Grammar and the Basic Variety'. *Second Language Research* 13: 348–66.

—— and Ewald Lang (eds.) (1989). *Dimensional Adjectives: Grammatical Structure and Conceptual Interpretation*. Berlin: Springer.

Blake, Barry J. (1994). *Case*. Cambridge: Cambridge University Press.

Blevins, James P. (1999). 'Productivity and Exponence' (commentary on Clahsen 1999). *Behavioral and Brain Sciences* 22: 1015–16.

Bloom, Paul (1994a). 'Generativity within Language and other Cognitive Domains'. *Cognition* 51: 177–89.

—— (1994b). ' Possible Names: The Role of Syntax–Semantics Mappings in the Acquisition of Nominals'. In Gleitman and Landau (1994: 297–329).

—— (1999). 'The Role of Semantics in Solving the Bootstrapping Problem'. In Jackendoff et al. (1999: 285–310).

—— (2000). *How Children Learn the Meanings of Words*. Cambridge, Mass.: MIT Press.

—— Mary A. Peterson, Lynn Nadel, and Merrill F. Garrett (eds.) (1996). *Language and Space*. Cambridge, Mass.: MIT Press.

Bloomfield, Leonard (1933). *Language*. New York: Holt, Rinehart & Winston.

Bock, Kathryn (1995), 'Sentence Production: From Mind to Mouth'. In J. L. Miller and P. D. Eimas (eds.), *Handbook of Perception and Cognition*, vol xi: *Speech, Language, and Communication*, 181–216. Orlando, Fla.: Academic Press.

—— and Helga Loebell (1990) 'Framing Sentences'. *Cognition* 35: 1–39.

Bolinger, Dwight (1961). 'Syntactic Blends and Other Matters'. *Language* 37: 366–810.

—— (1965a). 'The Atomization of Meaning'. *Language* 41: 555–73.

—— (1965b). *Forms of English: Accent, Morpheme, Order*. Cambridge, Mass.: Harvard University Press.

Booij, Geert (1999). 'Lexical Storage and Regular Processes' (commentary on Clahsen 1999). *Behavioral and Brain Sciences* 22: 1016.

Bowers, John (1975). 'Adjectives and Adverbs in English'. *Foundations of Language* 13: 529–62.

Bratman, Michael (1987). *Intention, Plans, and Practical Reason*. Cambridge, Mass.: Harvard University Press.

Brent, Michael (1994). 'Surface Cues and Robust Inference as a Basis for the Early Acquisition of Subcategorization Frames'. In Gleitman and Landau (1994: 433–70).

Bresnan, Joan W. (1973). 'Syntax of the Comparative Clause Construction in English'. *Linguistic Inquiry* 4: 275–344.

—— (1978). 'A Realistic Transformational Grammar'. In Halle et al. (1978: 1–59).

—— (ed.) (1982a). *The Mental Representation of Grammatical Relations*. Cambridge, Mass.: MIT Press.

—— (1982b). 'Control and Complementation'. In Bresnan (1982a: 282–390).

—— (2001). *Lexical-Functional Syntax*. Oxford: Blackwell.

—— and Jonni Kanerva (1989). 'Locative Inversion in Chicheŵa: A Case Study of Factorization in Grammar'. *Linguistic Inquiry* 20: 1–50.

—— and Ronald M. Kaplan (1982). 'Introduction'. In Bresnan (1982a: pp. xvii–lii).

—— and Sam Mchombo (1995). 'The Lexical Integrity Principle: Evidence from Bantu'. *Natural Language and Linguistic Theory* 13: 181–254.

Brooks, Rodney (1986). 'A Robust Layered Control System for a Mobile Robot'. *IEEE Journal of Robotics and Automation* 2: 14–23.

Brugman, Claudia (1981). 'Story of Over'. Bloomington: Indiana University Linguistics Club.

Bruner, Jerome S. (1974/5). 'From Communication to Language: A Psychological Perspective'. *Cognition* 3: 255–78.

Büring, Daniel (1993). ' Interacting Modules, Word Formation, and the Lexicon in Generative Grammar'. Cologne: Institut für deutsche Sprache und Literatur.

—— (1996) *The 59th Street Bridge Accent: On the Meaning of Topic and Focus*. Tübingen: Seminar für Sprachwissenschaft.

Busa, Federica (1996). *Compositionality and the Semantics of Nominals*. Doctoral dissertation, Dept. of Computer Science, Brandeis University.

Bybee, Joan, and C. Moder (1983). 'Morphological Classes as Natural Categories'. *Language* 59: 251–70.

Byrne, Richard W., and Andrew Whiten (eds.) (1988). *Machiavellian Intelligence: Social Expertise and the Evolution of Intellect in Monkeys, Apes, and Humans*. Oxford: Clarendon Press.

Calvin, William (1990). *The Cerebral Symphony*. New York: Bantam Books.

—— and Derek Bickerton (2000). *Lingua ex machina: Reconciling Darwin and Chomsky with the Human Brain*. Cambridge, Mass.: MIT Press.

Caramazza, Alfonso, and Michele Miozzo (1997). 'The Relation between Syntactic and Phonological Knowledge in Lexical Access: Evidence from the "Tip-of-the-Tongue" Phenomenon'. *Cognition* 64: 309–43.

Carey, Susan (1978). 'The Child as Word Learner'. In Halle et al. (1978: 264–93).

—— (1994). 'Does Learning a Language Require the Child to Reconceptualize the World?' In Gleitman and Landau (1994: 143–67).

—— and Xu, F. (1999). 'Sortals and Kinds: An Appreciation of John Macnamara'. In Jackendoff et al. (1999: 311–36).

Carnap, Rudolf (1964). 'Foundations of Logic and Mathematics'. In J. Fodor and J. Katz (eds.), *The Structure of Language*, 419–36. New York: Prentice-Hall.

Carroll, John B. (ed.) (1956). *Language, Thought, and Reality: Selected Writings of Benjamin Lee Whorf*. Cambridge, Mass.: MIT Press.

Carroll, Patrick J., and Maria L. Slowiaczek (1987). 'Modes and Modules: Multiple Paths to the Language Processor'. In Garfield (1987: 221–48).

Carstairs-McCarthy, A. (1999). *The Origins of Complex Language*. Oxford: Oxford University Press.

Casey, Shannon, and Robert Kluender (1995). 'Evidence for Intermediate Forms in the Evolution of Language'. In A. Dainora, R. Hemphill, B. Luka, B. Need, and S. Pargman (eds.), *Papers from the 31st Regional Meeting of the Chicago Linguistic Society*, vol. i: *The Main Session*, 66–80. Chicago: Chicago Linguistic Society.

Cela-Conde, Camilo J., and Gisèle Marty (1998). 'An Interview with Noam Chomsky'. *Syntax* 1: 19–36.

Chandler, Raymond (1953). *The Long Goodbye*. New York: Houghton Mifflin.

Cheney, Dorothy, and Robert Seyfarth (1990). *How Monkeys See the World*. Chicago: University of Chicago Press.

Chierchia, Gennaro, and Sally McConnell-Ginet (1990). *Meaning and Grammar: An Introduction to Semantics*. Cambridge, Mass.: MIT Press.

Chomsky, Noam (1951). 'Morphophonemics of Modern Hebrew'. Master's thesis, University of Pennsylvania.

—— (1957). *Syntactic Structures*. The Hague: Mouton.

—— (1959). Review of B. F. Skinner, *Verbal Behavior*. *Language* 35: 26–58.

—— (1965). *Aspects of the Theory of Syntax*. Cambridge, Mass.: MIT Press.

—— (1966). *Cartesian Linguistics*. New York: Harper & Row.

—— (1970). 'Remarks on Nominalization'. In R. Jacobs and P. Rosenbaum (eds.), *Readings in English Transformational Grammar*, 184–221. Waltham, Mass.: Ginn. (Also in Chomsky 1972a: 11–61.)

—— (1972a). *Studies on Semantics in Generative Grammar*. The Hague: Mouton.

—— (1972b). *Language and Mind*, 2nd edn. New York: Harcourt, Brace & World.

—— (1973). 'Constraints on Transformations'. In S. Anderson and P. Kiparsky (eds.), *A Festschrift for Morris Halle*, 232–86. New York: Holt, Rinehart & Winston.

—— (1975). *Reflections on Language*. New York: Pantheon.

—— (1977). 'On Wh-Movement'. In P. Culicover, T. Wasow, and A. Akmajian (eds.), *Formal Syntax*, 71–132. New York: Academic Press.

—— (1980). *Rules and Representations*. New York: Columbia University Press.

—— (1981). *Lectures on Government and Binding*. Dordrecht: Foris.

—— (1986). *Knowledge of Language*. New York: Praeger.

—— (1995). *The Minimalist Program*. Cambridge, Mass.: MIT Press.

—— (2000). *New Horizons in the Study of Language and Mind*. Cambridge: Cambridge University Press.

—— and Morris Halle (1968). *The Sound Pattern of English*. New York: Harper & Row.

—— and Howard Lasnik (1993). 'The Theory of Principles and Parameters'. Repr. in Chomsky (1995: 13–127).

Christiansen, Morten H., and Nick Chater (1999). 'Toward a Connectionist Model of Recursion in Human Linguistic Performance'. *Cognitive Science* 23: 157–205.

—— —— and Mark S. Seidenberg (eds.) (1999). *Connectionist Models of Human Language Processing: Progress and Prospects*: special issue, *Cognitive Science* 23(4).

Churchland, Patricia S. (1986). *Neurophilosophy: Toward a Unified Science of the Mind/Brain*. Cambridge, Mass.: MIT Press.

—— and Terrence J. Sejnowski (1992). *The Computational Brain*. Cambridge, Mass.: MIT Press.

Clahsen, Harald (1999). 'Lexical Entries and Rules of Language: A Multidisciplinary Study of German Inflection'. *Behavioral and Brain Sciences* 22: 991–1013.

—— and Mayella Almazan (1998). 'Syntax and Morphology in Williams Syndrome'. *Cognition* 68: 167–98.

Clark, Andy (1996). 'Linguistic Anchors in the Sea of Thought?' *Pragmatics and Cognition* 4: 93–103.

Clark, E. V., S. A. Gelman, and N. M. Lane, (1985). 'Compound Nouns and Category Structure in Young Children'. *Child Development* 56: 84–94.

Clark, Herbert H. (1996). *Using Language*. Cambridge: Cambridge University Press.

Clifton, Charles, and Fernanda Ferreira (1987). 'Modularity in Sentence Comprehension'. In Garfield (1987: 277–90).

Coleman, Linda, and Paul Kay (1981). 'Prototype Semantics: The English Verb *Lie*'. *Language* 57: 26–44.

Collins, A., and M. Quillian (1969). 'Retrieval Time from Semantic Memory'. *Journal of Verbal Learning and Verbal Behavior* 9: 240–7.

Coltheart, Max (1999). 'Modularity and Cognition'. *Trends in Cognitive Science* 3: 115–20.

Corballis, Michael C. (1991). *The Lopsided Ape*. Oxford: Oxford University Press.

Cosmides, Leda (1989). 'The Logic of Social Exchange: Has Natural Selection Shaped How Humans Reason? Studies with the Wason Selection Task'. *Cognition* 31: 187–276.

Crain, Stephen, and Mark Steedman (1985). 'On Not Being Led up the Garden Path'. In D. Dowty, L. Kartunnen, and A. M. Zwicky (eds.), *Natural Language Parsing: Psycholinguistic, Computational, and Theoretical Perspectives*. Cambridge: Cambridge University Press.

Crick, Francis (1994). *The Astonishing Hypothesis*. New York: Charles Scribner's Sons.

—— and Christof Koch (1990). 'Towards a Neurobiological Theory of Consciousness'. *Seminars Neurosc.* 2: 263–75.

Csuri, Piroska (1996). *Generalized Dependencies: Description, Reference, and Anaphora*. Doctoral dissertation, Program in Linguistics and Cognitive Science, Brandeis University.

Culicover, Peter (1972). 'OM-Sentences'. *Foundations of Language* 8: 199–236.

—— (1999). *Syntactic Nuts: Hard Cases in Syntax*. Oxford: Oxford University Press.

—— (2000). 'Concrete Minimalism, Branching Structure, and Linear Order'. In Proceedings of GLiP-2 (Generative Linguistics in Poland). Warsaw.

—— and Ray Jackendoff (1995). '*Something Else* for the Binding Theory'. *Linguistic Inquiry* 26: 249–75.

—— —— (1997). 'Semantic Subordination despite Syntactic Coordination'. *Linguistic Inquiry* 28: 195–217.

—— —— (1999). 'The View from the Periphery: The English Correlative Conditional'. *Linguistic Inquiry* 30: 543–71.

—— and Louise McNally (eds.) (1998). *The Limits of Syntax*. New York: Academic Press.

Curtiss, Susan (1977). *Genie: A Linguistic Study of a Modern-day 'Wild Child'*. New York: Academic Press.

—— (1994). 'Language as a Cognitive System: Its Independence and Selective Vulnerability'. In C. Otero (ed.), *Noam Chomsky: Critical Assessments*, vol. iv. London: Routledge.

—— and Stella de Bode (2000). 'Language Outcomes of 42 Hemispherectomies: If Neither Side nor Age Matters, then What Does?' Paper given at Boston University Child Language Conference, Nov. 2000.

Cutler, Anne (1994). 'Segmentation Problems, Rhythmic Solutions'. *Lingua* 92: 81–104.

Cutler, Anne, and Charles Clifton, Jr. (1999). 'Comprehending Spoken Language: A Blueprint of the Listener'. In C. M. Brown and P. Hagoort (eds.), *The Neurocognition of Language*, 123–66. Oxford: Oxford University Press.

Cutting, James (1981). 'Six Tenets for Event Perception'. *Cognition* 10: 71–8.

Dąbrowska, Eva (2000). 'From Formula to Schema: The Acquisition of English Questions'. *Cognitive Linguistics* 11: 83–102.

Dalrymple, Mary, Ronald Kaplan, John Maxwell III, and Annie Zaenen (eds.) (1995). *Formal Issues in Lexical-Functional Grammar*. Stanford, Calif.: CSLI.

Damasio, Antonio R. (1994). *Descartes' Error: Emotion, Reason, and the Human Brain*. New York: G. P. Putnam's Sons.

Darwin, Charles (1872). *The Expression of the Emotions in Man and Animals*, 3rd edn., with commentaries by Paul Ekman. New York: Oxford University Press, 1998.

Davidson, Donald (1967). 'The Logical Form of Action Sentences'. In N. Rescher (ed.), *The Logic of Decision and Action*. Pittsburgh: University of Pittsburgh Press.

Davis, Steven (1999). 'The Unity of Science and the Distinction among Syntax, Semantics, and Pragmatics'. In Jackendoff et al. (1999: 147–59).

Dawkins, Richard (1989). *The Selfish Gene*, new edn. Oxford: Oxford University Press.

de Waal, Frans B. M. (1996). *Good Natured: The Origins of Right and Wrong in Humans and other Animals*. Cambridge, Mass.: Harvard University Press.

Deacon, Terrence W. (1997). *The Symbolic Species*. New York: Norton.

Deane, Paul (1991). 'Limits to Attention: A Cognitive Theory of Island Phenomena'. *Cognitive Linguistics* 2: 1–63.

—— (1996). 'On Jackendoff's Conceptual Semantics'. *Cognitive Linguistics* 7: 35–91.

DeGraff, Michel (ed.) (1999). *Language Creation and Language Change: Creolization, Diachrony, and Development*. Cambridge, Mass.: MIT Press.

Dell, Gary S. (1986). 'A Spreading Activation Theory of Retrieval in Sentence Production'. *Psychological Review* 93: 283–321.

—— Lisa K. Burger, and William R. Svec (1997). 'Language Production and Serial Order: A Functional Analysis and a Model'. *Psychological Review* 104: 123–47.

—— Franklin Chang, and Zenzi M. Griffin (1999). 'Connectionist Models of Language Production: Lexical Access and Grammatical Encoding'. *Cognitive Science* 23: 517–42.

—— Myrna F. Schwartz, Nadine Martin, Eleanor M. Saffran, and Deborah A. Gagnon (1997). 'Lexical Access in Aphasic and Nonaphasic Speakers'. *Psychological Review* 104: 801–38.

den Besten, Hans (1977). 'Surface Lexicalization and Trace Theory'. In Henk van Riemsdijk (ed.), *Green Ideas Blown Up*. Instituut voor Algemene Taalwetenschap, University of Amsterdam.

Dennett, Daniel C. (1984). *Elbow Room: The Varieties of Free Will Worth Wanting*. Cambridge, Mass.: MIT Press.

—— (1991). *Consciousness Explained*. New York: Little, Brown.

—— (1995.) *Darwin's Dangerous Idea: Evolution and the Meanings of Life*. New York: Simon & Schuster.

Dennis, Maureen (1980). 'Language Acquisition in a Single Hemisphere: Semantic

Organization'. In D. Caplan (ed.), *Biological Studies of Mental Processes*, 159–85. Cambridge, Mass.: MIT Press.

Di Sciullo, Anna Maria, and Edwin Williams (1987) *On the Definition of Word*. Cambridge, Mass: MIT Press.

Donald, Merlin (1991. *Origins of the Modern Mind*. Cambridge, Mass.: Harvard University Press.

—— (1998). 'Preconditions for the Evolution of Protolanguages'. In M. C. Corballis and S. E. G. Lea (eds.), *The Descent of Mind*, Oxford: Oxford University Press.

Donnellan, Keith (1966). 'Reference and Definite Descriptions'. *Philosophical Review* 75: 281–304.

Downing, Pamela (1977). 'On the Creation and Use of English Compound Nouns'. *Language* 53: 810–42.

Dowty, David (1991). 'Thematic Proto-roles and Argument Selection'. *Language* 67: 547–619.

Dufva, H., and M. Lähteenmäki (1996). 'But Who Killed Harry? A Dialogical Approach to Language and Consciousness'. *Pragmatics and Cognition* 4: 35–53.

Dunbar, Robin (1998). ' Theory of Mind and the Evolution of Language'. In Hurford et al. (1998: 92–110).

Edelman, Gerald M. (1992). *Bright Air, Brilliant Fire: On the Matter of the Mind*. New York: Basic Books.

Elman, Jeffrey (1990). 'Finding Structure in Time'. *Cognitive Science* 14: 179–211.

—— (1993). 'Learning and Development in Neural Networks: The Importance of Starting Small'. *Cognition* 48: 71–99.

—— Elizabeth Bates, Mark Johnson, Annette Karmiloff-Smith, Domenico Parisi, and Kim Plunkett (1996). *Rethinking Innateness: A Connectionist Perspective on Development*. Cambridge, Mass.: MIT Press.

Emonds, Joseph E. (1970). 'Root and Structure-Preserving Transformations'. Doctoral dissertation, MIT.

Engelkamp, Johannes, and Ralf Rummer (1998). 'The Architecture of the Mental Lexicon'. In A. Friederici (ed.), *Language Comprehension: A Biological Perspective*, 2nd edn., 133–74. Berlin: Springer.

Erteschik-Shir, Nomi (1998). 'The Syntax–Focus Structure Interface'. In Culicover and McNally (1998: 211–40).

—— and Shalom Lappin (1979). 'Dominance and the Functional Explanation of Island Phenomena'. *Theoretical Linguistics* 6: 41–85.

Etcoff, Nancy L. (1986). 'The Neuropsychology of Emotional Expression'. In G. Goldstein and R. E. Tarter (eds.), *Advances in Clinical Neuropsychology*, vol. iii. New York: Plenum.

—— (1989). 'Asymmetries in Recognition of Emotion'. In F. Boller and J. Grafman (eds.), *Handbook of Neuropsychology*, vol. iii, 363–82. New York: Elsevier Science.

Fauconnier, Gilles (1985). *Mental Spaces: Aspects of Meaning Construction in Natural Language*. Cambridge, Mass.: MIT Press.

—— and Mark Turner (1994). 'Conceptual Projection and Middle Spaces'. La Jolla, Calif.: UCSD Cognitive Science Technical Report.

Fernald, Anne (1984). 'The Perceptual and Affective Salience of Mothers' Speech to Infants'. In L. Feagan, C. Garvey, and R. Golinkoff (eds.), *The Origins and Growth of Communication*. New Brunswick, NJ: Ablex.

Fiengo, Robert (1980). *Surface Structure: The Interface of Autonomous Components*. Cambridge, Mass.: Harvard University Press.

—— and Robert May (1994). *Indices and Identity*. Cambridge, Mass.: MIT Press.

Fillmore, Charles (1968). 'The Case for Case'. In E. Bach and R. Harms (eds.), *Universals in Linguistic Theory*, 1–90. New York: Holt, Rinehart & Winston.

—— (1982). 'Towards a Descriptive Framework for Deixis'. In R. Jarvella and W. Klein (eds.), *Speech, Place, and Action*, 31–52. New York: Wiley.

—— and Beryl Atkins (1992). 'Toward a Frame-Based Lexicon: The Semantics of RISK and its Neighbors'. In A. Lehrer and E. Kittay (eds.), *Frames, Fields, and Contrasts*, 75–102. Hillsdale, NJ: Erlbaum.

—— and Paul Kay (1993). *Construction Grammar Coursebook*. Berkeley: Dept. of Linguistics, University of California.

—— —— and Mary Catherine O'Connor (1988). 'Regularity and Idiomaticity in Grammatical Constructions: The Case of *Let Alone*'. *Language* 64: 501–38.

Fisher, Cynthia, D. G. Hall, S. Rakowitz, and Lila Gleitman (1994). 'When it is Better to Receive than to Give: Syntactic and Conceptual Constraints on Vocabulary Growth'. In Gleitman and Landau (1994: 333–75).

Fitch, W. Tecumseh (2000). 'The Evolution of Speech: A Comparative Review'. *Trends in Cognitive Sciences* 4: 258–67.

Flynn, Suzanne, and Wayne O'Neill (eds.) (1988). *Linguistic Theory in Second Language Acquisition*. Dordrecht: Reidel.

Fodor, Jerry (1970). 'Three Reasons for Not Deriving "Kill" from "Cause to Die" '. *Linguistic Inquiry* 1: 429–38.

—— (1975). *The Language of Thought*. Cambridge, Mass.: Harvard University Press.

—— (1983). *The Modularity of Mind*. Cambridge, Mass.: MIT Press.

—— (1987). *Psychosemantics: The Problem of Meaning in the Philosophy of Mind*. Cambridge, Mass.: MIT Press.

—— (1990). *A Theory of Content and Other Essays*. Cambridge, Mass.: MIT Press.

—— (1991). 'Information and Representation'. In P. Hanson (ed.), *Information, Language, and Cognition*, Oxford: Oxford University Press.

—— (1998). *Concepts: Where Cognitive Science Went Wrong*. Oxford: Oxford University Press.

—— (2000a). *The Mind Doesn't Work That Way*. Cambridge, Mass.: MIT Press.

—— (2000b). 'It's All in the Mind: Noam Chomsky and the Arguments for Internalism'. *Times Literary Supplement*, 23 June: 3–4.

—— Merrill F. Garrett, and David Swinney (1992). 'A Modular Effect in Parsing'. MS, Rutgers University.

—— —— Edward Walker, and Cornelia Parkes (1980). 'Against Definitions'. *Cognition* 8: 263–367.

—— and Ernie Lepore (1999). 'Impossible Words?' *Linguistic Inquiry* 30: 445–53.

Forster, Kenneth (1979). 'Levels of Processing and the Structure of the Language

Processor'. In W. Cooper and E. Walker (eds.), *Sentence Processing: Psycholinguistic Studies presented to Merrill Garrett*, 28–85. Hillsdale, NJ: Erlbaum.

Frank, Robert, and Anthony Kroch (1995). 'Generalized Transformations and the Theory of Grammar'. *Studia Linguistica* 49: 103–51.

Frazier, Lyn (1987). 'Theories of Sentence Processing'. In Garfield (1987: 291–308).

Frege, Gottlob (1892). 'Über Sinn und Bedeutung'. *Zeitschrift für Philosophie und philosophische Kritik* 100: 25–50. English translation in P. Geach and M. Black (eds.), *Translations from the Philosophical Writings of Gottlob Frege*, 56–78. Oxford: Blackwell, 1952.

Fromkin, Victoria (1971). 'The Non-anomalous Nature of Anomalous Utterances'. *Language* 47: 27–52.

Gallistel, Charles R. (1990). *The Organization of Learning*. Cambridge, Mass.: MIT Press.

Garfield, Jay (ed.) (1987). *Modularity in Knowledge Representation and Natural-Language Processing*. Cambridge, Mass.: MIT Press.

Garrett, Merrill (1975). 'The Analysis of Sentence Production'. In G. H. Bower (ed.), *Psychology of Learning and Motivation*, vol. ix, 133–77. New York: Academic Press.

—— (2000). 'Remarks on the Architecture of Language Processing Systems'. In Y. Grodzinsky, L. Shapiro, and D. Swinney (eds.), *Language and the Brain*, 31–64. New York: Academic Press.

Garrod, Simon, Gillian Ferrier, and Siobhan Campbell (1999). '*In* and *On*: Investigating the Functional Geometry of Spatial Prepositions'. *Cognition* 72: 167–89.

Gathercole, Susan E. (1999). 'Cognitive Approaches to the Development of Short-Term Memory'. *Trends in Cognitive Sciences* 3: 410–19.

—— and Alan D. Baddeley (1993). *Working Memory and Language*. Hillsdale, NJ: Erlbaum.

Gee, James, and François Grosjean (1983). 'Performance Structures: A Psycholinguistic and Linguistic Appraisal'. *Cognitive Psychology* 15: 411–58.

Gelman, Rochel, and C. R. Gallistel (1978). *The Child's Understanding of Number*. Cambridge, Mass.: Harvard University Press.

Ghomeshi, Jila, Ray Jackendoff, Nicole Rosen, and Kevin Russell (2001). 'Contrastive Focus Reduplication in English'. MS, University of Manitoba.

Gibson, Edward (1998). 'Linguistic Complexity: Locality of Syntactic Dependencies'. *Cognition* 68: 1–76.

Gigerenzer, Gerd (2000). *Adaptive Thinking: Rationality in the Real World*. New York: Oxford University Press.

Gillette, Jane, Henry Gleitman, Lila Gleitman, and Anne Lederer (1999). 'Human Simulations of Vocabulary Learning'. *Cognition* 73: 135–76.

Givón, Talmy (1995). *Functionalism and Grammar*. Philadelphia: John Benjamins.

Gleitman, Lila R., and Henry Gleitman (1970). *Phrase and Paraphrase*. New York: Norton.

—— Henry Gleitman, Carol Miller, and Ruth Ostrin (1996). 'Similar, and Similar Concepts'. *Cognition* 58: 321–76.

Gleitman, Lila R., and Barbara Landau (eds.) (1994). *The Acquisition of the Lexicon.* Cambridge, Mass.: MIT Press.

—— and Eric Wanner (1982). 'The State of the State of the Art'. In E. Wanner and L. R. Gleitman (eds.), *Language Acquisition: The State of the Art*, 3–48. Cambridge: Cambridge University Press.

Goddard, Cliff, and Anna Wierzbicka (eds.) (1994). *Semantic and Lexical Universals.* Amsterdam: John Benjamins.

Gold, E. M. (1967) 'Language Identification in the Limit'. *Information and Control* 16: 447–74.

Goldberg, Adele (1995). *Constructions: A Construction Grammar Approach to Argument Structure.* Chicago: University of Chicago Press.

Goldin-Meadow, Susan, and Mylander, C. (1990). 'Beyond the Input Given: The Child's Role in the Acquisition of Language'. *Language* 66: 323–55.

Goldsmith, John (1979). *Autosegmental Phonology.* New York: Garland Press.

—— (1990). *Autosegmental and Metrical Phonology.* Oxford: Basil Blackwell.

—— (ed.) (1995). *Handbook of Theoretical Phonology.* Oxford: Blackwell.

Goodall, Jane van Lawick (1971). *In the Shadow of Man.* New York: Dell.

Goodman, Nelson (1968). *Languages of Art.* New York: Bobbs-Merrill.

Gopnik, Myrna (1999). 'Some Evidence for Impaired Grammars'. In Jackendoff et al. (1999: 263–83).

—— and M. B. Crago (1990). 'Familial Aggregation of a Developmental Language Disorder'. *Cognition* 39: 1–50.

Gould, Stephen Jay, and Richard Lewontin (1979). 'The Spandrels of San Marco and the Panglossian Paradigm: A Critique of the Adaptationist Programme'. *Proceedings of the Royal Society of London* 205: 281–8.

Gray, C., M. P. König, A. K. Engel, and W. Singer (1989). 'Oscillatory Responses in Cat Visual Cortex Exhibit Intercolumnar Synchronization which Reflects Global Stimulus Properties'. *Nature* 338: 334–7.

Grimshaw, Jane (1979). 'Complement Structure and the Lexicon'. *Linguistic Inquiry* 10: 279–325.

—— (1990). *Argument Structure.* Cambridge, Mass.: MIT Press.

—— (1993). 'Semantic Structure and Semantic Content in Lexical Representation'. MS, Center for Cognitive Science, Rutgers University.

—— (1994). 'Lexical Reconciliation'. In Gleitman and Landau (1994: 411–30).

—— (1997). 'Projection, Heads, and Optimality'. *Linguistic Inquiry* 28: 373–422.

—— and Armin Mester (1988). 'Light Verbs and θ-marking'. *Linguistic Inquiry* 19: 205–32.

Groenendijk, Jeroen, Martin Stokhof, and Frank Veltman (1996). 'Coreference and Modality'. In S. Lappin (ed.), *The Handbook of Contemporary Semantic Theory*, 179–213. Oxford: Blackwell.

Gruber, Jeffrey S. (1965) 'Studies in Lexical Relations'. Ph.D. dissertation, MIT. Repr. in Gruber, *Lexical Structures in Syntax and Semantics.* Amsterdam: North-Holland, 1976.

Hagiwara, Hiroko, Yoko Sugioka, Takane Ito, Mitsuru Kawamura, and Jun-Ichi

Shiota (1999). 'Neurolinguistic Evidence for Rule-Based Nominal Suffixation'. *Language* 75: 739–63.

Hagoort, Peter, Colin Brown, and Lee Osterhout (1999). 'The Neurocognition of Syntactic Processing'. In Colin Brown and Peter Hagoort (eds.), *The Neurocognition of Language*, 273–316. Oxford: Oxford University Press.

Hale, Kenneth (1983). 'Warlpiri and the Grammar of Non-configurational Languages'. *Natural Language and Linguistic Theory* 1: 5–48.

—— and Samuel Jay Keyser (1993). 'On Argument Structure and the Lexical Expression of Syntactic Relations'. In K. Hale and S. J. Keyser (eds.), *The View from Building 20*, 53–109. Cambridge, Mass.: MIT Press.

Hall, D. G. (1999). 'Semantics and the Acquisition of Proper Names'. In Jackendoff et al. (1999: 337–72).

Halle, Morris (1973). 'Prolegomena to a Theory of Word-Formation'. *Linguistic Inquiry* 4: 3–16.

—— Joan Bresnan, and George Miller (1978). *Linguistic Theory and Psychological Reality*. Cambridge, Mass.: MIT Press.

—— and William Idsardi (1995). 'Stress and Metrical Structure'. In Goldsmith (1995: 403–43).

—— and Alec Marantz (1993). 'Distributed Morphology'. In K. Hale and S. J. Keyser (eds.), *The View from Building 20*, 111–76. Cambridge, Mass.: MIT Press.

Halpern, Aaron (1995.) *On the Placement and Morphology of Clitics*. Stanford, Calif.: CSLI.

Hankamer, Jorge (1989). 'Morphological Parsing and the Lexicon'. In W. Marslen-Wilson (ed.), *Lexical Representation and Process*, 392–408. Cambridge, Mass.: MIT Press.

—— and Ivan Sag (1976). 'Deep and Surface Anaphora'. *Linguistic Inquiry* 7: 391–428.

Hare, M., J. Elman, and K. Daugherty (1995). 'Default Generalization in Connectionist Networks'. *Language and Cognitive Processes* 10: 601–30.

Harris, Randy Allen (1993). *The Linguistics Wars*. New York: Oxford University Press.

Harris, Zellig (1951). *Methods in Structural Linguistics*. Chicago: University of Chicago Press.

Hauser, Marc (1996). *The Evolution of Communication*. Cambridge, Mass.: MIT Press.

—— (2000). *Wild Minds: What Animals Really Think*. New York: Henry Holt.

Hawkins, John A. (1994). *A Performance Theory of Order and Constituency*. Cambridge: Cambridge University Press.

Heim, Irena (1989). *The Semantics of Definite and Indefinite Noun Phrases in English*. New York: Garland.

Herskovits, Annette (1986). *Language and Spatial Cognition*. Cambridge: Cambridge University Press.

Hilferty, Joseph, Javier Valenzuela, and Oscar Vilarroya (1998). 'Paradox Lost'. *Cognitive Linguistics* 9: 175–80.

Hinrichs, Erhard (1985). *A Compositional Semantics for Aktionsarten and NP Reference in English*. Doctoral dissertation, Ohio State University.

Hirst, Daniel (1993). 'Detaching Intonational Phrases from Syntactic Structure'. *Linguistic Inquiry* 24: 781–8.

Hockett, Charles F. (1955). *A Manual of Phonology*. Baltimore: Waverly Press.

—— (1960). 'The Origin of Speech'. *Scientific American* 203 (Sept.): 88–96.

Hubel, David, and Torsten Wiesel (1968). 'Receptive Fields and Functional Architecture of Monkey Striate Cortex'. *J. Physiol. (Lond.)* 195: 215–43.

Huck, Geoffrey, and John Goldsmith (1995). *Ideology and Linguistic Theory*. Chicago: University of Chicago Press.

Hultsch, Henrike, Roger Mundry, and Dietmar Todt (1999). 'Learning, Representation and Retrieval of Rule-Related Knowledge in the Song System of Birds'. In A. Friederici and R. Menzel (eds.), *Learning: Rule Extraction and Representation*, 89–115. Berlin: Walter de Gruyter.

Hurford, James, Michael Studdert-Kennedy, and Chris Knight (eds.) (1998). *Approaches to the Evolution of Language*. Cambridge: Cambridge University Press.

Inkelas, Sharon, and Draga Zec (eds.) (1990). *The Phonology–Syntax Connection*. Chicago: University of Chicago Press.

Jablonski, Nina, and Leslie Aiello (eds.) (1998). *The Origin and Diversification of Language*. San Francisco: California Academy of Sciences.

Jackendoff, Ray (1972). *Semantic Interpretation in Generative Grammar*. Cambridge, Mass.: MIT Press.

—— (1973). 'The Base Rules for Prepositional Phrases'. In S. Anderson and P. Kiparsky (eds.), *A Festschrift for Morris Halle*, 345–56. New York: Holt, Rinehart & Winston.

—— (1974). 'A Deep Structure Projection Rule'. *Linguistic Inquiry* 5: 481–506.

—— (1975). 'Morphological and Semantic Regularities in the Lexicon'. *Language* 51: 639–71.

—— (1976). 'Toward an Explanatory Semantic Representation'. *Linguistic Inquiry* 7: 89–150.

—— (1977). *X-Bar Syntax*. Cambridge, Mass.: MIT Press.

—— (1983). *Semantics and Cognition*. Cambridge, Mass.: MIT Press.

—— (1987). *Consciousness and the Computational Mind*. Cambridge, Mass.: MIT Press.

—— (1988). 'Why Are They Saying These Things about Us?' *Natural Language and Linguistic Theory* 6: 435–42.

—— (1990a). *Semantic Structures*. Cambridge, Mass.: MIT Press.

—— (1990b). 'On Larson's Treatment of the Double Object Construction'. *Linguistic Inquiry* 21: 427–56.

—— (1991). 'Parts and Boundaries'. *Cognition* 41: 9–45.

—— (1992a). *Languages of the Mind*. Cambridge, Mass.: MIT Press.

—— (1992b). 'Mme. Tussaud Meets the Binding Theory'. *Natural Language and Linguistic Theory* 10: 1–31.

—— (1993). 'The Role of Conceptual Structure in Argument Selection: A Reply to Emonds'. *Natural Language and Linguistic Theory* 11: 279–312.

—— (1994). *Patterns in the Mind: Language and Human Nature*. New York: Basic Books.

—— (1995). 'The Conceptual Structure of Intending and Volitional Action'. In H. Campos and P. Kempchinsky (eds.), *Evolution and Revolution in Linguistic Theory: Studies in Honor of Carlos P. Otero*, 198–227. Washington, DC: Georgetown University Press.

—— (1996a). 'Conceptual Semantics and Cognitive Semantics'. *Cognitive Linguistics* 7: 93–129.

—— (1996b). 'How Language Helps Us Think'. *Pragmatics and Cognition* 4: 1–24.

—— (1996c). 'The Proper Treatment of Measuring Out, Telicity, and possibly even Quantification in English'. *Natural Language and Linguistic Theory* 14: 305–54.

—— (1996d). 'The Architecture of the Linguistic–Spatial Interface'. In Bloom et al. (1996: 1–30).

—— (1997a). *The Architecture of the Language Faculty*. Cambridge, Mass.: MIT Press.

—— (1997b). 'Twistin' the Night Away'. *Language* 73: 534–59.

—— (1999). 'The Natural Logic of Rights and Obligations. In Jackendoff et al. (1999: 67–95).

—— (2000). 'Fodorian Modularity and Representational Modularity'. In Y. Grodzinsky, L. Shapiro, and D. Swinney (eds.), *Language and the Brain*, 4–30. New York: Academic Press.

—— (in preparation). *The Ecology of English Noun–Noun Compounds*. Oxford: Oxford University Press.

—— and David Aaron (1991). Review of George Lakoff and Mark Turner, *More than Cool Reason*. *Language* 67: 320–38.

—— Paul Bloom, and Karen Wynn (eds.) (1999). *Language, Logic, and Concepts: Essays in Memory of John Macnamara*. Cambridge, Mass.: MIT Press.

Jackson, J. H. (1874). 'On the nature of the duality of the brain'. *Medical Press and Circular* 1: 19–41. Cited in J. Marshall, 'Biology of Language Acquisition', in D. Caplan (ed.), *Biological Studies of Mental Processes*, 106–48. Cambridge, Mass.: MIT Press, 1980.

Jakobson, Roman (1940). *Kindersprache, Aphasie, und allgemeine Lautgesetze*. English translation, The Hague: Mouton, 1968.

Johnson-Laird, Philip (1983). *Mental Models*. Cambridge: Cambridge University Press.

Joshi, Aravind (1987). 'An Introduction to Tree-Adjoining Grammars'. In A. Manaster-Ramer (ed.), *Mathematics of Language*, 87–114. Amsterdam: John Benjamins.

Jusczyk, Peter W. (1997). *The Discovery of Spoken Language*. Cambridge, Mass.: MIT Press.

Kager, René (1995). 'The Metrical Theory of Word Stress'. In Goldsmith (1995: 367–402).

Kahneman, Daniel, Paul Slovic, and Amos Tversky (eds.) (1982). *Judgment under Uncertainty: Heuristics and Biases*. Cambridge: Cambridge University Press.

—— and Anne M. Treisman (1984). 'Changing Views of Attention and Automaticity'. In R. Parasuraman and D. R. Davies (eds.), *Varieties of Attention*, 29–61. New York: Academic Press.

Kako, Edward (1999). 'Elements of Syntax in the Systems of Three Language-Trained Animals'. *Animal Learning and Behavior* 27: 1–14.

Kamp, Hans, and U. Reyle (1993). *From Discourse to Logic*. Dordrecht: Kluwer.

Katz, Jerrold (1966). *The Philosophy of Language*. New York: Harper & Row.

—— (1972). *Semantic Theory*. New York: Harper & Row.

—— (1977). *Propositional Structure and Illocutionary Force*. New York: Thomas Y. Crowell.

—— (1980). 'Chomsky on Meaning'. *Language* 56: 11–41.

—— (1981). *Language and other Abstract Objects*. Totowa, NJ: Rowman & Littlefield.

—— and Jerry Fodor (1963). 'The Structure of a Semantic Theory'. *Language* 39: 170–210.

—— and Paul M. Postal (1964). *An Integrated Theory of Linguistic Descriptions*. Cambridge, Mass.: MIT Press.

Katz, Nancy, Erica Baker, and John Macnamara (1974). 'What's in a Name? A Study of How Children Learn Common and Proper Names', *Child Development* 45: 469–73.

Kayne, Richard (1994). *The Antisymmetry of Syntax*. Cambridge, Mass.: MIT Press.

Kegl, Judy, Ann Senghas, and Marie Coppola (1999). 'Creations through Contact: Sign Language Emergence and Sign Language Change in Nicaragua'. In DeGraff (1999: 179–237).

Keil, Frank C. (1989). *Concepts, Kinds, and Cognitive Development*. Cambridge, Mass.: MIT Press.

Kelemen, D. (1999). 'Beliefs about Purpose: On the Origins of Teleological Thought'. In M. C. Corballis and S. E. G. Lea (eds.), *The Descent of Mind*, 278–94. Oxford: Oxford University Press.

Kempen, G., and E. Hoenkamp (1987). 'An Incremental Procedural Grammar for Sentence Formulation'. *Cognitive Science* 11: 201–58.

Kintsch, Walter (1984). 'Approaches to the Study of the Psychology of Language'. In Bever et al. (1984: 111–45).

Kiparsky, Paul (1969). 'Linguistic Universals and Linguistic Change'. In E. Bach and R.T. Harms (eds.), *Universals in Linguistic Theory*, 170–202. New York: Holt, Rinehart & Winston.

Kirby, Simon (1998). 'Fitness and the Selective Adaptation of Language'. In Hurford et al. (1998: 359–83).

Klein, Wolfgang, and Clive Perdue (1997). 'The Basic Variety, or: Couldn't Language be Much Simpler?' *Second Language Research* 13: 301–47.

Klima, Edward S., and Ursula Bellugi (1979). *The Signs of Language*. Cambridge, Mass.: Harvard University Press.

Kluender, Robert (1992). 'Deriving Island Constraints from Principles of Predication'. In H. Goodluck and M. Rochemont (eds.), *Island Constraints*, 223–58. Dordrecht: Kluwer.

Koenig, Jean-Pierre, and Daniel Jurafsky (1994). 'Type Underspecification and On-line Type Construction in the Lexicon'. In *Proceedings of the West Coast Conference on Formal Linguistics*. Stanford, Calif.: CSLI.

Koffka, Kurt (1935). *Principles of Gestalt Psychology*. New York: Harcourt, Brace & World.

Köhler, Wolfgang (1927). *The Mentality of Apes*. London: Routledge & Kegan Paul.

—— (1940). *Dynamics in Psychology*. New York: Liveright.

Kosslyn, Stephen (1980). *Image and Mind*. Cambridge, Mass.: Harvard University Press.

—— (1996). *Image and Brain: The Resolution of the Imagery Debate*. Cambridge, Mass.: MIT Press.

Koster, Jan (1987). *Domains and Dynasties*. Dordrecht: Foris.

Kripke, Saul (1972). 'Naming and Necessity'. In D. Davidson and G. Harman (eds.), *Semantics for Natural Language*, 253–355. Dordrecht: Reidel.

—— (1979). 'A Puzzle about Belief'. In A. Margalit (ed.), *Meaning and Use*, 239–83. Dordrecht: Kluwer.

Kroch, Anthony (1987). 'Unbounded Dependencies and Subjacency in a Tree Adjoining Grammar'. In A. Manaster-Ramer (ed.), *Mathematics of Language*, 143–72. Amsterdam: John Benjamins.

Kuhl, Patricia K. (2000). 'A New View of Language Acquisition'. *Proceedings of the National Academy of Sciences* 97 (22): 11850–7.

Kujala, Teija, Kimmo Alho, and Risto Näätänen (2000). 'Cross-modal Reorganization of Human Cortical Functions'. *Trends in Neurosciences* 23: 115–20.

Kuno, Susumu (1987). *Functional Syntax*. Chicago: University of Chicago Press.

Kuroda, Sige-Yuki (1965). 'Generative Grammatical Studies in the Japanese Language'. Doctoral dissertation, MIT.

Labov, William (1972). *Language in the Inner City*. Philadelphia: University of Pennsylvania Press.

—— (1994). *Principles of Linguistic Change*, vol. i: *Internal Factors*. Oxford: Blackwell.

Lackner, James (1981). 'Some Contributions of Touch, Pressure, and Kinesthesis to Human Spatial Orientation and Oculomotor Control'. *Acta Astronautica* 8: 825–30.

—— (1988). 'Some Proprioceptive Influences on the Perceptual Representation of Body Shape and Orientation'. *Brain* 111: 281–97.

—— and Paul DiZio (2000). 'Aspects of Body Self-Calibration'. *Trends in Cognitive Sciences* 4: 279–88.

Ladd, D. Robert (1996). *Intonational Phonology*. Cambridge: Cambridge University Press.

Lakoff, George (1970). *Irregularity in Syntax*. New York: Holt, Rinehart & Winston.

—— (1971). 'On Generative Semantics'. In D. Steinberg and L. Jakobovits (eds.), *Semantics: An Interdisciplinary Reader in Philosophy, Linguistics, and Psychology*, 232–96. New York: Cambridge University Press.

—— (1987). *Women, Fire, and Dangerous Things*. Chicago: University of Chicago Press.

—— (1990). The Invariance Hypothesis: Is Abstract Reasoning Based on Image-Schemas?' *Cognitive Linguistics* 1: 39–74.

—— and Mark Johnson (1980). *Metaphors We Live By*. Chicago: University of Chicago Press.

Lakoff, Robin (1968). *Abstract Syntax and Latin Complementation*. Cambridge, Mass.: MIT Press.

Lamb, Sydney (1966). *Outline of Stratificational Grammar*. Washington: Georgetown University Press.

Lambrecht, Knud (1994). *Information Structure and Sentence Form*. Cambridge: Cambridge University Press.

Landau, Barbara (1994). 'Where's What and What's Where: The Language of Objects in Space'. In Gleitman and Landau (1994: 259–96).

—— and Lila Gleitman (1985). *Language and Experience: Evidence from the Blind Child*. Cambridge, Mass.: Harvard University Press.

—— and Ray Jackendoff (1993). ' "What" and "Where" in Spatial Language and Spatial Cognition'. *Behavioral and Brain Sciences* 16: 217–38.

Langacker, Ronald (1987). *Foundations of Cognitive Grammar*, vol. i. Stanford, Calif.: Stanford University Press.

—— (1992). 'The Symbolic Nature of Cognitive Grammar: The Meaning of *of* and *of*-periphrasis'. In M. Pütz (ed.), *Thirty Years of Linguistic Evolution*, 483–502. Amsterdam: John Benjamins.

—— (1998). 'Conceptualization, Symbolization, and Grammar'. In M. Tomasello (ed.), *The New Psychology of Language*, 1–39. Hillsdale, NJ: Erlbaum.

Lappin, Shalom (ed.) (1996). *The Handbook of Contemporary Semantic Theory*. Oxford: Blackwell.

Larson, Richard (1988). 'On the Double Object Construction'. *Linguistic Inquiry* 19: 335–92.

Lashley, Karl (1951). 'The Problem of Serial Order in Behavior'. In L. A. Jeffress (ed.), *Cerebral Mechanisms in Behavior*, 112–36. New York: Wiley.

—— (1956). 'Cerebral Organization and Behavior'. In H. Solomon, S. Cobb, and W. Penfield (eds.), *The Brain and Human Behavior*, 1–18. Baltimore: Williams & Wilkins.

Lasnik, Howard (1989). *Essays on Anaphora*. Dordrecht: Kluwer.

Laurence, Stephen, and Eric Margolis (1999). 'Concepts and Cognitive Science'. In E. Margolis and S. Laurence (eds.), *Concepts: Core Readings*, 3–81. Cambridge, Mass.: MIT Press.

Lees, Robert B. (1960). *The Grammar of English Nominalizations*. The Hague: Mouton.

—— and Edward S. Klima (1963). 'Rules for English Pronominalization'. *Language* 39: 17–28.

Lenneberg, Eric (1967). *Biological Foundations of Language*. New York: John Wiley.

Lerdahl, Fred, and Ray Jackendoff (1983). *A Generative Theory of Tonal Music*. Cambridge, Mass.: MIT Press.

Levelt, Clara (1994). *The Acquisition of Place*. Leiden: Holland Institute of Generative Linguistics.

Levelt, W. J. M. (1989). *Speaking*. Cambridge, Mass.: MIT Press.

—— (1999). 'Producing Spoken Language: A Blueprint of the Speaker'. In C. M. Brown and P. Hagoort (eds.), *The Neurocognition of Language*, 83–122. Oxford: Oxford University Press.

—— Ardi Roelofs, and Antje Meyer (1999). 'A Theory of Lexical Access in Speech Production'. *Behavioral and Brain Sciences* 22: 1–38.

—— and Wheeldon, L. (1994). 'Do Speakers Have Access to a Mental Syllabary? *Cognition* 50: 239–69.

Levi, Judith (1978). *The Semantics and Syntax of Complex Nominals*. New York: Academic Press.

Levin, Beth (1993). *English Verb Classes and Alternations*. Chicago: University of Chicago Press.

—— and Malka Rappaport Hovav (1991). 'Wiping the Slate Clean: A Lexical Semantic Exploration'. *Cognition* 41: 123–51.

—— —— (1996). 'Lexical Semantics and Syntactic Structure'. In Lappin (1996: 487–507).

Levinson, Stephen C. (1987). 'Pragmatics and the Grammar of Anaphora'. *Journal of Linguistics* 23: 379–434.

—— (1996). 'Frames of Reference and Molyneux's Question: Crosslinguistic Evidence'. In Bloom et al. (1996: 109–70).

—— (2000). *Presumptive Meanings: The Theory of Generalized Conversational Implicature*. Cambridge, Mass.: MIT Press.

Lewis, David (1972). 'General Semantics'. In D. Davidson and G. Harman (eds.), *Semantics for Natural Language*, 169–218. Dordrecht: Reidel.

Lewontin, Richard C. (1990). 'How Much Did the Brain Have to Change for Speech?', *Behavioral and Brain Sciences* 13: 740–41.

Li, Peggy, and Lila Gleitman (2000). 'Turning the Tables: Explorations in Spatial Cognition'. Philadelphia: University of Pennsylvania Institute for Research in Cognitive Science.

Liberman, Alvin (1996). *Speech: A Special Code*. Cambridge, Mass.: MIT Press.

—— and Michael Studdert-Kennedy (1977). 'Phonetic Perception'. In R. Held, H. Leibowitz, and H.-L. Teuber (eds.), *Handbook of Sensory Physiology*, vol viii: *Perception*. Heidelberg: Springer.

Liberman, Mark (1975). 'The Intonational System of English'. Doctoral dissertation, MIT. Bloomington: Indiana University Linguistics Club.

—— and Alan Prince (1977). 'On Stress and Linguistic Rhythm'. *Linguistic Inquiry* 8: 249–336.

Lieber, Rochelle (1992). *Deconstructing Morphology: Word Formation in Syntactic Theory*. Chicago: University of Chicago Press.

Lieberman, Philip (1984). *The Biology and Evolution of Language*. Cambridge, Mass.: Harvard University Press.

—— (1991). *Uniquely Human*. Cambridge, Mass.: Harvard University Press.

Lillo-Martin, Diane, and Edward S. Klima (1990). 'Pointing Out Differences: ASL Pronouns in Syntactic Theory'. In Susan D. Fischer and Patricia Siple (eds.), *Theoretical Issues in Sign Language Research* 1: 191–210. Chicago: University of Chicago Press.

Linden, Eugene (1974). *Apes, Men, and Language*. New York: Penguin Books.

Lorenz, Konrad Z. (1952). *King Solomon's Ring*. New York: Thomas Y. Crowell.

—— (1966). *On Aggression*. London: Methuen.

McCarthy, John (1982). 'Prosodic Structure and Expletive Infixation'. *Language* 58: 574–90.

McCarthy, John, and Alan Prince (1986). 'Prosodic Morphology'. MS, University of Massachusetts, Amherst, and Brandeis University.

McCawley, James D. (1968). 'Lexical Insertion in a Transformational Grammar Without Deep Structure'. In B. Darden, C.-J. N. Bailey, and A. Davison (eds.), *Papers from the Fourth Meeting of the Chicago Linguistic Society*. Chicago: University of Chicago Dept. of Linguistics.

—— (1978). 'Conversational Implicature and the Lexicon'. In P. Cole (ed.), *Syntax and Semantics*, vol. ix, 245–59. New York: Academic Press.

—— (1988). 'The Comparative Conditional Construction in English, German, and Chinese'. In *Proceedings of the 14th Annual meeting of the Berkeley Linguistics Society*, 176–87. Berkeley, Calif.: Berkeley Linguistics Society.

McClelland, James L., and Mark S. Seidenberg (2000). 'Why do Kids Say Goed and Brang?' (review of Pinker 1999). *Science* 287 (7 Jan.): 47–8.

McElree, Brian, Mathew J. Traxler, Martin J. Pickering, Rachel E. Seely, and Ray Jackendoff (2001). 'Reading Time Evidence for Enriched Composition'. *Cognition* 78: B17–25.

McGurk, H., and J. MacDonald (1976). 'Hearing Lips and Seeing Voices'. *Nature* 264: 746–8.

McNally, Louise (1998). 'On the Linguistic Encoding of Information Packaging Instructions'. In Culicover and McNally (1998: 161–83).

Macnamara, John (1978). 'How Do We Talk about What We See?' MS, McGill University.

—— (1982). *Names for Things*. Cambridge, Mass.: MIT Press.

—— (1986). *A Border Dispute*. Cambridge, Mass.: MIT Press.

—— (2000). *Through the Rearview Mirror: Historical Reflections on Psychology*. Cambridge, Mass.: MIT Press.

—— and Gonzalo Reyes (eds.) (1994). *The Logical Foundations of Cognition*. New York: Oxford University Press.

MacNeilage, Peter (1998). 'Evolution of the Mechanisms of Language Output: Comparative Neurobiology of Vocal and Manual Communication'. In Hurford et al. (1998: 222–41).

Makkai, Michael (1999). 'On Structuralism in Mathematics'. In Jackendoff et al. (1999: 43–66).

Maling, Joan, and Sigriður Sigurjónsdóttir (1997). 'The New "Passive" in Icelandic'. In E. Hughes, M. Hughes, and A. Greenhill (eds.), *Proceedings of the 21st Boston University Conference on Language Development*, 378–89. Somerville, Mass.: Cascadilla Press.

—— Moira Yip, and Ray Jackendoff (1987). 'Case in Tiers'. *Language* 63: 217–50.

Malotki, Ekkehart (1983). *Hopi Time: A Linguistic Analysis of the Temporal Concepts in the Hopi Language*. Berlin: Mouton.

Marantz, Alec (1982). 'Re Reduplication'. *Linguistic Inquiry* 13: 483–545.

—— (1984). *On the Nature of Grammatical Relations*. Cambridge, Mass.: MIT Press.

—— (1992). 'The *Way*-Construction and the Semantics of Direct Arguments in English: A Reply to Jackendoff'. In T. Stowell and E. Wehrli (eds.), *Syntax and Semantics*, vol. 26, 179–88. San Diego, Calif.: Academic Press.

Marcus, Gary (1998). 'Rethinking Eliminative Connectionism'. *Cognitive Psychology* 37: 243–82.

—— (2001). *The Algebraic Mind*. Cambridge, Mass.: MIT Press.

—— U. Brinkmann, H. Clahsen, R. Wiese, and S. Pinker (1995). 'German Inflection: The Exception that Proves the Rule'. *Cognitive Psychology* 29: 186–256.

Markman, Ellen (1989). *Categorization and Naming in Children: Problems of Induction*. Cambridge, Mass.: MIT Press.

Marler, Peter (1984). 'Song Learning: Innate Species Differences in the Learning Process'. In P. Marler and H. S. Terrace (eds.), *The Biology of Learning*, 289–309. Berlin: Springer.

—— (1998). 'Animal Communication and Human Language'. In Jablonski and Aiello (1998: 1–20).

Marr, David (1982). *Vision*. San Francisco: Freeman.

Marslen-Wilson, William, and Lorraine K. Tyler (1987). 'Against Modularity'. In Garfield (1987: 37–62).

Marty, Anton (1918). *Gesammelte Schriften*, vol. ii, pt. 1. Halle: Max Niemeyer.

Massaro, Dominic (1997). *Perceiving Talking Faces: From Speech Perception to a Behavioral Principle*. Cambridge, Mass.: MIT Press.

Matthews, G. H. (1964). *Hidatsa Syntax*. The Hague: Mouton.

May, Robert (1985). *Logical Form: Its Structure and Derivation*. Cambridge, Mass.: MIT Press.

Meisel, Jürgen M. (1997). 'The L2 Basic Variety as an I-language'. *Second Language Research* 13: 374–85.

Merritt, M. (1984). 'On the Use of Okay in Service Encounters'. In J. Baugh and J. Sherzer (eds.), *Language in Use: Readings in Sociolinguistics*, 139–47. Englewood Cliffs, NJ: Prentice-Hall.

Michaelis, Laura, and Knud Lambrecht (1996). 'Toward a Construction-Based Theory of Language Function: The Case of Nominal Extraposition'. *Language* 72: 215–47.

Michotte, A. (1954). *La perception de la causalité*, 2nd edn. Louvain: Publications Universitaires de Louvain.

Miller, George (1956). 'The Magical Number Seven, plus or minus Two: Some Limits on our Capacity for Processing Information'. *Psychological Review* 3: 81–97.

—— and Noam Chomsky (1963). 'Finitary Models of Language Users'. In R. D. Luce, R. R. Bush, and E. Galanter (eds.), *Handbook of Mathematical Psychology*, vol. ii, 419–92. New York: Wiley.

—— and Philip Johnson-Laird (1976). *Language and Perception*. Cambridge, Mass.: Harvard University Press.

Miller, Philip, and Ivan Sag (1997). 'French Clitic Movement without Clitics or Movement'. *Natural Language and Linguistic Theory* 15: 573–639.

Millikan, Ruth (1984). *Language and Other Abstract Objects*. Cambridge, Mass.: MIT Press.

Milner, Brenda (1974). 'Sparing of Language Functions after Early Unilateral Brain Damage'. *Neurosciences Res. Prog. Bull.* 12(2): 213–17.

Minsky, Marvin (1975). 'A Framework for Representing Knowledge'. In P. H. Winston (ed.), *The Psychology of Computer Vision*. New York: McGraw-Hill.

Mithun, Marianne (1984). 'The Evolution of Noun Incorporation'. *Language* 60: 847–93.

Montague, Richard (1973). 'The Proper Treatment of Quantification in Ordinary English'. In K. Hintikka, J. Moravcsik, and P. Suppes (eds.), *Approaches to Natural Language*, 221–42. Dordrecht: Reidel.

Moravcsik, Edith (1978). 'Reduplicative Constructions'. In J. H. Greenberg (ed.), *Universals of Human Language*, vol. iii: *Word Structure*. Stanford, Calif.: Stanford University Press.

Nam, Jee-Sun (1996). *Lexicon of Korean Predicative Terms Classified by Morphological Ending Forms*, Vol. I/II (working papers 96–8, 96–9). Noisy-legrand, France: Institut Gaspard Monge, Université de Marne-la-Vallée.

Neisser, Ulric (1967). *Cognitive Psychology*. Englewood Cliffs, NJ: Prentice-Hall.

Nespor, Marina, and Irene Vogel (1986). *Prosodic Phonology*. Dordrecht: Foris.

Neville, Helen, and D. Lawson (1987). 'Attention to Central and Peripheral Visual Space in a Movement Detection Task: An Event-Related Potential and Behavioral Study. II: Congenitally Deaf Adults'. *Brain Research* 405: 268–83.

Newmeyer, Frederick J. (1969/75). *English Aspectual Verbs*. The Hague: Mouton.

—— (1980). *Linguistic Theory in America: The First Quarter-Century of Transformational-Generative Grammar*. New York: Academic Press.

—— (1998a). 'On the Supposed "Counterfunctionality" of Universal Grammar: Some Evolutionary Implications'. In Hurford et al. (1998: 305–19).

—— (1998b). *Language Form and Language Function*. Cambridge, Mass.: MIT Press.

Newport, Elissa (1990). 'Maturational Constraints on Language Learning'. *Cognitive Science* 14: 11–28.

—— Henry Gleitman, and Lila R. Gleitman (1977). 'Mother, I'd Rather Do it Myself: Some Effects and Non-effects of Maternal Speech Style'. In C. Snow and C. Ferguson (eds.), *Talking to Children: Language Input and Acquisition*. New York: Cambridge University Press.

Nikanne, Urpo (1990). *Zones and Tiers: A Study of Thematic Structure*. Helsinki: Suomalaisen Kirjallisuuden Seura.

—— (2000a). 'Some Restrictions in Linguistic Expressions of Spatial Movement'. In Emile van der Zee and Urpo Nikanne (eds.), *Cognitive Interfaces: Constraints on Linking Cognitive Information*, 77–93. Oxford: Oxford University Press.

—— (2000b). 'Constructions in Conceptual Semantics'. In Jan-Ola Östman (ed.), *Construction Grammar*. Amsterdam/Philadelphia: John Benjamins.

Nordlinger, Rachel (1998). *Constructive Case: Evidence from Australian Languages*. Stanford, Calif.: CSLI.

Nowak, Martin, David C. Krakauer, and Andreas Dress (1999). 'An Error Limit for the Evolution of Language'. *Proc. R. Soc. Lond. B* 266, 2131–6.

—— Joshua B. Plotkin, and Vincent A. A. Jansen (2000). 'The Evolution of Syntactic Communication'. *Nature* 404: 495–8.

Nunberg, Geoffrey (1979). 'The Non-uniqueness of Semantic Solutions: Polysemy'. *Linguistics and Philosophy* 3: 143–84.

—— Ivan Sag, and Thomas Wasow (1994). 'Idioms'. *Language* 70: 491–538.

Odden, David (1995). 'Tone: African Languages'. In Goldsmith (1995: 444–75).

Oehrle, Richard T. (1998). 'Noun after Noun'. Paper presented at the Annual Meeting of the Linguistic Society of America.

Oldfield, R. C., and A. Wingfield (1965). 'Response Latencies in Naming Objects'. *Quarterly Journal of Experimental Psychology* 17: 273–81.

Osgood, Charles E. (1984). 'Toward an Abstract Performance Grammar'. In Bever et al. (1984: 147–79).

Otero, Carlos (1983). 'Toward a Model of Paradigmatic Grammar'. *Quaderni di semantica* 4: 134–44.

Paivio, A. (1971). *Imagery and Verbal Processes*. New York: Holt, Rinehart & Winston. Repr. Hillsdale, NJ: Erlbaum, 1979.

Partee, Barbara (1975). 'Montague Grammar and Transformational Grammar'. *Linguistic Inquiry* 6: 203–300.

—— (ed.) (1976). *Montague Grammar*. New York: Academic Press.

—— (1979). 'Semantics—Mathematics or Psychology?' In R. Bäuerle, U. Egli, and A. von Stechow (eds.), *Semantics from Different Points of View*, 1–14. Berlin: Springer.

—— (1991). 'Topic, Focus, and Quantification'. In Steven Moore and Adam Z. Wyner (eds.), *Proceedings of the First Semantics and Linguistic Theory Conference* (Cornell University Working Papers in Linguistics, 10), 159–87. Ithaca, NY: Cornell Department of Modern Languages and Linguistics.

Payne, Katharine (2000). 'The Progressively Changing Songs of Humpback Whales: A Window on the Creative Process in a Wild Animal'. In N. Wallin, B. Merker, and S. Brown (eds.), *The Origins of Music*, 135–50. Cambridge, Mass.: MIT Press.

Perlmutter, David M. (ed.) (1983). *Studies in Relational Grammar*, vol. i. Chicago: University of Chicago Press.

—— and Carol G. Rosen (eds.) (1984). *Studies in Relational Grammar*, vol. ii. Chicago: University of Chicago Press.

Perry, Theresa, and Lisa Delpit (eds.) (1998). *The Real Ebonics Debate*. Boston: Beacon Press.

Pesetsky, David (1994). *Zero Syntax*. Cambridge, Mass.: MIT Press.

Piattelli-Palmerini, Massimo (1989). 'Evolution, Selection, and Cognition: From "Learning" to Parameter Setting in Biology and the Study of Language'. *Cognition* 31: 1–44.

Piñango, Maria Mercedes (1999). 'Syntactic Displacement in Broca's Aphasia Comprehension'. In R. Bastiaanse and Y. Grodzinsky (eds.), *Grammatical Disorders in Aphasia: A Neurolinguistic Perspective*, 74–89. Groningen: Whurr.

—— (2000). 'Canonicity in Broca's Sentence Comprehension: The Case of Psychological Verbs'. In Y. Grodzinsky, L. Shapiro, and D. Swinney (eds.), *Language and the Brain*, 327–50. San Diego, Calif.: Academic Press.

—— Edgar Zurif, and Ray Jackendoff (1999). 'Real-Time Processing Implications of Enriched Composition at the Syntax–Semantics Interface'. *Journal of Psycholinguistic Research* 28: 395–414.

Pinker, Steven (1989). *Learnability and Cognition: The Acquisition of Argument Structure*. Cambridge, Mass.: MIT Press.

—— (1994a). 'How Could a Child Use Verb Syntax to Learn Verb Semantics?' In Gleitman and Landau (1994: 377–410).

—— (1994b). *The Language Instinct*. New York: Morrow.

—— (1999). *Words and Rules*. New York: Basic Books.

—— and Paul Bloom (1990). 'Natural Language and Natural Selection'. *Behavioral and Brain Sciences* 13: 707–26.

—— and Alan Prince (1988). 'On Language and Connectionism: Analysis of a Parallel Distributed Processing Model of Language Acquisition'. *Cognition* 26: 195–267.

—— —— (1991). 'Regular and Irregular Morphology and the Psychological Status of Rules of Grammar'. In *Proceedings of the 17th Annual Meeting of the Berkeley Linguistics Society*, 230–51. Berkeley, Calif.: Berkeley Linguistics Society.

Plunkett, Kim, and Patrick Juola (1999). 'A Connectionist Model of English Past Tense and Plural Morphology'. *Cognitive Science* 23: 463–90.

—— and Virginia Marchman (1991). 'U-shaped Learning and Frequency Effects in a Multi-layered Perceptron: Implications for Child Language Acquisition'. *Cognition* 49: 21–69.

Pollack, Jordan (1990). 'Recursive Distributed Representations'. *Artificial Intelligence* 46: 77–105.

Pollard, Carl, and Ivan Sag (1987). *Information-Based Syntax and Semantics*. Stanford, Calif.: CSLI.

—— —— (1994). *Head-Driven Phrase Structure Grammar*. Chicago: University of Chicago Press.

Pollock, J.-Y. (1989). 'Verb Movement, Universal Grammar, and the Structure of IP'. *Linguistic Inquiry* 20: 365–424.

Postal, Paul M. (1962). 'Some Syntactic Rules in Mohawk'. Doctoral dissertation, Yale University.

—— (1964). 'Limitations of Phrase Structure Grammars'. In J. Fodor and J. Katz (eds.), *The Structure of Language*, 137–51. Englewood Cliffs, NJ: Prentice-Hall.

—— (1970a). 'On the Surface Verb "Remind" '. *Linguistic Inquiry* 1: 37–120.

—— (1970b). 'On Coreferential Complement Subject Deletion'. *Linguistic Inquiry* 1: 439–500.

—— (1971). *Crossover Phenomena*. New York: Holt, Rinehart & Winston.

—— (1974). 'On Certain Ambiguities'. *Linguistic Inquiry* 5: 367–424.

—— (1997). 'Islands'. MS, New York University.

Potter, Mary C. (1993). 'Very Short-Term Conceptual Memory'. *Memory and Cognition* 21: 156–61.

Povinelli, Daniel J., Jesse M. Bering, and Steve Giambrone (2000). 'Toward a Science of Other Minds: Escaping the Argument by Analogy'. *Cognitive Science* 24: 509–42.

Power, Camilla (1998). 'Old Wives' Tales: The Gossip Hypothesis and the Reliability of Cheap Signals'. In Hurford et al. (1998: 111–29).

Prasada, Sandeep, and Steven Pinker (1993). Similarity-Based and Rule-Based Generalizations in Inflectional Morphology'. *Language and Cognitive Processes* 8: 1–56.

Prather, Penny, Lewis Shapiro, Edgar Zurif, and David Swinney (1991). 'Real-Time Examinations of Lexical Processing in Aphasics'. *Journal of Psycholinguistic Research* 20: 271–81.

Premack, David (1976). *Intelligence in Ape and Man*. Hillsdale, NJ: Erlbaum.

—— and A. Woodruff (1978). 'Does the Chimpanzee Have a Theory of Mind?' *Behavioral and Brain Sciences* 4: 515–26.

Prince, Alan, and Paul Smolensky (1993). *Optimality Theory: Constraint Interaction in Generative Grammar*. Piscataway, NJ: Rutgers University Center for Cognitive Science.

Prince, Ellen (1998). 'On the Limits of Syntax, with Reference to Left-Dislocation and Topicalization'. In Culicover and McNally (1998: 281–302).

Pullum, Geoffrey (1981). *The Great Eskimo Vocabulary Hoax and Other Essays*. Chicago: University of Chicago Press.

Pulvermüller, F. (1999). 'Words in the Brain's Language'. *Behavioral and Brain Sciences* 22: 253–79.

Pustejovsky, James (1995). *The Generative Lexicon*. Cambridge, Mass.: MIT Press.

Putnam, Hilary (1975). 'The Meaning of "Meaning"'. In K. Gunderson (ed.), *Language, Mind, and Knowledge*, 131–93. Minneapolis: University of Minnesota Press.

Pylyshyn, Zenon (1984). *Computation and Cognition*. Cambridge, Mass.: MIT Press.

Quine, Willard van Orman (1960). *Word and Object*. Cambridge, Mass.: MIT Press.

Rappaport Hovav, Malka, and Beth Levin (1998). 'Building Verb Meanings'. In M. Butt and W. Geuder (eds.), *The Projection of Arguments: Lexical and Compositional Factors*, 97–134. Stanford: CSLI.

Rey, Georges (1996). 'Concepts and Stereotypes'. In E. Margolis and S. Laurence (eds.), *Concepts: Core Readings*, 278–99. Cambridge, Mass.: MIT Press.

Rickford, John (1999). *African American Vernacular English*. Malden, Mass.: Blackwell.

Ristau, Carolyn, and D. Robbins (1982). 'Language in the Great Apes: A Critical Review'. In J. S. Rosenblatt (ed.), *Advances in the Study of Behavior*, vol. xii, 142–255. New York: Academic Press.

Roberts, Craige (1996). 'Anaphora in Intensional Contexts'. In Lappin (1996: 215–46).

—— (1998). 'Focus, Information Flow, and Universal Grammar'. In Culicover and McNally (1998: 109–60).

Roberts, Sarah Julianne (1998). 'The Role of Diffusion in the Genesis of Hawaiian Creole'. *Language* 74: 1–39.

Rochemont, Michael, and Peter Culicover (1990). *English Focus Constructions and the Theory of Grammar*. Cambridge: Cambridge University Press.

Roelofs, Ardi (1997). 'The WEAVER Model of Word-Form Encoding in Speech Production'. *Cognition* 64: 249–84.

Rooth, Mats (1996). 'Focus'. In Lappin (1996: 271–97).

Rorty, Richard (1979). *Philosophy and the Mirror of Nature*. Princeton, NJ: Princeton University Press.

Rosch, Eleanor (1978). 'Principles of Categorization'. In E. Rosch and B. Lloyd (eds.), *Cognition and Categorization*, 27–48. Hillsdale, NJ: Erlbaum.

Rosch, Eleanor, and Carolyn Mervis (1975). 'Family Resemblances: Studies in the Internal Structure of Categories'. *Cognitive Psychology* 7: 573–605.

Rosen, Sara Thomas (1989). 'Two Types of Noun Incorporation'. *Language* 65: 294–317.

—— (1990). *Argument Structure and Complex Predicates.* New York: Garland.

Ross, John Robert (1967). *Constraints on Variables in Syntax.* Ph.D. dissertation, MIT. Published as *Infinite Syntax!* Norwood, NJ: Ablex, 1986.

—— (1972). 'The Category Squish: Endstation Hauptpoint'. In *Proceedings of the Eighth Meeting of the Chicago Linguistic Society.* Chicago: University of Chicago Department of Linguistics.

Ruhl, Charles (1989). *On Monosemy: A Study in Linguistic Semantics.* Albany, NY: State University of New York Press.

Rumelhart, David E., James L. McClelland (and the PDP Research Group) (1986a). *Parallel Distributed Processing,* vol. i: *Foundations.* Cambridge, Mass.: MIT Press.

—— —— (1986b). 'On Learning the Past Tense of English Verbs'. In J. McClelland, D. Rumelhart, and the PDP Research Group, *Parallel Distributed Processing,* vol. ii, 216–71. Cambridge, Mass.: MIT Press.

Russell, Bertrand (1905). 'On Denoting'. *Mind* 14: 479–93.

Ruwet, Nicolas (1991). *Syntax and Human Experience.* Chicago: University of Chicago Press.

Ryle, Gilbert (1949). *The Concept of Mind.* Chicago: University of Chicago Press.

Sadock, Jerrold (1991). *Autolexical Syntax.* Chicago: University of Chicago Press.

—— (1998). 'On the Autonomy of Compounding Morphology'. In S. G. Lapointe, D. K. Brentani, and P. M. Farrell (eds.), *Morphology and its Relation to Phonology and Syntax,* 161–87. Stanford, Calif.: CSLI.

Saffran, Jenny R., Richard N. Aslin, and Elissa L. Newport (1996). 'Statistical Learning by 8-month-old Infants'. *Science* 274 (13 Dec.): 1926–8.

Sag, Ivan (1997). 'English Relative Clause Constructions'. *Journal of Linguistics* 33: 431–84.

—— and Carl Pollard (1991). 'An Integrated Theory of Complement Control'. *Language* 67: 63–113.

Saussure, Ferdinand de (1915). *Cours de linguistique générale,* ed. C. Bally and A. Sechehaye. English translation: *Course in General Linguistics.* New York: Philosophical Library, 1959.

Savage-Rumbaugh, Sue, Stuart Shanker, and Talbot Taylor (1998). *Apes, Language, and the Human Mind.* Oxford: Oxford University Press.

Schank, Roger (1973). 'Identification of Conceptualizations Underlying Natural Language'. In R. Schank and K. Colby (eds.), *Computer Models of Thought and Language,* 187–248. San Francisco: W. H. Freeman.

—— and Lawrence Birnbaum (1984). 'Memory, Meaning, and Syntax'. In Bever (1984: 209–51).

Searle, John (1969). *Speech Acts.* Cambridge: Cambridge University Press.

—— (1980). 'Minds, Brains, and Programs'. *Behavioral and Brain Sciences* 3: 417–24.

—— (1995). *The Construction of Social Reality*. New York: Free Press.

Seidenberg, Mark S., and Maryellen MacDonald (1999). 'A Probabilistic Constraints Approach to Language Acquisition and Processing'. *Cognitive Science* 23: 569–88.

—— and Laura Petitto (1978). 'Signing Behavior in Apes: A Critical Review'. *Cognition* 17: 177–215.

Selkirk, Elizabeth O. (1982). *The Syntax of Words*. Cambridge, Mass.: MIT Press.

Selkirk, Elizabeth O. (1984). *Phonology and Syntax: The Relation between Sound and Structure*. Cambridge, Mass.: MIT Press.

Seuren, Pieter A. M. (1998). *Western Linguistics: An Historical Introduction*. Oxford: Blackwell.

Sgall, P., E. Hajičová, and J. Panevová (1986). *The Meaning of a Sentence in its Semantic and Pragmatic Aspects*. Dordrecht: Reidel.

Shallice, Tim, and Brian Butterworth (1977). 'Short-Term Memory Impairment and Spontaneous Speech'. *Neuropsychologia* 15: 729–35.

Shannon, Claude E., and Warren Weaver (1949). *The Mathematical Theory of Communication*. Urbana: University of Illinois Press.

Shanske, Alan, Diana D. Caride, Lisa Menasse-Palmer, Anna Bogdanow, and Robert W. Marion (1997). 'Central Nervous System Anomalies in Seckel Syndrome: Report of a New Family and Review of the Literature'. *American Journal of Medical Genetics* 70: 155–8.

Shastri, Lokanda, and V. Ajjanagadde (1993). 'From Simple Associations to Systematic Reasoning: A Connectionist Representation of Rules, Variables, and Dynamic Bindings Using Temporal Synchrony'. *Behavioral and Brain Sciences* 16: 417–94.

Shattuck-Hufnagel, Stefanie (1979). 'Speech Errors as Evidence for a Serial-Order Mechanism in Sentence Production'. In W. E. Cooper and E. C. T. Walker (eds.), *Sentence Processing: Psycholinguistic Studies Presented to Merrill Garrett*, 295–342. Hillsdale, NJ: Erlbaum.

Shatz, Marilyn (1982). 'On Mechanisms of Language Acquisition: Can Features of the Communicative Environment Account for Development?' In E. Wanner and L. R. Gleitman (eds.), *Language Acquisition: The State of the Art*, 102–27. Cambridge: Cambridge University Press.

Sher, Gila (1996). 'Semantics and Logic'. In Lappin (1996: 511–37).

Singer, W., A. K. Engel, A. K. Kreiter, M. H. J. Munk, S. Neuenschwander, and P. R. Roelfsema (1997). 'Neuronal Assemblies: Necessity, Signature, and Detectability'. *Trends in Cognitive Sciences* 1: 252–60.

Slater, Peter J. B. (2000). 'Birdsong Repertoires: Their Origins and Use'. In N. Wallin, B. Merker, and S. Brown, *The Origins of Music*, 49–64. Cambridge, Mass.: MIT Press.

Smith, Brian Cantwell (1996). *On the Origin of Objects*. Cambridge, Mass.: MIT Press.

Smith, Edward, and Douglas Medin (1981). *Categories and Concepts*. Cambridge, Mass.: Harvard University Press.

—— Daniel Osherson, Lance Rips, and Margaret Keane (1988). 'Combining Prototypes: A Selective Modification Model'. *Cognitive Science* 12: 485–527.

Smith, Neil V., and Iantha-Maria Tsimpli (1995). *The Mind of a Savant*. Oxford: Blackwell.

Smolensky, Paul (1999). 'Grammar-Based Connectionist Approaches to Language'. *Cognitive Science* 23: 589–613.

Spelke, Elizabeth, Gary Katz, Susan Purcell, Sheryl Ehrlich, and Karen Breinlinger (1994). 'Early Knowledge of Object Motion: Continuity and Inertia'. *Cognition* 51: 131–76.

Spencer, Andrew (1991). *Morphological Theory*. Oxford: Blackwell.

Sperber, Dan, and Deirdre Wilson (1986). *Relevance*. Cambridge, Mass.: Harvard University Press.

Stalnaker, Robert (1978). 'Assertion'. In P. Cole (ed.), *Syntax and Semantics*, vol. ix: *Pragmatics*, 315–32. New York: Academic Press.

—— (1984). *Inquiry*. Cambridge, Mass.: MIT Press.

Steedman, Mark (1994). 'Acquisition of Verb Categories'. In Gleitman and Landau (1994: 471–80).

—— (1999). 'Connectionist Sentence Processing in Perspective'. *Cognitive Science* 23: 615–34.

—— (2000). 'Information Structure and the Syntax–Phonology Interface'. *Linguistic Inquiry* 31: 649–89.

Steels, Luc (1998). 'Synthesizing the Origins of Language and Meaning Using Coevolution, Self-Organization and Level Formation'. In Hurford et al. (1998: 384–404).

Steiner, George (1997). *Errata*. London: Weidenfeld & Nicolson.

Stiebels, Barbara (1999). 'Noun–Verb Symmetries in Nahuatl Nominalizations'. *Natural Language and Linguistic Theory* 14: 783–836.

Stokoe, William (1960). *Sign Language Structure: An Outline of the Visual Communication System of the American Deaf*. Silver Spring, Md.: Linstok Press.

Studdert-Kennedy, Michael (1998). 'The Particulate Origins of Language Generativity: From Syllable to Gesture'. In Hurford et al. (1998: 202–21).

Sweet, Henry (1913). *Collected Papers*, arr. H. C. Wyld. Oxford: Clarendon Press.

Swinney, David (1979). 'Lexical Access During Sentence Comprehension: (Re)consideration of Context Effects'. *Journal of Verbal Learning and Verbal Behavior* 18: 645–59.

Tabor, Whitney, and Michael Tanenhaus (1999). 'Dynamical Models of Sentence Processing'. *Cognitive Science* 23: 491–515.

Talmy, Leonard (1978). 'The Relation of Grammar to Cognition: A Synopsis'. In D. Waltz (ed.), *Theoretical Issues in Natural Language Processing 2*: 14–24. New York: Association for Computing Machinery. Revised and enlarged version in Talmy (2000: i. 21–96).

—— (1980). 'Lexicalization Patterns: Semantic Structure in Lexical Forms'. In T. Shopen et al. (eds.), *Language Typology and Syntactic Description*, vol. iii. New York: Cambridge University Press. Revised version in Talmy (2000: ii. 21–146).

—— (1983). 'How Language Structures Space'. In H. Pick and L. Acredolo (eds.), *Spatial Orientation: Theory, Research, and Application*. New York: Plenum. Revised version in Talmy (2000: i. 177–254).

—— (1985). 'Force-Dynamics in Language and Thought'. In *Papers from the Twenty-first Regional Meeting of the Chicago Linguistic Society*. Chicago: University of Chicago Dept. of Linguistics. Revised version in Talmy (2000: i. 409–70).

—— (1996a). 'Fictive Motion in Language and "ception" '. In Bloom et al. (1996: 211–76). Repr. in Talmy (2000: i. 99–176).

—— (1996b). 'The Windowing of Attention in Language'. In M. Shibatani and S. Thompson (eds.), *Grammatical Constructions: Their Form and Meaning*. Oxford: Oxford University Press. Repr. in Talmy (2000: i. 257–310).

—— (2000). *Toward a Cognitive Semantics*. Cambridge, Mass.: MIT Press.

Tanenhaus, Michael, J. M. Leiman, and Mark Seidenberg (1979). 'Evidence for Multiple Stages in the Processing of Ambiguous Words in Syntactic Contexts'. *Journal of Verbal Learning and Verbal Behavior* 18: 427–40.

—— M. J. Spivey-Knowlton, K. M. Eberhard, and J. C. Sedivy (1995). 'Integration of Visual and Linguistic Information in Spoken Language Comprehension'. *Science* 268: 1632–4.

Tarski, Alfred (1936). 'The Establishment of Scientific Semantics'. In Tarski, *Logic, Semantics, Metamathematics* (trans. J. H. Woodger, 2nd edn., ed. J. Corcoran), 401–8. Indianapolis: Hackett, 1983.

—— (1956). 'The Concept of Truth in Formalized Languages'. In Tarski, *Logic, Semantics, Metamathematics* (trans. J. H. Woodger, 2nd edn., ed. J. Corcoran), 152–97. London: Oxford University Press.

Tenny, Carol (1994). *Aspectual Roles and the Syntax–Semantics Interface*. Dordrecht: Kluwer.

Terrace, H. (1979) *Nim*. New York, Knopf.

Tinbergen, Nikolaas (1951/89). *The Study of Instinct*. Oxford: Clarendon Press.

Toivonen, Ida (1999). 'The Directed Motion Construction in Swedish'. MS, CSLI, Stanford, Calif.

Tomasello, Michael (1995). 'Language Is Not an Instinct' (review of Pinker 1994b). *Cognitive Development* 10: 131–56.

—— (2000a). 'Do Young Children Have Adult Syntactic Competence?' *Cognition* 74: 209–53.

—— (ed.) (2000b). *Primate Cognition* (special issue). *Cognitive Science* 24 (3).

—— and William E. Merriman (eds.) (1995). *Beyond Names for Things: Young Children's Acquisition of Verbs*. Hillsdale, NJ: Erlbaum.

Tooby, John, and Leda Cosmides (1992). 'The Psychological Foundations of Culture'. In Barkow et al. (1992: 19–136).

Toulmin, Stephen (1972). *Human Understanding*, vol. i. Oxford: Clarendon Press.

Townsend, D. J., and T. G. Bever (1982). 'Natural Units of Representation Interact during Sentence Comprehension'. *Journal of Verbal Learning and Verbal Behavior* 21: 688–703.

Treisman, Ann (1988). 'Features and Objects: The Fourteenth Bartlett Memorial Lecture'. *Quarterly Journal of Experimental Psychology* 40A: 201–37.

Trubetzkoy, N. S. (1958). *Grundzüge der Phonologie*. Göttingen: Vandenhoeck & Ruprecht.

Truckenbrodt, Hubert (1999). 'On the Relation between Syntactic Phrases and Phonological Phrases'. *Linguistic Inquiry* 30: 219–55.

Tulving, Endel (1972). 'Episodic and Semantic Memory'. In E. Tulving and W. Donaldson (eds.), *Organization of Memory*. New York: Academic Press.

Twaddell, W. Freeman (1935). *On Defining the Phoneme*. Language Monograph No. 16. Repr. in part in M. Joos (ed.), *Readings in Linguistics*, i. 55–80. Chicago: University of Chicago Press.

Ujhelyi, Maria (1998). 'Long-Call Structure in Apes as a Possible Precursor for Language'. In Hurford et al. (1998: 177–89).

Vallduví, Enric, and Maria Vilkuna (1998). 'On Rheme and Kontrast'. In Culicover and McNally (1998: 79–108).

van der Lely, Heather (1999). 'Learning from Grammatical SLI'. *Trends in Cognitive Sciences* 3: 286–8.

—— and Valerie Christian (2000). 'Lexical Word Formation in Children with Grammatical SLI: A Grammar-Specific versus an Input-Processing Deficit?' *Cognition* 75: 33–63.

van der Zee, Emile (2000). 'Why We Can Talk about Bulging Barrels and Spinning Spirals: Curvature Representation in the Lexical Interface'. In Emile van der Zee and Urpo Nikanne (eds.), *Cognitive Interfaces: Constraints on Linking Cognitive Information*, 143–82. Oxford: Oxford University Press.

Van Hoek, Karen (1995). 'Conceptual Reference Points: A Cognitive Grammar Account of Pronominal Anaphora Constraints'. *Language* 71: 310–40.

van Turennout, Miranda, Peter Hagoort, and Colin Brown (1998). 'Brain Activity during Speaking: From Syntax to Phonology in 40 Milliseconds'. *Science* 280: 572–4.

Van Valin, Robert (1994). 'Extraction Restrictions, Competing Theories, and the Argument from the Poverty of the Stimulus'. In S. D. Lima, R. L. Corrigan, and G. K. Iverson (eds.), *The Reality of Linguistic Rules*, 243–59. Amsterdam: John Benjamins.

—— and Randy LaPolla (1997). *Syntax: Structure, Meaning and Function*. Cambridge: Cambridge University Press.

Vandeloise, Claude (1986). *L'espace en français*. Paris: Editions du Seuil.

Vargha-Khadem, Faraneh, Elizabeth B. Isaacs, Helen Papaleloudi, Charles E. Polkey, and John Wison (1991). 'Development of Language in Six Hemispherectomized Patients'. *Brain* 114: 473–95.

—— and R. Passingham (1990). 'Speech and Language Defects'. *Nature* 346: 226.

Verkuyl, Henk (1993). *A Theory of Aspectuality: The Interaction between Temporal and Atemporal Structure*. Cambridge: Cambridge University Press.

Watson, John B. (1913). 'Psychology as the Behaviorist Views It'. *Psychological Review* 20: 158–77.

Weinreich, Uriel (1966). 'Explorations in Semantic Theory'. In T. Sebeok (ed.), *Current Trends in Linguistics*, vol. iii. The Hague: Mouton. Repr. in U. Weinreich, *On Semantics*, 99–201. Philadelphia: University of Pennsylvania Press, 1980.

Weir, Ruth (1962) *Language in the Crib*. The Hague: Mouton.

Wertheimer, Max (1923). 'Laws of Organization in Perceptual Forms'. Reprinted in W. D. Ellis (ed.), *A Source Book of Gestalt Psychology*, 71–88. London: Routledge & Kegan Paul, 1938.

Wexler, Kenneth, and Peter Culicover (1980). *Formal Principles of Language Acquisition*. Cambridge, Mass.: MIT Press.

Wierzbicka, Anna (1985). *Lexicography and Conceptual Analysis*. Ann Arbor, Mich.: Karoma.

—— (1987). *English Speech Act Verbs: A Semantic Dictionary*. Orlando, Fla.: Academic Press.

—— (1988). *The Semantics of Grammar*. Amsterdam: John Benjamins.

—— (1996). *Semantics: Primes and Universals*. Oxford: Oxford University Press.

Wiese, Heike (forthcoming). *Numbers, Language, and the Human Mind*. Cambridge: Cambridge University Press.

Wilbur, Ronnie B. (1990). 'Why Syllables? What the Notion Means for ASL Research'. In S. D. Fischer and P. Siple (eds.), *Theoretical Issues in Sign Language Research*, vol. i, 81–108. Chicago: University of Chicago Press.

Williams, Edwin (1994). 'Remarks on Lexical Knowledge'. In Gleitman and Landau (1994: 7–34).

Wimmer, H., and J. Perner (1983). 'Beliefs about Beliefs: Representation and Constraining Function of Wrong Beliefs in Young Children's Understanding of Deception'. *Cognition* 13: 103–28.

Wittgenstein, Ludwig (1953). *Philosophical Investigations*. Oxford: Blackwell.

Worden, Robert (1998). 'The Evolution of Language from Social Intelligence'. In Hurford et al. (1998: 148–66).

Wynn, Karen (1995). 'Origins of Numerical Knowledge'. *Mathematical Cognition* 1: 35–60.

Yip, Moira (1995). 'Tone in East Asian languages'. In Goldsmith (1995: 476–94).

Zurif, Edgar (1990). 'Language and the Brain'. In D. Osherson and H. Lasnik (eds.), *An Introduction to Cognitive Science*, vol. i: *Language*, 177–98. Cambridge, Mass.: MIT Press.

Zwarts, Joost, and Henk Verkuyl (1994). 'An Algebra of Conceptual Structure: An Investigation into Jackendoff's Conceptual Semantics'. *Linguistics and Philosophy* 17: 1–28.

Zwicky, Arnold (1988). 'Morphological Rules, Operations and Operation Types'. *Proceedings of the Eastern States Conference on Linguistics* 4: 318–34.

—— and Geoffrey Pullum (1983). 'Phonology in Syntax: The Somali Optional Agreement Rule'. *Natural Language and Linguistic Theory* 1: 385–402.

Index

Lightning Source UK Ltd.
Milton Keynes UK
20 May 2010

154438UK00001B/2/P